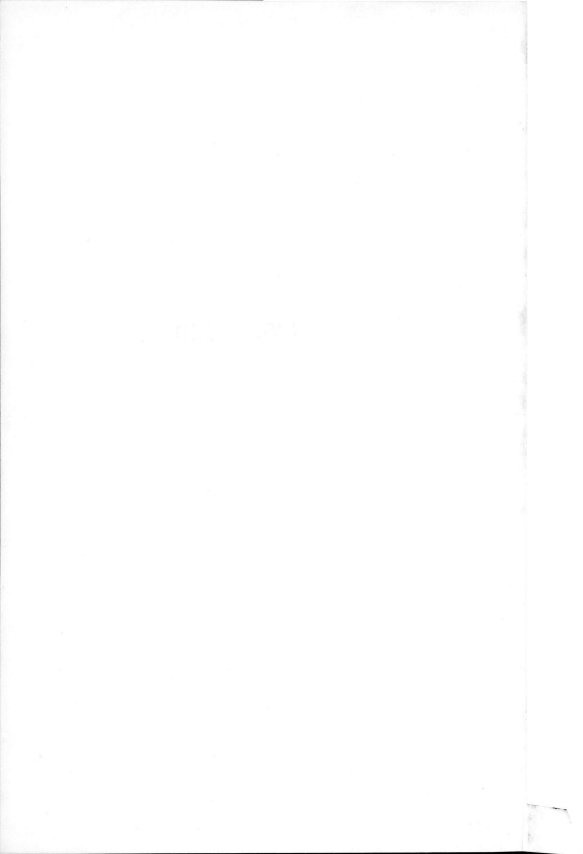

MANAGING ENGINEERING AND RESEARCH

MANAGING Engineering and Research

The Principles and Problems of Managing the Planning, Development and Execution of Engineering and Research Activities

DELMAR W. KARGER, B.S.E.E., M.S.G.E.

Dean, School of Management
Rensselaer Polytechnic Institute

Registered Professional Engineer, Penn.

ROBERT G. MURDICK, Ph.D.

Professor of Management, College
of Business and Public Administration
Florida Atlantic University

Registered Professional Engineer, N. Y.

SECOND EDITION

INDUSTRIAL PRESS INC., 200 Madison Ave., New York 10016

MANAGING ENGINEERING AND RESEARCH

Library of Congress Catalog Card Number: 77–91823

SBN 8311–1063–5

Contents

Preface

The purpose of this book is to provide a structure for the individual who wishes to master the state of the art of managing engineering and research. It combines the most recent concepts and practices available so that it can serve as a self-development book for the engineer or engineering executive and also serve as a textbook for students. We have attempted to blend basic management principles and new conceptual approaches and apply them to persistent engineering problems. The dimensions of the job of managing engineering and research have grown so rapidly that *many practicing managers are not even aware that they are not fulfilling their functions.*

Management of our technical resources has become a major activity and a national problem. The practice of managing engineering and research is based upon a fusion of the fields of management and engineering. While management principles apply to engineering management, just as they do to marketing management, production management, or financial management, there are special aspects of engineering and research which require both unique management techniques and consequent unique applications of fundamental principles.

Although dozens of books have been written on managing almost every other function of business, only a handful of books have recently appeared dealing with managing engineering and research. Many of these books, in our opinion, suffer from one or two basic deficiencies. They are either superficial or they reflect the lack of experience and insight of the authors. We have drawn on the wisdom and experience of many engineering executives, and have attempted to interpret and synthesize their findings on the basis of our own years of experience in this field. We also have drawn freely from the work and writings of many leaders in engineering and research. We greatly appreciate the assistance that they and their companies have provided.

Some chapters could obviously be expanded into lengthy books; in fact, books have been written on many chapter subjects. It is likely, however, that every manager has not read a book corresponding to each chapter. It is more likely that every manager needs an introduction to the subject matter of a number of the chapters. Thus, the chapters combined with their bibliographies are designed to point the way for further study. For the manager in engineering and research, then, this book is meant to provide both a convenient orientation to the many areas of technical management and to present solutions to many of his problems. However, it should be emphasized that we have not endeavored to present "cookbook" solutions or formulas; rather we have striven to present the underlying problems, facts, and principles so that the manager would better be able to develop a solution for his particular problems.

The authors are indebted to Mr. Enrico Petri for his contribution to Chapter 10 and his review which insures the validity of many aspects of this material. We also wish to express our appreciation to Emily Murdick, Margaret Watson, Dian Chartrand and Bertha Waters for translating scribbled copy and garbled tapes into neat manuscript. Mrs. Watson deserves special credit for keeping track of hundreds of manuscript pages and constant revisions. Professor Karger also wishes to acknowledge his wife Edith's encouragement and understanding during the writing of this revised edition.

Finally, the authors have prepared a manual for instructors who may utilize this book as a text. The manual contains a listing of applicable case studies which can be ordered from The Intercollegiate Case Clearing House. Most of this manual has been class-tested which should, in combination with the chapter bibliographies and the questions and problems, make this book valuable as a classroom text.

DELMAR W. KARGER
ROBERT G. MURDICK

August, 1969

CHAPTER 1

Business Strategy and the Role of Engineering and Research

INTRODUCTION

There are many people still living today who in their early childhood never saw an automobile, an airplane, an electric-light bulb, or a radio. Nuclear fission, nuclear fusion, space travel, lasers and masers have arrived in lightning succession, and make it almost impossible to shock our numbed minds with new technical advances.

Henry Adams, the American historian, was probably the first to recognize the "law of acceleration in history." He discovered that whether we plot power production or air speeds or invention generation, the curves rise geometrically rather than arithmetically. Almost any index of technological progress shows a similar acceleration.

Engineers and scientists have thrust upon the human race a gift that it is totally unprepared to accept. The gift is one that angers or frustrates those undeveloped countries that cannot participate. It places the power of world destruction in the hands of peoples with conflicting ideologies and varying degrees of maturity. Politicians and world leaders, many of whom could not pass a high school course in physics or algebra, are making decisions on allocating their nations' resources for research and the engineering employment of the products of technology. The real danger to mankind is the imbalance between the galloping advance of science and the slow, groping movement of man's understanding of man.

It would be of great benefit to society if, on the one hand, scientific and engineering leaders attempted to relate their work to society, and on the other hand if leaders in the behavioral fields would avoid the hypnotic gleam of technology. Managers of engineering or research activities should, therefore, take cognizance of social factors in order to provide leadership in a dynamic society. This means that managers should consider the social aspects of design—i.e., design equipment that does not pollute, select projects leading to products that serve the broader needs of man, such as rapid transport, better housing, etc.

The study of society has its roots in history. The profit contribution of the engineering manager may well be increased by his knowledge of historical trends. The great problems of industry have changed during the course of history. From the birth of our country until about 1900, the problem was how to produce enough goods. Almost anything that could be manufactured could be sold. About 1900, marketing began to be recognized as a growing problem by early scholars and businessmen such as Arch W. Shaw, Ralph Starr Butler, Fred Clark, and others. Soon businessmen began to realize that the new product was the most potent weapon available to them in the competition for the consumer's dollar—regardless of the product line(s).

One of the major subjects treated in this text is technology and its management, especially technological innovation that culminates in new products and new services. Technological innovation based upon scientific methods, as outlined by William D. Smith, was originated in the textile dye industry of Britain and Germany during the latter part of the 19th century. In the United States, it took root in the 20th century.[1]

Shortly after the turn of the century, such companies as General Electric and E. I. duPont deNemours opened industrial laboratories. By 1921, R & D (research and development) expenditures in the nation totaled about 150 million dollars or 0.2 percent of the gross national product.

The turning point in R & D efforts came with World War II. Following the war, the impetus continued, spurred by cold-war pressures. The realization that comparable methods of technical development could be adapted to civilian needs and a further recognition of the importance of the new product in the battle for an ever-increasing share of a growing market contributed to the rapid growth of R & D.

NEW DIRECTIONS FOR R & D

There are definite indications that some of our research effort is shifting from the physical sciences to social problems. As will be highlighted later, it is most important for technical managers of today to keep well aware of this and other such trends. Technical managers must bend more of their efforts to accommodate to social implications in order to have their organizations fully benefit from the activities of the technical function.

This means that technological and socioeconomic forecasting are becoming more critical to the development of E & R (engineering and research)

[1] William D. Smith, "In the World of Research, U.S. Has Biggest Empire," *The New York Times* (January 8, 1968), p. 137.

strategy. For example, Daniel V. DeSimone gives examples of periods of time required or estimated for major developments, past and future, in a chart (Fig. 1-1) entitled "What's Ahead in Technology."[2]

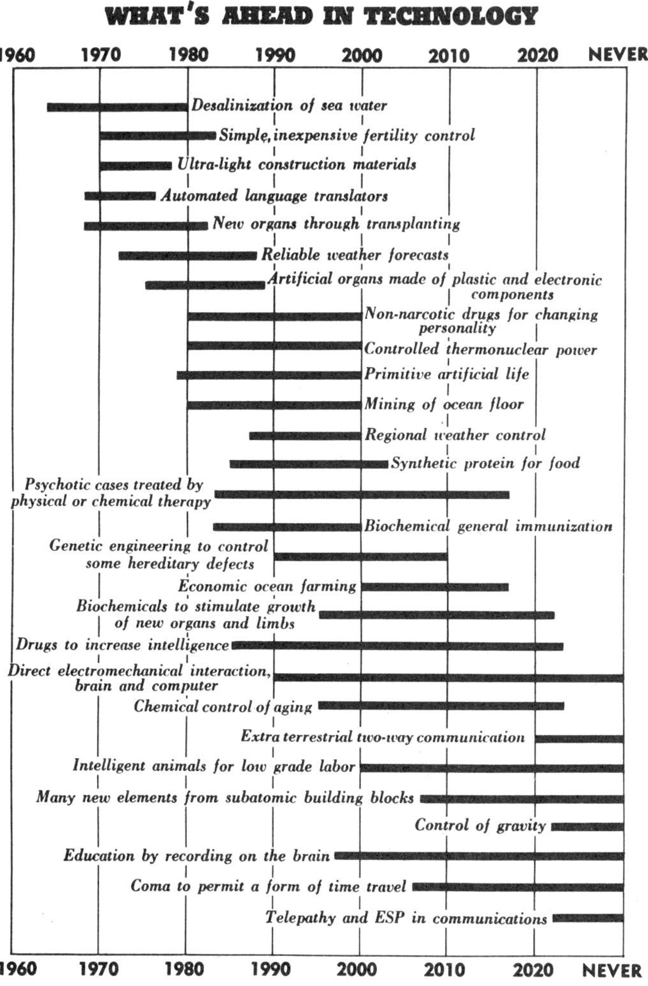

Fig. 1-1. This chart on anticipated future breakthroughs is based on predictions by panel of experts in Rand Corporation study by Olaf Helmer, a mathematician. Bar lengths represent range of time estimates by "middle half" of the panel, with one-quarter of group predicting earlier and one-quarter later dates. Helmer's findings appear in his "Social Technology" (Basic Books, Inc., 1966). *Source:* Daniel V. DeSimone, "Invention, the First Step, Is Often the Most Difficult," *The New York Times* (January 8, 1968). © by The New York Times Co. Reprinted by permission.

[2] Daniel V. DeSimone, "Invention, the First Step, Is Often the Most Difficult," *The New York Times* (January 8, 1968). © 1968 by The New York Times Co. Reprinted by permission.

More information on the future and where such information can be found is given in a three-part article by Dr. Spencer Hayden,[3] which appeared in the April, July, and October 1967 issues of the *Rensselaer Review*.

ECONOMICS AND INNOVATION

A majority of economists and students of our world are convinced that only a small fraction of economic growth, probably no more than 30 percent, can be accounted for by a quantitative increase in capital and labor. The rest is believed to stem from qualitative factors such as labor input and technical change. However, here opinion is divided as to how much of the growth is due to the educational level of the work force and how much is due to additions to the stock of technical knowledge. That each is significant is evident from the fact that there is at least 70 percent to divide between these two factors.

For the purposes of the following discussion, we shall consider innovation and invention as being synonymous. According to Jacob Schmookler,[4] "every invention is (a) a new combination of (b) pre-existing knowledge which (c) satisfies some want." Because invention is important to economic development and apparently affects social change, many people have speculated and developed strong beliefs concerning the factors that control it. Unfortunately, these are only speculations and usually appear as "obvious" propositions preliminary to the analysis of some other problem. They are seldom, if ever, based on serious study. One of the things Schmookler endeavors to accomplish is to consider in a rational manner two hypotheses: (1) that important inventions are typically induced by scientific discoveries; and (2) that inventions are typically induced by the intellectual stimuli provided by earlier inventions. For example, we often hear that one invention led to another, but a real study of the overall problem and data is seldom undertaken.

Space does not permit going into all the concepts advanced by Schmookler, his conclusions, and his reasons for reaching them. However, a few are especially important to R & D managers.

When both investment (or capital goods output) and the number of capital goods inventions are plotted against time for a single industry and compared, both the long-term trend and the long swings exhibit great similarities. There is one notable difference in that the lower turning points in major cycles or long swings generally occur in capital goods sales before they do in capital goods patents.

[3] Spencer Hayden, "The Year 2,000 A.D.," *Rensselaer Review,* Rensselaer Polytechnic Institute, Troy, N.Y. (April, July, October 1967).

[4] Jacob Schmookler, *Invention and Economic Growth* (Cambridge, Mass.: Harvard University Press, 1966).

According to Schmookler:

> The most reasonable explanation for the relation, an explanation consistent with the kinds of stimuli that led men to make important inventions, is probably the simplest. It is that: (1) invention is largely an economic activity which, like other economic activities, is pursued for gain; (2) expected gain varies with expected sales of goods embodying the invention; and (3) expected sales of improved capital goods are largely determined by present capital goods sales. . . .
>
> The possibility that the results reflect the effect of capital goods invention on capital goods sales is grossly implausible. In the time-series comparison, trend turning points tend to occur in sales before they do in patents, and long-swing troughs in sales generally precede those in patents. Moreover, trends and long swings in investment in the industries examined are adequately explained on other grounds. . . .
>
> Thus, while other phenomena may help cause the relation observed, its chief cause seems to lie in the simple fact that invention—and in all probability technological change generally—is usually not apart from the normal processes of production and consumption, but a part of them.[5]

Another related fact highlighted by Schmookler is that the more an industry spends on research and development, the greater the number of patents pending for that industry.

Business Week, which tends to take a practical and pragmatic view of economics, presented in 1960 a special report, "What Makes the U.S. Grow." The rationale developed in the article still holds true today. This article sets forth the concept that "there are two basic sets of causes of growth: one is the complex of cultural factors—including science, technology, population changes, religion, politics, social attitudes, class structure, and the intellectual and moral qualities of men: their skills, their imaginations, their drive, their courage."[6] The article gives the other cause of growth as economic factors. These two sets of factors, cultural and economic, must cojoin if growth is to occur and this cojoining of the two factors occurs in the act of investment—the genetic moment for economic growth. The greater the rate of investment, the higher the rate of economic growth.

It is not enough to stop here without calling attention to the two kinds of investment, autonomous investment and induced investment. Autonomous investment creates its own demand and results primarily from non-economic causes, from forces outside the economic system—usually from the action of cultural forces. Induced investment results primarily from economic factors such as interest rates, costs, prices, etc. As a growth producer, induced investment does little for us in the long run, whereas autonomous investment does cause long-term significant growth. It stems from the discovery of new techniques of production, new products, new resources, etc.

[5] *Ibid.*

[6] "What Makes the U.S. Grow," Reprinted from the January 23, 1960 issue of *Business Week* by special permission. Copyrighted © 1960 by McGraw-Hill, Inc.

The article leads to the conclusion that our rapid growth since World War II has not been based on any one or two innovations, such as textiles, iron making, and steam power in the period prior to 1840; or such as the railroads and steel prior to 1890. The present growth is based on literally thousands of new developments. As soon as one list of developments is compiled, it is obsolete because there are other new developments to be added.

THE PROCESS OF INNOVATION

The process of innovation, as outlined by Dr. Harvey Brooks,[7] Dean of Engineering and Applied Physics at Harvard University, is very elusive. Innovations may be as simple as a zipper or trading stamps, or as complicated as a giant computer.

Perhaps more important for the technical manager is a recognition that innovation in the presence of a strong science base tends to take on the character of a chain reaction. For example, the invention of the transistor in 1947 helped pave the way for magnetic memory cards, thin film memories, masers, lasers, and parametric amplifiers. It even impacted on ancillary technologies such as those dealing with pure materials and imperfection-free single crystals, because these were required to produce a commercially feasible transistor. The technologies to produce these made possible many advances in the understanding and use of the properties of solids. This in turn led to other devices, including a relatively simple and unsophisticated development such as the high-power vacuum circuit-breaker. Up to this time, such a circuit breaker had been an impossibility due to gas leaking from the metal surfaces exposed to the inside of the circuit breaker.

Dr. Charles R. DeCarlo, a mathematician with International Business Machines Corporation, with others, believes that invention is feeding upon itself. For example, he said that Alfred North Whitehead indicated "that the principal accomplishment of the last century was 'the invention of the method of invention.' " By this DeCarlo meant that science and technology had come to the point where the parts fed upon each other continuously and synergistically to enlarge the whole.[8]

The business corporation serves its mission in society by applying the uses of science and technology to expand its markets, increase its profitability, and insure its survival. It does this in several ways.

First, according to DeCarlo:

[7] Harvey Brooks, "Nation Turning to Science to Spur Economic Growth," *New York Times* (January 8, 1968).

[8] Charles R. DeCarlo, "Invention is Feeding Upon Itself," *The New York Times* (January 8, 1968).

By the direct use of scientific technique, it can extend, improve or provide more differentiations in its products and services. . . .

Secondly, markets can be expanded by invention-innovation that yield increased productivity, without changing the basic process. . . .

Thirdly, a market may be expanded by the adaptation of technologies that "fall out" of other enterprises. . . .

Finally, there is the creation of almost new markets and industries with the availability of new technologies.[9]

Television and biomedical engineering are examples of this.

The private business sector has been very successful in exploiting technology and innovation as outlined above. However, the market economy, to be truly successful in human terms, must involve total participation.

The current issues in the civil rights and poverty movements have their roots, at least partly, in the fact that by technological change, society has ripped apart old patterns.

The second problem, according to Dr. DeCarlo, "flows from the fact that the invention-innovation process has traditionally been exercised by private institutions that have generally the limited goal of providing a specific range of goods and services.[10] This, we believe, is a generally accepted fact.

The thrust of innovation in the past has been devoted to the needs of national security and of the private sector. The central issue today is how to redeploy some of our innovative skills to meet urgent public needs. For example, despite the most advanced biomedical research in the world, the United States has a poor record in the delivery of medical care to its population. Many nations surpass us with regard to low infant mortality rates, etc. Even our post offices are technologically backward in comparison with the rest of our communications network.

According to Dr. Harvey Brooks[11] we have an effective private marketing machine, but have yet to invent an analogous institution or a set of institutions to help solve our urgent public problems. If we do not provide this structure, our innovative push may well crash in upon itself.

What has this to do with the technical manager? It emphasizes the need to relate science and technology, the work of the research scientist and the work of the engineer, to the world of today. This can be done to some degree regardless of whether the work is being performed for profit or nonprofit organizations.

Our problem is to harness today's innovative thrust—to use it to build up national welfare, solve national and international problems. In doing so, the organizations involved will also benefit. The Soviets are trying to harness the same kind of thrust for their own purposes. Which holds the winning

[9] *Ibid.*

[10] *Ibid.*

[11] DeCarlo, "Invention is Feeding Upon Itself."

cards in such a competition—a free society or a controlled one? The answer is not entirely clear to many thinking individuals; however, the technical manager today is undoubtedly going to play a key role in the final solution.

We may be entering a new era, described by Dr. Kenneth Boulding,[12] an economist, as a new level of civilization—the postcivilized world. He believes that we in the United States and perhaps some of the other advanced countries are beginning to live in this new world that is as different and as far removed from the civilized world, as the civilized world is removed from primitive society. This is complicated by the fact that we still have in existence precivilized societies, civilized societies and so-called postcivilized societies. The problem of surviving so as to have everyone enter the postcivilized world is going to be most difficult.

RESEARCH AND TECHNOLOGICAL CHANGE

According to Dr. Edwin Mansfield,[13] there is surprisingly little known about the methodology by which new products and processes are invented, developed, commercialized, and accepted despite widespread attention. He attempted to summarize some of the findings of a continuing study of the process being conducted with the support of the National Science Foundation, the Cowles Foundation for Research in Economics at Yale University, the Ford Foundation, and the Graduate School of Industrial Administration at Carnegie Institute of Technology. As part of this inquiry, detailed studies were made of the chemical, petroleum, and steel industries. Some of these data are presented in a book by Schmookler.[14]

Calculations, based on crude data, suggest that, holding the size of the firm constant, the number of significant inventions carried out by a company seems to be highly correlated with the size of its research and development expenditures. This is in accord with the gross statistics alluded to above. Although the payout from an individual R & D project is obviously uncertain, it seems that there is a close relationship, over the long run, between the amount a firm spends on R & D and the total number of important inventions it produces.

Schmookler makes the surprising statement that, in most industries, when a company's R & D spending is held constant, it appears from available data that an increase in size of the company seems to be associated with a *decrease* in inventive output.

[12] Kenneth Boulding, *The Meaning of the 20th Century* (New York: Harper and Row, 1964).

[13] Edwin Mansfield, "Research and Technological Change," *Industrial Research* (February, 1964).

[14] Schmookler, *Invention and Economic Growth.*

THE ROLE OF GOVERNMENT IN ENGINEERING AND RESEARCH

Despite the vast and increasing amounts of engineering and research in which industry engages for the risks and gains of product development and innovation, government expenditures up to now have increased at a greater rate. In 1940, federal financing of research and development amounted to $74 *million,* less than one percent of overall federal expenditures and only 19 percent of the nation's total effort in R & D.[15] In 1975, the total outlay for R & D in the nation will total about $35 *billion.* Of this total, federal funds will account for well over 60 percent. Such a drastic increase in federal involvement in 26 years suggests that R & D is becoming nationalized and that science is becoming a ward of the United States government. The increasing rate of expenditure on R & D is graphically portrayed in Fig. 1-2.

In spite of these large increases in federal expenditures, the law of diminishing returns eventually must have its say. In fact, there are indica-

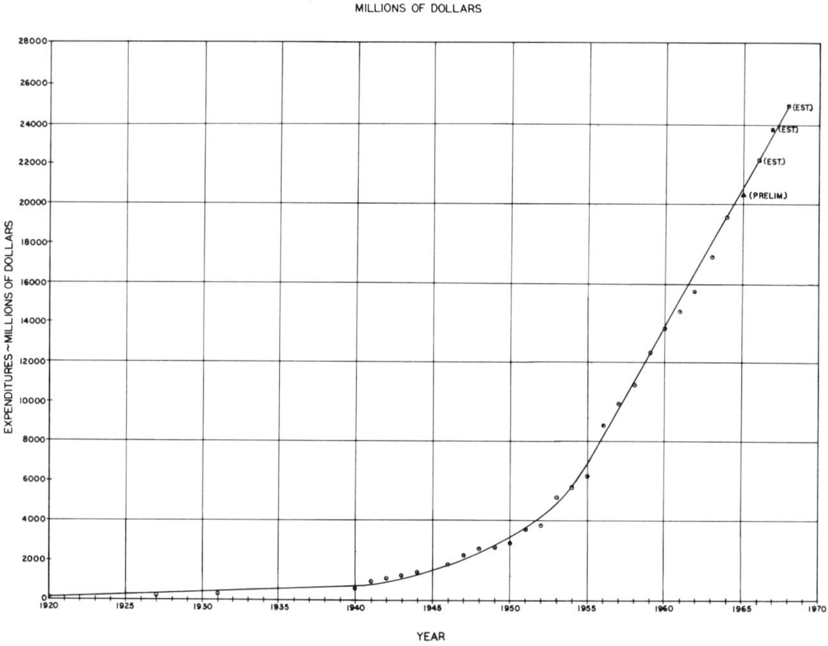

Fig. 1-2. Increasing expenditure of R & D.

[15] *Federal Funds for Science XI,* NSF Survey (Washington, D.C.: U.S. Government Printing Office, 1963), p. 49.

tions, while not readily apparent in the R & D growth curve, that the federal government's expenditures for R & D are in the incipient stage of a tapering-off process.

However, the above does not mean that industry-financed research has reached its zenith. As governmental R & D declines relative to GNP, industrial research could make up some or all of the difference. However, it should be realized that it is federal money that now gives the R & D growth curve its shape.

Whether governmental R & D funds will reach a plateau is important to the engineering and research manager. However, it is not as important as the fact that he must be well informed as to who is spending money and for what kinds of activities since it is and will be substantial in the foreseeable future. Finally, E & R managers must be aware that when the government talks of R & D expenditures, it covers everything from low-level engineering to basic research, as is attested by the chief compiler of R & D statistics, the National Science Foundation. The NSF definition of R & D is as follows: "Systematic and intensive study directed toward a fuller knowledge of the subject studied and use of that knowledge directed toward the production of useful material, devices, systems, methods, or processes."[16]

Government engineering and research may be divided into two classifications. The first is that which is actually carried out by government personnel at government-owned installations. The second is through grants and contracts with nonprofit organizations and universities, and through contracts with private industry. By far, the greater amount of funds is funneled out to private industry for engineering and development—not basic research.

With respect to research and development, the government has entered only those fields where its presence had some particular application to its constitutional duties, such as defense, public health, and the collection and spread of scientific information. Incidentally, the establishment of the agricultural research facilities under the Land Grant Act of 1862 probably did more to advance our civilization in the United States than most people imagine. It is why we can feed and clothe ourselves with only 5 to 10 percent of our total effort directed to this end.

Let us look at how the two-thirds of the federal funds that go to industry for R & D are divided and used. Most of the work is performed under contractual arrangements. The profit organizations doing the work are chiefly aircraft, missile, and electronic industries under Defense Department contracts, and a wide range of firms holding nondefense contracts with the National Aeronautics and Space Administration, the Atomic Energy Commission, and other agencies. Government, since it spends the most, has the controlling voice in national research and development as a whole.

[16] National Science Foundation, *Reviews of Data and Research and Development,* NSF 61-9, No. 26 (February 1961), pp. 61–69.

It seems obvious that E & R managers must be cognizant of the government's impact upon R & D since many will be involved in performing government-sponsored R & D. Of necessity, industrial and other organizations will need to seek some of these government funds. However, it is equally important for E & R managers to recognize the importance of spending some of their own organization's money on R & D.

THE MILITARY-INDUSTRIAL COMPLEX AND THE NEW INDUSTRIAL STATE

No discussion of the role of government in R & D would be complete without taking a broad look at what may be occurring in the United States. Galbraith, in *The New Industrial State*,[17] developed the premise that giant corporations have achieved such dominance that they can control their environment and immunize themselves from the discipline of all exogenous control mechanisms—especially the competitive market. This, of course, is amplified to discuss relationships with stockholders, financiers (the capital market), consumers, etc. Walter Adams of Michigan State University, in an article bearing the same title as the above subtitle, presents another hypothesis.[18] His position is the opposite of Galbraith's; he holds that industrial concentration is not the inevitable outgrowth of economic and technical forces, not the product of spontaneous generation or natural selection. Rather, he believes that concentration is often the result of unwise, man-made, discriminatory privilege-creating governmental action such as defense contracts, R & D support, patent policy, tax privileges, stockpiling arrangements, tariffs and quotas, subsidies, etc.

He goes on to say:

> My hypothesis is best explained in Schumpeterian power terms. According to Schumpeter, the capitalist process was rooted, not in classical price competition, but rather "the competition from the new commodity, the new technology, the new source of supply, the new type of organization—competition which commands a decisive cost or quality advantage and which strikes not at the margin of the profits and outputs of existing firms, but at their very foundations and their very lives."[19] The very essence of capitalism, according to Schumpeter, was the "perennial gale of creative destruction" in which existing power positions and entrenched advantages were constantly displaced by new organizations and new power complexes. This gale of creative destruction was to be not only the harbinger of progress but also the built-in safeguard against the vices of monopoly and privilege.

[17] John K. Galbraith, *The New Industrial State* (Boston: Houghton Mifflin Co., 1967).

[18] Walter Adams, "The Military-Industrial Complex and the New Industrial State," *American Economic Review* (May 1968).

[19] Joseph A. Schumpeter, *Capitalism, Socialism, and Democracy* (New York: Harper & Brothers, 1942).

Adams develops the obvious need for some kind of storm shelter for those who might suffer from the gales of change outlined by Schumpeter. His point is that this storm shelter is the government and that the unique buyer-seller relationship (government versus industry) defies analysis by conventional economic tools, and that it lies at the root of the military-industrial complex and the new power configurations generated by it. He goes on to say, "The complex is not a conspiracy between the 'merchants of death' and a band of lusty generals, but a natural coalition of interest groups with an economic, political, or professional stake in defense in space. . . . Every time the Congress authorizes a military appropriation, it creates a new constituency (i.e., propaganda machine) with a vested interest in its perpetuation and aggrandizement."[20]

These concepts all involve man-made policy and do not represent institutional inevitability. It is another facet of modern life that the R & D manager needs to understand in his role as a technically educated citizen.

NEW PRODUCT BASICS

In *Goals for Americans,*[21] the President's Commission credits private industry with making the United States the most productive nation in history. The report of the commission says specifically in this regard: "The magic ingredient is our competitive enterprise environment, the most powerful force ever known for stimulating individual and cooperative efforts to make innovations for the benefit of mankind. It encourages and rewards those enterprises which make successful changes, and punishes or eliminates the inefficient who fall behind."[22]

Innovation, then, must be the key to company growth and survival. Hence, engineering and research, which are responsible for the continual flow of new products, will have a more important bearing on the life of most manufacturing companies than ever before.

The necessity for, and the reasons behind, defense-oriented engineering and research are quite readily understood. However, to some, the reasons for conducting research and engineering in industrial organizations are not so obvious. What is not realized is that new products are basic to company growth; in fact, they are essential to its very survival. This is so even if a company has good products that are selling well, since almost all products have a finite life, most of them not exceeding two to five years. Only semi-basic materials, such as phosphor bronze, have significantly longer lives.

[20] Adams, "The Military-Industrial Complex."

[21] *Goals for Americans,* The Report of the President's Commission on National Goals (Englewood Cliffs, N.J.: Prentice-Hall, 1960).

[22] *Ibid.*

Some products, such as carnival novelties, may have a life cycle of only a few days. Since a company has no reason for existing if it does not have a product that it can make and sell at a profit, and since most products have a limited life, it is apparent that firms must develop new products (or product improvements) almost continuously. Related to the shortening product life cycle is the shrinking of the Discovery-to-Development Gap as illustrated in Fig. 1-3.

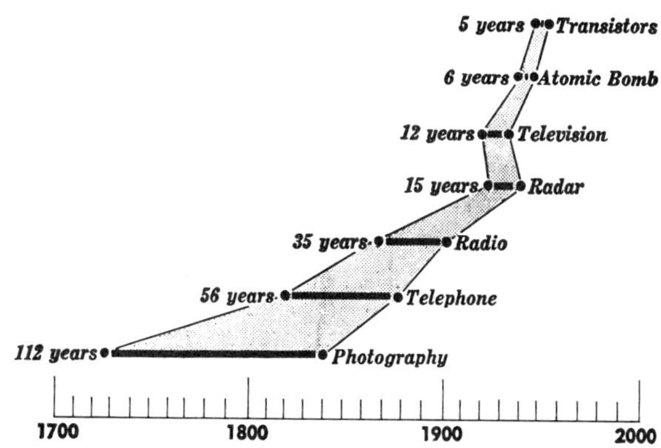

Fig. 1-3. Discovery-to-development gap. *Source:* By courtesy of *Science Journal*, London (September 1966).

That research and development projects, aimed at new products, are necessary to company growth is strongly indicated by growth data. If we plot the average percent of sales spent on R & D and compare it to plant growth for that industry over a ten-year period, we shall find that those firms that spend a greater percent of their revenues on R & D have experienced the greatest growth as measured by the increase in plant capacity. Comparison with other indexes of growth or size of firm shows a similar relationship.

Not only do almost all products have a finite life, but they have a life cycle similar to that indicated in Figs. 1-4a and 1-4b. It will be noted that the sales volume, profit margin, and monthly profit curves are similar in configuration but are dissimilar as to their phasing or time of maximization. While the phase relationship, the relative value, and the rates of change may vary, practically all products experience a similar variation and relationship.

The shape of the sales curve has been generally understood for many years; nevertheless, the identification of its phase relationship with the profit margin curve, the profit curve, and the investment recovery curve has not always been appreciated by management.

A primary economic conclusion that can be derived from the analysis

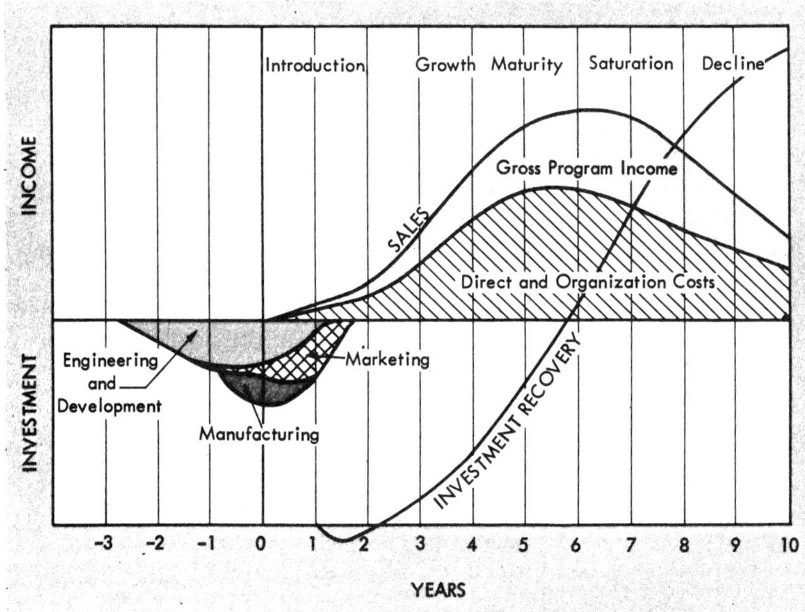

Fig. 1-4a. Product life cycle and investment recovery. *Source:* Harry L. Hansen, *Marketing: Text, Techniques, and Cases*, 3rd ed. (Homewood, Ill.: Richard D. Irwin, 1967).

of a typical product life cycle is that eventually every product is replaced by another or else, due to competition, it deteriorates into a profitless item. Consequently, new products must be continuously developed and introduced into the market if a company is to survive and grow. This statement is graphically illustrated by Fig. 1-5, which shows how profit contributions from a company's products vary with time. Furthermore, the increasing expenditure for E & R (Engineering and Research)* previously mentioned, is compressing and shortening the life cycle of almost every product, a fact that management in general must take into account.

The successful engineering and research manager must not only understand the significance of the facts so far presented, but he must also have an adequate grasp of the general business strategies involved and the overall business and organizational aspects of product planning. For example, he must know that a new product can be closely related to an antecedent product and that a "new" product does not always involve new markets or new technology. Table 1-1 shows the potential relationships between degrees of product newness and degrees of market newness. It explains how one can have a new product without affecting the firm's market and, con-

* E & R is used throughout this book to indicate that emphasis is placed on development in which research is, for the most part, applied research.

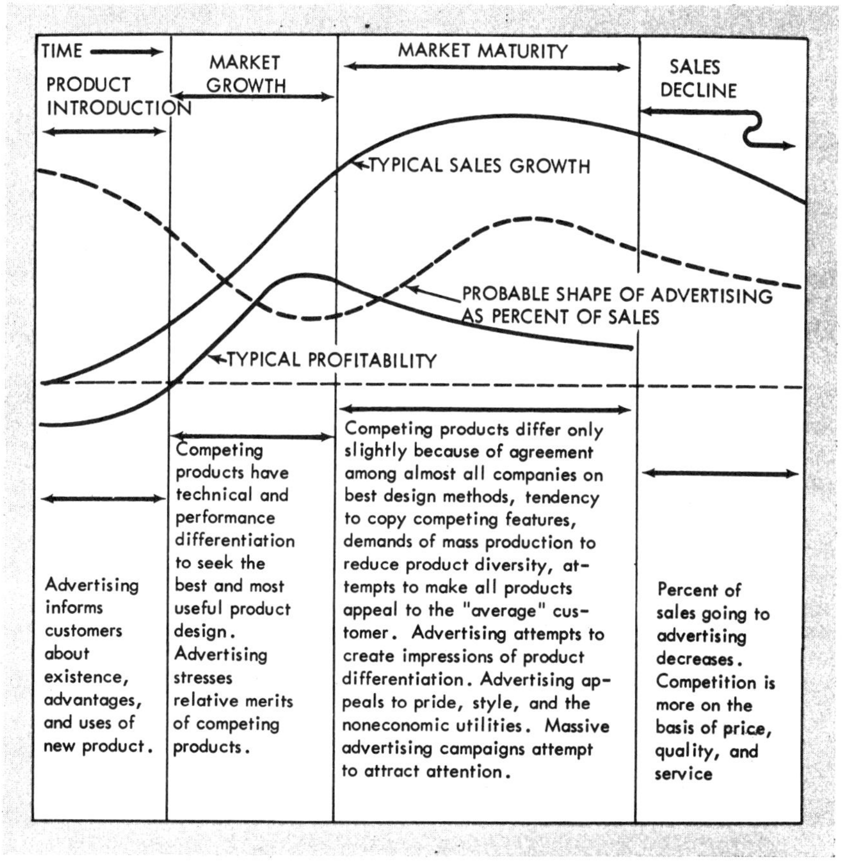

TIME
PRODUCT INTRODUCTION
MARKET GROWTH
MARKET MATURITY
SALES DECLINE
TYPICAL SALES GROWTH
PROBABLE SHAPE OF ADVERTISING AS PERCENT OF SALES
TYPICAL PROFITABILITY
Advertising informs customers about existence, advantages, and uses of new product.
Competing products have technical and performance differentiation to seek the best and most useful product design. Advertising stresses relative merits of competing products.
Competing products differ only slightly because of agreement among almost all companies on best design methods, tendency to copy competing features, demands of mass production to reduce product diversity, attempts to make all products appeal to the "average" customer. Advertising attempts to create impressions of product differentiation. Advertising appeals to pride, style, and the noneconomic utilities. Massive advertising campaigns attempt to attract attention.
Percent of sales going to advertising decreases. Competition is more on the basis of price, quality, and service

Fig. 1-4b. Product life cycle phases. *Source:* Harry L. Hansen, *Marketing: Text, Techniques, and Cases*, 3rd ed. (Homewood, Ill.: Richard D. Irwin, 1967).

TOTAL MONTHLY PROFIT
MONTHLY PROFIT
DOLLARS
PRODUCT A
PRODUCT B
PRODUCT C
PRODUCT D
TIME

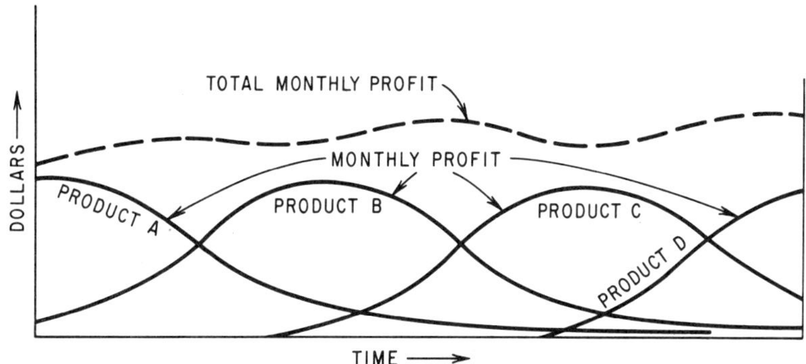

Fig. 1-5. How profit contributions from a company's products vary with time.

Table 1-1—Marketing versus

INCREASING MARKET NEWNESS →

Expand sales into new classes of customers.	No change in product, but new classes of customers reached. Probably involves finding some new uses for product. Can occur without expansion of sales to old classes of customers; can even occur when sales to old classes of customers are decreasing. Finding new uses for product may involve technical or new product assistance.	No change in product, but new classes of customers reached. Probably involves finding some new uses for product. Can occur without expansion of sales to old classes of customers; can even occur when sales to old classes of customers are decreasing. Finding new uses for product may involve technical or new product assistance.	Expanded sales to new classes of customers will not automatically occur. If such expanded sales occur it will be principally for same reasons and in same manner as those for an unchanged product.
Strengthened market in existing classes of customers.	Remerchandising and/or other sales effort to expand sales. Sell more customers of the same types previously served.	Remerchandising and/or other sales effort to expand sales. Sell more customers of the same types previously served.	Market coverage for present classes of customers likely to increase due to improvements in product characteristics and merchandisability. Since there is an effect on price, however, the general aim is always to reduce cost, increase profit margin, and only increase price when absolutely necessary.
No market change.	No change in product characteristics and no change in market penetration.	No change in product characteristics and no change in market penetration.	Positive market change likely to result; however, some adverse market parameters could hold sales constant, or even let them slip.
	No product change.	Product characteristics remain same but changes in components, formulation, production techniques, etc., made to keep costs in line and quality at same relative level.	Minor design modification. Improvements in product characteristics to yield greater utility to customers and/or increase merchandisability. Example: side-burn trimmer on Sunbeam electric shaver.

INCREASING PRODUCT

[23] D. W. Karger and R. G. Murdick, "Product Design, Marketing, and Manufacturing Innovation." Reprinted from the *California Management Review,* Vol. IX, No. 2 (Winter 1966). Copyright 1966 by the Regents of the University of California.

Engineering and Research[23]

In effect, the marketing function is here concerned with what is essentially a new product, complete with all the problems associated with a new product.	Opening of new markets because of introduction of a replacement product does not automatically follow. Unless changes in characteristics and/or resultant price obviously opens new markets, new applications must be actively sought and aggressively exploited when found in order to reach new classes of customers.	Addition of new product lines makes it possible to attract new classes of customers, especially where previously incomplete line made it necessary for certain classes of customers to buy from several manufacturers. New marketing programs involving promotion, channels of distribution, and emphasis required.	Addition of new product lines makes it possible to attract new classes of customers, especially where previously incomplete line made it necessary for certain classes of customers to buy from several manufacturers. New marketing programs involving promotion, channels of distribution, and emphasis required. If company is the first to use the new technology, coordinated marketing program may mean entirely new markets.
With major design modification of a product, is usually a strengthened market, because the sales department has new ideas to promote.	Replacement product usually lends itself to a remerchandising campaign resulting in greater penetration of existing markets.	If new product will be used by existing customers, the hold on them will be strengthened, especially if new product relates in some manner to existing product line.	If new product will be used by existing customers, the hold on them will be strengthened, especially if new product relates in some manner to existing product line. If company is the first to use the new technology, significant market gain may result.
Positive market change likely to result; however, some adverse market parameters could hold sales constant.	Product changes drastic enough to change market penetration. Example (possible little effect on market): synthetic resin instead of shellac in Johnson's Glo-Coat in 1950.	Not applicable.	Not applicable.
Major design modification. Example: IBM Selectric Typewriter.	Replacement of an existing product by new but related technology. Example: replacing tube-type portable radio with transistorized model.	Diversification: addition of a new product line (could be a new company introducing the product) involving existing technology, but new to the company. Examples: Bulova Accutron watches, Tensor lamps, G.E. computers.	Diversification or product line expansion using new technology. Involves development and/or expansion of the new technology.

NEWNESS ⟶

versely, how one can have or achieve new markets without a new product. Analysis of this figure will help the engineering and research manager to arrive at "sounder" business decisions in the new product area.

In a somewhat similar way, a relationship can be established between product newness and fabrication process newness, as well as a relationship between process newness and increasing market newness. The matrix illustrating increasing product newness versus increasing process newness is shown in Table 1-2.

There are interrelationships and interfaces between design and marketing, between marketing and production, and between production and design. This can be shown as an innovative three-dimensional matrix as illustrated in Fig. 1-6. Two of the outside interfaces have been shown in the previous illustrations.

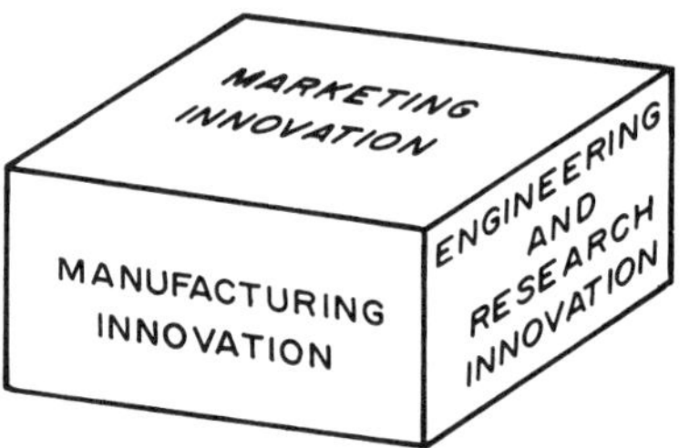

Fig. 1-6. Engineering and research manufacturing-market matrix. *Source:* D. W. Karger and R. G. Murdick, "Product Design, Marketing, and Manufacturing Innovation," *California Management Review* (Winter, 1966).

Some years ago, a study of eighty companies by Booz, Allen, and Hamilton (management consultants) disclosed that only one new product idea out of forty, on the average, is successful. Even when the idea reaches the market in the form of a new commercial product, it still has a hazardous existence. A study of 27,000 consumer and industrial products produced in 1964 was conducted by the staff of *Machine Design* magazine; they reported that four out of five products failed to even go over the break-even point.[24] The fact that many new products fail is supported by many other surveys. Failures ranged from television sets to catsup bottles. Figure 1-7 shows approximately how new product ideas fail in relationship to the five stages in the evolution of a new product idea. Each step or stage is a management decision point and, as shown in the graphical presentation, about half of the ideas existing at the beginning of the step are eliminated during its execution. (A preliminary step that is basic to new product evolution, but which is not indicated on this chart, is that of the exploration or search for new product ideas.)

[24] "New Products Called Risky But Necessary," *Machine Design* (December 22, 1966).

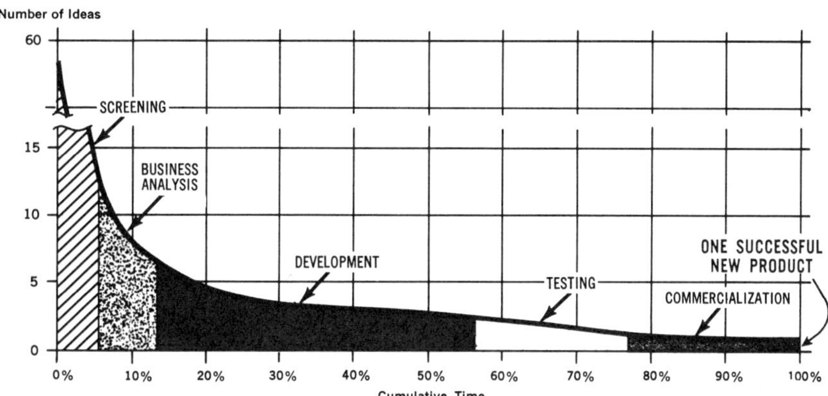

Fig. 1-7. Mortality of new product ideas by stage of evolution for 51 companies. *Source:* Booz-Allen & Hamilton Inc.

THE ROLE OF ENGINEERING AND RESEARCH WITHIN AN ORGANIZATION

Definition and Scope of E & R

The vast majority of government R & D dollars goes into engineering. Most of today's basic research is accomplished on the campuses of our country's colleges and universities. This was true in the past and is still true today. The only real exception was the secret Manhattan project. The associations formed then now account for half of the basic research done in the United States today. Perhaps it should also be mentioned that the Manhattan project certainly involved a host of university professors.

In 1953, industry performed about three-quarters of the nation's R & D—still controlled most of its own research. Over 60 cents of every dollar that industry spent in its laboratories came from corporate earnings. By 1968, the proportion was reversed. It is now the government that is supplying the 60 cents. (Industry's portion in 1968 was about 34 percent.)

The character of research in industry is changing—again because of the large flow of government funds and consequent government establishment of priorities. Even though a pattern and direction has not yet evolved, the relation between government and industry with respect to research is becoming a matter of great concern.

Although the scientific revolution is more than three centuries old, it was not until a little more than fifty years ago that a few pioneer corporations set out to organize their own search for new knowledge. They believed that this kind of risk-taking might turn out to be profitable. By 1941, industrial laboratories had been seeded all across the country and the World War II victories that were won in the laboratories of Britain and the United

Table 1-2—Manufacturing versus

INCREASING PROCESS NEWNESS →			
New - to - the - world manufacturing processes. Examples: "Float" plate glass. High energy metals forming. Use of lasers.	Not applicable.	Not applicable.	Not applicable.
Introduction of a new type of processing. Examples: Replacing electromechanical with electronic switching (assistance from engineering required). New products designed by engineering) to either expand existing line or begin a new line.	Not applicable.	Not applicable.	Not applicable.
Major modification of existing processing methods and/or materials. Example: batch vs. continuous production.	Not normally applicable. No change in basic product or its characteristics but changes in quantity or cost projections may necessitate reprocessing.	Not normally applicable.	Not normally applicable.
Minor modification of existing plant processing (materials and/or methods).	Minor modification in processing often made with consequent minor effect upon cost and/or quality.	No change in basic product characteristics, but minor changes in manufacturing methods to keep costs in line.	Production costs may increase or decrease. Major manufacturing process changes not usually required. Volume may increase and reduce costs.
No processing change.	No change in product or manufacturing.	Not applicable.	Not applicable.
	No change.	Product characteristics remain the same, but changes in components, formulation, production techniques, etc., to keep costs in line and quality at the same relative level.	Minor design modification. Improvements in product characteristics to yield greater utility to customers and/or increase merchandisability. Example: Addition of side-burn trimmer to Sunbeam electric shaver.

INCREASING PRODUCT

[25] D. W. Karger and R. G. Murdick, "Product Design, Marketing, and Manufacturing Innovation." Reprinted from the *California Management Review,* Vol. IX, No. 2 (Winter 1966). Copyright 1966 by the Regents of the University of California.

Engineering and Research[25]

Not applicable. Could be involved, but not usually.	Could be involved, but not usually.	Could be involved.	Required.
May be required.	May be required.	New - to - the - company processing or major modification is usually required.	Often required, sometimes in combination with above.
Major changes in processing usually involved and often is one of the major reasons for design modification. Cost quality, and/or product characteristics affected.	Major modification (or introduction of new processing) is required.	Major modification (or introduction of new processing) is required.	Major modification (or introduction of new processing) is required.
Major change in process usually involved.	Not applicable.	Not applicable.	Not applicable.
Not applicable.	Not applicable.	Not applicable.	Not applicable.
Major design modification. Example: IBM Selectric Typewriter.	Replacement of existing product by new but related technology. Example: Replacing tube-type portable radio with transistorized model.	Diversification: addition of new product or product line (could be new company introducing product) involving existing technology but new to the company. Examples: Bulova Accutron watches, Tensor lamps, G.E. computers.	Diversification or product line expansion using new technology. Involves development and /or expansion of the new technology. Examples: G.E. nuclear power plants. Douglas's rocket system.

NEWNESS ⟶

States dramatically changed both the character and significance of research and development in the postwar world.

The idea that R & D efforts could be profitable was emphasized by Dr. Max Tishler in a speech, when he said: "The concept that research can be harnessed for the benefit of industry and the economy is relatively new. Scientific research, long the exclusive province of the universities, has extended from the campus into the laboratories of industry. Scientists have learned that this new home can also be congenial and stimulating to the inquiring mind. In industry they find commensurate fulfillment and recognition, plus the new experience of translating the fruits of research into the satisfaction of human needs. On the side of industry, corporations have learned how to nurture the organized quest for knowledge for their own welfare and economy."[26]

If research had not been productive, corporations would never have supported it. Industry has learned that an enormous amount of research can be carried out for profit. Research and technological innovation have been a major factor in our postwar economic growth—probably America's most valuable asset in the highly competitive struggle for world markets.

Responsibilities of the E & R Organization

"The question is being asked with increasing persistence as to whether our priorities for research are leading to the placement of a disproportionate amount of our scientific and technical resources in line with the government's objectives. It appears that Switzerland, Sweden, Japan, and West Germany, unmotivated by Sputnik and unburdened by the needs of space and defense, spend a higher percentage of their gross national product than we do on R & D"[26] (for the private sector of the economy). Which policy will result in our country's capacity to maintain its broad leadership in in research? The Defense Department's claims of spin-offs appear to many to be unsubstantiated, while others feel that they are substantial.

Tishler also warns of another danger from present priorities. "Federal expenditures for research are endangering the future of industrial research and development by weakening the incentives for private investment in corporate laboratories. Now that three out of four dollars spent on R & D come from taxes, it is increasingly difficult to find a discovery untouched by public funds at some point during its development. If the government takes the position that we cannot permit a private company to have property rights in any such discovery, no matter how much of its own money the company risks in the research and development effort needed to turn it into a marketable product, we shall surely find companies less and less interested in taking that risk. Clearly, if all discoveries were in the public

[26] Excerpts from a speech entitled "The Government's Role and the Future of Discovery" by Dr. Max Tishler, President of Merck, Sharp & Dohme, delivered to the Society of Chemical Industry, September 26, 1963.

domain, there would be little incentive for private enterprise to make large investments for the development and commercialization of new products and for the support of the huge industrial laboratories that are among our most valued national assets."[27]

J. J. Servan-Schreiber has another view of the investment by the federal government in R & D that should not be overlooked. First, he emphasizes the contribution and role played by the United States government in *key* areas such as aviation, space, electronics, etc. This is then compared to the very much smaller contribution and role of the French government. Finally he concludes:

> We can now see how this dynamic cumulative process that characterizes today's America actually works:
>
> 1. Great size permits the development of an advanced scientific potential.
> 2. This potential in turn pushes the firm into new areas and thereby places it in a position of leadership.
> 3. The firm becomes useful to the government for carrying out various projects, and wins government contracts and tax-supported research grants.
> 4. This in turn increases its profit potential and its growth—the circle becomes a self-generating spiral.[28]

He further concludes that nothing of consequence would happen if the U. S. environment were not favorable. This favorable environment includes the education of its citizens and the talent of American industry—its knowledge of management and its ability to accept and master change.

The Vital Role of Engineering

The role of E & R within the company is to contribute to the profitability of the business (or the advancement of a nonprofit organization) by providing technical support in the formulation and implementation of the organization's objectives. To a great extent, the role of E & R is carried out through new product development activities.

Figure 1-8 illustrates the new product process from the Board of Directors all the way through to production and commercialization. The chart delineates the major phases of corporate activity, however it can be applied to virtually any kind of an organization.

The solid thin line flowing from "Sales" to "Corporate Objectives" indicates the contributions that sales make to the establishment of corporate objectives. The broken thin line between "Sales" and "Ideas" suggests the communication that should exist between sales and the E & R organization in the area of inspiring and/or evaluating ideas. The relative weights of the outlined dollar lines indicate the fact that new projects become progressively more expensive as they approach the production of commercialization stage.

The diamonds are major areas of corporate decision, and only corporate

[27] *Ibid.*

[28] J. J. Servan-Schreiber, *The American Challenge* (New York: Atheneum, 1968).

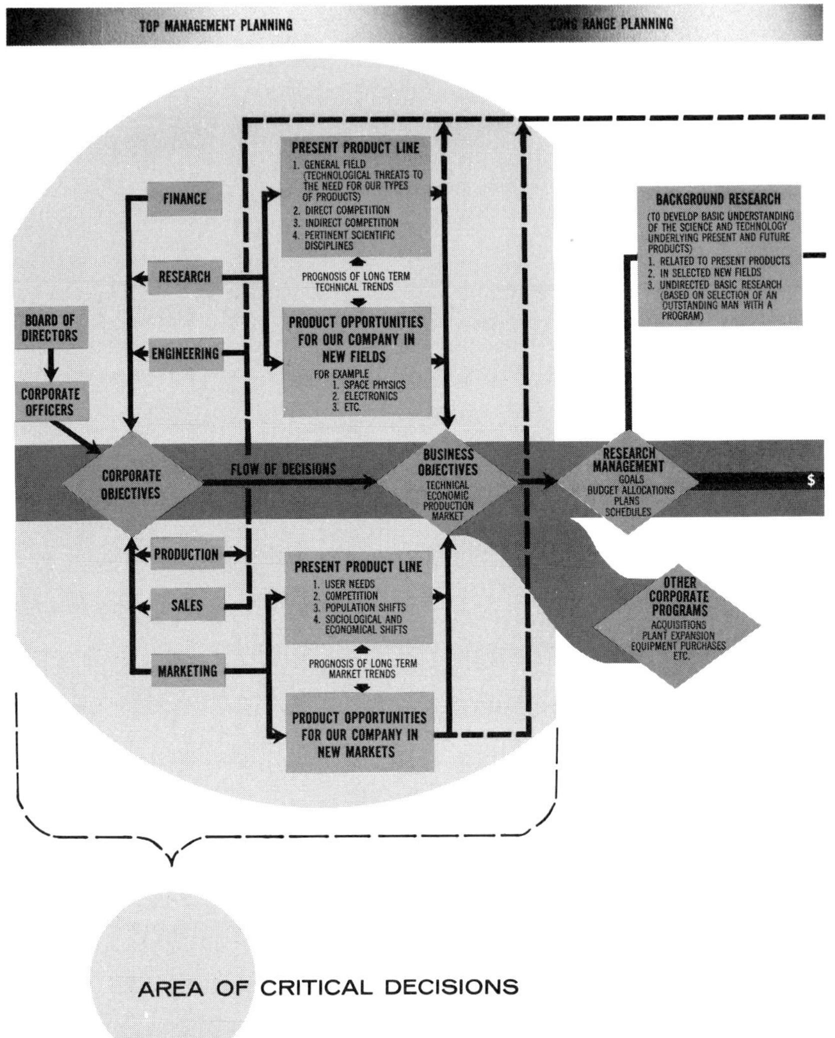

Fig. 1-8. Planning and management of Research & Development—integrated with Columbus

management can exercise this ultimate responsibility. However, top-level management seeks both internal and external help in meeting these responsibilities.

Note that the E & R activity participates in the very early stages of the process, and continues through to the very end. Most of the major activities will be examined separately later in this text. However, an understand-

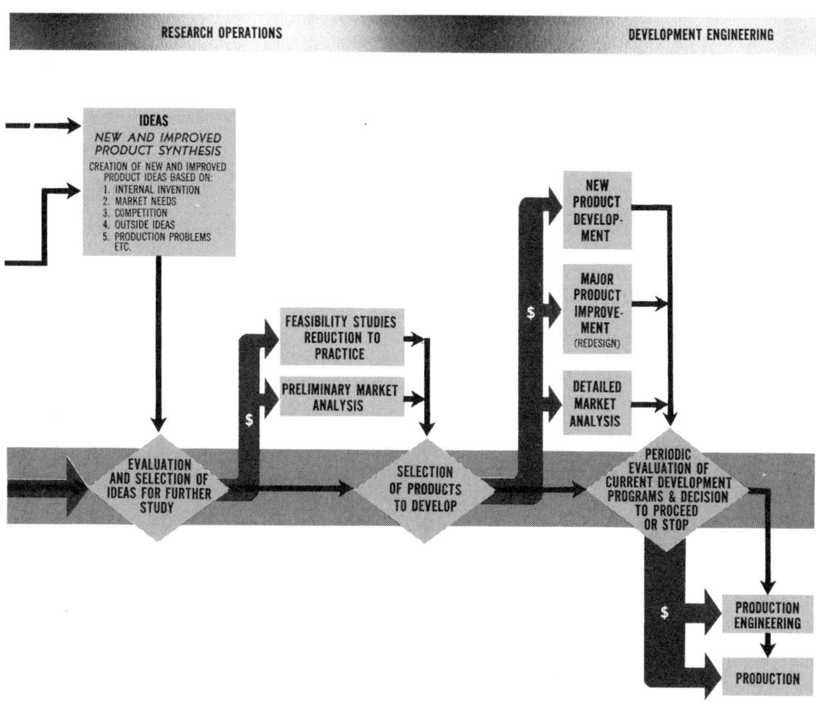

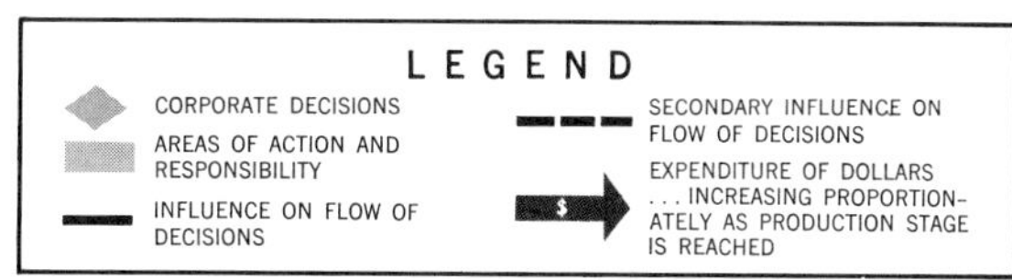

corporate objectives and overall operations. *Source:* Courtesy of Battelle Memorial Institute, Laboratories.

ing of the overall process as evidenced by the chart should be gained at this point for a better understanding of the material that will follow.

It cannot be overemphasized that the technical manager of today must be as aware of the sociological and psychological factors as he is of economics, or history, or managerial concepts. In essence, we have set the scene for a further discussion of the management of the technical function.

BIBLIOGRAPHY

ADAMS, WALTER. "The Military-Industrial Complex and the New Industrial State," *American Economic Review,* May, 1968.

ALGER, JOHN R. M., and HAYS, CARL V. *Creative Synthesis in Design.* Englewood Cliffs, N.J.: Prentice-Hall, Inc., 1964.

AMATAI, ETZIONI. "Chaos in Science," *Commonweal,* 84:494, July 9, 1965.

ANSOFF, H. IGOR. *Corporate Strategy.* New York, N.Y.: McGraw-Hill Book Company, 1965.

ASIMOW, MORRIS. *Introduction to Design.* Englewood Cliffs, N.J.: Prentice-Hall, Inc., 1962.

AZRAEL, JEREMY R. *Managerial Power and Soviet Politics.* Cambridge, Mass.: Harvard University Press, 1966.

BAKER, WILLIAM O. "Broad Base of Science," *The New York Times,* January 8, 1968.

BARZUN, JACQUES, and GRAFF, HENRY F. *The Modern Researcher.* New York, N.Y.: Harcourt, Brace & World, Inc., 1962.

"Big Money and High Politics of Science," *Atlantic Monthly,* August, 1965.

BOULDING, KENNETH. *The Meaning of the 20th Century.* New York, N.Y.: Harper & Row, Publishers, 1964.

BROOKS, HARVEY. "Nation Turning to Science to Spur Economic Growth," *The New York Times,* January 8, 1968.

BROUTON, HENRY J. *Principles of Development Economics.* Englewood Cliffs, N.J.: Prentice-Hall, Inc., 1965.

CANNON, J. THOMAS. *Business Strategy and Policy.* New York, N.Y.: Harcourt, Brace & World, Inc., 1968.

DANILORE, VICTOR J. "The Not-For-Profit Research Institutes," *Industrial Research,* February, 1966.

———. "25 Billion for Research," *Industrial Research,* January, 1968.

DEAN, BURTON V. Evaluating, Selecting, and Controlling R & D Projects, AMA Research Study 89. New York, N.Y.: American Management Association, Inc., 1968.

DECARLO, CHARLES R. "Invention is Feeding on Itself," *The New York Times,* January 8, 1968.

DECHARDIN, PIERRE TEILHARD. *The Future of Man.* New York, N.Y.: Harper & Row, Publishers, 1964.

DESIMONE, DANIEL V. "Invention, The First Step, Is Often The Most Difficult," *The New York Times,* January 8, 1968.

FRISCH, BRUCE H. "Brawl for Science Dollar," *Science Digest,* October, 1967.

GALBRAITH, JOHN K. *The New Industrial State.* Boston, Mass.: Houghton Mifflin Company, 1967.

Goals for Americans, The Report of the President's Commission on National Goals. Englewood Cliffs, N.J.: Prentice-Hall, Inc., 1960.

GREENBERG, D. S. "LBJ Directive: He Says Spread the Research Dollar," *Science,* 149: 1483–5, September 24, 1965.

———. "The Midwest: New Arrangement for Argonne Holds Promise of Greater Financial Aid for Region," *Science,* 145: 749–51, November 6, 1964.

HALLIGAN, C. W. "The Role of Government in Non-Profit Research Organizations," *Industrial Research,* July-August, 1963.

HANSEN, HARRY L. *Marketing: Text Techniques and Cases,* 3rd ed. Homewood, Ill.: Richard D. Irwin, Inc., 1967.

HAYDEN, SPENCER. "A Look at the Year 2000 A.D.," *Rensselaer Review,* Rensselaer Polytechnic Institute, April, July, and October, 1967.

HERTZ, DAVID B. "Science Giving New Tools for Thought," *The New York Times,* January 8, 1968.

HEYEL, CARL. *Handbook of Industrial Research.* New York, N.Y.: Reinhold Publishing Corp., 1959.

"High Energy Physics: Major Fight Brewing as Midwestern Legislators Take Stand on MURA Accelerator," *Science,* 142: 208–10, October 11, 1963.

JACKSON, THOMAS W., and SPURLOCK, JACK M. *Research and Development Management.* Homewood, Ill.: Dow Jones-Irwin, Inc., 1966.

JOHNSON, HAROLD W. "Education for Management and Technology in the 1970's," *Science,* May 10, 1968.

KARGER, D. W., and JACK, A. B. *Problems of Small Business in Developing and Exploiting New Products.* Troy, N.Y.: Rensselaer Polytechnic Institute School of Management, 1963.

KARGER, D. W. and MURDICK, R. G. "Product Design, Marketing and Manufacturing Innovation," *California Management Review,* Winter, 1966.

———. "Product Planning," *Machine Design,* Vol. 38:8, April 13, 1961.

KOROL, ALEXANDER. *Soviet Research and Development: Its Organization, Personnel and Funds.* Cambridge, Mass.: The M.I.T. Press, 1965.

KRANZBERG, MELVIN. "Research Shifting to Social Problems," *The New York Times,* January 8, 1968.

"Management Looks at R & D," *Chemical Engineering Progress,* April, 1966.

MANSFIELD, EDWIN. "Research and Technological Change," *Industrial Research,* February, 1964.

MATOUSEK, ROBERT. *Engineering Design.* New York, N.Y.: Interscience Publishers, Inc., 1963.

MURDICK, R. G. "Managerial Planning," *Machine Design,* Vol. 38:8, April 13, 1961.

National Science Foundation. *Reviews of Data on Research and Development,* NSF 61–9, No. 26. February, 1961.

———. *Federal Funds for Science XI,* NSF Survey. Washington, D.C.: U.S. Government Printing Office, 1963.

"New Products Called Risky But Necessary," *Machine Design,* December 22, 1966.

NEWTON, NORMAN T. *An Approach to Design.* Cambridge, Mass.: Addison-Wesley Press, Inc., 1951.

O'BRIEN, FRANK. *Crisis in World Communism (Marxism in Search of Efficiency).* New York, N.Y.: The Free Press, 1965.

PARSEGIAN, V. L. *Industrial Management in the Atomic Age.* Reading, Mass.: Addison-Wesley Publishing Co., Inc., 1965.

QUINN, J. B. "The Challenge of Effective Planning for Research," *Chemical Engineering News,* January 9, 1961.

REEVES, E. DUER. *Management of Industrial Research.* New York, N.Y.: Reinhold Publishing Corp., 1967.

———. "Research & Development: Is Business Getting Its Money's Worth Out of Research?", *Forbes Magazine,* Vol. 102, No. 10 (November 15, 1968), 34.

RICHMAN, BARRY M. *Soviet Management.* Englewood Cliffs, N.J.: Prentice-Hall, Inc., 1965.

———. *Soviet Management with Significant American Comparisons.* Englewood Cliffs, N.J.: Prentice-Hall, Inc., 1965.

ROMAN, DANIEL D. *Research and Development Management: The Economics and Administration of Technology.* New York, N.Y.: Appleton-Century-Crofts, 1968.

"Russia Upgrades Its Managers," *Business Week,* April 16, 1966.

SCHMOOKLER, JACOB. *Invention and Economic Growth.* Cambridge, Mass.: Harvard University Press, 1966.

SCHUMPETER, JOSEPH A. *Capitalism, Socialism, and Democracy.* New York, N.Y.: Harper & Brothers, 1942.

SERVAN-SCHREIBER, J. J. *The American Challenge.* New York, N.Y.: Atheneum Problishers, 1968.

SMITH, WILLIAM D. "In the World of Research, U.S. Has the Biggest Empire," *The New York Times,* January 8, 1968.

Stanford Research Institute. *An Exploratory Study of the Structure and Dynamics of the R & D Industry.* June, 1964.

TISCHLER, MAX. 1968. "Secrets of High Moment." An address before The Royal Society, London, England: November 19, 1968.

TRUNDLE, ROBERT C. "The Effective Rapid Scientific Advances on Profits," *Advanced Management Journal,* October, 1964.

TYBOUT, RICHARD A. *Economics of Research and Development.* Columbus, Ohio: Ohio State University Press, 1965.

WALKER, CHARLES R. *Technology, Industry, and Man.* New York, N.Y.: McGraw-Hill Book Company, 1968.

WEISS, HERBERT K. "Some Growth Considerations of Research and Development and the National Economy," *Management Science,* January, 1965.

WILSON, WARREN E. *Concepts of Engineering System Design.* New York, N.Y.: McGraw-Hill Book Company, 1965.

CHAPTER 2

The Nature of Managing

MANAGERS AND ORGANIZATIONS

The common formalized style of group activity in business is the hierarchal arrangement of responsibility, decision making, and communication. This pyramid arrangement has one manager at the top who is essentially the ultimate decision maker. Other managers report to him and, in turn, other managers report to them. Finally, at the bottom of the pyramid are the nonmanagers or functional individual contributors. Interwoven in the pyramid there are also staff managers and individual functional workers. This arrangement is so common that most practical businessmen have never thought of any other arrangement for organizing group activity.

The most obvious difference between managers and nonmanagers is that a manager is responsible for human resources in the accomplishment of his objectives. The manager is a communication center through which organizational objectives, policies, plans, and progress are passed downward while reports of progress and problems are passed upward. While there are many informal communication networks that permit rapid action and adaptability to new information, the managers occupy unique and important positions. Failure of a manager to apprise his group promptly of broad objectives, organizational goals, organizational changes, or other matters that members of the organization believe are important can have a devastating effect on group morale and cohesion.

The manager has often been viewed primarily as a decision maker. In modern organizations, he makes those decisions (1) that involve a specified level of resource allocation, or (2) that his subordinates refer to him in special cases of risk or broad impact on other organizational components, or (3) that represent conflicts among those reporting to him that cannot be resolved by "integration." Integration is the full development of conflicting positions, common analysis, and joint recognition of a good solution of differences.

It should be understood, however, that nonmanagers of the knowledge worker variety, such as engineers and scientists, often fill the role of decision makers. Also, it should be understood that decision making normally consumes but a small fraction of the manager's or executive's time.

The manager is often described as one who accomplishes his objectives through the work of others, his subordinates, in the hierarchal organization. Thus his work must be primarily intellectual rather than "hands on." For example, the manager of engineering and research would not normally

The Work of a Functional Individual Contributor	The Work of a Professional Manager
1. Responsible for *achieving* the objectives of the specific position.	1. Responsible for the *achievement* of all objectives of the component; responsible for his personal Professional Managerial contribution to the achievement of component objectives.
2. *Proposes* changes in the over-all objectives and broad function of the specific position and *participates* in their determination; *recommends* objectives for other positions, for the component and for the business.	2. Responsible for *deciding* on the over-all objectives and broad function of all positions in the component, except the Managerial position; *proposes* over-all objectives and broad function for Managerial position and for component and participates in their determination; *recommends* objectives for next larger component and for the business.
3. Includes responsibility, as assigned, to *recommend* and *suggest* to Manager on decisions involving other positions, for example: organizing, staffing, appraising.	3. Responsible for the organization of positions in the component; for example, designing and grouping positions, staffing, appraising, removing for cause (within authority).
4. *Proposes* policies and procedures for the component and the business and *participates* in their formulation.	4. Responsible for deciding on policies and procedures for the component within policies and procedures of the next larger component and the business; *proposes* policies and procedures for next larger component and for the business and participates in their formulation.
5. *Interprets* policies of own component and the business as these affect the responsibilities of the specific position, and of other positions as required.	5. *Interprets*, to those in the component, policies of larger component and the business as these affect the work of the component.
6. Responsible for *deciding* on specific objectives, plans and schedules of the position to meet agreed upon over-all objectives and broad function of the position; *recommends* objectives, plans and schedules for the component and for the business; can have responsibility for *deciding* on dispatching the work of other positions, when this responsibility has been designed into the specific position.	6. Responsible for *deciding* on objectives, plans and schedules for the component within agreed upon over-all objectives and broad function of the component; *recommends* objectives, plans and schedules for next larger component and for the business.
7. When designed into the specific position, has responsibility for guiding and counseling; and for *inspecting*, *measuring* and *evaluating* the work results of others; has responsibility to *recommend* on appraisals of others to the Manager to whom they report on request of Manager.	7. Responsible for *deciding* on appraisals of all those reporting to him in the component; can have responsibility to *recommend* on appraisals of others to the Manager to whom they report.
8. *Develops* and *recommends* standards for measuring work of the specific position; has responsibility for *recommending* standards for measuring work of other positions, as requested by the Manager; measures results of the work of the specific position.	8. Responsible for *deciding* on standards for measuring work of all positions in the component; *develops* and *recommends* standards for measuring work of the Managerial position; can have responsibility for *recommending* standards for measuring work of other positions in the business; measures results of the work of the component and of the Managerial position.
9. Responsible for *decisions* designed as necessary to achieve the objectives of the specific position, and for its contribution to the component, and the business.	9. Responsible for *integrating* or resolving conflicts in work occurring between positions in the component; and of personal conflicts, as required by the work.
10. Responsible for *appraising* own strengths and weaknesses; for *evaluating* and *deciding* on *own* self-development plans after receiving appropriate suggestions from the Manager of the component; responsible for *teaching*, *advising*, and *counseling* in his functional specialty as requested by others or as designed into the specific position.	10. Responsible for *creating* climate for the self-development of all in the component; for getting those in the component voluntarily to *appraise* their own strengths and weaknesses; responsible for *suggesting* plans for their own self-development; responsible for appraising his own strengths and weaknesses; for *evaluating* and *deciding* on *own* self-development plans after receiving appropriate suggestions from the Manager of the next larger component; responsible for *teaching* the work of managing to Managers in his component, and to other individuals in the component to the extent required by their work.
11. Responsible for direct communication with sources and recipients of necessary information, keeping Manager of component and others informed where their responsibilities are significantly affected.	11. Responsible for direct communication with sources and recipients of necessary information, keeping Manager of next larger component and others informed where their responsibilities are significantly affected.

Fig. 2-1. Some distinguishing characteristics. *Source: Professional Management in General Electric, Book Four, The Work of a Functional Individual Contributor* (New York: General Electric Co., 1959); p. 31.

perform lab tests or engineering design analyses. He might find it necessary to spot-check, but he should not be indulging in lengthy engineering design by himself. His primary job is to see to it that the work is done properly, economically, and on time to satisfy the business goals of the organization. An extension of this idea is that the engineering manager's fundamental role is not to conduct engineering but to contribute to the profitability of the company. Differences between the work of the manager and the individual contributor as developed by the General Electric Company are shown in Fig. 2-1.

THE BASIC FUNCTIONS OF MANAGERS

The basic functions of managers are the same in all organized activity. This does not mean that a manager of marketing may easily change over to become manager of engineering. It means that the functions performed in each case are the same, but the technical environment is different. This book deals primarily with the functions of managers in the engineering and research setting.

Despite some apparent variations, the functions of a manager as determined by different researchers are well agreed upon. These functions are shown in several forms below:

Planning	Planning	Planning	Planning
Organizing	Organizing	Organizing	Organizing
	Staffing		
Integrating	Activating	Directing	Initiating
	Coordinating	Motivating	
Measuring		Measuring	
	Controlling	Correcting	Controlling

The functions, both general and technical, are usually set forth in the manager's position description. (See Fig. 2-2.)

Planning

It is unfortunately true that most organizations operate on a crises basis. Managers seem to spend much of their time putting out "fires" instead of anticipating future events and making preparations to meet them effectively. Planning is the means with which the good manager guides the organization to prevent continuous short-range blind expediency. Planning is intellectual activity that precedes action. It is based on forecasts of alternative future events.

Planning precedes all other management functions and is the first step in carrying out the functions. In order to organize group activities, planning must be the first step. In order to direct, motivate, or integrate, the manager must first plan by establishing objectives and courses of action. In order to control, he must measure and take corrective actions. Standards of performance are necessary for meaningful measurement. Methods of implementing possible corrective actions must be planned ahead.

Organizing

Organizing is the process of defining and grouping the activities of the business, establishing responsibilities for the people who will carry out these activities, and setting forth the working relationships among these people. The structural and behavioral aspects of organizing with application to engineering and research components are discussed in Part II of this book.

Organizing requires that the manager ask and answer the following questions:

1. What work is to be accomplished and why?

VICE PRESIDENT–ENGINEERING AND RESEARCH

General Responsibilities

Under the direction of the President, be responsible for engineering in its broad aspects as it relates to the entire scope of the Company's activities. Direct the line supervision of the Company's central research, design, and development program. Furnish functional guidance to engineering and quality control activities in the various divisions of the Company.

Specific Duties

1. Organization Development. Develop and direct his supporting organization; and establish the duties and responsibilities for positions reporting directly to him.
2. Functional Guidance. Be responsible for functional guidance of all the Company's engineering activities.
3. Quality Standards and Control. Be responsible for seeing that quality and performance standards are established for all products sold by the Company; and be responsible for functional guidance of all quality control activities.
4. Research, Design, and Development. Direct the establishment and administration of a company-wide research, design, and development program to insure leadership in our fields of activity. Be responsible for the Research Laboratories. Be responsible for design and development of new products not closely allied with the work of, or assigned to, a product division. Work closely with Sales and Operations in matters pertaining to product development as related to the Company's sales position.
5. Technical Services to Divisions. Maintain adequate organization and facilities to render company-wide services in the fields of metallurgy, ceramics, chemistry, physics, and other similar technical fields involved in the Company's operations.
6. Technical Contacts. See that contacts are maintained with trade associations, professional societies, and educational institutions, as regards technical affairs, and with other outside technical organizations.
7. Engineering Personnel Development. Be functionally responsible for the technical development of engineering personnel.
8. Technical Information. Promote and be functionally responsible for insuring proper technical content of publications and oral presentations about the Company's products.

Fig. 2-2. Position description for Vice-President for Research and Development. *Source:* Reprinted by permission of the publisher from C. L. Bennet, *Defining the Manager's Job*, American Management Association Research Study No. 33 (New York: AMA, 1958), pp. 182–183. © 1958 by The American Management Association, Inc.

2. When is it to be done?
3. Where is it to be done?
4. What alternative ways are there for the work to be divided, classified, and combined into manageable packages?
5. Who will do the work?
6. What will be the relationships between individuals and components?

Directing, Motivating, and Integrating

Each manager must provide direction for the course of activities of his organization in order to fulfill company objectives. This direction is carried out by communicating fully with individuals in his organization, reflecting their views to higher management, and integrating the needs of individuals with the purposes of the company for the mutual benefit of both. It is thus a principal function of a manager to build a productive working climate.

Measuring, Controlling, Correcting

The manager must set standards of performance for his organization. The modern approach to establishing measurement is to have the individual participate in establishing his own goals and schedules; these agreed upon goals and schedules become the standard for measurement. The manager, in establishing goals, schedules, and objectives for his subordinates, takes into account organizational standards and objectives. The employee's personal goals and objectives must be in reasonable alignment with those of the organization. In intellectual activities such as engineering and research, it is difficult to establish objective measures of quality of work. Approaches to measuring performance in engineering and research are discussed in Chapter 13.

THE PROCESS OF MANAGING

The functions of a manager are related in an activity system that forms the *process* of managing. This process is best described by a diagram such as Fig. 2-3. It is important to recognize that the management process breaks down when the flow of information is interrupted between any two activities. The most common types of breakdowns occur because a manager withholds information on company objectives and plans from members of his organization or fails to insure feedback on performance from his people.

The lifeline of the management process is the flow of information. Some authorities believe that, at least in organizational components composed primarily of professional people, information flow is the necessary and sufficient condition for coordination, integration, and control. While management information systems (MIS) are usually planned on a company-wide basis, each functional manager must be concerned with developing that part of the system which serves him. An MIS in engineering and research is a system of procedures for planned collection, analysis, and dissemination of information for planning and implementing technical activities. The design of an MIS starts with asking questions such as:

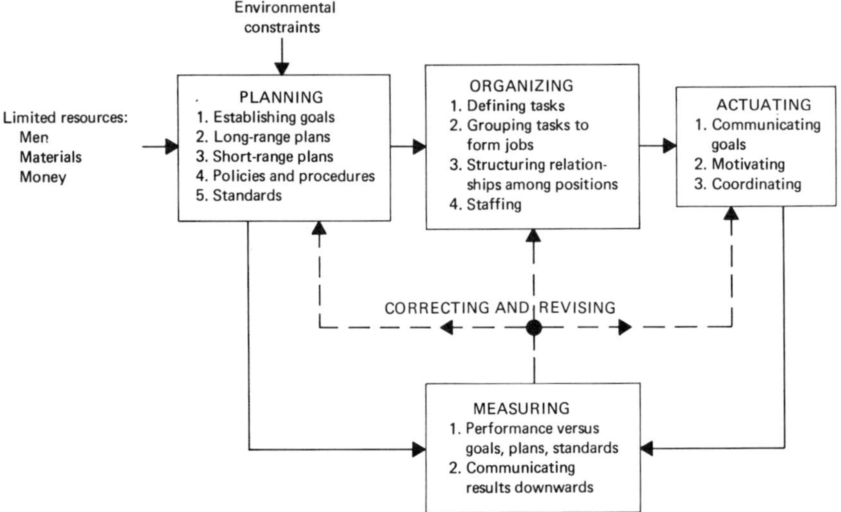

Fig. 2-3. The management process.

1. What kinds of planning, operating, and control problems does each manager face?
2. What data and information (processed data) do managers need to identify and solve their problems?
3. What is the most desirable and economically feasible data base for the MIS?
4. When do managers need the various types of information—real-time data, batch basis data, or data recall?

It is apparent from the above that storage and processing requirements are such that only the development of computers has made possible significant advances in information systems.

THE MANAGERIAL MIND

From the previous discussion, it might appear that anyone intellectually endowed could follow the precepts of managing and, theoretically, become a good manager. However, a cluster of certain attitudes and characteristics also appear to be necessary if a person is to be a successful manager—the evidence regarding this is overwhelming. Managers are dedicated to the accomplishment of organizational goals. They have a role to play before their subordinates in which they attempt to bridge the gap between the demands of higher management and the needs of the members in their particular organization.

The manager sees himself as a focal point of group confidence. In this role, he must maintain a constructive, indeed, optimistic outlook at all times. In a sense, his role is that of a teacher who must instill confidence in his people by encouraging their self-development and tolerating learning errors—however, he must also know when and how to be intolerant. If he permits serious failure in a subordinate, he himself will inevitably fail.

Managers are alert to interpersonal relationships within the total organization and seek to protect their own organizational component from external attacks. Yet the most typical characteristic of the manager is his dedication to the total organization.

More specific guides to playing the role of a manager for growth and advancement are given in Chapter 19.

SUMMARY

This chapter is a very brief introduction to the nature of management of all organizations. This book represents an amplification of these concepts in practice in the engineering and research activities of enterprises.

BIBLIOGRAPHY

ALBERS, HENRY H. *Principles of Organization and Management.* 2nd ed. New York, N.Y.: John Wiley & Sons, Inc., 1965.

BEACH, DALE S. *Personnel: The Management of People at Work.* New York, N.Y.: The Macmillan Company, 1965.

BEGED-DOV, AHARON G. "An Overview of Management Science and Information Systems," *Management Science,* August, 1967, pp. B817–29.

CARLSON, WALTER M. "A Management Information System Designed by Managers," *Datamation,* May, 1967, pp. 37–43.

DALTON, MELVILLE. *Men Who Manage.* New York, N.Y.: John Wiley & Sons, Inc., 1959.

DRUCKER, PETER F. *The Effective Executive.* New York, N.Y.: Harper & Row, Publishers, 1967.

EWING, DAVID W. *The Managerial Mind.* New York, N.Y.: The Free Press of Glencoe, 1964.

GREENWOOD, WILLIAM T., ed. *Management and Organizational Behavior Theories: An Interdisciplinary Approach.* Cincinnati, Ohio: South-Western Publishing Co., 1965.

HAMPTON, DAVID R.; SUMMER, CHARLES E., JR.; and WEBBER, ROSS A. *Organizational Behavior and the Practices of Management.* Glenview, Ill.: Scott, Foresman & Company, 1968.

KARGER, DELMAR W., and MURDICK, ROBERT G. "New Challenges and Responsibilities for Technical Managers," *Advanced Management Journal,* April, 1968, pp. 75–82.

MCFARLAND, DALTON E., ed. *Current Issues and Emerging Concepts in Management.* Vol. II. Boston, Mass.: Houghton Mifflin Company, 1966.

REEVES, E. DUER. *Management of Industrial Research.* New York, N.Y.: Reinhold Publishing Corp., 1967.

SCHODERBEK, PETER P., ed. *Management Systems: A Book of Readings.* New York, N.Y.: John Wiley & Sons, Inc., 1967.

SMALTER, DONALD J. "Management By Priority-of-Challenge," *Chemical Engineering Progress,* June, 1964.

TERRY, GEORGE R. *Principles of Management.* 3rd ed. Homewood, Ill.: Richard D. Irwin, Inc., 1960.

TILLES, SEYMOUR. "The Manager's Job: A Systems Approach," *Harvard Business Review,* January–February, 1963.

"What Is the Manager?", eds., *Harvard Business Review,* November–December, 1964.

CHAPTER 3

Planning the E & R Organization: Structural Logic

FUNDAMENTAL CONCEPTS

Purpose of Organization

The purpose of organizing a group of individuals is to achieve the most effective utilization of resources by the establishment of decision-making and communications processes designed to activate the full potential creativity and productivity of the members of the organization. "Organization is . . . a system of structural interpersonal relations. . . . Individuals are differentiated in terms of authority, status and role with the result that personal interaction is prescribed."[1]

Structural logic of organizations is a mechanistic classification of objectives, activities, positions, and roles designed to achieve clarity of authority, responsibility, and roles so that decision making and communication are expedited. The mechanistic formal organization is a rigid, hierarchical type of structure. Research on organizational behavior, particularly for creative professional people, has indicated that interpersonal relationships and organizational decision making must be quite different from the hierarchical arrangements shown on the company organization charts. However, the formal approach to the development of the E & R organization is useful because it is the first approximation to a rational working organization. Also, it provides a framework for last-resort and emergency decision making and action. The formal organization provides guidelines for the activities of people, without which gross inefficiency and chaos are likely to result.

Before the E & R organization can be effectively planned, top management of the company must first establish overall company goals and objectives. Unfortunately, in "real life" one must often proceed to organize by

[1] R. V. Presthus, "Towards a Theory of Organizational Behavior," *Administrative Science Quarterly* (June 1958).

guessing unstated goals and objectives. For example, what are the stated goals and objectives of the United States? E & R management has the responsibility to provide for:

1. E & R goals and objectives complementary to and supporting those of the firm.
2. A sound plan of organization based on the objectives.
3. Qualified personnel in all key positions.
4. Effective means of control that will permit top executives to delegate wide responsibility and authority, thus freeing themselves to concentrate on broad planning and direction.

The plan of organization must enable all members, individually and collectively, to function most effectively in achieving the common objectives.

Organizational Concepts

The skeleton of all organizations is called the "line" organization and represents the chains of superior-subordinate relationships. *Line* functions are those which are directly concerned with achieving the objectives of the organization. The "line" for line functions is a chain of command that runs from the top of the firm down to the lowest echelon. A typical line organization for a firm whose objectives are to design, produce, and sell products is shown in Fig. 3-1.

"Staff" refers to those individuals and functions that are not in the line-function chain of command. Staff positions do not bear direct responsibility for accomplishing the primary objectives of the organization. All that is not line is staff. The staff activities support the line organization in three capacities.

1. Advisory, to provide advice and counsel.
2. Service, to perform either broad scope work or specialized work.
3. Control, to regulate and constrain the activities of the line.

From an organizational viewpoint, staff positions appear as either personal or specialized.[2] Personal staff is created to provide advice and assistance to an individual manager. A personal staff assistant does not have any specific responsibilities except as assigned by his superior.

The personal staff assistant does not have any *official* authority over the line organization. However, because of his close and personal relationship with his superior (who does have authority over others) he does wield some "undelegated" authority. Subordinates of the manager may officially

[2] "Personal" and "specialized" correspond to "general staff" and "special staff" in the military organization. For an excellent exposition of this subject, see Col. Jack D. Nicholas, Col. George B. Pickett, and Captain (U.S.N.) William O. Spears, Jr., *The Joint and Combined Staff Officer's Manual* (Harrisburg, Pa.: The Stackpole Co., 1959).

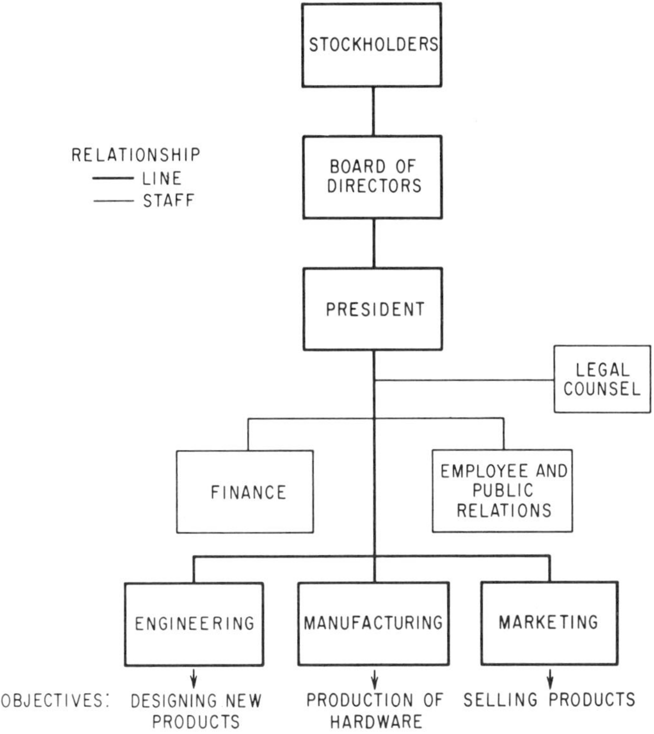

Fig. 3-1. Line organization.

choose either to accept or reject this authority although their actual choice varies with the particular situation. It is a difficult and potentially dangerous situation for all the participants. Because of this, there is a trend in modern management away from personal staff assistants. It is desirable to give every individual definite operations for which he can be held accountable and for which he can be rewarded if they are accomplished successfully.

Specialized staff groups (service personnel) advise, counsel, assist, and serve line personnel at all levels of the organization. Specialized staff groups have definite missions and responsibilities in the areas of research, planning, and measuring. The use of specialized staff is justified on the following grounds.

1. Some highly specialized skills are required which individuals can acquire only through long formal education and training. Line managers often do not have the characteristics or skills needed to obtain such knowledge. More importantly, they do not have the time to gain or to apply all the skills needed in the complex business system of today.

2. Continuous development and evaluation of plans or projects can be accomplished by specialized staff. The line manager can then concentrate on operations and utilize the data developed by the specialized staff.
3. Specialized staff can and do provide service and counsel to all members of the line on a continuing basis.
4. The staff may actually perform work *for* the line in specialized areas.

Besides line and staff, the committee is another organizational concept important to the manager. A committee may be either a permanent or temporary group charged with assignments that are usually broad in scope. The principal advantage of committees is that they permit an interchange of ideas and a judicious deliberation on problems considered too important, too difficult, or too broad for any one individual.

While the objections to using committees are numerous, the following are considered most significant:

1. There is a diffusion of responsibility and lack of accountability of the individual members.
2. Committee recommendations and actions must represent a thinking or decision process that is common to all members; hence, it must be representative of the lowest common denominator.
3. Committees can and do often delay and stifle line action and line initiative, particularly when committee approval of certain line actions is required.

In spite of the objections, committees are a popular form of organization. *In many cases they represent the only immediate and practical action that can be taken.* However, they are also often used as a device to permit a manager to avoid making a personal decision for which he must assume entire responsibility. In his mind, getting a committee to make a recommendation, which he in turn implements, provides an escape from responsibility for poor results and consequences. In reality, he must still bear the responsibility. The E & R manager should always review these facts before creating a committee.

Management rarely evaluates the cost incurred in committee deliberation and associated activities. If this were done realistically and recognition given to the fact that the salary-time charges are actual costs, then fewer committees would exist.

An outgrowth of the committee concept, which overcomes many of their disadvantages, is the "task force." Although a task force is basically a group of people charged with a very specific mission that usually is to be completed in a specified time, it differs from the committee concept not only by having a time limit set for the accomplishment of the objective, but also, and even more importantly, as to the men constituting the task force. The task force group *should* normally be the men who would be involved in accomplishing the mission, or men reporting to them whom *they* have nominated to the task force. The appointment or establishment of the task force emphasizes the mission and *forces* action. Responsibility tends to be more specific in the case of the task force, and institutionalized bureaucratic thinking does not get a chance to set in as with committees.

Centralization and Decentralization of Responsibility

In centralized organizations, all decision making is made at the highest possible level within the company. In a multiplant company having a centralized organization, all basic decisions and policies are made in the central headquarters. Exponents of this thinking believe that better decisions can be reached by having them made by the most *competent* officers in the company, which theoretically would be the highest ranking officers. Obvious theoretical strengths in this approach are:

1. The major decision makers are close to each other and it should, therefore, be easier for them to coordinate their efforts and have their individual decisions support the general effort or mission.
2. Subordinate managers do not need to be as competent as in the decentralized organization since they are not responsible for making major decisions.
3. Since each remote plant or function need not and should not be "self-sufficient," less total staff should be required.
4. Since subordinate managers need not be as competent, and somewhat less total staff is theoretically required, the cost of staffing the organization should be less.
5. Concentration of certain functions such as accounting, engineering, etc., in one place should help eliminate work duplication and make possible the use of better systems and methods.

A majority of modern management organizers favor highly decentralized authority and responsibility. In decentralized organizations, responsibility is delegated as far down as possible to permit individuals directly concerned with the work to make decisions related to their work.

Advantages attributed to the decentralized organization are as follows:

1. Decentralization of authority and decision making results in a more rapid response to changes in the work situation or economic environment.
2. It makes it possible for the decisions to be made by those with the greatest *knowledge* of local conditions.
3. It facilitates the personal development of individuals, and hence results in a "stronger" overall organization.

4. It provides a greater feeling of satisfaction to capable individuals than the centralized organization does.

Companies have achieved success with both the centralized and the decentralized organization approach. Furthermore, some of the nation's larger and older concerns have used each approach more than once. Also, it should be apparent that one could operate part of an organization such as the operation of the manufacturing facilities on a decentralized basis, and other parts such as engineering and accounting on a centralized basis.

Even though the general trend in modern management is towards decentralized organization, some functions of the firm logically continue on a centralized basis; for example, the treasury function is one of these which quite obviously should continue on a centralized basis.

Delegation

Since organizational components in business are formed to conduct activities beyond the capacity of a single individual, tasks must be distributed among the group. In the hierarchical organization, the tasks along with responsibility and authority for accomplishing them are delegated from the top of the organization down through lower echelons by means of subdivision into smaller elements at each level. That is, the E & R manager is given one portion of the total company's program to accomplish. He, in turn, subdivides his work to give a portion to each of the managers who report to him.

The technical manager who has dealt all his life with equipment and experiments where failure in any detail means failure in the final result may have difficulty in extensively delegating authority and responsibility. This fear of losing control of results causes him to attempt to maintain control of all details at all times. The effort conflicts with both the rational formal organization precepts and the behavioral nature of people in organizations.

Besides his fear of losing control, technical managers often have little understanding of the concepts of delegation, authority, responsibility, and accountability. Authority may be considered the "legitimate" right to command and to apply sanctions. Sources of authority are:

1. Institutional—accepted cultural practices
2. Subordinates—flow of acceptance through the organization maintained by the manager's ability to win support through his leadership
3. Organizational relationship—acceptance by members of the organization of the structured positions
4. Legal decree
5. Personal acceptance or consultative authority—subordinate acceptance of either charismatic leadership or specialized technical skill and reputation

6. Identification of members with the group so that through participative decision making, the group is the source of authority
7. Sanctions—the ability to dispense or withhold rewards. In almost all types of organizations, those with authority possess some such sanctions
8. Authority of the situation—consensus on action to be taken as achieved by discussion, mutual understanding, and "integration."

Responsibility is the duty to perform assigned tasks, and when the technical manager delegates responsibility he must also delegate authority along with it. Such authority is the "legitimatized" right to apply the necessary resources to carry out assigned functions. The manager who delegates a portion of his responsibility and authority should, therefore, not interfere with his subordinate's actions unless he wishes to revoke the assignment. While the subordinate is responsible for a task or activity assigned, the manager is always accountable to his superiors for results. That is, responsibility for work may be delegated, but accountability can never be relinquished. If a worker is given a task, every superior in the line above him is accountable to his superior for the performance. To be accountable means to be measured and rewarded or penalized accordingly.

Levels and Span of Management

How many people can a manager effectively direct? The manager's work consists of planning, organizing, initiating, coordinating, and controlling. To fulfill his functions, he must have contacts with his subordinates, with his own manager, and with others in the organization. If those reporting to the manager are doing quite different kinds of work, the manager may have to spend more time with each. However, if the individuals are highly competent professionals such as research workers, less contact between the manager and his people will be required. Furthermore, a manager may be able to manage many people who are doing the same type of work in the same field. The number of people reporting *directly* to a manager is called his span of management; it includes clerical as well as professional and managerial personnel.

The span of management throughout the organization has a very significant effect on the operation of the organization, other than from the decision-making viewpoint. If the span is small at all management levels, it causes many layers of management to be introduced. This is expensive in terms of number of managers required. Communications up and down the line become slow and suffer from greater distortion. Responsibility must be divided into many segments so that there is less responsibility at each level and at each position; consequently, there is less challenge to managers and workers. For these reasons, levels of management should be kept to a minimum. In the General Electric Company, one of the largest companies in the country, there are only six or seven levels from the president's office to the engineer or secretary just starting in at the bottom of the organization. An analysis of the R & D organization structures in the *American Management Association Research Study 72* shows the top R & D manager has a span of management of 6 or more in 40 percent of the 51 charts that show the span. The most frequent span is 5 and the spans vary from 1 to 16. It would be expected that the span would increase for lower levels of management.

Principles of Formal Organization

Some classical guidelines and checkpoints for planning the organization are given here:

1. Every component of the organization must be designed to contribute to the attainment of the company's and component's objectives.
2. The line organization should be established with logical subdivisions so that there is no overlapping or conflict of responsibility. Each position should report to only one other position so that no individual receives orders from more than one person. Individuals, however, may receive advice and assistance from staff.
3. There should be a clear line of authority and responsibility from top to bottom of the organization. Stated another way, there must be a scalar chain of authority. Individuals must have reasonable freedom of communication across the organization provided they keep their manager informed of any actions that may have a significant effect on their components.
4. Levels of management should be kept at a minimum by giving managers as wide a span of management as they can effectively handle.
5. Organization should precede the selection of people, their numbers, and qualifications.
6. Position design should determine the selection of personnel rather than personnel determining the organization. However, the capabilities of acquired and assigned personnel must be recognized. This will inevitably and logically require some adjustments in the preplanned organization.
7. Responsibility *and* authority should be delegated as near the point of action as it is possible to obtain sound decisions.
8. Authority must be delegated which corresponds to delegated responsibility.
9. An individual who delegates responsibility is not relieved of his accountability.
10. Organization planning would emphasize simplicity of work relationships concerning division of work.

11. Positions should be designed so that the work of managing is separated from the functional work.

STRUCTURING THE E & R ORGANIZATION

There are three basic and extremely important considerations in structuring the E & R organization. These are:

1. The subdivision of the work into tasks and regrouping into positions
2. The type of structure and arrangement of positions within the structure
3. The communications and control network, the motivational aspects of the organizational structure and climate, and the degree to which the psychological and social needs of the individuals in the organization are satisfied.

The first two considerations are the subject of this chapter; following chapters deal with the human or behavioral characteristics of organizations. The organization chart itself is only an approximation to the true organizational relationships and grows obsolete rapidly in most dynamic E & R organizations.

The E & R manager may be establishing a completely new E & R organization, restructuring his going organization in a continuous process of reappraisal and adaptation, or taking over a going organization. In each case, he should evaluate the present status and objectives, plan the future organization, and then start the implementation of his organizational plan. He must propose, and secure, acceptance by top management of development activities which he believes are appropriate. For example, he may seek responsibility for some or all of the following activities:

1. Assist the general manager by providing long- and intermediate-range plans for technical and product leadership.
2. Provide research (possibly), development, and design of new products.
3. Plan for further technical development of existing lines.
4. Supply adequate engineering test facilities. (Manufacturing normally establishes and maintains its own test facilities.) However, in the small company this is not practical, and the engineer should have cognizance of all test facilities.
5. Maintain or improve product reliability and value positions.
6. Set adequate quality standards.
7. Establish and/or administer technical service groups such as the technical information search center, centralized computer facilities, drafting and reproduction services, special laboratories, etc.

8. Establish and/or maintain application engineering and/or engineering service facilities.
9. Provide technical liaison with foreign subsidiaries and provide them with technical advice.

While it would be unlikely that a newly appointed manager of engineering would have either the desire or the opportunity to establish all of these broad objectives, circumstances vary so that any partial combination of the above objectives may be appropriate in a given organization. For example, in a small company there exist engineering functions and related activities that might be considered for combination, i.e., plant engineering, industrial engineering, quality control, etc. These are engineering functions of stature and importance parallel to those normally ascribed to E & R, but these functions should report to *engineering managers* who report to the *chief manufacturing executive*.

Another influence on the scope of engineering activities may be that the general manager has strong feelings regarding the engineering objectives and consequently imposes his views on the engineering manager. As a final thought, the manager of engineering should consider his own background and knowledge to ensure that in establishing his organization he does not take on more than he can efficiently manage.

Determine the Specific Work to be Performed

Once the broad objectives have been established, the engineering manager should determine more specifically the work to be performed. This selection depends upon the size and nature of the work, the type and number of products, the resources and facilities available, the freedom of choice available to the engineering manager, and the annual budget he may be able to get approved. Possible specific areas of engineering work might be:

1. Research
2. Advance engineering development
3. Engineering systems design
4. Engineering component design
5. Engineering development and proof testing
6. Technical supporting services
7. Package and style design
8. Application engineering
9. Field engineering.

In a relatively small company that cannot afford a large, or even any separate research group, a few scientists or highly trained engineers may conduct special investigations, be aware of pertinent scientific advances throughout the world, and serve as consultants to the rest of the engineering organization. An advance engineering development function may be included in the engineering organization to develop and demonstrate technical application possibilities of new concepts. If this is not done, such development work must be subcontracted if long-range new product development is not to be neglected or omitted. This latter course is an obviously dangerous alternative.

In the larger companies, technical supporting services are helpful in maintaining a high quality of engineering and product leadership. These services may include specialized groups of metallurgists, chemists, instrument engineers, laboratories with very specialized equipment, a digital and analog computer center, a technical information search group, etc.

Most engineering organizations today, even those of relatively small size, find that a computing center is a "must." This has come about because (1) electronic computers have been designed to fit almost any need and budget, and (2) the complexity of engineering work has grown to the point where much calculation work must be performed on electronic computers if they are to be done at all for a reasonable cost and within a reasonable time.

With regard to packaging and style designs, application engineering and field service engineering, the manager of engineering must be guided in his desires by the nature of the business and his relationship with the manager of marketing. When new products or new product lines are to be developed, the engineering manager must work closely with the marketing manager. The current and future products and engineering services sold have a close bearing on the manner in which the engineering functions are assembled.

The E & R manager must also interlock design work with manufacturing and process engineering. In the small firm, the engineering manager is likely to have responsibility for all of these activities. In the large firm, the E & R manager must take the initiative to work closely with the production management.

The definition of E & R responsibilities depends not only on technical tasks but also on significant product qualities to be achieved. These product qualities should be specified, as for example:

Performance	Features
Technical characteristics	Physical characteristics
Operating cost	Special functions
System cost	Base of installation and service
Reliability	Flexibility
Life	Accessories
Safety	Interchangeability
Environmental limitations	Transportability
	Safety
	Styling
	Compatibility

Obtain a Charter in Written Form

When appointed to a new position, an E & R manager should make certain he obtains a "charter" in writing. The purpose of a charter is to clarify objectives, relationships, responsibilities, and constraints for the E & R manager so as to provide him with a solid base for long-term operation. Dependence on good will, current incumbent superiors who may be transferred, and fallible human memory is a serious risk.

The charter may be in the form of a letter, a position description, or a functional organization description. The charter should outline the principal responsibilities of the manager of engineering and/or research and it should specify, in particular, responsibilities where possible conflicts with sales, manufacturing, or staff personnel may arise. There is no need for a charter to be a legal document describing every detail of the work. In fact, this would be both detrimental and a waste of time. Also, there is almost no piece of writing that cannot be nullified by some legalistic interpretation. The charter should serve as the framework within which good working relationships may be conducted by men of integrity. Moreover, it is a reminder of the original conditions on which the manager of engineering accepted his position.

Structure the Components and Define Key Positions

With specific work established and the general organizational pattern chosen, the components and subcomponents of the engineering organization should be drawn up on a structural organization chart, which, showing the component structure in block form, includes the following:

1. Component title
2. Position title of incumbent
3. Name of incumbents (when position is filled)
4. Key which relates each principal position to the functional description chart.

The functional description chart is in the form of *brief* descriptions (one or two paragraphs) of principal managerial and specialist positions. These descriptions of the primary functions and subfunctions should be detailed just sufficiently to show that practical "packaging" of work has been carried out.

Combine Work Elements into Positions

When the key positions have been established, each manager in the engineering organization must combine elements of work in his component to constitute subordinate positions. In combining work elements, a major consideration is the competence of the people available. Highly skilled engineers should be given highly challenging work. In many cases, the

Date ____________________

POSITION TITLE:	ACCOUNTABLE TO:
Manager - Thermal Design	Manager - Engineering & Research

BROAD FUNCTION

The Manager - Thermal Design has managerial and functional responsibilities for heat transfer and fluid flow characteristics of all designed equipment.

PRINCIPAL RESPONSIBILITIES

Managerial Objectives

1. Plan, organize, initiate, and measure the activities associated with the technical aspects, engineering design, development, construction, and operation of equipment as assigned to his component.
2. Recommend to the Manager - Engineering & Research programs and budgets within the policies and objectives of the Engineering & Research organization.
3. Promote the growth, enthusiasm, and effort of all personnel assigned to him by means of technical and general guidance, selection of assignments and personal contact.

Functional Objectives

1. Perform detailed heat transfer and fluid flow studies.
2. Assist in the preparation of test specifications for heat transfer and fluid flow tests.
3. Furnish surveillance over the design, manufacture, and installation of equipment to ensure compliance with thermal specifications.
4. Prepare progress reports and design-substantiating reports proving compliance of design with hydrothermal specifications.

Fig. 3-2. Position guide for a manager.

work can be so subdivided and combined that some of the resulting positions could be filled by technicians or persons not having an engineering education, ability, or the equivalent. This is an approach infrequently used, and is one of the reasons for the shortage of scientific and engineering personnel.

Engineering positions must be designed so that capable people are continually challenged. Inadequate position design is evident when the people available to a component have too high a level of competence for the positions. Scientific position design seeks homogeneity of skills and knowledge required to take necessary action.

Prepare Position Guides for Each Position

There are many formats for position guides, position descriptions, or position outlines as they may be called. The simpler the form and the more direct the language, the more likely it will be used as a living document and not just another piece of paper in some administrative file. The purpose of the position description is to detail the principal functions for which the incumbent is responsible. These delineated functions should be made the basis of the salary administration plan since an engineer or engineering manager should be paid for that work for which he is organizationally accountable. Examples of simple position guides for a manager, a specialist, and an engineer are given in Figs. 3-2, 3-3, and 3-4. A more detailed discussion of position descriptions will be found in Chapter 5.

Position Nomenclature

The organization is based on a dichotomy of workers: (1) managers and (2) individual contributors. All individual contributors report to only one manager although they may receive functional guidance from a technical or "team" leader.

The purpose of organizing the component and position structure of a company is to simplify operation. Position nomenclature is an integral part of such organization structure. Symptoms of poor nomenclature are apparent when the following conditions exist:

1. A great variety of vague titles
2. Different nomenclature for essentially similar positions
3. Lack of full company-wide uniformity
4. Lack of distinction between individual contributors and managers
5. Nomenclature identifying status, rather than component and work content.

In establishing a guide for sound nomenclature, four basic objectives should be sought. A nomenclature system should be:

1. *Rational.* To provide orderly and logical relationships among position titles
2. *Acceptable.* To satisfy the dignity of the individual by providing recognition of his work without accentuating status differences
3. *Comprehensible.* To facilitate understanding of the organization structure and position functions
4. *Flexible.* To fit special and future organizational requirements.

A sound nomenclature system will provide titles that indicate work content, mission, and possibly organizational component. Attempts to

Title: Engineer-Structural Evaluation

Accountable to: Manager-Mechanical Equipment

BROAD FUNCTION

The Engineer-Structural Evaluation is responsible for the structural evaluation of assigned components including technical surveillance, guidance and recommendations on design features, analytical and test programs.

FUNCTIONAL RESPONSIBILITIES

1. Provide technical surveillance of assigned components by performing analytical investigations and recommending and guiding experimental investigations.
2. Aid in establishment of operational procedures for assigned systems.
3. Recommend revisions in structural design basis and suggest criteria for the design of reactor components.
4. Provide consultation to engineers performing structural evaluation within the laboratory.
5. Participate in the development of improved methods for structural evaluation.
6. Seek and utilize to the fullest extent all available abilities and support within the laboratory as authorized, and direct such effort towards the fast and effective solution of new and major technical problems encountered in the execution of assigned projects.
7. Prepare letters, memoranda, and reports covering status, progress, and problems of work undertaken.

RELATIONSHIP RESPONSIBILITIES:

Normal responsibilities.

APPROVED BY: IMMEDIATE MANAGER: INCUMBENT: (sign)

________________ ________________ ________________

Fig. 3-3. Position guide for a specialist.

Date ______________

POSITION TITLE:	ACCOUNTABLE TO:
Engineer - Mechanical Equipment	Manager - Mechanical Equipment

BROAD FUNCTION

The Engineer - Mechanical Equipment is responsible for the engineering design, development test, and procurement of assigned components and equipment.

FUNCTIONAL OBJECTIVES

1. Prepare feasibility studies and development programs to establish optimum designs.
2. Prepare specifications and ordering information.
3. Analyze vendors' designs to assure that both steady-state and transient component requirements and service conditions can be met.
4. Review test results and evaluate performance of equipment components and make recommendations thereon for improvement of equipment.

Fig. 3-4. Position guide for an engineer.

include level of technical effort required tend to produce more friction than light. The formula for a title should permit a qualifying term, an action term, and work content term as illustrated below:

Qualifying Term	Action Term	Work Content
	Manager	Propellant technology
	Manager	Systems research
	Supervising engineer	Wood products
Consulting	Engineer	Analytical mechanics
Design	Engineer	Servomechanisms

E & R ORGANIZATIONAL PATTERNS

Functional Organization

The basic building block of all organizations is the functional specialty or discipline. In a functional organization, the work is partitioned according to subject or discipline and all similar work is performed within one component. In a purely functionally organized company, one engineering executive is responsible for all engineering work; one manufacturing executive is responsible for all manufacturing; and similarly for marketing and other functions. In multiplant and large multiproduct line companies, this represents an impractical centralization of responsibility. For small companies, functional organization is often desirable.

Within the E & R organizations of even large companies, it is quite common to find a functional type organization. Advantages accrue from bringing specialists in the same discipline together. It is easier to manage a homogeneous group and duplication of activities is eliminated. However, this form of organization is not so advantageous for cross-discipline development work. Figure 3-5 shows a simplified functional E & R organization

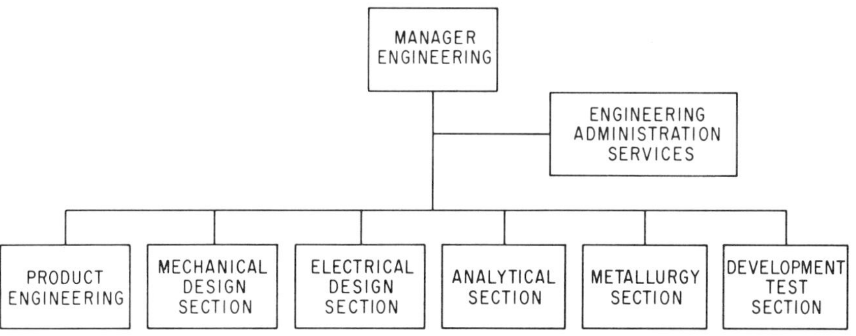

Fig. 3-5. Simplified functional engineering organization.

in which product designers "farm out" portions of design work to the functional sections. The product designers have responsibility for the coordination of design and the end product.

Product Organization

An entire company may be organized on a divisional basis so that each division is responsible for one product or product line. Each division may have its own E & R component organized in any fashion. If E & R is completely centralized, whether in a large or small company, it may be organized along product lines. A simplified product-type E & R structure is shown in Fig. 3-6.

Figure 3-7 shows the product organization for the engineering organization of a profit center component of a large company. The A-C Motor Section engineering organization is further divided functionally according to electrical design, mechanical design, and materials and insulation design activities.

One advantage of the product-type E & R organization is that there is one manager with line responsibility for all technical resources required

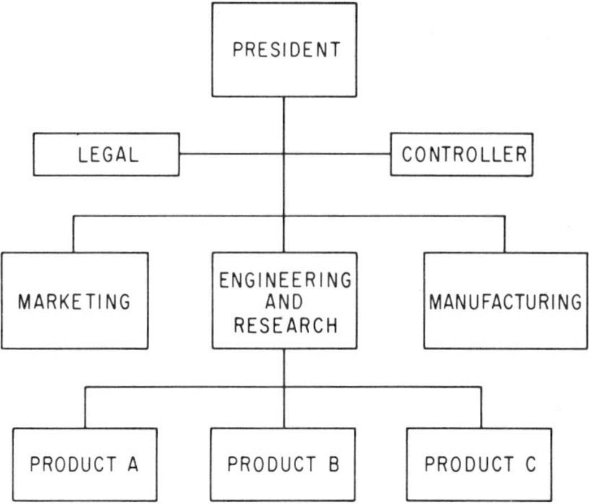

Fig. 3-6. Organization of E & R along product lines.

to develop and update products of a similar nature. Teamwork may be easily developed since the output of the group is matched to customer needs and profit measurements. A disadvantage is often the limited contact that each engineer has with others of his discipline. Motivation to keep abreast of his field is thus reduced. Varying numbers of specialists required from time to time either puts a strain on the organization or induces insecurity because of transfers out or transfers in. (The latter is a competitive threat to incumbents.)

Project Organization

With the growth of tremendous government research and development

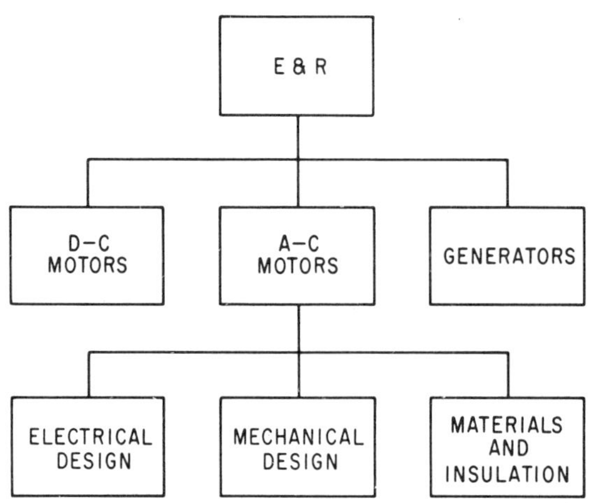

Fig. 3-7. Product organization of E & R with functional sub-units.

programs such as nuclear weapons and power plant, missile and space systems, detection and communications systems, and urban transportation systems, the project-type organization concept has evolved rapidly.

A project is a "one-shot," time-limited, goal-directed, major undertaking requiring the commitment of varied skills and resources. An E & R organization may carry on two or three multimillion dollar projects, at one extreme, to several hundred varied size projects at the other extreme. Projects follow "life cycles" in terms of commitment of resources and generally start with gradual growth, next increase rapidly to maximum size, and finally decline moderately and eventually tail away. The key to managing a project organization is to plan for a steady work load as projects grow and die. The "pure" project organization is illustrated in Fig. 3-8. Each project manager has all functional responsibilities for the success of his projects.

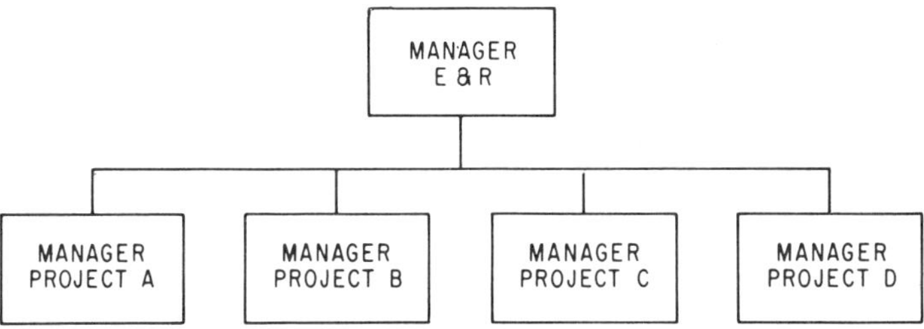

Fig. 3-8. "Pure" project organization of E & R.

Project organization has the following advantages:

1. The number and type of personnel assigned to the project to meet project demands can be changed rapidly.
2. Greater pressure can be exerted to overcome the inherent inertia in large projects.
3. Greater coordination and control of large jobs is possible with project-type organization.
4. Responsibility and accountability can be made more specific in the project-type organization.
5. Project organizations can shift personnel to meet the many difficult, unexpected, technical problems that arise. Like an organism, the project organization is self-healing.
6. Because of the continually changing internal organization of projects, it is easier to uncover leadership talent and transfer those who fail as leaders to other technical work without loss of status.
7. There is a high *esprit de corps* among project personnel because of close identification of individuals with the goals.

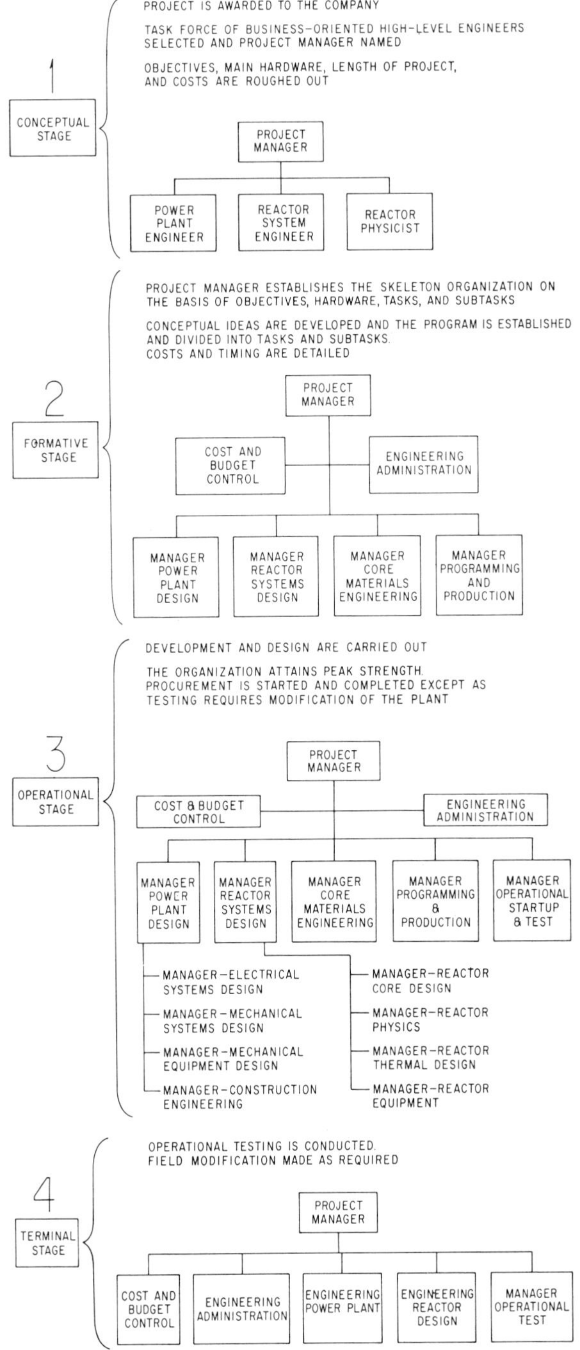

Fig. 3-9. Project life cycle.

8. The instability of project organizations and the continual regrouping of personnel tend to encourage original and creative thinking.

Since projects by their very nature finally terminate, they usually have a life cycle varying from several months to over five years. The stages of a project are:

1. *Conceptual.* A project manager is appointed to direct a small task force of highly competent business-oriented engineers, set broad objectives, approximate length of the project, and approximate cost.
2. *Formative.* The project manager establishes the project organization on the basis of the broad objectives and equipment that must be designed. Key personnel are chosen who then develop the basic concepts and detail the technical tasks, subtasks, organization, time, and costs.
3. *Operational.* The organization starts on the amplification of basic concepts and carries the engineering through completion of the design and procurement of equipment. The organization reaches peak strength in this stage.
4. *Terminal.* The organization is cut back drastically in the terminal stage. This is the cleanup stage when the final bugs are ironed out and the operation of the equipment is tested. Terminating a large project requires close control to prevent waste of manpower and heavy costs due to problems not corrected quickly.

As the work progresses through these four stages, the project organization changes in size and structure. Figure 3-9 depicts this change for a nuclear reactor power plant project. It may be noted that functional units are the basic blocks within the project organization. The organizations shown in Figs. 3-8 and 3-9 are essentially line organizations with responsibility for all aspects of the project vested in the project manager. Proper planning in multiproject E & R organizations requires that key men be shifted from mature and terminating projects to new projects by synchronization of all projects.

An alternative to the line project organization is the project-staff and functional line organization as shown in Fig. 3-10. The staff project managers coordinate and control the technical work, timing, and cost of technical work by staff relationships with line managers of the functional groups. Thus, engineers within a functional group are accountable to the project managers, a violation of traditional organizational principles.

Since each project manager is responsible for achieving his own project objectives, he exerts pressure on engineers, competes with other project managers for the services of the best engineers, and competes for priority of funds and supporting services. Lines of authority and communication are complex and much activity is dysfunctional (that is, working against achievement of organizational goals) in this situation.

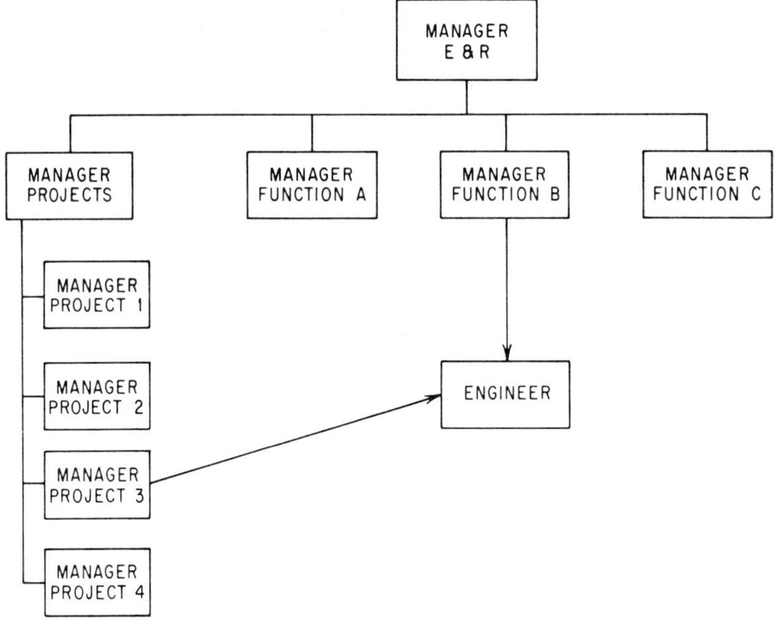

Fig. 3-10. Project staff organization.

System-Component Structure

The system and component basis for organizing is very effective when large, complex system projects of a similar nature occur repeatedly. For example, complex communications systems, weapon systems, ship and aircraft control and power systems, satellite systems, and nuclear power systems are typical. In order for a company to retain such business, it must have some means of sensing long range needs of very large customers and it must conduct advance development of systems in order to make proposals.

The systems engineers are responsible for the following:

1. Developing mission plans for new potential systems
2. Defining the system
3. Developing criteria for performance, specifying input and output limits throughout the system, and identifying constraints and trade-off prospects
4. Conducting advanced development of systems which have been "ordered" by customers
5. Maintaining surveillance over component design to assume integration and compatibility of all parts of the system during design and final acceptance testing.

The component engineers are responsible for either designing or procuring components that meet the system specifications. The total experience of both the systems groups and the component groups can be preserved and increased with this type of organization. A simplified example of such an organization is shown in Fig. 3-11. The organization within each block may be by function or by project.

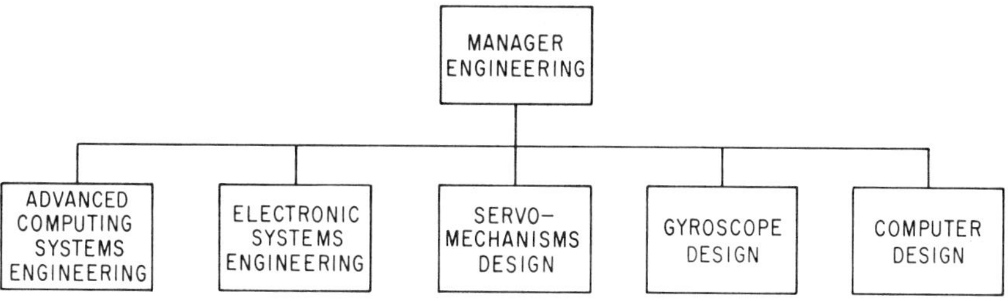

Fig. 3-11. System and component design organization.

Phase, Stage, or Process Organization

When the development and design work typically handled by the E & R organization can be conveniently divided into clear-cut chronologically ordered phases or stages, the phase-type organization may be very effective. In such cases, it serves to maintain well-defined subdivision of work and responsibility. In large companies, particularly, the innovative process covers a wide spectrum of technical effort ranging from research to concept development to advanced development to system and product design which appear to progress chronologically. Despite this appearance, however, it is rare that such clear subdivisions of work can be made because of feedback, overlapping, and need for integration. Thus the phase-type organization, except as approximated by the systems-component approach, is not very common.

Technical Support Units

It is often not economic to decentralize certain technical support activities such as highly trained researchers and consultants, drafting personnel, reproduction (drawing processing) personnel, and technical reports and instruction book personnel. The demand in subsections of the E & R organization is not constant nor large enough to support these activities in each subsection. Therefore, it is more economical and effective to centralize such support functions. Figure 3-12 shows specialists at two levels of the organization. Figure 3-13 shows technical support and administrative groups in the E & R organization.

Organizations in Operation

Although the structural logic for organizations has been developed so far, E & R organizations in actual operation show many deviations. In some

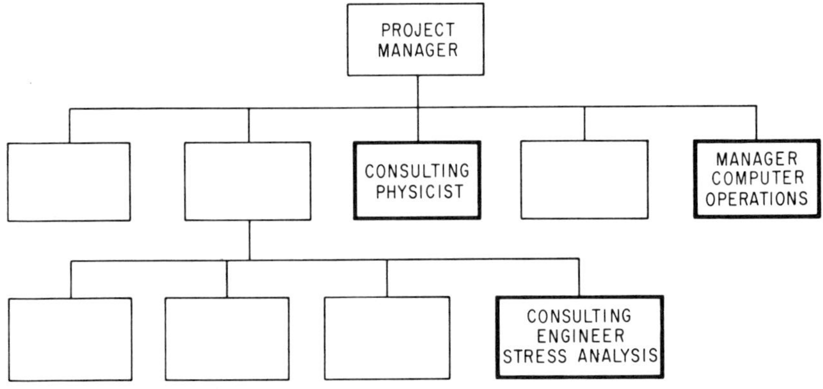

Fig. 3-12. Centralization of specialties.

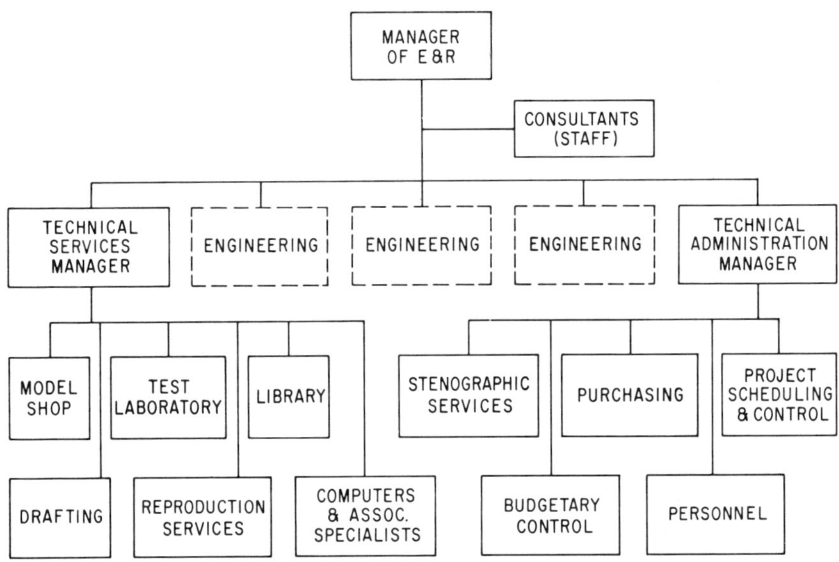

Fig. 3-13. Centralized technical and administration support groups.

cases, such deviations represent a flexible adaptation to the products, the customers, and the personalities of the managers which appear to yield best results. In other cases, the E & R organization is based on ignorance or power struggles among the managers. Figures 3-14 through 3-19 illustrate the nature of E & R organizations of some successful companies by showing how they were organized at one point in time. Since all organizations change specific structure almost continuously, these illustrations serve for illustrative purposes as well as any other similar set.

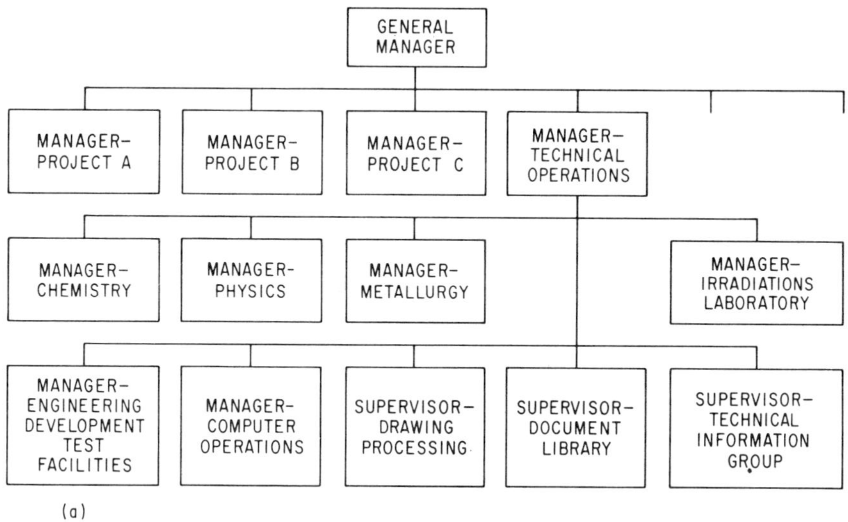

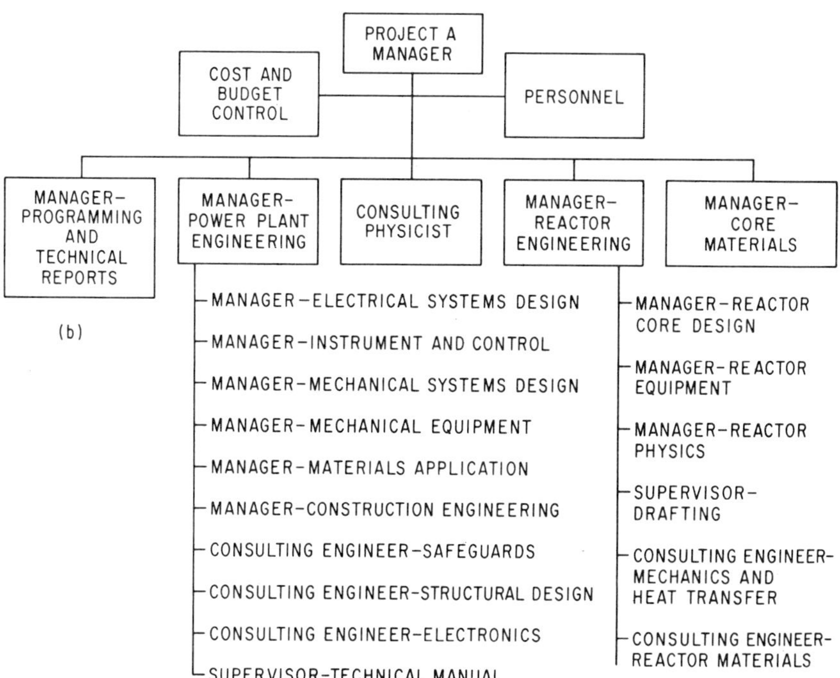

Fig. 3-14. (a) Project organization for reactor power plant design. (b) Another project organization for reactor power plant design.

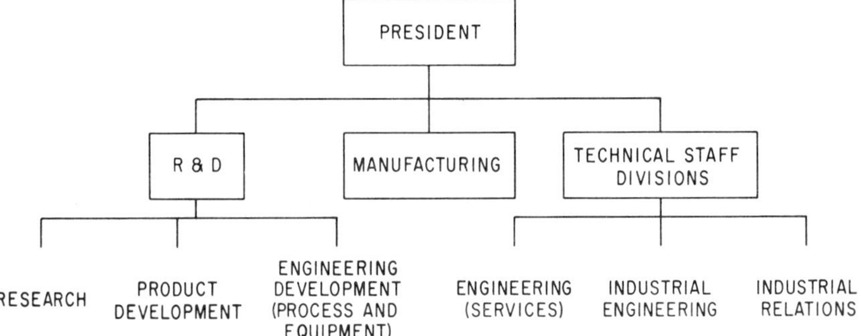

Fig. 3-15. Procter and Gamble technical organization.

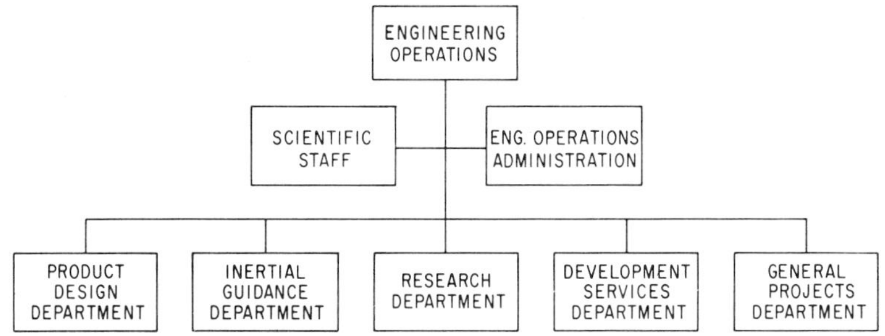

Fig. 3-16. Engineering organization of Arma Div. of American Bosch, Arma Corp.

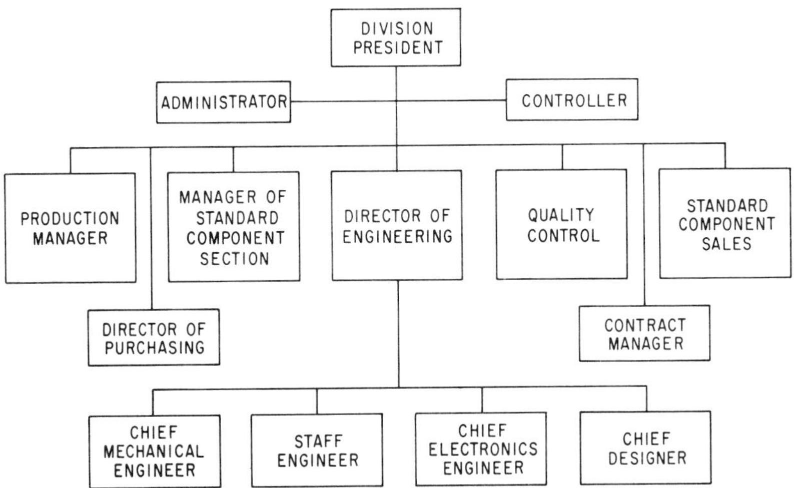

Fig. 3-17. A chart showing the engineering organization of the former Instrument Division of Sterling Precision Corporation. The Instrument Division has since been sold. It, however, illustrates a small company which was organized logically along functional lines. The span of managerial responsibility was broad so that there were only two levels of management separating an engineer from the president. It appeared to be a very good plan for the division.

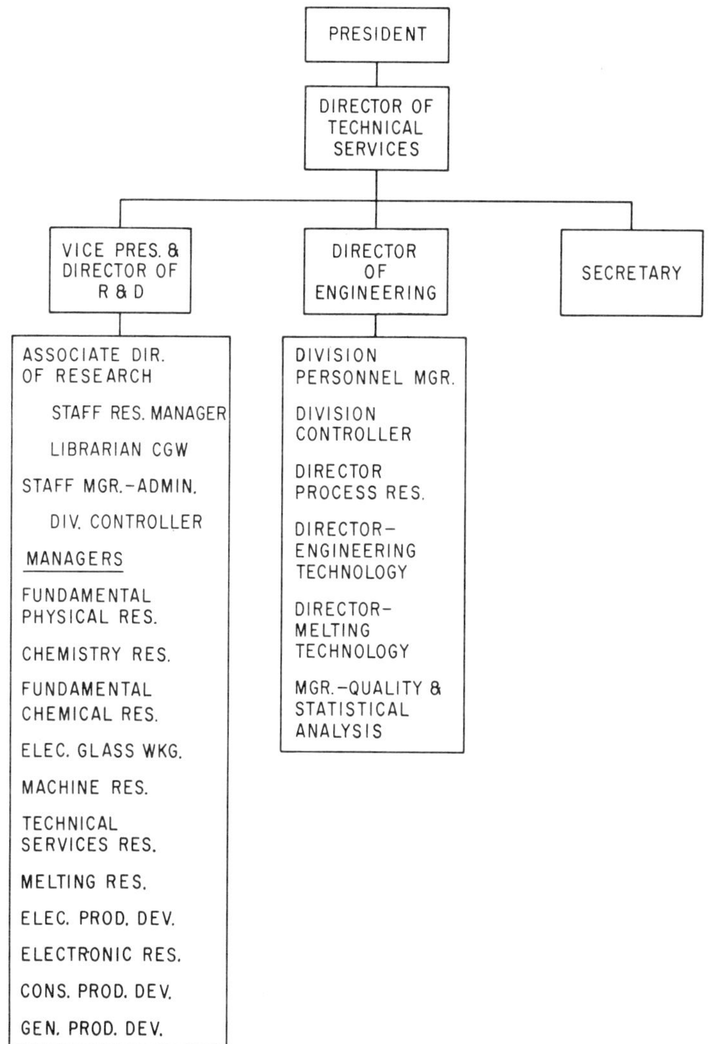

Fig. 3-18. Corning Glass Works organization chart.

ORGANIZATIONAL ANALYSIS THROUGH LINEAR RESPONSIBILITY CHARTING

The Linear Responsibility Chart (LRC) was developed by Ernst Hijmans of the Netherlands and introduced in the United States in simplified form by his friend.Serge A. Birn, management consultant in Louisville, Kentucky. The purpose of the chart is to identify in concise visual format all personnel, significant activities and processes, and responsibilities and relationships

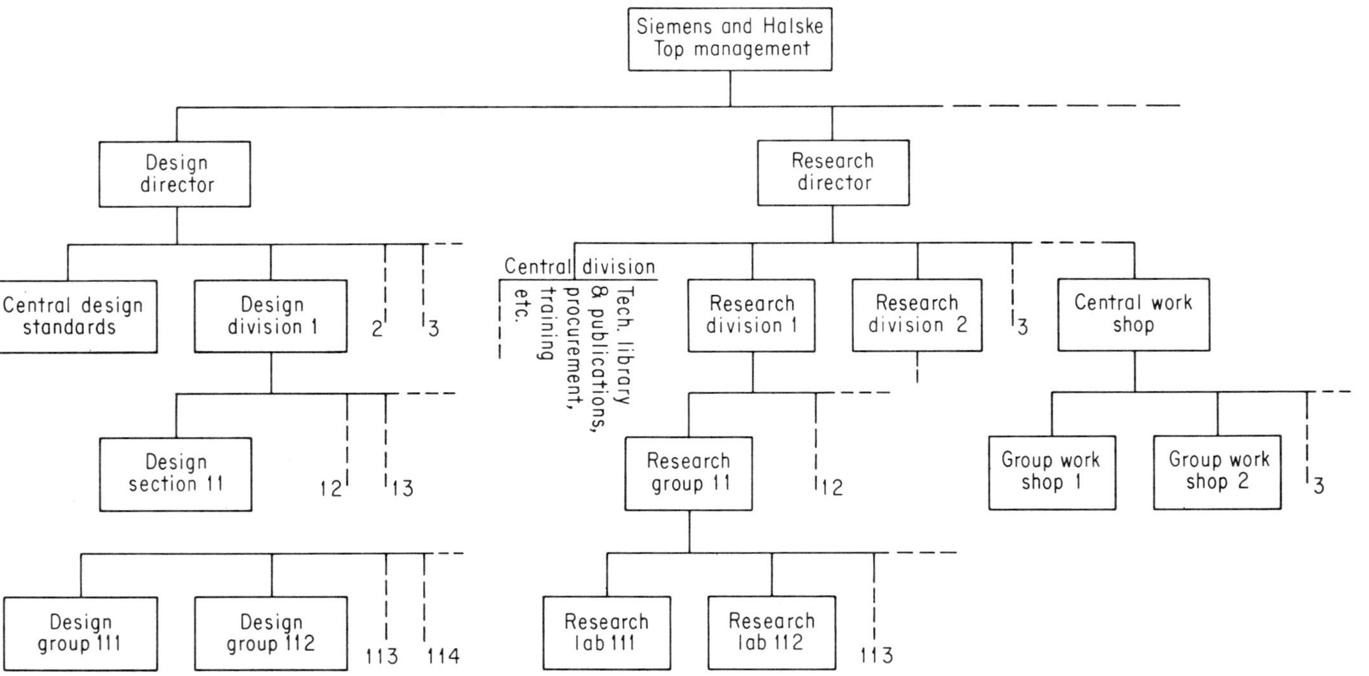

Fig. 3-19. Structure of E & R organization — Siemens and Halske, West Germany.

within the organization. The preparation of the LRC will uncover the answers to such questions as:

1. Are key men being bypassed?
2. Are work loads unbalanced?
3. To whom does a man report?
4. What persons must be notified of specific acts?
5. Who must be consulted?
6. Who has direct responsibility for performing specific tasks?
7. Who has supervision over the work and to what degree?

A typical LRC for an engineering department is shown in Fig. 3-20. Functions are listed down the left side and organizational positions across the top. The eight variations of responsibility are coded on the right side of the chart so that entries in the chart may be made and analyzed.

An overlay for the position of director of engineering is shown in Fig. 3-21. In practice, the overlay would line up just to the right of the vertical Column B in the original chart which denotes those acts for which the director of engineering is responsible. The overlay is shown positioned over the original chart in Fig. 3-22. The percents shown on the overlay in Figs. 3-21 and 3-22 correspond with those shown at the bottom of Column B for the director of engineering in Fig. 3-20.

A practical illustration of how the charting technique can be useful is shown in the before-and-after situation of Fig. 3-23.

> The "before" chart of this pair shows a situation that had grown up gradually over a long period and worked well as long as the company was operating under large, long-run contracts. However, too many production superintendents shared authority to make binding decisions on sequence of operations and other processing details. Time spent reconciling differences was great—often two hours per man weekly for as many as fifteen men. But, when competition forced the company to go out for new business aggressively, the old methods became suicidally cumbersome.
>
> Bids were late, friction increased among the many men who had authority to decide. Eventually, one week, it took six meetings, totalling twelve hours, for each of those involved, to come to a common decision. At this point, the Linear Responsibility Chart made clear why the company was falling behind.
>
> The conditions had existed before. Management knew something was wrong. But *what* was wrong, and in what way, did not become clear until a graphic display like this *made* it clear. The "after" chart, concentrating decision in a few hands—the proper ones—and giving only consultative authority to the others, straightened the problem out.
>
> One measure of the method's success was the reduction in "steps required" to settle methods from forty-one to twenty-one. Hours saved were almost geometrically proportional.[3]

[3] Alfred G. Larke, "Linear Responsibility Chart—New Tool for Executive Control," *Dun's Review and Modern Industry* (September, 1954). *Reprinted by special permission from Dun's Review and Modern Industry* (September 1954). Copyright, 1954, Dun & Bradstreet Publications Corp.

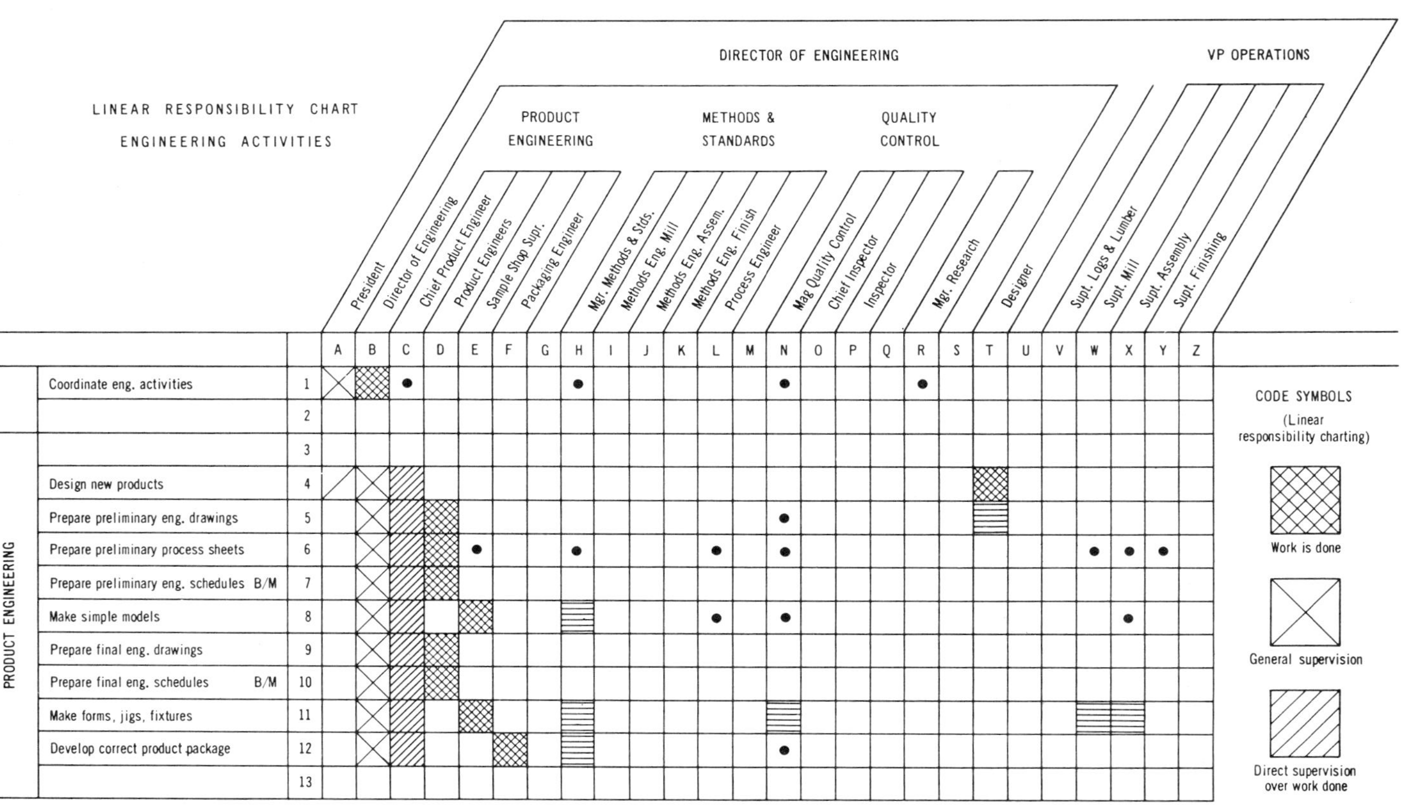

Fig. 3-23. Before-and-after situations shown on linear responsibility chart. *Source:* See Fig. 3-20.

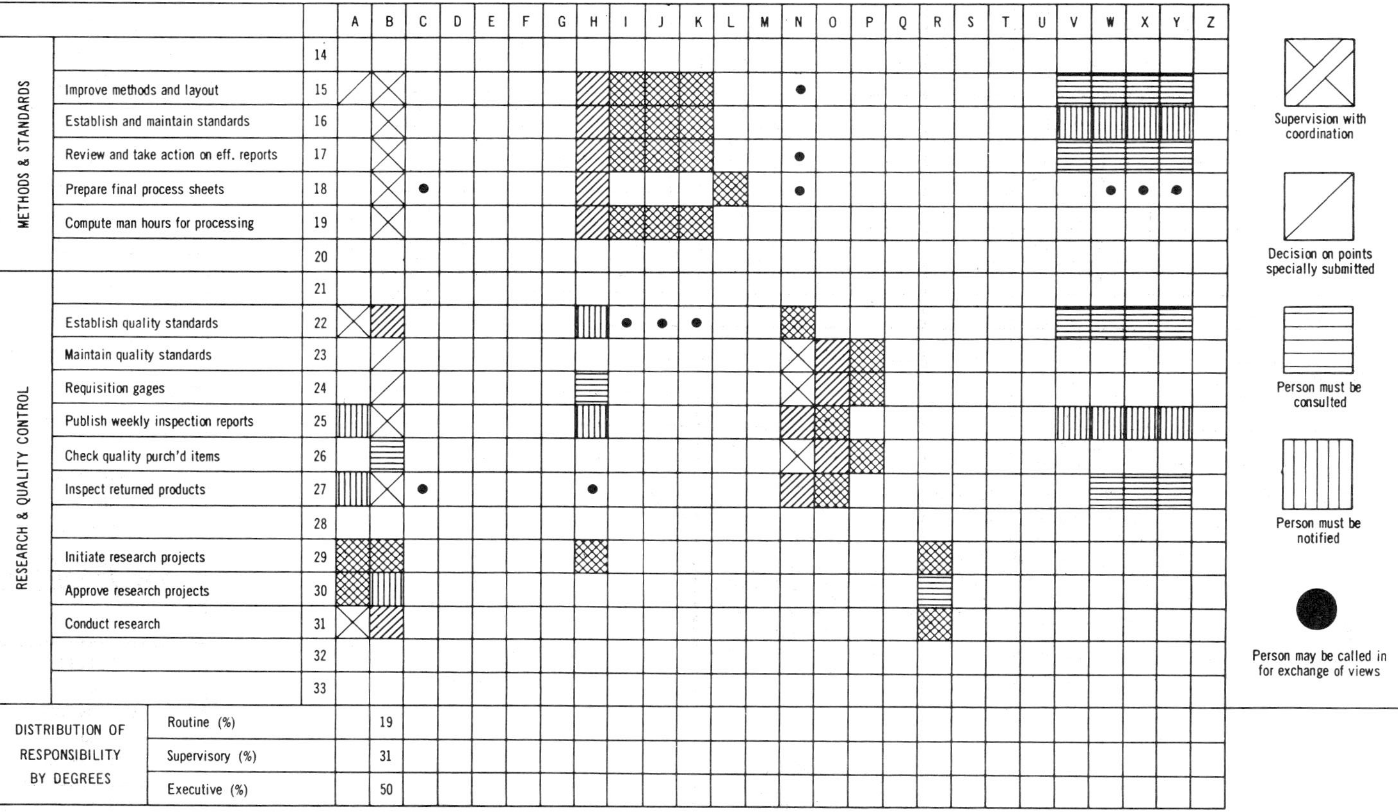

Fig. 3-20. Typical linear responsibility chart. *Source:* The basic distribution of functions shown in Figs. 3-20, 3-21, and 3-22, reproduced from "Linear Responsibility Charting," *Manufacturing and Industrial Engineering* (now *Plant Management*), February, 1957. The chart itself was developed by Leetham Simpson Limited, Montreal, Canada.

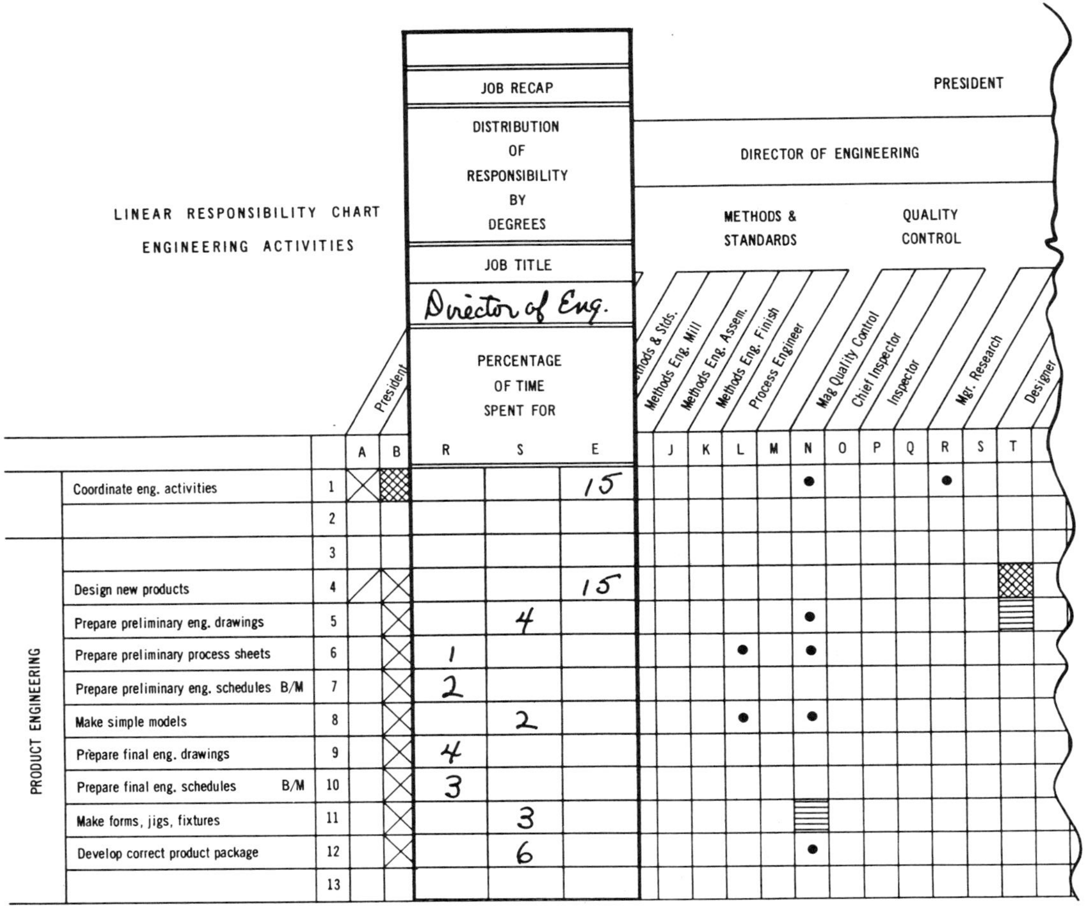

LINEAR RESPONSIBILITY CHART

ENGINEERING ACTIVITIES

PRESIDENT / DIRECTOR OF ENGINEERING / METHODS & STANDARDS / QUALITY CONTROL

JOB RECAP — DISTRIBUTION OF RESPONSIBILITY BY DEGREES — JOB TITLE: Director of Eng. — PERCENTAGE OF TIME SPENT FOR R, S, E

A = President; J = Methods & Stds.; K = Methods Eng. Mill; L = Methods Eng. Assem.; M = Methods Eng. Finish; N = Process Engineer; P = Mag Quality Control; Q = Chief Inspector; R = Inspector; S = Mgr. Research; T = Designer

	Activity	No.	A	B	R	S	E	J	K	L	M	N	O	P	Q	R	S	T
	Coordinate eng. activities	1	X	▩			15					●				●		
		2																
PRODUCT ENGINEERING		3																
	Design new products	4	/	X			15											▩
	Prepare preliminary eng. drawings	5		X		4						●						▤
	Prepare preliminary process sheets	6		X	1					●		●						
	Prepare preliminary eng. schedules B/M	7		X	2													
	Make simple models	8		X		2				●		●						
	Prepare final eng. drawings	9		X	4													
	Prepare final eng. schedules B/M	10		X	3													
	Make forms, jigs, fixtures	11		X		3						▤						
	Develop correct product package	12		X		6						●						
		13																

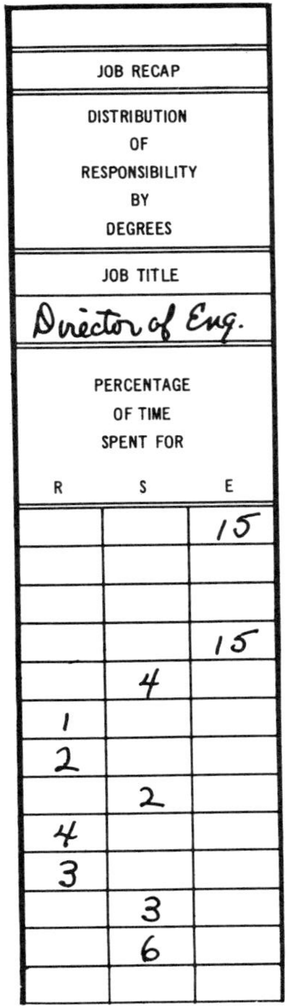

JOB RECAP — DISTRIBUTION OF RESPONSIBILITY BY DEGREES — JOB TITLE: Director of Eng. — PERCENTAGE OF TIME SPENT FOR

R	S	E
		15
		15
	4	
1		
2		
	2	
4		
3		
	3	
	6	

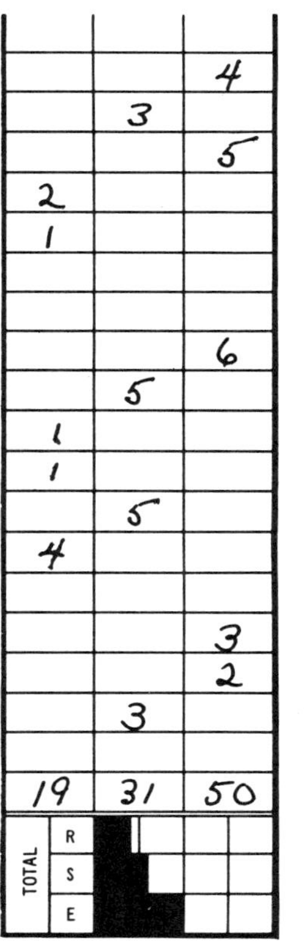

Section	Activity	No.	A	B	C–D	E–F	G–H
METHODS & STANDARDS		14					
	Improve methods and layout	15					4
	Establish and maintain standards	16				3	
	Review and take action on eff. reports	17					5
	Prepare final process sheets	18			2		
	Compute man hours for processing	19			1		
		20					
RESEARCH & QUALITY CONTROL		21					
	Establish quality standards	22					6
	Maintain quality standards	23				5	
	Requisition gages	24			1		
	Publish weekly inspection reports	25			1		
	Check quality purch'd items	26				5	
	Inspect returned products	27			4		
		28					
	Initiate research projects	29					3
	Approve research projects	30					2
	Conduct research	31				3	
		32					
		33			19	31	50
DISTRIBUTION OF RESPONSIBILITY BY DEGREES	Routine (%)			19	TOTAL R		
	Supervisory (%)			31	TOTAL S		
	Executive (%)			50	TOTAL E		

Column headings: A B C D E F G H I J K L M N O P Q R S T U

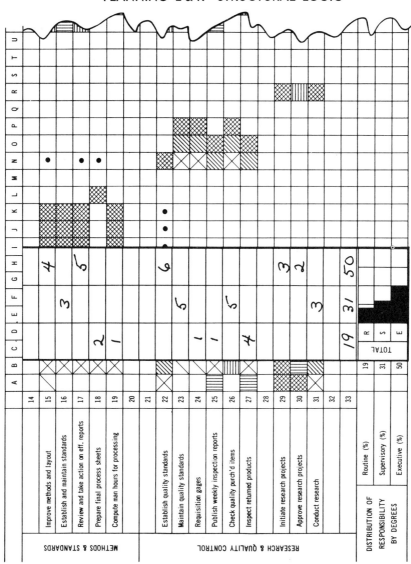

Fig. 3-21. (*Left*) Overlay for position of director of engineering. Fig. 3-22. (*Right*) Overlay in place on chart shown in Fig. 3-20.

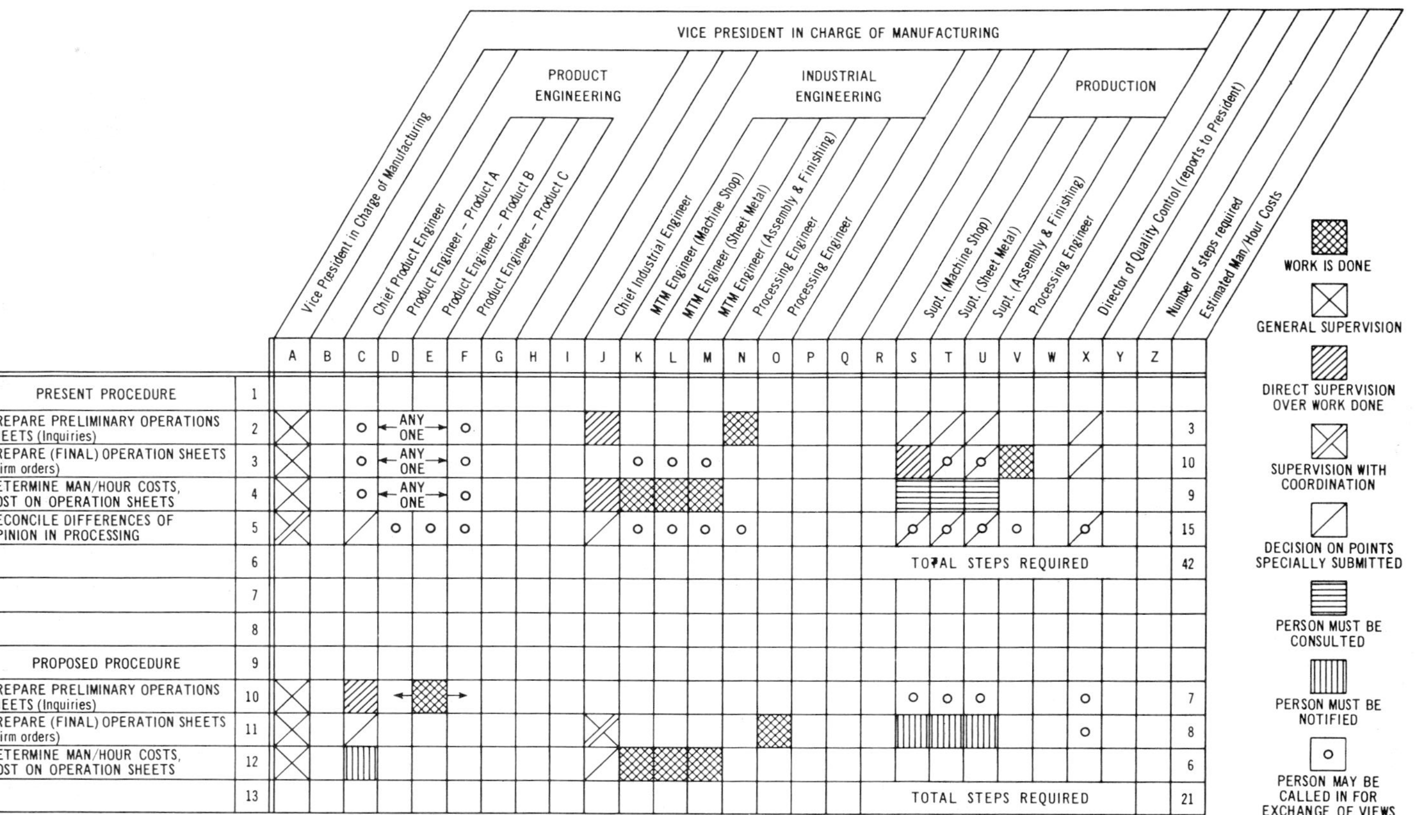

Fig. 3-23. Before-and-after situations shown on linear responsibility chart.

BIBLIOGRAPHY

ALBERS, HENRY H. *Organized Executive Action.* New York, N.Y.: John Wiley & Sons, Inc., 1961.

DALE, ERNEST. *Planning and Developing the Company Organization Structure,* AMA Research Report No. 20. New York, N.Y.: American Management Association, Inc., 1957.

DANIELSON, LEE E. *Characteristics of Engineers and Scientists.* Doctoral dissertation, The University of Michigan, 1960.

FRIED, GEORGE. "Convertible Engineering Organization," *Machine Design,* May 12, 1960.

GADDIS, PAUL O. "The Project Manager," *Harvard Business Review,* Vol. 37, No. 3, May–June, 1959.

———. "The Age of Massive Engineering," *Harvard Business Review,* January–February, 1961.

GREENWOOD, WILLIAM T. *Management and Organizational Behavior Theories: An Interdisciplinary Approach.* Cincinnati, Ohio: South-Western Publishing Co., 1965.

HAIRE, MASON. *Organization Theory in Industrial Practice.* New York, N.Y.: John Wiley & Sons, Inc., 1962.

JACKSON, THOMAS W., and SPURLOCK, JACK M. *Research and Development Management.* Homewood, Ill.: Dow Jones-Irwin, Inc., 1966.

KOONTZ, HAROLD, and O'DONNELL, CYRIL. *Management: A Book of Readings,* New York, N.Y.: McGraw-Hill Book Company, 1964.

LARKE, ALFRED G. "Linear Responsibility Chart—New Tool for Executive Control," *Dun's Review and Modern Industry,* September, 1954.

"Linear Responsibility Charting," *Manufacturing and Industrial Engineering* (now *Plant Management*), February, 1957.

LONGENECKER, JUSTIN G. *Principles of Management and Organizational Behavior.* Columbus, Ohio: Charles E. Merrill Books, Inc., 1964.

NICHOLAS, COLONEL JACK D.; PICKETT, COLONEL GEORGE B.; and SEARS, CAPTAIN WILLIAM O., JR. *The Joint and Combined Staff Officer's Manual.* Harrisburg, Pa.: Stackpole Books, 1959.

PRESTHUS. "Towards a Theory of Organizational Behavior," *Administrative Science Quarterly,* June, 1958.

"Research and Engineering Tailored to Fit the Times," *Engineering Opportunities,* October, 1964, pp. 8–11.

ROSSMAN, JOSEPH. *Industrial Creativity.* New Hyde Park, N.Y.: University Books, Inc., 1964.

SCOTT, WILLIAM J. "Organization Theory: An Overview and Appraisal," *Journal of the Academy of Management,* April, 1961.

STANLEY, ALEXANDER O., and WHITE, K. K. *Organizing the R & D Function,* AMA Research Study 72. New York, N.Y.: American Management Association, Inc., 1965.

STEINER, GEORGE A., and ROOT, EUGENE. "Linear Organization Charts," *California Management Review,* Winter, 1959.

TANGERMAN, E. J. "Engineering Organization in Transition," *Product Engineering,* May 11, 1959.

APPENDIX 3A

Personal Staff Assistants

Duties of Staff Assistants:

1. Prepare information and recommendations:
   a. Compile appropriate information.
   b. Make recommendations for action.
   c. Investigate proposals from other sources.
   d. Check on results obtained.
2. Aid in formulating instructions and making decisions:
   a. Give out orders for the chief.
   b. Make decisions in certain cases where policies and procedures are established.
3. Assist in contact work:
   a. Save the chief's time by arranging his interviews or interviewing individuals for him.
   b. Make reports on activities.
   c. Settle minor complaints.
   d. Disseminate information.
   e. Coordinate the division's activities and correlate its work with that of other divisions.

Among the things which a staff assistant should *not* do are:

1. Assume line duties.
2. Give advice as a specialist.
3. Merely make investigations without recommendations.
4. Only make suggestions when instead he should take some action.
5. Assume authority over subordinate line men.
6. Be guided by his own personal opinions.
7. Exceed his authority.
8. Talk too much or reveal confidential matters.

APPENDIX 3B

Committees

The real functions of a committee are to:

1. Interchange ideas.
2. Secure a meeting of minds.
3. Supply important information to the members or through them to the departments and the organization.
4. Receive and act on reports from committee members or from departments which have been asked for data or information.
5. Secure facts from many sources and assemble them into a combined plan.
6. Assay the results of operations, arrive at conclusions, and formulate reports or suggestions.
7. Make intelligent and expert studies of important factors, activities, or problems.
8. Develop and recommend procedures of operation.
9. Coordinate or set up time relationships between the operations or different departments.
10. Correlate or combine the activities of different departments.
11. Provide cooperation or special efforts in performance between the different departments.
12. Formulate and establish standards of various kinds.
13. Act as a clearing house for matters for which no other channel has been provided.

Advantages of Committee Organizations:

1. Under a strong executive chairman, a committee may quickly marshal many valuable points of view, since "two heads are better than one."
2. In conducting investigations, the several phases of the various questions may be quickly assigned to responsible members with a reasonable assurance of speedy action if a time schedule and proper follow-up are instituted.
3. Decisions arrived at are impersonal, leaving the chairman free from the personal criticisms so often leveled at a managing executive.
4. There is a stimulus toward cooperative action.
5. The members of the committee know better what is happening in the plant so that they can disseminate the information and team up with other individuals or departments.

Disadvantages of Committee Organizations:

1. Committees may be too large for constructive action since the number should seldom exceed three.

2. Committees are time-consuming and usually have to be prodded to prevent delays.
3. Important executives may be called so frequently from their work for meetings that the operations of the enterprise lag.
4. The members of the committee often are unfamiliar with important details of questions at issue and therefore may make wrong or ineffective decisions.
5. Action may often be superficial because of lack of time or interest of committee members.
6. Committees weaken individual responsibility resulting in compromise instead of clear-cut decisions.
7. The decisions often are made to conform to some executive's wants or to enable the members to avoid direct responsibility for unfavorable results.
8. Aggressive and outspoken members may dominate committee meetings and unduly influence the action, often adversely.

APPENDIX 3C

Check List to Test the Engineering Organization

1. Are the objectives, goals, and plans carefully defined and stated?	This will provide a sound, factual basis for determining the purpose, kind, and amount of work, as well as the number of positions which must be provided for both the long and short view.
2. Is the organization plan a compatible part of overall engineering planning?	Programs for growth, product innovation, introduction of new technology, new facilities or rearrangement, etc. will be most successful when work can be managed most effectively; when responsibility, authority and accountability are clearly assigned; when useful measurements exist; and when adequate manpower is available on time.
3. Is provision made for all engineering work?	Each engineering subfunction and its work elements must be performed (or procured) if a full engineering contribution is to be made. Voids will greatly jeopardize future success.
4. Have long-range and short-range work been clearly separated?	"Fire-fighting" type of work will crowd out important long-range work. Separation at higher organization levels reduces the number of people with responsibility for both.
5. Has decision-making been delegated to the point of action?	Day-to-day work aimed at immediate results against current commitments receives more prompt decision-making and action-taking. Channels of communication are unburdened to a greater extent. Higher organization personnel have more time for long-range planning and decision-making of broader scope.
6. Is there properly balanced attention and proper emphasis on all subfunctional work?	Each engineering subfunction represents an important part of the total work of engineering. To unbalance the emphasis invites distortion of the objectives of engineering. Undue emphasis on any subfunction risks important long-range work and a full engineering contribution to the success of the business enterprise.

7. Are there challenging managerial spans and minimum levels of organization?	Contributes to full utilization of high caliber people. Accelerates the flow and increases the accuracy of all communications.
8. Has managerial and functional contributor work been separated in defining positions?	Each is a specialized kind of work, and it will be performed more effectively if it receives the concentrated attention of different people. The work of the individual contributor can be made more challenging and satisfying.
9. Are there single lines of responsibility and a clear assignment of responsibilities and relationships?	A man deserves only one manager. Understanding is improved and confusion is avoided, if a. Each position derives responsibility from and is accountable to only one position. b. Responsibilities are not shared by two positions. c. Relationships within and without the component are clear and understandable to all concerned.
10. Have standards and measures of accountability been clearly established?	People give greatest attention to those things against which performance is measured and rewards are given. Clear measurements result in self-measurements, a most effective means of self-motivation. Teamwork is enhanced when "recommending" responsibilities are measured as well as "performing" responsibilities. A few, but balanced, measurements are more effective. A man deserves to know how well he is performing and what his opportunities are for self-development.
11. How flexible is the organization in meeting minor, medium, and major variations in work load?	Frequent reassignment of work is often damaging. Unrestricted reassignment of functional individual contributors to meet load fluctuations is desirable for training purposes. It can result in confusion and ineffectiveness if overdone. The organization structure should be such that minor and medium fluctuations have no significant effect on basic structure and that the effects of major fluctuations are reduced to a minimum.
12. Has the organization structure been designed to meet the total objectives of the business in the most economic manner?	Decentralization should not be carried to the point of creating positions that require only half of a man's real time. The number of managerial and functional individual contributor positions should be minimum.

	Positions should permit a maximum number of individuals to perform work requiring their full skill, in contrast to doing work of a lower skill simply because no one else is available in the organization component. Less measurable is the reduction in integrating or correlating work by higher organization levels when lower organization levels are assigned the work and "tools" necessary for maximum decision-making. However, this is of equal economic importance with the other items.
13. What geographical influences on the organization structure exist?	Minor distances between components should not govern or affect organization structure. A first-line manager in engineering preferably should manage work in an area easily within his vision, at least within easy walking distance. Geography should become less critical with each succeeding higher level of organization structure.
14. Is the organization structure best suited to your kind of engineering?	In mass production-oriented firms, where a product line consists of a number of types and sizes all produced in very high volume, the preponderance of effort takes place in the subfunctional fields of Manufacturing Engineering, Materials and Quality Control rather than in Shop Operations. In job shop businesses, where the unit volume of practically all products is very low, the preponderance of effort occurs in Shop Operations rather than Engineering. In mixed businesses with mass production for some products and pure job shop for others, the facilities should be separate for the two "kinds of manufacturing" for optimum overall results. Performance and profitability thus can be better measured individually. The organization structure of each should be most suitable for its particular problems.
15. In what respects has size influenced the application of principles of organization structuring?	Size itself is not a criterion for organization structuring. Size will not deter or prevent the application of sound principles. It merely affects the number of positions involved to perform individual work elements. Extreme size may demand maximum decentralization of work. Product diversity or complexity are of importance only as they affect the individual work elements.

16. What has been done concerning position guides, position evaluation, and nomenclature?	Position guides are useful only if they clearly define and describe the responsibilities, authorities, relationships, and accountabilities for the man, his manager, and for others with whom he has work relationships. Positions should be evaluated according to the value of the work, not according to the reporting level. Organization components and individual positions should be named to identify their primary work, they should not be named to indicate levels in the organization structure.
17. Does the plan of implementation represent a good "plan for action"?	Real progress will be made when there are target dates and associated interim organization structures by which it is possible to move towards the most desirable objective organization structure. Individuals should fully understand the organization changes sufficiently well in advance in order that they more fully contribute to successful implementation. Adequate manpower at the right time depends upon plans for manpower development and procurement. Recording the reasoning behind and explanations of major changes are required to evaluate progress and reappraise future needs.
18. Are there provisions for ensuring periodic review?	Implementation requires a reasonable period of time. It is more apt to remain on schedule if disciplined by the forcing action of regular review. Organization structuring is dynamic just as is research and design. It must continue to anticipate the changing needs of the business.

CHAPTER 4

Behavioral Characteristics of Organizations, Motivating and Leading

NEED FOR PERCEPTIVE LEADERSHIP

Technical managers usually rise from the ranks of engineers and scientists. For this reason their training and focus has been fixed on nonpersonal activities and achievements. As the engineer/scientist is first charged with directing a small group on a project, he is faced with learning administrative procedures at once. He may not be aware that he has also embarked upon another venture that is probably totally alien to his education and experience. This is the realm of the behavior of people in groups.

At whatever level the technical manager operates in the E & R organization, his ability to understand organizational behavior, to understand what motivates his particular types of technical employee, and to *apply* his knowledge is critical to the functioning and productivity of the E & R organization. Many managers believe they are naturally gifted with perceptive leadership when actually very few are. If he happens to be a newly created technical manager who rose from the ranks, he has spent most of his professional life dealing with "things" and/or materials, which certainly did little to prepare him for managing people. A study of research results on the nature of group behavior, motivation, and leadership styles and patterns represents a starting point for development of leadership qualities. This chapter highlights some aspects of the role of the technical manager in meeting company objectives and fulfilling the needs of his people.

Understanding the Engineer/Scientist as an Individual

It is essential for the E & R manager in dealing with his subordinates and associates to be aware that each perceives reality in a different way. The human mind is not a mirror of its environment but rather mirrors its own psychological, sociological, and cultural experience to yield an image that is unique. The manager must, therefore, seek to determine how others perceive "facts" in order to reconcile initial apparent differences and understand "irrational" behavior.

In addition, each individual is motivated by a "mix" of needs or wants. A. H. Maslow developed a hierarchy of these needs:

1. Physiological needs
2. Safety and security needs
3. Need for esteem by others, or social needs
4. Need for self-esteem, or ego needs
5. Need for self-fulfillment, or growing toward utilization of one's full potential.

What are the "on-the-job" needs of professional scientists and engineers? Eleven top R/D administrators gathered at the 11th Annual Industrial Research Conference at Columbia University and partially answered this very question. They stated that some of these needs are:

1. *Desire for professional stature*—A scientist/engineer may achieve more satisfaction by gaining status within his professional group than within the company organization. One of the primary means for his doing this is through published articles. A conflict between the scientist/engineer and the company may arise because the information for a proposed article may be considered "proprietary" information by the company. Also, companies are concerned with the time and cost involved in writing these articles. The result of the foregoing conflicts is the discouragement of the scientific/engineering writer. Thus, a company manager should make every effort to encourage these men and search for a solution when a conflict arises.
2. *Freedom*—Generally, a scientist/engineer wants to follow his project through to completion even though the company has determined that the project results cannot be economically advantageous to the company. Scientists/engineers also want to participate in the selection of their projects and to establish their own deadlines. In addition, the lack of freedom concerning working hours, dress, authorization of expenditures, etc., are sources of irritation to scientists/engineers.
3. *Promotion and advancement*—Scientists/engineers want promotion for a variety of reasons. The reasons vary from the desire for power to the desire to increase their effectiveness. Scientists/engineers feel that promotion should be based on technical knowledge and ability. They are discouraged when politics plays an important role in promotion. However, politics will always exist to some degree in every organization.
4. *Competent direction*—In general, scientists/engineers want to be managed by scientists/engineers. They tend to have less respect and

confidence in managers who have gained their position through administrative ability and/or personality.

5. *Corporate management understanding of technical problems*—Frequently, scientists/engineers feel that management is incapable of understanding technical problems.
6. *Disencumbrance from subprofessional tasks*—Scientists/engineers feel that their status requires that they should not be burdened with nontechnical tasks or routine technical tasks.
7. *Personal recognition and status symbols*—Money should not be considered as the only important source of status satisfaction for scientists/engineers. Some of the more commonly accepted sources of status for the individual are the location and size of one's office, the location of one's parking space, etc.[1]

Research results on the study of needs of technical professional people are conveniently summarized in Table 4-1.

Donald C. Pelz and Frank M. Andrews conducted extensive research on productive climates for R & D. They concluded that motivation, and hence productivity, depends vitally upon building the self-reliance and independence of the technical man. Yet the traditional systems of organizational rewards restrict the individual and foster dependence. The researchers feel that there are many alternative approaches creative management might employ and they suggest some ideas as a beginning.[2]

Individuals in organizations are often faced with conflicts of needs. Usually these conflicts arise between personal needs and organizational needs. Differences in value needs of the individual and the company have become more troublesome in recent years. Individuals must function in different roles which also gives rise to conflict within the individual. He must:

1. Fulfill the role to match his conception of himself as an individual
2. Fulfill the role expected of someone of his position in the organization
3. Fulfill the role of a given social position.

UNDERSTANDING PEOPLE IN ORGANIZATIONS

The individual in an organization interacts with other members of the organization so that each affects the behavior of the others. There is a great degree of interdependence among organizational variables such as group cohesion, functional and dysfunctional activities, rank and position of individuals in the organization, role expectations, coping patterns in response to conflict or ambiguity in perceived roles, and leadership patterns.

[1] "Reconciling Professional and Personal Goals and Needs With Company Goals and Needs," *Research/Development* (October 1960): 12–13.

[2] Donald C. Pelz and Frank M. Andrews, *Scientists in Organizations* (New York: John Wiley & Sons, 1966), pp. 90–111.

Table 4-1—Employee Needs (Rank Ordered)

SCHAFFER PROFESSIONAL MEN	HERZBERG, et al. ENGINEERS AND ACCOUNTANTS	MYERS					
		ENGINEERS	SCIENTISTS	MANUFACTURING SUPERVISORS	TECHNICIANS	FEMALE ASSEMBLERS	
1. Creativity and challenge	Achievement +	Work itself +	Responsibility –	Advancement +	Responsibility +	Competence of supervision	1.
2. Achievement	Recognition +	Responsibility –	Work itself +	Responsibility	Advancement +	Recognition –	2.
3. Social welfare ("need to help others")	Work itself +	Company policy and administration –	Company policy and administration +	Pay –	Pay –	Security –	3.
4. Moral value scheme (need to have behavior agree with this scheme)	Responsibility +	Pay –	Recognition +	Achievement –	Work itself –	Friendliness of supervision +	4.
5. Interpersonal relationships	Advancement +	Advancement +	Competence of supervision	Possibility of growth +	Company policy and administration +	Pay +	5.
6. Self-expression	Salary	Recognition –	Advancement +	Friendliness of supervision –	Achievement	Achievement +	6.
7. Dominance	Possibility of growth	Achievement	Achievement	Company policy and administration	Competence of supervision –	Work itself	7.

8. Recognition	Interpersonal relations (subordinates)	(Competence of supervision) –		(Competence of supervision)	Recognition	(Company policy and administration) –	8.
9. Economic security	Status	Friendliness of supervision –		(Peer relations)		(Peer relations) –	9.
10. Independence	Interpersonal relations (superior) –			Recognition +			10.
11. Socio-economic status	Interpersonal relations (peers)						11.
12. Dependence	Supervision-technical –						12.
13.	Company policy and administration –						13.
14.	Working conditions –						14.
15.	Factors in personal life						15.
16.	Job security						16.

Key: those in parentheses are nearly equal in rank; + lead to satisfaction (primarily); – lead to dissatisfaction (primarily); those unmarked are bipolar (primarily).

Reprinted from *Organizational Behavior* © 1965 by Philip B. Applewhite (pp. 16–17) with permission of Prentice-Hall, Inc., Englewood Cliffs, N.J.

In their attempt to integrate personal and organizational goals, people in organizations frequently "satisfice." That is, they perform safe tasks well enough to satisfy their managers but do not take initiative that may lead to outstanding performance and that also has the risk of failure attached to it.[3] It is apparent that the effective technical manager must create a climate that presents challenges but not threats, that recognizes both individual and group achievements, that extends individuals horizontally across disciplines and vertically through participative goal setting, and that evokes new responses through changing relationships. This is approximated by the collegial model of organizational behavior shown in Fig. 4-1.

PUTTING BEHAVIORAL KNOWLEDGE TO WORK

If the technical manager reads the results of research on organizational behavior, he will assimilate knowledge that will guide him. It is difficult to provide pat rules or generalizations for managing people in groups. Recent hypotheses and tests indicate that a "productivity orientation" and a "people orientation" are not opposite styles of management but may coexist together to produce highly effective organizations. R. R. Blake and J. S. Mouton have developed a highly successful training program around this concept exemplified by their "Managerial Grid." The highlights of the grid are shown in Fig. 4-2.[4]

Four Models of Organizational Behavior

	Autocratic	*Custodial*	*Supportive*	*Collegial*
Depends on:	Power	Economic resources	Leadership	Mutual contribution
Managerial orientation:	Authority	Material rewards	Support	Integration and teamwork
Employee orientation:	Obedience	Security	Performance	Responsibility
Employee psychological result:	Personal dependency	Organizational dependency	Participation	Self-discipline
Employee needs met:	Subsistence	Maintenance	Higher-order	Self-realization
Performance result:	Minimum	Passive cooperation	Awakened drives	Enthusiasm
Morale measure:	Compliance	Satisfaction	Motivation	Commitment to task and team

Fig. 4-1. Four models of organizational behavior. *Source:* Keith Davis, "Evolving Models of Organizational Behavior," *Academy of Management Journal* (March 1968), p. 29.

With considerable unexpressed qualifications, the following positive guides are suggested for the E & R manager:

[3] For a discussion of "satisficing," see Herbert Simon, *Administrative Behavior*, ed. 2 (New York: Macmillan, 1958), p. xxv.

[4] See Robert R. Blake, Jane S. Mouton et al., "Breakthrough in Organizational Development," *Harvard Business Review* (Nov.–Dec. 1964).

1. Promote your best men promptly. Promotion need not be in terms of steps up the hierarchy alone. Greater horizontal responsibility (job enlargement) and/or greater vertical decision-making responsibility (job enrichment) accompanied by organizational recognition and salary increases represent promotion.

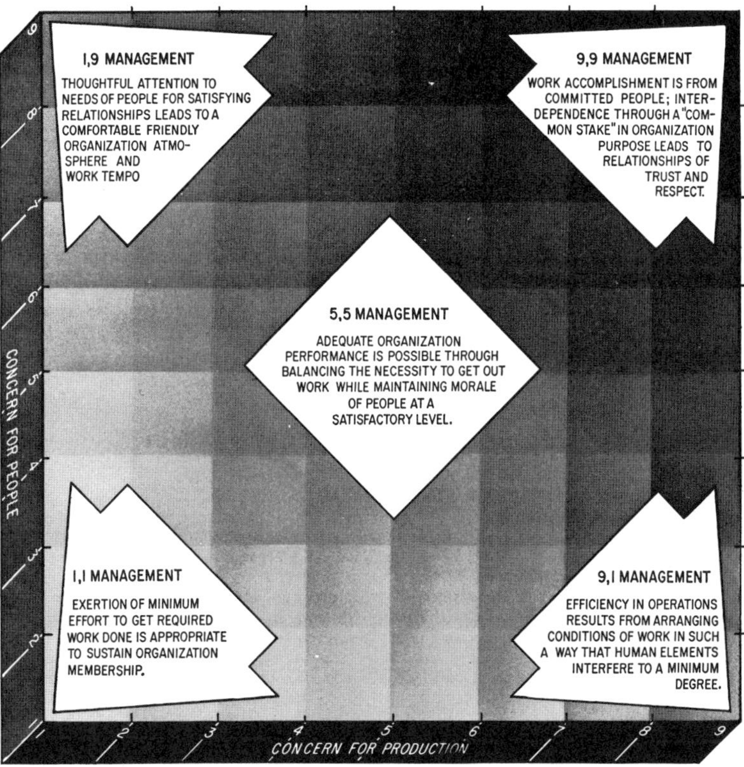

Fig. 4-2. The managerial grid. *Source:* Robert R. Blake and Jane S. Mouton; Louis B. Barnes and Larry E. Greiner, "Breakthrough in Organizational Development," *Harvard Business Review* (Nov.–Dec., 1964), p. 136.

2. Maintain good communications both downward, upward, and horizontally in the organization. Brief weekly meetings at every management level are advisable. Face-to-face contact between the manager and each of his subordinates should be held frequently enough so that the employee is fully aware of all activities relevant to his work and his manager's view of his performance. General meetings of the entire E & R organization (including clerical workers) should be held several times a year for a progress report and question and answer period. Thus, every worker is kept informed of general goals and progress as well as his own specific area of work. If people are not

kept fully informed, *they construct in their mind an image of reality* that may be greatly distorted. "Fully informed" does not mean that the lowest level worker must be informed of every detail of all E & R operations, but rather of the general goals and progress (the structure) and specifics relevant to his work.

3. Get each E & R member to participate in developing and setting his goals. This is done by first presenting the goals for the particular component of the E & R organization involved. The individual, in a two-way discussion with his manager, works out the part that he can play. Tasks and schedules should be established such that each individual faces work that meets his best expectations and aspirations. The plans should be the basis of measurement and appraisal and review should be a continuous process. Generally, high norms with firm follow-up provide higher incentive and greater self-discipline by the individual.
4. The manager should seek to help the members of his groups in practical ways such as expediting cross-organizational and higher organization level impediments to progress, obtaining resources, assisting with especially difficult problems when called upon, and providing timely information that bears upon his group's work.
5. The manager should seek to build strong group cohesion and yet maintain some intellectual competition among members. For example, he may be able to identify and report on a similar group in a competitive company for his group to excel. He should act as a buffer against pressures from above and yet make the group aware of the significance of its work to organizational goals. He must be willing to accept mistakes that are made by individuals attempting valuable achievements.
6. He should strongly encourage his people to report and publish their work and hence develop pride in their group because of its technical reputation.
7. The appraisal, evaluation, and reward structure should be established so that it is accepted as fair by the group. This means that the manager of the E & R organization must see that it is communicated to all members of his organization. Such communication should not be assumed to be a one-shot affair; rather it is particularly important to reinforce such communication regularly.

REVITALIZING THE E & R ORGANIZATION

E & R organizations may lose their productiveness and creativity due to the following:

1. Poor managers and hence poor leadership
2. Aging of the personnel
3. Stagnant organization structure.

Concerning managers, the manager of E & R is, of course, responsible for recruiting, selecting, and training his subordinate managers. E & R managers, regardless of their capabilities in technical work, must realize that their job demands a continual struggle against the status quo. Research itself requires a continual effort to do, to seek, and to uncover that which is different. As Merritt Williamson says, the "manager must initiate; fight the status quo . . . a real premium should be placed on that part of the manager's job which leads to continual disruption."[5] This, despite the fact that the engineering or research manager must maintain, to some degree, a smoothly running organization.

The aging of personnel within an E & R organization is more difficult to treat in many respects. The human brain in the upper intelligence groups does not reach maturity until about twenty-five years of age. Between twenty and forty is often the most creative period of a man's life even though the formulation of new ideas may extend over a much later period. Those few men who have trained their minds well may still maintain a high, though decreasing, level of creativity well into their senior years (Fig. 4-3). Obviously, one solution to this form of organization aging is to recruit

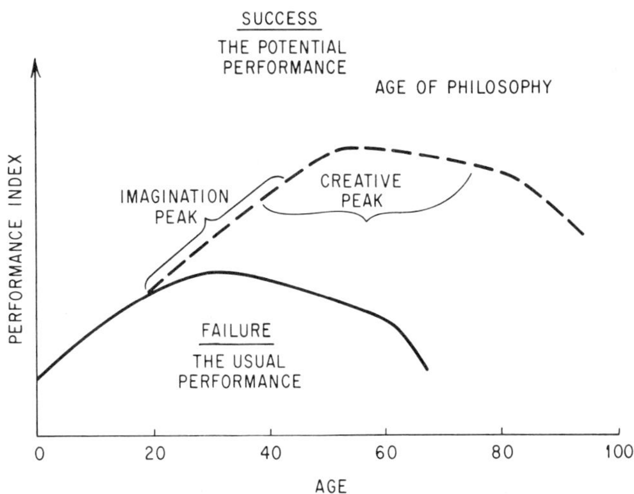

Fig. 4-3. Potential and performance of the individual scientist or engineer. *Source:* Adapted from chart by J. W. Still, M.D.

[5] M. A. Williamson, "Technical Research Management," *Reprinted by permission of the publisher,* F. D. Thompson Publications, Inc., from *Industrial Laboratories* magazine (now *Research/Development*), June 1958.

youth and discharge older engineers. This is difficult to do, even though the company would be ahead if it pensioned off some older men quite generously. The other alternative is to maintain a climate of youthfulness and challenge and continually create new organizational relationships as will be discussed below.

Not only do individuals age, but an organization does also. Symptoms of organizational aging are size, complexity, rigidity, and inertia. As organizations enlarge, communication becomes more difficult, staff functions appear to grow more numerous, and there appears a diminishing feeling of responsibility on the part of each individual.

Projects or activities of the E & R function best if not more than 500 to 1,000 people are directly involved, depending on the nature of the activity or project.

Complexity and rigidity of the organization structure and the engineering processes over a period of a year or more, and inertia in the organization due to lack of initiative and acceptance of responsibility are symptoms of aging.

What, then, can be done to counteract these tendencies? The project-type organization provides the answer automatically, i.e., it continually creates new teams, working relationships, and tougher goals. It emphasizes the need for creative thinking by creating a conducive climate; deemphasizes status symbols and long-service tokens. It encourages intuitive approaches to solutions since there will always be the methodical engineers who will want to check out such solutions by careful analysis to verify or disprove the daring and bold concepts often achieved by intuitive processes. It doesn't discourage the creative thinker before he has had a chance to transfer his ideas to paper. "Few human abilities play a greater role in engineering progress than the skilled ingenuity and creative thinking which underlie both inventiveness and resourceful leadership."[6] New situations, new organizational relationships, and new challenges can be introduced by the E & R managers to revitalize the aging organization.

DEVELOPING CREATIVE ENGINEERING

Creative Thinking

Creative thinking is the intuitive process by which an individual reaches a new (for him) solution to a problem that jumps over the step-by-step reasoning chain. Creative thinking calls upon all the previous knowledge of the individual, but not all in a conscious manner. Rather, there is a period of almost chaotic or aimless thinking followed by a new insight and restructuring of the problem and its elements.

[6] W. H. Easton, "Creative Thinking and How to Develop It," *Mechanical Engineering,* Vol. 68 (August 1946): 697–704.

A persistent myth about creative ideas is that they appear instantaneously as a sudden vision. Although this may occasionally happen, closer study shows that very few creative ideas and solutions have occurred at the beginning of the creative process. The creative process involves a time period in which a man combines and recombines his past experience in such a way that he arrives at a partial outline, a partial mental picture, which, when completed, has new elements and arrangements previously unknown to him.

Problems may be said to have three classes of solutions. One is the orthodox solution arrived at by analytical reasoning. In this case, the mental process is often merely a duplication of a known procedure with modified steps or quantities. The chief noncreative processes may be said to be:

Observation—noting and studying perceived objects, processes, and circumstances.

Remembering—retrieving information stored in the mind such as past facts, ideas, methods, processes, and circumstances.

Reasoning—selecting pertinent stored and observed information and determining the consequences of the assumed initial conditions within the constraints imposed by the pertinent assumptions.

Judgment—formulating decisions based upon the conclusions from reasoning in terms of the presently perceived environment and anticipated environment.

Another type of solution to a problem is that obtained by trial and error or by stubborn experimentation employing trial and error. It is true that there may be some small measure of analysis and creative thinking, but in the end the solution depends upon either luck or persistence.

The third type of solution is the creative solution. The process consists of the following steps:

Formulation of the problem. First the problem is formulated by observation, remembering, and communication from other people.

Reformulation of the problem. The first formulation of the problem is generally only a statement of what is and what is wanted. In the reformulation, the true nature of the problem is determined. For example, in making tennis balls, the first statement of the problem was how to pump air into tennis balls to pressurize them without leaving a sealing plug which unbalances the ball. As restated, the question was asked as to how a ball could be made with higher-than-atmospheric pressure on the inside. With the reformulation of the problem the creative solution in this case was relatively easy. Simply make the tennis balls inside a pressurized room without worrying about pumping them up and sealing them off.

Intensive concentration. Next is an intensive concentration on the problem for periods of time during which critical judgment is suspended.

Intermission periods. Creative solutions cannot be forced. After a period of intensive concentration, the creative person will put the problem aside temporarily although he may come back to it consciously from time to time. These "intermission" periods are what are sometimes called the "incubation" period. However, interest in the problem is maintained at a high level throughout.

Illumination or inspiration. Illumination is the event in which pieces of the solution fall into place with relative swiftness, often in a manner completely different from the former conscious structurings. It may occur when the mind is completely at rest and apparently unoccupied with the problem, that is, during a walk, in the middle of a dream, while playing golf, or while at a ball game. It is similar to the familiar emotional experience of failing to recall a familiar name or word. Intense effort to remember fails. Even though the individual relaxes his effort, the desire to remember remains and is accompanied by knowing discomfort. Then suddenly, at a later time, is the feeling that so often occurs during the illumination process—the feeling, "Why didn't I see that before?"

Creative Engineering

Creative engineering, as used here, means the achievement of a solution to an engineering problem by means of the creative thinking process. There is one other important constraint in this definition: the solution must represent an improved product, process, or method *resulting* in a new or better product. It is not enough simply to arrive at a completely new way of doing something or a new product if it is not better than before.

Crosby Field defines creative engineering in this way:

> May we define creative engineering, therefore, as the act of creating a new visualization of an application of established engineering principles? This does not necessarily include invention because many inventions are made which are not in accord with established engineering principles, nor does it absolutely exclude invention. However, this definition does include the activities of the constructive imagination of those skilled in the art of engineering, applied to new visualization of any type whatsoever. It certainly does include machine design even when the particular machine design does not include invention.[7]

Characteristics of Highly Creative Engineers

Much of the current scientific body of knowledge about characteristics of the creative individual is attributed to Dr. J. P. Guilford. Guilford divides the characteristics into two groups, that is, mental and emotional. The four basic mental attributes are as follows:

[7] C. Field, "Creative Engineering," address given at the Machine Design Division, ASME, semiannual meeting, Pittsburgh, Pennsylvania, June 20–24, 1954.

1. *Sensitivity to problems.* The highly creative individual sees problems around him and sees them far in advance of other people since he is continually observing and questioning.
2. *Fluency of thought.* The highly creative person has many ideas, not necessarily all good. But ideas come with high frequency because of the suspension of inhibiting judgment at the idea stage. Ideas breed more ideas.
3. *Flexibility of thinking.* This is the ability to avoid the rut of stereotyped thinking, to break away from habit and tradition. Dr. Guilford showed how flexibility of thought could be demonstrated by asking people to list as many uses as they could think of for a common brick. The flexible thinker would think of most of the fourteen possible categories. To illustrate, bricks could be used for their mass such as for paper weights, for their dimensions as book ends, or for throwing at enemies. They could be ground up to make red pigment for paint or be used as abrasives to sprinkle on icy walks. Moreover, they have thermal capacity and could be used as bed warmers, etc.

   Contrast this with rigidity of thinking described by John E. Arnold of MIT. Arnold was conversing with the director of research of a large power shovel company who proudly described the progress the company had made over the years. Their first shovel handled about one third of a cubic yard, and now as a result of research they have shovels that handle thirty cubic yards. Here was a case of only one question being asked: Can we make it bigger?
4. *Originality.* While the less creative person stops with one or two ideas as possible solutions to a problem, the more creative person thinks of numerous solutions. He is better able to assemble seemingly unrelated ideas and construct them into a new solution.

Some of the emotional attributes are high motivation, willingness of the individual to take a chance and stick his neck out, and persistence.

Other miscellaneous characteristics, or subclasses of those given above, which are easily identifiable in the highly creative engineer are:

1. The engineer places a greater emphasis on his desire for freedom and independence in thought and action.
2. Creative engineers show a personal recognition and acceptance of their special creative talents.
3. Creative engineers have a smaller number of close friends and are not "joiners" of organizations.
4. Creative engineers show a questioning approach to new things, new ideas, and to problems.
5. Highly creative people are apt to be more stable, less anxious, and display greater self-confidence.

6. More highly creative engineers think in more abstract and theoretical terms while others prefer the most practical.
7. The more creative show acute powers of observations and concentration.
8. The more creative can face ambiguous situations easily without becoming upset or anxious.
9. Some evidence shows that the most creative engineers come from the top decile and bottom decile of the engineering classes in school.

It may be of interest to the reader to note that a Kettering Foundation sponsored project to identify, through psychological tests, the creative engineer and scientist is being carried forward at Rensselaer Polytechnic Institute. It is still too early to report results. However, preliminary results indicate that the goal will be achieved.

Creative Engineering Courses and Seminars

A number of industrial firms believe strongly in the value of developing creative engineering potential. The General Electric Company has both a two- and three-year Creative Engineering Program for young engineers who qualify. In addition, General Electric Departments sponsor a thirteen-week course in creative engineering in which methods and attitudes are covered and actual engineering problems are solved. For technicians and other associated engineering personnel, a thirteen-week course is given covering the following:

1. Objectives
2. Problem recognition
3. Definition of the problem
4. Search for methods
5. Evaluation of methods and selection
6. Follow-through
7. Development
8. Attitudes
9. Ideation techniques
10. Group problems
11. Value analysis
12. Patents.

Also, General Motors, U. S. Steel, and other leaders in industry long ago inaugurated creative training programs.

Guide for Self-Improvement

The individual engineer who wishes to develop his creative ability on his own should first be aware of certain blocks or barriers to creative thinking. The most important of these barriers are:

1. *Perceptual blocks.* There are numerous blocks arising out of failure to recognize each element of a situation separately. That is, the individual becomes very familiar with some areas, and his mind slides over certain background details as obvious. Someone not familiar with the field would question each of these.

   Another example occurs when the individual affixes certain functions to an object. The association of a brick as only a building block would be an example. Here, he sees a brick as a brick, not as an object with mass, size, color, and other physical and chemical properties.
2. *Cultural blocks.* Cultural influences tend to repress certain ways of looking at problems and situations. Taboos bear upon certain fringe areas of thinking. Refinement of taste and intellectual training may obliterate whole areas of information and thinking patterns. In the present American culture, conformity, cooperativeness, and competitiveness all exert strong influence.
3. *Environmental blocks.* Environmental blocks emanate from influences affecting the individual's development. If his schooling has been of a rigid authoritarian type where "teacher knows all" and there is little class participation, he is apt to look to authority for his ideas.

   If his parents have fed him solutions to all his problems, he is apt to be dependent upon others for problem solving. Individuals need challenges that test them to the utmost and yet are solvable. Strength comes through a pattern of successes in such an environment.
4. *Emotional blocks.* Emotional blocks, which comprise the largest group, are the most serious of all. Some of these blocks are:

   1. Desire to succeed quickly with the result that the field of observation is limited, only those clues that seem relevant are seized upon, and not enough alternatives are examined
   2. Information from the outside world is distorted by the individual's frame of reference
   3. The basic attributes of perceived objects are not seen
   4. Fear of dreaming and desire to be practical
   5. Fear of ridicule by associates
   6. Preference for the logical over the intuitive approach
   7. Desire for security
   8. Bias for or against certain ideas
   9. Resistance to changing technology and methods
   10. Unwillingness to seek help from others in related specialties
   11. Self-satisfaction
   12. Lack of faith in one's self
   13. Over-cooperation.

There are certain patterns of behavior which the engineer should endeavor to cultivate. Concerning everything around him he should *question, observe, associate,* and practice *predicting.* To aid himself in these steps he should:

1. Keep a notebook with him at all times to jot down ideas that pop into his head as he questions and observes.
2. Keep a separate notebook at work or at home in which he lists problems he is now working on, problems he would like to work on, and the relative urgency of these.
3. At the beginning of each day, record the two or three most pressing problems and set a deadline for their solution.
4. Take the most urgent problem first and start working on it. Make a sketch or write something on a piece of paper since these are ways of initiating the thinking process at times. Collect pertinent facts and information.
5. Use a check list of idea stimulators as shown in Fig. 4-4.
6. Select a particular time of the day when you find you work most effectively. Work in the same place regularly. Occasionally, a great deal of quiet combined with feet on the desk and hands behind the head induces the relaxation which induces the flow of ideas.
7. Start with trying to give a true statement of the problem—not the statement as given. It may turn out that:
   a. There is no problem at all.
   b. The true statement of the problem gives the solution immediately as in the case of the pressurized tennis balls.
   c. An associated and more important problem may be uncovered and solved.
   d. The solution of the problem as restated may be seen to be analogous to a known problem and solution.
8. Seek a number of solutions *before* applying critical judgment. *Then* evaluate all solutions realistically.

The complete, thorough process, in summary, consists of: (1) Problem recognition; (2) Restatement of the problem; (3) Initial data collection and evaluation; (4) Synthesis; (5) Analysis of alternatives; and (6) Final complete interpretation.

Group Creativity

In group creativity sessions, sometimes called "brainstorming," from five to ten people gather together to develop creative ideas for solving a very specific problem. The general rules for such a session are:

1. Have a very specific problem defined; don't attempt to work on a broadly stated one.

IDEA STIMULATORS

1. Have I pinpointed the problem?
2. Have I searched books, reports, the trade magazines, patents?
3. How would I design it if I were to build it in my workshop at home?
4. Have I considered the physical, thermal, electrical, chemical, and mechanical properties of this material?
5. What other materials have the same properties required?
6. Have I looked for electrical, electronic, optical, hydraulic, mechanical, or magnetic ways of doing this?
7. Have I followed tradition, custom, authority, opinion blindly?
8. Have I looked at analogs for parallel problems?
9. Is this function really necessary?
10. How would other experts look at this problem?
11. Have I made this design accomplish its purpose?
12. Could I alter something already available to do the job?
13. Have I analyzed this in several ways?
14. Could I construct a model?
15. Why must it have this shape?
16. Could it be speeded up or slowed down?
17. Could this be turned inside out, upside down, or reversed?
18. Could this be changed to more of a three dimensional object, or could it be flattened out?
19. Could this be made cheaper, or should it be made more expensive?
20. What if this were made larger, higher, longer, wider, thicker, or lower?
21. What could be substituted? For what?
22. How could I rearrange or alter the parts, the subassemblies?
23. Has it been simplified as much as possible?
24. What new ways could it be used as it is?
25. What other forms of power would make it work better?
26. Where else can this be done?
27. Would this work better in the day, in the night, intermittently, or continuously?
28. Could this be put to other uses if it were modified?
29. Could several parts be combined?
30. Could standard components be substituted?
31. Could this be made easier to operate?
32. What if the order of the process were changed?
33. Can materials be salvaged or reclaimed?
34. Suppose this were left out?
35. How can this be made to appeal to the senses? Appearance improved?
36. Can it be made safer?
37. Can it be made more compact?
38. Should it be made more symmetrical or more asymmetrical?
39. Can I forget the specifications and get a better performance?
40. How about extra value?
41. Can this be multiplied, reduced, blown up, or carried to extremes?
42. What form could this be in — liquid, powder, paste, or solid? Rod, tube, polyhedron, cube, or sphere?
43. Can motion be added to it?
44. Will it be better standing still?
45. Can it be made better or cheaper for another production process?
46. Can cause and effect be reversed? Which is cause and which is effect?
47. Should it be put on the other end or in the middle?
48. Should it rotate instead of slide?
49. Should it slide instead of roll?
50. Could the package be used for something else afterwards?
51. What other method is there for separating the variables?
52. What if the speed were increased or decreased?
53. What if it were heat-treated, hardened, alloyed, cured, frozen, plated?
54. What if color were added or changed or it were made transparent or translucent?
55. What if it were twisted, streamlined, condensed?
56. How about blending or adding an assortment?
57. What if it were crushed, distilled, or compressed?
58. Would it be internally braced or externally braced?

Fig. 4-4. Idea stimulators.

2. Judicial judgment must be "ruled out" and any direct or implied criticism of ideas must be avoided until *after* the session.
3. "Free wheeling" must be welcomed. The wilder the idea the better; it is easier to scale down than up.
4. Quantity rather than quality of ideas is sought. The more ideas from which to choose the greater the likelihood for good ones to be introduced.
5. Combine and improve introduced ideas. Joining ideas or turning the ideas of other participants into even better ideas helps stimulate even more ideas.
6. Avoid including people of widely differing rank until the techniques have become very familiar.
7. The chairman of the group session should prepare a rough list of all ideas, see that they are clearly stated, and classify them into logical categories.
8. The list of ideas then should be screened by a group of executives who look for the best ones as well as for possible combinations or for ideas which could be improved by further development.
9. As soon as possible after the session, the responsible executive should report back to the group members the action taken.

Establish a Climate for Creative Engineering

There are a number of positive steps that management can take to ensure a climate for creative engineering. These are:

1. Try to give engineers a choice of problems to work on within their field of interest. In large corporations many problems needing solutions exist at almost any period in time; moreover, there usually are many aspects to each problem. Give the engineer a chance to match his interests to the problems.
2. Delegate considerable freedom to responsible engineers.
3. In the creative stage of design, allow time and freedom of thought for new ideas to incubate. Don't ask for justification of new ideas prematurely, or the complex process of developing many alternatives will be terminated. Management requires justification of new ideas, but the timing should be right, i.e., after the conceptual phase.
4. For the highly creative engineers foster a climate in which it is permissible to just sit and think without having such action being interpreted as a waste of time. What counts is the total number and value of new ideas per year and not the number of poor ideas per day.
5. Recognize all new ideas promptly by keeping the originators informed of action taken or reasons for not pursuing them.
6. Conduct seminars where informality rules, and where engineers and researchers can meet for cross-fertilization of ideas.

7. Don't resist major changes in technology or new ideas because they represent big leaps. Many managements crawl because of caution, are content to make progress with small changes, and don't take advantage of opportunities to make big gains by utilizing the ideas of their highly creative people.
8. Recognize personality differences and adapt the organization to allow for the "different" individual. This doesn't mean that the organization must bend to the whims of creative eccentrics, but rather that many creative individuals like privacy, like to set their own hours, and don't want to waste their time filling out administrative forms and reports.
9. Provide the highly creative engineers with tools and opportunity. Give them adequate physical facilities, high quality supplies that are easily available, the best in source materials and information service. Provide them with sufficient technicians, draftsmen, and clerical help because it's expensive to pay your most creative people for performing noncreative functions.

   Make off-hour facilities available since creative people don't work by the clock.
10. Send your highly creative people to technical society meetings and technical seminars for a "change of pace" so that they can meet other specialists, learn of new problems and techniques, and receive the stimulation that results from associating with the outstanding men in their field.
11. Give your highly creative engineers status and financial recognition comparable to managers rendering equally valuable contributions. An effective personnel audit system should include creativity factors and appropriate weighting of these factors. Periodic reviews of progress and contributions made by these gifted engineers offer the manager an opportunity to learn their problems and provide them with personal recognition.
12. Creativity will thrive in the E & R organization only to the extent that top management is creative itself and shows that it understands and values the creative process. Top management must feel the restless urge for new ideas, communicate this stimulation down through the ranks, and be willing to take more risks than most organizations presently do.

BIBLIOGRAPHY

Applewhite, Philip B. *Organizational Behavior.* Englewood Cliffs, N.J.: Prentice-Hall, Inc., 1965.

Argyris, Chris. *Personality and Organization.* New York, N.Y.: Harper & Brothers, 1957.

BARBER, B., and HIRSCH, W., eds. *The Sociology of Science.* New York, N.Y.: Glencoe Free Press, 1962.

BLAKE, ROBERT R., MOUTON, JANE S. et al. "Breakthrough in Organizational Development," *Harvard Business Review,* November–December, 1964.

DRUCKER, PETER F. "Twelve Fables of Research Management," *Harvard Business Review,* September–October, 1963.

EASTON, W. H. "Creative Thinking and How to Develop It," *Mechanical Engineering,* Vol. 68, August, 1946.

EVAN, W. M. "Conflict and Performance in R & D Organizations: Some Preliminary Findings," *Industrial Management Review,* Vol. 7, 1965.

———. "Harnessing the R & D Monster," *Fortune Magazine,* June, 1965.

GLASER, BARNEY S. *Organizational Scientists: Their Professional Careers.* Indianapolis, Ind.: The Bobbs-Merrill Company, Inc., 1964.

HAIRE, MASON. *Organization Theory in Industrial Practice.* New York, N.Y.: John Wiley & Sons, Inc., 1962.

HAMPTON, DAVID R.; SUMMER, CHARLES E., JR.; and WEBER, ROSS A. *Organizational Behavior and the Practice of Management.* Glenville, Ill.: Scott, Foresman & Company, 1968.

HERZBERG, FREDERICK. "One More Time: How Do You Motivate Employees?", *Harvard Business Review,* January–February, 1968.

HOUTON, F. V. "Work Assignment and Interpersonal Relations in a Research Organization: Some Participant Observations," *Administrative Science Quarterly,* 4, 1963.

HUBER, GEORGE P. "Implications of Organization Theory for Research Management," *Research Management,* September, 1967.

JACKSON, THOMAS W., and SPURLOCK, JACK M. *Research and Development Management.* Homewood, Ill.: Dow Jones-Irwin, Inc., 1966.

LOWIN, AARON. "Participative Decision Making: A Model, Literature Critique, and Prescriptions for Research," *Organizational Behavior and Human Performance,* February, 1968.

MARVIN, PHILIP. "Revitalizing the Engineering Organization," *Machine Design,* May 12, 1960.

ORTH, C. D.; BAILEY, J. C.; and WOLEK, F. W., eds. *Administering Research and Development.* Homewood, Ill.: Richard D. Irwin, Inc., 1964.

PELZ, DONALD C., and ANDREWS, FRANK M. *Scientists in Organizations.* New York, N.Y.: John Wiley & Sons, Inc., 1966.

"Reconciling Professional and Personal Goals and Needs with Company Goals and Needs," *Research/Development,* Vol. 11, No. 10, October, 1960.

ROSSMAN, JOSEPH. *Industrial Creativity, The Psychology of the Inventor.* New Hyde Park, N.Y.: University Books, Inc., 1964.

RUBENSTEIN, ALBERT H. "Organizational Factors Affecting Research and Development Decision-Making in Large Decentralized Companies," *Management Science,* July, 1964.

SCHEIN, EDGAR H. *Organizational Psychology.* Englewood Cliffs, N.J.: Prentice-Hall, Inc., 1965.

WILLIAMSON, M. W. "Technical Research Management," *Industrial Laboratories* (now *Research/Development*), June, 1958.

CHAPTER 5

Staffing and Developing the E & R Organization

PLANNING THE STAFFING PROGRAM

Long-range Requirements for Technical and Managerial Personnel

Staffing or manning an organization is concerned with the determination of manpower needs, the recruitment of people who can fill these needs, their placement within the organization, their training, and the retention of those who successfully fulfill the job requirements as incumbents. Long-range plans for staffing primarily depend upon the existence of realistic forecasts and the company's policy.

There are three important general objectives that should always be kept to the fore in connection with staffing:

1. Obtaining sufficient qualified men when needed
2. Minimizing staffing cost on a *long-range* basis
3. Maintaining ethical standards in recruiting, transferring, and severing employees.

Involved in the first objective listed above is the problem of obtaining the *right* quality of men, which does not always mean obtaining the most highly trained, experienced, or intelligent men. Actually, a combination of engineering skills, mature experience and youth should be sought out and brought together. The result of hiring only topnotch people may result in an unbalance of personnel who want only to manage, or design, or perform certain functions and who refuse to perform other *necessary work* that they consider "beneath them."

Satisfying the first and second objectives together is a major problem. The choice is often difficult to make between an all-out drive to fill requirements at a given time versus the lower costs associated with a continuous program to develop and maintain contacts with candidates.

The third objective of maintaining ethical recruiting standards is important to any company in the long run, especially where professional personnel are involved.

Establishing Policies with Regard to Hiring and Retention

The company must establish clear staffing policies dealing with both procedures and responsibilities so as to ensure that the entire process of staffing is accomplished without internal conflict between the E & R organization and Personnel or Employee Relations. A check list of areas where policies are needed is given below:

1. What are the responsibilities of E & R and Employee Relations in recruiting and selecting technical personnel?
2. What procedures and forms are required to ensure rapid processing of candidates and adequate records?
3. What sources for candidates shall be considered?
4. Will any age limits, geographical limitations, etc., be set?
5. What formula for starting salaries will be used to provide flexibility to meet market conditions but not upset the salary structure?
6. Should a continuous recruiting program be maintained or should all effort be concentrated at selected times?
7. How shall unsatisfactory personnel be handled?
8. Should effort be made to retain technical people with lengthy experience backgrounds or should emphasis be on keeping a young organization?
9. Should emphasis in hiring be on proven experienced engineers or inexperienced engineers with high potential?
10. What ratio of technicians to engineers is appropriate for the E & R organization to keep everyone working at their highest level of skill?
11. What is the policy with regard to keeping engineers, scientists, and technicians when business is bad?
12. Will policies be different with each of the groups—scientists, engineers, and technicians?
13. What policy will be followed concerning requests for internal transfers originating with the employee?
14. Should all higher jobs be filled by internal promotion?

Establishing Correct Policies Affecting Expenditures

The costs of staffing an organization are in two parts, i.e., hiring technical personnel and retaining them. The cost of hiring an engineer is so high that considerable, if not major, emphasis should be given to the retention aspect.

In a vast number of companies the emphasis could well be shifted to retention and not hiring. The incentive for this is easy to establish since each new man acquired represents an average expenditure of $3,000 to $5,000—in some cases the reported cost has been well over $10,000 per acquisition.

A. Q. Maisel writes:

> One contractor was spending $500,000 annually just for help-wanted advertising. Another firm's travel and moving expenses, which were charged back to the Pentagon, came to $540,000. A third firm spent $907,560 to recruit and relocate 193 engineers, but in the same period lost 134 engineers to other companies—thus scoring a net gain of only 59 men. For each engineer added to this plant's staff, the Treasury had to pay out $15,380![1]

Had the latter firm shifted the emphasis to retention, the net gain of fifty-nine men at an average cost of $4,660 (based on recruiting 193 engineers) would have only cost them about $275,000, thereby saving $625,000 from the $900,000 originally spent. Wouldn't $625,000 go a long way in any company to provide a better atmosphere for the engineers, pay for technical society dues, provide for pay raises where an inequity existed, and generally improve the lot of the engineers in the company so that they would be less likely to leave?

Admittedly, this is an oversimplification of the problem and, even in the company concerned, the line of reasoning might not be entirely correct. However, this amount of money in almost any size company, if intelligently used, could have a beneficial effect on the retention rate.

Know What the Professional Employees Want

In view of the costs just described, it is obviously important to know what the professional technical people are seeking in a job. Some ideas concerning this can be obtained through survey results. For example, in several Deutsch & Shea (New York consultants) surveys seeking the reaction of engineers to various factors believed to be involved in an engineer's reaction to a job, salary is not first in importance, although it is high ranking. In the survey results shown in Fig. 5-1 only five surveys showed salary ranked first.

These survey results are amplified and at the same time substantiated in another survey in which over 3,000 engineers participated. The results of this survey (showing percent of times a factor was mentioned) are illustrated in Fig. 5-2. It clearly shows that the type of work was considered of prime importance, even surpassing salary which ranked second. Also, salary and location appear to be of approximately equal importance.

Location has become an influential factor in the hiring of engineers. Among the material attractions, it runs a close second to salary. Although

[1] A. Q. Maisel, "Let's Stop This Shocking Waste of Manpower," *Reader's Digest* (May 1957).

MOTIVATING FACTORS WHICH INFLUENCE ENGINEER JOB SELECTIONS

Factors (In order of importance)	Number of Surveys in Which Factor Was Ranked: First	Second	Third	Fourth	Fifth	Sixth
Salary	5	2	4	-	2	1
Challenging opportunity	3	3	2	-	1	-
Interesting work	3	2	-	1	-	-
Opportunity for advancement	2	4	1	-	-	-
Location	1	-	6	3	-	-
Type of work	1	1	3	-	2	-
Potential growth of company	1	1	-	3	-	1
Company prestige and reputation	1	-	-	1	1	2
Progressive research and development program	-	1	-	3	1	-
Regular salary increases	-	1	-	-	3	1
Job security	-	-	-	2	-	-
Opportunity for advanced study	-	-	-	-	1	-

Fig. 5-1. Motivating factors that influence engineer job selection. *Source:* Eugene Raudsepp, "Why Engineers Work," *Machine Design* (February 4, 1960).

MOTIVATING FACTORS BY FIELDS OF ENGINEERING

Factors (In order of importance)	Total	Research	Development	Design	Operation	Production	Admin. Mgt.	Sales	Other	No Answer
	(per cent)									
Type of work, interesting, diversified	45.0	52.1	45.7	45.0	42.8	41.8	41.1	43.9	46.5	41.7
Salary	33.9	31.3	39.5	37.8	25.2	32.9	34.0	31.1	23.2	16.7
Location, good place to live, family	31.2	33.6	37.3	30.2	27.7	33.6	27.1	13.5	24.5	50.0
Opportunity for advancement	29.8	22.6	25.6	27.7	27.0	32.2	39.5	36.5	22.6	8.3
Challenge, more responsibility, chance to use creative ability	16.9	18.5	15.5	17.0	20.1	19.2	18.7	22.3	25.8	25.0
Reputation, prestige of company	13.7	9.1	13.5	13.6	13.8	15.8	14.9	12.8	11.6	8.3
Working conditions, personnel policies	11.7	14.0	12.1	11.9	13.2	10.3	9.6	14.9	7.7	8.3
Growing organization, growing field	6.9	6.4	9.3	5.8	5.7	7.5	8.4	6.1	5.8	-
Security, retirement plan, benefits	6.8	7.2	7.3	6.3	12.6	3.4	6.9	5.4	3.2	8.3
Opportunity to learn, broaden experience, training programs	6.6	11.3	7.9	6.0	5.0	7.5	5.9	2.7	6.4	-
Small company	4.1	2.6	3.3	4.3	4.4	6.2	4.3	4.1	3.9	8.3
Job was available	3.4	2.6	2.6	4.9	3.1	4.8	2.8	3.4	3.2	-
Progressive research and development program	2.8	8.7	3.5	3.6	3.8	2.1	2.6	3.4	1.9	-
Own business, partnership, independence	2.7	2.6	2.0	4.0	4.4	2.1	3.5	6.8	3.9	-
Type of product	2.5	0.8	2.6	2.7	1.3	0.7	1.6	4.1	2.6	8.3
Previous association with company	1.8	2.6	1.5	1.6	1.9	3.4	1.0	1.4	1.9	8.3
Public service, humanistic reasons	1.3	1.5	0.7	0.9	2.5	2.1	1.2	2.7	1.9	8.3
Opportunity to travel	1.3	-	0.4	1.8	1.9	-	1.0	4.1	1.9	-
Regular salary increases	0.4	0.8	0.4	0.7	-	0.7	0.6	-	1.9	-
All others	1.9	1.9	2.2	1.3	1.3	0.7	2.8	2.0	1.9	-
No answer	2.7	1.5	1.5	2.7	4.4	3.4	2.4	0.7	2.6	8.3

Fig. 5-2. Motivating factors by field of engineering. *Source:* Eugene Raudsepp, "Why Engineers Work," *Machine Design* (February 4, 1960).

climate seems to be the most important feature of a desirable location, other factors such as the availability of educational facilities and professional and cultural opportunities are also a large part of the picture. A married engineer has as one of his main concerns the finding of a suitable environment for his family.

Fringe benefits, which generally rank low, are not decisive factors. According to Eugene Raudsepp, a research consultant with Deutsch and Shea, they have never ranked higher than seventh in any of their surveys. However, the company that does not offer at least some benefits is at a definite disadvantage. Dr. Raudsepp endeavored to summarize an engineer's needs as shown below:[2]

The engineer wants:

1. Programming and scheduling of his work assignments, clearly defined objectives, and planning in detail
2. A set pattern to follow, but devoid of the tendency to routinize his job
3. Competent supervisors
4. Adequate credit from his company for his ideas and accomplishments
5. Security in his job—based on his attainments
6. Favorable regard of top management for his work
7. Compensation, concrete awards, and economic advancement
8. Assurance that his supervisors know how well he is doing
9. Opportunity to influence work on technical projects
10. Follow-through, performed by himself, on the job he has started
11. Participation in decisions that affect him
12. Opportunity to see his ideas put to use
13. Freedom to maintain an independent, self-directing attitude on how to tackle any particular problem
14. The right work assignment
15. Variety of professional work
16. Work that is challenging and stimulating
17. Planned programs or opportunities for self-development and advancement
18. Information which explains how his work fits into the entire project or product
19. Adequate facilities to get his work done
20. A well-organized supporting staff and adequate technical assistance
21. Employment in a company that is known for its excellent products and reputable professional staff
22. Association with a company which clearly defines authority and responsibility.

[2] Eugene Raudsepp, "Why Engineers Work," *Machine Design* (February 4, 1960).

ORGANIZING FOR EFFECTIVE STAFFING

The Personnel Function in Hiring and Retention

Basically, the functions of the personnel department in the staffing process are to:

1. Locate candidates according to man-specifications and schedules supplied by E & R.
2. Make preliminary screening of candidates and supply resumes of applicants to E & R management.
3. Enhance the reputation of the company through prompt and fair processing of, and dealing with, all applicants. This includes eliminating, or at least trying to minimize, bias in all personnel activities.
4. Initiate and help conduct company manpower development and training programs.
5. Observe personnel activities throughout the entire organization to ensure that company policies with respect to personnel are followed in the line organization.
6. Conduct exit interviews when employees terminate to uncover problems and retain good will of those leaving.

The E & R Responsibility in Hiring

The E & R management has the following responsibilities in the staffing process:

1. Make careful forecasts of future and present manpower requirements.
2. Prepare position descriptions with the personnel department for all positions and supply Personnel with staffing requirements and specifications.
3. Carefully evaluate all resumes and promptly notify Personnel of any interest.
4. *Be available promptly for the interview* when candidates arrive.
5. Notify Personnel promptly of E & R's decision regarding hiring a candidate.
6. Keep Personnel up to date on cancellation of job openings.

Establish Clearly Defined Relationships

E & R management and Personnel management should work out clearly defined procedures for each step of the way in staffing. Personnel people must know whom they must deal with in E & R, what constitutes an official notification of desire to interview or hire, and to whom to bring candidates when they arrive for interview, etc. There are tendencies in many cases for Personnel to usurp some of the important decision-making responsibilities of E & R management unless the responsibilities of each organization are carefully established. On the other hand, engineering management often negates the efforts of the personnel department by keeping candidates waiting for hours for scheduled interviews or by failing to notify Personnel of cancellation of job openings. In general, Personnel will, however, set up the various forms for processing and maintaining files on candidates.

CARRYING OUT THE STAFFING JOB

Sources of Technical Personnel and How to Reach Them

There are many sources of technical personnel and many ways of reaching them. The time and cost per man hired are usually deciding factors in selecting a recruiting "mix." A list of possible sources of technical personnel are:

1. Recent graduates of colleges and technical institutes
2. People with good technical aptitudes who dropped out of college or school for financial or other nonscholastic reasons
3. Graduate students
4. Faculty members
5. People employed by other firms
6. People unemployed but seeking employment
7. Aliens
8. Handicapped unemployed technical personnel
9. Retired technical personnel
10. Minority groups with adequate training who are having difficulty finding employment
11. Personnel within the company seeking transfers and promotions
12. Walk-ins.

Methods of reaching and locating technical personnel (not necessarily recommended) are:

1. Advertising
2. Alumni Placement Services
3. Answering ads of people seeking employment
4. College recruiting
5. Conferences and conventions
6. Contacts with technical personnel by managers making speeches
7. Contacts with technical schools and professors
8. Cooperative engineering programs
9. Direct contact of known individuals employed by other firms
10. Employees' recommendations and bonus programs
11. Employment agencies—private and government
12. Executive recruiting and management consulting firms

13. Field recruiting campaigns
14. Internal manpower inventory system
15. Speaker Bureau lists
16. Subscription to lists such as those of Decision, Inc., Careers, etc.
17. Technical meetings
18. Vendors' and customers' recommendations.

One way of acquiring personnel that is often overlooked involves looking in your own company first before searching outside. Also involved in this concept is not just giving "lip service" to upgrading employees, but doing something about it.

When looking for a senior man, the first inclination is to look outside because it brings in new talent; moreover, it eliminates upsetting a smooth-working team by the removal of a promising man and putting him in the new job. What the manager fails to consider is that the man he did not want to disturb is probably going to leave because he was not offered the opportunity; consequently, instead of looking for one person he has to look for two. Failing to upgrade an employee because of the fear of upsetting a smooth-working group often forces one to face a greater problem than the one he tried to avoid.

One company reduced their recruiting costs substantially through the use of employee referrals. For each professional or subprofessional person hired, the employee was awarded a $100 savings bond. It was surprising the number of good people who were brought in by this method. Certainly, one can argue that it was the responsibility of the employee in the first place to help the company, but it took the extra incentive to make it a reality.

This highlights the fact that there are two basic approaches to staffing—internal and external. An integral part of any internal recruiting program is the device normally identified as a personnel or management audit. To be effective, the audit should be periodically revised and reviewed. It should make available information such as name, age, length of service, education, work experience, training courses attended, health evaluation, results of psychological tests, and performance appraisal. A related technique, which goes one step further, employs the replacement table. This table shows the individual's background and rating, and also the projected promotions. Audits are useful tools that can assist in determining resources available and can be screened quickly with the use of data processing equipment.

One of the first external places one goes to look for a new man is the local employment agency. Almost as popular are employment agencies in the major cities. It is the job of the employment agencies to bring together prospective employees and qualified applicants. The results obtained with an employment agency depend on several factors: (1) the capability of the man handling your inquiry, (2) the degree to which you have been able to inform him of your needs (here is where the position description is of paramount importance), and (3) the number of applicants available and qualified for the open position.

It is a great help if the company recruiter knows the employment interviewer personally. Such a relationship will result in the interviewer's doing a better job of matching the applicant and the job. Also, it is possible that the agency will give the company first chance at a desirable applicant if the agency manager knows the company representative well enough; however, the agency would hesitate to admit this.

In case a suitable employment agency is not known to the company, a good procedure is to buy the weekend papers, particularly the Sunday papers, in the cities to be explored and see which agencies do the best job of advertising and apparently have the best list of jobs covering the professional areas involved. A large number of open positions generally indicates an active and successful employment agency.

Do not depend on telephone calls or letters to place the order with the agency; visit the agency personally. Personnel Department recruiters can and should do much of this, but it is also often advisable for the E & R manager to go along on a few visits. Not only does this get the agency acquainted with the man who is going to interview applicants, but it also gives both of the parties a chance to thoroughly explore the open positions and the associated requirements of both the job and the man desired. Don't forget to take along the man-job specification or position description which will be later described. It is one of the first things that the employment interviewer at the agency will request. Also, the man-job specification will save money by eliminating many undesirable applicants—applicants which the company would otherwise have to pay to come to the plant to be interviewed.

Another equally popular method used to attract new employees is that of advertising in local and national newspapers as well as professional journals. This does secure some applicants if you have glamour jobs to advertise; but for the ordinary everyday kind of job offering, the results are anything but spectacular.

Advertising in a city's newspapers in conjunction with a visit to the city to interview applicants produces somewhat better results, but normally they are not particularly good unless you have one or two glamour jobs to include in the ad. This additional personal effort will bring in marginal applicants for the glamour jobs who are willing to be considered for the others.

In writing the advertisement, don't forget the major concerns of the engineer. For example, if the job location is in an extremely good climate, say so. If the job makes possible advanced graduate study, stress this since it is important to applicants for engineering and research positions. Also, don't forget the man's interest in providing the proper environment for his family. It is these personal touches in the advertisement that can help you find applicants you really want.

If you haven't the talent available in your plant to write the proper kind of advertising, there are specialists to whom you can turn. In fact, the ad agency working with your marketing division can give you some help. However, some companies prefer to work with agencies that specialize in employment matters.

If you are seeking managerial talent, then you will probably consider going to one of the many professional management recruiters. A comparatively complete list is given in the American Management Association's directory of consultants. Professional journals, the business sections of major city Sunday newspapers (especially the *New York Times*) provide additional sources of managerial recruiting firms.

The problem of seeking and obtaining good technical and managerial personnel is complex. While there is no single ideal approach, careful study of the firm's individual problem, careful planning, and implementation of plans by trained personnel pays off in a big way.

MATCHING THE EMPLOYEE AND THE JOB

The very factors affecting retention can also help pick the right man for the job and increase the possibility that he will stay with the company for a substantial period of time. Also many of the factors involved in hiring a satisfactory man can be of major help to a firm in retaining its men and in establishing high morale among its professional employees.

The hiring of an engineer by a company is comparable to a marriage. The most successful marriage of an engineer with a new firm occurs when:

1. The engineer's personality, education, and professional background fit the requirements for the job
2. He likes the kind of work offered
3. The engineer and the company mutually agree that he will fit well with his co-workers and associates
4. The community offers the kind of living that the engineer and his family enjoy.

These are basic major considerations; therefore, failure to meet the conditions of any one of them can cause an ultimate failure of the marriage. The first three affect the employee and his company directly and are personally important to him since he spends most of his day at the plant. Even at home he will consider his plant's problems and challenges; thus, the man and the job must suit each other.

In seeking to fill a position the company should define the position in detail and in writing. Without a man-job specification, the prospect can't really make a sound decision, nor can the people involved in the hiring find the right person or properly evaluate those applicants which they do locate. If the man-job specification is not defined as precisely and accurately as possible, the Personnel Department will likely give the prospective new engineer a second- or even third-hand garbled verbal description of the job.

Even when the engineering or research manager talks to the man personally, he is not likely to get through to the candidate completely because the candidate will only make incomplete notes of the very voluminous information which is given him. The result is that he usually goes away with an incorrect impression of what he is being hired to do.

To illustrate, nobody would even remotely consider buying a highly technical product without receiving a detailed engineering specification of what the product will do, its characteristics, its performance, etc.

Man-Job Specification

Defining the job can best be accomplished by developing a document discussed earlier, the "Position Description" or "Position Guide," and combining it with a specification of the characteristics of the man who could fill such a job. This document is a man-job or recruiting specification and two forms of this kind of document are illustrated in Fig. 5-3 and Fig. 5-4. A Linear Responsibility Chart would also serve. The definition of jobs and man-specifications is not a "cure-all," nor will it solve all employee recruitment problems; nevertheless, it is of great help.

Most companies assign the development of such man-job or recruiting specifications to the personnel department. This is a satisfactory procedure, but if the E & R manager and his management team do not play a leading role in their development, the results are of little value. Generally, technical and scientific managers try to escape working on the development of a recruiting specification. However, delegating the responsibility to men who aren't even remotely acquainted with what is being done or who do not know exactly what the job requires results in a document containing fuzzy definitions, incorrect concepts, etc. If engineering specifications were written along the same lines by an employee, he would either be severely reprimanded or dismissed. There is only one logical answer as to what should be done, and that is for the supervisor or manager needing the man to participate actively in the development of the position description. In fact, the manager usually must do a major share of the work if the recruiting specification is to be of real value in the hiring procedure.

Man-job or recruiting specifications are vital to any recruitment effort. They are needed not only for a company staffed recruitment program, but more particularly if employment agencies, recruitment specialists, etc., are to be used. They have another value since they assist in the elimination of work duplication, job evaluation programs, development of systems and procedures, and in personnel training.

Complete man-job specifications consist of three main sections: (1) the personal, educational, and professional requirements of the job, (2) the duties and responsibilities encompassed in the job, and (3) a general designation of interdepartmental relationships that will be encountered by the employee.

RECRUITING SPECIFICATION

Position Title____________________ Incumbent(s)__________

Department____________________ __________

Section____________________ __________

Reports to: Name________________ Prepared by______ Date____

Title________________ Approved by______ Date____

---

1. Knowledges and skills required to perform the job in a normal manner:
   a. Education (level of formal schooling and major degree, if required).

   b. Experience (kinds required and years of each kind).

   c. Other significant knowledge and skills, and extent of command required by incumbent.

2. Decision making:
   a. List typical examples of decisions made, and potential risks involved.

   b. List typical examples of recommendations for decision making, and extent of risks involved.

3. Planning, problem solving, and creative activity:
   a. List typical examples of planning required including long-range.

   b. List typical examples of problems solved, indicating analysis and creative activity required, lack of precedent, etc.

4. Special tasks and unusual features (list examples that will aid in distinguishing this position from others like it, without repeating information in the Position Guide or in other parts of this supplement).

5. Company programs, projects, and products (summarize the actual or potential results with which this position is concerned and their relation to over-all objectives. List typical examples).

6. Human resources (list the categories and numbers of personnel supervised, directly and through subordinates).

Fig. 5-3. One type of recruiting specification.

Position Description:

Project Engineer (Electronic)

I. PERSONAL, EDUCATIONAL AND PROFESSIONAL REQUIREMENTS:

AGE: 30 - 45

PHYSICAL CONDITION: Good.

HOME ENVIRONMENT: Good to excellent.

APPEARANCE: Good to excellent.

EDUCATION: College graduate. B.S. in EE with electronics major minimum educational level. M.S. in EE with some formal training in management preferred. The specific area of the major such as semi conductors, computer circuitry, etc. is relatively unimportant (in this company the work area is broad and several openings almost always exist).

MOTIVATION: Should have an intense desire to succeed.

PERSONALITY (IMPORTANT): Must be excellent.

Man must have the personality that makes it possible for him to sell:

(a) Himself,
(b) His department,
(c) His work.

STABILITY: Must be able to perform well under consistent and extreme pressure.

REPORT WRITING: Must be good to excellent. The ability to develop concise, to the point, reports is a must.

WORK EXPERIENCE: Eight (8) Years minimum experience.

His professional engineering experience should logically be drawn from the following areas:

(A) Trainee
(B) Design
(C) Test
(D) Quality Control
(E) Administration (Engineering)
(F) Teaching (Electronics)
(G) Research
(H) Student (Company or University classes in electronics and/or management)

At least part of his experience should include the successful direction of technical design and development of projects - a minimum of several minor or one major project.

II. DUTIES AND RESPONSIBILITIES:

A. GENERAL

Carry forward to completion, with only minor direction, major and minor projects. The general objective and the general scope of projects to be supplied by the department head.

The engineer will have assigned to him other engineers and professional personnel needed to accomplish the assignments.

B. SPECIFIC DUTIES AND RESPONSIBILITIES.

1. Play a "leading role" in the formulation of project objectives.
2. Devise and establish schedules of accomplishment for all major tasks and all definable subtasks.
3. Assist in the estimation of all costs.
4. Devise and secure necessary approval for project organization and a schedule of manpower by personnel classification vs. time.
5. Implement the project organization and assume responsibility for all aspects of the project under the general direction of the engineering manager.
6. Assure attainment of schedules and cost objectives.
7. At all times keep abreast of all significant aspects of the project and provide the major guidance to its accomplishment.
8. Provide all necessary reports to management and any involved contractor.
9. Assure attainment of specifications from an engineering "point of view".
10. Provide technical leadership to the project.
11. Shrink project personnel as rapidly as needs decrease.
12. Provide for attainment of objectives and goals at minimum cost.
13. Coordinate the establishment of any special facilities.
14. Negotiate for and direct any required consultants or specialists.
15. Evaluate personnel and recommend appropriate management action.

III. RELATIONSHIPS:

The incumbent will have relationships with the managers and/or personnel of the following functions:

1. Drafting
2. Model Shop
3. Testing Laboratory
4. Quality Control
5. Industrial Engineering
6. Advanced Development Engineering
7. Contract Administration
8. Sales
9. Personnel
10. Security
11. Purchasing
12. Accounting
13. Production Management

Fig. 5-4. Another type of recruiting specification.

Figure 5-4 shows a typical recruiting specification (often referred to as a Position Description) for a Project Engineer in a project-oriented E & R Department that is usable for all of the purposes indicated. It differs substantially from the position descriptions mentioned previously because of its possible multiple usage.

Section 1, covering personal, educational, and professional requirements, to the uninitiated, appears relatively simple, unimportant, and very easy to develop. This assumption is the first error commonly encountered; in fact, the whole development of the man-job specification is usually approached on this basis. The results are sloppy definitions and statements.

The professional needs no guidance as to the statement of job title and educational requirements. However, this is not true of many of the other items. For example, consider motivation. Almost everyone, before thinking about the subject, will immediately specify that they want the employee to be highly motivated and ambitious; for example, the E & R manager may specify that he wants a highly motivated, ambitious, driving, and self-starting individual. However, he shouldn't fail to recognize that this type of person will expect more responsibility in a short period of time, at most in one or two years. If he doesn't get it, he will leave or become a problem. Once again the job must be filled. All this relates to the earlier discussion about the proper mix or combination of employees.

It is true that a company does need *some* highly motivated people, but at the same time, a company needs and can use advantageously a fair number of individuals who are not highly motivated in order to get the more routine tasks accomplished. If the job to be filled is routine and is not ordinarily used as training ground for more responsible positions, don't request an ambitious and highly motivated individual.

The example specification indicates the need for a personality which would enable the man to sell himself, his department, and his work. If the desired employee is to be used in capacities involving this kind of activity, then by all means specify it. However, don't eliminate a competent engineer by putting the need for this characteristic into the specification and rigidly adhering to it if someone else could do the selling chore.

A similar comment could be made concerning report writing. A man may be a good engineer but may be very poor in expressing himself or explaining what he has done. Why ask for something that isn't really needed? Most engineering departments have one or two individuals on their staff who are good at writing or in presenting engineering material to outsiders. Also, it is common in the larger engineering groups to actually have a technical writing group who can be used to develop the necessary reports. In other words, it is important to ask for what is actually needed. Don't complicate the job by demanding what is not required in the performance of the job.

It is even more important to be precise in the development of Section 2—the list of duties and responsibilities. Here should be listed all of the major tasks that the recruit is likely to perform. This section then becomes extremely useful to the interviewers in evaluating the applicant and by the applicant in evaluating the job. Remember that marriage is a two-way contract, and both parties must keep this in mind. Too often the employer overlooks this aspect of the hiring procedure. The duties and responsibilities offer *both* parties the opportunity to evaluate each other as well as the job offer as to: (1) the applicant's qualifications, (2) the applicant's ultimate satisfaction with the work, and (3) the degree of professional development and opportunity offered.

The Applicant's Plant Visit

It is standard procedure today to invite a candidate to visit the company as its guest before the final interview and selection. Too often the company carefully isolates the applicant from contact with all except the recruiting specialist in the personnel department and one or two engineering supervisors or managers. He is given no opportunity of meeting with his potential co-workers and talking with them privately. Earlier it was mentioned that one of the four keys to a successful marriage of an engineer with a new firm occurs when "the company and the engineer mutually agree that he will fit well with his co-workers and associates." Why try to "second-guess" something that can be actually explored firsthand? Let the applicant meet with several of his prospective co-workers. Then, he can evaluate the situation from his own viewpoint, and they can evaluate it from theirs. In addition, the company's employees can do two things for the manager. First they can evaluate the man for the job, and secondly they can help sell the company and the job to the applicant. If your personnel policies are reasonably good and your employee morale is reasonably high, they will do a good job for you in both respects; in fact, you will increase their job satisfaction and status by taking such action. If the manager can't trust his employees to do these two things for him, he had better correct the conditions in his department or function before starting to hire additional people.

Psychological Tests

Many books and articles have been written on psychological testing, and most modern companies do utilize some psychological tests. The manager need not be a test expert, but rather he should recognize that this is an area in which a specialist is needed to plan, administer, and interpret the tests. However, this does not eliminate the need to know certain concepts and basic facts concerning them—especially the basic types, their proper usage, and the interpretation of results.

Psychological tests are an important *adjunct* to personal interviews, but they should not be allowed to supplant the personal interview and personal selection techniques. *The results of such tests are indicators, and it should be recognized that the indications are not always correct.*

The danger of relying entirely on test results was emphasized to one of the authors in connection with a search for tool designers and draftsmen. The company test experts suggested using a spacial relations test as one of the selection tools. This test purports to evaluate the individual's ability to visualize objects in space. It was discovered that successful tool designers do not necessarily score high on this test; in fact, most of them scored about average. The best tool designer acquired actually scored below average. This statement is not made to disparage test results, but it is given to introduce a word of caution to the inexperienced.

Most psychological test batteries include an intelligence test, a personality test, and an interest test. While the intelligence test is certainly the most useful and important test, personality and interest tests help to verify your impression of the prospective employee's make-up and how well he will fit into the organization.

It now appears that because of the increasing sensitivity to the rights of individuals, some legal hazards can arise from a testing program. Therefore, it is advisable to consult a legal specialist in this area before instituting a psychological testing program.

Things to Check

When interviewing a new employee, do not fail to explore the prospective employee's family life. This is especially true for managerial and major staff positions. Many firms today consider it essential to meet the wife as an aid in evaluating the man's family relationships and to determine whether she would assist or hinder her husand in his position. An unhappy wife can certainly destroy the morale, ambition, and output of almost any employee.

Reference checking is important and should not be delegated to a subordinate. If an applicant is being considered for a professional position, the reference checking should be done by telephone. Very few people will express their true feelings about an employee in writing unless the employee was either a genius or else a complete "stinker." A reasonably reliable impression of the man's past performance on other jobs can be gained only by personally talking to his immediate superior on past jobs. Press the reference for points of weakness as well as strengths. It will be found that it is very difficult to extract a statement as to a man's weakness if the employee's work was reasonably good. Only perseverance will get an answer. Once such an answer is obtained, it is equally important to recognize that it was difficult to secure and under no circumstances should it be given undue emphasis since all of us have weaknesses. Be only concerned with those weaknesses that have special relevance to the job for which the applicant is being considered.

Consider the Applicant's Needs

Keep the applicant's needs in mind. He and his family are going to want to know about the city and the geographical area into which they are being asked to move. Chamber of Commerce brochures, state booklets, and other brochures should all be given to the prospective employee.

While salary is not always the prime consideration, as previously mentioned, it is of great importance. The financial aspects of the job should be discussed candidly with the applicant. The specific salary offer may be given to him verbally; however, it should later be confirmed in writing. Having a standard salary schedule showing minimum, maximum, and any specific intermediate salary levels helps not only with the job applicant but also with your existing staff. To tell your job applicant that the salary for the job has a practically unlimited ceiling does not present a realistic picture. Instead, the candidate should be shown the company's salary plan. In this case it is obvious that the limits should be reasonable and fair. If they aren't, it is a matter that the E & R manager had better rectify before starting a recruitment program to replace men who have been lost.

Professional development, as previously mentioned, is a prime consideration for any prospective engineer. An engineer who has been out of school several years soon finds that his only real security is the knowledge and skills that he has acquired and will acquire in the future. The position description can serve as a starter on the discussion of professional development. Not only are the engineers interested in how this job will bring about further professional development because of work specified (this is where the position description comes in), but he also will be interested in promotion channels, company training programs, and especially in advanced degree programs available to him in the area. It is advisable to have local college catalogues and brochures available as well as descriptions of any company educational-subsidy plan.

If there are no local colleges or universities, the company obviously has a problem in meeting this employee requirement. This problem can be partially overcome by emphasizing professional society meetings in the area and by having copies of past and future programs to give him. In fact, there is no reason why the company could not bring in outstanding specialists to present seminars to company professional employees as a substitute for the lack of formal college and university programs. Also, few people are aware of the vast variety of college credit correspondence courses available from many of our major universities and colleges. These college credit courses and the participating universities are listed in a booklet which can be obtained from the Office of the Secretary, National University Extension Association, Bloomington, Indiana.

Promotional prospects and future advancement opportunities are one of the important items that must be discussed with a job applicant. However, this must be done in relation to the discussion of professional development since they usually are related. Not only should advancement and promotional channels be shown in relation to organization charts, but they also should be illustrated by giving past specific examples.

Do not overlook the fact that design engineers and scientists would ordinarily prefer to advance by performing exactly the same general kind of work, but at a more advanced level. Most of these individuals are not primarily interested in moving over into management. This is a difficult concept for the "dyed-in-the-wool" manager to understand. Is the company prepared to discuss candidly this aspect of the engineering or research job? Most companies give "lip service" to the idea that one can advance doing engineering work without moving into straight managerial activities. However, a careful examination of their personnel discloses that very few men doing design engineering or research work are really being paid a salary equivalent to that generally given to their managers.

MANPOWER INVENTORY

Purpose of the Manpower Inventory

A company does not have to grow very large before it needs some systematic method for keeping track of talent within the company. The Manpower Inventory (MI) is a method for ensuring both that the company has an opportunity to make maximum use of the skills of its personnel and that its scientific personnel may be recognized and promoted as responsible openings occur. Morale is accordingly increased greatly in a company where every effort is made to place people in the right jobs and advancing them to better positions when they are found to be equipped for greater responsibility.

The primary purpose of the MI, then, is to expose every engineer and scientist to company-wide opportunities and to provide every E & R manager with pertinent information about the best qualified candidates for any openings in his organization. Any growing company could benefit by establishing the following policies, or some similar to them:

1. Every position should be filled with a fully qualified employee.
2. Every employee should be considered for a better position when he is qualified to fill such.
3. When an opening occurs, at least three candidates, if possible, should be considered and their respective qualifications appraised.

4. Personnel considered in filling a position should include the best qualified people in the component which has the open position and a number of individuals from other organizational components.
5. Every manager should cooperate completely in making employees from his group available for evaluation by other managers who have better or more suitable positions in their components.
6. Any employee should not generally be considered for a transfer until he has had time to prove himself in his present job (usually in a period of two years) and can suggest one or two more suitable successors.
7. A manager who has to deny a significant opportunity for advancement to one of his people because it would disrupt his operations greatly should see to it that this condition does not last more than one year and that his employee is given another equivalent opportunity within this time.

Operation of the Manpower Inventory

The Manpower Inventory consists basically of some kind of file system whereby upon specification of a group of characteristics of an individual, information on all personnel with these characteristics can be retrieved quickly and economically. This relates to the previously mentioned personnel or management audit; in fact, it may be synonymous with it. It has been estimated that there are as many as 18,000 possible characteristics that could be used to describe a person's qualifications. Only that information which would actually be used to search for and compare people with positions should be included in the file.

Access to the file may be either direct or indirect. Types of files lending themselves to direct access are:

1. *Resumes.* A list of resumes is maintained and manual sorting is carried out. This is very cumbersome as the number of resumes approaches 100.
2. *Edge-sort cards.* Resume information is written right on the cards, but key specifications or access information is coded by punches on the edge of the cards. Rapid searching is possible up to several thousand cards.

An indirect access type of file is primarily represented by punched cards. All data are punched into one or more cards. Much of the data must be coded in order to keep the number of cards per individual to a reasonable number and to permit machine searching. A similar approach could be to use magnetic tape in combination with a computer.

Types of files employing indirect access are desirable where the number of personnel is large. The coded cards can also be used in combination with resumes. Mechanical sorting is used to identify the desired individuals and the resumes can then be removed from an ordinary letter file for more information. These resumes in a personal file may either be in a standard format or prepared in any manner desired by the individual employee. One reason for the latter method is that this resume provides a more complete profile of this employee.

Placement Service

There is, of course, a matching service that the company may have in conjunction with the Manpower Inventory for filling open positions. This service is the Placement Service to find positions for employees who may seek transfers for any of the following reasons:

1. Their component has been reorganized, contracted, or abolished
2. An individual may be involved in a serious difference of philosophy with his manager, or there may be a basic personality clash
3. An individual may find that he is not suited for the type of work in his particular component
4. A man may have long mastered his job and find himself stagnating.

Either the employee or his manager may by agreement seek the assistance of a placement service under these conditions if such a service exists. In addition, such a placement service is useful in making direct placements from college recruiting teams and for experienced outside applicants. Through the use of the manpower inventory and the placement service, a company maximizes its likelihood of achieving optimum short- and long-range utilization of its engineering and scientific personnel.

DEVELOPMENT OF TECHNICAL PERSONNEL

Objectives

Nearly every engineer, scientist, or technician considers two questions when he thinks of his job future. These are: "Where do I stand?" and "How do I grow?" The primary objectives of the company's personnel development program should be to provide the motivation, opportunity, and means for each person to develop to his full potential. Such development will enable the individual to achieve greatest satisfaction on his job through improved performance, greater earning power, and increased long-term advancement within the company.

Not only do the employees gain through such a personnel development program, but the company does as well. For the company, increased employee competence leads to greater productivity, higher morale, and a more favorable competitive position. Training must, therefore, be considered an integral part of every man's job, rather than a separate appendage that can be omitted when business conditions are unfavorable.

Principles Underlying the Development Program

The company which is establishing a new personnel development program or reviewing the present one must consider the basic principles which underlie any such program if it is to be successful. These principles are reviewed briefly below:

1. *Self-development is the basis of personnel development.* A man cannot be trained unless he is self-motivated and recognizes the need for development.
2. *Climate for development must be present.* Managers at all levels must realize the need for and importance of developing their men as part of their jobs. They must encourage each man to seek his higher level of performance by offering training opportunities and challenging assignments.
3. *Provide opportunity for all.* Everyone should be given an opportunity to augment his contribution. The program should not be for just a few selected engineers and scientists, but for all personnel from managers to technicians.
4. *Improve present performance.* The initial effort of personnel development should be directed towards improving the employee's present performance. If a man's work is not improving, consideration should be given to reassigning him to work where he is more highly motivated and which is more in line with his particular talents. In short, try to find the best in every man.
5. *Build future increased capability.* While the emphasis in most cases should be on improving present performance, under unusual circumstances the accent may be on the future. Moreover, one should always consider the future in planning a development program.
6. *Development must be planned.* Intelligent management does not depend on the old theory that all good men are bound to rise. Systematic and planned development of all personnel will ensure achieving the maximum growth of the individual, thereby providing the company with the greatest organizational strength.
7. *Self-development requires assistance.* Each individual must look to his manager for guidance and opportunity. Besides the manager, each outstanding specialist, as part of his professional responsibilities, has the responsibility of helping to guide and train the men around him in his field.
8. *AAA: Assign—Appraise—Assign.* Development must be guided by performance appraisal. Also involved is the concept of promotion when abilities match a job opening to be followed by another performance appraisal on the new job for both evaluation *and* guidance.
9. *Learning on the job plus formal training is needed.* Neither on-the-job training nor formal training by itself is sufficient for developing the

individual to his fullest. However, continued formal training, especially in combination with on-the-job training, is of vital importance to the professional development of scientific people.

Self-development means that the individual must arrive at a realistic evaluation of his own performance and needs. There exists a tendency on the part of many managers and company development specialists to concentrate heavily on overcoming the individual's weaknesses; this may be a completely incorrect approach. Rather, emphasis should be placed on developing and exploiting each person's strengths with secondary attention to correcting "weaknesses." Correcting weaknesses often implies trying to make a man what he is not or cannot be. Developmental action must be tailored to each individual; it should not be a mass or common program.

One problem which occurs in many companies is that a man's immediate manager may be very little removed from his men in age, experience, and professional standing. At the lower levels of management, the managers may simply not have the seasoning which invokes the confidence of their men in terms of long-term career planning. One practical way of overcoming this problem is to have the immediate manager and either the next higher level manager or a highly respected professional leader meet with the individual when long-term development plans are discussed.

From these reasons and based on the previously outlined principles, it is possible to enumerate the action to be taken in a one-year cycle of appraisal and development:

1. *Contractual Relationship*
   The manager and the concerned professional employee (including technicians) review the individual's position and reach agreement on duties, responsibilities, and accountability.
2. *Performance Appraisals*
   a. The manager appraises the man's performance.
   b. Employee makes a self-evaluation of his performance to self-determine his developmental needs for discussion with his manager at the time of his performance appraisal.
3. *Salary Determination*
   Salary of the man is established within the bounds of the job evaluation plan on the basis of performance and is reviewed by at least one higher level of management.
4. *Manager–Employee Conference*
   a. Manager and employee discuss appraisal and salary action.
   b. Development program for the employee is reviewed relative to self-development activity, "coaching" on the job, company training courses, and participation in external educational programs.

TRAINING THE ENGINEER IN INDUSTRY

Why Industry Trains Engineers

There was a time when many companies (and many engineers) thought that when the engineer had obtained his degree, school was over. This concept has now almost vanished for three principal reasons. First, there is a realization that the four-year engineering program cannot provide a man with both the breadth and the depth which are needed to embark upon an engineering career. Second and equally important, the frontiers of knowledge are moving ahead so rapidly that engineers must continue to be trained to use new concepts and techniques. The third reason that engineers require further technical training is that their diverse backgrounds do not usually match the equally diverse needs of the particular company. This is particularly true in the larger companies where many professional men are hired regardless of their specialty on the basis that the company will train them in work which satisfies both their interests and those of the company.

There are approximately a dozen basic or principal engineering degrees, although one can find two or three dozen different ones if all U. S. schools are considered. This is further complicated by the fact that companies have and develop even more varieties of specialists. For example, one company specializing in reactor engineering design has over forty-eight different recognized specialists.

It would not be unusual in such a company, for example, to find a man with a degree in marine engineering working in any one of a number of areas such as manufacturing facilities and testing, mechanical and thermal design, electrical and electronics engineering, or physics and nuclear engineering.

Besides additional technical training, many companies also believe that engineers benefit by formal courses in communications skills as well as in managerial principles, concepts, and techniques. Such courses will later be discussed.

TRAINING THE TECHNICIAN IN INDUSTRY

A very valuable source of technical skill that managers often overlook is the engineering technician. Skills of technicians cover a wide range—in some cases complementing those of the degree-holding engineer and in other cases overlapping them.

Technicians fall roughly into two categories—those who apply a specialized craft to the development and test of hardware and those who perform scientific and technical supporting calculations and design work. The U. S.

Department of Health, Education, and Welfare defines a technician as "an individual who assists with technical details in a trade or profession; uses tools, instruments, and/or special devices to design, illustrate, fabricate, maintain, operate and test objects, materials or equipment; performs mathematical and scientific operations, reporting on and/or carrying out a prescribed action in relation to them; examines and evaluates plans, designs, and data; determines action to be taken on the basis of analysis; assists in determining or interpreting work procedures and maintaining harmonious relations among groups of workers."

The technician of today may well be better grounded in the fundamentals of mathematics, engineering, and science than the engineer of twenty-five or thirty years ago. Technicians desire identification with the engineering group and its accomplishments. Many are graduates of technical institutes or have taken several years of engineering; moreover, most want to progress into the engineering ranks. Consequently, progressive companies have established programs which raise the technician's educational level. A training program may be directed towards developing exceptional technicians through a combination of on-the-job training and company courses. Normally, engineers and technicians do not take the same courses or attend the same classes in company training programs. Another approach is to offer a tuition-refund program which will permit ambitious technicians to complete the formal requirements for an engineering degree at a local college or university.

As a general rule, the development of technicians tends to be more specific than that of engineers; otherwise, the principles are essentially the same.

HOW TO ORGANIZE FOR TRAINING

The organization of the training function must be tailored to meet the needs of the particular company. Fortunately, there are a few guides for establishing the technical training function within a company. The large multiplant company requires a central training director or technical service as well as training specialists in each plant or laboratory. (*See* Fig. 5-5.) In the large company, a centralized group is required to establish over-all policies, develop certain types of courses, and provide coordination and interchange of information among the plant training directors. Here will be located specialists in technical and scientific training as well as the other areas of training involved at both the corporate and plant level. The training directors in each plant develop the particular type of courses and training methods required in his plant. The relationship between the corporate engineering education staff and the product department or plant training directors is shown in Fig. 5-6.

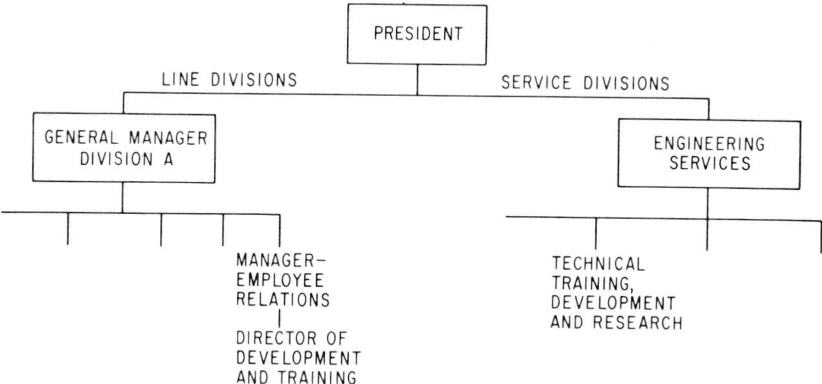

Fig. 5-5. The training function in the large organization.

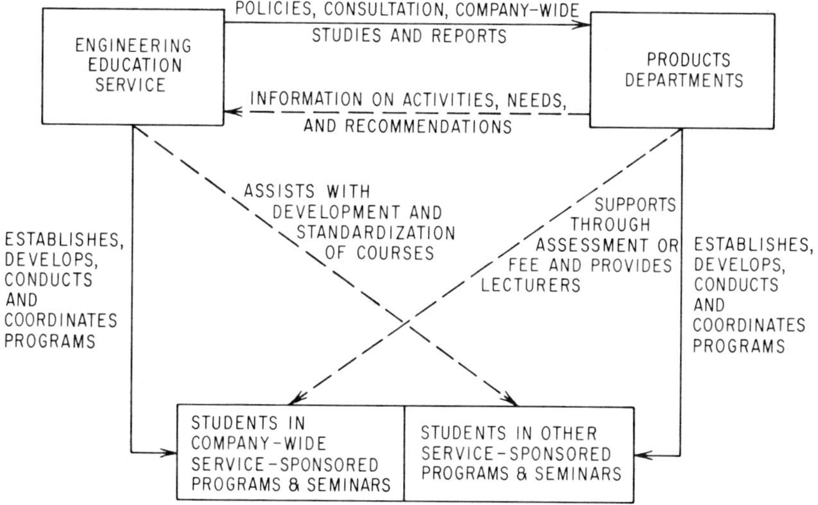

Fig. 5-6. Schematic diagram of functional relationships in technical training.

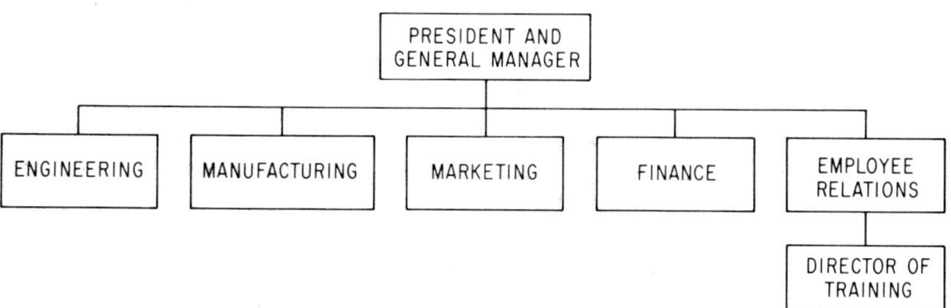

Fig. 5-7. The training function in the small organization.

In the smaller company, the training director may report to the engineering manager, the employee relations manager, or even to the production manager when there is a strong industrial engineering function. Figure 5-7 depicts the training function as one of the auxiliary services in the plant. In this case, all training functions—engineering, marketing, manufacturing, financial, and managerial, etc.—are usually grouped together.

HOW TO SET UP THE TRAINING PROGRAM

Elements of the Program

A main duty of the training director is to analyze both the needs of the company and the resources available to prepare a suitable program. The broad program of training engineering personnel may consist of any combination of the following elements:

1. Long-term intensive and integrated company technical programs
2. Individual company technical courses
3. Company managerial courses
4. Nontechnical courses
5. Short company technical seminars or courses
6. Seminars, work shops, or courses sponsored by groups outside of the company
7. College tuition-refund programs leading to bachelor's and advanced degrees
8. Formal on-the-job training programs (e.g., apprentice programs).

An explanation of some of these elements may be warranted. The first, the long-term intensive program, is found usually in the medium-size and large companies. General Electric's three-year Advanced Engineering Program is perhaps one of the best known throughout industry.

Nontechnical courses are those such as conference leadership, human relations, reading improvement, and report writing.

The widespread use of workshops, symposiums, or seminars has grown with the urgent need for more communication both within and among the rapidly advancing sciences and technologies. This type of training permits face-to-face exchange of problems, and intensive and usually well-organized question-and-answer sessions, which may or may not utilize experts to provide answers.

In college tuition-refund courses and programs leading to bachelor's and/or advanced degrees, the company refunds to the employee the tuition or some fraction thereof upon successful completion of each course. These programs are becoming popular for several reasons. For example, the smaller company may not find it economical to set up a variety of company courses on a continuing basis. Also, engineers feel a sense of accomplishment in working towards an advanced degree rather than taking a number of company courses, however well-designed they may be to meet their immediate and future needs.

Determining the Needs

Despite the fact that it is the company which pays, the training director must satisfy two customers—the company *and* the engineer. A particular training program will not be successful if the employees do not enroll in the program of their own volition but rather are drafted into the courses. Therefore, after the training director has determined his management's opinion as to the skills and knowledge which need to be developed, the training director should make a survey of the engineers to secure their attitudes on the subject. Since the training program should take care of short-, intermediate-, and long-range requirements, the training director should obtain the above-mentioned reactions from management and the engineers in this frame of reference. Moreover, this means that priorities can and must be established for each training need.

Researching the needs for technical training is best determined by personal interviews with the managers and engineers rather than by survey letters. However, an appointment letter may be used to prepare the way for the interview. Considerable probing and commentary by the training director are often needed to help the managers crystallize their thinking with respect to engineering training.

In determining the needs for specific training courses or programs, the training director and management must consider and evaluate the following:

1. Size and organization of the company and the engineering function
2. Type of research, development, or design being conducted
3. Short-range (one to two years), intermediate-range (three to five years) or long-range company objectives for developing men
4. Engineers' interests and enthusiasm (or lack of it) for various types and areas of training.

Evaluating Alternative Programs

Cost is a major factor in the selection of a suitable training program. If there is a nearby university which provides adequate and needed courses, the training director must evaluate the advantage of company-sponsored courses against those of a tuition-refund program. Engineers generally prefer the university courses; however, the cost to the company may be higher if full tuition is refunded. Seminars and workshops serve a different purpose than courses, and they can also be employed to supplement either company or university courses. Sometimes company or area-wide cooperative study groups can be formed to fill gaps in the available training courses.

The advantages and disadvantages of company-sponsored courses are:

Advantages

1. May be tailored exactly to company needs
2. May be given at any time of day or evening
3. May be less expensive
4. Promotes technical interchange among engineers in the classes
5. May be taught conveniently in the company plant
6. All employees needing the course can practically be forced to participate.

Disadvantages

1. Often more narrow and oriented to "company line."
2. Competent instructors may not be available.
3. Adequate facilities may not be available.
4. Non-accreditation may result in poor enrollment; if "pressure" is used to get participation, the results will be poor and morale may be lowered.
5. Companies are not in business to compete with universities so that parallel courses result in poor public relations.
6. Attendance is often harder to maintain.

The advantages and disadvantages of tuition-refund programs are:

Advantages

1. Fundamentals rather than narrow training are emphasized.
2. Adequate facilities and trained instructors are employed.
3. Cross-fertilization of ideas with engineers from other companies is possible.
4. Courses are accredited and may form part of an advanced degree program.

Disadvantages

1. Desired courses may not always be given each year.
2. Courses may be given only on company time or only in the evening, either of which may be considered undesirable.

OTHER PROFESSIONAL ACTIVITIES

In addition to training programs and educational aid, practically all companies engage in other kinds of developmental activities for their technical personnel. In a survey of 148 executives the Bureau of National Affairs, Inc. found that the companies represented by these executives carried out such activities as shown in Fig. 5-8.

Professional society meetings, conferences, seminars, workshops, and

DEVELOPMENTAL PROGRAMS

	All Cos. (%)	Larger Cos. (%)	Smaller Cos. (%)
Encourage professional licensing	49	49	49
Encourage membership in professional or technical societies	85	80	95
Encourage attendance at conventions, seminars, etc.	92	88	100
Pay for subscriptions to professional or technical publications	96	96	97

Fig. 5-8. Developmental activities in large and small companies. *Source:* Reproduced by permission from Personnel Policies Forum, Survey No. 62, Copyright 1961, by The Bureau of National Affairs, Inc., Washington 7, D. C.

symposia all must be an integral part of the training program if it is to be realistic, effective, and practical. The programs available are outstanding; however, it is difficult to predict exactly how much of the employee's educational needs can be realized by utilizing these educational aids.

Some professional employees don't belong to a professional society; others belong but don't attend meetings. Still others should and would like to belong to several because of their interests or needs but can't afford to do so. Many companies will pay the membership dues in a second society if it is considered important to the employee's work or because of certain public relations objectives. Also, companies often pay the dinner assessment which is a part of most professional society meetings.

The supervisor or manager of a group can do a great deal to influence his men to join and to attend the local meetings. However, the training director obviously finds it difficult to appraise the value of such unscheduled education. Furthermore, local professional society meetings can never substitute for a formal course.

The attendance situation with outside symposia, conferences, seminars, and workshops is entirely different. Here, one can send specific people and request them to write a report on what they learned. If the employee must be sent to another city to attend, and this is the usual situation, then the cost can be high. Nevertheless, the program quality is usually equally high. Many companies have found it to be advantageous to encourage their employees to attend. Moreover, they are simultaneously helping to create the working conditions appreciated by professional employees.

The chief disadvantage associated with such affairs is that it takes the employee away from his work for an extended period. On the other hand he has the opportunity to talk over his problems with men in his profession and often returns with solutions to specific work-associated problems. If a relatively large group can't attend, at least specialists and prospective instructors should be sent to appropriate conferences, seminars, etc. In any event, such affairs are definitely a part of the training spectrum.

The money involved in the activities just described usually does not appear on the training budget, although such activities are definitely a part of training. The fact that the funds involved are neither in the training budget nor under the control of the training director both complicates his task and makes it easier.

HOW TO ADMINISTER THE TRAINING PROGRAM

Educational and training programs should be planned to encompass the full spectrum of activities and will ordinarily include a combination of company courses, tuition-refund offerings, and external technical meetings and seminars. The first problem is to maintain a proper balance between courses, the men to be trained, and the available money.

To balance these factors, it is first necessary to carry out the market survey covering managers and professional personnel previously outlined under "Determining the Needs." The training needs can then be listed in the order of the priorities established during the survey. Opposite each, list the number of men to be trained.

Now an even more difficult task must be faced, that is, the cost estimation for each training need. Cost will be related to the subject matter, the number of men involved, and the method selected to impart the required knowledge (the director may not be able to utilize the most effective or the lowest cost approach because of a lack of opportunity, facilities, and/or instructor). Subsequently, the estimated costs should be listed opposite each training need as well as the training method.

The final step before implementing the program is to equate the available budget against the needs. This may require lengthy discussions with top management regarding the funds to be allocated to the training function as well as some reconsideration of priorities and training methods. Once this has been accomplished, the program is ready to be implemented.

MEASUREMENT

Measurement of the *profitability* of training engineers in industry in management terms, i.e., dollars, poses a very difficult problem in most cases. However, comparing money spent to the originally estimated cost is comparatively simple and should always be done.

ESTABLISHMENT OF STANDARDS

Standards for Scope of Training Program

1. Degree of need for program
2. Degree to which short-and long-range goals are planned for
3. Are any major needs not being met? Is anything being done about it?
4. Is the program being continuously reviewed and revised?

Administration of the Training Program

1. Is the training function clearly defined and responsibility properly assigned within the organization?
2. Are the proper kinds and number of people assigned to the training function?
3. Are there adequate facilities, space, equipment and materials?
4. Does the training group receive periodicals, books and information to maintain contact with advances in industry training?
5. Does the training get done on time and as planned?
6. Does the training director publicize training activities and make his services understood by management and engineers alike?

Teaching and Learning Process

1. Does the course actually present the material outlined?
2. Is the material covered in proper depth and breadth?
3. Do the engineers participate actively by means of discussion and problem solving?
4. How effective is the instructor?
5. Were the students properly selected relative to background, knowledge, need for course, ability, and interest?

Direct Results

1. Did the training succeed at the intended level of teaching - learning?
2. To what extent did the engineers learn what was intended to be taught?
3. Are the engineers more effective in problem-solving on the job in the area covered by the course?
4. To what degree are the engineers satisfied with the course?
5. To what degree are the managers satisfied with the immediate results? The result of a long period of time?

Fig. 5-9. Establishment of training standards.

Evaluation of the educational program in terms of meeting the needs of the organization is more feasible than putting a dollar value on the profit contribution of the training program. Such evaluation is based upon (1) establishing goals, (2) establishing standards, and (3) comparing performance with the standards. Goals, of course, are the direct consequence of organizational deficiencies and needs. Standards provide a yardstick for measurement by comparison of actual performance with standard performance.

There are basically four broad areas in which goals may be established:

1. The scope of the over-all program relative to the needs
2. The administration of the training program
3. The teaching and learning process itself
4. The ultimate effects of the program towards increasing the effectiveness of the engineers.

Standards in turn may be established in detail for these four broad areas by further development such as indicated in Fig. 5-9.

BIBLIOGRAPHY

ALLISON, D. "Sending Engineers Back to School," *Management Review,* 52. July, 1964.

BEACH, DALE S. *Personnel: The Management of People at Work.* New York, N.Y.: The Macmillan Co., 1965.

BEESON, WILLIAM B. "Ethics and Executive Search," *Michigan Business Review,* May, 1965.

BROWNE, D. E. "Building Defense Against Obsolescence," *Financial Executive,* Vol. 25:1, August, 1967.

BUNIN, SANFORD. "The Campus Recruiter," *Advanced Management,* January, 1960. Vol. 25:1, Bureau of National Affairs, Inc., The. "Solving the Shortage of Specialized Personnel," *Personnel Policies Forum, Survey No. 62*, September, 1961.

CROSBY, CHARLES H. 1958. "Concepts of Job Assignment in the Project-type Engineering Department." Paper No. 58–SA–48, read at semiannual meeting of American Society of Mechanical Engineers, June 15–19, 1958, in Detroit, Mich.

CUMMINGS, K. C. "Characteristics of the Technician as an Engineering Aide," *Journal of Engineering Education,* 47:443–9, January, 1957.

DANIELSON, LEE E. "Characteristics of Engineers and Scientists." Doctoral dissertation, The University of Michigan, 1960.

———. "The Engineer and the Technician," *Chemical Engineering Progress,* May, 1967.

EVANS, W. M. "The Problem of Obsolescence of Knowledge," *IEEE Transactions on Engineering Management,* March, 1963.

FERDINAND, T. N. "On the Obsolescence of Scientists and Engineers," *American Scientist,* Vol. 54, March 1966.

HERZBERG, FREDERICK. "One More Time: How do You Motivate Employees?", *Harvard Business Review,* Vol. 42, No. 1, January–February, 1964.

HEYEL, CARL. *Handbook of Industrial Research Management.* 2nd ed. New York, N.Y.: Reinhold Publishing Corp., 1968.

HINRICHS, JOHN R. *High Talent Personnel.* New York, N.Y.: American Management Association, Inc., 1966.

Industrial Research Institute. "Continued Development of Technical Personnel—Prevention of Obsolescence," *Research Management,* Vol. VIII, No. 3, May, 1965.

JACKSON, THOMAS W., and SPURLOCK, JACK M. *Research and Development Management.* Homewood, Ill.: Dow Jones-Irwin, Inc., 1966.

KANTER, STUART ALLEN. "The Social Psychology of Premature Occupational Choice: An Investigation of Student Careers in an Undergraduate Engineering School." Doctoral dissertation, University of Michigan, 1967.

KARGER, DELMAR W. "Engineers: How to Get Them, How to Keep Them," *Machine Design,* January 4, 1962.

KRIGEL, M. W. Updating the Training of R & D Personnel—The Industrial Viewpoint. Paper presented to the 16th National Conference on the Administration of Research, Denver, Colo., 1962.

LAWRENCE, PAUL R., and SEILER, JOHN A. *Organizational Behavior and Administration.* Homewood, Ill.: Richard D. Irwin, Inc., and The Dorsey Press, 1965.

LEVINSON, H. "What Management Should Know about Scientists," *Air Force Magazine & Space Digest,* December, 1965.

LITTERER, JOSEPH A. *The Analysis of Organizations.* New York, N.Y.: John Wiley & Sons, Inc., 1965.

LOEBELSON, R. M. "Cutting Down on Recruitment Costs," *Space/Aeronautics,* Vol. 25:2, February, 1961.

LUPTON, D. KEITH. "The Oversell in Staff Recruiting," *Personnel Journal,* February, 1966.

MAISEL, A. Q. "Let's Stop This Shocking Waste of Manpower," *Reader's Digest,* Vol. 70:421, May, 1957.

MARGULIES, N., and RAIA, A. R. "Scientists, Engineers and Technological Obsolescence," *California Management Review,* Vol. 10, Winter, 1967.

MURDICK, R. G., and SMALLWOOD, G. L. "Training Engineers on the Job," *Machine Design,* December 8, 1960.

"The 'Obsolescent' Engineer and the New Engineers," *Space/Aeronautics,* April, 1962.

ORTH, CHAS. D.; BAILEY, JOHN C.; and WOLEK, FRANCIS W. *Administering Research and Development.* Homewood, Ill.: Richard D. Irwin, Inc., 1964.

PEIZ, DONALD C., and ANDREWS, FRANK M. *Scientists in Organizations.* New York, N.Y.: John Wiley & Sons, Inc., 1966.

RAUDSEPP, EUGENE. "Why Engineers Work," *Machine Design,* February 4, 1960.

ROSOW, JEROME M. "The Growing Role of Professional and Scientific Personnel," *Management Record,* National Industrial Conference Board, February, 1962.

URIS, AUREN. *The Executive Job Market.* New York, N.Y.: McGraw-Hill Book Company, 1965.

CHAPTER 6

Compensating and Rewarding Technical Personnel

ESTABLISHING A POLICY

From an overall viewpoint, E & R management and the company should establish a policy with respect to compensating and rewarding technical personnel. The policy should:

1. Ensure reasonable starting rates
2. Compensate technical personnel within the organization equitably with respect to each other as well as to similar employees in other firms and industries
3. Promote the retention of high-quality engineers and scientists, thereby reducing turnover costs
4. Motivate the technical organization to put forth its best effort
5. Recognize and provide rewards in proportion to the degree of performance
6. Encourage misplaced personnel to seek work for which they are better qualified
7. Permit planning for total salary costs.

While technical personnel, like other groups of workers, are motivated by other than monetary compensation in varying degrees as outlined in Chapter 5, monetary compensation always ranks as a most important factor. It is significant not only for itself, but because it is inextricably associated with status and achievement.

Establishing a reliable and creative compensation policy is easier said than done. Tradition plays such a strong role in this area that most companies fail to even consider some of the approaches that would fully motivate their engineers and scientists.

Because of the many possibilities for integrating financial and nonfinancial compensation factors to achieve various combinations of objectives, management must first establish a basic policy that can be detailed and implemented. Since every company differs from all others with regard to such factors as resources, long-range goals, objectives, philosophy, areas of technical competence, profit experience, sales trends, etc., it would be impossible to present a policy with related objectives that would have general applicability. It is possible, however, to touch upon the factors, financial and otherwise, which management must consider in establishing its master compensation plan.

SALARY COMPENSATION FOR E & R PERSONNEL

Salary

Managements have adopted various approaches to setting salaries for engineers. Among the most commonly practiced are:

1. No formal compensation plan—negotiated increases
2. No formal plan—"administered" compensation
3. Formal salary review based on "replacement cost"
4. Salary administration plan—ranking system
5. Salary administration plan—maturity curve
6. Salary administration plan—job evaluation and weighted performance appraisal
7. Any of the above combined with an incentive system.

Regardless of the method used, it is important to recognize that employers carefully study the market prices of engineers even though any single employer has little effect on the going rate. As one executive of a large chemical company said:

> Our policy, like that of most major corporations, is to pay the kind of competitive salaries necessary to attract and retain our share of the most capable personnel in American science. To do this, it is necessary to know how our rates compare with those of firms in competition with us for research personnel. Therefore, we participate with many companies in surveys and studies of salary rates and trends.[1]

Another executive writes about engineers:

> Pricing the levels of professional work is accomplished primarily by the salary-

[1] Reprinted with permission from George L. Royer, "Salary Administration of Research Personnel," *Research Management* (Summer, 1958).

survey technique because we are trying to relate the pay of professionals within the company in some predetermined manner to the pay received by comparable professionals in other selected companies[2]

Negotiated Increases

In some firms, mostly the smaller ones, there is no formal salary plan or any system of appraisal and review. The engineer works at the same salary until he becomes dissatisfied or receives a better offer elsewhere. Then he goes to his supervisor and asks for an increase. In a sense, this is the truest form of unrestricted bargaining, although both sides do not necessarily have equal bargaining strength. The employer is probably well aware of market rates and the fringe factors which tie the individual to his present position and location. Moreover, he probably has in mind a figure at which he would rather hire another engineer.

Administered Compensation

In the administered salary plan, the *individual* is the basis of the plan rather than a formal job and salary structure. Subjective judgments of the engineer's worth to the company are made in terms that relate his contributions to those made by other employees.

In this kind of approach to compensation, the supervisor always plays a key role by providing data or judgments. However, the final salary decisions are generally made by a high-ranking officer or by a small group of key individuals. It is possible under this plan to regularly review all men once a year as in other more formal plans.

In this kind of plan, it is vitally important that the supervisor speak up for his men; if not, they obviously will fare poorly. While a supervisor may "go to bat" for his men under almost any kind of plan, it is of much greater importance under this plan—in fact, it is one of its major weaknesses. Nevertheless, it is widely used, especially in the smaller companies where the duties falling under any position title are flexible and where the individual, therefore, tends to make the job.

Replacement Cost

The replacement-cost method of reviewing and compensating engineers is probably the least used in a formal or recognized manner. However, the concept, in a subjective manner, enters the picture in almost all of the plans.

The replacement-cost method corresponds to the idea in economics of paying only enough to call forth the workers. In this case, management reviews the engineers regularly to compare their salaries against the esti-

[2] Robert E. Sibson, "Establishing Formal Pay Programs," *Optimum Use of Engineering Talent* (New York: AMA Management Report, American Management Association, 1961).

mated cost of replacing them at the lowest price possible. If a man has improved his productivity and value significantly, he will be given an increase which it is believed will be just equivalent to that of a replacement. In fact, he may be paid slightly less since management knows that workers will not usually seek employment elsewhere until their salary falls about 10 per cent below the general market rate.

Ranking Plan

One of the simplest approaches to a systematic and logical method of establishing position and salary levels is the ranking plan. Each supervisor, at the annual review time, ranks the engineers in his organization. The engineering manager at the next higher level then meets with these supervisors and tries to get agreement on an over-all ranking of all engineers. Often he may get agreement on only certain key men and he, then, makes the decision as to the final ranking of all others. Salaries for key individuals at various levels of ranking are established, and the remaining men are evaluated for raises relative to these.

Maturity Curve Approach

Another basis for compensation is the maturity curve approach. Although it has become unpopular as the concept of factor analysis and pay proportional to contribution has been developed, some companies still use maturity curves.

The maturity curves are based first of all on surveys of the market to determine what engineers get paid versus years of experience. The data is plotted in the form of a scatter diagram; then curves are drawn to represent quartiles, deciles, or some other arbitrary salary division. Figure 6-1 illustrates the kind of curves used in this approach; moreover, the company can adjust these curves upward or downward, depending on the policy it wishes to establish.

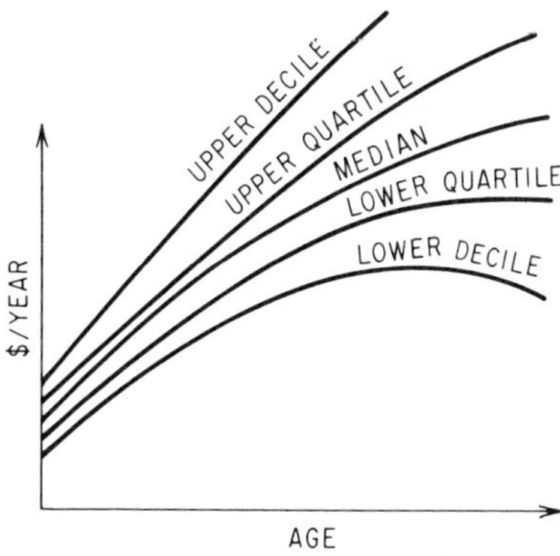

Fig. 6-1. Maturity curves.

During the first year or two that an engineer is with a company, he is closely observed to determine where he fits relative to the maturity curves. Once he is slotted in position, he finds it almost impossible to advance to another curve, as those who have had experience with this system can report. On the other hand, management is slow to drop him to a lower curve if his performance does not continue to match position. Each year, the engineer is reviewed to determine if a significant raise in salary is required to keep him in place on the curves.

Usually a merit rating system accompanies this plan to keep the engineer informed of his strengths and weaknesses. However, because of the very nature of the system the merit rating serves little purpose as far as helping the engineer accelerate his rate of growth.

Often the maturity curves themselves, which are kept by the top engineering manager, are unavailable for inspection. The continually increasing engineering salary scales make this kind of plan difficult to administer and probably is one of the major reasons for companies' abandoning it.

Salary Administration

Salary administration plans are attempts to apply scientific methods to compensating engineers (and other employees) fairly with respect to salary levels within the industry and with respect to payment for the relative contributions of individuals within the company. This is in accord with the concept that the best morale in the organization can be achieved only if there is a fair and consistent system for giving and withholding rewards which is based on performance.

Salary administration, therefore, must be concerned with the application of rational methods to the compensation of employees. To establish a salary plan fair to all, management must deal with the following problems:

1. Salary structure, which concerns the relationships between salary ranges for different kinds of jobs. (A job identifies a group of positions which are essentially identical with respect to their major or significant tasks.)
2. Salary level, which is the level of the entire salary structure relative to the general job market, both within the industry and with respect to local conditions.
3. Determination of the individual's salary.
4. Fringe benefits.
5. Control of the total labor cost and of the policies of salary administration.
6. Cost of administering any plans evolved by salary administration.

Salary administration plans in general,place considerable emphasis upon the separation of the job from the man. Therefore, any one job is considered a series of tasks or responsibilities which must be carried out, and the compensation structure is primarily based upon these tasks.

The first big problem in salary administration is establishing the relationship among jobs, i.e., their relative worth. Job evaluation has been developed by industrial and management engineers to achieve this objective. The steps taken in a job evaluation are:

1. A study is made of the jobs in the organization through the collection of facts regarding the duties, responsibilities, and work requirements for successful performance. This study is conducted by a job analyst who must be primarily concerned with the work actually accomplished rather than what the man thinks he perhaps should be doing in the future.
2. From the data collected, one must determine in a job evaluation study what the company is paying for, by determining which factors place one job higher than another. These factors are called "compensable factors."
3. Develop a system of job appraisal so that the jobs containing greater amounts of compensable factors are consistently ranked above those containing lesser amounts.

It is a practice in large companies not to analyze all jobs since it is impractical. Therefore, only key jobs are selected for determining compensable factors. The factors chosen, however, must be present to a varying degree in all jobs, and it is important that they do not overlap. The latter is achieved by very careful definition of each factor. Also, only the most significant compensable factors should be chosen, and they should have job significance to both the employee and management. Examples of compensable factors are shown in Tables 6-1 and 6-2. Table 6-1 is a plan developed by the National Electrical Manufacturers Association (NEMA), and Table 6-2 represents a company plan. Salary administra-

Table 6-1—Compensable Factors Developed by NEMA

Skill	Effort	Responsibility	Working Conditions
Job knowledge	Physical effort	Equipment and process	Surroundings
Judgment and ingenuity	Mental or visual effort	Material and product	Unavoidable hazards
		Safety of others	
		Directing work of others	

Table 6-2—Compensable Factors for a Typical Company

Knowledge and Skill Required	Application of Skill	Character and Scope
Specialized and technical knowledge	Final decision making	Human resources
Skills of persuasion and negotiation	Planning, problem solving, and creative ability	Physical and financial resources
Managerial and administrative skills		Company programs and products
		Special assigned tasks

tion, to be successful, must also be concerned with the more general objectives, the most important of which are as follows:

1. To provide compensation and opportunities which will attract and hold personnel of all qualifications and which will motivate each individual to increase his value.
2. To ensure periodic review of the development and progress of individuals so that the high-performance employees will be recognized and encouraged and other employees can be guided towards types of work in which they can utilize their full capacities.
3. To maintain frank and clear two-way communication on salary matters at all levels of organization.

Once the compensable factors have been determined, the evaluation of each job relative to another may be made in various ways including the ranking method previously described. More rational and scientific approaches are:

1. *The Classification Method.* In this method, a number of classifications are established and carefully defined. The classifications are described in terms of the level of compensable factors. Each position is studied individually and assigned to the appropriate class.
2. *Factor-Comparison Method.* The compensable factors of all jobs are isolated, and the major ones selected. Each factor is weighted for relative performance; subsequently, each position is considered factor by factor so that it may be ranked against other positions. Finally, the money paid for each position is distributed by factor. The result can be expressed as a table in which the rank value of the compensable factors can be compared with the money value ranking. A simplified form of such a table is shown in Table 6-3.

Table 6-3—Factor-Comparison Evaluation of Compensable Factors

	Compensable Factors							
	Mental		Skill		Responsibility		Relationships	
	Difficulty Value	Money Value	Difficulty Value	Money Value	Difficulty Value	Money Value	Difficulty Value	Money Value
Engineer A	2	2	4	5	1	1	2	2
Engineer B	1	1	3	3	2	2	1	3
Engineer C	4	3	1	1	1	5	4	5
Engineer D	3	4	2	2	3	3	3	1
Engineer E	5	5	5	4	4	4	5	4

3. *Point-Rating Method.* Here a suitable number of factors, which are common to all positions considered, are selected. Each factor is divided into a number of degrees ranging from high to low, and each degree is assigned a number of points according to its relative worth. The difference in points from one degree to another for a given factor is usually not a linear relationship. Jobs are rated by determining the appropriate degree of each factor present in the job. The number of points corresponding to each degree is recorded and summarized. A typical point-rating plan for an engineering organization is shown in Table 6-4. Table 6-5 shows the ratings for a position using this plan which requires a Master's Degree, nine years of experience, team leadership qualities, and the ability to solve complex problems having little precedent, plus internal relationships with people of higher status and guidance of seven or eight other engineers.

   A major advantage of the point plan is its stability. While jobs may change, the point system tends to improve with age. The influence of differences in human judgment tends to be minimized. Its biggest disadvantage is the difficulty in developing the point system. The factors and their breakdowns must be carefully defined, weights must be allocated to the factor strictly in accordance with their importance, and point values must be assigned to each degree.

The development of a salary structure and its pricing should be accomplished by people with specialized training in the area. Amateurish attempts to establish a salary plan can wreck any organization, especially the E & R organization. The final result in a carefully planned salary program will be a structure rate, a minimum rate, and a maximum rate for each job level as illustrated in Fig. 6-2. A promotion occurs when an engineer's job is reconstructed and rated at a higher level. While on the same job, he can still receive salary raises based on performance up to the maximum rate for his job level.

Since salary is a reward for job performance, former methods of evaluating employee's "traits" are disappearing. That is, rating engineers on their "persistence," "personality," "aggressiveness," "ability to get along with other people," etc., is not considered to yield a good measure of their per-

Table 6-4—Point-Rating Method of Job Evaluation

	Points
A. EDUCATION REQUIRED	
1. High school graduate	35
2. 2 years of college	65
3. College graduate	112
4. M.S.	125
5. Ph.D.	190
B. EXPERIENCE REQUIRED	
1. Less than 1 yr	39
2. 1–2 yr	49
3. 2–3 yr	60
4. 4–5 yr	71
5. 5–7 yr	88
6. 8–10 yr	105
7. 10–15 yr	130
8. Over 15 yr	150
C. SCOPE OF RESPONSIBILITY	
1. Engineer responsible for providing directed effort in conducting designated assignments.	48
2. Engineer responsible for undirected effort on lesser tasks.	63
3. Engineer, group leader, or manager responsible for a moderately broad engineering task.	90
4. Specialist or group leader responsible for broad engineering recommendations or tasks. Manager responsible for a broad engineering task.	110
5. Consulting engineer responsible for broad technical recommendations, technical advice in his field of specialty and establishment of engineering base. Manager responsible for a major technical activity.	151
6. Unusually broad consulting and advising responsibility. Managerial responsibility for more than one technical activity.	189
D. COMPLEXITY OF PROBLEMS	
1. Logical answer can be obtained with little analysis.	45
2. Analysis is required, but precedent and principles determine general approach.	59
3. Considerable investigation and analysis is required, but precedent or principles provide a guide.	75
4. Complex problems with little precedent.	92
5. Complex problems with no precedent.	121
6. Analysis and synthesis dealing with many intangible factors.	155
E. SCOPE AND COMPLEXITY OF RELATIONSHIPS	
1. Internal relationships with others of same status.	10
2. Extensive internal relationships with others of higher status.	26
3. Customer contact on products or progress.	48
4. Extensive internal relationships with others of higher status and customer contact on products or programs.	55
F. NUMBER OF ASSIGNED PERSONNEL	
1. 2–5	30
2. 6–10	51
3. 11–20	62
4. 21–30	74
5. 31–50	90
6. 51–100	110
7. 101–150	135
8. 151–300	164
9. 301–500	201

Table 6-5—Point-Rating Score for an Engineering Position

Factors*	Points
A4	125
B6	105
C3	90
D4	92
E2	26
F2	51
Total	489

* See Table 6-4.

formance on the job. The "results approach" to evaluation, which is preferable, is based upon a contractual relationship between the man and his manager. In the light of organizational goals, the engineer and manager seek agreement on the work the engineer should accomplish and when he should complete various tasks and/or goals. This is an objective approach which gives the engineer responsibility for a defined area. Successful completion of the work carries with it the implication that the engineer possesses those personal traits required and to the degree desired.

In summary, then, the responsibilities of the job are outlined in the position guide, the man and his manager agree upon specific tasks to be accomplished by given times, the manager reviews with the engineer his relative success in meeting his work objectives, and the engineer is rewarded financially according to his output.

There are certain obstacles to the administration of a salary plan which

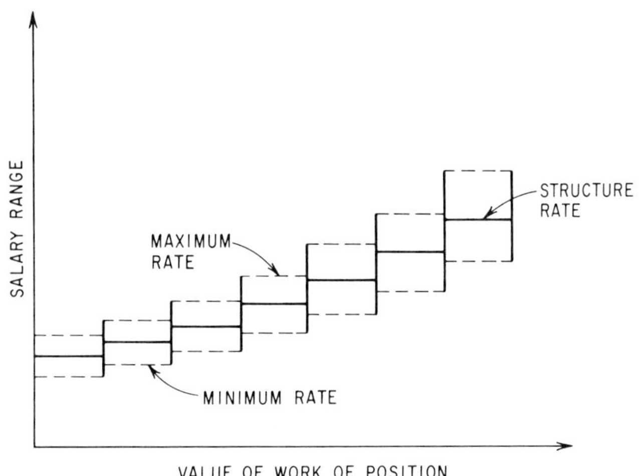

Fig. 6-2. Salary structure.

are not highly publicized among engineers or even lower level managers. Most companies plan to spend a relatively fixed amount of money on engineering salaries if the number of engineers is to remain constant; in fact, this statement can be applied to each element of the organization. Thus, the company may establish a limit of a 6 per cent increase in total engineering labor costs each year. Even this modest increase cannot be continued indefinitely unless the output of the engineers increases considerably each year. The company looks not so much at the absolute value of the individual engineer as at the cost of an engineer to replace him.

Salary and Bonus

The bonus form of financial payment is well known. It only remains to point out that it may be given according to two general plans. In the first method, only the key personnel are eligible for a bonus. In the other plan, a blanket bonus is often given just before Christmas or at the close of the fiscal year to all personnel in certain categories. Bonuses in either case are not usually specified in advance.

Practically all bonus plans are tied to company profit performance. If there aren't sufficient profits, there is no bonus. Also, most bonus systems are not formally established in writing, which means that the board of directors or an executive committee decides each year whether there will be a bonus and how much will be available to divide among those who are to receive it. In the unspecified plan, the total is usually divided among the organizational units on some basis such as the relative number of employees who are to receive a bonus or the relative total monthly or annual salary in the various organizational units. The head of each unit then sits down with his managers and allocates the amount to be received by each man.

If it is a formal plan specified in writing, a fixed and/or variable percentage of the profits is usually related to salary level in some specified way to arrive at the bonus.

Salary Plus Incentive

Combination salary and incentive plans are usually created to attract and hold highly paid key personnel. Such plans, which usually offer tax advantages, may include such items as profit sharing, stock options, retirement provisions, etc.

Management Awards

So-called management awards are somewhat misnamed since they are usually given at the end of the year by management to individual contributors who performed some outstanding job. Such an accomplishment might be completing an important and difficult task ahead of schedule, producing some ingenious design to break a bottleneck or effecting a large cost reduction, etc. The management awards may be a combination of monetary payment and a framed certificate. Newspaper articles and pictures usually result from the giving of such awards. The monetary amounts are usually small, i.e., $100, a share of stock, or some other nominal compensation.

FRINGE BENEFITS AS SUPPLEMENTARY COMPENSATION FOR E & R PERSONNEL

Fringe benefits are discussed under the topic of financial compensation because they have a significant cash value to the recipient. There are many such benefits, most of which are well known, and a few are listed here to show the variety:

1. Pension plans
2. Stock option plans (qualified, unqualified,or "phantom")
3. Matching stock or bond savings plans (the company matches the employee's savings up to a certain amount)
4. Vacation plans (longer paid vacations based on service with the company)
5. Health, life insurance (ordinary and/or split-dollar), and unemployment plans
6. Tuition-refund plans, some involving time off from work as well
7. Interest free or guaranteed loans
8. Pension and profit sharing trusts
9. Variable annuities
10. Profit sharing
11. Retained interest in inventions
12. Salary continuation after retirement
13. Use of the Scientific Foundation approach to provide for sabbaticals, etc.
14. Company-furnished automobiles
15. Moving expenses and bonuses for transfers
16. Time-and-a-half and/or double-time pay for overtime work and/or holiday work.

Available space will not permit discussing all of the fringe benefits, their effect upon employees, the way they can be implemented, etc. However, here are a few of the listed items that are unusual enough to warrant some elaboration.

Scientific Foundations

A scientific foundation set up by a company can provide incentives for scientists and, at the same time, offer ways to save on taxes. Such a foundation could grant sabbaticals and use the foundation's facilities to do pure research. This certainly is an excellent way to recruit and keep scientists. This same foundation could provide funds for travel to universities and other centers of learning, funds and facilities to enable engineers and scientists to do independent research in their spare time, etc. Second, it can be used to provide undergraduate and graduate scholarships and fellowships less expensively than by direct grants from the corporate treasury. Many corporations have set up scientific foundations to handle the scholarship and fellowship program but have not considered using them for the purposes mentioned earlier. These and many other creative suggestions for compensating and rewarding scientists were advanced by Gustave Simons, a noted tax lawyer.[3]

Pension and Profit-Sharing Trusts

While the contributions of a company to a trust aren't taxable, in the case of a profit-sharing trust the firm can only deduct contributions up to 15 percent of the average annual pay of the people participating in the trust. Since there is no limitation in contributions from a company tax view toward a pension trust, it often permits providing more adequately for employees in the older age brackets, providing the payout is related to social security payments, i.e. these must be taken into account by deduction of the employee's social security benefits from the amount he is to receive from the trust.

Pension trusts also make possible variable annuities where part of the proceeds are invested to provide a fixed return and another part is invested in securities that hopefully will increase in value and more than compensate for inflation.

Profit-sharing trusts do give employees greater incentive to produce and are particularly valuable for rewarding younger employees—because the more the company earns, the more the participating employee earns. Sears and Roebuck has combined this approach with its stock bonus plan by setting up a stock bonus trust. Apparently it has worked well in making it possible to hold onto executives. Instead of contributing cash, the company contributes stock. Trusts can be a combination of pension and profit-sharing. Still another way is to tie the trust to an affiliate which might be the R & D laboratory. Here the rewards provided the participants (in our example the R & D laboratory, set up as an affiliated company) might be high in comparison to those provided direct or to regular employees of the parent company. Limiting the high benefits through a trust set up by an affiliate may not incur the wrath and displeasure of employees in the remainder of the company.

[3] Gustave Simons, "How to Attract and Reward Good Scientists." From the October 1963 issue of Business Management magazine with permission of the Publisher.

Retained Interest in Invention

Employees with inventive ability would be favorably impressed by a provision for retained interest in inventions. Incidentally, this is a common arrangement in Europe. The IRS permits an inventor to treat royalties like a capital gain and this could prove to be a potent incentive. According to Simons[4] the company can easily protect itself against the inventor/scientist leaving its employ with rights to its invention by retaining an option to buy his rights on a formula basis.

Salary Continuation After Retirement

The above could be accomplished by the company insuring the life of a given scientist and naming itself as the beneficiary. With the proper policy, it can be paid up by the time the scientist retires. The annuity received from the insurance company can then be used to compensate the scientist. If the company borrowed to pay the premiums on the policy, it can deduct the interest whereas it could not deduct the premiums. According to Simons, "If enough people are included in such a plan the proceeds from the insurance which are not taxable, will soon amount to more than the cost of the policies, the cost of the loan that pays the policies, and the after-tax cost of the supplementary annuity. Thus, in one fifteen-million program I know of, the annual gains soon exceeded the annual cost by $12,000 per year."[5]

Health, Life Insurance, and Unemployment Plans

There is an endless variety to the benefits covered by this topic.

One particularly interesting idea is that of split-dollar insurance for engineers and scientists. It involves the company advancing an interest free loan to pay the premiums on an insurance policy up to the policy's cash value. The problem here is that in the early years of a whole life or a "paid-up" (in a fixed number of years) policy at the end of, say, 20 years, the employee's share would be burdensome in early years since the cash value had not built up to any significant proportion. However, in later years the difference between the cash value and the premium is minimum. If the company first establishes an insured deferred compensation program and then shifts to a split-dollar plan later on, it can keep down the cost of the split-dollar insurance to the employee.

Stock Option Plans

In addition to the ordinary qualified (in the IRS sense) plan, one can offer phantom stock options to engineers and scientists. Ordinarily, the

[4] *Ibid.* [5] *Ibid.*

objection to stock options is that one cannot deduct the cost of the plan. With phantom stock option plans the company credits the employee with a certain amount of stock without actually giving him the stock. It also credits him with any subsequent increase in the price of the stock and with any dividends it pays. When the employee retires, the company then pays him the accumulated credits without giving up the stock itself. According to Simons,[6] if the company finances such a program through tax-deductible insurance, it can keep the cost of the program reasonable enough to make it attractive.

Interest-Free or Guaranteed Loans

Often a company will provide second mortgages for property purchases. This is quite conventional and interest may or may not be charged.

Mr. Simons advances a more thought provoking idea: "Consider making interest-free loans of good size—say of 50,000 dollars or more. Your scientists won't have to pay taxes on such a loan. They may be able to invest them to such good advantage that they can repay the principal within 5 years—yet make a profit for themselves."[7]

Vacation Plans

In addition to the conventional vacation plans, the company may arrange special tours for groups of employees. These can provide vacations that are far superior to those the employee is able to arrange for by himself. It also develops an *esprit de corps* among the employees and loyalty for the company.

AN OVERVIEW OF ENGINEERING SALARIES

Anyone who has had a close working relationship with salary administration in an engineering and research organization will be aware of certain management restrictions on salary increases. For example, a directive may be issued to managers at each level that the total dollar increase in engineering payroll must be limited to a fixed percent. Here some will get an increase and some will not obtain any increase. Does this mean that all of those receiving no increase have shown no improvement in performance in one year's time? Does salary really correspond to performance as salary administrators claim? Or are there underlying economic factors such as management's inability to pay more than the marginal productivity of labor in combination with the factors of production?

Do salary administration plans really accomplish their purpose in paying individual engineers according to their performance? These are interesting and valid questions for serious consideration.

[6] *Ibid.* [7] *Ibid.*

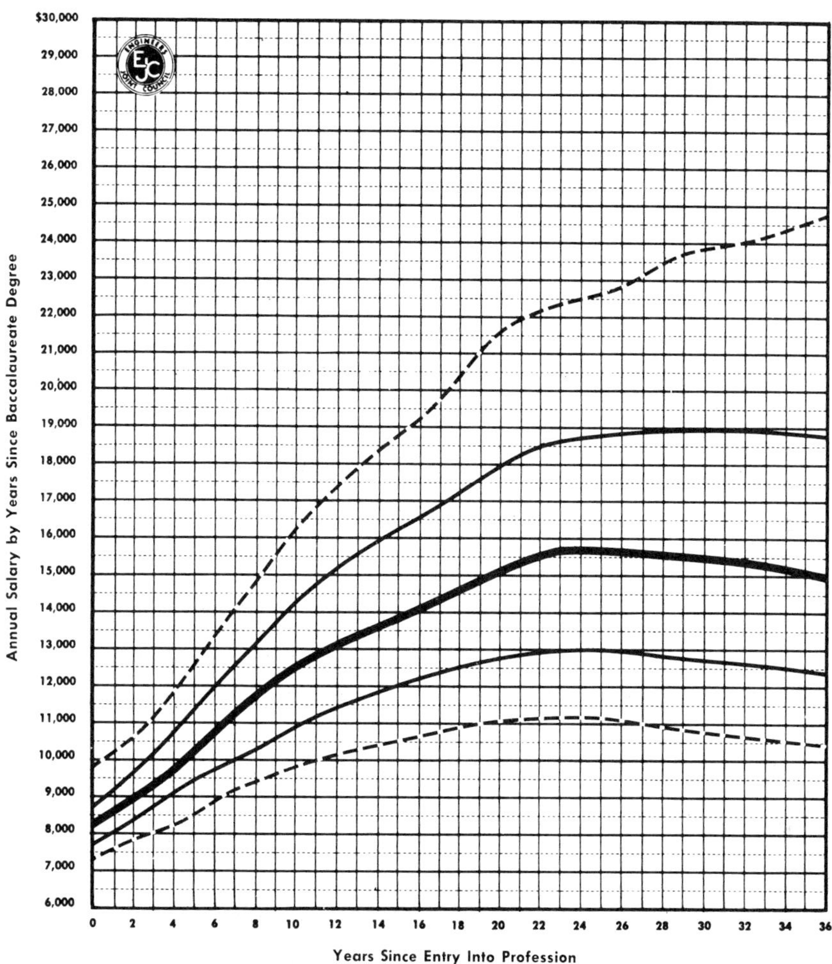

Fig. 6-3. Annual salaries in 1966–1967 of all graduate engineers in all industries by year of entry into profession. Number of engineers covered, 189,127. *Source:* Figs. 6-3 to 6-5 were taken from *Professional Income of Engineers, 1966–67*, New York: Engineering Manpower Commission of Engineers Joint Council, June, 1967.

With demand for engineers expected to increase and supply expected to decrease in the next few years, the information which follows is interesting since it relates to where engineering salaries now stand. Figures 6-3, 6-4, and 6-5 present this information. The new survey for the Engineering Manpower Commission of Engineers Joint Council indicates that the overall median salaries of all engineers, regardless of degrees or year in which the Bachelor's degree was obtained, was $12,500 in 1966–1967.

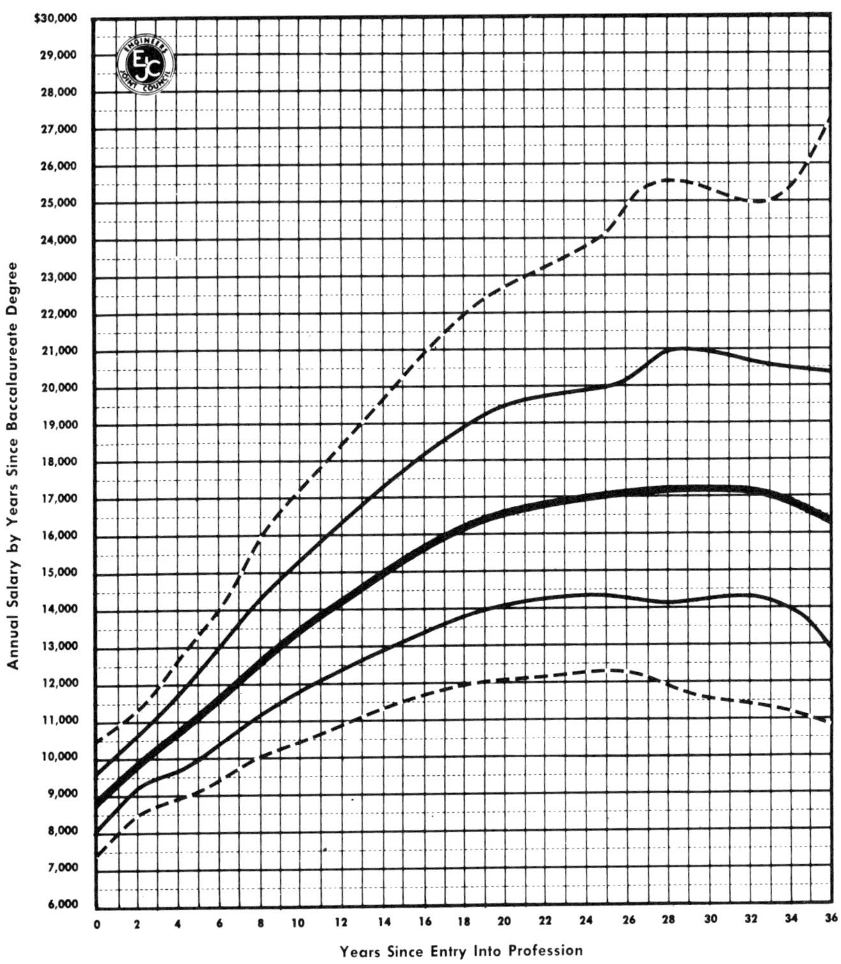

Fig. 6-4. Annual salaries in 1966–1967 of Masters of Science graduates in all industries by year of entry into profession. Number of engineers covered, 27,622. *Source:* See Fig. 6-3.

NONMONETARY REWARDS FOR E & R PERSONNEL

Salary is, of course, not the only means by which management can reward and motivate engineers and scientists. As the illustrious economist Alfred Marshall phrased it in 1890:

> The true reward which an occupation offers to labour has to be calculated by deducting the money value of all its disadvantages from that of all its

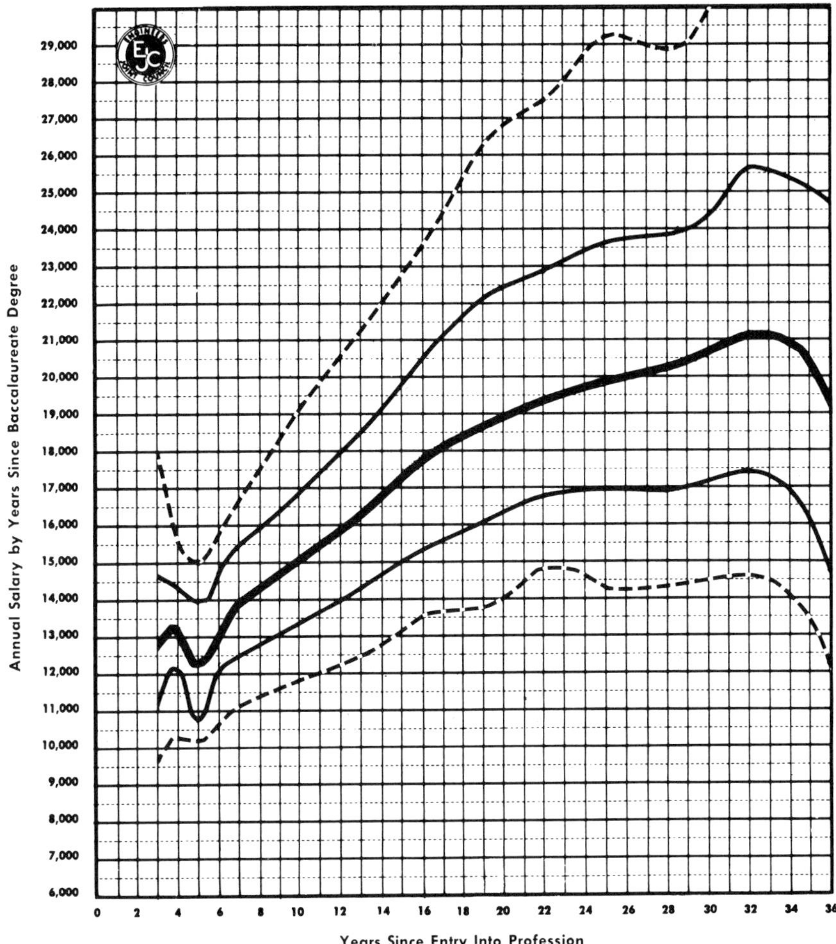

Fig. 6-5. Annual salaries in 1966–1967 of Doctors of Science and Doctors of Philosophy in all industries by year of entry into profession. Number of engineers covered, 8,736. *Source:* See Fig. 6-3.

advantages; and we may describe this true reward as the *net advantages* of the occupation.[8]

Some of the non-monetary motivating factors or positive advantages of a particular engineering job, many of which were ranked as to importance in Chapter 5, are listed as follows:

1. Climate for creativity
2. Professional challenge, responsibility, and recognition

[8] Alfred Marshall, *Principles of Economics,* 8th ed. (New York: Macmillan, 1948), p. 73.

3. Opportunity for self-development
4. Opportunity for promotion or advancement
5. Parallel paths and identification with management
6. Physical facilities
7. Good service organizations and technical and clerical assistance to technical journals, attendance at technical society meetings, professional license fees, and reprints of articles
8. Status symbols
9. Geographical location of plant and climate
10. New, growing organization working in a new field
11. Type of product.

Climate for Creativity

The importance of establishing a climate for creativity has been discussed in Chapter 4. It only remains to emphasize that a "creative climate" must be based upon the *actions* of engineering management, not *words,* if it is to represent a plus factor to the engineer or scientist.

Professional Challenge, Responsibility, and Recognition

All too often, the technical contributor finds that he is part of a huge team or machine, and that his assignments which are narrow in scope are handed to him without explanation. His responsibility for carrying out even so specialized a task as developing or engineering a new product may be diluted by team assignments or by constant close supervision. Whatever success the whole E & R organization achieves is attributed mainly to top management, and less and less responsibility is attributable to each lower level of management.

While it is true today that many technical projects are so broad that many individuals must work together to bring them to fruition, each individual should be informed about the broad objectives, and each individual should be given specific responsibilities for a broad enough area to make him stretch. Although he should be held accountable for his accomplishing his job, he should be given reasonable latitude in choosing the processes or method used to accomplish his task. At the conclusion of the work or at periodic intervals, his work should be appraised and his contribution recognized by proper financial and/or other types of nonmonetary rewards.

Opportunity for Self-Development

Technical personnel are acutely aware of how rapidly knowledge becomes obsolete. Consequently, most of them consider opportunities for self-development as a necessary facet of a job. This aspect of the job has been discussed in two previous chapters.

Opportunity for Promotion or Reassignment

In both small and large companies, E & R people want to know answers to such questions as: "What are the chances for promotion?" "What are the chances for reassignment within the company if I wish to change jobs for any reason?" Within the small company, knowledge of the organization and its philosophy are enough to provide the answers. In the large company, the technical person must look for some formal organized procedure to provide such opportunities.

The degree to which there is an opportunity to change jobs within a company is in part related to the manpower inventory discussed in Chapter 6. Its primary purposes are to expose every engineer and scientist to company-wide opportunities and to provide every E & R manager with pertinent information about the best qualified candidates for any openings in his organization.

Parallel Paths and Identification with Management

A major problem which the manager of the larger engineering and research organization faces is keeping highly competent and creative people working directly on research and engineering projects. Most young technical professionals entering industry today are aware of the two separate paths of progression—the managerial and the specialist. Top management has, in the past, put a considerable premium on advancement through the ranks of management. It is only natural that the most competent technical people would seek to leave the technical area to attain the status and monetary rewards of management. It was bad enough that in many cases such people were unsuited for managerial work by their temperaments, but now the drain upon the ranks of much-needed competent specialists has become obvious.

As a result, there has been the development of "parallel paths" of opportunity. Just as there is a hierarchy of management, a hierarchy of technical positions may be established. As the engineer or scientist climbs the specialization ladder, he actually becomes more of a generalist in technical matters and acquires a business orientation. He becomes a counselor and advisor to management and may exert considerable influence over major management decisions. The pay scale from the lowest to the highest level of technical contribution has thus been broadened enormously.

As a further inducement, top management has in many cases encouraged technical people to identify themselves with the management group. This has been done by explicit statement of policy regarding professional engineers and scientists and management, that is, by communicating management objectives, problems, and viewpoints to professional people; providing common exclusive or executive company dining rooms; and by holding special combined meetings. All of these and similar steps help create a climate where the professional worker feels that his contribution is equally important to that of the manager's.

Physical Facilities

The more competent engineers and scientists may be rewarded with bigger offices, better furniture, location near key activities, personal technical equipment, etc.

Technical Assistance

The progressive manager of E & R will try to supply his organization with technical service groups and administrative and clerical assistance so that his people can concentrate on creative research and engineering.

Technicians, laboratory assistants, engineering administrators, and skilled clerical people performing work which challenges them can remove much of the burdensome work from the engineer or scientist—work that does not utilize his unique abilities.

Other Miscellaneous Benefits

Other benefits are those which give the technical contributor the feeling of status. These could in addition to those things already mentioned, include such items as attending professional meetings, a parking space identified by name, the privilege of buying certain major items through the company, desk or office name plates, acceptance into managerial circles, etc.

Opportunity to participate in a rapidly growing technology is a bonus which some managements fortunately may be able to provide. Also, management can deliberately establish its plants and laboratories in geographical areas which offer an attractive climate, recreational, and/or educational facilities.

BIBLIOGRAPHY

AMA Management Report No. 58, Optimum Use of Engineering Talent. 1961. New York, N.Y.: American Management Association, Inc.

BRALLEY, JAMES A. "Job Status as an Award for Scientific and Administrative Accomplishment," *Research Management,* Vol. 3, No. 4, The Proceedings of the Industrial Research Study Meeting No. 2, Winter, 1960.

Bureau of National Affairs, Inc., The. "Solving the Shortage of Specialized Personnel," *Personnel Policies Forum, Survey No. 62,* September, 1961.

Engineering Manpower Commission of Engineers Joint Council. *Professional Income of Engineers, 1966–1967.* New York, N.Y., June, 1967.

LEAMER, FRANK. "Professional and Administrative Ladders—the Advancement of Broad Classification in a Research Organization," *Research Management,* Vol. 2, No. 1, Spring, 1959.

National Science Foundation. *Scientific Manpower 1960.* Papers of the Ninth Conference on Scientific Manpower, NSF 61–34, May, 1961.

RIEGEL, JOHN W. Administration of Salaries and Intangible Rewards for Engineers and Scientists. Paper for the Bureau of Industrial Relations, The University of Michigan, Ann Arbor, Mich., 1958.

ROYER, GEORGE L. "Salary Administration of Research Personnel," *Research Management,* Vol. 1, No. 3, Summer, 1958.

SIMONS, GUSTAV. "How to Attract and Reward Good Scientists," *Business Management,* October, 1963.

CHAPTER 7

Identifying New Product Opportunities

INTRODUCTION

The purpose of building an engineering organization is to execute the technical actions necessary to develop a profitable business. The activities to be executed by the engineering and research organization range from providing long-range counsel to top management to the identification, selection, and development of new product concepts. The chapters in this section are concerned with these primary responsibilties of technical management. The focus is on execution of the operational activities of the E & R organization.

The activities discussed relate directly to the inventive process which has been described as the following four-step sequence:

1. Defining the problem
2. Evaluating technological and economic factors
3. Achieving insight
4. Performing a critical revision.

It should be emphasized that *all* the steps are necessary, not just the third. History is full of examples proving this point. The steam engine, the steamboat, radio transmission, the telephone, and the electric light are just a few of the examples. Every one had been conceived as an idea by other than the commonly known inventor. Many of the "firsts" claimed for the USSR are rooted in some fact. For example, Polznov did operate a steam engine before Watt, but no one could repair a leak in his boiler. Popov transmitted a radio signal three miles in 1896, but no one cared. Edision was the most productive inventor in American history with 1,093 patents to his credit. His success was based upon a *combination* of good management, financial expertise, technical ingenuity, and inventiveness. These four factors represented by the four steps must be present for inventions to be successful.

TECHNOLOGICAL THREATS

The most significant phenomenon of modern society is the increasing rapidity with which nature is being made to serve man. Progress in technological developments far outpaces social, political, and economic advances. The diffusion of the results of technological advances has a great impact on these other activities of man. From the specific viewpoint of the firm, advances in science and technology offer both an opportunity and a threat to its economic well being. A single new development may propel a firm to great success as was the case with the electrostatic copier and Xerox. On the other hand, the development of integrated circuits imbedded in plastics has seriously and adversely affected a number of electronic components firms.

For single-product firms or firms receiving most of its revenues from only one of its products, an unforeseen technological innovation can be devastating. Multiproduct firms, despite the apparent security from diversification, must also be on guard against changes in the environment leading to new products. One of the major failures of management is its lack of identification of challenges by a systematic approach. Management should have a formal program for technological forecasting, needs research, selection of major product areas, and development of specific product concepts. It is obvious that research and engineering personnel must play a major part in such an effort.

TECHNOLOGICAL FORECASTING

It is not enough that the E & R organization simply design improved products. It must also set the *direction* of product development and innovation to satisfy new market needs in terms of technological advances. The E & R organization must work with the marketing organization to forecast technological changes that will be produced by a combination of socio-economic pressures and growth of knowledge in science.

Technological forecasting is growing rapidly in importance as an organized way of predicting scientific and engineering progress over a span ranging from about three to twenty-five years ahead. Such forecasting is essential to long-range planning despite the fact that techniques for such forecasting are still primitive.

There appear to be five basic approaches to technological forecasting* which the E & R manager may select from:

* More information on a somewhat new approach to technological forecasting is found in a Ph.D. thesis by Dr. Simons of Rensselaer Polytechnic Institute. It is entitled *Technological Forecasting: The Identification and Selection of High Priority Solutions.*

1. Obtain a number of technological forecasts from published articles and private and government reports and evaluate and reconcile these. For most small and medium size companies, this is the most practical method.
2. Forecast major socioeconomic changes and technological milestones, and then fill in the gaps in technology required to achieve these. This means a sort of PERT diagram of the future is prepared. Major milestones might be farming and living on the ocean bottom, personal flying devices that are small and light enough for individuals to carry around with them, intercontinental commercial passenger rockets, electronically controlled highways, and enclosed, air conditioned cities. TRW, Inc. uses such an approach by listing over 400 product prophesies in its "Probe" technique.
3. Forecast trends in growth of physical characteristics. For example, such characteristics as the increase in speed of transportation, increase in power/cubic foot obtainable, increase in food yield/acre, changes in metallic properties obtainable, and changes in synthetic fiber characteristics obtainable.
4. List a large number of technological fields. In each field, select materials, processes, and products that appear to be continually evolving yet are basic enough so that they will still be important in the future predicted time span. Forecast results of such continuing changes and relate these by cross-checking among fields. Where the needs for specific scientific advances are the same for several fields or industries, more rapid progress may be anticipated.
5. Prepare a matrix listing technical development down one side of a chart, product functions across the top of the chart, and time as a third dimension. Fill in the blocks in the chart with estimates for combinations of technical developments and product functions for the company's field(s) of interest.

Technological Forecasting at TRW*

TRW, Inc.'s method for predicting technological advance as far as 20 years ahead has received much favorable attention. This method, called Probe, is based on the following ground rules as actually employed in Probe (A second study, Probe II, is now under way):

1. Each of four group vice-presidents nominated five of his most creative and knowledgeable technologists to participate

* The authors wish to express their appreciation for the ready courtesy and assistance on every occasion they have called upon TRW. The description of Probe is a brief condensation of the extensive material supplied by Dr. Harper Q. North, V. P., Research & Development, and Mr. Donald L. Pyke, Assistant to the Vice President, both of whom were responsible for the development of Probe.

2. Each participant was asked to list—independently—those technical events that he felt might take place over the next 20 years and which would have a substantial impact on the current or potential product lines of his group

3. He was then asked to indicate the date for which he felt there was a fifty percent chance for occurrence of each event

4. He could consult freely throughout the company but events and dates were to be *his* judgments

5. A few published general and economic forecasts were supplied each participant.

The first-round questionnaire being used for Probe II is shown in Fig. 7-1. The first round results of Probe I were edited, combined, and grouped according to technologies. The draft was returned to each panelist with the request that he edit freely in areas of his own expertise. A sample page from Probe I is shown in Fig. 7-2. Probe II, a much larger study, will undoubtedly revise the predictions which are now several years old.

Probe Category ______________ Panel Member ____________ TRW Division ______________

	Desirability			Feasibility			Timing		
1. List below all anticipated technical events (indicating source, if external to TRW) which will have a significant effect on TRW in the above category. 2. Evaluate each predicted event with respect to the three factors at the right in view of the anticipated environment.	Needed desperately	Desirable	Undesirable but possible	Highly feasible	Likely	Unlikely but possible	Year by which the probability is χ that the event will have occurred. χ = .20	χ = .50	χ = .90

Fig. 7-1. TRW's Probe II: First round questionnaire.

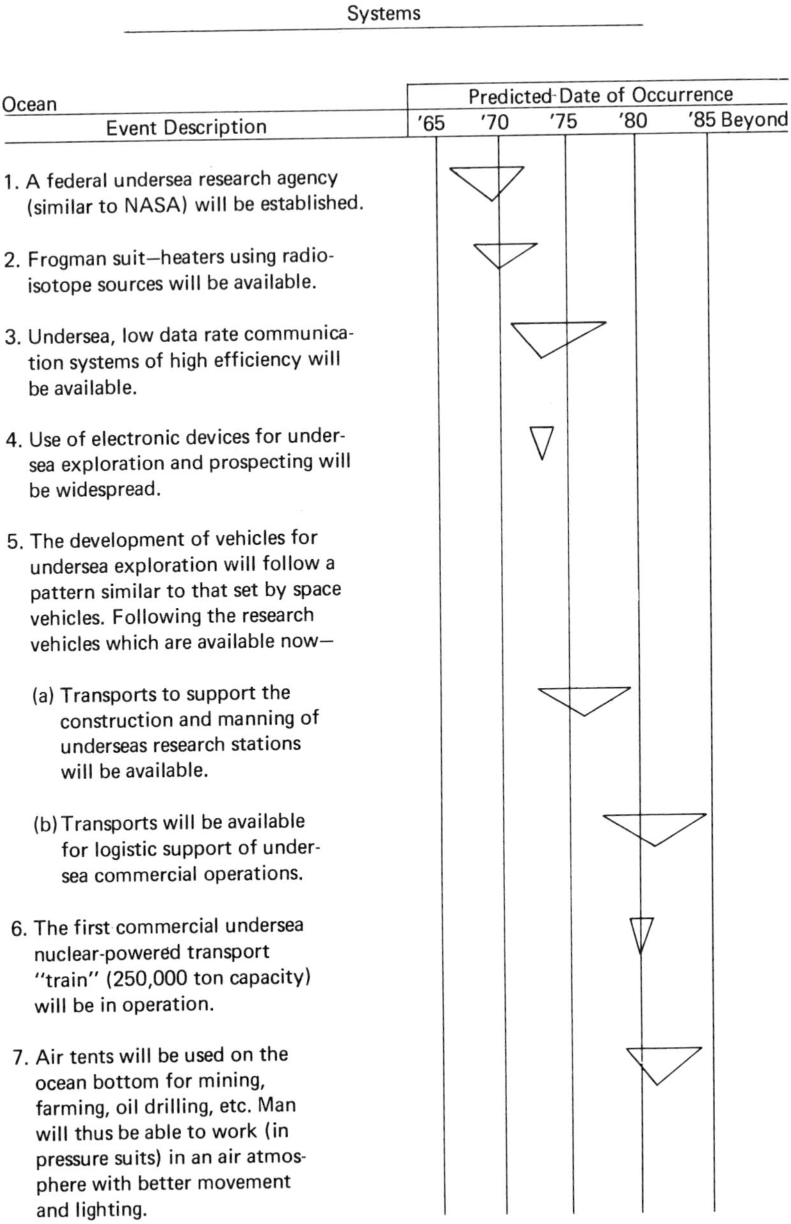

Systems

Ocean Event Description	Predicted Date of Occurrence '65 '70 '75 '80 '85 Beyond
1. A federal undersea research agency (similar to NASA) will be established.	
2. Frogman suit—heaters using radio-isotope sources will be available.	
3. Undersea, low data rate communication systems of high efficiency will be available.	
4. Use of electronic devices for undersea exploration and prospecting will be widespread.	
5. The development of vehicles for undersea exploration will follow a pattern similar to that set by space vehicles. Following the research vehicles which are available now—	
(a) Transports to support the construction and manning of underseas research stations will be available.	
(b) Transports will be available for logistic support of undersea commercial operations.	
6. The first commercial undersea nuclear-powered transport "train" (250,000 ton capacity) will be in operation.	
7. Air tents will be used on the ocean bottom for mining, farming, oil drilling, etc. Man will thus be able to work (in pressure suits) in an air atmosphere with better movement and lighting.	

Fig. 7-2. Sample TRW projection format.

NEEDS RESEARCH AND VENTURE OPPORTUNITIES

Once a technological forecast has been prepared, the next step toward developing new product concepts is to perform *needs* research. Although the marketing organization carries the major responsibility for this, the E & R manager must work closely with the marketing people in order to clarify technical possibilities. Needs research attempts to define as broadly as possible a set of customer needs that can be satisfied by a rational program of the company.

Needs research, subsequent to technological forecasting, leads to the following questions:

1. What are possible alternative fields of endeavor that should be considered for the company?
2. What major product areas should be considered?
3. What are the potential growth and revenue for each product area?
4. What resources and restraints affect the alternatives?
5. Is internal growth possible or should the firm seek venture opportunities for expansion to meet technological and marketing challenges?

The contribution of needs research to identification of E & R objectives and project selection has been presented by Donald J. Smalter, Director of Strategic Planning for International Minerals and Chemical Corporation as shown in Fig. 7-3.

Note that needs research is important to defining E & R objectives in the conceptual, exploratory, and development cycles in this figure.

E & R IN LONG-RANGE PLANNING

In order to satisfy the identified needs, the company's top management must plan long-range as well as short-range actions to achieve specific objectives. The manager of E & R along with other functional managers must work out such long-range plans for review by the company's top management.

The manager of E & R must keep himself informed so that his objectives and plans are directed toward fulfilling corporate objectives and are compatible with the plans of the other functional areas. The long-range plan represents a predetermined course of action over a specified period of time (usually 5 or more years) consisting of a projected response to an anticipated environment in order to accomplish a set of objectives. The long-range plan encompasses the very detailed short-range (one-year) plan.

Engineers and scientists,by the nature of their work.like facts and data. Long-range planning requires a risk-taking entrepreneurial orientation.

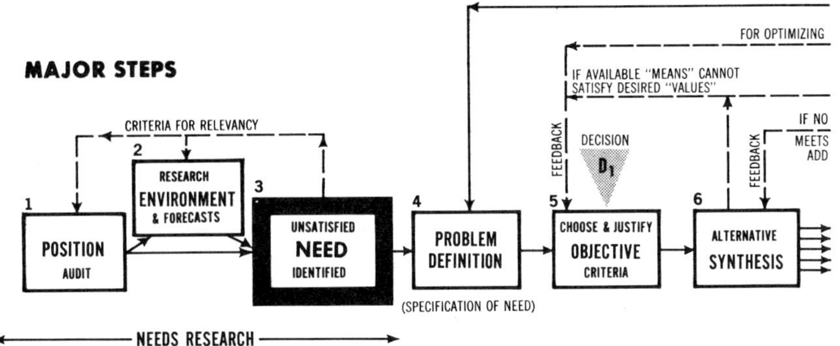

ANALYTICAL COMPONENTS

1. POSITION AUDIT
RESOURCES
CAPACITIES
PROFIT SOURCES
INVESTMENT
FINANCIAL CONSTRAINTS
MARKET SHARE
ATTRIBUTES
- Strengths
- Weaknesses

FLEXIBILITY
MOMENTUM

2. RESEARCH ENVIRONMENT & FORECASTS
SOCIO-ECONOMIC FORECASTS
REGULATORY CONSTRAINTS
FUNDAMENTAL SCIENTIFIC REVIEW & RESEARCH
TECHNOLOGY FORECASTS
NEEDS-OF-USER STUDY
MARKET POTENTIAL
POSITION OF COMPETITION
- Strengths
- Weaknesses

3. UNSATISFIED NEED IDENTIFIED
POSE CRITICAL QUESTION
EXAMPLES
- A Business Need
- Problem Requiring Solution
- Goal Desired
- A Marked Demand, Lack, or Desire
- A Competitive Threat
- An Apparent Opportunity ·

OFFICIALLY INITIATED BY "REQUEST-FOR-PROPOSAL"
IDENTIFIED BY FORMALLY ORGANIZED SEARCHING

4. PROBLEM DEFINITION
DESCRIBE SITUATION
- Economics
- User Requirements
- Policy
- Input/Output Analysis

LIST BOUNDARY CONSTRAINTS
- Tolerance
- User Desires
- "Spillover" Effects
- State-of-the-Art
- Urgency, etc.

MINIMIZE INTERACTION WITH OTHER "SYSTEMS"

5. CHOOSE & JUSTIFY OBJECTIVE CRITERIA
LIST VALUES DESIRED (i.e., "ENDS" to be satisfied)
- Economic
- Convenience
- Psychological
- Legal
- Ethical

EVALUATE MERITS & SCREEN-OUT
- Assign Measure-of-Value
- Check for Realizability
- Test for Consistency

RANK PREFERENCES IDENTIFY DECISION-CRITERIA FOR PICKING OPTIMUM ALTERNATE
CLEARLY JUSTIFY THE NEED
"FIT" WITH FIVE YEAR GOALS
STATE PREMISES WHERE LACKING FACTS
QUANTIFY CRITERIA WHEREVER POSSIBLE

6. ALTERNATIVE SYNTHESIS
COMPILE / INVENT / CREATE } ALTERNATIVES
TAKE IDEA CENSUS
APPLIED CREATIVITY
- Check Listing
- Attribute Listing
- Morphological Analysis
- Brainstorming Sessions

LIST AVAILABLE "MEANS"
- Inputs/Outputs
- Boundary Conditions

UNDERTAKE FUNCTIONAL SYNTHESIS
- Block Diagram Design
- Construct "Model"

7. ANALYSIS
DEDUCE CONSEQUENCES AGAINST OBJECTIVES
- Performance
- Risk
- Quality, etc.

Fig. 7-3. Methodology for Project Exploratory Planning (P-E-P).

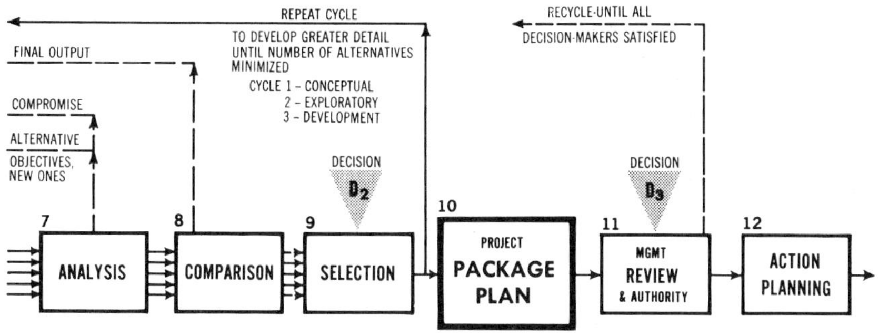

ESTIMATE PROBABILITIES
OF SUCCESS
Objectively Established
Subjectively Judged
"A Degree of Belief"
PREDICT MOVES BY
COMPETITION, (USING
"GAME THEORY")

8. COMPARISON

CONSEQUENCES GROUPED
Annual Cost
User Satisfactions
Goodwill Values
Legal Constraints
Safety
ASSIGN "MEASURE-OF-VALUE" TO CONSEQUENCES—As Possible
COMPARE AND RANK
IDENTIFY QUALITATIVE PRO & CONS

9. SELECTION

EVALUATE AGAINST
Decision-Criteria
Objectives
SELECT OPTIMUM USING MOST APPLICABLE TYPE OF DECISION
Trial and Error
Appeal to Authority
arbitrary power
intuition
ethical precepts
Mathematical
maximum expectation
statistical, etc.
Semi-Automatic

10. PROJECT PACKAGE PLAN

PRECISE DESCRIPTION OF ANTICIPATED
Performance
Economics
Schedule
TYPICAL "PROSPECTUS" CONTAINS:
WHAT?
Need to be Satisfied
Specification of Need
Goals to be Achieved
Functional Description (Scope) of Chosen Alternative
Premises (if analytical depth sacrificed in order to expedite solution, state assumptions)
Background
our position at present
significant history
WHY?
Why Solution Desirable
"Values" Described & Justified
Project Economic Justification
what replaced
Chief Environmental Factors & Significance
forecasts
competitions' response
HOW (WHERE)?
Input/Output Detail
features
constraints
tolerances
Project "Cradle-to-Grave" Costs
Options & Sequence
Risk Estimated
Identification of Critical Aspects
Resource Requirements in FIVE YEAR PLAN
Alternates
why not chosen
preference ranking
WHEN (WHO)?
Preliminary Schedule

11. MANAGEMENT REVIEW & AUTHORITY

PRIORITY AMONG OTHER PROJECTS
DESIRED TIMING ESTABLISHED
LEAD RESPONSIBILITIES ASSIGNED
EFFECT OF CHANGE ON FIVE YEAR PROGRAM-PLAN

12. ACTION PLANNING

APPLICATION OF PERT SCHEDULING AND CONTROL TECHNIQUE

Source: D. J. Smalter, International Minerals & Chemical Co.

Forecasts, expectations, and assumptions replace facts in the development of alternatives and selection from among them. Flexibility must be a characteristic of the plans so that annual revision is possible without description of short-range operations.

From the viewpoint of the technical manager, long-range planning must focus on:

1. Conception of profitable product ideas
2. Mobilization of resources to develop these products.

The development of new product concepts is a critical aspect in the implementation of long-range plans.

MANAGEMENT OF NEW PRODUCT DEVELOPMENT

The stages in new product evolution as identified in Chapter 1 are as follows:

1. *Exploration*—the search for product ideas *to meet company objectives*
2. *Screening*—a quick analysis to determine which ideas indicate potential thus meriting careful investigation
3. *Business analysis*—detailed examination of the idea involving the full application of market research techniques and the further scrutiny of the idea by the other functions of the business, especially the scientific and general management
4. *Development*—converting the idea into a potential product that is demonstrable and producible
5. *Testing*—the commercial experimentation necessary to verify earlier business judgments
6. *Commercialization*—committing the company's reputation and resources by the production and sales of the product.

Another very important characteristic of the product evolution is that each stage is progressively more expensive. Figure 7-4 shows how cumulative costs increase rapidly with time for the average project in a sample of companies. The exploration phase is not shown in this figure.

This, coupled with the high mortality rate of new product ideas, emphasizes the need to effectively manage the new product process. That the process can be successfully managed is an established fact even though it is very difficult. However, before this can be accomplished by top management (not by engineering and research management) with any real degree of assurance, there are three tasks concerning the entire company that they must complete. They are:

1. Determine and evaluate company strengths and weaknesses

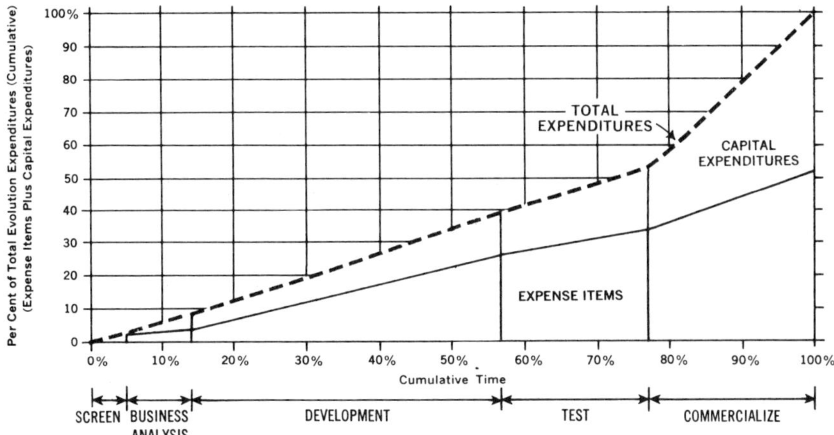

Fig. 7-4. Cumulative expenditures and time for new product by stage of evolution — all-industry average. *Source:* Booz-Allen & Hamilton Inc.

2. Determine long-range, overall company goals; including financial, technical, production, and marketing objectives
3. Organize for product planning.

Only after the first two tasks have been completed should step 3, the organization of the product-planning function, be attempted. These three actions are the direct concern of engineering and research management, and it is important that they participate by providing technical counsel in the first two instances and sharing functional responsibility for the third activity. Both engineering and research separately play vital roles in setting the technological direction of the company.

While the scope and detail of the problems presented by each step will vary between companies, they will hinder progress on new product development and act as a roadblock to successful engineering and research management if they are not resolved satisfactorily. Also, without accomplishing these three basic steps, any product-planning group which is established will waste much of its effort. These are losses few firms can afford.

Basic Step 1. Evaluation of Strengths and Weaknesses. The determination and evaluation of corporate strengths and weaknesses is certainly fundamental. This analysis should include, but not be restricted to, the following:

a. Corporate Board
b. Executive talent
c. Quantity and quality of general and professional manpower, including special strengths in pertinent areas such as scientific, engineering, skilled craftsmen, common labor, etc.

d. Financial position and capabilities
e. Facilities
f. Markets and marketing positions
g. Corporate image and reputation.

Basic Step 2. Establishment of Goals. Only after making a determination of corporate strengths and weaknesses and then thoroughly analyzing and evaluating them, is it possible for top management to realistically establish long-range, over-all business goals. These must include long-range financial, technical (of primary concern to the engineering and research manager), production, and marketing objectives. They should be related to anticipated company capabilities and future environment changes. Here are some of the main items to be established in determining goals for five and ten years.

1. Business prospects and directions
2. Financial condition and structure of business in view of projected product plans
3. Technical objectives as related to facilities, manpower, organization, and finance
4. Physical facility and manpower requirements taking into account projected new products, raw materials, and markets
5. Marketing objectives by product line.

The first item mentioned under long-range goals was the determination of the business prospects and direction. This is elaborated on below since it is of particular importance to E & R managers. The considerations involved are as follows:

a. Projected technological, sociological, economic and market trends
b. Horizontal and vertical diversification of product lines
c. Expansion of present product lines
d. Entry into new related and unrelated fields
e. Entry into frontier fields such as atomic energy, space flight, solar energy. Decisions on this often stem from 1 and a.

Basic Step 3. The Organization of the Product Planning Function. Merely determining a company's strengths and weaknesses and defining its objectives will not result in the development of new products that can be sold at a profit. It is an important step, but something must be done to implement and carry out the objectives. What is needed is a sound new product organization, the establishment of which is called for in Basic Step 3. The new product organization being referred to is not normally a part of engineering and research, although it is always of great importance to them. This should be remembered in determining the responsibility for engineering and research assignments.

Successful organization of the new product function requires a careful and thorough consideration of the company and its organization. What is best for one company is wrong for another. The nature and duties of any organizational element to whom this responsibility is delegated, the function's status, the scope of its activity, and relation with the other organizational elements of the company are not easy to arrive at, but there are some guiding principles that have proven successful. In fact, a definitive program, having as its nucleus the following concepts, has repeatedly provided successful manageability of the new product function.

These guiding principles for new product organization are as follows:

1. Top management must recognize that new products are their responsibility.
2. The new product process must and can be managed.
3. The new product function must be organized as a top executive staff activity.
4. Both the organization and the control must be established in accordance with the stages of new product evolution.
5. Full usage must be made of the interdepartmental product team concept.
6. The new product evolutionary process involves a continuing series of evaluations—one evaluation at each stage.
7. The marketing considerations must be kept "in sight" at all stages, especially in establishing general product specifications.

Not only must top management set the objectives in relation to the company's strengths and weaknesses, it must also make a continuing series of decisions about each new product going through the development process, i.e., whether to: (1) field test the product, (2) test market it, or (3) enter into full-scale commercialization. New product development is truly a top management responsibility.

The organization of the new product function has evolved into one principal approach—a separate new products or product-planning department. To date, this separate department, in combination with the product team approach, is the best general approach that has been developed. The product team consists of one representative from each of the functions concerned with a given product. They are organized under a project leader, usually a representative of the new product department. Sales, engineering, manufacturing, and industrial engineering are always represented.

That the separate department is a logical approach is readily apparent when one stops to consider what has happened in numerous companies. Originally the chief executive, assisted by the manager of research or engineering, made the new product decision. When he became overburdened, the responsibility was transferred to the executive committee or a special new products committee. The executive committee, if it assumed the responsibility, usually became deluged with work, a dilemma which it tried to escape by forming a subcommittee. These two approaches did have the advantage, as does a separate new product committee (another early approach) of representing all functions of the business. However, the subcommittee or the separate new product committee, has the inherent weakness of any committee; it usually is not an effective approach. A committee basically is not an action-oriented activity and is best used by management for investigative, fact-gathering, evaluation, and recommending roles.

With this as a background, a separate new product department under a chief executive was a logical development. Such new product departments usually report directly to one of three top executives. The executive offices involved and the approximate distribution of new product departments reporting to them are as follows:

A majority report to the chief executive officer

About 50 percent of the remainder report to the engineering and research director (usually in a science- and/or engineering-oriented company having technical products)

And 50 percent report to the marketing office (ordinarily in a marketing oriented company with consumer products).

The new product department normally contains only a few people; in fact in the very small company, there is only one man. Usually the larger departments include men with experience in market research, engineering and research, and general administration. This latter area is represented because reports must be developed, budgets must be watched and controlled, and the paperwork can't be allowed to accumulate. The need for representative engineering and research, as well as market research skills is quite obvious. A combination of these skills is needed for the one-man department that makes the staffing extremely difficult. The balance of the required man power evolves from the various product teams established for each new product.

HOW TO OBTAIN IDEAS FOR NEW PRODUCTS

There are two basic sources for ideas for new products:

1. Creation of ideas by people assigned the responsibility for developing new product ideas
2. Ideas or products suggested by other people within and outside the company.

No one individual, or even groups of individuals, within the company can afford to depend on themselves alone for new product ideas. The major problem is how to find ideas created by others, both recorded and unrecorded. To achieve this goal, the company must search among its employees, outside among many sources within the country, and finally among foreign sources.

IN-COMPANY SOURCES OF NEW IDEAS

Direct Creation of Ideas

There are three creative processes which are used by everybody:

Imagination or synthesis. This is a process of rearranging, reforming, recombining, or weaving ideas into new combinations during deliberate thinking about a problem. It is usually based on easily remembered ideas. For example, the ordinary automobile engine is considered by some as a triumphant monstrosity because of the use of explosions driving reciprocating pistons to produce rotary motion. It would seem desirable to obtain a rotary motion directly. This objective is attained in the concept of the Wankel engine which is one based on a synthesis of well known ideas into a new form.

Two or more well-known ideas or products may be combined into a new idea. The invention of the vacuum cleaner is an example. The vacuum cleaner was invented by a person suffering from asthma who wanted to find some way of cleaning without raising great amounts of irritating dust. The vacuum cleaner represents a combination of the electric motor, a turbine pump, and a collector system that allows the air to escape at low velocity but traps the dust particles within the container.

Inspiration. Inspiration is the result of an accidental stimulus that triggers a new idea or solution to a problem. For example, Dr. Edward Benedictus dropped a chemical flask that he had neglected to clean. Instead of the pieces flying all over the lab, the plastic film coating the interior held the broken pieces together. Several days later he witnessed the collision of two automobiles in which one occupant was seriously injured. Benedictus related this occurrence to the previous incident with the flask and the result is today's safety glass.

The engineer can deliberately improve his creativity by observing unusual phenomena and seeking transfers or applications to his work.

Illumination. Illumination occurs after long intense thinking about a problem, rather than immediate inspiration. It results from the surfacing of long-forgotten ideas or the learning of a complex of new knowledge. Illumination may occur after the conscious effort on the problem has been temporarily put aside.

How To Seek In-Company Sources of New Ideas

Very few companies make a systematic effort to seek new product ideas from all employees in the company. It is true that suggestion systems are common, but these are not directed at uncovering new product ideas so that few turn up. Actually, there is no reason why a company cannot set up a new product suggestion system to parallel the usual work improvement suggestion system. Every idea submitted through such a system should be promptly acknowledged by the product planner or engineering department. Evaluation of ideas should be made at regularly scheduled meetings and the results communicated to the employee.

Besides this mass approach, a member of the E & R department may be assigned the task of periodically seeking out new ideas from technical, marketing, and manufacturing personnel. This duty requires an individual who can gain the confidence of others by a nonjudgmental manner. It is much easier to dry up an idea source than keep it flowing. If he ridicules or even mildly discourages a contributor at any time, he will not be likely to obtain the free-wheeling thoughts on new products.

Typical general approaches to querying individuals are:

1. A direct and unrestricted request for a new product idea
2. A request for the other person to describe any unusual features of equipment being designed. This is followed by questions as to why or how this portion of the project could be converted into a new product
3. A direct question as to which components, subsystems, or mechanisms developed in the past were unusual, and then following up again with questions as to why or how such items could be converted into new products
4. As a last resort (if the previous approaches did not dredge up any ideas), ask them to describe the equipment they are now engineering. Here, skill in posing the proper follow-up questions is of paramount importance. In other words, the idea searcher must act as a catalyst, and perhaps even, on his own, synthesize ideas.

Some specific questions which might be asked are:

1. What products can they see as a real need that the *industry* should develop and offer for sale? (If they are consumers of the product, ask them to consider it as a consumer rather than as a producer.)
2. What new equipment, gadget, or mechanism would they like to see developed to help them in their work? What is needed to help someone else on the job?
3. What safety device is needed?

4. What have they heard others say was needed as a new product?
5. What operation(s) on their or someone else's job seems unnecessarily difficult? Such situations can often lead to a new product idea.
6. What would help them reduce costs in their particular function of the business? (Some people need the dollar concept to trigger their thoughts.)
7. What job have their friends complained or talked about as being most difficult or expensive?
8. What piece of equipment is not performing correctly? Why?

Employee Invention Records

Well-organized companies record ideas which are patentable and file for patent coverage on many of these. These records should be regularly scanned by the engineering management and the product planning function to see if new product ideas are involved. More will be said later in this chapter about the availability of these ideas from other companies.

Reports

Salesmen reports can be a fruitful source of ideas, particularly if the salesmen are encouraged to listen and look for new product ideas. It is surprising how rarely this request is made of salesmen; nevertheless, they can be a most fruitful source if efforts are made to develop them in this area.

Any company engaged in organized technical engineering research and/or development usually requires regular submission of technical notebooks to management. These reports should be carefully screened for new product ideas, not merely for the presence of engineering problems.

Make-Buy Decisions

Every company continuously screens the parts and materials which it makes and which it purchases on either a formal or informal basis to determine whether to make or purchase the item in the future. Obviously, this must be done for the entire parts list of a new product to be produced. If one can make an item at less cost than the money required to buy it, there certainly exists the possibility of making and selling this item to someone else. The company already has an internal market and apparently can be competitive in the external market, providing an outside market does exist for the item. It does not always follow that one can be competitive in the external market if one can make a product at less cost than it takes to buy it, but at least there is a good possibility that this may be so. The advantages of having a captive market, one's own company, is always attractive. In fact, large companies sometimes acquire another firm primarily to ensure that the latter will use their product, thereby resulting in increased profits, expansion of the product line, etc.

Credit and Collection Departments

A percentage of almost any firm's delinquent accounts stems from deficiencies in the company's products. Collection personnel should be trained to notify Product Planning of complaints encountered, especially if numerous complaints are received about a particular defect. A pattern of complaints might very well reflect a basic widespread need that a new product could satisfy.

In smaller companies, the company president often looks at samples of letters from delinquent customers to eke out complaints about product performance. Similarly, these should be seen by the product planner, regardless of the company's size, in order to obtain clues for new products.

Service Department

Company servicemen have intimate contacts with the final users, which enables the serviceman to fill two "new product" roles. First, a portion of the service calls stems from weaknesses in the product. In a similar manner to the complaints previously mentioned regarding the credit and collection department, the serviceman when he finds weaknesses in the product can often give suggestions as to how an improved product could be built. The second new product role of the serviceman is perhaps of even greater importance. He often is in the position to observe an adaption of the company's equipment by some ingenious mechanic to fit a peculiar operating condition or job requirement. Such adaptions may well reflect a need that exists among other prospective customers for a new kind of equipment.

In connection with the second new product role, it is suggested that a special place on the serviceman's report be provided to list unusual applications or uses for the company equipment. Another approach would be to have him prepare a special report on breakdowns resulting from legitimate attempts to use the machine as well as from usage in ways for which it was not intended. Some people have even suggested establishing a bonus system for any such ideas that are converted into new or improved products.

Sales Department

As previously mentioned, salesmen as well as other company personnel should be approached for new product ideas. They have many opportunities for talking with the customer about new applications for existing equipment, modifications that the customer feels should be made on the equipment, and, in fact, new product suggestions.

Some companies ask each salesman annually to visit a specified number of customers, picking representative samples, and working through a simple questionnaire aimed at discovering new product ideas. He will find that customers are eager to express their ideas if they feel that the salesman is genuinely interested in their point of view and not simply looking for phrases which can be used as testimonials in selling products.

Other companies have used sales meetings to staff brainstorming sessions geared at developing new product ideas. Out of one such session came 226 ideas, ten percent of which received careful study and six of which were put into production.

It is suggested that there be a specific place on the salesman report form for new ideas, suggestions, reports on competitors' new products, and on customers' complaints. New products and new product ideas should be stressed; in fact, one could even run special new product contests among salesmen.

Purchasing

Vendors are continually bringing the attention of your purchasing agents to new products which they are trying to introduce. Some of these might be produced by your company with a distinct advantage over the competing firm because of peculiar facilities or abilities which you have within the plant. In other cases, vendors often mention to the purchasing agent that a great need exists for a product having certain characteristics; therefore, the help of the purchasing department should be secured. In a similar manner, your advertising agency could easily suggest possible new product ideas.

Company Acquisition

While this, properly, is a subject that is usually outside the realm of engineering or research, it is a route that many companies take in acquiring new products. In many respects, there is little difference in the end result obtained when a company secures new product ideas by acquisition and when it develops the idea internally. The advantages in company acquisition are great since company growth is achieved in the shortest possible time. Not only does the purchaser obtain new products, he also secures facilities to produce, personnel to research, engineer, manage, and operate, in addition to obtaining a marketing organization and the associated marketing and distribution channels.

EXTERNAL SOURCES OF IDEAS

Solicited and Unsolicited Ideas

It is possible to actively solicit suggestions from outside sources. However, great care should be taken in inviting suggestions. Otherwise, many difficulties will be encountered including that of being swamped with a thousand old ideas that have been previously reviewed and discarded. Moreover, as will be shown in Chapter 17, it is dangerous to consider ideas from the outside especially if they are not covered by a patent which is still in force. If the patent has expired, the company still is involved in a hazardous procedure if it uses the idea—provided it was called to the company's attention through a suggestion from outside. Great care must be taken in even considering such an idea. Otherwise, the company may incur major liabilities for something that is either unpatentable or even for something that has been patented but on which the patent has expired.

Practically all companies receive unsolicited new product ideas. Chapter 17 presents ways in which such ideas must be handled if the company is to protect itself from major damage or liability claims.

Other Companies

It does make sense to look to other industrial firms which may have patented certain products or processes that are outside of the area of their normal operation. Such patents are filed away and only brought out if they are needed to defend them from a patent litigation. The companies holding these patents may be perfectly willing to license others to use them; furthermore, such companies are often interested in supplying basic materials needed to make the end item. An example of this latter situation was the Fansteel Metallurgical Corporation who were interested in expanding the use of tantalum. Since electrolytic capacitor manufacturers were slow in exploiting the properties of this metal, Fansteel started the production of tantalum electrolytic capacitors. While Fansteel was still producing capacitors, they were even more interested in having other firms join in the production of such capacitors and were perfectly willing to license responsible firms.

The principal difficulty encountered in soliciting other industrial firms is that the company often insists that the prospective client disclose rather specifically what product or type of product or technical area he is interested in and why. Also, unless you are affiliated with a well-known firm, they will want some reasonable proof that your company is capable of and intends to manufacture and sell any product that shows good potential and which falls in the desired product line or category.

If information is desired on research facilities of big firms, the *Research Centers Directory* of the Gale Research Company, Detroit, Michigan, is one source for such information.

Research Laboratories

If new product ideas are to be solicited, one should be sure to include in the solicitation an approach to the various industrial research laboratories—both nonprofit and profit organizations. Examples of such organizations will be found in Chapter 16.

In a similar manner, most of the country's educational institutions providing degrees in engineering and/or science are possible sources of new product ideas and therefore should be solicited; in fact, many of them have separate research institutes similar to the nonprofit institutions previously mentioned. These educational institutions often have patented ideas which can be used as profitable new products by appropriate firms. In fact, many universities are deriving substantial income from royalties collected on items produced by companies. Some of these universities have tried to simplify licensing their patented ideas by cooperating with the Research Corporation of New York City.

Many research institutes and research laboratories, in addition to being sources of already developed or defined new product ideas, will also find and/or develop new products. This is especially true for the nonuniversity affiliated laboratories. The independent research laboratories or institutes, which are established to do research, have no other major objective. The institutes affiliated with colleges and universities usually have other goals, at least to a minor degree, such as promoting the university, providing part time employment for professors and/or students, etc. Such university laboratories or institutes will generally have a less commercial orientation, which may be good or bad depending upon the project involved. Almost every college or university that offers a technical curriculum will accept some outside research projects. One major problem with university affiliated laboratories is that they generally reserve the right to publish all findings.

All of these research laboratories or institutes do work on a contract basis, and it is advantageous to define the work to be done as precisely as possible if costs are to be minimized. If merely the product category is specified, maximum expense will be incurred; at the same time, it could well be worth the cost. The reasons for going to such research institutes, laboratories, or university research activities for a service are quite numerous. Some of the more usual reasons are:

1. The firm's engineering or research staff is loaded and cannot accept additional work without expansion.
2. The staff cannot be expanded to accomplish the desired work in the time available.
3. The existing engineering and/or research skills in the company are not well suited to the desired product or product category.
4. Facilities are needed which would necessitate a large and undesirable capital expenditure.
5. The laboratory or institute has the required specialized personnel and/or facilities.

Table 7-1—Types of Patents Available and Useful in New-Product Development[1]

Types of patents	Terms of use	Are lists of patents available?	Are abstracts available?	Review copy of patent at—	Purchase copy of patent from—	Make application for use to—
Expired	Free	Numerical only; see Gazette.[2]	No; see selected claim in Gazette.	Patent Office and some public libraries.[3]	Patent Office, Washington 25, D. C., or photocopy from some libraries.	None required.
Dedicated	do	No; see Gazette	do	do	do	Do.
Available for license or sale	By royalty or outright purchase.	Yes; in Gazette	No; see Gazette prior to June 30, 1954; otherwise see patent.	do	do	Patent owner.
Foreign-owned (United States patents issued to nationals of other countries).	do	No; see Gazette	No; see Gazette or patent.	do	do	Do.
Design	Same as other patents above.	do	do	do	do	Do.
Government-owned	Ordinarily free	Yes; Superintendent of Documents, Washington 25, D. C.	Yes; at Commerce field offices, SBA field offices, or Government Patents Board, Washington 25 D. C.	Patent Office or Government Patents Board, Washington 25, D. C.	Patent Office, Washington 25, D. C.	Government agency having jurisdiction.
Government-licensed	Dependent upon terms of license accorded to Government.	Yes; Government Patents Board, Washington 25, D. C.	Yes; Government Patents Board, Washington 25, D. C.	do	do	Do.
Acquired from enemies	Licensed upon application.	Yes; Office of Alien Property, Washington 25, D. C.	Yes; Office of Alien Property, Washington 25, D. C.	Commerce field offices and some public libraries.	do	Office of Alien Property, Washington 25, D. C.
Foreign (issued by countries other than United States).	(4)	Some lists available: Write to Patent Office, Washington 25, D. C.	Generally, not in the United States.	New York Public Library or Patent Office.[5]	Photostat from New York Public Library or Patent Office.	Patent owner.

[1] Any expired patent for invention is available to the public for use; provided, however, there are no later patents applicable to the original invention.

[2] Official Gazette (Selected Reference No. 1): A weekly publication of the Patent Office. Copies are available in many public libraries and from the Superintendent of Documents, Government Printing Office, Washington 25, D. C.

[3] Public libraries which have patents for public inspection:

Albany, N. Y., University of State of New York.
Atlanta, Ga., Georgia Tech Library.[a]
Boston, Mass., Public Library.
Buffalo, N. Y., Grosvenor Library.
Chicago, Ill., Public Library.
Cincinnati, Ohio, Public Library.
Cleveland, Ohio, Public Library.
Columbus, Ohio, Ohio State University Library.
Detroit, Mich., Public Library.
Kansas City, Mo., Linda Hall Library.[a]
Los Angeles, Calif., Public Library.
Madison, Wis., State Historical Society of Wisconsin.
Milwaukee, Wis., Public Library.[a]
Minneapolis, Minn., Public Library.[a]
Newark, N. J., Public Library.
New York, N. Y., Public Library.
Philadelphia, Pa., Franklin Institute.
Pittsburgh, Pa., Carnegie Library.
Providence, R. I., Public Library.
St. Louis, Mo., Public Library.
Toledo, Ohio, Public Library.

[a] Collections incomplete but copies of patents issued subsequent to July 1, 1946, should be available.

[4] No general statement possible except that foreign patents protect only in country of issuance. Their use in United States restricted only if United States patent has been issued.

[5] Copies in classified order at Patent Office only. Copies in numerical order at Patent Office and New York Public Library.

6. The company has a partially developed idea that apparently has great potential but which the firm's own designers have been unable to make work satisfactorily or have been unable to production engineer the idea so that it can be produced at a competitive cost.
7. The company desires to see the results from scientists who are not as rigidly controlled as those within the company.

Nonplant Personnel

Exactly the same approaches and practically all of the questions used for company employees will work equally well for almost any individual. The principal change is that one must recognize that nonplant personnel may have a moral or actual obligation not to disclose certain information because of their employment. This is especially true for government personnel or for people working on military projects or for those producing products going to the Armed Services. One must always recognize that other people may have a primary loyalty and responsibility that is committed to another firm.

Government Sources

There are many government sources of new product ideas. Since the United States Government sponsors a major portion of the research and development conducted in this country, obviously they control an increasingly large number of patents. A vast majority of these patents are available for license to the general public; however, it must be understood that an exclusive license cannot be obtained.

There is a publication entitled *Patent Abstracts of Government Owned Inventions Available For License*. The licenses can be obtained from the government agency having cognizance over the patent. At present, there are more than six books covering different classifications of inventions, plus at least eight books of supplementary patents. The total number of available patents is approximately 7,000. The books are available from the Office of Technical Services (OTS) of the Department of Commerce. OTS also publishes a Bibliography of Scientific and Industrial Reports.

NASA has the Office of Technology Utilization to help speed their developments into industrial applications.

Patents of various kinds represent a prolific source of new product ideas. One helpful summary of such sources is reproduced from the U. S. Department of Commerce and Small Business Administration Guidebook entitled *Developing and Selling New Products.*

One of the best sources of new product ideas is a monthly bulletin called *Products List Circular* which is published by the Production Assistance Division of the Small Business Administration, Washington, D. C. This bulletin contains abstracts of inventions which the owners are willing to sell or to license the manufacturer of the new product.

The United States Patent Office has a register of patents available for license and sale; moreover, it has a list of dedicated patents.

Other government publications which contain ideas that can be helpful in new product development are *U. S. Government Research Reports* (this is actually a catalogue of reports), and *Technical Reports Newsletter* (a monthly digest of research reports).

There is no central publication listing all federal research. One commercial publication that provides brief reports on federal activity in many areas is *Data,* 1346 Connecticut Avenue, N.W., Washington 6, D. C.

By now, you have recognized that a major distributor of government research reports is the Office of Technical Services, Washington 25, D. C. OTS publishes many items including reports on atomic energy research.

The Armed Forces maintain their own information center for the exchange of information among defense agencies and contractors. This center is the Armed Services Technical Information Agency. Declassified ASTIA documents are distributed through the Office of Technical Services. At the present writing, a nine-volume listing is available and is entitled *The Subject Index to Unclassified ASTIA Documents* (PB151567).

The Battelle Memorial Institute is a clearinghouse and research center for materials research for defense. Individual reports on BMIA research conducted by Battelle is available from OTS, and defense contractors and subcontractors may obtain many of these free reports directly from BMIA, Battelle, 505 King Avenue, Columbus 1, Ohio.

The National Academy of Sciences–National Research Council is a major source of scientific reports covering research conducted under the auspices of the National Academy as well as outside research which it sponsors. A major guide to its publications is *Publications of the National Academy of Sciences,* National Research Council, Printing and Publishing Office, 2101 Constitution Avenue, Washington 25, D. C.

The National Science Foundation in Washington has established the National Referral Center for Science and Technology.

The National Bureau of Standards also is a source of government research data. Included in the publications available from this bureau is the *Technical News Bulletin Monthly.* It also issues six important journals of research covering major scientific areas such as physics, mathematics, chemistry, etc. Titles and prices can be obtained from the National Bureau of Standards. Similarly, the Bureau of Mines and the Atomic Energy Commission issue research data.

Other Outside Sources

Technical and trade journals, both domestic and foreign, often carry advertisements which offer a new product for sale or for license. Similar advertisements often appear in *The Wall Street Journal* or the financial section of major metropolitan newspapers. *The New York Times* is a very good source for such advertisements.

There are a number of professional marketing firms which make a business of developing and licensing inventions. Some of these are:

Ladd & Little, Inc.
789 Walt Whitman Road
Huntington Station
Long Island, New York 11749

Research Corporation
405 Lexington Avenue
New York, New York 10017

Inpak Systems
441 Lexington Avenue
New York, New York 10017

Tainton Company
3100 Elm Avenue
Baltimore, Maryland

Institute for Corporate Diversification, Ltd.
135 East 44th Street
New York, New York 10017

Some popular magazines contain a feature which lists product needs expressed by their readers. Some of these needs would be especially helpful to consumer-product-oriented companies. The annual Congress on Better Living run by *McCall's Magazine* is a good example of such help.

Technical and trade journals often have a new product section; in fact, some trade publications are devoted entirely to listing new products. Most manufacturers find it advisable to carefully examine the new products presented in such magazines. One can often see how they could improve on one of these new products by incorporating in it some developments which the company has already made, thereby resulting in a very salable new product. Even if another company's development cannot be directly incorporated or, even more importantly, improved by harnessing the energy of one's own company to introduce a better new product, one will often find that a picture and/or description of a new product will stimulate ideas for another new product. *Business Publications Guide* lists about 2500 U.S. and Canadian business publications giving a breakdown by industry.*

FOREIGN SOURCES OF NEW PRODUCTS

There are two ways to find new products in foreign markets. The most satisfactory method is to conduct a personal search abroad. However, it is also possible to discover new products by staying home and utilizing trade information and European agents.

* Obtainable from *Industrial Marketing,* 740 Rush St., Chicago, Ill.

The European Search

Probably the best way of scouting for new products in Europe is to attend the spring and early summer trade fairs. A complete list of European Trade Fairs is published annually in January in *The New York Times*. The list may also be obtained from consulates of the principal European countries and the major European airlines. Many of these trade fairs, which have no counterpart in the United States, are of mammoth proportions.

It is possible to attend six to eight fairs in three to six weeks by starting in the southern part of Europe, for example, with the Milan Samples Fair in April, and then progressing northward. Once one has decided upon the fairs he wishes to attend, it is advisable to write in advance for a detailed program stating that he is a prospective buyer. Most of these fairs extend to buyers special privileges and lures, including free entrance fees. Generally, one should plan on attending the first days of each fair when there are ample supplies of literature and samples. One should make the acquaintance of the exhibitors and indicate the field(s) in which one is interested.

One may generally assume that any product which is shown in an industrial trade fair or which is reported in the literature is really not new; nevertheless, such items may not be at the commercial stage. The earliest knowledge of new products is best obtained by personal contact with leaders in the field, and this can only be done by a trip to Europe or by utilizing the services of a technically trained European representative, as later outlined in this chapter.

Additional important new product information can be obtained by visiting government institutes and universities in the principal European countries. It is usually advisable that attendance at not more than two fairs be scheduled in one week in order to allow for side trips to scout for interesting leads or to visit the aforementioned government institutes and universities.

Our commercial and industrial research laboratories have no counterpart in Europe. However, several United States firms such as the Stanford Research Institute, Arthur D. Little, Inc., and the Battelle Memorial Institute, etc., have European laboratory affiliates. You probably would find it advisable to visit the directors of the European laboratories because they are frequently aware of new products which have not yet reached the exhibition stage.

General Sources of Information

The principal source of foreign new product ideas is found in Europe. Regardless of whether one goes to Europe or remains at home, it is essential to know the European markets and the principal sources of new product information. A very useful report entitled *Researching Foreign Markets* is published by the National Industrial Conference Board, Inc., 460 Park Avenue, New York, New York 10022. It describes sources and methods for collecting foreign market information.

Generally, it is advisable to check the publications of the World Trade Information Service of the U. S. Bureau of Foreign Commerce. This bureau publishes economic and statistical reports, which include basic economic data, reports of recent economic developments, methods of establishing foreign business, and patent and trade-mark regulations of the various foreign countries.

For certain specific countries such as France and Sweden, this same bureau has combined market studies under a single title, *Doing Business in Sweden.* Also, the Bureau's Investment Handbook series includes such reports as *Investment in Australia.* More than seventeen countries have been covered in these reports.

Other publications of the Bureau of Foreign Commerce which may be useful are *Foreign Commerce Weekly, World Trade Directory,* a *Directory of Foreign Development Organizations for Trading and Investment,* and a *Guide to Foreign Business Directories.* Somewhat related is a 1961 publication of the U. S. Department of Commerce entitled *Checklist of Bureau of Foreign Commerce Publications.*

Finally, the UNESCO Division of the United Nations has many helpful publications. For information on Europe, you should also consult the quarterly publication of the Organization for European Economic Cooperation which covers the productivity of the major European countries. Names and addresses of competing firms can be obtained from *World Trade Directory* published by the Bureau of Foreign Commerce. Foreign producers are usually willing to supply samples of new products to American licensees or, under certain conditions, to prospective licensees.

Foreign Patent and Literature Searches

One way of getting advance notice of new European products is to scan foreign patents and applications. Of the foreign patents, Belgian patents are open to the public before any others; furthermore, they are abstracted regularly in a bulletin entitled *Revue Des Brevets Belgiques* published by the Office Des Inventions, SPIRL, 26 Rue de Naples, Brussels. In addition to the monthly abstract bulletin, there is available *Derwent's Patents Report* which is published by Derwent Information Service, 54 Tenterden Drive, London, Northwest 4, which contains abstracts of patents issued by the German, British, and Belgian Patent Offices. The French patents are reported in a publication of the French Patent Office. Moreover, a search in chemical abstracts or in the abstracts published by the Maison de la Chimie of Paris may reveal new products relating to specific fields of chemistry.

Finding European New Products without Going There

Although one can find new products in the European market without traveling to Europe, the use of a foreign technical representative is almost essential. To implement such a program, the following steps should be taken:

1. Become familiar with the European products and markets via information sources such as those previously mentioned.
2. Become familiar with foreign new inventions via information sources on patents.
3. Contact U. S. commercial research laboratories who have foreign subsidiaries or affiliates. Several of these have previously been mentioned. Frequently, such firms carry on development work for European clients on new products which the client would like to exploit in the United States.
4. Subscribe to periodic reports which cover new European products such as the *Import Bulletin* published by the *Journal of Commerce*.
5. Contact firms which specialize in the introduction of foreign developments into the United States. Examples of such firms are Marc Wood International, Inc., 30 Rockefeller Plaza, New York, and Advance House, Inc., Suburban Square Building, Ardmore, Pennsylvania.
6. Obtain the services of a foreign representative and instruct him in the fields of your interest. Names and addresses of prospective representatives can be obtained from the Bureau of Foreign Commerce of the U. S. Department of Commerce.

BIBLIOGRAPHY

ABBOTT, ROBERT E. "It's Not Too Soon To Look to the 21st Century," *Product Engineering,* February 26, 1968.

AMES, CHARLES B. "Payoff From Product Management," *Harvard Business Review,* November–December, 1963.

BRIGHT, JAMES R. "Can We Forecast Technology?", *Industrial Research,* March, 1968.

———. "Opportunity and Threat in Technological Change," *Harvard Business Review,* November–December, 1963.

———. *Technological Forecasting for Industrial Government.* Englewood Cliffs, N.J.: Prentice-Hall, Inc., 1968.

BUCHANAN, WILLIAM, ed. *Industrial Research Laboratories Directory.* 12th ed. New York, N.Y.: R. R. Bowker Co., 1965

CALDER, NIGEL, ed. *The World in 1984.* Baltimore, Md.: Penguin Books, Inc., 1965.

CHEANEY, EDGAR S. "Technological Forecasting by Simulation of Design," *Battelle Technical Review,* Vol. 16, No. 5, May, 1967.

CLARKE, A. C. *Profiles of the Future.* New York, N.Y.: Harper and Row, Publishers, 1962.

DALKEY, N. *Delphi.* p–3704. Santa Monica, Calif.: The Rand Corp., 1967.

EWING, DAVID W., ed. *Long Range Planning for Management.* New York, N.Y.: Harper and Row, Publishers, 1964.

FURNAS, CLIFFORD C. *The Next Hundred Years: The Unfinished Business of Science.* New York, N.Y.: Reynal and Hitchcock, 1936.

GILMORE, FRANK F., and BRANDENBURG, RICHARD G. "Anatomy of Corporate Planning," *Harvard Business Review,* November–December, 1962.

GORDON, THEODORE J. *The Future.* New York, N.Y.: St. Martin's Press, Inc., 1965.

GORDON, THEODORE J., and HELMER, OLAF. *Report on a Long Range Forecasting Study.* p–2982. Santa Monica, Calif.: The Rand Corp., 1964.

GROSSMAN, ADRIAN J. 1963. "An Approach to Formalizing Entrepreneurial Processes in Business." In *Symposium C6,* Paper No. C6c, C105 XIII. New York, N.Y.: General Electric Co., 1963.

HALL, ARTHUR D. *A Methodology For Systems Engineering.* Princeton, N.J.: D. Van Nostrand Co., Inc., 1962.

ISENSON, RAYMOND S. "Technological Forecasting in Perspective," *Management Science,* October, 1966.

JANTSCH, ERIC. *Technological Forecasting in Perspective.* Washington, D.C.: OECD Publications Office, 1967.

KARGER, D. W. *The New Product.* New York, N.Y.: The Industrial Press, 1960.

KRANZBERG, MELVIN. "Men, Myths & Inventions." Paper presented to The Presidents Association, New York, N.Y., Summer, 1968.

LEVY, ROBERT. "The Go-Go World of the Risk Manager," *Dun's Review,* November, 1967.

LIEN, ARTHUR P.; ANTON, PAUL; and DUNCAN, JOSEPH W. *Technological Forecasting: Tools, Techniques, Applications.* AMA Bulletin 115. New York, N.Y.: American Management Association, Inc., 1968.

MARTING, ELIZABETH, ed. *New Products: New Profits.* New York, N.Y.: American Management Association, Inc., 1964.

MCGLAUCHLIN, LAURENCE D. "Long Range Technical Planning," *Harvard Business Review,* July–August, 1968.

MURDICK, ROBERT G. "Nature of Planning and Plans," *Advanced Management Journal,* October, 1965.

"New Products: Setting a Time Table," *Business Week,* May 27, 1967.

PALMER, ARCHIE N., and KRUZAS, ANTHONY P., eds. *Research Centers Directory,* also quarterly supplement, *New Research Centers.* Detroit, Mich.: Gale Research Company, 1965.

PESSEMIER, EDGAR A. *New Product Decisions: An Analytical Approach.* New York, N.Y.: McGraw-Hill Book Company, 1966.

PETERSEN, RUSSELL W. "New Venture Management in a Large Company," *Harvard Business Review,* May–June, 1967.

PYKE, DONALD L. 1968. Technological Forecasting. Paper presented to the 5th Engineering Economy Summer Symposium of the American Society for Engineering Education, June 21, 1968. (Discussion of PROBE at TRW, Inc.)

QUINN, JAMES B. "Technological Forecasting," *Harvard Business Review,* March–April, 1967.

RUBENSTEIN, ALBERT H. "Studies of Idea Flow in Research and Development," *Some Theories of Organization,* rev. ed., edited by A. H. Rubenstein and C. J. Haberstroh. Homewood, Ill.: Richard D. Irwin, Inc., and The Dorsey Press, 1966.

SCHEUBLE, PHILIP A., JR. "ROI for New Product Planning," *Harvard Business Review,* November–December, 1964.

SCHON, DONALD A. *Technology and Change: The New Heraclitus.* New York, N.Y.: Delacorte Press, 1967.

SIMONS, GENE R. "Technological Forecasting: The Identification and Selection of High Priority Solutions." Doctoral dissertation, Rensselaer Polytechnic Institute, Troy, N.Y. 1969.

SMALTER, DONALD J. "The Managerial Lag," *Chemical Engineering Progress,* June, 1964.

SMALTER, DONALD J., and RUGGLES, RUDY L., JR. "Six Business Lessons From the Pentagon," *Harvard Business Review,* March–April, 1966.

"Trends and Forecast: For '68 and Far Beyond," *Product Engineering,* January 29, 1968.

TWEDT, DIK WARREN. "How Long Does It Take to Introduce New Products," *Journal of Marketing,* January, 1965. pp. 71–72.

U.S. Air Force. *Technological Forecasting,* Report No. ASD-TDR-62-414, June, 1962.

U.S. Bureau of Labor Statistics. *Technological Trends in Major American Industries.* Washington, D.C.: U.S. Government Printing Office, 1966

U.S. Department of Commerce. *Long Term Economic Growth, 1860–1965.* Washington, D.C.: U.S. Government Printing Office, 1966.

WEINBERGER, ARTHUR J. "Estimating Sales and Markets," *Chemical Engineering,* January 20, 1964.

CHAPTER 8

Selecting Projects and Establishing Technical Objectives

A PROBLEM IN DECISION MAKING

A well-balanced, product-planning research organization will have more ideas for products and improvements than can be exploited within the limitations of economics and time. Normally, these ideas or projects will be carried forward to different degrees of completion in proving feasibility, determining market potential versus price, estimating costs, and generally evaluating the worth of the project. One of the most critical and most difficult problems in business, and one especially involving E & R, is one that has received little attention by authorities—the decision-making process involved in the selection of technical objectives for the E & R organization over a one- to three-year period from a hodgepodge of current ideas and programs that are in various stages of advancement.

It is true that there has been much study on how to develop a specific new product. Also new techniques have been evolved for selecting products or programs for development when considerable information is available or can be easily estimated. But how far should the E & R and Marketing Department proceed with an idea (i.e., how much money should be spent) before it is totally adopted? At what rate should the money be spent? How is one idea to be compared to another? What are the criteria for evaluating ideas? Are technical objectives established by intuition, hunch, experience, with assistance from quantitative approaches or are they based wholly on quantitative facts? What elements are involved in decision making in the critical early stages of product development? *The nature of this "screening" step is the most critical stage of the entire E & R process.*

It is the point at which the company places its chips upon the winners and losers, endeavoring to minimize the losses and to maximize the gains.

The purpose of this chapter will be to outline approaches that a company may take in selecting and evaluating projects for development in order to achieve maximum future profits. The emphasis, of course, will be placed on the part played by E & R. A detailed treatment of decision theory is beyond the scope of this chapter, but the new concepts of this field will be mentioned to introduce them to the E & R manager. In other words, a managerial approach rather than the specialist's approach is taken in this chapter—however, the discussion indicates the kind of specialist approaches and ideas that may apply.

SOME RELATIONSHIPS AND IDEAS

The manager of E & R has the responsibility of developing a sound program based upon technical objectives which are market-oriented. Others could correctly state that the technical objectives must be in line with, and support, the business or organization objectives. Such a program is characterized by the following:

1. Business, marketing and technical objectives and assumptions are clear, explicit, and logically related
2. The program is technically feasible and attainable within the established schedule
3. The program is in reasonable balance with respect to utilization of resources
4. The program is flexible so as to permit adjustment for changed conditions.

The E & R manager is responsible for developing and making recommendations that help form overall company business objectives. In a reverse flow, he must accept the final company objectives and from these establish the specific E & R goals needed to make E & R's contribution towards their success.

The greatest engineering development ever devised is worthless if there is nobody who will buy it or if it can't be made and sold at a profit. It is, therefore, evident that the marketing section may well have a major influence on company and technical objectives. Manufacturing also is involved, but *after* the marketing has been involved. The extent of these influences depends upon the type of business in which the company is engaged, the size of the company, etc. If the company is going to make something to put on the shelf or if it can see exactly what the customer wants, then Marketing is in the saddle. If the company is going to sell something before it is built, then E & R must be the major influence. It would be appropriate for the reader at this time to review that portion of Chapter 1 which relates E & R, Marketing, and Manufacturing as to product newness. Figure 8-1 shows schematically how this effort is divided between E & R and marketing by type of business.

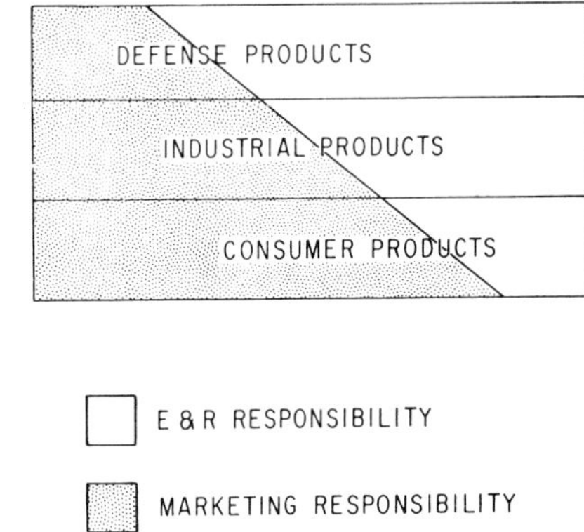

Fig. 8-1. Responsibility for determining product program objectives for the three classes of products.

The elements which the manager of E & R deals with in the process of establishing technical objectives can now be given as follows:

1. Specific company objectives related to or otherwise involving the area of E & R
2. Resources of the E & R organization, i.e., men, facilities, money and time
3. Product ideas or programs
4. Status of each product idea or program relative to:
   a. E & R
   b. Marketing
   c. Manufacturing.

It is from these elements that the manager of E & R makes decisions which result in the specific E & R program, which contains the technical objectives as noted earlier. These technical objectives must be expanded or "exploded" into subdivisions to the point where responsibilities are assigned to individual engineers.

THE DECISION PROCESS

The decision process for selecting projects to be included in the E & R program has gone through a rapid evolution in recent years. To a degree some of these elements still occur as a company grows from a one-man operation. Originally, the top manager or owner of the company simply makes the decision to develop and sell specific products. Then there develops a group approach whereby the top manager and his functional managers get together and "hash out" the new product programs. The next step in the evolution is the recognition that detailed "paper studies" or analyses in all areas, and even some explanatory engineering work, could improve the decision-making process tremendously. Apparently, even with the same data, evaluations can differ greatly. The criteria and decision processes for all people participating in the evaluation of projects simply are not the same.

Attempts to reduce the evaluation process to a common denominator follow four paths after a purely technical evaluation. The first is a formal or semiformal evaluation of subjective and/or objective business and scientific data—usually a somewhat unorganized process. A second involves the development of business criteria or factors for comparison. A third path involves the use of simple mathematical models. Finally, there is the operations research approach which involves the use of a systems model, forcing an organized consideration of all factors.

In all these methods, there is no escape from the necessity of making judgments. These methods provide means for making better judgments, however, by clarifying the problem and establishing common specific criteria for judgments to be made from fine subdivisions of the principal factors. An outline or discussion of these various methods for evaluating E & R projects will now be given.

Before looking at project evaluation from a managerial view, there is one aspect of project evaluation that should override all other considerations. This all-important aspect is timing, particularly from the technical viewpoint rather than the managerial viewpoint.

One view of timing is that a project may be too early or too late from a business or marketing view. If the need for the project result has already passed (that is few if any customers exist) or if the need can be seen at some distant point in the future (but not at present); then don't proceed with the project.

It is the technical side of timing as outlined in an address by Dr. Guy Suits which deserves special consideration by the manager of E & R. Dr. Suits first says one of the most difficult problems for E & R management is the general problem of timing, both business and technical. Looking at the almost purely technical timing problem, Dr. Suits recommended that we should:

1. Identify the key or pivotal problems early.
2. Concentrate on these problems and determine if they can be solved now—often their solutions are so far beyond the present "state of the

art" that it would be impossible or impractical to try and solve them now. A massive attack now would not result in a positive "pay-off," in fact it likely would also result in a technical failure. Moral: Don't beat your head against a stone wall unless you find a few loose stones.

3. If the overall project is important, review the pivotal problems from time to time—keep to the fore that the solution may come from developments in fields not directly related to the problem. Moral: Don't bury your head in the sand. If you can't do it today, and the problem is still important, don't forget it.[1]

Objective and Subjective Considerations

As mentioned in the chapter on performance measurement, *both* objective and subjective criteria should be used in evaluation. Also, just because objective criteria exist, we should not discard the subjective because they are often the most important. Finally, it is important to *consciously* use both types of data.

Rather subtly, with respect to planning and strategy creation and evaluation, we are involved in relating business or general organization (in the case of a nonbusiness organization) considerations or strategy to E & R programs and projects, including the results of exploratory research. This is difficult, because while business or organization strategy can be (and sometimes should be) based upon exploratory research, it is rare that a scientific breakthrough produces a general organization strategy. Whether this is even possible in an organization depends upon how cleverly the organization constructed its basic objectives and strategies.

There must be a convergence of the business and research inputs before one is likely to find a research input important enough to motivate a general organization strategy. The E & R group must understand that a convergence has not occurred until it has been established that:

1. The proposed strategy can be executed.
2. The technical portion is not only feasible, but that it has been demonstrated that:
   (a) the process will work,
   (b) it will produce the desired product or result, and
   (c) reasonable yields can be obtained under practical operating conditions.
3. The new substrategy is consistent with the general overall objectives.

Another factor that makes this process most rare is that new knowledge concepts (and, therefore, often programs) usually arise or have their origins at the lower organizational levels in the E & R group (the place

[1] This material is paraphrased and in part quoted from an address by Dr. Guy Suits, former Vice President and Director of Research, General Electric Company, at the Industrial Research Institute, Colorado Springs, Colorado, May 15, 1962.

where most of the up-to-date professionals are located), whereas general policies and plans are almost solely top management thoughts.

EVALUATING PROJECTS (STRATEGIES) ON THE BASIS OF ORGANIZED BUSINESS DATA

Once a project or strategy appears, on the basis of preliminary investigations, to be feasible and to likely be attractive to some degree, a model of the project that can be analyzed from business (or organizational), economic, and technical standpoints should be developed. This can be very simply conceptualized for a new product oriented project in a business as illustrated in Fig. 8-2. This all-inclusive model should be broken down into a series of similar models to show properly the effect of time and the status at different stages of development.

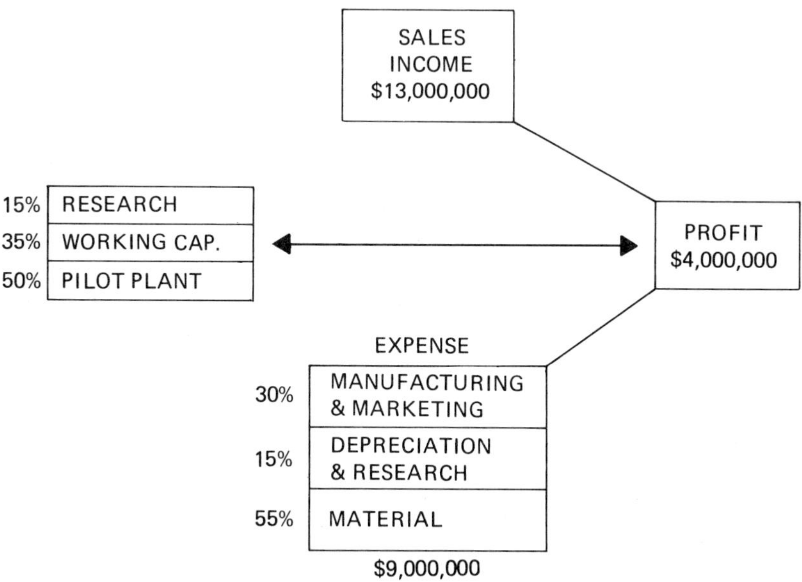

Fig. 8-2. Model for a new product strategy.

A company should develop for its guidance the minimum level of attractiveness in the term of some common yardstick such as return on investment. Of course, time must also be taken into consideration. In a rather simple manner, if financial models and some yardsticks are available for measurement, a group of prospects could be compared in a manner similar to Fig. 8-3.

Project "A" obviously starts out poorly and even if the technical effort succeeds it barely meets the minimum standard. Project C is a far superior choice from a business view. What is lost in this view is the total return, unless this is the basis of the ordinate.

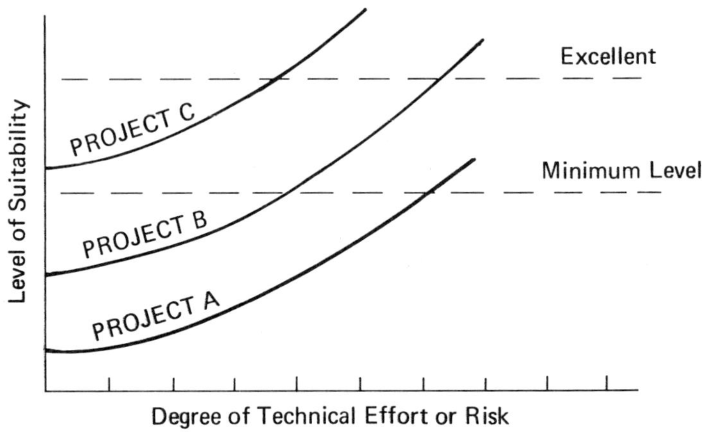

Fig. 8-3. Model for comparison of projects.

Another approach to evaluating projects on the basis of organized business data is the factor rating or profile technique. One that has been devised by John S. Harris of Monsanto Chemical Company and used by that company for several years is summarized in Figs. 8-4 to 8-6. This system reflects the belief that there are a number of criteria in the selection of a new product or project upon which managerial judgment must be based, and that this judgment is best rendered when the criteria are not assembled or averaged but are presented simply, separately, and simultaneously.

A somewhat more elaborate rating procedure has been developed by C. M. Mottley and R. D. Newton of Chas. Pfizer & Company. They propose five basic criteria for the selection of industrial research projects in a paper presented before the Operations Research Society of America (May, 1959). These are summarized in Fig. 8-7 and an illustration of their application is given in Fig. 8-8. By plotting the project score against the proposed budget expenditure for the coming year and by accumulating these expenditures beginning with the highest score project, a product mix of programs can be determined. Obviously one stops when the cumulative financial requirements match available money. However, just looking at the coming year's costs associated with the projects being considered could be fatal to the company since some of the projects in future years could eventually require expenditures beyond the means available to the company in any one or all areas (E & R, marketing, manufacture, service, etc.).

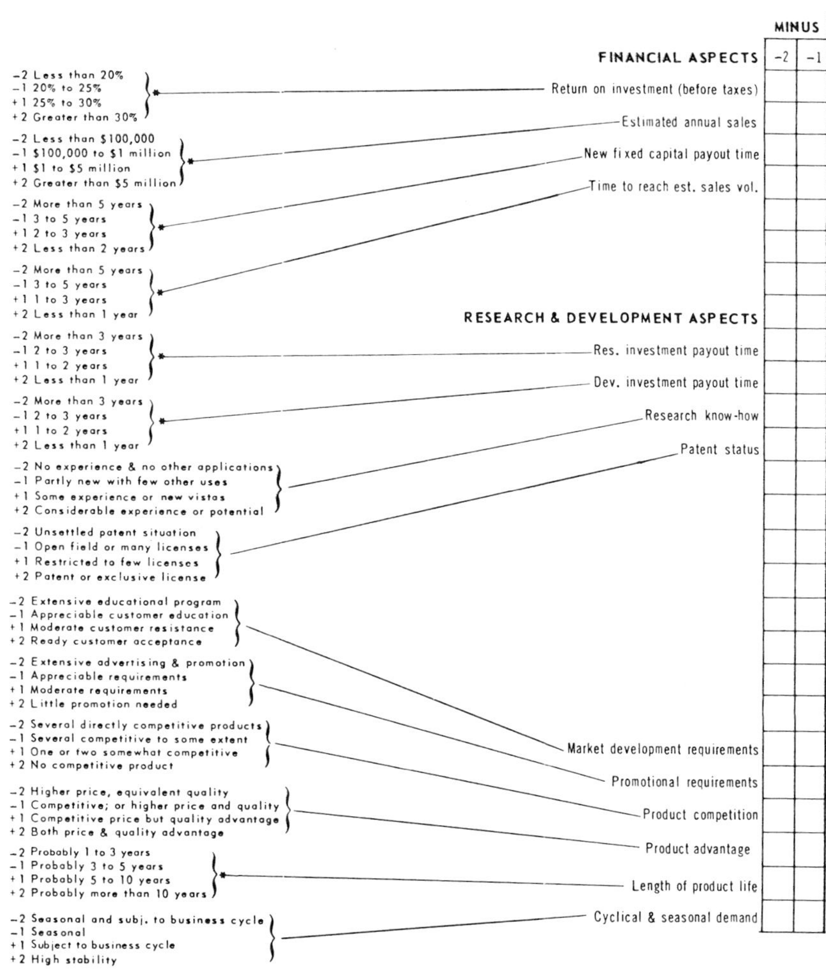

*(*The ratings for this aspect will depend on the individual company's type of business, accounting methods, and financial objectives. The values shown above are estimated on the basis of various published information to bracket the averages for large chemical companies.)*

Fig. 8-4. Profile chart used in overall evaluation of a new product. (Continued on next page.) *Source:* Figs. 8-4 to 8-6 were reprinted from *Chemical and Engineering News* by their permission and that of author, John S. Harris, Vol. 39, No. 16 (April 17, 1961), 110. Copyright 1961 by the American Chemical Society and reprinted by permission of copyright owners.

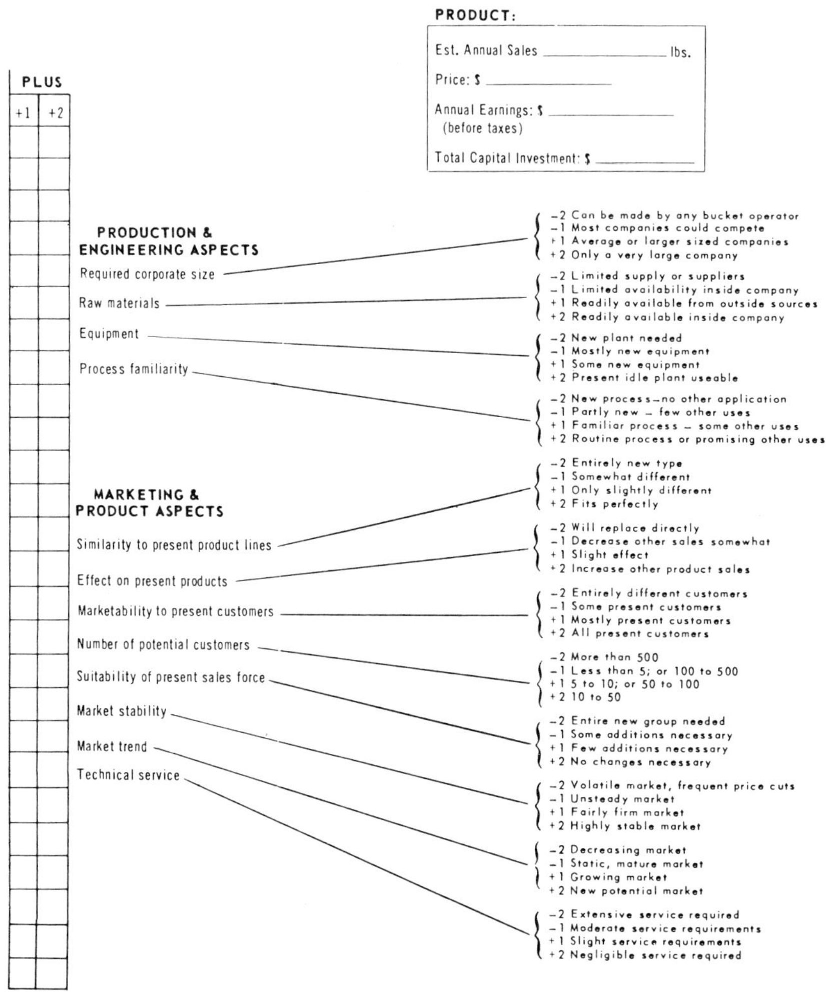

Fig. 8-4 (Continued). Profile chart used in overall evaluation of a new product. (For examples of complete chart see pages 193–196.)

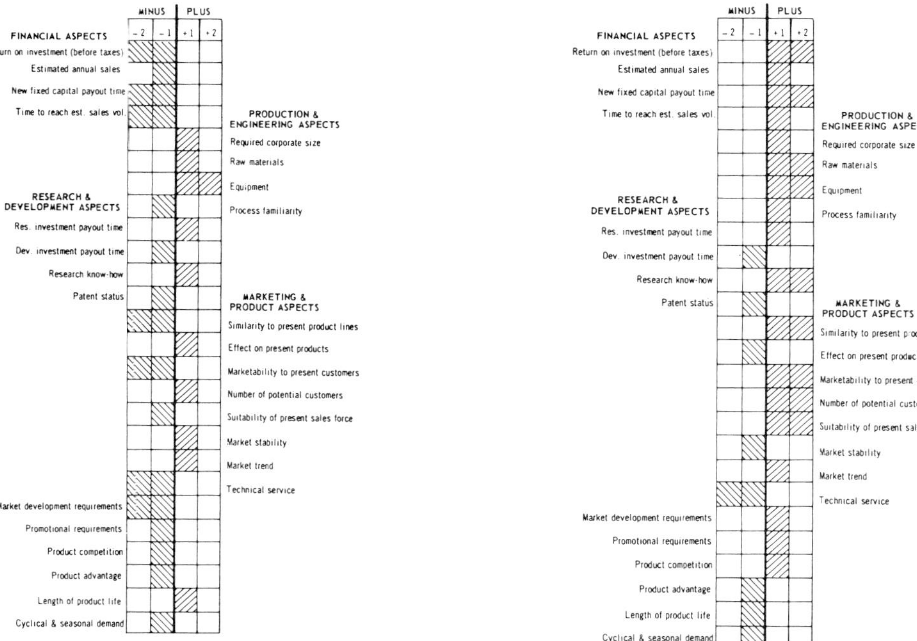

Fig. 8-5. (*Left*) Before the chart shown in Fig. 8-4 was put into use, it was tried out on several products previously put on the market by Monsanto Chemical Company. One of these was Textile Preservative-B which had been a market failure due primarily to poor profitability and heavy technical service and marketing demands. As shown, this chart would have emphasized these points and could have saved much time and expense. (*Right*) Insecticide-N, unlike Textile Preservative-B, proved to be a market success. Based on developmental data, the chart missed what actually happened only on annual sales and length of product life; both were underestimated. (These two charts reflect only the information available during development of the products.) *Source:* See Fig. 8-4.

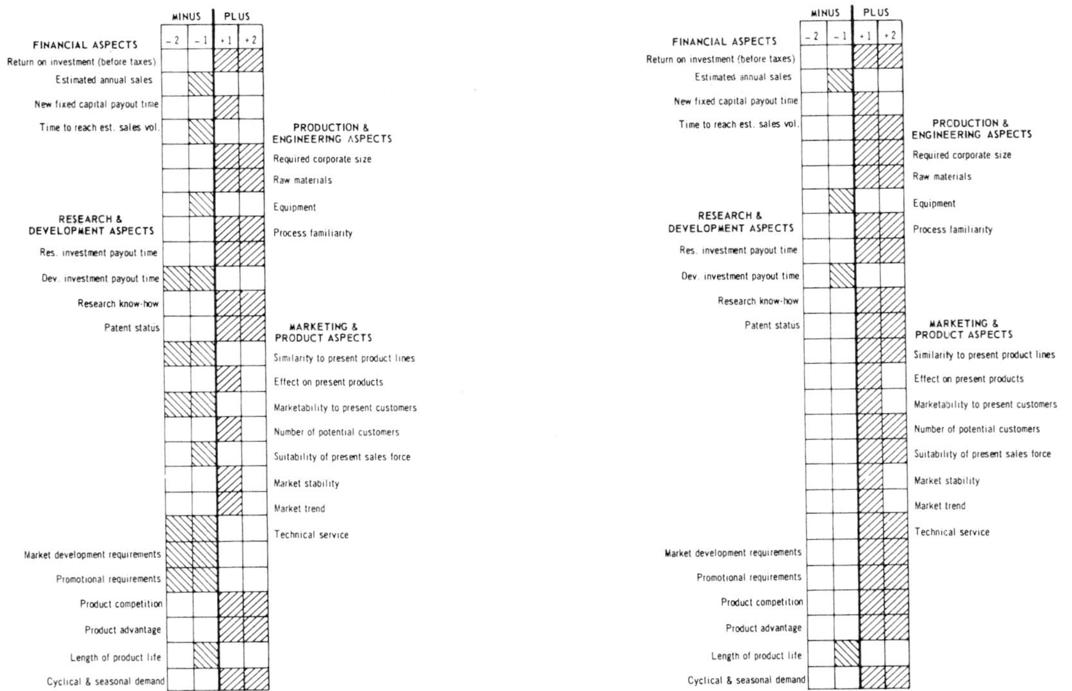

Fig. 8-6. Where alternatives are available, such as in marketing methods, the profile chart provides a comparison of which is better. Drilling Additive-R could have been marketed in either of two ways. Case I (*left*) shows the effect of direct sales to the many drilling mud companies. Case II (*right*) shows what happens when the product is sold through a distributor specializing in additives to drilling mud companies. Clearly, marketing is a controlling factor. *Source:* See Fig. 8-4.

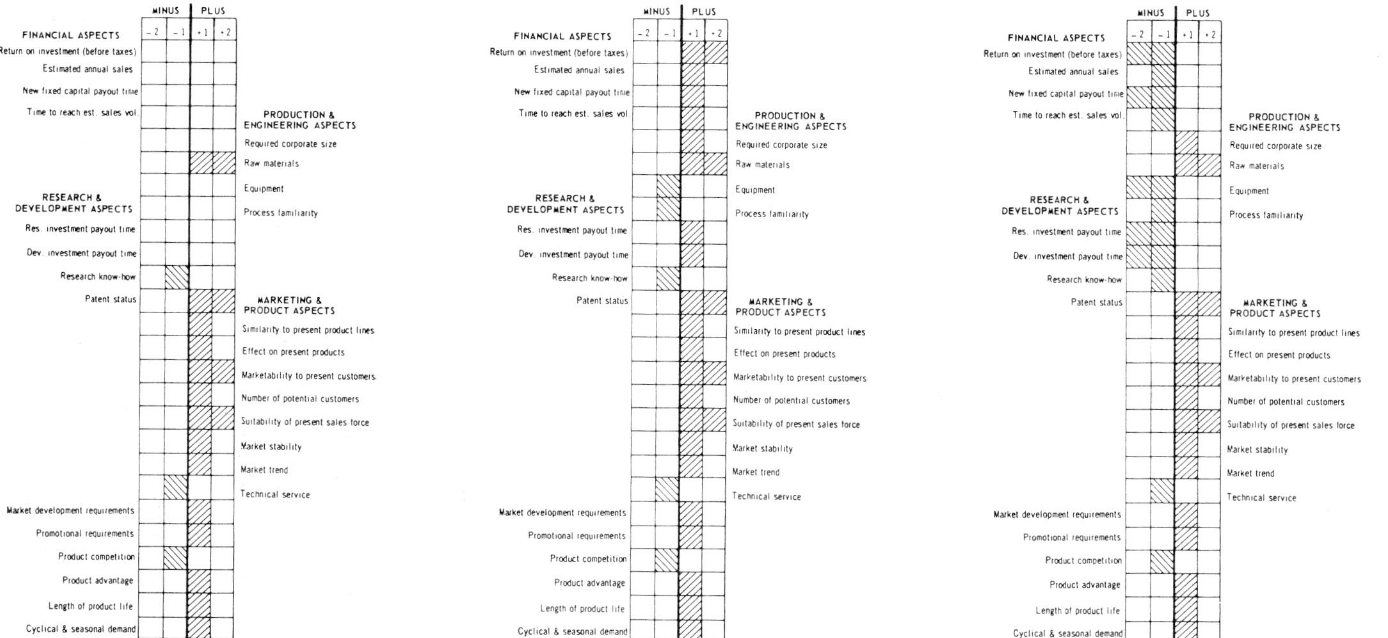

Fig. 8-6 (*Continued*). Plasticizer-D provides an example of how a profile chart can change during the development of a product. At Stage I (*left*) it has shown promise in screening tests. Process work has not been started as yet — thus, neither the process nor economics is known. Several months later, during process research, the chart at Stage II (*center*) still rates the product high. Economics look good. An unavoidable by-product has been found, but it is expected to sell at a profit. Stage III (*right*) shows a much different picture. More work has shown that the by-product will not sell. This depresses financial aspects, and necessary pricing lengthens the time to reach volume sales. Process research shows the need for a new plant. At this point, Plasticizer-D was dropped. *Source:* See Fig. 8-4.

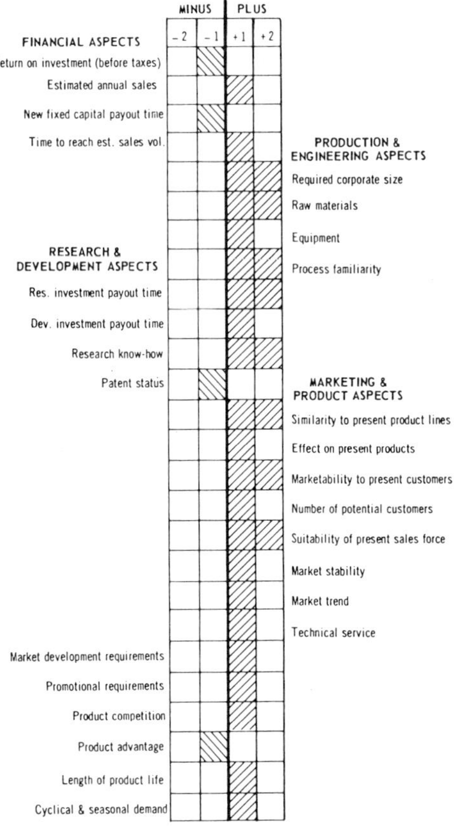

Fig. 8-6 (*Concluded*). This chart shows that Resin Intermediate-H, still in commercial development, has less than promising financial aspects. However, the production and marketing areas of the chart are favorable, providing reasons for trying to commercialize the product. *Source:* See Fig. 8-4.

SIMPLE MATHEMATICAL MODELS

A simple index for comparing projects which was developed a number of years ago by Fred Olsen of Olin-Mathieson is shown below:

$$\text{Index of Return} = \frac{\begin{matrix}\text{Estimated Value of Research} \\ \text{If It Succeeds}\end{matrix} \times \begin{matrix}\text{Estimated Chance} \\ \text{of Success}\end{matrix}}{\text{Estimated Cost of Research}}$$

A formula which takes into consideration the fact that money is worth more now than later is given by Sidney Sobelman of Picatinny Arsenal. As a first approximation,

$$z = pT - ct$$

RATING SYSTEM

Criterion	Question	Range of answers	Numerical rating
Promise of success (P)	What is the best estimate of the promise of technical success consistent with known economies and the state of the art?	Unforeseeable	1
		Fair	2
		High	3
Time to completion (T)	How long will it take to complete the research effort from this time forward?	Greater than 3 years . .	1
		1 to 3 years	2
		Less than 1 year.	3
Cost of project (C)	How much will it cost to complete the research effort from this time forward?	Greater than $1 million .	1
		$100,000 to $1 million. .	2
		Less than $100,000 . . .	3
Strategic need (N)	To what extent is successful research needed from a market standpoint?	No apparent market application; must be developed.	1
		Desirable to maintain, reinforce, or expand position within market applications currently served	2
		Essential in relation to current or projected markets within market applications not currently served.	3
Market gain (M)	What is the net market gain potential for the company after taking into account losses through product replacement?	Less than $1 million/yr.	1
		$1 to $10 million/yr. . .	2
		Greater than $10 million/yr.	3

Fig. 8-7. Rating system for selection of industrial research projects. *Source:* C. M. Mottley and R. D. Newton, "The Selection of Projects for Industrial Research," *Operations Research* (November–December 1959).

where z = product value or decision-making factor, p = average net profit/year, T = market or useful life in years, c = average development cost/year, and t = years of development. All dollar values should be discounted to the present time by multiplying by $1 \div (1+i)^n$ where i is the rate of interest and n is the year of occurrence. This formula can be used for periodic evaluation at different steps of a product's development.

If average development time $\bar{t}$ and average useful life $\bar{T}$ are known for a class of products, then projects which have a shorter than average development time or longer than average market time can be recognized and rewarded.

EVALUATION OF PROJECTS
IN RELATION TO
PROPOSED BUDGET EXPENDITURES

Project no.	Rating of criteria					Project Score	Budget request for next year	
							By project	Cumulative
	P	T	C	N	M	S	$ thousand	$ thousand
3	3	3	3	3	2	162	0	0
19	3	3	2	3	3	162	200	200
10	3	2	3	3	2	108	25	225
5	2	3	3	2	3	108	100	325
21	3	3	2	2	2	72	100	425
23	2	2	2	3	3	72	400	825
30	2	2	2	3	2	48	40	865
2	2	2	2	3	2	48	40	905
4	2	2	2	3	2	48	50	955
14	2	2	2	3	2	48	50	1,005
1	3	2	2	2	2	48	130	1,135
15	2	2	2	2	3	48	350	1,485
25	1	2	3	3	2	36	40	1,525
8	2	1	2	3	3	36	75	1,600
29	2	1	2	3	3	36	75	1,675
28	2	2	2	2	2	32	50	1,725
12	2	2	2	2	2	32	100	1,825
13	2	2	2	2	2	32	150	1,975
6	2	2	2	2	2	32	175	2,150
17	1	2	2	2	3	24	100	2,250
22	3	1	2	2	2	24	125	2,375
16	1	1	2	2	3	12	60	2,435
27	1	1	2	3	2	12	60	2,495
11	1	1	2	3	2	12	100	2,595
26	1	1	2	3	2	12	100	2,695
20	1	1	1	3	3	9	375	3,070
18	1	1	2	2	2	8	60	3,130
24	2	1	2	1	2	8	75	3,205
7	1	2	2	2	1	8	100	3,305
9	1	1	1	2	3	6	400	3,705

Fig. 8-8. Examples of project evaluation in relation to proposed budget expenditures based on system shown in Fig. 8-7. *Source:* See Fig. 8-7.

Let

$$T^* = T + \bar{T}(1 - t/\bar{t})$$

$$t^* = t + \bar{t}(1 - T/\bar{T})$$

Then the revised formula is:

$$z = pT^* - ct^*$$

C. Huetten and L. Sweany of P. R. Mallory & Company, Inc. have developed a model which permits evaluation of a project at any one of seven steps after the idea stage. Basically, a company which spends a dollars on a new product expects a total return of b dollars for a net gain of c over the lifetime of the product. The solution of this complex problem is achieved by reducing it to a number of smaller problems which can be attacked more easily. The general problem is therefore divided into seven steps as shown in Fig. 8-9, the estimates *a* and *b* being made for each step on an individual basis and then modified to take into account interactions between steps. These must then be periodically reevaluated in order to correct the estimating error on the steps completed and to adjust the estimates, where required, for the steps still to be completed. These steps are as follows.

1. The product is named, its objective and scope are defined, and general requirements are written.
2. Detailed requirements are written, and a "paper approach" solution that appears to satisfy the detailed requirements is proposed.
3. Perform the exploratory work needed to prove the feasibility of the "paper approach."
4. Initiate a formal research and development project and complete it to the point that the development of the product is complete.
5. The product is tooled for production, and final engineering is completed.
6. Production is started and continues to the "break-even" point in the financial history of the product. (The income from the product at this point equals all of the expenses incurred on the product at this point.)
7. The production rate is geared to the life cycle of the product—this takes into account the gradual obsolescence of the product.

This analysis results in the determination of the gain *c* over the full life of the product. Obviously, it is important to any investor to be aware of the relation between the money he risks and that which he gains. If the potential and/or probable margin is too slim, he will look for a better bargain. However, some ratio of gain to risk will always be acceptable to him. Since the company is the investor, it should set minimum standards on the gain to risk ratio for a proposed new product. This ratio can then be used as one index of merit on which to base advancing a new product to the next step or rejecting it and holding it for review. The minimum acceptable gain to risk ratio will vary with the type of company, but on the average, *a net gain ratio of 2.5 is often acceptable.*

Another factor that will usually be considered as an acceptance criteria is *the estimated annual dollar volume from the new product;* of course, there must be an associated profit. It is possible that other acceptance factors may also be considered as indicators as to whether an item should be advanced to the next step. If the dollar volume of business from a new product represents too small a percentage of the overall goals set by the

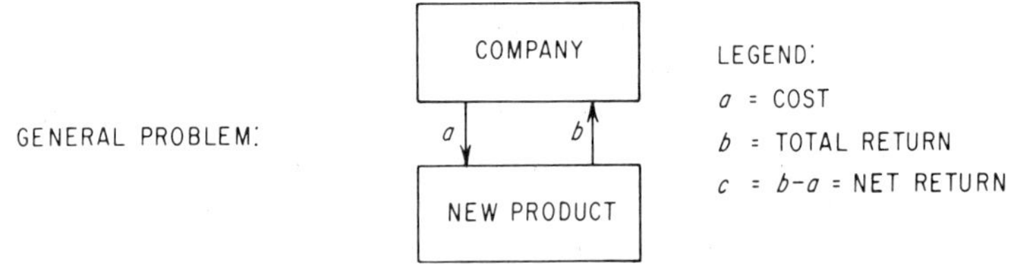

SEVEN STEP BREAKDOWN:

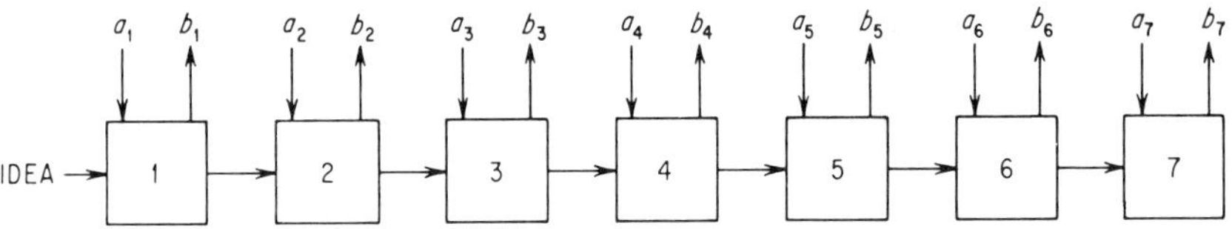

Fig. 8-9. Breakdown of general problem of project evaluation.

company, it may be possible or appropriate to consider several new products having substandard dollar volumes but with similar manufacturing processes and sales areas, as a group to form an acceptable new product package. The minimum acceptable amount for each new product will depend upon the company objectives.

"Break-even" time may also be a criteria in deciding the acceptance of a new product. A company may not want its money tied up in excess of a certain period of time because of financial reasons. If the company needs or wants to conserve its resources, a break-even time acceptance criterion is indicated.

The factors described are not by any means the only ones that can or should be used as criteria for measuring the acceptability of a product and its advancement to the next step. Other decision factors usually include marketing and manufacturing considerations.

To analyze a new product based upon the seven steps just described requires certain factors to be estimated and others to be calculated. The accuracy of the estimates will depend upon the experience of the estimators and the amount of supporting information that is available as a guide. Following an often-used procedure in mathematics, simplifying assumptions have been made in developing expressions used to calculate the remaining factors in the analysis. A look at the analysis factors that must be estimated and calculated will be helpful.

Figure 8-10 shows an analysis summary sheet for Product X that follows the a and b concept with additional information required to complete the analysis. The \$1.50 selling price, p, of Product X has been either estimated directly or developed through costing and profit calculations. Assuming that something is known about the potential market for this product from pub-

Subject: PRODUCT X		No. / Date:
	ESTIMATE	REMARKS
p	$1.50	Selling price
V_m	1,300,000	Unit volume per year (max)
f_m	1,950,000	Dollar volume per year (max)
t_c	2	Acceleration time, years
a_1	COSTS 50	Preliminary analysis
a_2	250	Analysis and paper-approach
a_3	2,500	Analysis and exploratory
a_4	35,000	Research and development
a_5	108,916	Tooling, pre-production, interest, etc.
a_6	1,891,169	Expenses during break-even period
a_7	9,963,429	Expenses during remaining production time
a	12,001,314	Total Expense (sum of a_1 thru a_7)
b_1	INCOME 0	None expected
b_2	0	None expected
b_3	0	None expected
b_4	0	None expected
b_5	0	None expected
b_6	2,037,885	To break even
b_7	10,736,454	During remaining production time
b	12,774,339	Total Income (sum of b_1 thru b_7)
t_1	TIME	Analysis
t_2	0.2	Analysis and paper-approach
t_3		Analysis and exploratory
t_4	1.0	Research and development
t_5	0.5	Tooling and product engineering
t_6	1.9	To break even
t_7	6.4	Remaining production time
t	10.0	Total Time (sum of t_1 thru t_7)
c = 773,025 (net gain)	d = 146,716 (risk)	c/d = 5:1 (gain/risk)

Fig. 8-10. Sample of an analysis summary sheet which provides information necessary for making product decisions. Data are shown for a typical product X at Stage 1. Here, the a's, b's, c and d are in dollars; the t's are in years. Similar sheet is used for each stage, providing complete history of product. *Source:* Clarence Huetten and Louis Sweany, "Does Your New-Product Idea Measure Up?", *Product Engineering* (May 9, 1960).

lished market figures, an estimate is made as to what portion of this market the company might be expected to obtain at the estimated selling price. Since most products have a growth period, a relatively stable period of production, and then a period of decline, it is appropriate to estimate the maximum expected volume V_m, which in the case of Product X is 1,300,000 units per year. The maximum yearly dollar volume f_m is then \$1.50 × 1,300,-000 or \$1,950,000.

The estimation of the acceleration time, t_a, completes this segment of the analysis giving the estimated price, unit and dollar volume, and the time required to reach maximum production. For Product X, it was estimated that maximum production would be realized two years after the beginning of production. The rate of production increase over this two-year period might be considered as linear to simplify calculations, or a curve which would be more representative of the actual rate increase based on past experience could be used.

The remaining segments in Fig. 8-10 are self-explanatory. At the bottom of the figure, c is the total of the b's minus the total of the a's. In the analysis, the maximum risk is the sum of all the expenses incurred up to the beginning of production plus certain expenses incurred during initial production. In Fig. 8-10, d is the sum of a_1 through a_5.

MODERN DECISION THEORY

Certainty, Risk, and Uncertainty

In the previous discussion of selection of alternative projects, there was an implicit assumption regarding the future. That is to say, if two products were compared on the basis of return on investment, then the action of competitors, the state of the economy, the growth of the industry, the possibility of war or peace, etc., were assumed to be taken into account. Actually, the manager of E & R and other members of the management team make decisions under conditions of varying knowledge about the future. Some things are known with *certainty*. In other situations, the probabilities of various conditions are known so that the decisions are made under *risk*, an obvious example of this latter condition is the everyday operation of insurance companies. Where no basis at all exists for estimating the probability of future events, the decisions are said to be made under *uncertainty*.

Developments in modern decision theory make it advisable for the manager of E & R to have a basic understanding of the subject. Applications of decision theory to selection and evaluation of projects are being reported in current literature.

Certainty and Risk Criteria

If the manager of E & R had five projects under contract, each of which he could assign to a different engineer, each of whom would require different known times to complete any one of the five contracts and each of whom receives a different salary, he could assign any one of the five contracts to Engineer A, any of the four remaining to Engineer B, any of the three remaining to Engineer C, etc., so that there are 120 ($5 \times 4 \times 3 \times 2 \times 1 = 120$) ways of assigning the jobs. It would be necessary to obtain the total cost of engineering work for each strategy and then select that arrangement of assignments with lowest associated cost. This shows that even under conditions of certainty, the decision problem can involve such large numbers of strategies to evaluate that it is not always simple.

Under conditions of risk, the decision-maker is assumed to have certain strategies which he may follow and that his "payoff" or reward depends upon events which may occur with known probabilities. Suppose, for example, management must select between Strategy 1, the development of a new, high-volume, simple product and Strategy 2, the development of a low-volume, complex, highly engineered product. Their main competitor, it is known from past experience, will follow one of three courses of action. He will duplicate the products 50 percent of the time, he will develop a slightly improved product to sell cheaper 40 percent of the time, and he will develop a much improved product 10 percent of the time. The payoffs which the company will receive in the face of each of these competing strategies can be calculated, it is assumed. The simple table of payoffs shown below helps summarize this whole discussion.

	C 1	C 2	C 3
Probabilities	0.5	0.4	0.1
Strategy 1	$10,000	$9,000	$12,000
Strategy 2	14,000	8,000	6,000

The management, under these conditions, should select the strategy which provides the highest average payoff. This is often called the "expected value" of the payoff and is obtained by multiplying each payoff by its probability and adding the results.

$$\text{Expected value for Strategy 1} = 0.5 \times \$10{,}000 + 0.4 \times \$9{,}000 + 0.1 \times \$12{,}000 = \$9{,}800$$

$$\text{Expected value for Strategy 2} = 0.5 \times \$14{,}000 + 0.4 \times \$8{,}000 + 0.1 \times \$6{,}000 = \$10{,}800$$

With this criterion, management would select the second strategy.

Decision trees involving the use of probabilities are another kind of model used in arriving at correct decisions. In a presentation of this approach, Edward A. McCreary in *Think* wrote the following:

As part of an overall decision study involving research and development possibilities, the Pythagoras Parts Company of New York determined that for one particular $1,000,000 investment in a new process and product, the company stood a 70 percent chance of developing high sales over a period of time and net cash flow of $4,000,000. However, there was also a 30 percent chance of relatively low sales and a negative cash flow of (—)$1,000,000. Project managers were anxious to get a yes or no on this decision . . .[2]

They developed a decision tree model, which is shown in Fig. 8-11.

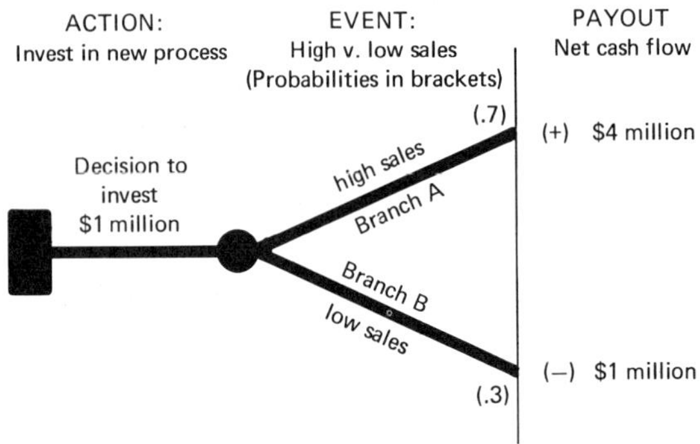

Fig. 8-11. Decision tree for new product investment. *Source of Figs. 8-11 through 8-14:* Edward A. McCreary, "How to Grow a Decision Tree," THINK (March–April 1967). Reprinted by permission from THINK Magazine, published by IBM, copyright 1967 by International Business Machines Corporation.

In this simple decision tree, analysts would modify the return in each branch by the probability (estimated) that the event would occur. Therefore, the composite value* for branch "A" is 2.8 million (.70 × $4,000,000) and for branch "B", —0.3 million [.30 × (—)$1,000,000]. From these two figures one could determine that the composite value of the project was 2.5 million by algebraically adding the branch composite values ($2,800,000 — $300,000 = $2,500,000). The tree could now be simplified to look as in Fig. 8-12.

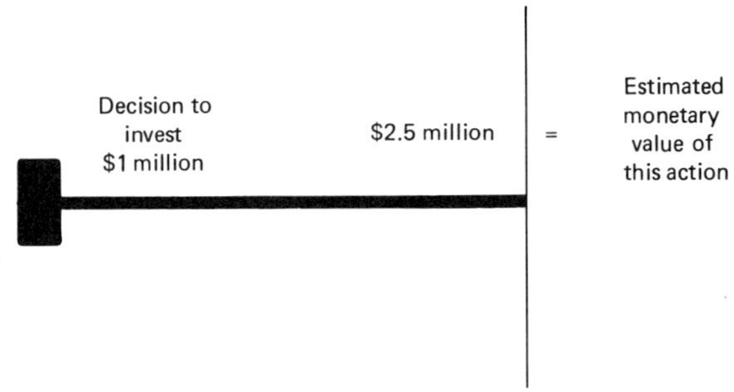

Fig. 8-12. Expected value for the project. *Source:* See Fig. 8-11.

[2] Edward A. McCreary, "How to Grow a Decision Tree," THINK (March–April 1967). Reprinted by permission from THINK Magazine, published by IBM, Copyright 1967 by International Business Machines Corporation.

* Other writings use the term "conditional payoff."

As McCreary notes, in real life the composite return is not achieved on a single venture; either the $2.8 million is gained or the $300,000 is lost. In other words, regardless of the probability of success or failure, the outcome is a success or failure and not a combination. However, it was hypothesized (not at all unrealistically) that another company approached Pythagoras and opened negotiations to buy the development—they had heard rumors regarding the project. The bargaining started at about $2 million and gradually rose. At this point the hypothetical $2.5 million value ceased being nearly so hypothetical and unrealistic.

In real life, decision trees usually have many branches when time and the various alternatives are shown. Such bushy trees need to be trimmed before exposing them to top management. In order for the reader to better understand the concepts expressed, imagine a process oriented company looking at the year ahead. The sales manager says there is a 60 percent chance that sales will rise 20 percent, and a 40 percent chance that sales will drop 5 percent. In the first case, it was then determined the purchase of that set of new process equipment would generate a positive cash flow of $460,000 and that this would be reduced to $340,000 in the event of a sales drop. The alternative, and it was a possible one, was to use the existing equipment and go to overtime. This approach would generate a $440,000 positive cash flow in the case of a sales rise and $380,000 profit would be the net result in the event of a sales drop. The simple decision tree showing this condition is as shown in Fig. 8-13. On the basis of this model, the best decision is to solve the problem by going to overtime. However, when looking further into the future the sales manager believed the product to have excellent prospects and forecast that even if sales dropped 5 percent in 1969, that the odds were 8-in-10 that sales would increase by

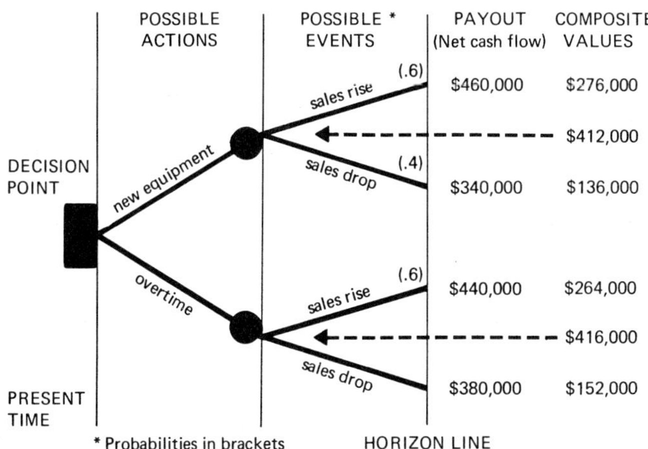

Fig. 8-13. Decision tree for a risk venture. *Source:* See Fig. 8-11.

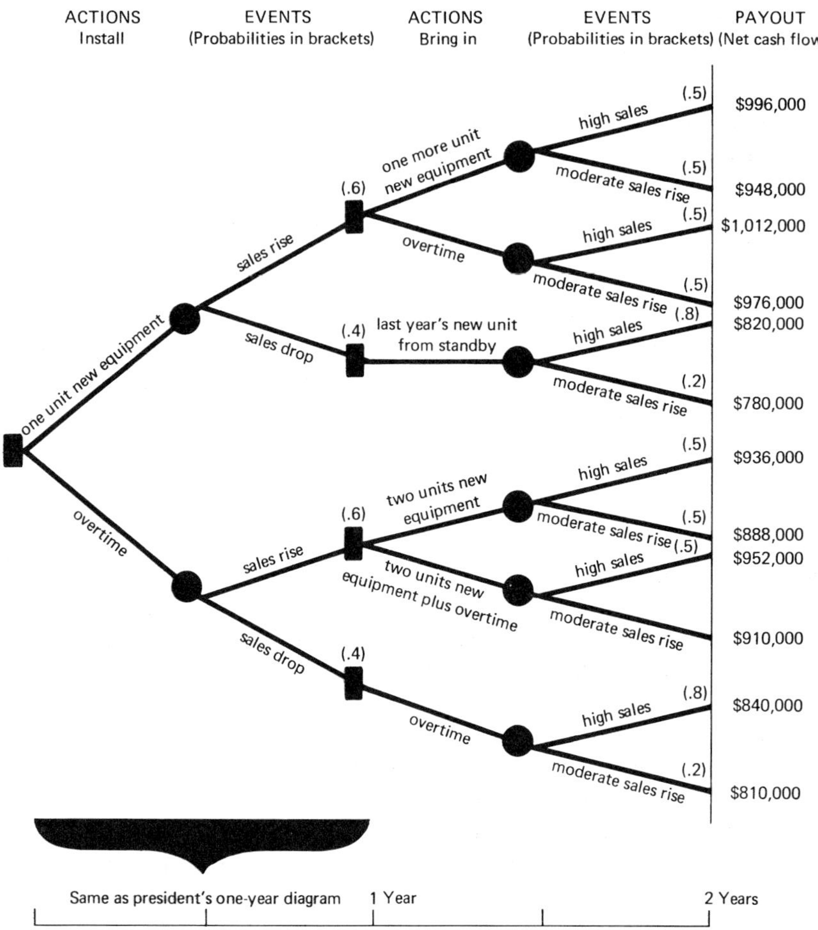

Fig. 8-14. Extended decision tree. *Source:* See Fig. 8-11.

at least 10 percent in 1970. Moreover, if sales rose as hoped in 1969, the odds were 50-50 that they would further increase by either 20 *or* 10 percent in 1970. The resultant decision tree now appeared as shown in Fig. 8-14. The cash indicated flows are calculated for each branch. If you work out this problem, you will find overtime to be the wrong long-range decision.

Decision Making Under Uncertainty*

Maximin—The Criterion of Pessimism. This criterion was proposed by Abraham Wald. When the decision maker must select a strategy in the

* For a rather complete discussion of some aspects of this problem, with applications to contracting, the reader may want to review a doctoral dissertation by E. J. Fisher of Rensselaer Polytechnic Institute entitled *Parametric Uncertainty in Military Research & Development Decisions.*

face of future events or "states of nature" whose likelihood he cannot even guess, he may choose to assume that the worst will befall him. The representation of his strategies in the face of these events represented as N 1, N 2, and N 3 may be summarized as in the example below. Payoffs are shown in thousands of dollars.

	N 1	N 2	N 3
Strategy 1	$ 50	$200	$ 1
Strategy 2	210	−10	75
Strategy 3	300	10	−1

The minimum payoff for each strategy is:

S 1	1
S 2	−10
S 3	−1

The maximum of these minimum payoffs is associated with Strategy 1. It is noted that this approach is one of timidity, since possible large profits associated with Strategy 3 are foregone by assuming that nature will be malevolent. The term "maximin" can now be seen to be derived from the choice of the maximum of the minimum payoffs.

Maximax—The Criterion of Optimism. Leonid Hurwicz suggests a criterion based on optimism. There is no reason for the E & R manager to feel that all the breaks will go against him. If he doesn't get the worst break, he may obtain much higher payoffs for all other possibilities. Perhaps he feels lucky and wants to shoot for the big gain. In the table given directly above, the maximum payoffs for each strategy are:

S 1	200
S 2	210
S 3	300

The maximum of these maximum payoffs indicates that Strategy 3 is preferred. Like the maximin criterion, this criterion is based on extreme values and ignores the intermediate payoffs.

Weighted Payoff Criterion—Hurwicz. As a compromise between optimism and pessimism, the minimum payoff with its emphasis on security could be weighted, say, ⅔, and the maximum payoff as ⅓. The values associated with each strategy in the above table would be:

S 1 $\frac{2}{3} \times 1 + \frac{1}{3} \times 200 = 67\frac{1}{3}$
S 2 $\frac{2}{3} \times (-10) + \frac{1}{3} \times 210 = 63\frac{1}{3}$
S 3 $\frac{2}{3} \times (-1) + \frac{1}{3} \times 300 = 99\frac{1}{3}$

Laplace (Bayes) Criterion. The Laplace criterion, sometimes known as the criterion of insufficient reason, is one that has been subject to much debate which still continues. It assumes that since the probabilities of the various states of nature aren't known, they can be assumed to be equal. Using the same table as before, the three states of nature would be assigned a probability of occurrent of ⅓. Using this criterion, Strategy 3 would be the choice.

S 1 $\frac{1}{3} \times 50 + \frac{1}{3} \times 200 + \frac{1}{3} \times 1 = 82\frac{2}{3}$
S 2 $\frac{1}{3} \times 210 + \frac{1}{3} \times (-10) + \frac{1}{3} \times 75 = 91\frac{2}{3}$
S 3 $\frac{1}{3} \times 300 + \frac{1}{3} \times 10 + \frac{1}{3} \times (-1) = 103$

Minimax—Savage's Criterion of Least Regret. The criterion of least regret is that of the Monday morning quarterback. Regret is measured by the difference between the payoff the company actually receives and that which they could have received if they had known the state of nature which would occur. Again, the same table of payoffs will be considered and it is repeated below for convenience.

	N 1	N 2	N 3
S 1	50	200	1
S 2	210	−10	75
S 3	300	10	−1

Suppose that N 1 actually occurred. Also, if the decision maker had chosen strategy S 1, he would experience a regret because he had not chosen S 3. The amount of regret quantitatively expressed would be 300 − 50 = 250. If he had chosen S 2, he would have experienced a regret of 300 − 210 = 90. If he had chosen S 3, he would have experienced no regret since he received the largest payoff possible for this state of nature. Using this process, the regrets associated with the three strategies for the other two states of nature may be calculated. The results of such calculations can be summarized in a table of regrets as has been done below for the example:

	N 1	N 2	N 3
S 1	250	0	74
S 2	90	210	0
S 3	0	190	76

The maximum regret for each strategy is:

S 1	250
S 2	210
S 3	190

The minimum of these maximum regrets indicates that the third strategy should be employed for this table of payoffs.

Mixed Strategies

Suppose the decision maker feels that "nature" is trying to outguess him. This could occur when competitors exert an unknown influence on future markets based upon their estimate of what the decision maker of the present firm will do. The decision maker could then select his strategies on a probability basis, say, by employing S 1 20 percent of the time, S 2 40 percent of the time, and S 3 40 percent of the time. The table of payoffs could be extended to show the expected payoffs for this mixed strategy as shown below:

	N 1	N 2	N 3
S 1	50	200	1
S 2	210	−10	75
S 3	300	10	−1
.2 × S 1 + .4 × S 2 + .4 × S 3	214	40	29.8

These odds for each strategy could be changed until the set is found which will yield the largest minimum payoff. This strategy is called the "optimal" mixed strategy.

Concluding Remarks on Project Selection

All of the approaches discussed have been used or experimented with by various technologically advanced companies. In fact, Monte Carlo simulation that uses continuous probability distributions associated with variables in the decision and random process model is currently being adopted by many companies.

The development of high speed and large memory electronic computers has led to the development of complex models of companies and of probabilistic simulations. Managers are provided with pay-off versus risk curves for alternative projects which are much more meaningful than a simple deterministic point estimate of payoff.

One other point is very important and has been largely neglected so far in the interest of simplicity. Project outlays and returns usually take place over a long period of time. For comparison purposes, *it is extremely important that all cash flows be discounted or compounded to the same point in time* for all alternative projects.

ESTABLISHING TECHNICAL OBJECTIVES

The E & R Program in Relation to Technical Objectives

Before the manager of E & R can recommend a technical program to top management, he must have completed an evaluation of the potential projects from both the technical and commercial viewpoints. To accomplish the commercial evaluation, he must have secured the assistance of the marketing manager and probably other members of the top management team. He may have developed and presented his technical objectives in much detail; yet when he reviews his program with top management, it is possible that major changes may be made by them for over-all business reasons. Top management will not provide detailed technical direction—only general guidance. Therefore, modification of the presented E & R program may occur because of new directions provided by general management. These new directions will be phrased in general terms. Similarly, management may relay to E & R a major project which has been outlined only generally by a customer. Many situations arise in which the E & R manager is ultimately faced with the reduction of broad or general objectives to specific technical objectives. Thus, while the E & R manager may play a large part in identifying and selecting areas for technical development, eventually he receives a written formulation of broad objectives agreed upon by top management and himself. A big part of the E & R job is to analyze these broad objectives, translate them into specific objectives, select from alternative approaches, subdivide the big projects into tasks and subtasks, and finally make sure that individual responsibilities are assigned for all parts of every project.

Usually, technical objectives will be formulated in one of the following forms:

1. General brief objectives for a complex system
2. Detailed plus general specifications for complex systems and equipment
3. General broad objectives for a specific product line or product
4. General objectives required to implement various company goals.

The technical objectives often need to be expanded and clarified to bring out the objectives and implications of the customer's problems. This may be accomplished by definition of the objectives in terms of specific tasks or, in case of some products, by formulation of a set of engineering specifications.

General Brief Objective

In the case of a defense project, the Armed Services may have considerable confidence in a certain company, the work may require a highly imaginative approach, and the contractor may wish to give the research organization considerable leeway. When all the contractual language is eliminated, the technical objective is apt to appear in a short paragraph similar to the following hypothetical one:

Design a one-man flying device weighing not more than x pounds which will rise vertically to h feet in t minutes. It must be capable of hovering, and of moving in any horizontal direction. It must have a forward speed of v miles per hour.

The development of such a machine may require over several hundred scientific personnel. Various broad approaches must be defined. The type of propulsion system, type of fuel, materials, etc., offer many possibilities under such a brief description of the technical objectives. E & R management must isolate major technical tasks to be performed, examine combinations of current technical solutions to each major problem, and seek possible breakthroughs in the over-all problem.

General and Special Specifications

In the development of a large, new complex product such as a nuclear-powered ship, insistence on producing a brief paragraph for the technical objective might result in considerable delay before the technical objectives or conceptual approach could be amplified to the point where the work could be divided into logical packages or tasks for assignment to engineering groups. In such a situation, the practice is to spell out the more orthodox parts of the work in detail and specify the hoped-for characteristics in the areas where research and advance engineering must be performed. The entire set of specifications, which may make up a good size volume, is occasionally called "General and Special Specifications." Quite often, of course, it is found as the work progresses that the specifications required cannot be met within the time and budget limitations; consequently some engineering compromises must be made. As the work progresses, difficulties are recognized, and the general specifications may be relaxed to something which is within practical reach. In the beginning, however, such general specifications represent technical objectives which call forth the best possible capabilities of the E & R organization.

Broad Objectives for a Product Line or Product

A particular company may have one or several clearly-defined product lines, or perhaps just products, upon which its very existence depends. The E & R and the marketing sections should be closely allied to determine the direction that research and product improvement are to take. This effort should result in the formulation of broad E & R objectives.

Such broad objectives are not spelled out in detail; only the desired end result is generally spelled out. This end result could relate to any one or any combination of product performance items or product features.

General Objectives to Implement a Company Goal

Technical objectives may have to be formulated from an interpretation of specified company goals rather than being based upon expected technological advances or marketing needs. For example, a company goal may be to establish the company firmly in a certain type of business. Suppose, for example, the company manufactures vacuum cleaners and toasters. The company may set as a goal, leadership in the manufacture of portable appliances. E & R and marketing organizations must then establish their technical objectives to achieve this goal.

The company may be experiencing seasonal sales and want to overcome this handicap. For example, if the firm manufactures electrolytic capacitors for home radio and television sets, sales will generally peak the last six months of the year. A possible E & R goal would therefore be to develop a line of alternating current motor starting capacitors since they exhibit an opposite sales variation.

Another possibility is that the company wishes to increase its profit-to-sales ratio. E & R must then propose new products or cost reduction objectives for present products.

Again, many companies feel that growth is a necessary condition for survival; therefore company goals may specify an increasing sales volume which perhaps can only be achieved by expansion of E & R activities in development of new products or by the company acquiring other companies through purchase or merger.

ANALYZING TECHNICAL OBJECTIVES TO ESTABLISH TASKS AND SUBTASKS

The Problem

When the technical objectives have been formulated, it is usually necessary to translate broad objectives into concrete tasks or work packages. The interpretation of broad objectives calls for the highest level of technical and managerial competence. Obviously there are many ways in which the objectives might be implemented, but the difficult problem is to define the engineering and research jobs so that they offer a real challenge to the technical people, yet do not seem impossible to them. Depending upon the nature of the objectives and the company's products, three approaches to the formulation of technical objectives into work assignments may be considered.

Systems Approach

A system is an aggregate of elements (equipment components) which function together in time-dependent response to inputs in order to achieve a set of desired outputs. The design of systems, therefore, involves establishing overall system parameters and dynamic characteristics as well as component specifications. If the technical objectives are such that a new equipment system must be engineered, the approach to translating the objectives into work assignments would be as follows:

Overall system requirements would first have to be specified to serve as a "reference" design. These requirements would include inputs and outputs, performance characteristics, and any other features and technical characteristics judged appropriate. The work would then be divided into (1) system engineering and research and (2) component engineering and research. The requirements and characteristics of the system as laid out in the reference design would place certain demands upon the characteristics of the subsystems and components characteristics.

With each step of the process, there is an amplification of requirements and refinement of all aspects—technical research and engineering, testing, costs, personnel, etc. Whereas the broad overall technical objectives may have been outlined in one or two pages, each major task to be performed may require several pages to specify it, and each subtask probably will require even more space to properly state its specifications. In general, the system tasks and subtasks, as well as the subsystem tasks and component tasks may be assigned to either groups of technical personnel or to individuals, depending upon the amount of research and engineering required. The ultimate responsibilities given to the individual engineer may be in the form of a complete specification.

Consider, for example, the design of a gun-fire control system for a new bombing plane. The state of the present art is known, the improved speed and maneuverability characteristics of the new bomber and its assumed target are given, and the objectives of the new and supposedly improved gun-fire control system are given in some form of specification. The first problem is to reduce the technical objectives to work packages which can be assigned to engineers and scientists for development and design.

In the systems approach, a serial method would be to set up the differential equations which would solve the problem of directing the guns to hit the target on the basis of input information regarding the relative positions, velocities, and accelerations of the bomber and the target as well as ballistic information. These equations may be set up in a number of forms, but the one believed best suitable for "mechanization" must be chosen by the systems engineers. The next step would be to prepare a block diagram of the mechanization of the equations. The block diagram would show the inputs, outputs, feedbacks, servos, adding, multiplying, resolving circuits, and components required (assuming that an analog computer is to be used). At this point the necessary components could be specified, and component engineers could be set to work developing or adapting available components. In actual practice, a parallel method is used whereby some component design work is carried out at the same time as the systems work.

Thus the technical objective might first be divided into four tasks—the development of the equations for the system, the development of the block diagram showing the mechanization, the development of systems requirements for the components, and the development and design of the components. As a simple example of subtasks, similar components could be grouped together and the development of a group of like components would constitute a subtask. For example, a number of servos with differing requirements would need to be developed and this work would form a subtask. Individual engineering responsibilities within the framework of the subtask could be assigned on the basis of each servo or on the basis of similar problems.

Product Approach

In the product approach to analyzing technical objectives and establishing tasks, the first step is to list the "new" products and their characteristics. The new products may be completely new or simply modified and improved products.

The tasks are defined as the new product design or the old product improvements. If considerable research and engineering are required for a particular task, this task would be broken down into subtasks. As before, the purpose of breaking the work down in small-size packages is to permit the work to be: (1) more clearly defined in greater detail; (2) more accurately budgeted; (3) more carefully evaluated with regard to technical difficulty; and (4) scheduled more accurately.

An example of dividing the development of a product into tasks and then the tasks directly into responsibilities is illustrated by Fig. 8-15. Some fabrication steps are shown.

Programmatic Approach

In the case of large projects, the development of a program of tasks based on a generalized set of technical objectives is quite complex. There are many ways of reaching the end result in a large project. Moreover, if one particular technical path is chosen, there is then the further problem of subdividing the work into tasks which are suitable for the present or some proposed organization to handle. In addition, on large projects, tasks must be established in some cases for alternative approaches to the most difficult problems foreseen. This parallel effort is required to ensure that the project can be completed on time.

The preparation of tasks based upon technical objectives for large projects is no one-man show. The project manager may make his own version, but he should also have the most experienced and technically competent engineers and managers in his organization contribute. The drafts of plans should be thoroughly rehashed until the project manager is satisfied that no major points have been overlooked. The final project plans should be documented in some such form as shown in Fig. 8-16.

Figure 8-16 provides a space for indicating the individual responsible

TECHNICAL OBJECTIVE					SCHEDULE NO.
Design new and improved model of X - 13 Washing Machine					10.1
RESPONSIBLE	TARGET DATE	REV. DATE NO. 1		REV. DATE NO. 2	REV. DATE NO. 3
A. G. Bonnie Project Engineer	May 1, 1971	June 1, 1971, as of 9/15/70			

TASK SUBJECT NO.	TARGET DATE	SCHEDULE DATE		RESPONSIBLE
		Orig. Extension	Status	
1. Establish objectives, timing, and responsibilities	6/1/70		C	Manager - Design Engineering
2. Establish X - 13 specification	7/1/70		C	G. Smallwood
3. Establish X - 13 functional design	8/1/70		C	G. Smallwood
4. Propose manufacturing methods for optimum productivity	8/7/70	8/31/70	C	R. Hope
5. Establish X - 13 design drawings and instructions taking into account No. 4	10/1/70	10/31/70	X	E. Gross
6. Construct prototype	12/15/70			A. Corbeau
7. Test prototype and adjust design as required	2/15/71			I. M. Drott
8. Change drawings as required and issue to Purchasing and Manufacturing	3/15/71			D. R. Smith
9. Make 24 units for the use of Manufacturing and Sales	5/1/71			S. Moore
10. Test assemblies and deliver models.	6/1/71			I. M. Drott

Status Legend C - Completed X - Slippage

Fig. 8-15. Schedule form showing product technical objective and the assignment of responsibilities.

for a task. Normally a manager is given the prime responsibility for a task, although he may, of course, delegate the task or any part of it to an individual. The problems arise when the tasks, because of their nature, require the effort of several organizational components. To simply assign responsibility for the task to a group of managers would be too vague an assignment. It would be difficult or impossible to measure performance and responsibility for failure of accomplishment.

SUMMARY OF OBJECTIVE ESTABLISHMENT

This phase of establishing technical objectives and interpreting them is sometimes called the "study" phase. One company considers the technical study phase as consisting of the following steps:

PROJECT ______ PROJECT NO. ______

TASK ______ TASK NO. ______

Assigned to Department ______ Date ______ Dept. No. ______

Cognizant Engineer ______ Date ______

Description & Purpose of Task (General) ______

Work Divisions By Subtasks:
Subtask No. 1 ______
Subtask No. 2 ______
Subtask No. 3 ______
Subtask No. 4 ______

ESTIMATED COSTS

	19__				19__				
	Labor	Indirect	Other Direct	Total	Labor	Indirect	Other Direct	Total	Grand Total
Subtask 1									
Subtask 2									
Subtask 3									
Subtask 4									
Totals									

ESTIMATE OF MANPOWER

	Engrs.' Grade	Engrs.' Grade	Technicians' Grade	Other	Engrs.' Grade	Engrs.' Grade	Technicians' Grade	Other
Subtask 1								
Subtask 2								
Subtask 3								
Subtask 4								
Totals								

Anticipated completion date by "major milestone" for each subtask.

Subtask No. 1 ______
Subtask No. 2 ______
Subtask No. 3 ______
Subtask No. 4 ______

Fig. 8-16. Form for documenting final project plans.

1. Establish customer requirements
2. Establish product design philosophy
3. Select preliminary design approach
4. Identify critical problems and alternative approaches to these problems
5. Plan feasibility program and resources required
6. Estimate the resource requirements for design and production
7. Estimate an end date for the program as an objective.

The first important point to remember about establishing technical objectives is that it is necessary to find out as completely as possible what the customer *desires* and what his requirements really are. The second important point is that the interpretation of the objectives depends greatly on the type of service desired from E & R. By *service* is meant any of the following: research and engineering alone (report of analytical and experimental studies), design of a single component, or the design and construction of a prototype of an integrated system.

BIBLIOGRAPHY

ALLEN, D. H. "Credibility Forecasts and Their Application to the Economic Assessment of Novel Research and Development Projects," *Operations Research Quarterly,* March, 1968.

ANDERSEN, SIGURD L. "Venture Analysis, A Flexible Planning Tool," *Chemical Engineering Progress,* March, 1961.

ASHER, D. T. A Linear Programming Model for the Allocation of R & D Efforts. Paper presented at the 1st Joint ORSA–TIMES Meeting, November, 1961.

BAKER, N. R. and POUND, W. H. "R & D Project Selection," *IEEE Transactions on Engineering Management,* EM 11, December, 1964.

BAUMOL, WILLIAM J. *Economic Theory and Operations Analysis.* Englewood Cliffs, N.J.: Prentice-Hall, Inc., 1961.

BERG, T. L., and SHUCHMAN, ABE, eds. *Product Strategy in Management.* New York, N.Y.: Holt, Rinehart, & Winston, Inc., 1963.

BRIGHT, JAMES R. *Research, Development, and Technological Innovation: An Introduction.* Homewood, Ill.: Richard D. Irwin, Inc., 1964.

———, ed. *Technological Forecasting for Industry and Government.* Englewood Cliffs, N.J.: Prentice-Hall, Inc., 1968.

BUSHNELL, J. L., et al. *An Annotated Bibliography on the Management of Research and Development,* Technical Memorandum No. 100. Cleveland, Ohio: Operations Research Department, Case Western Reserve University, March 1, 1968.

COLLCUTT, R. H., and READER, R. D. "Choosing the Operational Research Programme for B.I.S.R.A.," *Operations Research Quarterly,* Vol. 18, No. 3, September, 1967.

DEAN, B. V., and SENGUPTA, S. S. "Research Budgeting and Project Selection," *IRE Transactions on Engineering Management,* EM 9, December, 1962.

DECISCO, ROBERT W. "Economic Evaluation of Research Projects—By Computer," *Chemical Engineering,* June 3, 1968.

DIMSDALE, B., and FLATT, H. P. "Project Evaluation and Selection," *IBM Systems Journal,* September–December, 1963.

ENKE, STEPHEN. *Defense Management.* Englewood Cliffs, N.J.: Prentice-Hall, Inc., 1967.

ENRICK, NORBERT LLOYD. *Management Operations Research.* New York, N.Y.: Holt, Rinehart & Winston, Inc., 1960.

FISHER, E. J., "Parametric Uncertainty in Military Research & Development Decisions." Ph.D. thesis, Rensselaer Polytechnic Institute, Troy, N.Y., 1969.

FABRYCKY, W. J., and TORGENSEN, PAUL E. *Operations Economy.* Englewood Cliffs, N.J.: Prentice-Hall, Inc., 1966.

FISHBURN, PETER C. *Decision and Value Theory.* New York, N.Y.: John Wiley & Sons, Inc., 1964.

FREIMER, MARSHALL, and SIMON, LEONARD S. "The Evaluation of Potential New Product Alternatives," *Management Science,* February, 1967.

GREEN, PAUL E. "Decision Making in Chemical Marketing," *Industrial & Engineering Chemistry,* September, 1962.

LEDLEY, R. S., et al. "Methodology to Aid Research Manning," *IEEE Transactions on Engineering Management,* June, 1967.

LYTLE, A. A. "The Yardsticks for Research Success," *Product Engineering,* October 19, 1959.

MAGYAR, WILLIAM B. "Economic Evaluation of Engineering Projects," *The Business Quarterly* (University of Western Ontario), Spring, 1968.

MCCREARY, EDWARD A. "How to Grow a Decision Tree," *THINK* (IBM), March–April, 1967.

MEYERSON, MARTIN. "Price of Admission into the Defense Business," *Harvard Business Review,* July–August, 1967.

MILLER, DAVID W., and STARR, MARTIN K. *Executive Decisions and Operations Research.* Englewood Cliffs, N.J.: Prentice-Hall, Inc., 1960.

— —. "A Major Shift in Emphasis," *Developing a Product Strategy,* AMA Report No. 39. New York, N.Y.: American Management Association, Inc., 1968.

MOTTNEY, C. M., and NEWTON, R. D. "The Selection of Projects for Industrial Research," *Operations Research,* November–December, 1959.

MULLINS, PETER LAKE. "A Systems Analysis Approach to Research Allocations for Research and Development Activities." Ph.D. dissertation, Stanford University Business School, August, 1967.

O'MEARA, JOHN T., JR. "Selecting Products," *Harvard Business Review,* January–February, 1961.

REEVES, E. DUER. *Management of Industrial Research.* New York, N.Y.: Reinhold Publishing Corp., 1967.

ROBERTS, E. B. *The Dynamics of Research and Development.* New York, N.Y.: Harper and Row, Publishers, 1964.

ROMAN, DANIEL D. *Research and Development Management.* New York, N.Y.: Appleton-Century-Crofts, 1968.

RUBENSTEIN, ALBERT H., and DEAN, B. V., eds. *Operations Research in Research and Development.* New York, N.Y.: John Wiley & Sons, Inc., 1963.

SEILER, ROBERT E. *Improving the Effectiveness of Research and Development.* New York, N.Y.: McGraw-Hill Book Company, 1965.

SIMON, H. A. *The New Science of Management Decisions.* New York, N.Y.: Harper and Row, Publishers, 1960.

SOBELMAN, SIDNEY. *A Modern Dynamic Approach to Product Development.* Department of Commerce, Office of Technical Services, No. PB151649. Washington, D.C.: U.S. Government Printing Office, 1958.

SOUDER, WILLIAM E. "Selecting and Staffing R & D Projects via Op Research," *Chemical Engineering Progress,* November, 1967.

SPROW, FRANK B. "Evaluation of Research Expenditures Using Triangular Distribution Functions and Monte Carlo Methods," *Industrial and Engineering Chemistry,* July, 1967.

VILLERS, RAYMOND. *Research and Development: Planning and Control.* New York, N.Y.: Financial Executives Institute, 1964.

WEINBERGER, ARTHUR J. "Estimating Sales and Markets," *Chemical Engineering,* January 20, 1964.

CHAPTER 9

Project Management

With the advent of large defense systems and the rapid advances in science and technology, new management techniques were required to manage the development of such complex systems. The traditional stable E & R organizational patterns proved inadequate for the giant steps in engineering design. Neither were such organizations able to compress time schedules, maintain work on different design phases in parallel, or control the myriad of details in large projects.

WHAT IS PROJECT MANAGEMENT?

Project management is a form of organization and a philosophy of action that focuses responsibility on a project manager for attainment of project objectives. The goals of the project are specific, the time limitations for the project are defined, and the resources to be employed are negotiated by the project manager with his superiors.

Projects usually cut across many disciplines and draw upon many resources within the company. They are concerned with "systems" or complex products so that project management is sometimes referred to as "systems management," "program management," or "product management."

The need for a project management approach is evident when:

1. The scope of the present organization does not contain the technical resources required so that outside vendors and suppliers are required
2. Integration of the project's activities will disrupt the work schedules of the present organization
3. Coordination with either a customer with larger system responsibilities

or major suppliers of subsystems suggests the establishment of a parallel project organization
4. Compressed time schedules and fixed fee or penalty contracts require extremely close control and clearly defined responsibility for results
5. Major innovation is required so that creative people who prefer stimulation to security will be attracted.

It should be emphasized that the techniques developed for management of large projects can be cut down and tailored to small projects in smaller companies to yield lower costs and higher profits.

DISTINGUISHING CHARACTERISTICS

The distinguishing characteristics of a project management approach are:

1. Goal, task and subtask responsibilities well defined
2. Limited life
3. Project oriented organization
4. Dynamically changing organization and responsibilities
5. Frequent reporting for coordination and progress evaluation
6. Tight cost control tied in with technical progress by task, subtask, and shop order
7. Participants outside the company over which project management has only weak control.

A number of major advantages of the project management approach were given in Chapter 3. A summary of these and others are:

1. Better control and measurement of project progress
2. Clearly defined responsibility and full time effort of individuals on the project
3. Shorter product development time and hence usually lower cost
4. Improved quality and reliability
5. Opportunity to identify leaders and creative individuals in shorter time span. Also, weeds out the weaker engineers and scientists who cannot work under pressure
6. Higher morale because of group cohesion in striving towards challenging goals within compressed time schedules
7. Changing organizational relationships stimulates many engineers and scientists and broadens their understanding of related disciplines
8. Improves customer and vendor relationships
9. Configuration control is more easily attained.

The major disadvantages are:

1. The difficulty of finding or training good project managers

2. Complexity of organizational planning and hence possible lower utilization of personnel
3. Necessity to synchronize transfer of resources from dying projects to growing projects
4. Any snag that delays the coordinated design operation of the project can cause snowballing cost overruns
5. Time-pressure may stifle creativity
6. Competition among project managers for services of key men and common resources such as engineering laboratory work
7. Duplication of functional skills among projects and lack of close association of people with similar skills.

PROJECT ORGANIZATION

The two basic types of project organization, project line organization and project staff organization were discussed in Chapter 3. The life cycle of the project organization, in more detail, consists of six phases:

1. *Exploration phase.* A small group of key engineers investigate or develop general specifications, attempt to identify major problem areas, and classify the major tasks to be performed. This group may be a loose coalition or be guided part time by the future project manager. Their job is primarily technical exploration and their output is a report.
2. *Startup phase.* When a project manager is assigned full time after the exploratory phase and a commitment to the project has been made by management, the project starts up. This may be at a low rate of commitment of resources during what is essentially a critical planning stage.
3. *Growth phase.* When the planning and programming are well advanced, implementation of plans takes place by means of a rapid buildup of the project organization. Key men to head task-based organizational components are chosen and they in turn seek to complete the staffing of these components.
4. *Maturity phase.* When the project organization reaches its peak strength, it is likely to remain close to this level for an extended period of time to accomplish the design goals. Shifts in organization within the project are continuous as emphasis shifts from one aspect of the design to another.
5. *Decline phase.* As the major design problems are overcome and the design becomes well advanced, the project is able to gradually free some of its people until finally only a few are left to handle communication and customer problems. Careful planning and consid-

eration of each individual engineer must be involved as transfers to other projects are made.

6. *Phase out.* When delivery of the system has been accepted by the customer, the project may be officially terminated. Often, however, one or two men may be assigned to follow up the performance of the equipment over a period of a year and be available to assist the customer throughout this period.

Although the line project organization form offers greater control than staff project management and functional hierarchies for large projects, the project manager must still be capable of applying nondefined persuasion and power. He must be able to influence the quality of work and the time schedules of many vendors supplying engineering service and system components. He must be able to negotiate with top management and other project managers for utilization of centralized in-house services when he needs them. He must also deal with the customer as development proceeds and negotiate such changes in specifications as appear justified by new knowledge.

PLANNING AND PROGRAMMING

Project planning is concerned with developing the major goal and tasks of the project, the resources required, the organization, and the information decision and control system. Planning must be tied into a master budget.

Programming is the up-dated detailed planning for implementing the basic project plan. Programming is a basic tool of management for gathering, integrating, and interpreting available information with respect to objectives, manpower, materials, facilities, cost, and time. In addition, variances of actual from planned performance can be identified and depicted. In a slightly more detailed fashion, programming can aid in the following areas of managerial concern:

Project objectives. Programming is concerned with assisting management in obtaining the specific technical, cost, time, and manpower objectives of the project within the framework already established by management.

Manpower. Efficient utilization of manpower is of major importance in a project where many highly skilled people are employed. The programming staff can aid in preparing and integrating manpower projections and in preparing related records used for control and measurement.

Materials and facilities. Lead time for ordering materials must be taken into account. When scarce materials must be made available, plans must be made for special following and expediting. Allocation of facilities among projects should be planned to avoid critical delays or idle

facilities. If construction of special buildings or installations are required, these must be planned for in terms of men, money, and time.
Costs. Of course, costs are of vital importance in any business. The fact that greater detail concerning management-established project objectives and the manpower and hardware requirements are available makes it possible to be far more accurate in budgeting and cost estimation than by using the old rule-of-thumb and experience methods. Also of help is the fact that the programming staff is in an excellent position to correlate the historical data and analyses of the accounting group with project objectives and progress.
Time. This basic element of programming is expressed by time schedules. The master schedule shows the time objective for each major task. The detailed schedules show the time required to accomplish each major and/or minor step in the project plan. The element of time must be tied closely to manpower requirements, to the budget, and to progress—all leading up to the eventual delivery of designs, data, and hardware.
Measurement and control. Programming, if properly carried out, permits management control by exception. Management must be kept informed about variances of actual performance from planned progress. Potential trouble spots can be detected early through the control aspects of programming so that management can take action to avert serious problems.

Programming should be conducted at two levels:

1. Programming the entire E & R work by making sure that entire projects are phased properly with respect to each other. New projects or product developments must be planned so that as the old ones draw towards completion, the new ones are started up.
2. Individual projects or product programs must be planned and scheduled.

The purpose of programming is the optimum allocation of resources so as to achieve E & R objectives within specified constraints such as those of cost and time. In any engineering project, programming is carried out whether it is done by: (1) scribbling notes on a calendar pad; (2) documenting by letters; (3) conducting elaborate investigating and reporting techniques; or (4) a specially trained staff using operations research and large electronic computers. The underlying process in any case should be as shown in Fig. 9-1.

In fundamental structure, a research and engineering program is similar to any other program such as, for example, a factory production program. In each case, a series of events or tasks must be defined and accomplished in a logical sequence so as to achieve an ultimate goal.

Three factors, however, apply to research and engineering which have

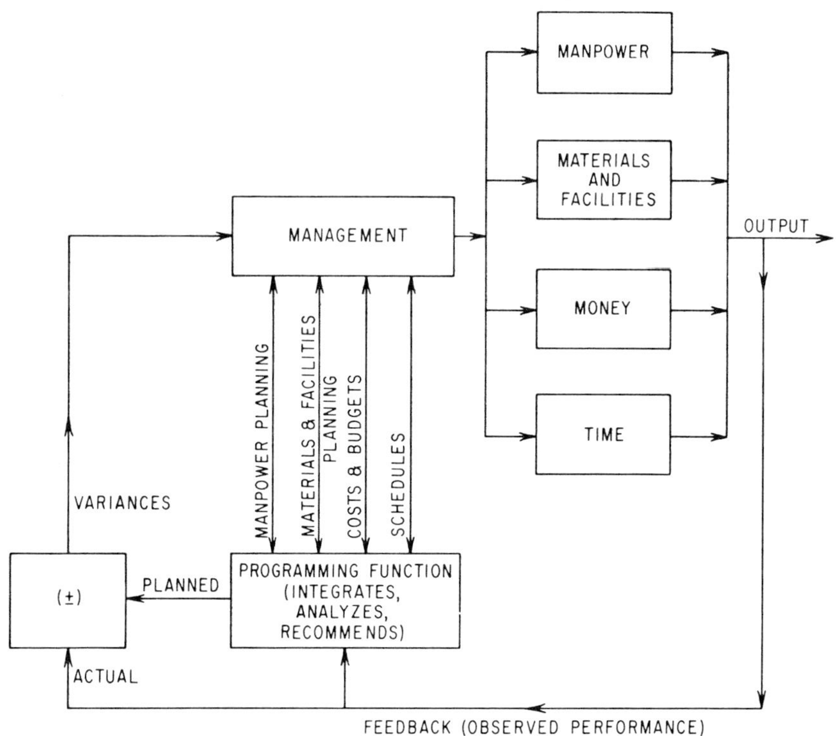

Fig. 9-1. The programming process.

in the past made attempts at programming such work a matter of intense controversy. First, research and engineering are primarily creative and intellectual activities rather than physical activities, and opponents of such programming attempts have claimed that creativity cannot be scheduled. Secondly, there are no guides to scheduling since research and engineering are pioneering by nature, nonrepetitive, and therefore involve events or tasks never before experienced—in fact, many times involving not even similar experiences. Thirdly, the results of research and engineering are unpredictable so that frequent changes in program emphasis and detail are required.

Fortunately, a number of factors contribute to make possible an orderly approach to planning. Despite the unpredictability of results and the unknown time for a particular solution to be reached, if ever, it must be recognized and conceded that *some* problems can be scheduled on the basis of past experience. Where difficult problems are foreseen, alternative approaches can be carried out in parallel and a time schedule for each approach can be estimated. Furthermore, there has always been the compromise factor in engineering—usually it involves settling for a less desirable solution within the time constraint rather than trying for a perfect solution in the indefinite future. Finally, massive concentration on critical problems through careful planning will be apt to achieve project objectives that cannot be reached in any other way.

ORGANIZING FOR PROGRAMMING

In a very small engineering organization of up to about ten engineers, the manager may simply establish start and completion dates, roughly estimate costs, and work out task assignments and schedules with his engineers. In slightly larger organizations, the individual engineers may program their own jobs as assigned and submit the programs to the manager of E & R for integration, approval, and control purposes.

It costs anywhere from $25,000 to $50,000 a year to support an engineer or scientist. This includes his salary, overhead, and supporting technical personnel.[1] In 1965 the average cost was $40,600. It is evident that poor programming can result in major losses. In a ten-man organization of engineers, a schedule slippage of 5 percent would be equivalent to the annual salaries for two programmers. The project manager of even small projects should, therefore, give serious consideration to employing at least one full-time programmer.

There are basically three ways to organize for programming. In a functional organization, the programmer or manager of programming is on the same organizational level as the functional managers and reports as they do to the manager of E & R.

In the line project organization, the manager of programming may report directly to the manager of E & R just as the project managers do. A second approach is to have programmers assigned to the project organization and to report to the individual project managers. While the second method does not permit easy integration of all projects, it does make the work of the programmers more effective. They are viewed as part of the project organization rather than "spies" from outside.

In organizing the programming group itself, it often pays to study the major engineering organizational components that will be served and to parallel these as much as possible. The advantages of this are:

1. A minimum number of people from the programming group will be contacting each engineering component.
2. The programmer who works constantly with one engineering function will become well-versed in this type of work and be of maximum service.

[1] The "performance cost" or total E & R performance funds divided by the total number of engineers and scientists is given for the Federal Government, private industry, universities, and other non-profit groups is given in *National Patterns of R & D Resources,* 1953–1968, NSF 67–7 prepared by The National Science Foundation.

3. The work of the various programming specialists can be easily integrated within the programming group.

PROGRAMMERS

Although a number of companies employ engineers as programmers, others have been highly successful using technicians or high-caliber women college graduates. For women with a degree in mathematics, physics, chemistry, or some similar background, programming provides a stimulating and challenging job. Companies that use engineers often find the engineers overqualified and unwilling to serve long in such a capacity. Also, there is a competitve feeling between the programming engineers and the design engineers. Friction may develop when the programming engineer attempts to influence the design or make suggestions. Women, on the other hand, generally possess the tact and perseverance required to dig details out of design engineers who are reluctant to take time out from the design job; at the same time they usually won't try to compete on the engineering level.

PROGRAMMING FOR COMPLEX PROJECTS

Whether the program information is analyzed and shuffled by means of charts and trial and error or whether modern mathematical methods are used, the basic work of the programmers remains the same. For the sake of simplicity and clarity, programming is first described as it was and still may be carried out without using the relatively new mathematical methods. In actual practice, the gap between the old and the new is not as great as has been implied. The old methods have been used by skilled programmers to plan parallel efforts, to shorten time schedules, to locate long lead times, to determine critical paths, and to shorten over-all schedules by showing where crash programs are needed. The disadvantage of the old method is that changes cannot be made as rapidly as they can with methods employing computers; the programmers themselves have to recompute and shift schedules.

The programming work is, for simplicity, first amplified upon by following the programming process by the old method. For further simplification, the effort is described in terms of the following phases of a project:

1. Conceptual phase
2. Formative phase
3. Operational phase
4. Terminal phase.

Programming in the Conceptual Phase

A project is first conceived when a customer or potential customer states his requirements in general terms. The interested company responds by finding out as much as possible about the customer's objectives and then prepares a proposal. If the order is received, the project is next initiated, usually by establishing broad objectives and by appointing a project manager.

At this point, the project will develop in either of two ways. In one case, a small study team of senior engineers may make feasibility studies of various conceptual designs. With such a small group, this preliminary work can run from a few months to one or more years, depending on the size of the project. In the other case, the project may be staffed rapidly to near-peak strength. The personnel are first grouped into study teams, each to develop and evaluate the feasibility of a concept.

In this conceptual phase, the technical-programming group plays a big part. Programmers establish reasonable schedules from skimpy assumptions, supply data to assist in making sound manpower estimates, evaluate costs and equipment requirements, and generally assist in developing a convincing and logical presentation to the customer.

The customer usually has the right to evaluate the basic conceptual work. If the customer accepts the proposed concept and a contract to proceed is involved, the conceptual phase of the project usually continues for a while longer. During this period, conceptual engineering-design work is carried on. Concurrent with conceptual design, the programming groups prepare a preliminary list of tasks—specific work "packages." After the Preliminary Task List is developed, a brief description of the scope of the work and the specific goals for each task is prepared. This Task List may show preliminary manpower requirements and cost estimates.

Programming in the Formative Phase

Once the conceptual design is developed, the project begins to take shape and enters the formative phase. Programming in the formative phase aids in firmly establishing the major tasks, which are then divided further into subtasks for easier planning and following.

Having established the major tasks, the programmers, working with the engineers, plan the major steps or "milestones" for completion of the tasks. Figures 9-2a and 9-2b show in outline form what is involved in establishing milestones for a task. Each item must be examined carefully to determine its effect on other related items with respect to both initiation and completion.

Detailed schedules are then made up for each milestone in each subtask, Fig. 9-3. If there are conflicts in the over-all Milestone Chart, this

MILESTONE PROGRAM

Subtask 6.5 Control Units

Milestones	Date
1. Issue the application specification.	________
2. Complete component evaluation tests to establish design.	________
3. Issue firm equipment specification for prototype units to customer for approval.	________
4. Place order for prototype unit and final units.	________
5. Order materials for prototype unit.	________
6. Release manufacture of prototype unit.	________
7. Perform acceptance tests on prototype unit.	________
8. Order long-delivery materials for production unit.	________
9. Start manufacture of production units.	________
10. Start acceptance tests of production units.	________
11. Deliver production units.	________

Fig. 9-2a. Milestone program for one subtask. *Source of Figs. 9-2a to 9-5:* R. G. Murdick and A. B. Oppenheim, "Programing for Complex Projects," *Machine Design* (October 2, 1958).

CHECK LIST FOR MILESTONES

1. Do scheduled completion dates for each milestone appear reasonable?
2. Does the last milestone date meet the deadline for the total job?
3. Are these milestones the most significant among all the steps to be performed?
4. Are they definable and reportable facts?
5. Do they concisely represent progress (or lack of progress if not accomplished on schedule).
6. Are they in the proper chronological sequence, and do they disclose an effective process for successfully accomplishing the total job?
7. Are these milestones which will permit attainment of the stated purposes?
8. Do these milestones generally relate to the total job to be done, rather than to the major components?

Fig. 9-2b. Check list for milestone. *Source:* See Fig. 9-2a.

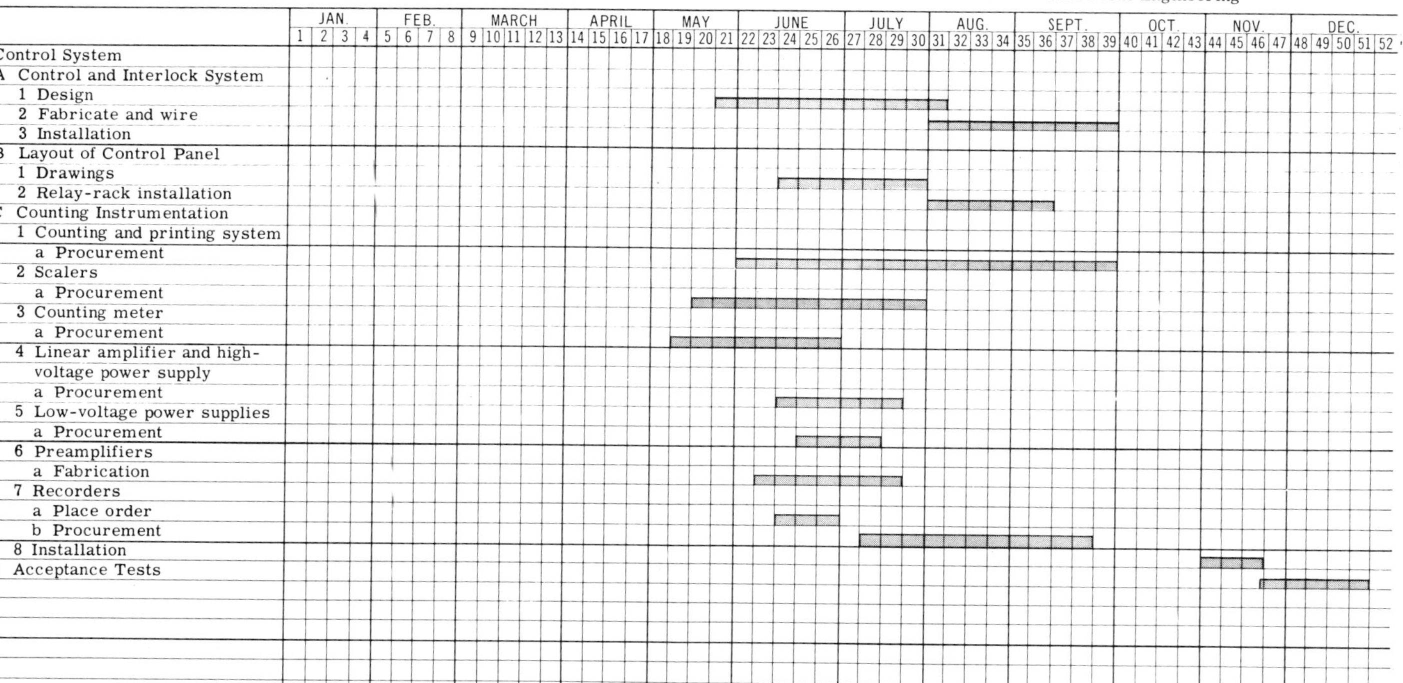

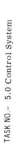

Fig. 9-3. Detailed schedule dovetails the milestones for all subtasks. *Source:* See Fig. 9-2a.

final detailing will expose them. Detailed schedules are important for both control and measurement purposes.

Detailed schedules are revised as necessary so that people working from them will be assigned to jobs in proper sequence. Typical detailed steps leading up to a normal first milestone, "Design Specifications, Customer-Approved," are:

1. Complete the preliminary investigation
2. Establish the direction of the design
3. Prepare specification and initiate quotations for the development unit
4. Order the development unit
5. Fabricate and test development unit
6. Evaluate test data and establish design requirements for production units
7. Prepare production unit specifications
8. Obtain appropriate internal specification comments
9. Complete final specifications and submit to customer for approval
10. Receive customer approval of specifications.

As soon as feasible, prepare a bill of materials listing each system, its components, and the quantity required. The involved organizational elements should be given copies. The bill of materials should be kept up to date as the project progresses since it is used as a control and for the placement of orders.

There are three major problems that arise in project organization:

1. Achieving build-up of manpower as the project starts to accelerate
2. Obtaining personnel with the required specialized training and experience
3. Redistributing people to other projects as the project tapers off.

The programming group, by integrating all available information and preparing short- and long-range forecasts, helps management deal with these problems more effectively.

Budgeting and cost control are important for any profit-motivated company. Programming relates costs to tasks, manpower, materials, and time. The milestones and milestone dates are worked out by the programming group in discussions with the task leaders. Next, the manpower and material required to accomplish each milestone are estimated by the cognizant engineer. Programmers and engineers next develop the manpower and material required each quarter, or even each month, for each task and for the entire project. This information is used to calculate the funds required for such a program.

At this stage, the complete program for the project will have been worked out in some detail. This program should now be reviewed by the programming staff and by the engineers by asking questions such as:

1. Are the milestones and milestone dates for each task consistent and tight—but not too tight?
2. Is the manpower build-up by numbers and kinds of personnel reasonable and possible?
3. Are the costs of the tasks and over-all program reasonable and economical?

When the program is reviewed in this critical manner, some changes are usually required. Programming has the function of continuously monitoring in this critical manner throughout the life of the project.

Because the programming group must maintain an intimate knowledge of all work of the project, it is desirable to include the project reporting and project procedures functions within this group. Although periodic and special reports for each task must be written by the responsible engineers, the programming group can integrate these into a consistent report, prepare summaries for management, and edit and handle the publication of the project reports.

For the same reasons, the programming staff is in the best position to detect procedural problems and prepare, for management approval, procedures for efficient and consistent project operations. This is no small chore, since many procedures must be prepared early in the project and should serve as long as possible. Although procedures are continually changed throughout the life of the project, each change or new procedure usually produces a temporary faltering in some portion of the operation. Therefore, it is desirable to keep new procedures to a minimum and to depend upon the previous experience of the programming group to maintain good continuity with previously satisfactory procedures.

Programming in the Operational Phase

A leveling off of the total number of people in the project is a characteristic of the operational phase. At this time the program is fairly well-stabilized with respect to objectives, milestones, and detailed schedules.

During the operational phase the prime function of the programming group is to provide the tools of measurement to the project manager. Programmers will follow all details of the project—design, fabrication, construction, costs, and schedules; they report variances and the effects of such variances immediately to management. Proper use of programming permits the project manager to take preventive or corrective action before the variance damage becomes serious.

Programming provides more than a guide for the path ahead. It provides a measure of how closely the path has been and is being followed and to what degree goals have been attained. It answers such questions as:

1. Was each function, task, and component well organized?
2. Are the number and types of people available when needed?
3. Was the original schedule reasonable, or was performance poor as measured by a good schedule?
4. What critical items jeopardize the entire schedule at any given time?
5. Is there failure in meeting milestone dates in one particular area, and if so, why?
6. Were the cost estimates good?
7. Were and are the costs within the budget, and if not, which tasks are running in excess?

Project Design, Construction, and Installation

Weighted Percentage-

Complete Report

Milestones	Cumulative Percent Complete
1. Establish conceptual design of equipment	14
2. Obtain customer approval of conceptual design	17
3. Develop new or specialized mechanical components	25
4. Develop new or specialized electrical components	30
5. Build prototypes and breadboard models of new or specialized components	36
6. Complete test facilities	--
7. Complete tests of prototypes and breadboard models	--
8. Initiate procurement of long lead items	--
9. Complete production drawings and obtain approval as required	--
10. Complete material ordering	--
11. Complete equipment assembly	--
12. Complete performance tests	--
13. Ship equipment and instruction books	--
14. Supervise installation of lead equipment	--

Fig. 9-4. Weighted percentage — complete report. *Source:* See Fig. 9-2a.

Besides the charts discussed for planning, supplementary charts and reports are used for measuring and controlling. The Critical-Items Report, a weekly report on items seriously affecting the overall schedule, may be used. Another helpful report is the Weighted Percentage-Complete Report, Fig. 9-4. Two useful control charts shown in Fig. 9-5 relate to costs. One is a plot of monthly cost versus the budgeted cost for each month. The other is the cumulative cost to date plotted on the same chart with the budgeted cumulative cost. A breakdown of indirect costs

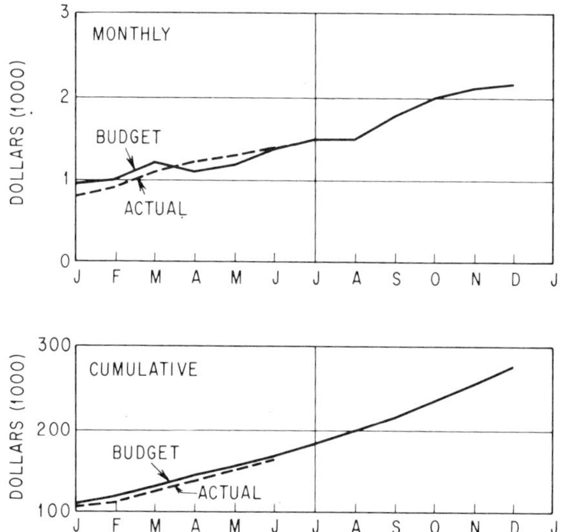

Fig. 9-5. Monthly and cumulative budget plots. *Source:* See Fig. 9-2a.

and a comparison of indirect expense with the applied rate can also be handled by the programming activity. It is not implied that programming takes over accounting functions, but rather that from prompt, well-planned accounting reports, programmers can analyze, evaluate, and prepare reports for management.

Programming in the Terminal Phase

The terminal phase of a project requires, perhaps, the most careful or closest planning by the programming staff. Design engineering work drops off rapidly while construction proceeds at peak rate until it is completed. The mix of types of expenditures changes rapidly. It is at this time that bottlenecks or "bugs" may occur which require increased efforts. The programming staff must follow schedules, procurement, and construction especially closely to anticipate problems far enough in advance to permit forestalling them.

When the entire project is completed, programmers review the project performance, prepare an analysis of variances from plans, and make recommendations for succeeding projects.

PROGRAM EVALUATION REVIEW TECHNIQUES (PERT)

Purpose

The need for better ways of allocating resources in research and engineering projects has grown as these projects become more complex and costly. For defense contracts, time is often the most critical factor—not the dollar cost. The manager of a large project today must be able to follow rapid changes in progress, costs, schedules, delivery dates, etc., in order to guide an "army" of engineers and scientists towards successful completion of the project. Intuition is helpless in the face of such complexity.

Logic systems have, therefore, been developed which interrelate the many activities and events of a project so as to permit achievement of project goals. These systems require the use of high-speed computers with large storage capacity if they are to be of practical assistance. There are actually two basic systems which have been developed, PERT and CPM. PERT is the abbreviation for Program Evaluation Review Technique and CPM stands for Critical Path Method. PEP, Program Evaluation Procedure, is similar to PERT and was developed by the Air Force.

PERT was originally conceived of as a project monitoring device. It was developed in 1958 by a team composed of members from Booz, Allen & Hamilton, Lockheed's Missile and Space Division, and the Special Projects Office of the Navy. The objectives of PERT, as given by the Navy, are as follows:

1. The fostering of increased orderliness and consistency in the planning and evaluating of all areas of the project
2. The providing of an automatic mechanism for the identification of potential trouble spots in all areas which arise as a result of a failure in one
3. The structuring of a method to give operational flexibility to the program by allowing for experimentation in a simulated sense
4. The speedy handling of an analysis of the integrated data in order to permit timely preventive or corrective action.

PERT has had several generations of improvement. The first generation was that used for the development of Polaris. It was concerned with scheduling and controlling *time* and is now usually identified as PERT/time. Second and third generations of PERT have been completed which deal with the problems of cost and reliabilty. PERT methods dealing with cost are now referred to as PERT/cost. Cost, or resource, information is integrated with the time information in an attempt to evaluate performance or reliability measurement and control. The aim is to provide an early look at reliability problems in order to make the most useful allocation of resources.

Definitions

Some definitions are first introduced in order to explain PERT. These definitions will themselves take on greater significance as the explanation continues.

ACTIVITY—An activity is a time-consuming process in research and engineering. It is the work-in-process between two points or events in time. Activities may include design, analyses, fabrication, testing, etc. An activity is represented by an arrow in PERT network diagrams. The length of the arrow has no significance at all.

ACTIVITY TIME—Estimates of the time required to complete an activity in a specified manner are called activity times. There are three kinds of estimates:

1. *Optimistic time* which is the shortest time in which an activity can be completed if there are no "hitches" or misfortunes.
2. *Most likely time* which is the best estimated time to complete the activity under normal working conditions. This is the modal estimate or the time that would occur most often if the activity were repeated under exactly the same conditions many times.
3. *Pessimistic time* which is the longest time an activity would take if major changes in approach or design were required, i.e., the project was more difficult than appeared at first study.

CRITICAL PATH—A particular sequence of activities from the beginning to the end of the project for which there is no slack and, therefore, a slippage of any event would be expected to produce the slippage in the final event.

EVENT—An event is a specific accomplishment recognizable as a particular instant in time.

FLOW CHART, NETWORK, OR FLOW PLAN—A network is a diagram or topological representation of the project made up of one or more series of sequential events joined by activity lines to show the time interrelationships among events.

SLACK OR FLOAT TIME—Excess of time available over the time required to complete an activity.

Slack Paths—Slack paths are sequences of activities which have excess time as opposed to critical (or zero) slack paths. It is also possible to have negative slack. Positive slack means that there is flexibility within the path.

Pert Times—

t_e—*expected interval* of time which an *activity* will require

T_E—*expected point* in time at which an *activity* will be completed This is identical with "earliest time" for an event and is obtained by adding the t_e's for each path to the event in question and finding the path for which this sum is maximum.

T_L—*latest point* in time (latest date) at which an event can be reached without delaying the schedule

T_S—*scheduled time* for an event established independently of PERT, against which progress is measured.

Milestone—Milestones are significant events or selected points on which progress information is needed in order to evaluate performance with regard to meeting final project objectives.

How PERT Works

Drawing the Network. In applying PERT to a project, the project must be represented by a network of interdependent activities and events. As the first step, the project manager must define the objective of the project. Programmers then work with the engineering organizations to dig out information and help define tasks and subtasks. When the project has thus been subdivided in detail, programmers then prepare a summary network with major milestones as events. This summary network is presented to engineering management for review before a detailed network is prepared.

An alternative approach to developing the networks is the team approach. A typical team would include a leader from the electrical engineering field, one from mechanical engineering, a drafting supervisor, plus representatives from manufacturing, quality control, and purchasing. A workable team should be limited to about eight people. A programmer should chair the meetings. The time required of this team for planning, network development, and time estimating is about two to three hours per 100 events. Later, networks can be developed and refined by programmers on the basis of decisions and information developed at the team meetings.

To draw the networks, the program lists every detailed subtask to be accomplished. Then, starting with the final objective he works *backward* in developing the network. Each event should be labeled or coded, and all events should be checked to make sure that they are in the proper sequence. An illustration of a simple coded network is given in Fig. 9-6.

To be sure that all activities are represented and in proper sequence the following questions should be asked about each:

1. What activities immediately follow this activity?
2. What activities can be performed concurrently?
3. What activities immediately precede this activity?

It is also important to note that:

1. Every network can have only *one* beginning event.
2. Every network can have only *one* ending event, and all activities must lead to this event.
3. Two or more activities which are performed concurrently after a single event cannot be represented by the same arrow. A dummy event (38) must therefore be introduced as shown in Fig. 9-6 with a dummy activity requiring zero time to complete. The concurrent activities are *a* and *b*.

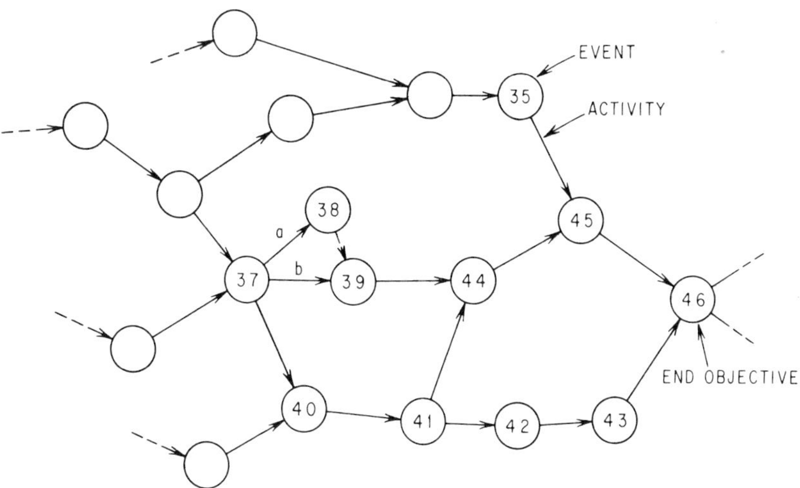

Fig. 9-6. PERT network.

Estimates of Activity Times. Three estimates of time are required—the earliest, the most likely and the latest or most pessimistic. These time estimates deal with the future, and the further into the future these times extend, the higher will be the uncertainty and the lower the validity. In order to make them as accurate and valid as possible, one view holds that these estimates should be obtained from the person responsible for carrying out the activity. Another view is that a higher degree of objectivity should be introduced, such as having the estimates developed within a group consisting of all of the people involved. While much more could be said about these estimates, they are the most authoritative available.

From these three times (earliest, most likely, and latest), the "expected" or mean time to complete the activity and the variance of the expected time (expected time as defined in PERT) can be calculated. Figure 9-7

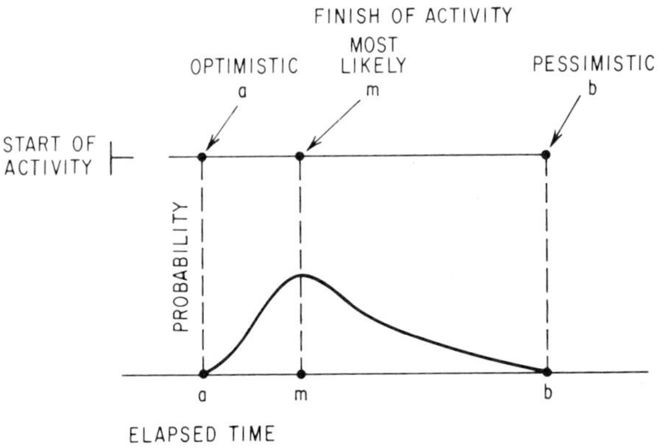

Fig. 9-7. Estimating the time distribution for completion of an activity.

shows a probability distribution for the estimated time for completing an activity. Note that the most likely time locates the peak of the curve. Figure 9-8 shows the computation of the expected time, t_e. For practi-

The four curves below show conceivable probability distributions of anticipated completion times. Essentially all possible completion times will lie between a to b. The calculated mean times fall near the center of the range except as affected by lack of symmetry of the distribution.

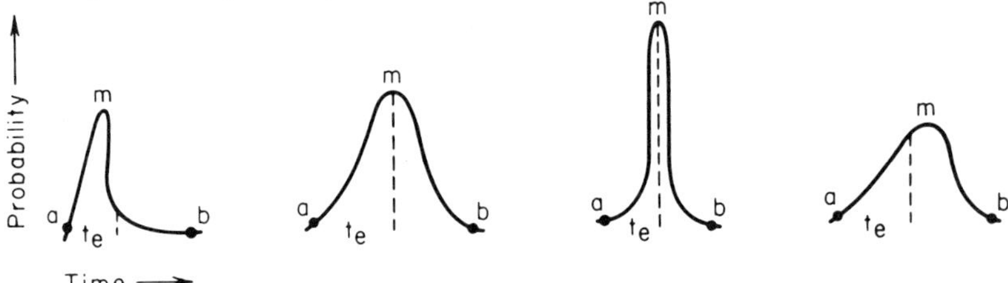

Activity time estimates:

a = optimistic

m = most likely

b = pessimistic

Mean time to complete activity is:

$$t_e = \frac{a + 4m + b}{6}$$

(A computer is often used to calculate this for each activity)

Fig. 9-8. Calculation of mean activity time from activity time estimates.

cal purposes, it is assumed that the standard deviation is one-sixth of the range between the pessimistic and optimistic times.*

Halcomb Associates of Sunnyvale, California, markets a pocket-sized plastic, circular, slide rule which is designed to handle all necessary computations for a PERT project (shown in Fig. 9-9). This device, known as PERT-O-Graph II, Critical Path Computer, brings PERT's efficiencies to companies other than those engaged in developing huge systems where computers arc essential. It is a useful tool in small project management and new

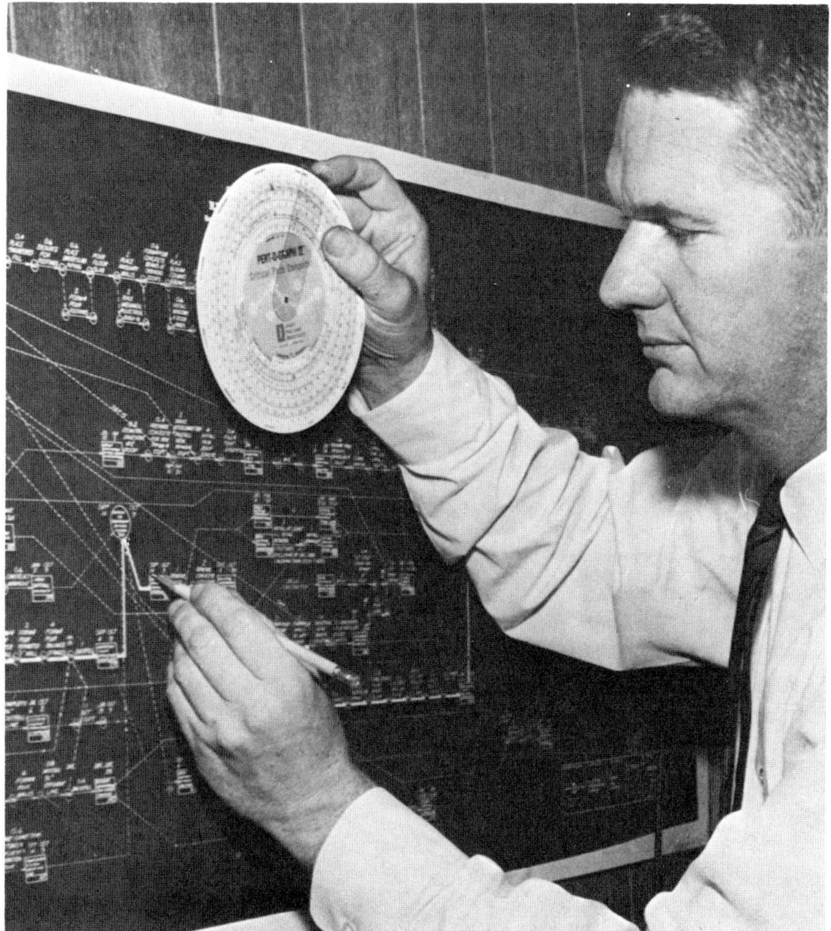

Fig. 9-9. Simple disk-type computer for PERT calculations.

* The probability distribution of the expected (in the statistical sense of average or mean) time of an activity is assumed to be the beta distribution $f(t) =$ (constant) $(t - a)^{\alpha} (b - t)^{\gamma}$ where α and γ are functions of a, b, and m.

product development. A Project Manager's PERT/CPM Handbook is also supplied as part of a kit.

By using the standard deviation as calculated above (which, together with the expected time, establishes a normal probability curve), the probability of meeting scheduled dates can be estimated. See Fig. 9-10.

The slack time is calculated simply as $T_L - T_E$, the latest time an activity can be completed minus the earliest time an activity can be completed. Any complete path from the beginning event to the end event which has zero slack, i.e., $T_L = T_E$, is a critical path.

Shaded area is an estimate of the chances:

1. Determine $= \dfrac{T_S - T_E}{\sigma_{T_E}} = Z$

   where: T_S = Scheduled date

   T_E = Expected date

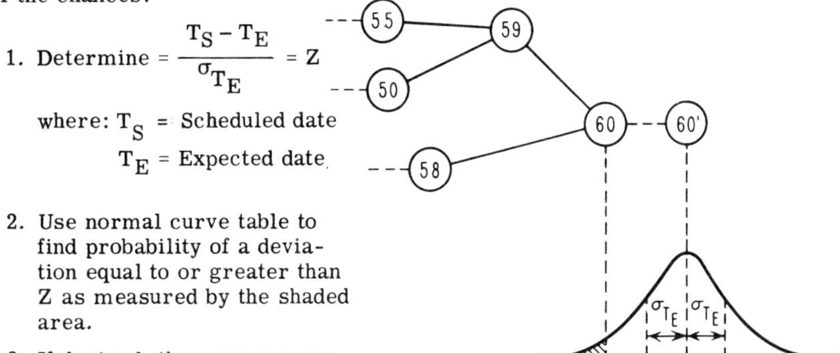

2. Use normal curve table to find probability of a deviation equal to or greater than Z as measured by the shaded area.
3. If desired, the programmer may use the normal curve table and determine the probability that T_E falls between two selected limits such as $T_E \pm \sigma_{T_E}$.

Fig. 9-10. Estimate of probability of meeting scheduled date, T_s.

A typical computer report, which might be issued weekly or biweekly, is shown in Fig. 9-11. Through such reports as these, the project may be monitored. Reports indicate where slack exists, where the probability of meeting schedules is getting low, and suggest where trade-off of resources tc gain time is advisable. Thus, PERT is a tool for management by exception.

"PerTree"

Detailed PERT charts, computer "print-outs," etc. are so detailed that management usually wants some kind of summarized report. The "PerTree," apparently devised by AEC and NASA, is one way of summarizing the results of PERT programming. It utilized concepts borrowed from PERT, Gantt charting, and conventional flow charting. Its main features are illustrated in Fig. 9-12.

The same general approach can also be utilized in summarizing Critical Path Programs, the next technique to be described in this text.

PROJECT STATUS REPORT												
PROJECT: MARK 93 GROUND SUPPORT					CONTRACT NO. 98-7865				REPORT DATE: 11/30/61			
IDENTIFICATION				TIME STATUS					COST STATUS			
Charge or Summary No.	Level*	Begin Event No.	End Event No.	Sched. Elapsed Time (weeks)	Date Com-pleted	Earliest Completion Date (S_E)	Latest Completion Date (S_L)	Activity Slack (weeks) (S_L-S_E)	Actual To Date $	Contract Estimate $	Latest Revised Estimate $	Overrun (Underrun) $
71831070	6	598	599	9.0	1/30/71	12/21/71	12/30/71	1.3	5,600	5,600	5,600	
71831072	6	601	602	1.0		05/03/72	03/30/72	-4.8		1,450	1,650	200
670057		590	602			05/03/72		-4.8	5,600	28,300	24,200	(4,100)
71831083		565	568			04/02/72	04/27/72	3.6				
		577	578			05/09/72	04/27/72	-1.7				
	6	565	578			05/09/72		-1.7	2,740	14,700	14,700	
670037	5	590	610			05/27/72		-1.7	129,000	660,000	657,900	(2,100)
670016	4	001	999			01/31/73		-4.8	889,000	3,640,000	3,665,200	25,200

*SUMMARY LEVEL
- 6. Charge Level
- 5. Time and Cost Summary at Major Hardware Level
- 4. Time and Cost Summary at Subsystem Level

Fig. 9-11. Project status report. *Source:* Based on *PERT Cost Systems Design*, DOD and NASA Guide, Office of the Secretary of the Defense, National Aeronautics and Space Administration, Washington 25, D.C. (June 1962).

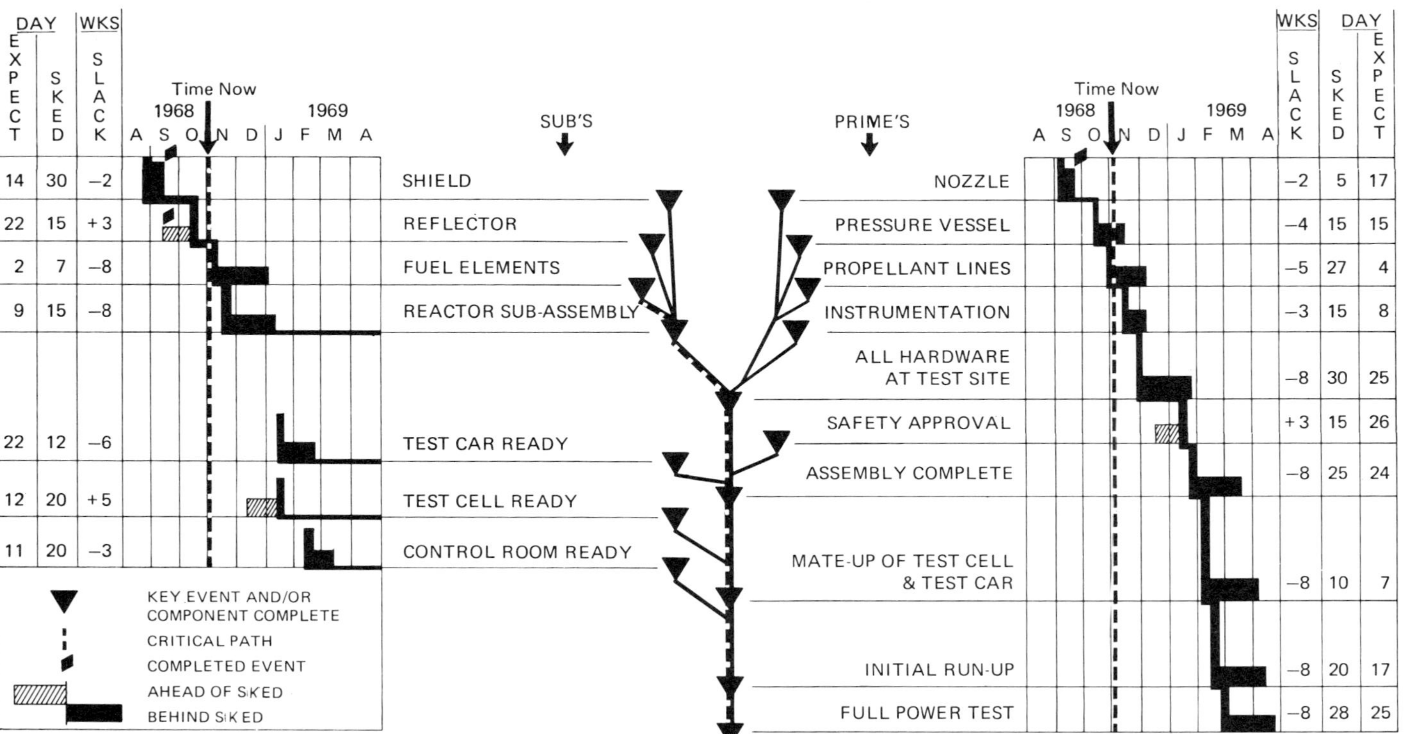

Fig. 9-12. PerTree for experimental nuclear engine. *Source:* Brief 67-10568, AEC-NASA Space Nuclear Propulsion Office, U.S. Atomic Energy Commission, Washington, D.C. 20545.

Summary of PERT

In summary, the PERT system involves:

1. Selection of specific, identifiable events that must occur before the project can be completed
2. Sequencing of the events and establishing interdependencies between these events in the development of a project network
3. Estimating the time required to achieve these events and a measurement of the uncertainties of the estimates
4. Designing an analysis and evaluation procedure based upon this data
5. Establishing information channels to notify all personnel concerned of achievements and changes
6. Applying electronic data processing equipment to the analysis and providing the necessary reports.

CRITICAL-PATH METHOD (CPM)

General Method

In late 1956, E. I. du Pont de Nemours & Co. started a study to find more efficient ways of planning and scheduling plant construction. The first recognized need was to have a master plan which integrates all efforts towards a single objective. The next requirement of the system was to separate the planning function from the scheduling function. Planning in this instance refers to the statement of the required activities and the order in which they must take place. The next step was to develop a network showing the interrelationships of the activities and the execution time and the cost of each activity. If the maximum time available for a job equals its duration, the job is called critical. A delay in a critical job will cause a similar delay in the project completion time. There is normally at least one continuous path of critical jobs from beginning to end of the project network and this is called a critical path. A job is said to have float time, or simply "float," if the maximum time available for a job exceeds its duration.

The duration of a job or activity may be varied in many cases by applying more manpower, working longer hours per day and more days per week, etc. Every set of job durations, of course, may lead to a different length of time for a project to be completed. Thus management must have some criterion for evaluating the different possibilities. Cost is one such criterion.

When the direct cost (direct labor and materials) of a typical engineering job varies with elapsed time, the cost curve is as shown in Fig. 9-13. Under "normal" conditions, the costs would be at the minimum point or normal limit. A job may be expedited with resulting higher costs. There is inevitably a limit to how fast a job may be performed, and this is called the crash limit. The cost slope can be approximated by a straight line connecting the crash limit and the normal limit. For any given project duration, a series of schedules may be established of which one will give a minimum cost. These minimum costs may be plotted against project duration time to show how cost and time may be traded as circumstances require (Fig. 9-13).

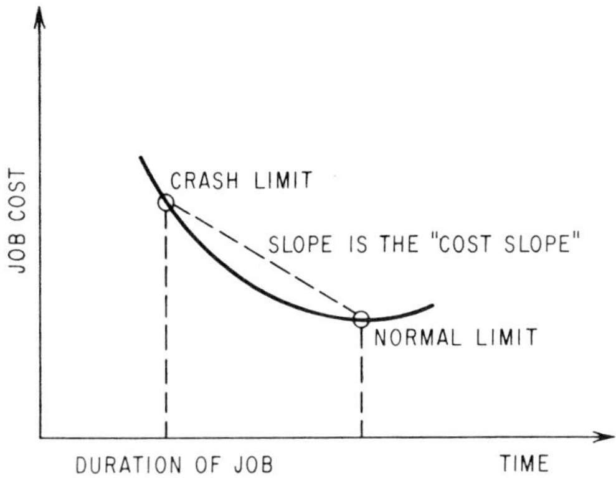

Fig. 9-13. Typical job curve in terms of time of job.

An illustration of CPM which shows in more concrete fashion how this system works is given below. This example also shows how, for small projects, manual computations may be used.

Scheduling a Small Project

In order to illustrate CPM, a simple problem is analyzed in detail. An excellent example of such a problem has been worked out by Charles J. Lynch, Associate Editor, *Product Engineering* (McGraw-Hill Publishing Co.) and is reproduced here by the kind permission of Mr. Lynch and *Product Engineering*.

For this example, we've chosen a gearbox—actually, the scheduling of a prototype gearbox for a new machine tool. The diagram is simple, there is no need for a computer, but the steps in the critical path method are the same no matter how large or small the project.

Here's how it's done. The project engineer starts with the gearbox specification prepared by the machine design group. Drawing on his experience with similar projects, he lists all the jobs that need to be done to deliver an assembled unit meeting these specifications. The list contains 15 jobs. He then calls in his chief designer, drafting-room supervisor and shop foreman, and they estimate time and cost of each job on both a normal and "crash" basis, as shown in Fig. 9-14. In making the estimates for crash time and cost, they consider such expediting measures as overtime work, hiring additional manpower, and subcontracting special jobs.

	Normal			Crash		
	Time, Weeks	Total Float, Weeks	Cost $	Time, Weeks	Cost, $	Cost Slope, $/week
A Design	2.5	0	450	1.5	700	250
B Drafting	0.8	1.0	140	0.5	200	200
C Check drawing	0.2	1.0	35	0.1	45	100
D Deliver special materials	2.0	0	10	1.0	30	20
E Deliver bearings, oil seals	1.5	3.3	10	0.5	20	10
F Inspect purchased parts	0.1	3.3	20	0.05	25	100
G Pattern for housing	2.3	0	350	1.3	550	200
H Cast housing	0.2	0	50	0.1	75	250
I Machine housing	0.4	0	100	0.3	150	500
J Turn shafts	0.8	1.8	175	0.3	375	400
K Heat treat shafts	0.3	1.8	75	0.3	75	...
L Machine gear blanks	0.8	0.6	175	0.4	325	375
M Cut gears	1.0	0.6	250	0.5	450	400
N Heat treat gears	0.5	0.6	125	0.5	125	...
P Assemble	2.0	0	300	1.0	600	300
TOTALS			2265		3745	

Fig. 9-14. Job listing for completing gear box. *Source:* Charles J. Lynch, "How to Schedule a Small Design Project," *Product Engineering* (September 18, 1961).

The next step is to prepare the arrow diagram. (See Fig. 9-15.) The first job is obviously "design," so an arrow is drawn to represent this. This is followed by three jobs, all of which can be started as soon as the design is complete: (B) drafting, (D) ordering special materials, (E) ordering bearings, oil seals and other purchased parts. Three arrows sprouting from the head of the first show this relationship. Shop work can't begin until the drawing is checked and special materials arrive, so both these arrows terminate at the beginning of the shop work (4).

Shafts, housing and gears can all be made during the same time interval so these are shown as parallel arrow paths. All arrows terminate at the begin-

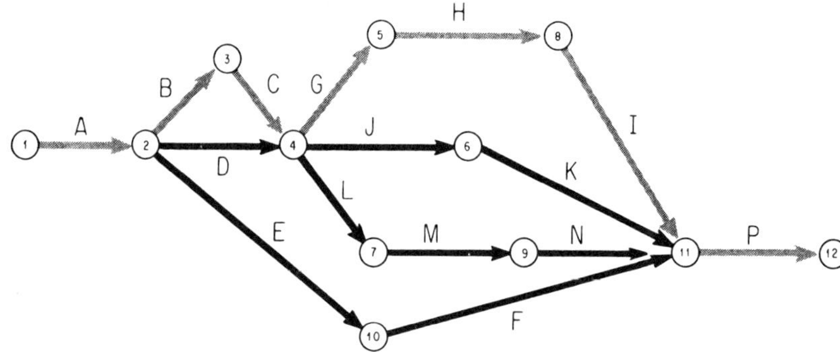

Fig. 9-15. Arrow diagram for critical-path method. *Source:* See Fig. 9-14.

ning of the assembly phase where they meet the arrow representing delivered and inspected purchased parts.

Now, referring to the normal job times previously agreed upon, it is easy to establish the critical path—the one requiring greatest total time. And these critical times tell how much float is available in parallel paths.

The project engineer is now ready to estimate how much time he can squeeze out of the project and what it will cost. Subtracting crash time from normal time and normal cost from crash cost and dividing the two gives him the cost slope which he enters as another column of the table. This is a measure of how costly it will be to speed up each job. Looking first at the job with zero float and lowest cost slope, and then moving on to more expensive critical jobs, he finds his expediting steps break down like this. (For purposes of computation—though this may not be true in practice—he assumes that it is possible to expedite a job to any desired point between the normal and crash times at a pro rata portion of the cost for an all-out crash program on that job.)

- The least expensive critical job is D. Because of the allowable float in parallel jobs B and C, he can cut *one week* at a cost of $20. Now B, C and D are all critical. But no more time can be pared from these because D has already been reduced to the allowable minimum.
- He can save *0.6 weeks* by speeding up G. This costs him (0.6) (200) or $120. He could have saved a full week but there is only 0.6-week float in jobs L, M and N. With this compression, G is still the least expensive critical job. But to cut any more from G, he would have to cut an equal amount from L (the least expensive job in the parallel critical path) at a cost of $200 + $375 = $575 per week.

Continue to shave time from critical jobs and re-examining non-critical jobs as they become critical, he finds he can save

- *1 week* in A at a cost of $250
- *1 week* in P at a cost of $300
- *0.4 weeks* by trimming G and L at a cost of 0.4 (575) = $230
- *0.1 weeks* by compressing H and M at a cost of 0.1 (650) = $65
- *0.1 weeks* by expediting I and M at a cost of 0.1 (900) = $90

At this point the project has been reduced to the minimum. Total time is 5 weeks, which is equal to the time of an "all-crash" project. But total cost is $3340 compared with $3745 for the "all-crash" project.

The curve in Fig. 9-16 shows the relationship between project cost and time. This is combined with the curve for indirect project costs, using the established overhead figures for the departments involved. The total cost curve has a minimum point at 7.6 weeks, meaning he can produce the gearbox at minimum cost by expediting jobs D and G while allowing the other jobs to proceed on a normal schedule. This adds only $120 to the direct cost.

Use of Boards and Charts

The use of charts or schedule boards to represent the major phases of a project is desirable under some circumstances. Careful consideration should be given to the need before such boards are used to show detailed schedules. The detailed schedules and performance are readily available through the computer reports. The maintenance of detailed boards and

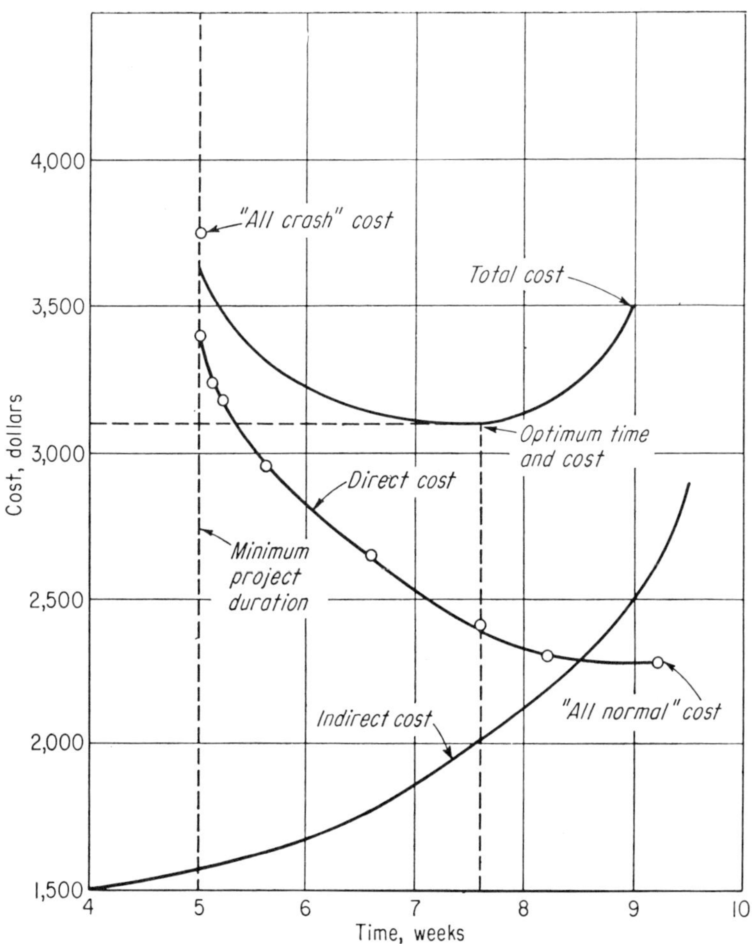

Fig. 9-16. Relationship between gear-box project costs and time. *Source:* See Fig. 9-14.

charts showing progress are expensive to set up and maintain. They are often abandoned after they are established for the following reasons:

1. Those actually following the work in detail and setting up the boards don't need the boards and are diverted from their main work.
2. Immediate supervisors obtain detailed information from computer reports and discussions with programmers and engineers concerned with the work.
3. Higher management and visitors are not familiar enough with the codings on the boards to understand what they mean without getting a further explanation and evaluation in any case.

COORDINATION

"To coordinate" means to bring elements into common action. Coordination consists of *planning for* and *obtaining* unified action *during* the process of carrying out engineering work as opposed to *controlling* which is correcting *after the fact* for deviations from established standards or limits. Coordination is a positive concept implying cooperative effort towards common goals. Controlling concerns itself with the restricting or confining of work within established limits. Because of the basic difference between coordination and control, they are treated separately.

Objectives of Coordination

The coordination of E & R projects has its own set of specifics. With regard to objectives:

1. The desires of the customer and the direction taken by the engineering work as the technical work unfolds must be coordinated. Modifications of the customer's viewpoint will occur on two- to five-year projects as new knowledge either closes doors or opens doors to new opportunities.
2. In large organizations particularly, E & R management must be concerned with keeping the many engineers and technicians fully cognizant of the broad commercial or defense objectives of their project and the present broad interests of the company. Without coordinated effort there will be "drift," schedule slippages, and missed opportunities for innovation. "Backing and filling," and indecision will result in frustration of the engineers.
3. Engineers must be kept informed of new test and analytical data and design changes made by others in the organization during the progress of a project. The larger the project, the greater is the problem of making sure that all engineers are proceeding on the same basis. This is

a main purpose of the reference designs discussed in an earlier chapter.

4. Another objective of coordination is to keep the *applied research* scientists and engineers working on problems pertinent to the company's interests. Lack of coordination may result in fostering pet projects of the researchers or of some company executive which have dubious potential commercial values.
5. Obtaining the results of applied research and advance engineering in time to be of value is another major objective. People in engineering and research tend to be perfectionists—they are interested in proven and thoroughly researched or engineered projects rather than results that involve an element of risk. The objective is to coordinate the work of these researchers with the needs of the engineers so that reasonable conclusions or results are available on time instead of having carefully proven results available a year yater.
6. Coordination of E & R personnel is also concerned with obtaining an optimum interchange of ideas. Such an interchange regarding difficult problems helps crystallize thinking generally and secures agreement on the best approaches to the obtaining of solutions.
7. Coordination must occur with respect to the use of facilities such as test laboratories, test equipment, model shops, computer facilities, etc. Despite the most careful advance planning, there are constant minor shifts in schedule which must lead to changes in the scheduling of the use of such facilities. Obviously it is undesirable for such facilities to be idle if there is work to be done. Related to this problem is the fact that variations in rates of design progress will result in two or more groups wishing to use the same facility simultaneously.
8. Engineering documentation groups must be staffed so that their outputs coincide with the needs of users.
9. Proper timing of the rate of progress by various groups working on a project is essential. Research, advance development, or design in one area will proceed faster than that in another area which will result in changes of the phasing between related tasks. Temporary and/or permanent shifts of manpower to lagging tasks may be desirable. Overtime work, of course, is another possible solution. Coordinated use of outside consultants may be another solution. However, where the work between various tasks is interdependent, a coordinative effort is required.

Basic Methods of Coordination

Successful coordination of E & R rests upon six basic principles:

1. *Acceptance by most individuals* of the plans, goals, and the part the individuals will play in achieving them
2. *Advance planning* to organize the entire E & R effort and its timing

3. *Communication downwards* of plans, goals, and procedures to all people in the organization
4. *Free interchange of information* among engineers and scientists at all working levels
5. *Feedback up the line* of progress and problems
6. *Documentation* of engineering work.

Specific Methods

Coordination, to a great extent, is essentially a communication process. Therefore, specified methods or techniques used to coordinate E & R activities may be classified under "verbal" and "written" as follows:

Verbal Techniques

1. Regular staff meetings at each organizational level
2. Design review meetings
3. General project informational meetings
4. Conferences or technical meetings
5. Committee meetings
6. Manager–individual-contributor daily working relationships
7. "Grapevine."

Written Techniques

1. Organization charts
2. Operating and policy manuals
3. Engineering instructions
4. Memos and reports
5. Letters
6. Minutes of meetings
7. Engineering and manufacturing drawings
8. Specifications
9. Bulletins for general announcements.

Staff Meetings. Staff meetings provide an excellent means of coordinating E & R since they provide two-way communication, both up and down the line. In one company, the general manager meets regularly on Monday afternoons with all people who report directly to him. He informs them of new developments in all areas and regarding problems relating to customers. Each of his staff is given an opportunity to introduce items of significant interest concerning projects or other current problems of general interest. Discussion of all items and problems is kept brief, but if assignment of effort groups is required, the representative at the meeting is so notified by the general manager.

The next morning, Tuesday, the managers who attended the general manager's staff meeting hold staff meetings of their own for managers, consultants, etc., who report directly to them. Items of interest from the general manager's meeting are relayed, as well as making subassignments of any work assignments emanating from the general manager's meeting. The pattern of these meetings follows that of the general manager's, except that these meetings have a narrower interest and are more oriented to the work problems of each group. The reason for this is that the managers, consultants, and specialists will be talking about their own work and work problems, rather than items of broad general significance.

That afternoon, the managers who attended the morning meetings hold similar meetings with the engineering and technical support people in their organizations.

The staff meetings, to be successful, must be held regularly at the scheduled times. Usually, there is the tendency to put the functional work first and start skipping the meetings. It must be recognized that good communication is a fundamental requirement for getting the right work done in the right way at the right time and is, therefore, worth the effort and time required.

Design Review Meetings. The responsibility of the design engineer has increased rapidly as equipment has grown more complex and costly. He is often responsible for decisions involving thousands of dollars in test and development effort; moreover, he must incorporate the specialized knowledge of many fields into the design. For these reasons, the Design Review Meeting has emerged as a technique used to assure the incorporation of the best thinking into design work without essentially altering the responsibility of the design engineer for the final product. The design engineer, subject to the decisions of his manager, still is responsible for the design, regardless of whether or not he elects to use one or more of the ideas presented at Design Review Meetings.

Design Review Meetings are held at key times in the development of the product such as at the conclusion of the conceptual design, at the time proposed reference designs are completed, and at a time when the design is fairly well-advanced so that layouts, some detailed drawings and a substantial design basis are available. Design Review Meetings are also often held when any particularly crucial decision must be made or when some major problem persists.

The participants in the Design Reviews are the design engineer, selected mature engineers from any part of the E & R organization whose specialties relate to the problem, and possibly representatives from Manufacturing, Marketing, or Research. The chairman of the meeting may be the project manager or even the manager of E & R.

There should be thorough preparation for such meetings which may last a full day. All participants should be invited well in advance. A formal statement of the problems or items to be discussed as well as drawings and supporting material should be supplied to them sufficiently in advance so that the participants can study them carefully before the meeting. Participants are supposed to come to the meeting well-prepared to criticize, question, and offer well-thought-out suggestions based on some engineering analysis of their own. As a result, it is quite usual to have free discussions which uncover new ideas at the meeting.

General Informational Meetings. General meetings of all personnel in E & R serve a useful purpose. They provide the manager of E & R with an opportunity to present the direction of the engineering and research directly to all technical people without the distortion which inevitably occurs when communication passes through several levels. Moreover, such meetings provide an opportunity for the technical personnel at the lower organizational levels to get to know the manager of E & R. Ordinarily such general meetings are restricted to one to four per year. Also, one or more of them are usually dinner meetings.

Conferences or Technical Meetings. The technical meeting is probably the most misused device for coordination existing. Although entire books are available on the subject, a few key rules are given to avoid the great waste of time (and hence money) which occurs in technical meetings in even the best managed companies. The chairman who calls the meeting should:

1. Invite only participants who can contribute.
2. Make sure that those who are to present papers or head discussions are competent to do so and will come fully prepared.
3. Invite only those participants needed to accomplish the purpose.
4. Notify each participant of the precise purpose of the meeting. Do not plan to cover more than about three main items.
5. Give the participants adequate advance notice.
6. Keep the meetings on the track and keep them short. If no progress is being made and the meeting is getting nowhere, terminate it.
7. Nail down the conclusions for each point and decide whether they are tantamount to recommendations, solutions, or decisions.
8. Document the purpose and the results of the meeting.

Committee Meetings. Committees have been discussed in Chapter 3. Guides for holding committee meetings are similar to those for technical meetings just described.

Manager–Individual-Contributor Relationships. The engineer, through direct contact with his manager, is kept informed of the direction of the work. An engineering manager may have, perhaps, twenty engineers reporting directly to him. In the last analysis, it is the engineers and researchers who are the "doers"; therefore, management must fully coordinate the work of these people. The principal coordination occurs through planning and guiding in face-to-face discussions.

"Grapevine." The grapevine is a modern industrial device which surpasses the jungle drums. If the manager of E & R wishes to transmit or

prevent transmission of any exceptional piece of news throughout his organization, he should consider the grapevine. A word dropped to some key carrier will spread through the organization at sonic velocity.

Written Techniques

Organization Charts and Operating and Policy Guides. Organization charts are often included in Operating and Policy Guides since both relate to the formal aspects of coordination. Organization charts, if kept up to date, are valuable in large organizations to keep people notified of whom they should approach to obtain information or to process work. Large, growing organizations may have frequent shifts of personnel so that organization charts, while difficult to keep up-to-date, serve a vital need.

The Organization and Policy Guides, which are often referred to as "manuals," are kept in loose-leaf form for easy revision. These guides are characterized by a high degree of authority, a formal and centralized preparation, and a distribution usually limited to managers and key administrative personnel. Although such guides are issued for the company as a whole, naturally many of the policies and procedures contribute towards coordination. The policy guides usually contain both policies and procedures. A policy can be defined as the statement of common purposes for organization components in matters where, in the interests of achieving both the component and over-all company objectives, it is necessary that those responsible for implementation adhere to uniform standards of application. A procedure is a series of detailed steps telling employees how to accomplish a task or goal, after the decision to accomplish the particular task or reach the particular goal has been made.

Company organization, policy and/or procedure manuals are often classified into categories, and individual directives or procedures are identified by numbers. A typical classification of the contents is as follows:

Administration and Legal	Manufacturing
Employee Relations	Finance
Engineering and Research	Health, Medical, and Safety
Marketing	Procurement and Stocking

In project-type organizations where the projects are large, a Project Operating Instructions Manual should be set up which is designed to provide all the specific procedures required to successfully run a project. For example, procedures for engineering changes, procedures for design changes, procedures for drawing approval, etc., are typical of the coordinating instructions which may be peculiar to each project. Examples of the format which has been used for this purpose are given in Fig. 9-17.

Engineering Instructions. The Engineering Instruction is simply a formalized method of documenting an engineering request, instructions, or

SYSTEMS DEPARTMENT		PROGRAM PROCEDURE
SUBJECT	CLASSIFICATION	NO.
Program Instruction	Engineering Documents	

I GENERAL

A. Purpose - This instruction establishes policy, responsibilities, and procedure relative to the use of Program Instructions, Form 102.

B. Policy - Program Instructions will be used to:

1. Authorize funds or transfer funds.
2. Serve as a formal commitment and/or agreement for materials and services.
3. To order materials, components, hardware, and equipment other than resource equipment which should be ordered in accordance with Program Procedure No. 11.03.
4. Announce drawings for ordering materials, hardware, etc., and for the manufacture thereof.
5. Communicate to Development Manufacturing or Quality Control and Test Operations special engineering instructions not covered on the engineering drawings, such as:
   a. Specifying special engineering requirements, special tests, or manufacturing instructions when needed.
6. To transmit needed information or instructions to a vendor or subcontractor through Production Control or Development Manufacturing, who, in turn will request Purchasing or Subcontracts to issue an Instruction Sheet to the vendor or subcontractor.
7. To re-schedule, revise, or cancel instructions already released.

II RESPONSIBILITIES

A. Issuance - Any engineering organizational component in the department has the authority to issue Program Instructions in accordance with this procedure to facilitate their responsibilities that require implementation with other organizations.

Issued By	Date Issued	Supersedes Issue Dated	Page 1
Manager-Operations Planning & Admin.	January 10, 1969	October 2, 1968	of 4

Fig. 9-17. Operating instruction policy and responsibilities.

transfer of information. It is highly flexible since it may be used whenever it is convenient. Subject to his securing the needed signed approval for the particular Engineering Instruction, any engineer may issue an Engineering Instruction within the area of his responsibility. As examples, an EI may be issued: (1) to request that a certain test be performed by the test group, (2) to ask another engineering component or consultant to supply specified analyses or information, (3) to give the go-ahead on an approved program, or (4) to supply "official" values of paramcters or design features to a requesting engineering component. A format for the EI is shown in Fig. 9-18.

Memos and Reports. Memos or informal technical reports and other types of technical and budgeting reports contribute greatly to coordination of E & R through dissemination of the results of work performed throughout the engineering organization. More will be said on this topic later in the chapter.

Letters. Letters, if properly employed, can be very helpful in coordinating E & R. Unfortunately, many engineers are not good letter writers. Ambiguity, digression, and verbosity are frequently characteristics of engineers' letters. Consequently, some organizations prefer the use of the structured EI which serves the same purpose in most cases.

Minutes of Meetings. Minutes of meetings are useful not only to document the results, but also to distribute the results of the meeting to engineers concerned throughout the entire E & R organization. Minutes of meetings should not be detailed verbatim reports of everything which occurred. Rather, they should record concisely the purpose of the meeting and results obtained.

Engineering and Manufacturing Drawings. The value of drawings as the most important means for coordinating engineering work requires little explanation. Approval procedures should be established for drawings and drawing changes so that only "official" drawings are in circulation. There must be an allowance for the informal type of drawings which are identified as sketches and are sometimes given a separate numbering system.

Specifications. Like drawings, specifications serve as a common basis for the E & R effort. They provide guides to both engineering and production work. Specifications in E & R relate to commodities, materials, products, and equipment. Specifications may be classified by function as relating to engineering, design product performance, manufacturing, test, and purchase. Specifications may be divided into two classes—general specifications and detail specifications. General specifications cover the requirements common to a number of products so that these requirements may be easily referenced. A detail specification covers all the requirements necessary to define the characteristics of a specific product. Detail specifications may require reference to general specifications for some requirements.

SPC - 102 PROGRAM INSTRUCTION

FROM			TO	CUSTOMER
TASK			SUBTASK	REQUISITION
SPECIFICATION NUMBER			PROJECT NUMBER	PROGRAM
DATE OF ISSUE			REVISION	SHOP ORDER
REVISED	ITEM NO.	QTY.	INSTRUCTION	( ) PRIME EQUIPMENT ( ) DEVELOPMENT PROGRAM
DISTRIBUTION			PREPARED BY & DATE	P.I. NUMBER
			APPROVED BY	DATE
				SHEET NUMBER

Fig. 9-18. Engineering instruction form. *Source:* Robert G. Murdick, "Coordinating Engineering Activities," *Machine Design* (June 7, 1962).

The requirements for both general and detail specifications may be presented either according to performance requirements or design requirements. Performance specifications express requirements in the form of output, function, or operation without specifying anything about the details of the design. Conversely, design specifications specify the information necessary to produce the item such as material, composition, physical and chemical requirements, weight, size, and dimensions.

There is no one standard format for specifications; however, the format for military specifications is widely used and available. The outline for the military specification is as follows:

1. Scope
2. Applicable documents
3. Requirements
4. Quality assurance provisions
5. Preparation for delivery
6. Notes.

In setting up a system for the preparation of specifications, it is well to assign responsibility for coordination, approval, and maintenance of files to a central committee or a mature engineer. Procedures should be established to cover:

1. Format
2. Origination and preparation
3. Reviews and approvals
4. Assignment of identifying number
5. Final approval, publication, and distribution
6. Changes and revisions.

A list of eleven rules for preparing technical specifications is shown in Fig. 9-19.

REPORTING TECHNICAL PROGRESS

Reports of technical progress are essential for technical coordination and control purposes. Without detailed technical reports, financial reports for control are meaningless. Although PERT techniques permit ready grasp of progress and delays, once again the detailed technical report is necessary to substantiate the validity of PERT reports and control techniques.

Further, the engineering and research job is not complete until it is properly and adequately documented. Unfortunately, many engineers and research people fail to recognize the most important purpose of reporting their work, that is, the dissemination of scientific knowledge so that others do not

11 PRACTICAL RULES FOR PREPARING TECHNICAL SPECIFICATIONS

1. Avoid writing a new specification whenever possible. Try to adopt one already in existence. This practice can save time and money. National organizations which maintain current information in important subject areas are listed under Sources of National and Industry Specifications, Standards, and Practices.

2. Amend an available specification when it connot be used "as is." If, for example, the existing spec is too specific where it should be general, and general where it should be specific, the spec should be amended as necessary and all suitable paragraphs copied as is. It is good practicc to mention the basic specification in the "Applicable Documents" section of the company spec with the following note: "The following specification No. XXXXX is a part of this specification to the extent specified herein."

3. For each requirement of the specification indicate a corresponding test procedure, cross referenced whenever practical. For example:

Requirement	Requirement Paragraph	Test Method Paragraph
Temperature Cycling	3.8	4.8
Plating Thickness	3.9	4.10
Moisture Resistance	3.10	4.12

4. Avoid devising test methods for internal company use only. Use the standards developed by ASTM, government, or other organizations as much as possible.

5. Assign a tolerance to each requirement or characteristic expressed as a numerical value. If the requirement is merely stated as 10 w, 100,000 psi, or 100 F., it does not tell the inspector what to do if the measured values are 10-1/2 w, 999,999 psi, or 99 or 101 F. For example; pressure tolerances may be expressed as:

100,000 psi ± 1000 psi	100,000 psi max
100,000 psi min to the nearest 100 psi	100,000 psi min

Tolerance to the nearest 100 psi means that all values over 99,950 are rounded off to 100,000 psi and accepted. All values less than 99,950 are rounded off to 99,900 psi and rejected.

The more selective the vendor must be to satisfy the specification, the more costly will be the product.

6. Specify only those requirements necessary to do the job. Each requirement will affect inspection procedures and ultimate cost. Be prepared to justify each requirement and to explain how it affects the end product. The following items should be carefully determined:

Characteristics of the product to be controlled.
Degree of control.

A partial list of environmental conditions and other requirements which might be covered in a specification is:

Fig. 9-19. Practical rules for preparing technical specifications.

Temperature range	Explosion proofing
Altitude	Life test
Vibration	Service test
Shock	Shelf life
Humidity	Radio interference
Sea	Size and weight
Sand and dust	Cooling
Sun and weathering	Components application and quality
Air and waterproofing	Human engineering

Requirements for materials may include the following:

Chemical composition: Texture, color, odor

Physical Properties:

a. Density	h. Compression strength
b. Melting point	i. Yield strength
c. Thermal expansion	j. Creep strength
d. Specific heat	k. Shear strength
e. Modulus of elasticity	l. Elongation
f. Hardness	m. Impact
g. Tensile strength	n. Endurance limit

7. Specify a sampling plan, indicating how test specimens will be selected and inspected. For information on sampling procedure, the following publications are recommended:

MIL-STD-105 – Sampling Procedures and Tables for Inspection by Attributes
MIL-E-5272 – Environmental Testing, Aeronautical and Associated Equipment
MIL-STD-414 – Sampling Procedures and Tables for Inspection by Variable for Per Cent Defective
MIL-STD-109 – Inspection Terms and Definitions
ASTM – Manual on Quality Control of Materials

8. Be specific and aim for simplicity and clarity of expression. Specifications are read by all kinds of people – draftsmen, designers, purchasing agents, vendors, sales clerks, sales engineers, etc. A specification must be understood by everybody who will have to read it as a part of his job. It must be specific enough to avoid multiple interpretations of its requirements.

9. Never rely on catalogue information alone when writing a specification. Component requirements are not always clearly spelled out in catalogues or similar literature and often require amplification.

10. When nonstandard or little known terms are used, do not hesitate to define them. For example:

Room temperature shall be 75 ± 12 F.

Sea level shall be to 10,000 ft.

11. Keep in mind that a poorly written specification is better than none. Its shortcomings will not go unnoticed very long. In practice, feedback from those who use the spec will usually provide the information necessary for amendment or revision.

Fig. 9-19 (*Continued*). Practical rules for preparing technical specifications. *Source:* A. J. Fitzgerald and Rowen Glie, "A Guide to Technical Specifications," *Machine Design* (July 6, 1961).

have to duplicate the research elsewhere. Scientific research effort is a limited resource which management cannot afford to waste. Beyond this basic reason for reporting progress, achievement, and failure, there are, of course, other highly important business reasons. These include customer requirements, internal communication, and legal and patent considerations.

There are a number of types of engineering and research reports, and it is important in preparing them that the primary purpose and nature of each be thoroughly understood by management. These reports are:

1. Internal memo or the topical report
2. Formal technical engineering and research report
3. Project progress report
4. Technology or functional progress report
5. Test section progress report
6. Summary periodic report to management
7. Terminal project reports.

Internal Memo

The purpose of the internal memo is primarily one of facilitating timely internal communication. It usually covers preliminary or tentative results that are needed by other technical groups. It is sometimes called a topical report because results of a special study that are urgently needed may be covered. At the other extreme, some interesting result that is incidental to the direction of the main research effort may be reported by this means.

The style of the internal memo should not be restricted, but rather the author should be allowed freedom of expression, use of idiom, and opportunity to express his opinions when he so identifies them. The author, however, should not forget that the primary purpose of the report is to communicate to his peers, not confuse or entertain them.

While freedom in style is recommended, some restrictions in format are also recommended. The member of scientific reports has been growing at an exponential rate until the annual rate is of the order of 100,000. In one year over sixty million pages or the equivalent of 465 man-years of steady round-the-clock reading is being turned out by the laboratories and research centers throughout the world. It is difficult even to keep up with the abstract publications in some technical fields. All this argues for a more or less standardized format so that readers can quickly determine the subject matter of the report and whether it may contain information of use to them. The report might typically have:

1. An identification or serial number, a very specific title, the author's name, the company's name, and the date on the cover
2. A title page with a three-by-five-inch box with information such as report no., date, author, title, company name, number of pages, and a very brief abstract of a few lines

3. Distribution page showing distribution of the report
4. Table of contents and, if appropriate, a list of illustrations
5. Contents arranged to state the purpose of the report and give the conclusion first. For example:

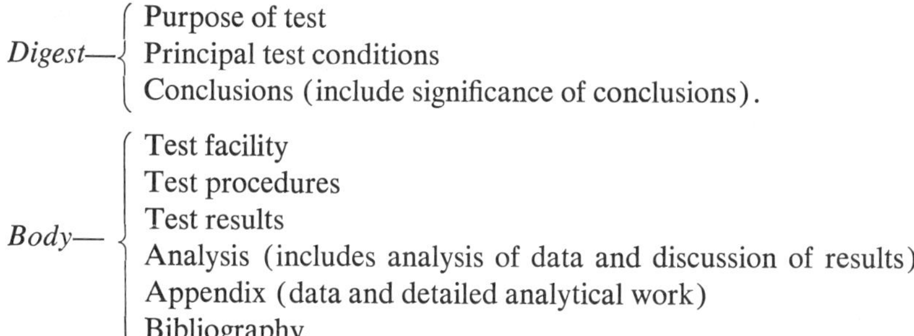

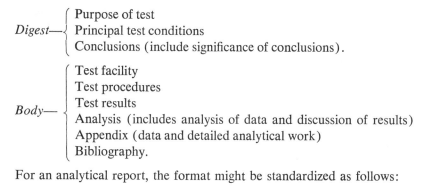

Digest—
- Purpose of test
- Principal test conditions
- Conclusions (include significance of conclusions).

Body—
- Test facility
- Test procedures
- Test results
- Analysis (includes analysis of data and discussion of results)
- Appendix (data and detailed analytical work)
- Bibliography.

For an analytical report, the format might be standardized as follows:

Digest—
- Purpose of investigation
- Principal assumptions
- Conclusions (includes significance of conclusions).

Body—
- Analysis (includes all assumptions, analytical work, and discussion of results)
- Appendix (data used and detailed derivations needed for the main analysis)
- Bibliography.

The timing of the internal memo is very important. Every small advance or interesting but irrelevant discovery should not be issued with fanfare. The deciding factors are: (1) Is this *vital* information needed by the design group at this time to help them maintain their schedule? *or* (2) Has work on this line of investigation now been carried as far as it will be? *or* (3) Has a major milestone in a long investigation been completed?

When the time is ripe for such a report, it should be written forthwith. Three obstacles often prevent this in the E & R organization. The press of new work often prevents the author from working on the report. It is up to the author's manager to see that the report is not held up for this reason. Another cause for delay, and perhaps complete neglect, is that many scientists dislike to write up their work. Again, it is up to their manager to educate them on the necessity for reporting results and show them how they will benefit from the development of the important skill of report writing. A third obstacle to timeliness in production of reports may be the shortsightedness of higher management or some cost-reduction committee in maintaining a typing and reproduction group which is inadequate to handle the volume of reports. In the latter case the engineers and scientists at first prepare their reports on time and then see them held up for weeks or months in production until their value is completely lost. The authors, as a result, then write fewer reports and depend upon casual, personal contact as a means of interchanging technical information. Obviously, this is a poor and inefficient method of disseminating vital information. The cost-cutters feel happy because the low volume of reports justifies their claim that the production staff and facilities are adequate. Unfortunately, this situation is all too common.

What about the quality of production of the topical report? Because of its nature, the topical report is usually prepared by a very inexpensive method such as fluid duplicators, xerography or diazo reproduction. Sometimes when the distribution is large, the offset process of reproduction is used. Illustrations may be freehand sketches, photographic prints, or available engineering drawings.

The distribution should be limited to people who have a need for such information; often, there is the tendency to send one's masterpieces to everyone in the organization directory. The author should be made to realize that if this were done in every case, the cost of printing, distributing, and the review and rejection by uninterested readers would be staggering. Often standard distribution lists are established for certain categories of these reports. While this may be a time-saver and efficient in operation, it does have the drawback that the lists must be revised from time to time, plus the fact that, of necessity, it is designed to fit the general situation.

Terminal Technical Report

The terminal technical report is a formal and final report of some investigation or project. Whereas the internal memo or topical report covers preliminary results, often when further confirmation will be required, the terminal report is the culmination of a scientific investigation or test. It is often called a formal report because it represents the finished exposition of the author or authors and may be circulated outside the organization to the customer, to other divisions within the company, and occasionally to other companies in the industry. The latter is particularly true for reports of work prepared under defense or other government contracts.

Project Progress Report

The "progress report," while known for years, has grown in importance in parallel to the rise of defense and government contracts. Once the progress report was a method of letting the customer know at irregular intervals how things were progressing. Now the progress report must roll out of the engineering and research group with a regularity of products off an assembly line. The progress report has been brought to a stage of art and science that is remarkable. Its purpose is usually to allow layers of government officials to examine minutely each microscopic activity of the contract work.

The project progress report is usually issued to report the progress on large multimillion dollar projects throughout their lives. While it may be issued quarterly or every other month, it is common to find that the customer requires a monthly report.

The format, the content, and the style are inextricably woven together in the concept of the progress report. The format may be based upon dividing the entire project into tasks, subtasks, and jobs; or it may be based upon a division of topics parallel to the engineering echelons and groups that comprise the engineering organization. Often these are practically identical in the project-type organization. The format with all the headings and subheadings is usually prepared initially by a technical editor or coordinator working with engineering management. From time to time, minor revisions will be required as investigations are completed and new ones started throughout the life of the project. There may be as many as five levels of subheadings since the customer often wants to put his finger right on a very small segment of the work.

Obviously, with such a detailed format, the content of the report must be different in nature from other types of reports. Both content and style are designed to provide the following information on each item as concisely as possible in each issue:

1. Progress made since the last report. If none, why not.
2. Problems encountered, what is being done about them, and if nothing has been done, what and when will something be done.
3. Results of tests or analysis in condensed form.
4. Significance of such results to the technical progress and to the schedule of the project.
5. Whether the work of each item is on schedule, if not, why not, and what is being done to bring it back on schedule.
6. Sometimes budgeted costs and costs-to-date must be included.

At the request of the Navy, several companies print the instructions shown in Fig. 9-20 on the inside of the front cover of every progress report as a constant reminder to authors.

The progress report is often a source of friction between the customer and the contractor. The contractor can only do his best to assign good personnel to getting the dozens of individual reports from engineers throughout the organization by the time of each monthly deadline. The customer, in turn, lets his wishes be known very often by "letters of comment" addressed to top management in which he asks for further information on individual items or points out inadequacies of the most recent progress report.

Considerable friction with the customer may be avoided if a positive approach is taken in presenting technical progress. The engineer-author may

GUIDELINES FOR WRITING A PROGRESS REPORT

Purpose:

The primary purpose of this report is to provide the reader doing work related to the________________________ project with current knowledge of the project and with the progress that was made during the reporting period. The secondary purpose is to provide others interested in________________________ _____development with information on the technical progress made on this project.

Use:

Management uses the report to guide the direction and scope of the program and to coordinate it with other related work. Technical people use the report to keep informed on work which is outside of their particular responsibility, to gain a perspective of the job as a whole, and to learn how their work fits into the overall picture.

Audience:

In general, the reader can be assumed to have an engineering college education and a broad familiarity with this type of equipment and technology, physics, and power plant engineering.

Report Methods

Be Concise - Use as few words as possible to convey the thought.
Be Specific - Avoid statements such as "a study was made" or "work progressed." State what was studied and what progress was made.
Report Only Facts - A technical report should contain no opinions unless they are clearly indentified as such. It should not convey a mood, either optimistic or pessimistic.

Report Scope:

In writing up a subject which is being reported upon for the first time, the items described below should be covered. For subjects which have been covered in previous reports, the writer should exercise judgment in determining which of the itmes below should be covered.
Responsible Person and Project Proposal Number - At the beginning of each section of the report, give the name of the person responsible for the work and the identifying reference number of the document which justifies and authorizes the work.
Statement of the Problem and Background - State why this work is being done; when started; when to be completed.
Description of Work - State what was accomplished during period. If tests were run, give pertinent test data. Always give the duration of the test as well as the number of cycles of repetitive tests. Includes curves, photographs, and drawings with captions, where applicable. Photographs should always include a person or other appropriate scale-establishing aid. If this work ties in with other work, reference the page on which the other work is described. If backup efforts are involved, briefly describe them.
Future - Tell when the next step in this work will be reached, i.e., completion of test work, completion of one phase of the work and entering the next, etc.
Decisions - If a decision is made as a result of the work, give a full account of the facts and reasoning on which the decision was based. If practical, optimizing curves should be included.
Evaluation - Evaluate and interpret the results of the work as to its significance to the work reported and to the project as a whole. The results of some experiment may have been achieved after great effort on the experimenter's part but its contribution to the whole problem is what is significant, not the experiment itself.
Problems - Always report problems, particularly those which might cause delays. Small hidden problems often develop into large serious ones. Give an estimate as to the possibility of a solution being reached in time. If the solution is not forthcoming in time, state what is holding it up.
Suggestions - What could be done to improve the progress of the work?

Fig. 9-20. Guidelines for writing a progress report.

consciously recognize before he communicates that what he is about to say or write is either favorable or unfavorable to the person who is listening or who will be reading his words. However, he may feel that the "facts" or the "situation" warrants using direct, blunt language. Representing unpleasant situations in direct negative terms often erects a barrier between the engineer and the people with whom he is dealing. It isn't necessary to have a "happy-happy" attitude in the face of all circumstances, but it is necessary to find the positive elements and build upon them in order to be most effective in reaching the real engineering goals.

Technology Progress Report

Often engineering and research organizations have a supporting group of scientists carrying on long-range continuing investigations, the interim results of which are used by the engineering organization from time to time. Such research is not directed toward the accomplishment of short-range goals on a specific schedule. The work is of an applied research nature and is recognized as such.

Progress in the technology area is likely to be reported in a monthly or quarterly report. This report is not so likely to be subject to the close analysis and criticism of the customer. The outline is more variable and free, and the scientists report the results which they think are of most interest. This is, of course, a formal report so that the production quality should be good.

Development—Test Report

Often there is a central test section in the E & R organization which conducts all engineering development tests at the request of the various engineering groups. If proper control is to be maintained, the test group should submit a monthly progress report to the engineering sections. Each test may be identified by a serial number and title. The report on each test should include information such as the responsible initiating engineer, the responsible test engineer, the estimated cost of the test, cost-to-date, starting date and scheduled completion date, and a very brief summary of progress. This is an internal progress report, and economy is the objective. By careful planning of the reproduction process and format, this report may be prepared by simply adding information on to old masters each month. In one organization, when the report was run off using offset masters, a new master was printed from the old master. This new master was then modified at the next report period.

The timely issuance of this report is most important both from a technical viewpoint and a cost viewpoint. It is difficult for engineering labor costs to rise rapidly without a big recruiting program; however, because of the equipment and outside contract work often involved in development tests, costs may get out-of-hand within a few months if careful control is not exerted.

Summary Business Report to Management

There are numerous ways in which the general manager or laboratory manager and his staff may be kept informed of what is going on throughout the plant or laboratory. Staff meetings, memos, letters, special reports, and informal contacts all serve this purpose admirably. However, there is nothing quite as good for getting precision of expression as having each manager on the general manager's staff prepare a one- to three-page summary of activities and problems in his organization for the past month. It gives each manager a chance to lay on the line his accomplishments. At the same time, the general manager and those managers on the staff can get a good over-all view of the operation. Such a report may be circulated on up to company officers in the larger companies.

While the summary business report is not primarily an engineering report and the manager of engineering prepares only the material covering his function, his contribution is a very significant one. The monthly progress report which his projects prepare are of great value in providing the manager of engineering with much of the data and information upon which he will base his summary of progress.

Terminal Project Progress Report

The terminal report at the conclusion of a major project should be a technical report, not a cost and schedule review. There are always many others who can do a poorer job faster and cheaper, and, of course, a few who can do a *better* job faster and cheaper. New methods plus technical advances made it doubtful that cost and time comparisons of jobs between good engineering firms have much meaning. From a marketing viewpoint, people forget after a while how much they paid, but they never forget how good or bad the product is.

The terminal report does offer a company an opportunity to show its technical power. This report should clearly delineate the original goals and the final accomplishments. Development problems and their solutions should be shown. Assembly drawings of major equipment, additional art work, and adequate tables and graphs should back up the technical story. For a large project, this terminal technical report may require several volumes. The production should be a high quality job in a durable binding.

Technical Publications Group

The assembly of technical information, editing, and production of reports are too important for control of engineering work for the project manager to assign these responsibilities to disinterested engineers on a part-time basis. Publications work requires professionally trained people. These people should receive proper recognition of their skills.

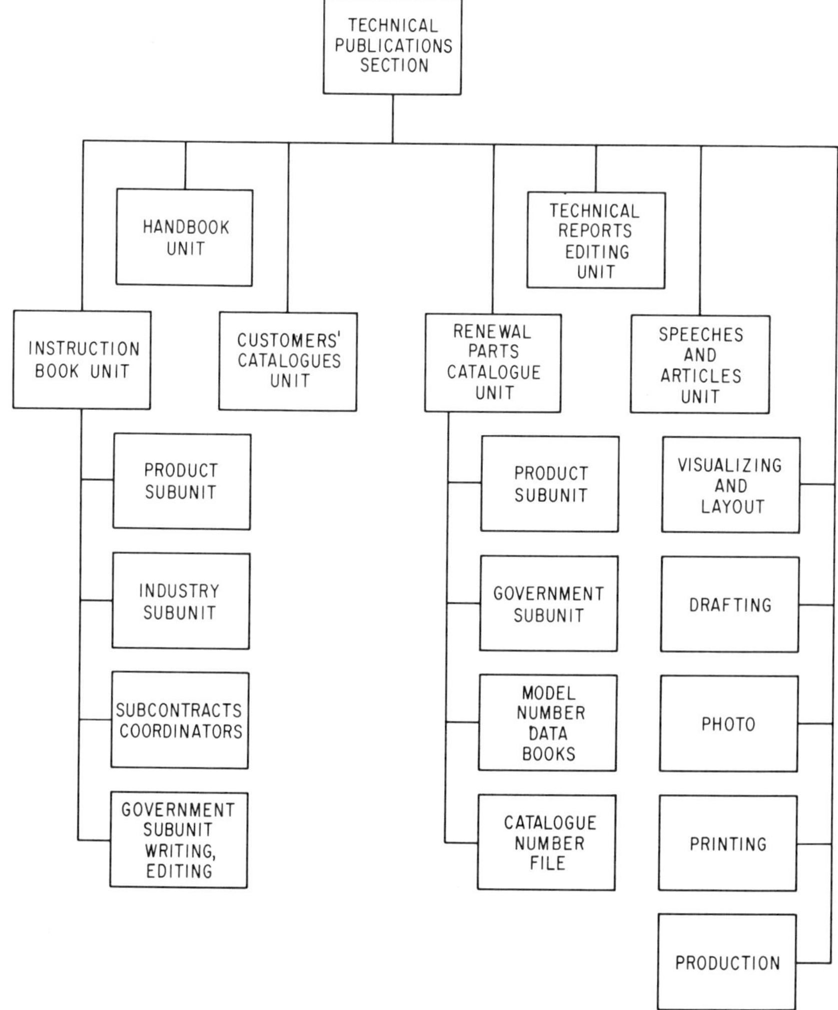

Fig. 9-21. Organization of the technical publications section. *Source:* R. G. Murdick, "Producing Technical Publications," *Machine Design* (February 1, 1962).

A technical publications group may handle reports, instruction books, catalogs, and possibly, technical advertising copy. Once the broad objectives have been outlined, the services to be performed have been listed, and the make-or-buy decisions have been made, organization of the technical publications group may proceed. A complete technical publications organization would be similar to that shown in Fig. 9-21.

As mentioned in Chapter 14, the Technical Publications Group is often an integral part of an Engineering Administration Activity. Some further comment on the work of a Technical Publications Group will also be found in Chapter 14.

BIBLIOGRAPHY

Air Force Systems Command. *System Engineering Management Procedures,* AFSCM 375–5, 1964.

———. *System Program Management,* AFSCM 375–4, 1965.

ALFANDARY-ALEXANDER, MARK, ed. *Analysis for Planning Programming Budgeting.* Washington, D.C.: Washington Operations Research Council, 1968.

ARCHIBALD, R. D., and VILLORIA, R. L. *Network-based Management Systems (PERT/CPM).* New York, N.Y.: John Wiley & Sons, Inc., 1967.

BAUMGARTNER, JOHN S. *Project Management.* Homewood, Ill.: Richard D. Irwin, Inc., 1963.

———. "Project Management." In *Handbook of Business Administration,* edited by H. B. Maynard. New York, N.Y.: McGraw-Hill Book Company, 1967.

BOOZ, ALLEN & HAMILTON. *Project Manager's Handbook.* Loose-leaf. Chicago, Ill., 1967.

BURGESS, JOHN A. "Making the Most of Design Reviews," *Machine Design,* July 4, 1968.

CLELAND, DAVID I. "Organizational Dynamics of Project Management," *IEEE Transactions on Engineering Management,* December, 1966.

———. "Why Project Management?", *Business Horizons,* Winter, 1964.

CLELAND, DAVID I., and KING, WILLIAM R. *Systems Analysis and Project Management.* New York, N.Y.: McGraw-Hill Book Company, 1968.

DEAN, BURTON V. *Evaluating, Selecting and Controlling R & D Projects,* AMA Research Study 89. New York, N.Y.: American Management Association, Inc., 1968.

DEAVIES, EMMETT G. 1964. "Management of the Project Staff." Unpublished paper, School of Management, Rensselaer Polytechnic Institute, April, 1964.

Department of Defense, Office of the Secretary of Defense. *Standardization Manual M205—Military Outline of Form and Instructions for the Preparation of Specifications.* Washington, D.C.: Superintendent of Documents, U.S. Government Printing Office, 1953.

FITZGERALD, A. J., and GLIE, ROWEN. "A Guide to Technical Specifications," *Machine Design,* July 6, 1961.

FLEISCHMANN, WALTER L. "Specifications, Their Preparation and Use," special report from *Metal Progress,* undated.

FRIED, GEORGE. "Convertible Engineering," *Machine Design,* March 3, 1960.

GADDIS, PAUL O. "The Project Manager," *Harvard Business Review,* May–June, 1959.

GILMAN, WILLIAM. *The Language of Science.* New York, N.Y.: Harcourt, Brace, & World, Inc., 1961.

HANSEN, JOHN V. E. "How to Use Technical Writers to Increase Efficiency of Engineering Functions," *Machine Design,* November 28, 1957.

HOWELL, ROBERT A. "Multiproject Control," *Harvard Business Review,* March–April, 1968.

JOHNSON, R. A.; KAST, R. E.; and ROSENZWEIG, J. E. *The Theory and Management of Systems.* New York, N.Y.: McGraw-Hill Book Company, 1963.

LANIER, H. F. "Organizing for Large Engineering Projects," *Machine Design,* December 27, 1956.

MANDEL, SIEGFRIED, ed. *Writing in Industry.* New York, N.Y.: Polytechnic Press of the Polytechnic Institute of Brooklyn, 1959.

MARTINO, R. L. *Project Management and Control.* 3 vols. New York, N.Y.: Presidents Professional Association, American Management Association, Inc., 1964–65.

MCGEE, A. A., and MARKARIAN, M. D. "Optimum Allocation of Research/ Engineering Manpower Within a Multi-Project Organizational Structure," International Business Machines Report No. 61-907-171, December, 1961. Oswego, N.Y.: International Business Machines Corp., 1961.

MIDDLETON, C. J. "How to Set Up a Project Organization," *Harvard Business Review,* March–April, 1967.

MODER, J. J., and PHILLIPS, C. R. *Project Management with CPM and PERT.* New York, N.Y.: Reinhold Publishing Corp., 1964.

MORRISON, EDWARD J. "Defense Systems Management: The 375 Series," *California Management Review,* Summer, 1967.

MURDICK, R. G. "The Cognizant Engineer," *Machine Design,* April 25, 1963.

———. "Engineering and Research Reports," *ibid.,* August 31, 1961.

MURDICK, R. G., and OPPENHEIM, A. "Programming for Complex Projects," *Machine Design,* October 2, 1958.

National Aeronautics and Space Administration and Office of the Secretary of Defense. *DOD and NASA Guide—PERT Cost.* Washington, D.C.: Superintendent of Documents, U.S. Government Printing Office, June, 1962.

PAIGE, HILLIARD W. "How PERT-COST Helps the General Manager," *Harvard Business Review,* November–December, 1963.

QUADE, E. S. *Systems Analysis Techniques For Planning-Programming-Budgeting.* P-3322. Santa Monica, Calif.: The Rand Corp., 1966.

RUBIN, IRWIN M., and SEELIG, WYCKHAM. "Experience as a Factor in the Selection and Performance of Project Managers," *IEEE Transactions on Engineering Management,* Vol. EM-14, No. 3, September, 1967.

SADOW, R. W. "How PERT Was Used in Managing the X-20 (Dyna-Soar) Program," *IEEE Transactions on Engineering Management,* December, 1964.

THOMAS, A. M. "The Product Design Review Committee," *Machine Design,* January 7, 1960.

CHAPTER 10

Financial Planning and Cost Control

RELATIONSHIP BETWEEN TECHNICAL AND FINANCIAL PLANNING FOR E & R

In a company in which engineering and research are the only products sold, it is immediately apparent that closely integrated technical and financial planning is necessary. Profits depend on maintaining costs below the selling price of the service that is sold. In the more complex case of development projects in which hardware must be delivered, poor financial planning may often obscure the proper allocation of costs so that project overruns produce either financial losses or loss of future business.

Finally, in many companies, the engineering and research work is considered an overhead expense. E & R is devoted primarily to evolutionary product improvement or new product development. While control of costs is maintained by a fixed budget, the connection between financial planning and technical productivity is tenuous at best. The hazard in this instance is that on a long-range basis the company will either fall behind technically or sustain disproportionate costs for its E & R.

The project management techniques such as PERT/Cost have been developed to permit careful technical planning and cost reporting of E & R. Reporting of costs and subsequent attempts at correction are not enough by themselves. The real key to cost control lies in forecasting technical activities and costs on a very short-range basis (month-to-month in most cases, but even week-to-week in some) as well as for a year ahead. Monthly forecasts and cumulative annual forecasts based on actual plus forecast data will allow managers to anticipate problem areas in advance. Variances of any kind may be related directly to the technical areas. The basic relationships and lines of communication connecting technical and financial activities are illustrated in Fig. 10-1.

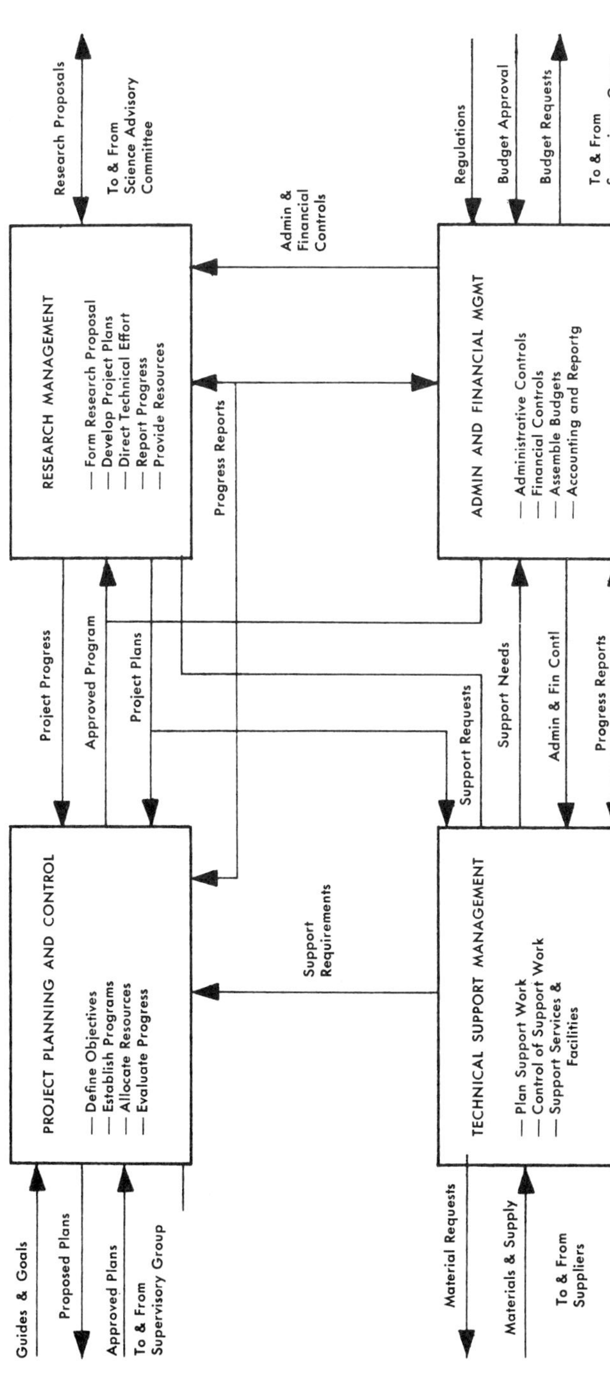

Fig. 10-1. Areas of and relationships between major responsibility groups. *Source:* Harold M. Sollenberger, *Major Changes Caused by Implementation of a Management Information System,* NAA Research Monograph 4 (New York: National Association of Accountants, 1968), p. 35.

PROFITS AND COSTING BASICS

The basic accounting (and economic) formula for a profit oriented enterprise is simply:

$$\text{Profit} = \text{Revenue} - \text{Expense}$$

This is the essence of the Profit and Loss (P & L) statement of accounting. Revenue comes primarily from sales of goods and services (operating income) and miscellaneous income such as interest and sales of items the company has used but no longer needs.

Expenses are usually shown on the P & L statement as (1) Cost of Goods Sold, (2) Selling Costs, and (3) General and Administrative Costs. E & R costs are often buried in the latter, but when they apply to specific products they are included in Cost of Goods Sold.

Allocation of E & R costs requires the combined efforts of the technical organization and the accounting department. Therefore, it is advisable for all engineers having responsibility for expenditure of funds to have a basic knowledge of cost elements. Those cost elements which may contribute to E & R costs are:

1.* Research and advance development engineering
2.* System and/or pre-production product engineering
3.* Product support engineering
4. Facility cost
5. Equipment cost
6. Tool, jig, fixture, and miscellaneous materials handling equipment cost
7. Purchased materials cost
8. Direct labor cost (manufacturing)
9. Shrinkage
10. Scrap
11. Transportation
12. Overhead
13. Selling expense
14. General and administration expense
15. Patent license cost
16. Special taxes.

These costs should be segregated into Direct Costs and Indirect Costs (or Overhead or Burden). Direct Costs consist primarily of salaries of technical people working on the particular job plus materials used for the job (Direct Materials). The trend is to charge all salary-related items and

* Includes direct labor, overhead, other applied charges, etc., as later outlined in detail.

benefits to Direct Costs to reduce the overhead costs. The reason for this is that Direct Costs are controllable by the technical personnel, whereas indirect costs extending over a period of time such as insurance, taxes, administrative salaries, and company-wide assessments are beyond the control of the technical personnel. It is particularly important that budgeting and cost reporting in technical organizations be in terms of direct costs. "Accounts" or "Shop Orders" identified by titles and code numbers are established to permit collection of costs at the smallest subdivision of element costs desired. At the other end, a summary cost analysis is usually prepared for recosting old products or costing new products or proposals. (See Fig. 10-2.)

Accounting Treatment of E & R (by Enrico Petri)

The cost of E & R referred to alternatively as Research and Development by accountants and Research and Experiment by the Treasury Department has been subject to varied treatment in both accounting and taxation.

Accounting treatment is conceptually based on the determination of whether the expenditure gives rise to an asset or an expense and whether the asset is tangible or intangible in nature. An asset is created if the expenditure generates revenue beyond the year of its incurrence. The uncertainty associated with this determination has encouraged accountants to expense E & R costs as incurred. Recording an asset is known as "capitalizing" the cost. If the E & R cost directly results in the creation of a tangible asset, it is added to the asset's cost and ultimately appears as an expense in the form of a periodic depreciation charge, if the direct costing[1] approach is used. Under absorption costing, depreciation (and other fixed overhead) is added to the cost of units produced, thereby entering the expense stream as a "cost of units sold."

E & R costs may also contribute to the creation of intangible assets. Intangible assets are classified as follows:

(a) Those having a term of existence limited by law, regulation or agreement, or by their nature (such as patents, copyrights, leases, licenses, franchises for a fixed term, and goodwill . . . of limited duration);

(b) Those having no such limited term of existence and as to which there is, at the time of acquisition, no indication of limited life (such as goodwill generally, going value, trade names, secret processes, subscription lists, perpetual franchises, and organization costs).[2]

[1] Direct costing (or variable costing) charges all fixed costs each year as an expense of that period. Absorption costing creates fixed manufacturing costs as a product cost, that is, adds it to the cost of units produced.

[2] AICPA Committee on Accounting Procedure, Accounting Research and Terminology Bulletins, Final Edition, Chapter 5, p. 37.

___ Cost Estimate
___ Bid Estimate
___ Engineering
___ C.P.F.F.
___ Fixed Price
___ Cost Indication
___ Make-Buy

THE NEW PRODUCT COMPANY
Plant - New York, New York

BR. or Est. No. 2536
Date January 5, 1969
Page 1 of 1

Distribution	Customer: Manufacturers of Military Electronic Equip. Customer No.:	Item #	Qty.	At	Amount
H. B. Allen	Article: Special high-temperature elec-				
G. M. Clark	trolytic capacitor having extremely low			(unit cost)	
J. E. West	electrical leakage				
I. Newman	Representative unit	1	150M	$6.70	$405,000.00

		%	1					
1	Material		2.78					
2	Shrinkage	2	.06					
3	Procurement	5	.14					
4	Transportation	1	.03					
5	Total Material		3.01					
6								
7	Labor		.34					
8	Efficiency	90	.03					
9	Total Labor		.37					
10								
11	Overhead	181	.67					
12	Pre-Prod. Engr.		not charged					
13	Tools Etc.		.19					
14	Prod. Support Engr.		.13					
15	Engineering Labor		4.37					
16	Engineering O/H							
17	Total Mfg. Cost							
18	Interest							
19	Gen. & Admin.	5	.22					
20	Institutional Adv.	1	.04					
21	Royalties							
22								
23								
24	Total Cost		4.63					
25	Desired Profit		2.07					
26	Des. Selling Price		6.70					
27	Actual Profit		2.07					
28	Act. Selling Price		6.70					

Delivery and F.O.B. Point: New York, N. Y.

Comments: The above cost estimate is for a typical capacitor with a current selling price of $6.70 each.
Pre-Production engineering is considered as a legitimate charge against company R & D budget.
Pre-Production engineering is amortized over estimated first year's production for costing purposes.
Tool and Facilities are lumped into one charge and amortized over a three-year period for costing--
therefore one-third (1/3) of total charged to first year's production.

J. Blow — Product Manager   J. E. West — Engineer   Cost Estimating   J. Adams — Estimator

GL319-2 M-1705-2

Fig. 10-2. Sample cost analysis form for costing new products. *Source:* Delmar W. Karger, *The New Product* (New York: The Industrial Press, 1960).

The costs of limited life intangibles (Type a) are systematically charged to expense on the income statement over the periods benefited. This periodic write-off of an intangible asset is called "amortization."[3]

[3] However, the Treasury Department designates the periodic writeoff of intangibles of *determinable life* as DEPRECIATION. Sec. 1.167 (a)(3) Federal Regulations.

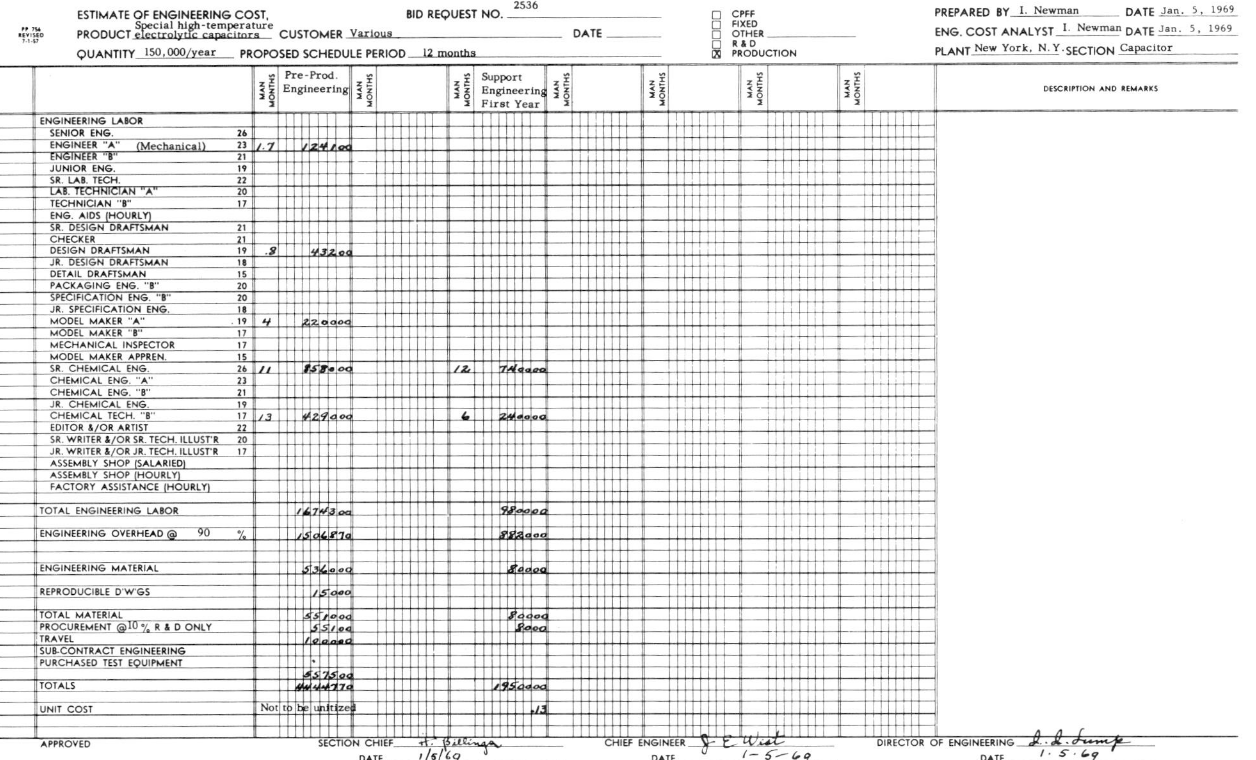

PP 756 REVISED 7-1-57

ESTIMATE OF ENGINEERING COST,   BID REQUEST NO. 2536
PRODUCT Special high-temperature electrolytic capacitors   CUSTOMER Various   DATE
QUANTITY 150,000/year   PROPOSED SCHEDULE PERIOD 12 months

☐ CPFF
☐ FIXED
☐ OTHER
☐ R & D
☒ PRODUCTION

PREPARED BY I. Newman   DATE Jan. 5, 1969
ENG. COST ANALYST I. Newman   DATE Jan. 5, 1969
PLANT New York, N.Y.   SECTION Capacitor

		MAN MONTHS	Pre-Prod. Engineering	MAN MONTHS		MAN MONTHS	Support Engineering First Year	MAN MONTHS		MAN MONTHS		MAN MONTHS		MAN MONTHS		DESCRIPTION AND REMARKS
ENGINEERING LABOR																
SENIOR ENG.	26															
ENGINEER "A" (Mechanical)	23	1.7	124100													
ENGINEER "B"	21															
JUNIOR ENG.	19															
SR. LAB. TECH.	22															
LAB. TECHNICIAN "A"	20															
TECHNICIAN "B"	17															
ENG. AIDS (HOURLY)																
SR. DESIGN DRAFTSMAN	21															
CHECKER	21															
DESIGN DRAFTSMAN	19	.8	43200													
JR. DESIGN DRAFTSMAN	18															
DETAIL DRAFTSMAN	15															
PACKAGING ENG. "B"	20															
SPECIFICATION ENG. "B"	20															
JR. SPECIFICATION ENG.	18															
MODEL MAKER "A"	19	4	220000													
MODEL MAKER "B"	17															
MECHANICAL INSPECTOR	17															
MODEL MAKER APPREN.	15															
SR. CHEMICAL ENG.	26	11	858000			12	744000									
CHEMICAL ENG. "A"	23															
CHEMICAL ENG. "B"	21															
JR. CHEMICAL ENG.	19															
CHEMICAL TECH. "B"	17	13	429000			6	244000									
EDITOR &/OR ARTIST	22															
SR. WRITER &/OR SR. TECH. ILLUST'R	20															
JR. WRITER &/OR JR. TECH. ILLUST'R	17															
ASSEMBLY SHOP (SALARIED)																
ASSEMBLY SHOP (HOURLY)																
FACTORY ASSISTANCE (HOURLY)																
TOTAL ENGINEERING LABOR			1674300				980000									
ENGINEERING OVERHEAD @ 90 %			1506870				882000									
ENGINEERING MATERIAL			536000				80000									
REPRODUCIBLE D'W'GS			15000													
TOTAL MATERIAL			551000				80000									
PROCUREMENT @10 % R & D ONLY			55100				8000									
TRAVEL			100000													
SUB-CONTRACT ENGINEERING																
PURCHASED TEST EQUIPMENT			557500													
TOTALS			4444770				1950000									
UNIT COST		Not to be unitized					.13									

APPROVED   SECTION CHIEF H. Billinga   DATE 1/5/69   CHIEF ENGINEER J. E. West   DATE 1-5-69   DIRECTOR OF ENGINEERING L. L. Lump   DATE 1.5.69

Fig. 10-3. Preproduction engineering estimate shown on a typical engineering estimating form. *Source:* See Fig. 10-2.

Unlimited life intangibles (Type b) are not subject to amortization until it becomes evident that their term of existence has become limited.[4]

Preliminary to capitalizing or expensing E & R cost, the accountant seeks to determine whether the purpose of the expenditure is to maintain a competitive position or to expand the firm's position in the market. Continuing E & R expenditures to improve or replace an existing line are of the former type; they simply maintain current levels of revenue and hence are expensed. E & R expenditures whose benefits are indeterminate or uncertain are also expensed currently. E & R expenditures incurred to develop a new product line or major changes in old lines are expected to generate future revenue streams and should be capitalized.

Some firms whose E & R expenses remain a relatively constant percentage of revenue expense their E & R costs annually. Annual expensing under these conditions tends to offset the problem of cost and revenue not being matched from a time viewpoint. Net income is, therefore, not significantly different from what it would be if costs were capitalized and amortized.

Whether to "expense" or "capitalize" is sometimes settled by the nature of the contract, cost plus, for example, where the firm is assured of recapturing E & R costs as well as a stipulated rate of return.

While accountants list numerous factors as guidelines to "capitalizing" or "expensing," the final determination must be made on the particular facts involved and an appraisal of the benefits to be obtained.

Tax Aspect. Research and experimental expenditures are defined for tax purposes in Sec. 1.174-2(a)(1) of the Federal Regulations as follows:

> (a) In general. (1) The term "research or experimental expenditures," as used in section 174, means expenditures incurred in connection with the taxpayer's trade or business which represents research and development costs in the experimental or laboratory sense. The term includes generally all such costs incident to the development of an experimental or pilot model, a plant process, a product, a formula, an invention, or similar property, and the improvement of already existing property of the type mentioned. The term does not include expenditures such as those for the ordinary testing or inspection of materials or products for quality control or those for efficiency surveys, management studies, consumer surveys, advertising or promotions. However, the term includes the costs of obtaining a patent such as attorney's fees expended in making and perfecting a patent application. On the other hand, the term does not include the costs of acquiring another's patent, model, production or process, nor does it include expenditures paid or incurred for research in connection with literary, historical, or similar projects.

Under Section 174 I.R.C., the taxpayer has the option of treating E & R either:

1. As an expense fully deductible in the year incurred or,
2. As a deferred item to be amortized over a period exceeding 60 months.

[4] When Type (b) intangible life becomes limited, it becomes subject to Type (a) treatment. It is written off over the remaining life.

Failure to exercise the option will result in it being treated as a charge to capital. This means that the taxpayer will be unable to deduct the expenditure until the project is terminated or abandoned.[5] The tax definition of a capital asset is different from that in accounting. Section 1221 I.R.C. defines a capital asset as, among other things, *not including,*

> property . . . subject to an allowance for depreciation . . . or real property used in a trade or business.

This tax treatment is similar to the accounting treatment of an unlimited life intangible.

An election[6] by the taxpayer to defer E & R expenditure will permit their amortization over any *arbitrary period* selected by the taxpayer of not less than 60 months. Deferral, even though elected, will not be permitted where the property resulting from the E & R expenditure has a *determinable useful life.* In this instance, the expenditure *must* be amortized or depreciated over its *determinable useful life.*[7]

Tax versus Accounting Approach. E & R is one of the areas where tax and accounting treatment need not agree. Thus, the taxpayer may "expense" E & R for taxes and "capitalize" them on the books and statements.[8]

Research, Development, and Product Engineering (Preproduction)

E & R costs can be summarized on a form similar to that shown in Fig. 10-3, with one column allocated to each major portion of the engineering effort associated with a particular proposal and/or product. Involved in the E & R effort that is required prior to production are such items as the following:

1. Salaries of scientists and/or engineers to conduct research and other investigations of the problem
2. Salaries of scientists and/or engineers to produce preliminary and final designs

[5] Sec. 1.167(a)-3, Regulations state that an intangible whose life is limited may be depreciated. Charging E & R to a capital account obviously treats it as an intangible of unlimited life.

[6] An election, once made to expense E & R expenditures, is applicable to all such costs incurred unless, on request, the Commissioner of Internal Revenue allows a change. Sec. 174(b)(2) I.R.C., 1.174-3(a), (b)(3) Regs.

[7] For illustration see Sec. 1.174-4(a)(4) Regs.

[8] Revenue Ruling 57-58, 1958-1 CB, p. 148. Of course such a procedure will result in taxable income different from accounting income. When this occurs, generally accepted accounting principles require recognition of deferred tax effect in the accounts and on financial statements. See: H. Black, Accounting Research Study, No. 9, "Interperiod Allocation of Corporate Income Taxes," American Institute of CPAs, 1966; Opinion of Accounting Principles Board, No. 11, "Accounting for Income Taxes," American Institute of CPAs.

3. Salaries of engineers working on standardization and reliability problems
4. Junior engineer and/or technician labor to support the above work
5. Industrial design and/or packaging engineering costs
6. Internal and external consulting engineering or technical specialist costs
7. Production engineering
8. Drafting labor
9. Specification engineering costs
10. Library research for or by any of the above classes of personnel
11. Craft and/or model-maker labor costs required to construct simulated and working models
12. Technical publication costs for writers, illustrators, etc.
13. Subcontracted engineering and experimental work
14. Subcontracted labor (internal or external to the company)
15. Cost of blueprints, photostats, etc.
16. Engineering material—raw, semifinished, and finished
17. Cost of special machines, special test equipment, etc., that should be charged directly to the project
18. Procurement and/or transportation cost chargeable against the material purchased
19. Engineering overhead on the labor
20. Travel of engineering personnel caused directly by the project
21. Patent license fees and associated legal expense
22. Telephone, telegraph, and other telecommunications
23. Miscellaneous expenses.

The above can serve as a partial checklist of the more commonly encountered costs associated with an engineering project. It would be virtually impossible to cover every possible category or kind of cost that might be encountered. However, it is vitally important not to overlook any hidden costs such as the necessity to manufacture in the engineering department a small number of samples or test pieces that must be submitted to the government or to prospective customers for evaluation and possible destruction testing.

Production Support Engineering

For new products, after the development and documentation have been completed, further engineering is usually required to support initial manufacturing. These costs should be segregated from development costs even though the elements may be similar and the same cost form is used.

Facility Cost

Facilities are capital items (but not all capital items are facilities) ranging from buildings to work benches. Definitions vary from company to company, but generally it is advantageous to consider facilities as being those items which could have a future use for other product development as opposed to special-purpose items for single-shot use.

Buildings are accounted for as capital expenditures and must be depreciated over the period of economic usefulness of the assets. Such depreciation is charged into an overhead account. If the E & R organization is utilizing a building, the depreciation will be charged to the E & R overhead account.

Some items which are normally charged as a lump sum or expense for the year may sometimes be capitalized and amortized *for the purpose of product costing*. In practice, plant and industrial engineering departments help in establishing ordinary facility costs.

Equipment Cost

E & R equipment consists of tangible items, other than plant used for research, development, or engineering design or support purposes. Equipment is generally a capital item, but in some cases may be used up in a year or destroyed in the process of using it and hence may be an expense.

The manager of E & R may also be concerned with estimating the total cost for a new product. In such a case, he will need to consider choices between purchase of manufacturing equipment at different levels of automation and alternative cost of fabrication. Such choices also affect the type and cost of raw materials used. Engineering will be called upon to consider concessions on tolerances, materials, shapes, and processes. The purchasing department and value engineers or analysts can provide considerable help in developing improved methods and lower cost estimates.

Tool, Jig, Fixture, and Miscellaneous Materials Handling Equipment Costs

This cost element is normally associated with the manufacturing effort and especially the first item, tool costs, can be subdivided into two categories:

1. Vendor tool costs
2. Internal company tool costs.

Purchased Material Costs

In connection with the above comment on tool costs, it is wise for the E & R manager to know that if a company needs to manufacture special tools in order to produce a part for either the engineering or the manufacturing effort, that vendors will sometimes "bury" the special tool cost in the cost per part. On other occasions they will quote the tool cost as separate from the piece part cost. This latter approach is advantageous to the company requesting the quotation because, first, one knows exactly what the tooling costs are, and secondly, since the tool is paid for as a separate item, it becomes the property of the purchaser once a job is completed. If this approach is not taken, the part is delivered and the supplier keeps the tool for either its scrap value or for use on future jobs. It is for this reason that it is wise to have vendor quotations on parts and/or equipment to be segregated into:

1. Special tool costs
2. Selling price for the material or product desired.

In summary, this action has these advantages:

1. Facilitates analysis of the quotation
2. Usually yields a lowest quote on repeat orders
3. Results in control of the toolings so as to:
   a. Prevent the vendor from using it to make parts for a competitor
   b. Make possible the removal of the tooling from the vendor in the event that the company decides to make the part itself or to give future orders to another vendor.
4. Permits the greatest degree of flexibility in handling the tool charges since it makes possible a choice of:
   a. Charging to the first order (which the vendor would probably do if the tool cost was not covered as a separate item)
   b. Amortization over any arbitrary quantity *for product costing* (not permissible from a *tax* view)
   c. Taking the cost out of future profits
   d. Deferring and amortizing over current and future runs.

One facet that must be considered in the analysis of material costs in an estimate is that actual purchases usually can be made at five to ten percent under the quotations obtained for the cost estimate. While much depends upon the types and kinds of materials involved, the previous statement is generally true if the purchased material portion of the estimate is considered in its entirety.

Direct Labor Cost

For purposes of E & R planning, budgeting, and controlling, salaries of technical people contributing directly to the development and design of a product are treated as direct labor by the E & R organization. Since the total of the E & R costs represent a lump sum, they are not related to the number of items manufactured in an industrial firm. Therefore, E & R costs, from the accountant's viewpoint, are usually liquidated as indirect expenses over a period of time.

From the manufacturing and accounting viewpoint, labor which is used directly in the manufacture of the product is considered direct labor or prime labor. If engineering work is to be conducted throughout the life of the product, such engineering salary costs may also be considered as direct labor costs.

In project management, the manager of E & R may estimate direct labor costs on the basis of technical tasks and organization. That is, the project is divided into tasks and subtasks and the man-months or man-years to complete each task are estimated. The quality of engineers as well as quantity will affect direct labor costs, so that more refined estimates should take this into account. Further, the amount of indirect labor support such as secretaries, clerks, and administrative workers can reduce the number of technical manhours required.

In functional organizations where many small projects are worked on by different groups, estimates of direct labor costs for a product are more difficult to make and costs are more difficult to control. Engineers do not work continuously on a single project so that startup time is required each time they shift back to a particular product problem. Liaison is often more difficult and time consuming. If possible, actual calendar times should be established for work on a particular product, so that control of direct costs is made easier.

The E & R manager should also recognize that competitive products play an important part in his design. The total E & R costs and the direct labor costs for manufacture cannot be allowed to be so large that the product would be priced out of the market.

Shrinkage

While this generally relates to the manufacturing area of a business, it can apply to E & R. Also, E & R personnel can affect manufacturing's material shrinkage. Many kinds of problems can be buried under this term. It is intended here to cover the ordinary material losses, over-buys, over-shipments accepted, etc. It is not intended that this item cover such losses as can be incurred when whole units or sections of a unit must be scrapped due to destructive testing or where the construction of the unit is such that it cannot be repaired if it happens to fail after assembly and adjustment. These latter instances should be covered under the cost element—"Scrap." Other material losses classified as shrinkage are bound to occur because of pilferage, carelessness in handling or because incorrect or incomplete records were kept of items actually used. Engineering and research personnel often contribute to such losses by unauthorized usage of parts for experimental purposes. It is, unfortunately, a habit of many engineers to visit the factory and take parts off the production floor to use in engineering without charging them out properly.

Another kind of shrinkage loss occurs because vendors, when shipping certain types of parts, are normally permitted to over- or under-ship by a small percentage of the total quantity ordered. Such permissible over-shipments (the usual case) cause unbalanced inventory and increase the cost of the product. Other parts are damaged in processing due to errors or accidents. All these situations cause a shrinkage in inventory that must be compensated for in the cost structure.

It is usual for the cost estimating section of the cost department in cooperation with Material Control to apply a percentage factor, based on guess and experience, against the unit material cost sufficient to compensate for shrinkage. Shrinkage varies from a fraction of a per cent up to 5 to 10 per cent of the material cost, depending upon the product, the class or kind of parts, the complexity of the product, the number of parts, etc. One way of reducing shrinkage to the minimum is to pay particular attention to controlling the usage of the more expensive parts and keep the shrinkage on these to a minimum. Often this can be kept down to a tenth of one per cent; then, one can allow the control imposed on low-priced items to be somewhat relaxed since shrinkage in these will only have a minor effect on overall costs.

Scrap

When scrap exists, it affects *both material and labor.* Scrap, like shrinkage, can and does occur in *both* E & R and in Manufacturing. While it can often be handled as a percentage factor in the cost analysis in a similar manner to shrinkage, it is often necessary to cost it out separately if actual units must be constructed and later destroyed.

More importantly, it should be remembered that if a unit is scrapped, it contains not only material which costs money but also labor and its associated overhead which costs money. Moreover, there is always the labor associated with the actual scrapping of the part with a possible minor return from salvaged material. Another cost element that can be considered under this subject is the cost of repairing damaged or bad units. Scrap is an item that the E & R manager and the cost department cannot afford to overlook.

Transportation

This cost element appears to be deceptively simple. The expense of transporting materials, equipment, tools, jigs, fixtures, etc., are the charges involved. Both Engineering and Manufacturing incur transportation charges.

A common way for cost accountants to handle this element is to increase the base material cost by a percentage. However, it is usual to segregate the transportation costs associated with capital or special equipment and estimate these separately so that they usually become an integral part of such equipment cost.

Transportation costs for the manufacturing activity normally range from 1 to 2 per cent of the material cost. However, they can be considerably more or less depending upon the kind of material involved. Transportation costs become even more involved and difficult when one or more plants of a company are shipping material to another which in turn assembles the item. In connection with E & R budgets, this accounting classification often covers the moving expenses associated with both old and new personnel.

Overhead

Overhead in E & R is almost universally handled as a percentage application against direct labor cost. It is designed to cover indirect costs associated with the personnel whose labor is classified as direct. It is not designed to cover indirect expenses such as advertising, general administrative, interest, selling, etc.

Precisely which accounts are classified as overhead varies with the company. In the engineering department, the following items or functions have been classified as overhead:

Maintenance
Drafting
Model shop
Tool room
Blueprint department
Dues and subscriptions
Library
Operating supplies
Travel
Telephone and telegraph
Secretarial and clerical
Employee service expense
Memberships
Books and subscriptions for personnel
Professional services
Publications and cataloguing
Electricity
Water
Gas
Stationery and office supplies
Freight, express, and cartage
Operation and maintenance of company automobiles
Postage
Fuel
Laboratory visits
Donations
Compressed air
Outside stenographic services
Rent
Depreciation
Buildings and grounds charges
Allocated charges from Accounting, Personnel, etc.
Purchasing
Legal staff.

While all of the above have been classified as overhead accounts in some companies, many of them have also been classified as direct costs in other firms. The E & R manager should become very familiar with which cost elements are actually included in overhead in his company and which are to be classified as direct. The actual practice within a given company may vary because of special clauses in contracts.

The accounting department will establish a special code number for each type of expense so that they can be properly allocated to product, to function, and to overhead or to expense. Proper coding of actual charges is as important to the E & R manager as a proper estimation of costs. Improper coding can cause the budget forecast for his activity or the estimated cost on a project to be out of line. This kind of error can be as embarrassing as when actual charges get out of line due to a lack of proper control or because of poor estimating.

Overhead can be divided into two fundamental divisions. One of these divisions is known as fixed overhead charges. While it is true that virtually nothing in industry actually remains fixed, it is a fact that many indirect overhead charges are essentially constant within a relevant range of activity. A sample of such charges are rent, building upkeep (landlord expense), certain salaries such as those of the E & R manager and other similar functional managers, heat, etc.

The other fundamental division of overhead contains the variable expenses. Examples of variable expenses are supervisors' salaries, general clerical salaries, accounting salaries, receiving and shipping department operating costs, etc. The greater the level of direct labor activity, the more personnel for the supporting functions are required; hence, the greater the associated expense from items such as those listed above.

Sometimes companies take advantage of this fundamental division in overhead charges in costing new products. Management will sometimes agree to only charge the variable overhead against the direct labor during the initial product activity.

Selling Expense

If the product being developed is similar to, or a part of, the current product line, marketing expense may be estimated as a percent of selling price on the basis of past ratios.

If a new product is being introduced, assumptions must be made regarding the marketing effort which will be made to sell the product. Detailed estimates should be made of marketing research costs, promotional costs, distributional costs, and service costs. The manager of E & R may help in identifying customers, selecting channels of distribution, and preparation of advertising and technical manuals, if the product is primarily an industrial item.

General and Administrative Expense

G & A, as the above is commonly referred to, like selling expense, is self-explanatory and is usually a percentage application against total manufacturing cost or total cost as defined by line 24 of Fig. 10-2. It involves the cost of maintaining the top management echelon of the company and distributes the cost of such activity over the entire product line and services offered by the company.

Patent License Costs

This is sometimes included in G & A. In any event, it is usually a percentage application against either total manufacturing cost or cost of sales (essentially line 24 of Fig. 10-2). As mentioned under legal considerations, royalty payments are usually determined by applying the royalty percentage against the cost of the product or the selling price.

Special Taxes

This cost element usually appears where a state sales tax is involved. If any special tax is levied, it is usual to levy it against selling price although it could involve the application of a percentage against such items as labor, manufacturing cost, total cost, material only, etc.

E & R and the Costing Problem

It is not enough to merely know about the various cost elements and how each one contributes to the over-all cost. Neither is it enough to merely know ways of reducing specific cost elements. In order to effectively handle the costing problem, the E & R manager must see to it that Engineering provides complete cooperation and assistance to all elements in the organization. Costing is an onerous chore, and normally engineers do not like to be involved. Unfortunately they must be involved, and they must participate in a cooperative manner. If they do not assist in the cost estimating effort to the best of their ability and try in every possible manner to help all elements of the organization "beat the cost into line," the cost will be too high and the contract will not be obtained or the product will never reach the market in a successful manner.

BUDGETS, COST REPORTING AND CONTROL

Budgets represent the economic and time quantification of the technical plan. Budgets that are closely tied to technical task descriptions represent the basis of good planning. The reporting of performance against budget goals and standards permit measurement of performance and control of E & R activities. Budgets can only succeed, however, if their purpose is made clear to engineers and scientists and their impact on daily activities of technical personnel is minimized by competent financial personnel. From the viewpoint of the engineers and managers with responsibility for expenditures, budgets and reports offer a means for them to do a better job and perhaps prevent disastrous failure.

Budgeting and cost reporting lead to better definition of objectives, more effective evaluation of work in progress by each level of management, and better measurement of performance at every level. Budgeting and cost reporting may be fairly general or very detailed, according to the size of the organization, the size of the budgets, the needs of the organization, and the benefits desired. For example, a small E & R organization that does no service work for other departments and that does not sell or license its products to other companies will require very little effort in the budgeting area. On the other hand, a large research department working on numerous projects with responsibilities delegated to several project managers and to others at lower management levels will find it desirable and necessary to prepare quite detailed budgets.

The process of budgeting and cost reporting is an important phase of measuring and evaluating engineering and research, as discussed in Chapter 13. The gathering of information, the preparation of preliminary budgets, the consolidation of budgeting information, and the distribution of cost reports received from the accounting department are functions which may be carried out by the engineering administration organization. The remainder of this chapter will be concerned with some of the mechanics of this process and certain related principles and philosophical considerations.

In budgeting for E & R work there must be a close relationship between the organizational structure, the budget, and the cost reporting system. That is, clear-cut responsibility for packages of work must be related to clear-cut responsibility for expenditures to accomplish this work.

Budgets should be prepared for at least one year in advance. This does not mean that there will be no allowance for changed conditions. A quarterly or semiannual review may be made, and if changed circumstances warrant, the budget for the year should be revised. However, there should be a careful justification for major changes. In this way, the budget becomes a tool, not a master.

Budgeting assists E & R operation and planning in several specific ways:

1. It insures periodic program review
2. It requires that programs be planned completely and effectively
3. It helps coordinate research activities by:
   a. Balancing activities within the program
   b. Encouraging the exchange of information
   c. Coordinating current and long-range plans
4. It establishes checkpoints for both projects and organizational units for later application of control actions
5. It encourages information exchange between E & R, management, and operating groups.

The E & R budget forecast and reporting system helps to control expenses before, rather than after, they have occurred. Preparation of budgets forces managers to review progress periodically and to replan the program where such action is required. Budget reviews have two beneficial effects:

1. The overall program cannot grow haphazardly
2. Project budget reviews provide a stimulus to show progress.

At budget reviews which usually occur quarterly or semiannually as well as annually, managers must justify their performance and any request for new project funds. Justification of any expenditure, whether within budget or out of budget, rests on proving the productivity of the group and the benefits to be ultimately derived by the company from the activities which were carried on during the budget period.

In the process of developing budgets, research managers are forced to plan their program in a concrete fashion. The careful planning and scheduling required by the budgeting effort helps orient the E & R staff to the nature and the magnitude of the technical problems they will face and to interrelate the various parts of the various projects to the whole technical program.

The budget is a planning device that coordinates the detailed technical plans into one overall picture. It helps planners to see the aggregate impact of detailed man-hour schedules, equipment schedules, personnel-acquisition schedules, etc., in addition to forcing a consideration of these for each project or program. Budgeting tends to eliminate "firefighting" and the introduction of pressure projects. The overall management review of the E & R budget also will help eliminate duplication of effort.

The Capital Budget

The capital budget may be prepared under two general headings—capital requirements and capital contingencies. Under the heading of capital requirements would be listed a brief description and the estimated cost of each item which the E & R activity can foresee as necessary during the budget period. Under the heading of capital contingencies would be listed a brief description and estimated cost of those items that the department thinks it might become necessary to acquire and which depend upon the outcome of work in progress or the completion of plans in development. Ordinarily these items would concentrate in the latter part of the budget period, and some of them would be transferred to capital requirements in the preparation of subsequent budgets.

The capital budget for E & R can be divided into two categories:

1. Equipment needed in order to complete a particular project
2. Equipment which generally makes it possible for E & R to work more effectively and efficiently.

Examples of the former kind of equipment might include radiation and/or soundproof rooms, special test equipment, laboratory space, etc. If equipment is absolutely required in order to complete a particular project or program, management can evaluate its worth by considering the potential value of the results expected from the particular program or project. Here, the evaluation of the whole program in its entirety is involved, and approval of any required capital facilities must be on the basis of the attractiveness of the individual programs and projects involved.

If the equipment or capital improvements are intended to increase the over-all efficiency of the E & R activity, it can often be evaluated by determining how soon the additional costs will be recovered by increased efficiency, what kind of return on investment will be possible, etc. Also, there is a tendency in recent times to use discounted cash flow techniques in evaluating returns on capital investments. Since the costs of such capital improvements will be recovered over a period of years, consideration must be given to the fact that our dollar is regularly being inflated and that a dollar earned five years from now will have less value than a dollar earned today. In any event, the problem with this kind of equipment is to assess the cost savings which typically involve decreasing the time that E & R personnel consume in setting up and making experiments, producing models, etc. Since established cost systems rarely isolate the costs related to such cost savings, the savings must be estimated on a broad basis. When capital improvements are of a very general nature such as improved lighting, air conditioning, etc., it is even more difficult to estimate their effect upon cost. Here, subjective management judgments are involved.

In establishing the cost for a capital equipment item, there are associated costs in addition to the cost of the equipment itself. These associated costs include such items as freight and transportation, installation costs, and there may even be associated building and foundation costs. All or portions of these may be capitalized or expensed depending upon the policies and accounting practices of the company.

Project and Program Budgets

Only the very smallest of engineering organizations budget their total E & R expenditures without breaking down by specific projects and programs. Each project must have a dollar target figure *or* an absolute maximum figure associated with it. Experience has shown that actual expenses almost always exceed budgeted expenses in projects because of the unknowns of development engineering and related research. *When funds are strictly limited, the planned work should be tailored down to cost below the assigned funds by as much as 10 to 50 percent.*

Further controls are achieved by project budgeting, by breaking the total project work into tasks, subtasks (and subsubtasks, if necessary), and budgeting these small pieces of work in complete detail. Budgeting should start at the bottom and the individual budgets combined to form the total budget. Then tasks may have to be revised by lowering objectives, omitting or revising test programs, or reducing time spent on analysis. Obviously, lower budgeted projects will have either lower objectives or higher risks or both.

Organizational Budgets

One method of evaluating E & R is by the performance of the organized groups to meet their budget forecasts. This means that the accounting activity of the company or else a sub-accounting activity located in the administration component of E & R must not only show budget forecasts but also performance against the forecast for project and program budgets. Also, this must be done for all organizational total budgets. The managers must be required to explain significant variances from the forecasts.

From an overall view, applied research or specific engineering projects can generally be budgeted in greater detail than more fundamental research projects. Often, fundamental research is budgeted only on the broadest of bases, and it is seldom that result schedules are tied closely to budgets. In some organizations, fundamental studies are budgeted on a "slush fund" basis. The E & R manager is allowed 5 to 15 per cent of his total budget to assign as he sees fit. This is passed along to researchers so as to allow them to spend a certain portion of their time on fundamental studies or else interested and capable men in the organization are asked to submit proposals for a specific project to be covered by these funds.

Budgeting starts with the scheduling of scientific effort through the manpower schedules. The manpower schedules are converted to expense projects by multiplying scheduled man-hours, man-days, or man-years by estimated salaries. It is common to take into account merit and/or general increases, fringe benefits, overtime premiums, etc.

In addition to labor, one must give consideration to material and other expenses associated with projects or programs in each organizational unit, the organizational unit budgets, and the total E & R organizational budget. Both forecasts and variances are again involved. The kind of things that must generally be considered are those previously enumerated under the cost estimating and costing section of this chapter. Some of these can be classed as direct costs and others as indirect or overhead items. Many of the indirect or overhead costs are controllable and are, therefore, usually budgeted separately. Typical indirect costs which are partially or wholly controllable include such items as professional society dues, subscriptions, library costs, maintenance expense, operating supplies, normal travel, normal telephone and telegraph expense, etc.

Overhead costs such as rent, depreciation, insurance, taxes, heat, light, and power are frequently not shown on departmental budget reports because the individual unit manager can exert little or no control over them.

Each organizational unit for which a budget forecast is prepared is normally known as a cost center and is assigned a control number by the accounting department. This control number is usually the department number. Such action facilitates the accrual of actual costs for comparison against budget forecasts. In addition, subcontrol numbers identify costs allocated to specific projects and/or programs.

"Learning" in E & R Projects

The "Learning Curve" or "Manufacturing Progress Functions" which appear to hold true for manufacturing also appear to hold true for engineering and research on sequences of similar projects. A simple example of a learning curve would show that each successive similar project required, say, 80 percent of the number of man-hours required by the previous one. This reflects such factors as specialized knowledge gained by the engineers, improvement in available equipment, building of information files, better teamwork, and improved management procedures. This learning obviously has important implications for budgeting and cost estimating. If the E & R and financial managers are not aware of the uses of such progress curves, particularly when they are concerned with proposals for initial and follow-on contracts involving production of hardware items, the company may continually overbid.[9]

Accuracy of Budgets

It is essential that both management and E & R recognize certain attributes of E & R budget forecasts:

1. The research budget will not be accurate as to detail but can be accurate in the aggregate.
2. Detailed research program budgets are accurate only in the short run.
3. Forecasts must allow for project and program flexibility.
4. Effort expended on a research project can be projected, but the results secured cannot be predicted.

The aggregate E & R expenditure for a budgetary period can be quite accurately forecast, and it can be controlled to meet the budget forecast. This is true because the major element in most E & R activity is personnel cost. This cost element can be simply controlled by either hiring the number of people covered by the budget; or else, if the number already available is too large or will become too large at some point in the budgetary period, the excess personnel should be released. It is common to find only minor variances from total E & R budgets—in fact, many managers say that they can stay within the budget almost all the time.

While aggregate accuracy is common, the detailed organizational budget forecast cost as well as the forecast cost of particular projects or programs quite frequently deviate from the forecasts.

[9] For a discussion of manufacturing progress models, see W. J. Fabrycky and Paul E. Torgersen, *Operations Economy: Industrial Applications of Operations Research* (Englewood Cliffs, N. J.: Prentice-Hall, 1966), pp. 95–120.

Because of the unpredictability of E & R projects, project budgets tend to be accurate only in the short run; consequently, some organizations replan and rebudget their technical programs quarterly. Others adjust project budgets semiannually, although their aggregate fund delegations may be made on an annual basis. The farther into the future a general or project budget extends, the less accurate it is likely to be as to detail.

Above all, there is a need for flexibility in budget development and in interpreting budget details. Project and program appropriations are estimates which are to be used as guides and cannot be used to set rigid limits. It is impossible to predict exactly what will be needed, especially on more fundamental research projects.

Appropriation Requests

In some firms, budgets are based upon "Appropriation Requests." A form entitled "appropriation request" similar to the one shown in Fig. 10-4 is used for the recommendation of expenditures to be made during the year. These forms may be made out at any time during the year, but the total of such appropriations must not exceed the budget established at the beginning of the year without special action by the executive committee. As finally approved, it becomes the standard for work to be performed and is completely made out before each task is started. Such requests are invariably required for capital expenditures.

CASE STUDY OF A BUDGET AND COST REPORTING SYSTEM

An example of an E & R organization with a total annual budget of over $25 million is provided to show how a highly detailed system works. Smaller firms will find ideas which they may apply, but most firms will not have so elaborate a system.

Subdivision and Costing of Work

Subdivision of Work. The laboratory under discussion is organized along project lines with engineering sections of 50 to 200 people reporting to the project manager. The projects buy the development and test services of the service groups in a manner similar to the way they would buy vendor services. The difference is that rapid changes to peaks and recessions in the purchase of labor (scientists and engineers) from the services cannot be tolerated. Therefore, budget changes for procurement of such labor can only follow long-range trends. In budget terms, labor purchased from within the laboratory is referred to as "sources of labor."

In its most simplified form, the work required to accomplish the objectives of a project is broken down as follows:

- Project work in total
  - Tasks
    - Subtasks
      - Job or subprograms
        - Shop orders

REQUEST FOR APPROPRIATION

Appropriation No. ________

1. Component Initialing Request:

2. Brief Description of Work and/or Facility:

3. Amount of Appropriation Request - Plant Investment ____________

   Expense ____________

   Total ____________

4. Justification of the Proposed Expenditures Should Be Explained on Blank Hecto Master

5. Detailed Cost Estimate - (If Additional Space Required Use Blank Hecto Master)

6. Project Engineer Responsible For Works:

7. Work to be Performed by - Contract   Subcontract   Purchase Order

8. Est. Starting Date   Est. Completion Date

9. Source of Funds

10. Shop Order or Account Distribution (To Be Assigned By Financial Section)

Estimates and Date Prepared: ____________

Appropriation Approved or Reviewed By:

____
Section or Function Manager

____
Project Manager (If Applicable)

____
Manager - Finance

____
Space & Property Management

____
Secretary - Appropriations Comm.

Appropriation Recommended By: ____________

____

Distribution:
- Project Manager
- Section or Function Manager
- Secretary - Appropriations Committee
- Manager - Finance
- Manager - Contracts and Purchasing
- Plant Engr. & Constr.

____
General Manager

Fig. 10-4. Request for appropriation form.

A section is assigned a portion of the project work. This work associated with each project in turn can be subdivided naturally into tasks corresponding to major pieces of equipment and unit organizations. Additional not-so-obvious tasks are instituted as required. Tasks in turn are divided into subtasks for purposes of separating out manageable packages of work and assigning funds. In order to accomplish the fairly permanent subtasks, jobs or subprograms must be initiated according to the way the design progresses. These jobs may last from a few weeks to a year and hence are short-lived compared to the subtasks.

Shop orders or appropriations are opened to allow charging of funds to the different parts of the jobs. Thus the shop order essentially describes the smallest unit of work.

Costing. Roughly speaking, the laboratory is concerned with costs segregated in all of the following ways:

Form 1—Direct and indirect expense
Form 2—Applied (direct) labor and other applied charges (i.e., materials and subcontracts)
Form 3—The application of costs for each unit or responsible individual.

It is necessary therefore to establish a costing system which will permit segregation of charges according to these three classifications. The first step is to give each organizational component an identifying code number so that whenever a component either does work for itself, buys labor or material, or sells its own services, charges can be accumulated accordingly. Figure 10-5 shows how the code numbers for each component in

PROJECT ORGANIZATION CODES

Component Title	Code No.
Component Design Section	
Mechanical Design	521
Service Equipment Design	522
Thermal and Hydraulic Design	523
Structural Analysis	524
Materials Application	525
Systems Design Section	
Mechanical Design	531
Instrumentation Systems	532
Control Design	533
Systems Analysis	534
Field Engineering	535
Engineering Administration	590

Fig. 10-5. Project organization codes.

the laboratory can be set up. These codes, plus the task and subtask codes, form the basis of the shop order system.

Costing—Direct Costs. A shop order (S.O.) in this system is composed of two parts, the master file number and the working shop order. Both the acceptor of the work and the fund owner are identified. When a shop order is opened in a unit below the section level, a copy of the complete shop order and title goes to the accounting department. Thus, in all future correspondence and reports, only the working shop order portion needs to be used. Laboratory personnel charge these working shop orders on weekly or monthly time cards.

Materials purchased may be charged to the same S.O. as the labor on a job. For more detailed reporting, however, a separate S.O. may be opened for materials and subcontractors. A job or subtask may be small enough so that only one S.O. is required or large enough for twenty or more S.O.'s. Before any S.O. opened in a section is sent to the accounting department, the project financial analyst reviews the form which opens the S.O. He countersigns it to show that money has been budgeted for this item, and that there is enough money left in the budget to cover it. It is then possible for managers to sign material requests (purchase requisitions) using this S.O. up to the amount allowed by the manager's position as published in a Laboratory Operating and Policy Guide. For large subcontracts, as many as eight to ten people may be required to sign the material request form.

The policy of the laboratory is to charge everything possible to these direct cost shop orders. Labor of first-line managers, drafting labor, expenses to attend technical society meetings, and almost all travel expenses are examples of items classified as direct costs.

Costing—Indirect Costs. An index gives the laboratory account numbers including the indirect account numbers. The indirect account numbers are tacked on to the component number to make up an account number. If an individual in the component whose code is 721 wishes to make a telephone call, he gives the operator the charge number 721-315. When an employee in the component takes a company course or tuition-refund course, he uses the charge number 721-313. Secretaries, staff people, and higher level managers charge their time to the 311 (indirect expense) account.

The accounting group combines laboratory general service costs with indirect costs incurred by the engineering and technical organizational components to develop an applied overhead rate as a per cent of direct salaries for each component. This rate is used in making short-term budget forecasts.

Budgets and Forecasts

All budgets for the laboratory start with budgets made out at the section level. These are combined to form project budgets which in turn are combined to form the laboratory budgets.

All budgeting for the laboratory starts with a form, similar to those shown in Figs. 10-6 and 10-7. This form is used to make the first rough cut to see how the totals estimated by the managers add up and compare with available funds for the coming fiscal year. After the project proposals have been reviewed by top management and the amounts revised, the details of the budget for the coming fiscal year are worked out at the section level. There are perhaps thirty to fifty budget forms and reports required by the accounting department during the year. These forms and the dates they are due are published in a one-inch-thick volume.

The first step in working out the details of the section budget is to summarize the information from the final project proposals. Notice that most budgeting is concerned with *direct* costs consisting of internal laboratory labor and materials and subcontracts. The summary budget form is therefore called the Budget by Elements of Cost.

When the section budgets by elements of cost, it must obviously do this by task also. The task budget total dollars must therefore equal the total dollars in the Elements of Cost Budget. In fact, it is most logical to start budgeting with the jobs by elements of cost and proceed upward to the tasks. The final step is to spread the budget over each month for the coming six months by task and elements of cost.

In E & R work, the expenditure of money must change as the technical developments dictate. Although some investigations, jobs, tasks, etc. follow nicely along budgeted lines, considerable flexibility is required in other areas. For this reason a three-month rolling forecast is prepared each month.

Cost Reports and Analyses

Budgeting by itself is a weak tool without some method of obtaining actual costs rapidly at the end of the selected reporting periods. The usual reporting period is the end of the month. At the laboratory, the fiscal month is the unit of time, and cost reports are issued about ten days after the end of the period.

The direct cost reports are provided for the:

1. Fund owner
2. Fund acceptor
3. Section
4. Project
5. Laboratory.

HSF 774 1G 8 67

WORK PACKAGE ☐ SUMMARY ☐ INSTRUCTION

CARD CODE	ORIG. DEPT. CODE	TYPE CONTRACT	PROGRAM - WPI NO.

TO	ACCOUNT NO. (Mat'l / Labor)	CATEGORY MFG. EST.	SPLIT SALE	ACTIVITY CODE

COPIES SR. PROJ. ENG., FIN. CONT. ADM., OTHERS AS DESIGNATED	PROGRAM PLAN NO. & DESCRIPTION	WPI DATE	WPI COMP. DATE
	WPI DESCRIPTION		

FUNCTION											TOTALS
LABOR $											
LABOR HRS											
PURCH. $											
TOTAL WITH O.H.											Grand Total with Overhead
COMP. DATE											
ACTIVITY											
RATE PER HOUR											

INSTRUCTIONS:

CONTRACT NUMBER

TOOLING OWNERSHIP

CUSTOMER MARKING

FUNCTION CODES & DESCRIPTIONS

A - Multi Function
B - Design
C - Drafting
D - Checking - Dimensional Analysis
E - Reliability
F - Analysis - Technical Staff
G - Project Engineering
H - Program Adm. Control
J - Tool Design
K - Quality Assurance & Engineering

L - Production Control
M - Mfg. Control & Engineering
N - Model Shop (S)
7 - Model Shop (H)
P - Lab Facilities (S)
5 - Lab Facilities (H)
Q - Lab Instrumentation (S)
3 - Lab Instrumentation (H)
R - Lab Operations (S)
4 - Lab Operations - Test (H)

S - Centralized Publications
T - Services (School, Training, etc.)
W - Mechanical Design
X - Systems Evaluation
Y - Sales & Marketing

1 - Inspection
6 - Assembly & Test
8 - Manufacturing
0 - Tool Manufacturing

These instructions are within the scope of the Engineering Program Plan referenced above and will not exceed authorized cost.

PREPARED BY	DATE	PROJECT ENG. PROGRAM MGR.	DATE	PROG. CONT. FIN. CONT. ADM.	DATE
ASST. CHIEF CHIEF ENG.	DATE	ENG. DEPT. AUDITOR		ASST. ENG. MGR. ENG. MGR.	DATE

Fig. 10-6. Form for documenting project plans. *Source:* Copyright 1965, United Aircraft Corporation. Used with permission.

The direct reports given to the fund owner (usually the first-line managers) are:

1. *Owner* reports of amounts spent by S.O. subtask and task
2. *Details of Applied Labor* showing who performed work on each S.O.
3. *Owner Other Applied Charges Details*

4. *Acceptor* report showing S.O.'s on which the component accepted work for other components
5. *Acceptor Applied Labor Details*
6. *Acceptor Other Applied Charges Details.*

PROJECT ______________________ PROJECT NO. __________

TASK ______________________ TASK NO. __________

Assigned to Department ______________ Date ________ Dept. No. __________

Cognizant Engineer ______________ Date ________

Description & Purpose of Task (General) ______________________

Work Divisions By Subtasks:
Subtask No. 1 ______________
Subtask No. 2 ______________
Subtask No. 3 ______________
Subtask No. 4 ______________

ESTIMATED COSTS

	19___				19___				
	Labor	Indirect	Other Direct	Total	Labor	Indirect	Other Direct	Total	Grand Total
Subtask 1									
Subtask 2									
Subtask 3									
Subtask 4									
Totals									

ESTIMATE OF MANPOWER

	Engrs.' Grade	Engrs.' Grade	Technicians' Grade	Other	Engrs.' Grade	Engrs.' Grade	Technicians' Grade	Other
Subtask 1								
Subtask 2								
Subtask 3								
Subtask 4								
Totals								

Anticipated completion date by "major milestone" for each subtask.

Subtask No. 1 ______________
Subtask No. 2 ______________
Subtask No. 3 ______________
Subtask No. 4 ______________

Fig. 10-7. Form for documenting final project plans.

SUMMARY

The financial aspects of E & R are significant because they bear upon:

1. Project or functional planning. In this connection, financial plans are the quantitative representations of the technical plans.
2. Project or functional control and employee motivation. Budgets must be such that they provide standards and incentives, not strait-jackets.
3. Taxes which the company must pay. Proper accounting and financing decisions in E & R can result in substantial savings for the company.

Milestone Legend

1. Com. Prel. Des.
2. Test FDM Motor
3. Award S.D. Con.
4. App. Sys. Des.
5. Initial F.T.
6. Final PFQT Test
7. Award Site Dev. Con.
8. Final Qual. Test
9. Award Prod. Con.

IMPACT PROGRAM AND COST SCHEDULE

WS No. xxx
CONTRACT NO. xxxxxx
Large Solid Motor

By Project & Task

NO. 1
DATED 2-2-65

REV. NO. 0
PREPARED BY

Description	Program Number		1965: 1	2	3	4	1966: 1	2	3	4	1967: 1	2	3	4	1966	1967	Total
																	MOTORS
System Definition	1																
Feasibility Dem.	2			1 1	1*												3
System Development	3																36
Design		1				1	2 2 1										6
PERT		2						1 1 2	2 1 1								8
Continuing Dev.		3								1 1	1						3
Qualification										1	1 1 2	22					9
Flight Test								1	1 1	1	1	1	2 2				10
Production	4														50	100	150
																	189
Key Program Milestone				2	3	4		5	6	7		8	9				

Description	Program Number		1965: 1	2	3	4	1966: 1	2	3	4	1967: 1	2	3	4	1966	1967	Total
System Definition	1		$ 35.000														$35.000
Feasibility Dem.	2		10.000	$20.000	$15.000	$ 5.000											50.000
System Development	3																
Design		1		5.000	10.000	20.000	$20.000	$ 5.000									60.000
PERT		2			5.000	5.000	20.000	35.000	$25.000								90.000
Continuing Dev.		3							15.000	$20.000	$10.000						45.000
Qualification		4								30.000	30.000	$20.000					80.000
Flight Test		5					10.000	10.000	10.000	10.000	10.000	20.000	$15.000	$ 5.000			90.000
Production	4												15.000	35.000	$250.000	$200.000	500.000
TOTAL			$45.000	$25.000	$30.000	$30.000	$50.000	$50.000	$50.000	$60.000	$50.000	$40.000	$30.000	$40.000	$250.000	$200.000	$950.000

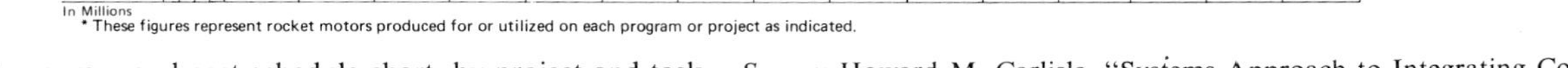

In Millions
* These figures represent rocket motors produced for or utilized on each program or project as indicated.

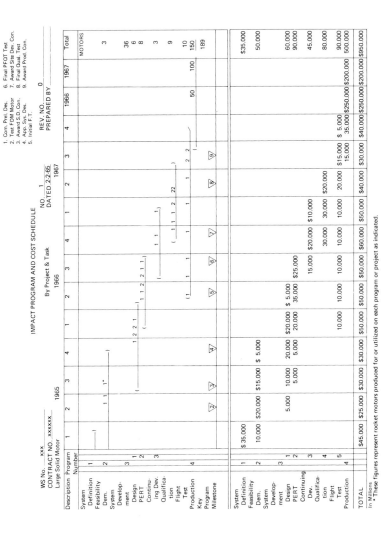

Fig. 10-8. Impact program and cost schedule chart, by project and task. *Source:* Howard M. Carlisle, "Systems Approach to Integrating Costs and Technical Data," *Management Services* (July–August 1967).

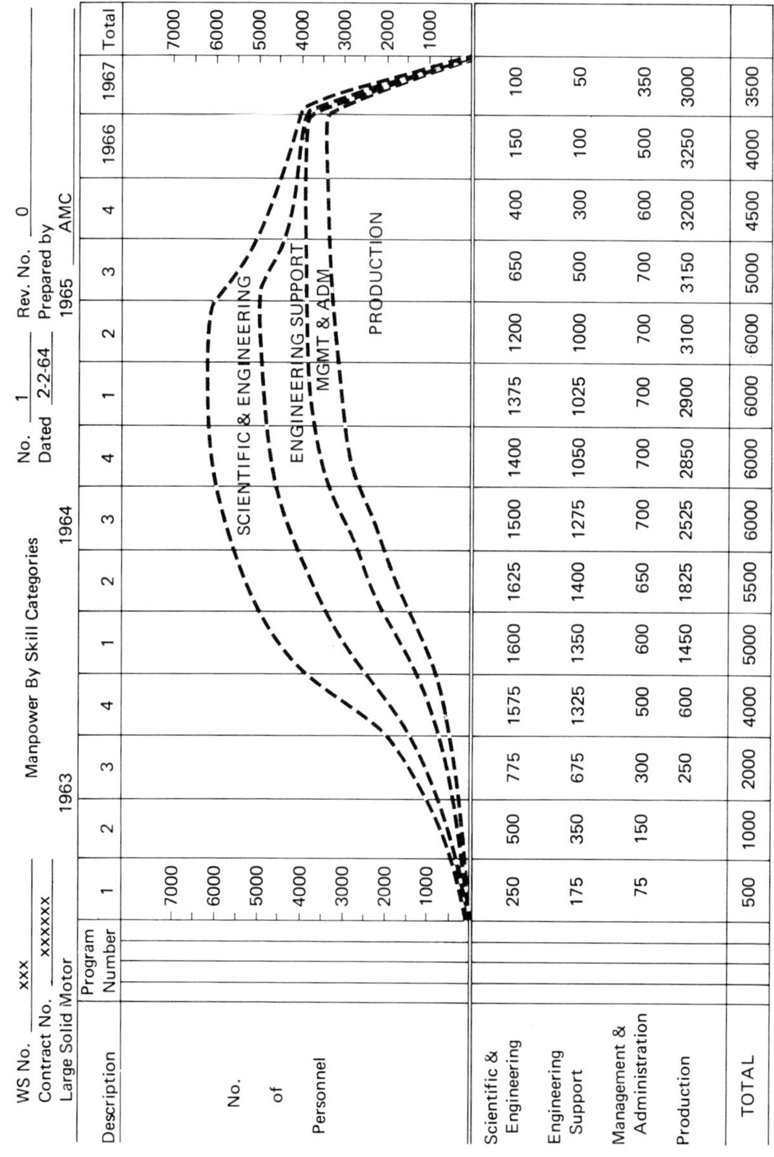

Description	Program Number	1963: 1	2	3	4	1964: 1	2	3	4	1965: 1	2	3	4	1966	1967	Total
Scientific & Engineering		250	500	775	1575	1600	1625	1500	1400	1375	1200	650	400	150	100	
Engineering Support		175	350	675	1325	1350	1400	1275	1050	1025	1000	500	300	100	50	
Management & Administration		75	150	300	500	600	650	700	700	700	700	700	600	500	350	
Production				250	600	1450	1825	2525	2850	2900	3100	3150	3200	3250	3000	
TOTAL		500	1000	2000	4000	5000	5500	6000	6000	6000	6000	5000	4500	4000	3500	

Fig. 10-9. Impact program and cost schedule chart, manpower by skill categories. *Source:* See Fig. 10-8.

4. One most significant development has been the relating of technical work to financial systems by ever improving techniques. One example of a planning, controlling, and reporting technique is shown by Figs. 10-8 and 10-9. Here a wealth of information has been compressed into a form which managers can grasp at a glance in what is known as Management Program Analysis (IMPACT) charts.

Reports are also provided to service groups which do not have funds allocated but which perform work on the many shop orders of fund owners.

Summary reports of monthly costs are distributed to upper levels of management. Detailed reports are distributed to lower levels of management and are circulated among group leaders responsible for specific engineering jobs.

BIBLIOGRAPHY

ANDERSON, M. L., and ESCHRICH, J. "Economic Analysis of R & D Projects," *Chemical Engineering Progress*, July, 1965.

BONCHONSKY, JOSEPH P. "Cost Control for Program Managers," *NAA Management Accounting*, May, 1967.

CARLISLE, HOWARD M. "Systems Approach to Integrating Cost and Technical Data," *Management Services*, July–August, 1967.

CLELAND, DAVID I., and KING, WILLIAM R. *Systems Analysis and Project Management*. New York, N.Y.: McGraw-Hill Book Company, 1968.

DURO, RICHARD A. "A System of Research and Development Cost Control," *NAA Management Accounting*, May, 1967.

FABRYCKY, W. J., and TORGERSEN, PAUL E. *Operations Economy: Industrial Applications of Operations Research*. Englewood Cliffs, N.J.: Prentice-Hall, Inc., 1966.

GALLANTIER, ALEXANDER J. "Accounting Reports on Research and Development," *NAA Management Accounting*, November, 1967.

JORDAN, RAYMOND. *How To Use the Learning Curve*. Boston, Mass.: Materials Management Institute, 1965.

KARGER, DELMAR W. *The New Product*. New York, N.Y.: The Industrial Press, 1960.

KRAIG, HARRY J. "The Milepost Approach to Control of Research and Development Projects," *NAA Bulletin*, January, 1960.

MYERS, LARRY R. "Effective Engineering Budgets," *Machine Design*, December 8, 1966.

National Science Foundation. "Decision-making on Research and Development in the Business Firm," *Reviews of Data on Research and Development*, NSF 64-6, February, 1964.

RASMUSSEN, SVEIN G. "Budgeting and Control of Development Projects," *Machine Design*, August 29, 1968.

SCHMIEG, HARRY J. "Control of Overhead With a Variable Budget in a Research Operation," *NAA Bulletin*, August, 1959.

SEILER, ROBERT E. *Improving the Effectiveness of Research and Development.* New York, N.Y.: McGraw-Hill Book Company, 1965.

SHILLINGLAW, GORDON. *Cost Accounting, Analysis and Control.* Homewood, Ill.: Richard D. Irwin, Inc., 1967.

SOLLENBERGER, HAROLD M. *Major Changes Caused by the Implementation of a Management Information System,* NAA Research Monograph 4. New York, N.Y.: National Association of Accountants, 1968.

VILLERS, RAYMOND. *Research and Development: Planning and Control.* New York, N.Y.: Financial Executives Research Foundation, 1964.

WILLIAMS, E. L., and WILSON, G. A. "Project Cost Control at Raytheon's Wayland Laboratory," *IEEE Transactions on Engineering Management,* September, 1963.

CHAPTER 11

The Design Steps from Conception to Production

THE MANAGEMENT VIEW

The tendency in American business is for managers to depend upon experience and "muddling through" rather than upon studying the structure and functions of processes. Two views are commonly held by E & R managers; either the design process is the same for all products or it is distinctly different in every case. Yet the search for similarities and differences based upon an understanding of the characteristics of design processes is the key to effective management of the E & R organization. The pattern of organization, the quality of the end product, the economy of design and manufacture, and the potential for automation of design are all dependent upon management's insight into the processes of design.

NATURE OF THE DESIGN PROCESS

The basic design process may be set in motion as a result of one of three events:

1. A customer states a general need or specifies a particular problem or requirement.
2. The marketing or E & R department identifies a problem or a need which requires the development of a new or improved product.
3. As a result of a technological advance, an engineer or scientist proposes an application. The positive commercial prospects are subsequently confirmed by market research and economic analysis.

The purposes of design, according to G. A. Francis, are:

1. Developing new products for new markets
2. Developing new products for existing markets
3. Developing new uses for existing products
4. Improving the quality of present products
5. Reducing costs of using an existing product
6. Minimizing dangers or nuisances associated with a product or with the use of a product
7. Eliminating difficulties associated with the production or with the use of a product
8. Standardizing a product or product line
9. Improving customer relations
10. Improving public relations.[1]

Another and unique viewpoint of the purpose of design is that of D. E. Chambers. Engineering design is described as an essential part of the process by which materials or other products are raised from a lower to a higher stage of *value added*. Starting with natural-resources raw materials as zero, Chambers develops a scale of value added ranging up to nineteen.[2]

Engineering may be considered to be primarily the creating and processing of information of a combined technological and economic nature and documenting and communicating this information. Design thus appears to consist of two basic types of activities:

1. Mental analytic and creative activity
2. Processing of information.

The mental analytical activities consist of: identifying subproblems, selecting types of information to be accumulated, analyzing such information to determine that which is pertinent, conducting analytical investigations employing scientific principles, analyzing the results at each step of the design process, and "debugging" equipment. The mental creative activities consist of: envisioning the ultimate product, the possible approaches, the aggregation of "black boxes" required for a complex system—identification of potential problems, conception of wholly new solutions to problems, planning of non-routine tests, and syntheses of new ideas—analyses, and test results to provide a new product.

Processing Information

Processing of information consists of: retrieving, computing, analyzing, documenting, converting, transporting, reproducing, sorting, and storing.

[1] Gerald A. Francis, "Engineering Analysis of Existing Products," *Battelle Technical Review*, November 1967, p. 14.

[2] D. E. Chambers, *What is Engineering?*, Internal report, General Electric Company, Engineering Services Research, New York, 1963, p. 3.

The retrieval of information involves searching for and identifying pertinent data from such sources as:

1. Handbooks, catalogs, journal articles, technical information systems, data banks, and other published information
2. Company data such as: files, reports, standards, samples, test results, field service reports, procedure manuals, and cost information.

The processing of information occurs:

1. *Among* engineers, draftsmen, technicians within the E & R activity, and among other people outside the E & R organization. In general, it usually involves a form of information as the design progresses.
2. *From* engineers and draftsmen *to* others outside of E & R who are concerned with fabrication, selling, operation, and servicing.
3. *To* engineers and draftsmen *from* others outside of E & R who are directly concerned with the projects.

Originating Information

Except for the data retrieval from the minds of engineers, which could be minimized, machines would soon take over if there were nothing more to design work than the processing of information. However, any existing data or information can be traced back to its birth and hence to some point in time when it did not exist in any form. New ideas, data, or information *must be created* or born in the design process. That is, information must result from the mental efforts of human beings based upon *observation* and *cogitation*. What are the situations which lead to observation, cogitation, and the birth of new ideas, concepts, and hence, data or information? Some of these situations are as follows:

1. Customers go through the observation-cogitation process and *originate* information which is then documented in the form of needs and specifications
2. Other engineers and scientists outside the company *originate* ideas which constitute technological advances.
3. Engineers within the company *originate* ideas and data as a result of:
   a. Observation of the transformation of materials in the construction of models, prototypes, and production items
   b. Observation of operation of equipment in testing and actual customer use
   c. Discussions with associates, consultants, subcontractors, vendors, and customers.

FACTORS AFFECTING THE DESIGN PROCESS

Product Characteristics

A list of attributes which must be considered in the design of a product, with varying degrees of emphasis for different products, is:

1. Performance of basic and subsidiary functions
2. Accuracy of performance
3. Speed of performance
4. Cost
5. Reliability
6. Environmental adaptability
7. Maintainability
8. Replaceability by successive models
9. Safety and fail-safe features
10. Producibility
11. Optimum materials and process for size of manufacturing run
12. Simplification, standardization, preferred sizes, and modular construction
13. Weight
14. Size and shape
15. Styling and packaging
16. Compatibility with other systems or auxiliary equipment
17. Ease of operation (human engineering)
18. Balanced design through tradeoffs
19. Ease of transporting and installing
20. Legality
21. Social aspects (pollution, radiation, sound blasts, etc.).

Type of Product

Each field of engineering has its own peculiarities. These peculiarities are reflected in the design process. For example, in electronic design, the breadboard usually represents one stage. In aerodynamics, the wind-tunnel test of a model may be said to correspond roughly to the breadboard. In mechanical design, the scale model is a characteristic of this field. Therefore, the type of product being designed is a factor which influences the design process. Typical product types may be categorized as:

1. Electrical
2. Electronic
3. Mechanical
4. Nuclear
5. Chemical
6. Optical
7. Biological.

The major categories often are divided into subcategories; for example, mechanical products can be divided into static and dynamic. A static product has no moving parts, and is essentially "passive," such as a desk. A dynamic product has moving parts as, for example, a bicycle or automobile. Chemical products or processes can be divided into organic and inorganic. In addition, the designer will have to deal with many combinations of the major categories and subcategories. This has a significant effect upon the designer's job and hence, upon the basic design steps.

System versus Component Design

System Design. A system is a collection of components, equipment, and/or subsystems related by lines of communication (in a broad sense) so that all parts and lines of the system contribute to some overall purpose. A system accepts inputs and transforms these into outputs. A system may be said to be a *closed system* if it adjusts itself by feeding back part of its output to be compared with corresponding input, and corrects its output. It is said to be an *open system* if there is no corrective feedback.

Systems vary from small and subsystems to supersystems. Complex systems are those in which a change in one variable will affect many other variables in the system, usually in a nonlinear manner. In complex systems there are usually subsystems and feedback loops within feedback loops.

The systems engineer is concerned with the interactions of the parts of the systems. Therefore, his function is to specify inputs, output, and the requirements for components which make up the system. Component engineers then attempt to design components to meet these specific requirements. The systems engineer must analyze and design not only for steady-state operation but for transient conditions such as surges, step-inputs, oscillating inputs, startups, and shutdowns. In systems engineering design, optimization of system performance is sought by tradeoffs in performance among components and/or subsystems.

Component Design. The "component" approach to design refers to the design of any simple product as well as a component in a system. A component is distinguished, for this definition, as a piece of equipment with a single function in which the parts are physically close together. Such equipment may produce an output of some kind as a direct functional response to an input.

Many so-called "components" in systems are actually subsystems. For example, a boiler on a ship has temperature- and pressure-sensing devices which compare the actual output with the scheduled output, resulting in an error signal being fed back to the input control. Such sensing devices may have remote sensing and control circuits; hence they would not qualify under the above definition of a component.

In the design of a simple product or a component, an approximation of the sequential design process is likely to be used. This is because the entire product can be carried along as a "lump" from one phase to the next. The design steps require relatively short periods compared with those for complex equipment so that a more orderly and uncomplicated approach becomes appropriate.

Innovation and Complexity

The degrees of innovation and complexity of the product will affect the design process since the higher the degree of either, the less well-defined are the design processes. For low innovation or complexity, the design process is mainly an information processing activity; for high innovation or complexity, creative thought is required. Figure 11-1 shows scales for innovation and complexity. Note that automated design encompasses products low on both scales, i.e., transformers and capacitors.

INCREASING INNOVATION ↑	Elemental parts and static, simple form end products	Simple devices, and components	Subassemblies of the first-order and simple end products	Functional modules and assemblies of the second order	Equipments	Systems	Supersystems
Giant step forward	Transparent steel windows				Antigravity device, flying saucer	Portable, low cost, mass two-way TV transmission system	Transmigration transportation system
New product representing a major breakthrough never before conceived		Ball point pen, electric light bulb	Xerox copiers		Nuclear powered submarine, jet aircraft		
Replacement of an existing product by use of new technology	Plastic ashtray, plastic hose and piping				Transistorized computers		
Major design improvements				Integrated circuit chips			
Minor design improvements to yield greater utility	Teflon coated cookware		Printed circuits	Automobile safety features			
Custom design of a regularly carried product		Capacitors, transformers					
"Borrowed" improvements by adapting from existing products		Felt-tip pens, rechargeable-battery flashlights		Portable TV sets			
"Face-lift"	Colored handles on screw drivers	Streamlined fountain pens					
No product change	Bolts, wheels, ashtrays, hand tools	Fountain pens, spark plugs, gears, lamps	Gear trains, portable radios	Automobile engines, modular computer circuits	Radio & TV transmitters, automobiles, N/C machine tools	TV networks, long lines telephone system, nuclear reactor power plants	National defense early warning radar systems, satellite communication systems

INCREASING COMPLEXITY →

Fig. 11-1. Innovation and complexity.

Sequential versus Concurrent Approach

In a strictly sequential design approach, one step would be fully completed before the next step is undertaken. There would be no feedback from later steps to earlier steps, i.e., no recycling. In practice, it is doubtful that a purely sequential process is ever carried out. There is always continual readjustment and change in the design as evaluations are made of analysis, tests, prototype construction, etc.

It is apparent that a sequential process represents the longest time for the design. The time for each step is added to obtain the total time for the job.

The emphasis on concurrency in the design process arose because of the need for compressing the total time for the design process. (See Configuration Control in Chapter 14.) Concurrency in design means that later steps are initiated before the earlier steps are completed. It represents a time overlap of steps. The greater the degree and amount of overlap the more compressed is the total schedule. Some steps in the design process are thus underway before required information is available from the "earlier" steps. Assumptions must therefore be made and continuously corrected as information becomes available. There is a continual recycling of information between phases of the design work.

Required versus Available Personnel

The type and number of personnel required, as well as the contribution of each type, have a bearing upon how the design work is conducted. Types of personnel normally involved in the design process are:

1. Researchers of various kinds and grades
2. Research assistants
3. Engineers of various kinds and grades
4. Computer programmers
5. Engineering technicians
6. Engineering assistants
7. Designer-draftsmen
8. Draftsmen of various grades
9. Craft personnel
10. Shop workers of various levels of skills
11. Managerial personnel.

In certain types of mechanical design, the greatest part of the design work is carried out by skilled designer-craftsmen. For example, the N. A. Taylor Company, specializing in boating accessories and hardware, utilizes talented craftsmen to do the major part of developing such items as convertible tops for boats, ski-tow rigs, etc.

In certain types of products depending heavily upon chemical and/or complex physical processing for their production, most of the design work may be done by scientists or research-level personnel. For some products involving complex electro-mechanical combinations, most of the designing may be done by engineers and/or engineering technicians on laboratory or prototype models. In all cases, the experience, knowledge and native intelligence of the individuals as well as their ability to work together as a team affect their contributions.

Unfortunately, it is unlikely that the ideal mixture of number and quality of personnel required to do a specific job at optimum cost is readily available. Even if available within the E & R organization, because of scheduling problems, some other combination will probably be used. Moreover, it is not an easy task to identify the best mix; therefore, this factor will have a bearing upon how well each step of the design process is carried out.

Organization

The manner in which the E & R organization is established exerts a considerable influence on the design process. The contrast in approach between a functional organization and a line project organization is considerable.

Facilities Required and Available

Office space, office equipment, drafting space and equipment, test facilities, calculating machines and computers, and shop facilities which may be required obviously affect the length and depth of effort of each step of design work. Shortage of any of these facilities or substitution of lower quality facilities for those required will affect the emphasis in the design process.

THE GENERAL DESIGN PROCESS

The Basic Steps and Feedbacks

If it is assumed that customer desires and requirements have been articulated in the form of technical objectives, the basic steps in design are:

1. Thinking and visualization
2. Accumulation of information
3. Development of conceptual alternatives
4. Engineering exploration or feasibility program
5. Reference design
6. Analytical investigations
7. Specification, construction, and tests of materials, components, breadboards, and mock-ups
8. Drawings and initial engineering specifications
9. Construction of development model

10. Test of development model (May be concurrent with 9.)
11. Drawings and specifications of prototypes
12. Construction of prototype(s)
13. Test of prototype(s)
14. Construction of field test models and/or pilot production run
15. Field tests, if appropriate
16. Final production design
17. Modification of design due to customer or production problems.

These steps are generally sequential but not entirely. Some may be carried out in parallel. In most cases there is a recycling of steps as further information is acquired. The complete process is shown schematically in Fig. 11-2.

Accumulation of Information

Information is usually accumulated regarding the state of the art, attempts to develop predecessor systems, new developments in materials and components, and problems encountered by others attempting to design similar systems and components. A preliminary search is usually made at the time a proposal is prepared.

Development of Conceptual Alternatives

The development of alternative conceptual designs is the phase in which creativity pays off. It is the time in which blue-sky thinking should be indulged—the time for breaking away from the orthodox, the traditional, and the routine mediocrity so common in large organizations.

The conceptual phase is the time when it is the most economical to change, rearrange, and try out all types of promising new ideas. This is because, in the conceptual phase, engineering is carried only far enough so that judgment may be passed on the most likely designs. It is often purely a "paper design," although sometimes a few simple tests may be performed in a number of areas.

One of the most important steps in the conceptual design phase is to assemble all data and information that can serve as an input to the design process. Thorough literature and patent searches should be conducted during this period.

The conceptual design period should be limited to a specified time. Since researchers and engineers tend to be perfectionists, they will usually continue the search for the best overall design beyond the point of maximum practicality. If the time is extended, the original burst of creativity may taper off, or such a profusion of ideas may flow forth that it is impossible to develop and/or evaluate them within the resources of the E & R organization.

Any excess of ideas or ideas on other subjects that are not used should

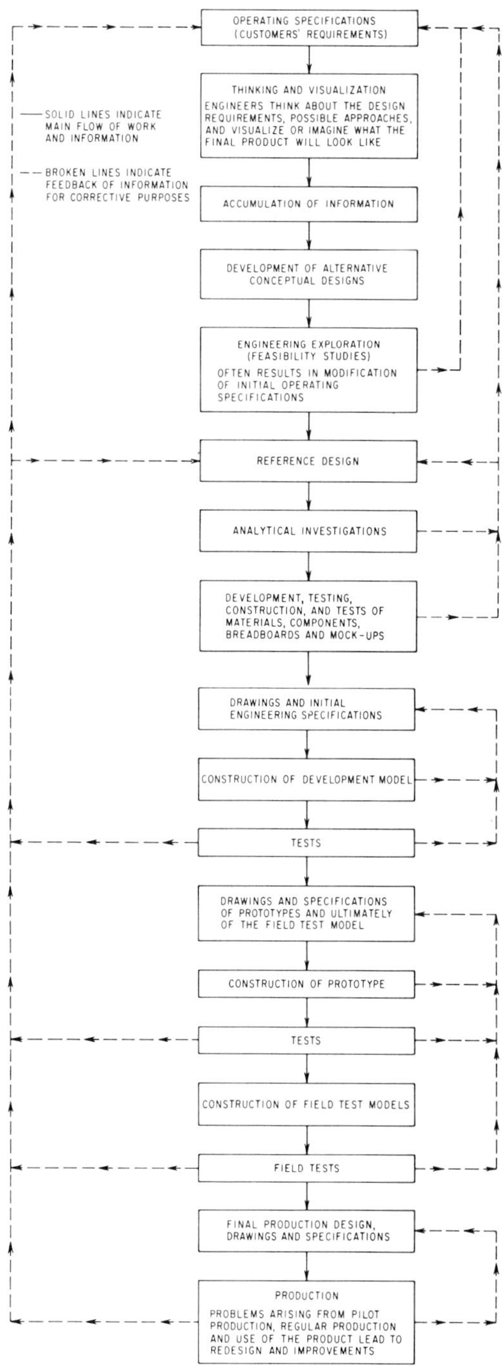

Fig. 11-2. Schematic portrayal of the general design process.

be recorded so that they do not become lost forever. There will be future design programs where many of them can be used.

The alternative conceptual designs should be worked into a formal presentation. If a design review committee exists, and this is a very desirable and worthwhile approach, it should have the opportunity of evaluating the various approaches. The broad and varied experience of the members can spell the difference between utimate success or failure. The designs should be evaluated from all angles, and the best three or four should be ranked. The ultimate decision as to which design offers most promise and is worth developing is made by the E & R manager, of course. Even if a design review committee does not exist, the formalization of the various designs will be of much help in arriving at a good decision.

Engineering Exploration or Feasibility Program

In the conceptual stage, the engineering is approximate or rough in nature. There is neither time for investigation of all problems, for thorough, detailed analysis, nor time and money for research or engineering design testing.

In the feasibility stage of the engineering design process, various problems recognized in the conceptual stage must be investigated. Analysis is carried to the point where either a solution is achieved on various problems, or alternative further programs may be evaluated. Similarly, this is true for research on specific basic problems. Testing of materials, components, and assemblies will be conducted. Rather than build expensive prototype assemblies, mock-ups and "breadboards" will be built for testing feasibility of design and accumulating design information. The information gained may necessitate some modification of the original specifications—the point of origin for the first information "feedback circuit" in the design process illustrated in Fig. 11-2.

Reference Design

The result of the exploratory design process is the *reference design,* which specifies product parameters and characteristics in sufficient detail to serve as the base for design of the prototype. A reference design report is issued which establishes the functional feasibility of the product concept and all engineers working on various components, parts of the product, or engineering analysis use the reference design data as the basis for their assumptions. Any refinements or changes which are required thereafter must be carefully justified, documented, and promptly communicated to all engineers concerned with the product or project.

Analytical Investigations

Starting with the reference design which provides parameters at system interfaces, systems engineers conduct analytical studies of each subsystem and the total system. Such studies cover system operation and response, limitations, ranges of variables, and reliability. These studies will almost always result in modifications of the reference design and occasionally in the operating specifications—another information feedback in the design process. At this stage areas are identified where testing will be required to check analysis and calculations.

Development Tests

Once the feasibility has been established and the reference design documented, thorough investigation of mechanical, electrical, hydraulic, thermal, reliability, and other characteristics may need to be tested. Test programs may be required to supply data for the detailed design and to determine various operating characteristics. Environmental studies and tests may be required. Materials tests are often required. In this phase of the design process, every aspect of design is investigated preparatory to building the prototype. It is possible, and often economical, to build some subassemblies which are to be tested just as they will be in the prototype so that these subassemblies may later be used there. Moreover, it should be realized that here another information feedback can occur.

Drawings and Initial Engineering Specifications

At this time, the first complete documentation is made of all information required to construct the system. Drawings and written engineering specifications will now provide a complete description of the system.

Construction and Test of a Development Model

This step may not always be carried out. Very often parts of the system may be constructed and other parts simulated. It is possible that the entire system may be simulated; the simulation may make use of computers, breadboards, etc., or a combination of various such approaches. This may be the first time that the operation of the system as a whole may be tested and/or analyzed. Simulation provides a means to:

1. Research the system principles and engineering analysis
2. Determine system response to the complete range of inputs and/or possible expected transient phenomena
3. Determine the effects of modifications of components on system operation
4. Determine the effects of man-machine and other types of trade-offs on system performance.

Refer to Fig. 11-2 for an identification of possible information feedbacks.

Drawings and Specifications of Prototypes

The specification of the prototype is the phase of the design process in which all previous information is combined and detailed drawings are prepared along with further amplification of the various specifications.

Construction and Tests of Prototypes

The work of the design engineer is not done when he hands over specifications to the model shop or to technicians and/or mechanics assigned to the design engineer. He must continue to follow the construction of the prototype through to the conclusion. Thus, the construction of the prototype is carried out with close liaison between the engineer and the shop and vendors,and the engineer usually ends up by personally participating in the assembly.

The prototype testing may take place in both the laboratory and the field; however, it is usually initially tested in the laboratory. When field-testing a unit, it is usual to construct several modified versions of the prototype which are generally identified as field-test models. This aspect of systems or product design is clearly discussed in an appendix to this chapter.

Standard test specifications should be established and statistical techniques employed to obtain measurements and data which will be useful in analyzing the operation. The design is reviewed in light of the prototype tests to determine what changes should be made for field-test models or for a pilot run in the factory. Prototype tests are sometimes called "proof" tests. In the evaluation of *any* tests, the customer's viewpoint must be considered throughout. If it is forgotten, the entire project could end in ultimate failure. All of these steps activate information feedbacks as shown in Fig. 11-2

Final Design, Drawings, and Specifications

It is only after evaluation of all prior laboratory and field tests that the final production design as well as the necessary drawings and specifications are established.

Pilot Production Model Test

Prior to the start of production, it is quite common to make a pilot or limited number of the production model using as much production tooling as possible. The pilot run should usually be made by the production department; nevertheless, engineers should work closely with them. Sometimes the pilot run models replace field testing.

Pilot models should receive laboratory testing and sometimes additional field testing. Manufacturing problems may arise which dictate design changes. The tests should evaluate performance against the previously established production or final specifications. The results of engineering laboratory tests should be compared to and reconciled with tests made on production test equipment. All tests should be carefully planned in advance, specified in writing, evaluated, and reported on in a formal manner. It is common to have information feedback generated in this phase.

Production and Customer Use

It is quite common for production to find that certain components or subsystems do not or cannot be made to conform exactly to specified parameters. Sometimes this is found as a result of product usage in the field, rather than by production testing. Such occurrences always generate necessary information feedback for needed design modification and/or changes in over-all specifications.

OTHER VIEWPOINTS OF THE DESIGN PROCESS

Other writers in covering the design process include the earlier steps of setting objectives, the parallel marketing effort, and the manufacturing engineering that are all certainly part of the broad design engineering effort. These aspects are included in this book separately in order to focus on the heart of the design process discussed in this chapter. The views of other writers are summarized in Figs. 11-3 and 11-4.

POST-DESIGN

While creative engineering pays off at any point in the design process, it usually provides the greatest gains in the conceptual stage and in a review period. Although design engineering must take cost into account, its primary goal is usually to get something built that is below a certain prescribed cost figure. Time prevents an elaborate search for the most economical design. Consequently, progressive companies—particularly those engaged in high quality production—are introducing *Value Engineering* (originally called Value Analysis) to search for ways of getting equivalent value at lower cost. Because a high element of creativity is required in Value Engineering, a brief discussion is given here to present the management aspects of this technique or procedure.

First, what is Value Engineering? Value Engineering is the creative study of every item of cost in every part or material used in a product with the objective of attaining equivalent value at a lower cost. It must consider substitute materials, newer processes, the abilities of special suppliers, and the possibility for engineering redesign. Value Engineering focuses Engineering, Manufacturing, and Purchasing on one objective—*equivalent performance at lower cost.* Value Engineering may be part of the E & R organization or, in some cases, of manufacturing, purchasing, or industrial engineering groups. Their *modus operandi* is to analyze and make recommendations. Value Engineers should not play the role of critics but should associate themselves with the design team.

As defined at American Machines & Foundry Co., the stages in the evolution of an experimental engineering project, together with the principal types of work normally performed under each stage, are:

Stage 1 – Engineering Analysis: An engineering survey to evaluate the technical feasibility of the project, concurrent with or subsequent to commercial analysis. Includes:

1. Study and evaluation of requirements, including performance, appearance, size, weight, service, cost, and other pertinent factors.
2. Study and evaluation of prior technical art, including a review of patents and competing products or processes, both existent and potential.
3. Study and evaluation of possible alternative schemes of developing product or process, including:
   - 3.1. Preliminary estimate of the time and cost of developing each alternative.
   - 3.2. Engineering opinion of the approximate tooling and manufacturing cost of each alternative.
   - 3.3. Engineering opinion of possible financial return.
4. Preparation of a report to include:
   - 4.1. Summary of findings.
   - 4.2. Analysis of critical and limiting technical elements.
   - 4.3. A set of preliminary specifications.
   - 4.4. Detailed recommendations as to course of action to be followed, including estimate of funds required for Stage 2, and appropriation request, if any, for Stage 2.

Approximately 30% of this effort may be assigned to technicians; for example, collection of information on prior art and estimates, discussions with manufacturing and other engineering departments such as design.

Stage 2 – Engineering Exploration: An investigation to select the most practicable scheme of developing the product or process, and to prove the technical feasibility of the principles involved. Includes:

1. Thorough study of possible alternative development schemes.
2. Preparation of schematic diagrams and sketches.
3. Design, construction and test of jury rigs, or experimentation with processes and test of process samples, or other similar work that may be required to prove the feasibility of principles involved.
4. Check for potential patents and/or infringements.
5. Preparation of a report to include:
   - 5.1. Revised estimate of time and cost to complete the project.
   - 5.2. Revised engineering opinion of the approximate tooling and manufacturing cost.
   - 5.3. Revised engineering opinion of possible financial return.
   - 5.4. Summary of work completed and results obtained.
   - 5.5. Evaluation of potential technical success.
   - 5.6. Revised specifications for approval, including cost, performance, appearance and design specifications, such as size, weight, maintenance, service, etc.
   - 5.7. Recommendations as to future action, including estimate of funds required for remaining stages of project, and appropriation request, if any, for Stages 3, 4, and 5.

One or more technicians might be assigned full time to follow design and construction of jury-rigs or process tests, and to gather information for project engineer's analysis. (item 3)

Technician can assist project engineer in compiling information. (item 5.6)

Fig. 11-3. Engineering project stages. *Source:* Jay H. Bergen, "Putting the Technicians to Work in Research and Development Projects," *Machine Design* (May 14, 1959).

Technician may spend up to 100% of his time conveying jury-rig information to design, following job progress, working on model construction, and carrying on liaison with manufacturing.

Stage 3 – Prototype Design: Incorporation of principles established under Stage 2 into a practical design which will meet the approved specifications, and preparation of detailed drawings for manufacture of prototype. Includes:

1. Preparation of layouts.
2. Construction of a scaled dummy model (when necessary).
3. Consultation with industrial designer.
4. Consultation with factory engineers.
5. Preparation of detail drawings.
6. Check for potential patents and/or infringements.
7. Preparation of a bill of material.
8. Preparation of report to include:
   - 8.1. Evaluation of progress to date and outlook for the future.
   - 8.2. Tentative tooling and manufacturing cost estimate.
   - 8.3. Comparison of design with specifications.
   - 8.4. Recommended future action.

Major portions of shop and purchasing department liaison and operational testing may be assigned to technicians.

Stage 4 – Prototype Construction: Fabrication of prototype in accordance with the drawings and bill of material prepared in Stage 3. (Costs collected against this stage will include shop costs only; cost of engineering liaison and changes will be charged to Stage 3). Includes:

1. Shop labor and materials for fabrication.
2. Operational tests by shop personnel.
3. Modifications necessitated by engineering changes.
4. Engineering liaison with shop.

Approximately 50% of these four steps may be performed by a technician under direct supervision of an engineer.

Stage 5 – Prototype Test: Prototype testing in shop under simulated operating conditions and/or in the field under actual operating conditions. Includes:

1. Establishment of standard test specifications.
2. Installation and operation of prototype.
3. Compilation and evaluation of test data.
4. Minor alterations as required to conduct tests.
5. Preparation of a report to include:
   - 5.1. Evaluation of test results and comparison with specifications.
   - 5.2. Recommended design changes.
   - 5.3. Recommended specifications for pilot production models.
   - 5.4. Revised tentative tooling and manufacturing estimates.
   - 5.5. Recommended future action, including appropriation requests, if any, for Stage 6.

30 to 60% of the work in this stage may be done by technicians. Major assistance is provided by following the items checked.

Stage 6 – Pilot Production Model Design: Design modification to incorporate changes approved from Stage 5, and to reduce manufacturing costs to the minimum. Includes:

1. Consultation with industrial designer.
2. Consultation with factory engineers.
3. Preparation of layouts.
4. Preparation of detail drawings.
5. Preparation of assembly drawings.
6. Check with Patent Department.
7. Preparation of a bill of material.
8. Reduction in costs through simplification of design and methods, substitution of materials, etc.
9. Preparation of manufacturing and tooling cost estimates by factory.

Fig. 11-3 (*Continued*). Engineering project stages.

10. Preparation of a report to include:
    10.1. Evaluation of progress to date and outlook for future.
    10.2. Tooling and manufacturing cost estimates.
    10.3. Comparison of design with specifications.
    10.4. Recommended future action, including appropriation request, if any, for Stages 7, 8, and 9.

Stage 7 – Pilot Production Model Construction: Fabrication of pilot production models by the factory in accordance with the manufacturing drawings and bill of material prepared in Stage 6, and using tools prepared for the production run, to insure that all engineering errors are corrected and to check manufacturing cost estimates, before a large lot is built. (Costs collected against this stage will include shop costs only; cost of engineering liaison, changes and report will be charged against Stage 6.) Includes:

Here, the technician may handle about 90% of the shop liaison and can do most of the legwork involved.

1. Factory labor and materials for fabrication.
2. Operational tests by factory personnel.
3. Modifications necessitated by engineering changes.
4. Engineering liaison with factory.
5. Preparation of report to include:
    5.1. Evaluation of design, particularly from manufacturing standpoint.
    5.2. Estimation of actual manufacturing cost compared with previous estimates.
    5.3. Recommended future action.

Stage 8 – Pilot Production Model Test: Pilot production models testing in factory under simulated operating conditions and/or in the field under actual operating conditions. Includes:

Probably 70 to 80% of the work in these four areas can be performed by technicians under the supervision of engineers.

1. Establishment of standard test specifications.
2. Installation and operation of pilot production models.
3. Check with Patent Department.
4. Compilation and evaluation of test data.
5. Minor alterations as required to conduct tests.
6. Impartial evaluation.
7. Preparation of a report to include:
    7.1. Evaluation of test results and comparison with specifications.
    7.2. Recommended design modifications, classified into those required for first production lot and those deferable.
    7.3. Recommended final specifications.
    7.4. Recommended future action.

The technician also can assist in reviewing progress to firm up these recommendations.

Stage 9 – Preparation for Manufacture: Final revision and checking of drawings, bill of material, and other instructions for economic lot manufacturing, and compilation of technical data for sales and service. Includes:

Technicians would be able to handle the major effort in these areas.

1. Checking and finalizing of drawings and bill of material.
2. Preparation of engineering-manufacturing instructions.
3. Preparation of technical data folio including necessary information for installing, operating, and servicing unit.
4. Training of service personnel, including establishment of form desired for field reports.
5. Release of drawings for manufacture.
6. Preparation of final report to include:
    6.1. Review and evaluation of engineering performance of the project.
    6.2. Recommendations as to handling of other development projects.

Fig. 11-3 (*Concluded*). Engineering project stages.

	Manager	Marketing	Engineering	Manufacturing
PHASE I - STUDY				
1. Establish Business Objectives, Timing and Strategy	R			
2. Define Responsibilities and Relationships	R			
3. Establish Customer Requirements		R		
4. Establish Specific Product Requirements and Schedules	R			
5. Establish Product Design Philosophy			R	
6. Establish Manufacturing Philosophy				R
7. Establish Marketing Philosophy		R		
8. Select Preliminary Product Design Approach			R	
9. Identify Critical Problems and Alternate Approaches			R	R
10. Plan Feasibility Program Including Resource Requirements		R	R	R
11. Estimate Design and Production Program Resource Requirements		R	R	R
12. Review and Authorize Feasibility Program	R			
PHASE II - FEASIBILITY PROGRAM				
13. Establish Subsystem and Component Functional Design Requirements			R	
14. Establish Component Design Approaches			R	
15. Make Electrical Schematics and Mechanical Layouts			R	
16. Preliminary Product Design Review			R	
17. Propose Possible Manufacturing Methods for Critical Components			R	R
18. Determine Design Alternatives for Critical Components			R	
19. Producibility Review for Critical Components				R
20. Establish Design Specifications for Critical Components			R	
21. Determine Design Alternatives for Critical Manufacturing Processes			R	
22. Prove Feasibility of Critical Manufacturing Processes				R
23. Establish Design of Critical Manufacturing Processes				R
24. Plan Design Program Including Resource Requirements			R	R
25. Re-estimate Production Program Requirements		R	R	R
26. Review and Authorize Design Program	R			
PHASE III - DESIGN PROGRAM (PRODUCT AND PROCESS)				
27. Review Product Design Approach			R	
28. Revise Electrical Schematics and Mechanical Layouts			R	
29. Product Design Review			R	
30. Propose Possible Manufacturing Methods			R	R
31. Determine Product Design Alternatives			R	
32. Producibility Review				R
33. Complete Product Design Evaluation			R	
34. Finalize Product Design Specifications for Initial Production			R	
35. Complete Production Process Design				R
36. Establish Market Plan for Distribution and Service		R		
37. Prepare Production Program Plan Including Resource Requirements		R	R	R
38. Review and Authorize Production Program Plan	R			

Fig. 11-4. Integrated program plan.

PHASE IV - INITIAL PRODUCTION	Manager	Marketing	Engineering	Manufacturing
39. Release Product Design to Manufacturing			R	
40. Interpret Product Design Specifications			R	
41. Establish Production Equipment Methods and Procedures				R
42. Build Products to Established Product Design Specifications				R
43. Establish Product Installation, Maintenance and Operating Procedures		R		
44. Distribute and Service Products		R		
45. Evaluate Adequacy of Product Design Specifications			R	
46. Evaluate Production Samples			R	
47. Evaluate Manufacturing Process from Product Viewpoint			R	
48. Evaluate Manufacturing Process from Capability and Productivity Viewpoint				R
49. Evaluate Distribution and Service System		R		
50. Evaluate Customer Satisfaction		R		
51. Evaluate Business Performance of Initial Production	R			
PHASE V - CONTINUING PRODUCTION				
52. Propose Design Changes to Improve "Quality" or Reduce Costs			R	R
53. Propose Process Changes to Improve "Quality"			R	R
54. Propose Process Changes to Reduce Cost				R
55. Evaluate Proposed Design and Process Changes from Product Viewpoint			R	
56. Evaluate Required Process Changes from Productivity Viewpoint				R
57. Evaluate Proposed Design and Process Changes from Marketing Viewpoint		R		
58. Propose Design Change Program		R	R	R
59. Review and Authorize Design Change Program	R			
60. Establish Revised Product Design Specifications			R	
61. Establish Necessary Process Changes				R
62. Produce Redesigned Products				R
63. Evaluate Redesigned Products			R	
64. Distribute Redesigned Products, Spare Parts, and Service Information		R		
65. Evaluate Productivity of Redesigned Manufacturing Process				R
66. Evaluate Business Performance	R			

R - Primary Responsibility for Result

Fig. 11-4 (*Continued*). Integrated program plan. *Source:* "An Integrated Approach to Product Quality and Producibility," *Engineering Services* (Schenectady, N. Y.: General Electric Company).

The process of Value Engineering is based upon examining each *part* and each *function* and asking such questions as:

1. What is it?
2. What does it cost per year?
3. What does it do?
4. Does its use contribute value?
5. Is its cost proportionate to its usefulness?
6. Does it need all of its features?
7. Is there anything better for the intended use?

8. Can a usable part be made by a lower cost method?
9. Can a standard product be found which will be usable?
10. Is it made on proper tooling considering the quantities made?
11. Do material, reasonable labor, overhead, and profit total to its costs?
12. Will another dependable supplier provide it for less?
13. Is anyone buying it for less?

A specific project could be divided into five stages:

1. *Information Phase.* Secure all basic facts including drawings, engineering, purchasing, and manufacturing information.
2. *Speculative or Creative Phase.* Generate all possible solutions, consult others, systematically explore the questions in the above list.
3. *Functional Analysis.* Divide the job into functional areas such as a fastening job, an electrical job, a dust protection job, etc. Obtain expert consultation in each area.
4. *Cost Analysis Phase.* Estimate the dollar value of the most likely solutions.
5. *Status Summary and Conclusions.* Issue a *concise* suggestion sheet covering each part which has possibilities of being improved or deleted and send to the appropriate personnel.

Figure 11-5 shows examples of cases where Value Engineering was put into practice.

CONCLUSION

The tremendous power for achievement which is possible through creative engineering has hardly been tapped. Too often the uncreative stifle the creative people. The creative engineer needs to learn to persist in the face of such comments as:

It won't work.
We tried that before.
It will never get by the Underwriters.
We can't pay for the tools.
It is patented.
We haven't had a failure in fifty years; why change it?
There's no other source of supply.
Cost doesn't count—just get it shipped.
It can't be done.
It's a government job.
We can't help it—that's the policy.
We don't have enough time.
Our business is different.
We'll come back to it later.
It leaves me cold.

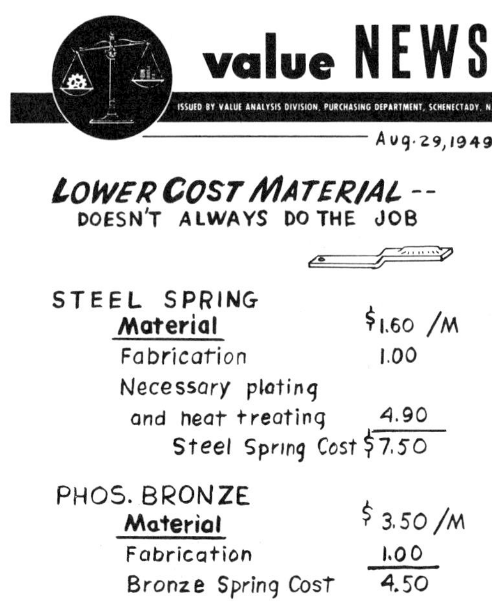

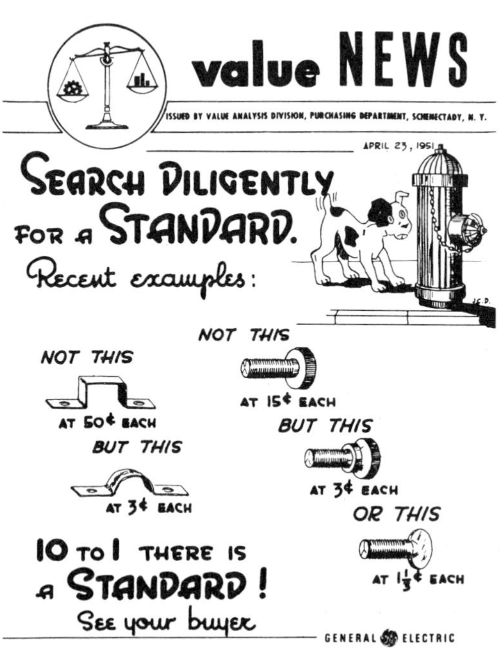

Fig. 11-5. Examples of applied Value Engineering. *Source:* General Electric Co., Value Analysis Div., Schenectady, N. Y.

Let's think about it some more.
This isn't the right time for it.
We can't hold up production for that.
Cost is not important—just get it out the back door.
We don't do it that way.
It costs too much.
That's not my responsibility.
No one else knows as much about it as we do.

AUTOMATION OF DESIGN

The processes of engineering development and design consist of (1) conceptualization and (2) information processing. Processing of information may be considered to be:

1. Data processing
   a. Converting
   b. Transporting
   c. Reproducing (documentation)
   d. Sorting
   e. Storing
   f. Retrieving
2. Computing
3. Programmed reasoning.

Much of the work of design that was once considered to be creative and only to be performed by human beings is now performed by computers. Once a logic network has been constructed by an engineer, computers can "design" various modifications of simple products. Slowly the creative area is shrinking as larger computers can store more technological, economic, and marketing data and are able to search, compare, evaluate, and make decisions on the basis of criteria specified by engineers and others in the company.

The advance in automation of engineering design has followed the pattern of automation in manufacturing. "Islands" of engineering automation have been established as, for example, in information searching, computing, documentation, evaluating alternative designs, and designing simple components. Automation is also a matter of degree since any significant replacement of human labor by machine represents an advance in automation. For this reason, levels of automation applicable to E & R work need to be defined. Two examples of such scales are shown in Figs. 11-6 and 11-7.

Since definitions of degree of automation are very useful, each step in the process of design can be listed and a level of automation assigned. It is then possible to draw a profile chart of automation so that activities with relatively low levels of automation may be highlighted.

<table>
<tr><th>Initiating Control Source</th><th colspan="2">Type of Machine Response</th><th>Power Source</th><th>Level Number</th><th>LEVEL OF MECHANIZATION</th></tr>
<tr><td rowspan="9">From a variable in the environment</td><td rowspan="6">Responds with action</td><td rowspan="3">Modifies own action over a wide range of variation</td><td rowspan="15">Mechanical (Nonmanual)</td><td>17</td><td>Anticipates action required and adjusts to provide it.</td></tr>
<tr><td>16</td><td>Corrects performance while operating.</td></tr>
<tr><td>15</td><td>Corrects performance after operating.</td></tr>
<tr><td rowspan="3">Selects from a limited range of possible prefixed actions.</td><td>14</td><td>Identifies and selects appropriate set of actions.</td></tr>
<tr><td>13</td><td>Segregates or rejects according to measurement.</td></tr>
<tr><td>12</td><td>Changes speed, position, direction according to measurement signal.</td></tr>
<tr><td colspan="2" rowspan="3">Responds with signal</td><td>11</td><td>Records performance.</td></tr>
<tr><td>10</td><td>Signals preselected values of measurement. (Includes error detection.)</td></tr>
<tr><td>9</td><td>Measures characteristic of work.</td></tr>
<tr><td rowspan="4">From a control mechanism that directs a predetermined pattern of action</td><td colspan="2" rowspan="4">Fixed within the machine</td><td>8</td><td>Actuated by introduction of work piece or material.</td></tr>
<tr><td>7</td><td>Power tool system, remote controlled.</td></tr>
<tr><td>6</td><td>Power tool program control (sequence of fixed functions).</td></tr>
<tr><td>5</td><td>Power tool, fixed cycle (single function).</td></tr>
<tr><td rowspan="4">From man</td><td colspan="2" rowspan="4">Variable</td><td>4</td><td>Power tool, hand control.</td></tr>
<tr><td>3</td><td>Powered hand tool.</td></tr>
<tr><td rowspan="2">Manual</td><td>2</td><td>Hand tool.</td></tr>
<tr><td>1</td><td>Hand.</td></tr>
</table>

Fig. 11-6. Levels of automation. *Source:* Taken from Automation and Management, James R. Bright, Division of Research (Boston, Mass.: Harvard University Press, 1958).

	Function Performed by Machine	Characteristics
L 1	None	All work performed by humans. Manual aids are used.
L 2	Supplies action energy	Mechanical or electrical energy is supplied for the basic process action.
L 3	Supplies all action energy	Energy is supplied for all control functions, auxiliary functions, and basic functions.
L 4	Stores the control instructions	Machine follows established step-by-step stored instructions.
L 5	Controls intermediate and auxiliary actions	Feedback in minor loops assists in control.
L 6	Controls output by main loop feedback	Closed loop feedback produces controlled output by iterative process.
L 7	Modifies or creates control instructions	Machine determines what to do and requires no human control.

Fig. 11-7. Seven levels of automation in engineering work.

For lower costs and higher quality from automated design, the E & R manager should look for:

1. Repetitive work
2. Work requiring constant revision whose changes in other areas of activity can be programmed
3. High physical operations
4. Slow, high cost, or poor quality communication and documentation.

BIBLIOGRAPHY

Air Force Systems Command. *Configuration Management During the Acquisition Phase*, AFSCM 375–1, June 1, 1962.

———. *System Program Management Procedures,* AFSCM 375–4, May 31, 1966.

ALGER, JOHN R. M., and HAYS, CARL V. *Creative Synthesis in Design.* Englewood Cliffs, N.J., Prentice-Hall, Inc., 1964.

ALLEN, THOMAS J. "Studies of the Problem-Solving Process in Engineering Design," *IEEE Transactions on Engineering Management,* Vol. EM-13, No. 2 (June, 1966), pp. 72–83.

ASIMOW, MORRIS. *Introduction to Design.* Englewood Cliffs, N.J.: Prentice-Hall, Inc., 1962.

BASNETT, R. T. "How to Increase and Encourage Engineering Productivity," *Product Engineering,* July 5, 1965.

BERGEN, JAY H. "Putting Technicians to Work," *Machine Design,* May 14, 1959.

BOLZ, ROGER W. "Manufacturing Engineering," *Automation,* October, 1958.

BROADBENT, D. E. "Aspects of Human Decision-Making," *Computers and Automation,* XVII, No. 5 (May, 1968), pp. 30–39.

BUNNELL, T. R. "Manufacturing Engineering," *Automation,* September, 1959.

CHAMBERS, D. E. *What is Engineering.* General Electric Company, Engineering Services Research, February 18, 1963.

CHESTNUT, HAROLD. *Systems Engineering Methods.* New York, N.Y.: John Wiley & Sons, Inc., 1967.

"Computers Speed the Design Cycle," *Business Week,* November 7, 1964.

DAVIS, BENJAMIN G. "Manufacturing Planning Parallels Product Development," *Machine Design,* February, 1963.

DEAN, MARVIN A. "Costs and Consequences from Idea to Hardware," *Research/Development,* December, 1961.

DEVLIN, T. J. "Putting Information to Work," *Chemical Engineering Progress,* March, 1965.

"Engineering Managers Face Up to Automation," *Proceedings 12th Annual Joint Engineering Management Conference.* Cleveland, Ohio, September 17–18, 1964.

EYRING, HENRY B. "Sources of Uncertainty and Their Consequences in Engineering Design Projects," *IEEE Transactions on Engineering Management,* Vol. EM-13, No. 4 (December, 1966), 167–180.

FEIST, HERMAN J. "Developing Schematics," *Machine Design,* November 11, 1965.

FITZGERALD, A. J., and GLIE, ROWEN. "A Guide to Technical Specifications," *Machine Design,* July 6, 1961.

FRANCIS, GERALD A. "Engineering Analysis of Existing Products," *Battelle Technical Review,* November, 1967.

FRICK, HENRY. "Design Guide to Value—II," *Product Engineering,* March 2, 1964.

GIESLER, BRYAN E. "Maintainability." Paper submitted for course in Research and Design Management, April 22, 1966.

GREGORY, S. A., ed. *The Design Method.* New York, N.Y.: Plenum Publishing Corporation, 1966.

HALL, ARTHUR D. *A Methodology for Systems Engineering.* Princeton, N.J.: D. Van Nostrand Co., Inc., 1962.

HEYSON, ALLEN E. "Classification of Product Characteristics," *Machine Design,* June 20, 1963.

HOLSTEIN, DAVID. "Decision Tables," *Machine Design,* August 2, 1962.

HOPKINS, R. C. "A Systematic Procedure for Systems Development," *IRE Transactions on Engineering Management,* June, 1961.

HUGGINS, R. TROY. "Second Lesson in Value Engineering," *Product Engineering,* March 30, 1964.

"IBM Buys its Own Sales Pitch," *Business Week,* October 30, 1965.

International Business Machines Corporation. 1963. "Automated Design Engineering," *General Information Manual.*

———. "Engineering Design Data Processing at IBM." *General Information Manual.* Undated.

———. "The Survey and Implementation of an Automated Design Engineering System." *Reference Manual,* 1963.

JOHNSTONE, DENVER T., JR. "The Management of Quality Control and Reliability," *Machine Design,* March 14, 1963.

KOPP, CARL G., and WERTZ, JAMES B. "Designer and Computer: An Engineering Partnership," *Battelle Technical Review,* February, 1968.

LANDERS, RICHARD R. "Reliability Audits," *Machine Design,* March 2, 1961.

———. *Reliability and Product Assurance.* Englewood Cliffs, N.J.: Prentice-Hall, Inc., 1963.

LANGEFORS, BORJE. "Automated Design," *International Science and Technology,* February, 1964.

LANGIENWALTER, D. F., and CHALUPA, R. *Product Design Structure Manual.* General Electric Company, December 15, 1960.

LESLIE, HOWARD L. G. "Design Guide to Value," *Product Engineering,* December 23, 1963.

MATOUSEK, ROBERT. *Engineering Design.* New York, N.Y.: Interscience Publishers, 1963.

MCCOLM, E. M. "Experimental Design: A Technique for Getting Most Information at Least Cost," *Research Management,* Spring, 1958.

MORSE, CHARLES W. "Manufacturing Engineering Today," *Automation,* July, 1961.

MORTON, MICHAEL S. S. "Interactive Visual Display Systems and Management Problem Solving," *The Industrial Management Review,* Fall, 1967.

MURDICK, R. G., and KARGER, D. W. 1966. "Guidelines for Engineering Automation." Unpublished paper.

NADLER, GERALD. "Investigation of Design Methodology," *Management Science,* June, 1967.

NEWTON, NORMAN T. *An Approach to Design.* Cambridge, Mass.: Addison-Wesley Publishing Co., Inc., 1951.

NOSAL, MELVIN A. 1967. The Role of Automation in Engineering and Research. Paper submitted for course in Research and Design Management, May 16, 1967.

"Now—It's Fabric Design by Electronics," *Textile World,* January, 1967.

"Organization and Management of R and D," *Semi-annual Progress Report #78-64,* Alfred P. Sloan School of Management, Massachusetts Institute of Technology, June 30, 1964.

PALLADINO, NUNZIO J., and DAVIS, HAROLD L. "The Engineering Design of Power Reactors," *Nucleonics,* June, 1960.

PERLMUTTER, D. D. "What is Systems Engineering?", *Chemical Engineering Progress,* May, 1962.

POHS, HENRY A. "Materials Specification System," *Machine Design,* October 10, 1963.

"Report on Engineering Design," *Journal of Engineering Education,* April, 1961.

"Research Scientist's Proposal Envisions 'Chemical Shorthand,'" *Engineering Opportunities,* May, 1965.

ROSSNAGEL, W. B. "Methods of Solving the Reliability Problem," *Product Engineering,* September 2, 1963.

RUGGLES, WAYNE F. "First Lesson in Value Engineering," *Product Engineering,* December 23, 1963.

"Selecting Business Opportunities," *Battelle Technical Review,* October, 1966.

SEMINARA, JOSEPH L., and TEVIS, JACK M. "Mockups: Plain and Fancy," *Machine Design,* June 20, 1963.

SHEA, GORDON F. "A Guide to the Structure of Military Specifications," *Machine Design,* July 19, 1962.

SOBELMAN, SIDNEY. *A Modern Dynamic Approach to Product Development.* United States Department of Commerce, PD 151649, December, 1958.

———. "Speeding Product Development," *Machine Design,* April 14, 1960.

SWAIN, ALAN D. "Design Practices to Reduce Human Errors," *Machine Design,* April 23, 1964.

TAYLOR, MORRIS P. "Design is More Than Nuts and Bolts," *Product Engineering,* March 10, 1958.

THOMAS, A. M. "The Product Design Review Committee," *Machine Design,* January 7, 1960.

TRIPOLI, PHILIP. "Value Engineering," *Machine Design,* October 12, 1961.

VARGO, FRANK J. "Lowest Life Cycle Cost (L^2C^2) Program," *Engineering Opportunities,* March, 1968.

VIITANEN, V. K. *Product Development—From Research to Production. Part 2 The Teamaker from Prototype to Production.* Contributed by the Machine Design Division for presentation at the ASME Annual Meeting, December 1–6, 1957, at New York, N.Y.

WARNER, C. E., and BERG, R. L. "Producibility Designing for Production," *Mechanical Engineering,* May, 1961.

WEIR, I. R. "Industrial Standardization—A Valuable Tool for Economic Progress," *The Magazine of Standards,* February, 1961.

WILSON, WARREN E. *Concepts of Engineering System Design.* New York, N.Y.: McGraw-Hill Book Company, 1965.

WOODSON, THOMAS T. *Introduction to Engineering Design.* New York, N.Y.: McGraw-Hill Book Company, 1966.

YOUNG, GORDON, "What is a 'Test'?", *Machine Design,* July 22, 1965.

CHAPTER 12

Managing for Standardization, Variety Control, Producibility, Reliability, and Maintainability

In managing for standardization, variety control, producibility, reliability, and maintainability, the manager faces the problem that each of these fields has become or is becoming highly specialized. It is too much to expect the design engineer to be thoroughly knowledgeable in each field; yet he is usually the individual responsible for the end product, whether it is a complete system, a complex product, or some small component. In the case of systems, the problem is even more complex because the attainment of these aspects in the design of the components does not necessarily yield these qualities in the system in which the components are used.

That these characteristics of a product are important will be seen from a discussion of each. Some approaches to achieving technical objectives for such characteristics through organization and procedures will also be discussed.

TECHNICAL STANDARDS

Development of Standards

A standard is the means by which measurement is made possible. A standard can apply to a process, an object, or an abstract concept such as time. H. W. Robb of General Electric defined standards in a broad sense:

> Standardization is the activity concerned with the conceiving, formulating, distributing, revising and promoting the use of standards. Standardization is

the organized solution of common problems, and standards are the records of such solutions to avoid waste of creative effort in the repetitive consideration of the same problems.

Standards are as old as man, and the spoken word (standards of sound, symbol, and gesture) is probably the oldest of all. With the development of standards there arises the accompanying problem of maintaining them. Many unperceptive individuals view standardization as being the antithesis of creativity. Yet without standards our present-day technology could not have developed.

Generally a standard is that which has been established as a model to which an object or an action may be compared. These standards may be in the form of:

1. Physical models
2. Written descriptions
3. Devices for making specified comparison—i.e., a "Go-Nogo" gauge
4. Any combination of implements and instructions to be used in decision making.

The basis of the pound was first established in 1266 when Henry III of England defined the coinage and commercial pound in terms of the English penny which was to weigh "32 grams of wheat taken from the middle of the ear." Another of the oldest standards whose definition has also been changed is the unit of length. In 1875, the standard of length was established as a meter. This was defined as the distance between two lines engraved on a platinum-iridium bar stored in a special vault in France. Due to the modern need for more accurate measurement, the meter is now defined as 1,650,763.73 wave lengths in vacuo of the orange-red light given off by electrically excited Krypton-86. Many of our common standards changed with our advancing technology, i.e., with our ability to measure accurately and with our need for a more precise standard.

In the United States, the backbone of the development and maintenance of standards is the United States of America Standards Institute. The membership of the Institute consists of government departments and technical organizations plus over 2,000 individual company members. The USASI does not establish standards, but provides itself as an independent agency having the machinery to establish standards by a consensus. The USASI doesn't have the authority or purpose of enforcing standards; it simply labels the accepted standards as United States of America Standards. It is also the United States' representative in the International Organization for Standardization. While many older technologies have barely started to use the services of USASI, the many new technologies such as electronics, plastics, and atomic energy have increased the demand for its services.

The government bureau which plays a very important part in the development of standards is the National Bureau of Standards. The National

Bureau of Standards conducts basic research and provides: (1) information, (2) measurements, (3) technical help in developing testing methods, and (4) technical assistance to other groups attempting to develop standards. The NBS will take on special standard studies for industry as well as initiate projects of its own.

Standardization is concerned with the conception, formulation, and dissemination of standards. Enforcement and revision are also concerns in the Standardization Department of an organization, especially in industrial organizations. In the design process, standardization is concerned with components, materials, testing, and engineering procedures. Standards are interrelated with cost, reliability, maintainability, specifications, and producibility. The question can be raised as to why components should be standardized, i.e., why shouldn't each company's product be completely different from that of another? If there were no use of standardization in design, every company would use different sizes and types of screws, for example, that would make repairs difficult or impossible. Without standardization in everyday life, light bulbs would probably not fit lamp sockets, electrical connector plugs would not fit all outlets, and replacements for batteries, tires, etc., would be both difficult and costly to find. The idea of the importance of interchangeability of parts originated with Eli Whitney when he demonstrated the concept in the manufacture of rifles during the Revolutionary War. Automation has accentuated standardization and will further do so, as well as broaden the base of technical standards.

What Should be Standardized?

The principle which guides standardization applies equally to procedures, components, and end products—standards should apply both to the routine and to the repetitive. Also, standards should keep pace with new knowledge and advancing technology. Thus, standardization will not suppress creativity, but instead, permit people to spend more time on creative work—especially if a reasonable procedure is available when deviation should become necessary.

To illustrate, suppose a firm is in the business of control circuit design and production. If every time a potentiometer were required, an engineer had to design it and the draftsman had to draw it, the cost of the potentiometer would be closer to twenty dollars than two dollars. Each of these highly skilled people would be diverted from doing truly creative work—work that is new and useful. Thus, once something basic and simple has been invented and improved by the best engineering talent over the years and performs adequately in all respects, standards should be established for its use in design. In this case, potentiometer standards relate to physical size and shape, resistance, wattage, accuracy, and life. It is not true that engineers should never try to improve a component or product once a standard has been set. When a technological or commercial need arises, then creativity can be applied to the specific product again. Standardized products can become obsolete rapidly due to technological change in particular. For example, tube fittings which were used in fuel lines of older aircraft were standardized. However, with the advent of jet engines, fuel flow requirements are often twenty times as large as formerly. If the old standards were used, the hex portion would have required a wrench of the size used on locomotives. There isn't enough room to put such a large fitting or turn a wrench of that size in most aircraft. Consequently, a new approach to such components was taken and new standards were established.

Standardization can apply not only to parts and end products, but also to intermediate assemblies. Particularly in electronics, the manager of E & R should consider the use of standard modules which are interchangeable among various types and styles of end products. Standardization in such cases not only reduces cost of design, but it minimizes manufacturing and service costs as well as simplifying and speeding service.

Varieties of Standardization

Standardization activities can generally be placed into one of five categories:

1. Horizontal standardization
2. Specific standardization
3. Area standardization
4. Functional versus logistical standardization
5. Cooperative versus unilateral standardization.

Horizontal standardization could be called general or commodity standardization. In this category the item being standardized is anticipated to be used in a wide array of projects or products and often also to fill various needs, i.e., bolts, nuts, bearings, diodes, etc.

Specific standardization is also known as system or vertical standardization. Specific standardization amounts to what could be called project or product standardization. It covers all aspects of a project or product from design to operation. It must take full advantage of horizontal (general) standards.

The key to success in this type of standardization is advance planning so that the various designers will be provided with the same lists of standards selected, those selected for that system or project. It is a pervasive type of standardization that must be utilized at the project's inception and terminated only when the "product" is retired.

Area standardization is used to achieve maximum economy in a firm whose plants or places of business are widely scattered geographically. In cases such as these there is usually more than one supplier of a given kind of equipment, part, or material. Therefore, a variety of similar objects (but not exactly the same) will be used by such an organization—hence the need to establish standards for each geographic area.

Functional standardization is primarily concerned with performance criteria. Items built to a common functional standard may differ greatly in appearance, but share the same use or function. *Logistical standardization,* on the other hand, specifies a part in complete detail. Each part, process, and configuration is expressly detailed. If a system has been logistically standardized then each spare part must be identical to the unit it replaces. A functionally standardized system will operate with items from different sources which may differ in internal structure but will be identical in form, fit, and function.

Cooperative standardization has resulted in standards for such things as threads, fitting sizes, etc. Imagine the hardship if manufacturing standards did not exist.

Scope of the Engineering Standards Program

The scope of a typical engineering standards program might consist of the following:

1. Formulate plans for the development and improvement of common standards used in engineering
2. Prepare and disseminate Engineering Standard Practice Instructions covering such things as design practice, manufacturing standards, and drafting practice
3. Prepare and disseminate *Materials Standard Practice Instructions* giving properties and applications of materials, preferred sizes and grades, processes to be used, costs, etc.
4. Provide a Manual of Standard Parts listing standard electrical and mechanical components recommended and available, costs, applications, and technical data
5. Assist with the preparation of standard specifications used for purchasing, manufacturing, and testing
6. Provide a suitable classification, distribution, and promotion (also, in many cases, enforcement) of standards
7. Maintain liaison with outside organizations concerned with standards such as the USASI
8. Provide for the periodic review of standards for revision and/or canceling.

For purposes of classification, General Electric standards are set up with a numbering system. Four series are assigned to materials, one each to finishes and test methods, and three to design data and standard practice according to the following:

Series	Classes of Standards
A	Nonmetallic materials
B	Metallic materials
C	Machine parts
D	Supplier and ingredients
E	Test methods
F	Finishes
G	Design data
K	Drafting practice

The manuals are distributed separately to departments according to their needs.

A modern and up-to-date standards program can encourage designers to utilize technical advances. Without such a program, some designers, left on their own, would fall behind with respect to modern engineering and science. Conversely, an inferior set of standards will hold back good men.

Organization for the Standards Program

In large companies, much standardization work is carried out at the corporate or headquarters level, but also some must usually be performed at the product department level. Committees are frequently employed to establish company standards since a number of viewpoints, particularly in engineering, manufacturing, and purchasing, must be represented.

The engineering standards program within the product department, or in a small company, may be located within a technical services or an engineering administration organization. Besides developing the standards required for the particular product line, the standards group in the product organization is concerned with the daily problems of disseminating catalogue information, up-dating manuals, and keeping engineers and draftsmen "standards-conscious."

An example of a standards organization is shown in Fig. 12-1.

Summary of Benefits of Standardization

The benefits from standardization include the following:

1. Assurance of availability—the right item available at the right time, in adequate quantities.
2. Assurance of interchangeability. This is extremely important, since many manufacturers contribute to any given product or project.
3. Assurance of reliability—products and components made to standards that assure adequate performance.
4. Assurance of producibility—products and components designed to adequately meet all requirements including those of producibility engineering.

5. Assurance of optimum sizes or varieties.
6. Proper utilization of resources. This benefit can only be realized if adequate use is made of standardization.

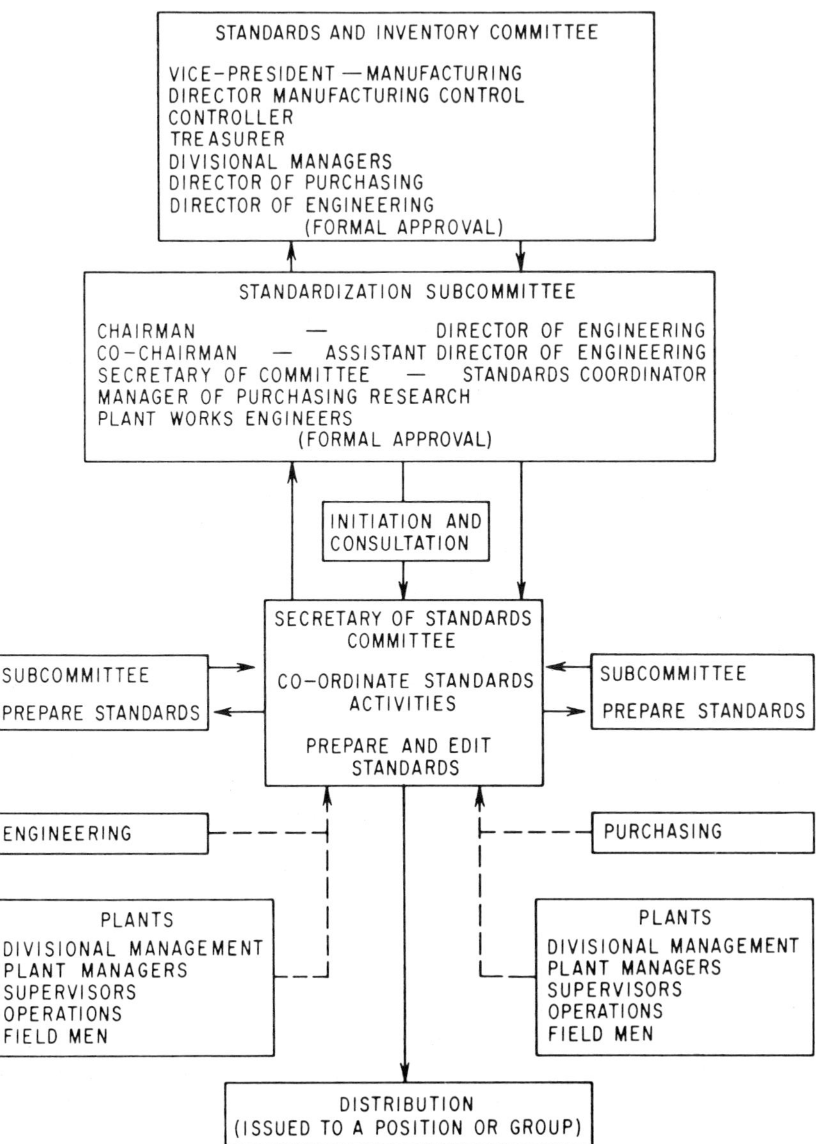

Fig. 12-1. A standards organization chart. *Source:* B. Scott Liston, "How to Set Up a Standards Program for a Small Company," *The Magazine of Standards* (December 1958).

VARIETY CONTROL FOR SIMPLIFICATION, STANDARDIZATION, AND PRODUCIBILITY

Variety Control is a procedure that can aid standardization by limiting the kinds and/or sizes of parts and components, as well as the number of models. This helps maximize the producibility of the product or system. It is a technique generally identified in Europe as variety control and reduction; in the U. S. and Canada the work is largely carried out under the guise of simplification, standardization, and producibility. Many European countries from England to Israel which are utilizing the technique are deriving major benefits from it.

Variety Control can best be described and explained through the citation of a few examples* describing results and/or benefits obtained from the *application* of the technique.

One would imagine that relatively new industry such as exists in Israel would have little need for variety (remember that the terminology refers to parts and components, as well as to products) control and reduction, since in addition to being new, the firms were generally founded by knowledgeable industrialists.

Two Israeli plants, Lodzia and Adin-Neufeld, manufacture knitwear. Applying variety reduction concepts, they questioned the logical basis of the intervals between adjacent sizes in the standard size ranges of knitwear—standards of the Israel knitwear industry. In the 28- to 44-in. range, the steps were 2-in. intervals. The 2-in. interval between 28 in. and 30 in. represented an increase of 7.1 percent above the 28-in. size, while the 2-in. interval between the 42- and 44-in. size represented an increase of only 4.8 percent above the 42-in. size. The *irrationality* of such a size range structure was emphasized by the fact that (1) the knitted garments had a large amount of stretch and (2) the amount of change between sizes was not proportional, as previously explained. By developing a more logical range structure fixed percentage size (8 percent was a reasonable step) around a present 36-in. midpoint, the theoretically exact sizes would be: 28.5 in., 30.8 in., 33.3 in., 36 in., 38.9 in., 42 in., and 45.3 in. These would cover the same range of requirements with seven instead of nine sizes, thereby reducing the number of different sizes to be manufactured by 22 percent. The theoretical sizes could be labeled as: 28-29, 30-32, 33-34, 35-37, 38-40, 41-43, and 44-46. As a result of this work the Israel Productivity Institute and the Standards Institute of Israel are withholding the standard previously mentioned until a further study can be made so as to recommend more rational national standard size specifications for the knitwear industry.

* The firms drawn from Israeli industry were participants in a study and work project conducted by Prof. Harold W. Martin of Rensselaer Polytechnic Institute.

The first reaction of the reader to this example will probably be to minimize its importance to U. S. industry thinking that it is too simple, and that we are generally far more sophisticated in designing or engineering a product. However, the message and lesson should be heeded.

A somewhat unsophisticated application of this technique occurred in Israel Cycle Manufacturers Ltd. For manufacturing economy, a decision was made to break with tradition and to standardize on one chain-wheel and sprocket for both twenty-six- and twenty-eight-inch cycles. Similarly, it was decided to standardize on the four-inch pedal for both ladies' and men's cycles. In both cases of departure from traditional practice, there was no adverse reaction from either the distributors or users. In other words, don't let tradition stop you from attempting to reduce the variety of component parts.

In a computer memory development project, directed by one of the authors, the concept of variety control was introduced into the initial design with the practical effect that an entire solid state computer memory system was constructed by using essentially only two kinds of transistors, one diode, six resistors, and three fixed capacitors. It was only in auxiliary portions of the memory system that similar parts of other values or types were used. In a similar way a standard basic "and/or" circuit, and a standard basic "flip-flop" circuit were used throughout the entire system. The required varied characteristics were obtained by usage of the different values of resistors and capacitors.

To a degree, variety reduction and/or control is a procedure that must be implemented by management; furthermore, it involves a balancing of unification versus diversification. Its philosophy and management problems are quite similar to those of standardization.

RELIABILITY

The Growing Importance of Reliability

In the past decade, reliability has suddenly assumed major importance. Not only has it become of primary concern in the development of large weapons systems, but its emphasis is beginning to be reflected in the civilian market. Examples of the latter are the extended time guarantees on automobiles, refrigerators, etc. Industry has become reliability-conscious due, in part, to advancing technological developments and, in part, to recent wars which vividly emphasized the consequences of unreliability.

Unreliability results in excess costs, time wasted, introduces the psychological effect of inconvenience, and in certain instances jeopardizes personal and/or national security. The cost of unreliability is not only the cost of the failing item but also that of the associated equipment which is damaged or destroyed as a result of the failure. More importantly the primary equipment is worthless (for its intended purpose) until the failure has been repaired. This shutdown usually represents the greatest cost when dealing with a complex system. All of these result in losses of man hours which also may be very costly.

The failure of a transistor in a home radio ordinarily would be of little consequence from the standpoint of downtime or cost. On the other hand, the failure of a similar transistor in a space vehicle might prevent a staging from occurring, which would lead to the subsequent loss of the total missile at a tremendous cost and possibly, the loss of human life. Another expense arising from unreliability of machines and equipment in service, however a little less obvious, is the expense of maintenance. Although, here, the immediate results of unreliability may not be as disastrous as the missile example, the necessity of having trained personnel continuously check out the equipment is obviously expensive and may result in "down time" when operation is badly needed.

Time wasted is a frequent consequence of unreliability. In industry, time wasted is almost always synonymous with money wasted. For example, the cost of down time on machines or computers certainly results in excess cost. In a similar vein, an airliner removed from service because of mechanical or electrical failure results in a delay of departure which may not only cost the airline revenue, but there is the excess cost of providing overnight lodging, extra meals, etc., for passengers who could not be delivered to their destination as scheduled.

An almost classical example of the psychological effect of unreliability was that of the ill-famed Vanguard satellites, which involved the United States' effort to compete with Russia's success with Sputnik I.*

Perhaps the most important consequence of unreliability is in its effect upon national security. For example, when we discuss the number of missiles on the launching pads, the number of airplanes in the Strategic Air Command, or the number of radar stations, we usually think of the actual physical number and not the effective number which depends upon the reliability of the particular weapons system.

Unfortunately, there is no panacea for unreliability. A reliability equal to unity (100 percent) will not be obtained as long as its factors are fallible human beings, imperfect communications, incomplete understanding, and requirements beyond current technological experience. The degree of reliability obtainable, however, can be generally predicted and, to a large extent, controlled if the proper techniques and methods are used.

Employing such qualitative terms as "rugged," "shock resistant," "a long life expectancy," etc., is not enough. Only by the use of reliability techniques, which supply numbers as a measure, and through the use of statis-

* The third attempt to launch a Vanguard satellite on March 17, 1958 was very successful.

tics and analysis of data, will a valid basis for describing key characteristics of complex products and/or systems be obtained.

Fundamentals of Reliability

Reliability can be defined[1] as the probability of a device delivering adequate performance for the length of time desired under specified operating conditions. The four factors: probability, adequate performance, time and operating conditions are each necessary parts of the definition of reliability.

Probability, the first element in the definition, allows us to express numerically, the number of times we can expect an event to occur out of a total number of trials. Thus, the statement that the probability of survival, P_s, of a device operating for 50 hours is 0.75, indicates that only 75 times out of 100 trials would we expect the device to be functioning after a 50 hour operating period.

Adequate performance, the second element of the reliability definition, indicates that definite performance criteria must be established so that all concerned will know what is to be considered a satisfactory performance.

Time as an element in the definition is necessary because it represents a measure of the period during which we can expect a certain degree of performance. In order to establish its reliability, we must have knowledge of the length of time we wish the device or system to function.

Operating conditions are those functional and environmental conditions under which we expect a device to function. Common examples of these conditions are: temperature, humidity, shock, and vibration.

An expression of reliability does not mean very much unless the prevailing physical or environmental conditions under which the reliability was assessed are included as part of the statement of reliability. Since reliability is expressed as a number, its value will change with changing operating conditions. For example, a claim by an automobile manufacturer that his cars can go 100,000 miles between brake changes does not mean much unless the conditions are specified, i.e., steady operation over toll roads is a far different matter than is stop and go city driving.

The most common measures of reliability are failure rate r, probability of survival P_s, and mean time between failures ($MTBF$). The failure rate is commonly expressed in terms of failures per hr., per 100 hrs., per 1,000 hrs., or percent of failures per 1,000 hrs. The probability of survival is expressed as a decimal fraction or percent which indicates the probable or expected number of devices that will function for a required period of time. For example, suppose in military terms, the mission time was 50 hours, suppose further that a large number of units were tested and all of them equaled or exceeded 50 hours of operation. We would then have an

[1] For definitions associated with reliability, see MIL-Std-721.

example of 100 percent reliability. However, if only 70 percent of the devices equaled or exceeded 50 hours of operation, we would conclude that their reliability for this mission is probably 70 percent. Statistical methods are used to determine degrees of confidence for the predicted results.

The mean time between failures is measured in hours. The larger the value of *MTBF,* the greater the reliability. The *MTBF* is the ratio of the total test time of a device to the total number of failures.

The failure rate is the reciprocal of the *MTBF.* Therefore, the smaller the numerical value of failure rate, the greater the reliability of the device being described from a reliability view.

The basic reliability equation, if it is assumed that an exponential distribution of random failures during the useful life period will occur is:

$$R = e^{-t/MTBF}$$

$$\text{or } R = e^{-\lambda t}$$

where R = reliability or probability of success
t = mission time, in hours

$$MTBF = \frac{\text{operating hours}}{\text{failures}}$$

$$\lambda = \text{failure rate} = \frac{1}{MTBF}$$

Reliability can be determined from the same basic equation when the mean cycles between failure (*MCBF*) is known. Here it is important that the cycle be carefully defined in any *MCBF* calculation.

$$t = \text{mission cycles required}$$

$$\lambda = \frac{1}{MCBF} = \frac{\text{failures}}{\text{operating cycles}}$$

To convert from one failure rate unit to another can easily be accomplished by relocation of the decimal point as shown in this example:

$$0.06\%/1{,}000 \text{ hrs.} = 0.0006/1{,}000 \text{ hrs.} = 0.6/10^6 \text{ hr.}$$

It perhaps should be noted here that when the *MTBF* or *MCBF* is equal to the required operating time t, then only 37 percent of the units can be expected to be still operating at time t (or the probability of one unit operating to time t, is 37 percent). This is based on no wearout failures occurring before time t. When the *MTBF* is four times as large as t, 78 percent of the units can be expected to be still operating at time t.

Reliability recognizes three *types* of failures which may be inherent in the equipment and occur without fault on the part of any person.

*First, there are the "**early failures.**"* These are the failures which occur early in the life of a component as a result of poor manufacturing and quality control techniques during the production process. It is extremely difficult to prevent few substandard items from eventually getting through the assembly cycle. Early failures can be eliminated by the "debugging process" and/or the "burn-in" process. The debugging process consists of operating an equipment for a number of hours under conditions simulating actual use. When weak or substandard components fail in these early hours of operation, they are replaced by good components. Only then is the equipment released for service. The "burn-in" process consists of operating a lot of components under simulated conditions for a number of hours and then using the components which survive for the assembly of the equipment.

The second type of failure is caused by **wearout of parts.** Wearout failures are symptoms of aging. These failures can be prevented in most cases by proper maintenance. In continuously operated systems, one method is to replace at regular intervals the accessible parts which are known to be subject to wearout, and to make the replacement intervals shorter than the mean wearout life of the parts. When parts are inaccessible, the usual method is to design these parts for longer life than the intended life of the equipment.

The procedures just described, relative to minimizing wearout failures, are really a part of good preventive maintenance that has been correctly scheduled. Reliability engineering is, therefore, concerned with wearout failures and their prevention by observing the statistical distribution of wearout occurrences and then determining the overhaul or preventive replacement time periods for the various parts during their design life. Then, if failures still occur during the operational life of a system, they will almost certainly be chance failures which are the "heart" of reliability engineering.

The third type of failure is referred to as **"chance" failure.** This type of failure cannot be eliminated by good debugging techniques or the best maintenance. These failures are caused by chance factors beyond the design strength of the component.

Chance failures occur at random intervals, irregularly and unexpectedly; but over a sufficiently long period of time their frequency of occurrence is relatively constant and can, therefore, be determined. There is little one can do to eliminate chance failures, but it is possible to reduce the chance of system breakdown due to chance failures by employing statistical techniques and predictions to select or determine the most reliable components and to use them in the proper place(s) at the right time.

Related to all kinds of failures, but especially important to "chance" failures are the reliability facts of series and parallel operation.

When units are in series, the failure of any one of the units will cause failure of the end item and system reliability can be expressed as follows:

If the system $= 1 + 2 + 3 + \cdots + n$

then $$R_{\text{system}} = R_1 \times R_2 \times R_3 \times \cdots \times R_n$$

$$MTBF \text{ system} = 1 \div \left(\frac{1}{MTBF_1} + \frac{1}{MTBF_2} + \frac{1}{MTBF_3} + \cdots + \frac{1}{MTBF_n} \right)$$

When units are in parallel reliability is increased through redundancy. The system reliability can be expressed as follows (if one neglects, for simplicity, the reliability of the decision-making device, the switchover function, and the fail-safe requirements):

$$R_{\text{system}} = R_1 + R_2 - (R_1 R_2)$$

Figure 12-2 represents the essential facts related to exponential distribution of random failures.

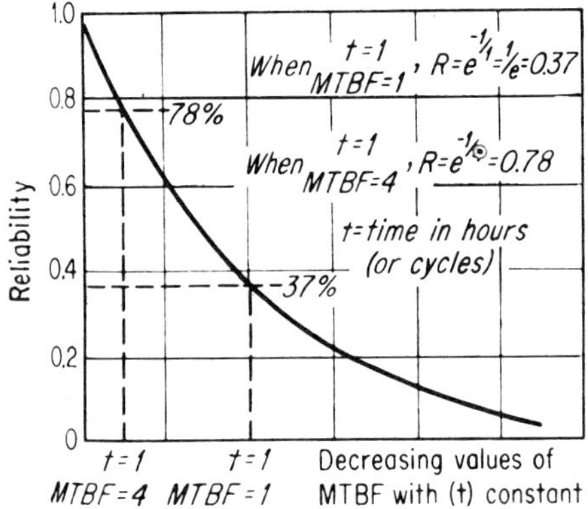

Fig. 12-2. Exponential reliability. *Source:* W. B. Rossnagel, "Methods of Solving the Reliability Problem," *Product Engineering*, Sept. 2, 1963. Copyright 1963, McGraw-Hill, Inc. Used by permission of Product Engineering.

The so-called "bathtub curve" in Fig. 12-3, illustrates how desired reliability performance is generally expressed.

The nomograph in Fig. 12-4 can help the reader to understand the relationship between *MTBF,* reliability, and operating time. Also, it is a quick way to arrive at a reliability, if *MTBF* and operating time is known. If the desired reliability is known, then the nomograph can be used to determine either *MTBF* or operating time, if one of these two terms is known.

There are two kinds of confidence: intuitive and statistical. Intuitive confidence is usually not objective and can, at times, be very misleading. Statistical confidence is the best technique for estimating how sure we are that the reliability is within a given range.

If correct basic assumptions are made for distribution of failures and randomness, *confidence* indicates the percentage of time in which the reli-

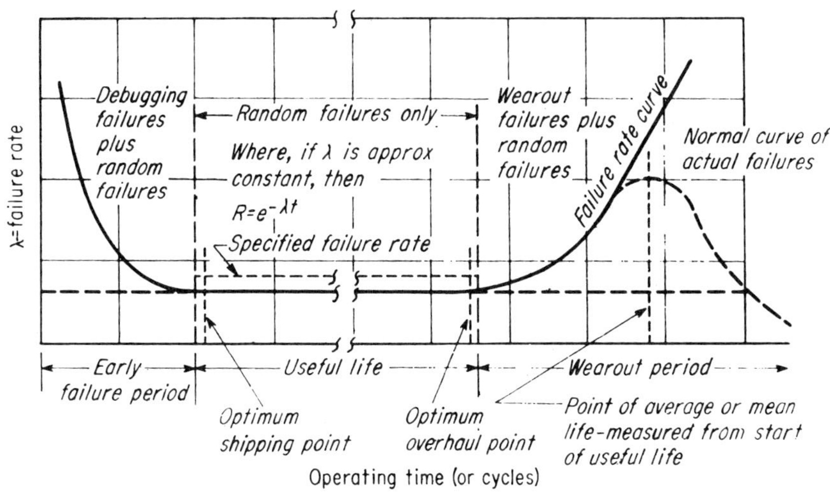

Fig. 12-3. Idealized bathtub curve. *Source:* See Fig. 12-2.

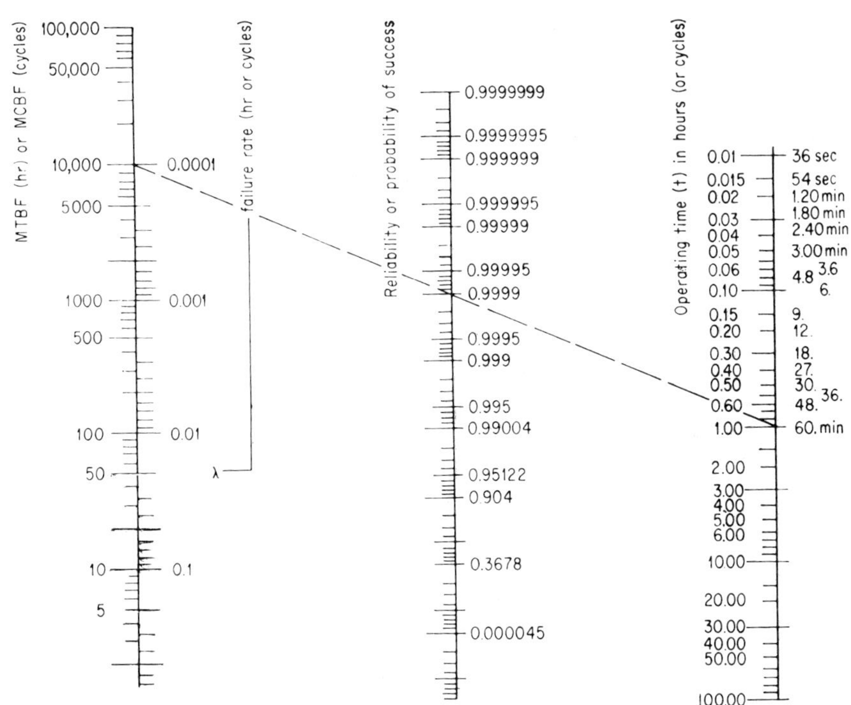

Fig. 12-4. The basic reliability equation. *Source:* See Fig. 12-2.

ability estimate is expected to fall in the correct (specified) range. This range is the *precision* of the estimate. The *confidence interval* is the range between the upper and lower reliability values. The interval is often described by *confidence limits*.

The relation between number of failures, operating hours, and confidence limits is illustrated in Fig. 12-5. An example of its use now follows:

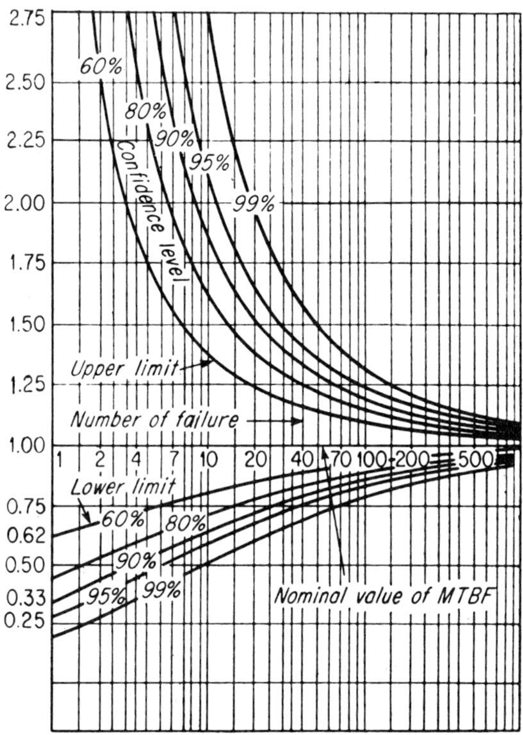

Fig. 12-5. Relation between number of failures, MTBF confidence limits and operating hours. *Source:* See Fig. 12-2.

Assume that a nominal value of *MTBF* of 1,000 hrs. has been obtained from field use, or a simulated testing, in which 10 failures have occurred. If we are asked to indicate a "confidence" in this *MTBF*, then referring to the confidence chart, we can say we are 90 percent confident that, in similar data, the *MTBF* will be above 640 hrs. (1,000 hrs. × 0.64), or 9 out of 10 times we expect the *MTBF* to be above 640 hrs.

Or we could be less "sure," say, 60 percent confident, in a higher minimum *MTBF* value. At a 60 percent confidence level we could expect the *MTBF*, in similar data, to be above 800 hrs. (1,000 hrs. × 0.80), 6 out of every 10 times.[2]

[2] W. B. Rossnagel, "Methods of Solving the Reliability Problem," *Product Engineering,* September 2, 1963. Copyright 1963, McGraw-Hill, Inc. Used by permission of *Product Engineering.*

The upper limit can also be determined by using Fig. 12-5. However, it is not often of significant interest.

The Causes of Unreliability

While the specific causes of unreliability are many, the root of the problem is due to the dynamic complexity of system development concurrent with a background of urgency and budget restrictions. However, *Time* magazine, in its February 24, 1958 issue, indicated that Russian weapons tend to be simpler in design and more mobile; also, that the West believed that the Soviets made simple weapons because they were unable to make complex ones. Now *Time* indicated that we were beginning to realize that simplicity bespeaks a high state of engineering skill. Sir Isaac Newton never forgot that the ultimate of sophistication is simplicity, and it would be well for the modern engineering manager constantly to keep this thought before his designers.

The fact that equipment is being designed and built at the very limits of technological knowledge and experience is a causative part of the problem of unreliability. In the last few decades technical abilities have improved to such an extent that engineers are creating or are on the verge of creating systems and devices which previously existed only within the realms of scientific imagination. Examples of this include: space travel, space probes, communications satellites, navigation satellites, computers, etc. Although the basic laws were known, engineers in the past could not produce the systems needed to perform these feats. At the same time, it should be obvious that what is feasible and possible is not necessarily reliable. We may know how a system or component works in one environment, but not necessarily how it will function in another, or how it might interact with a second system. In other words, engineers often work at the limits of their technological knowledge and ability. At the same time there is an urgency to probe the unknown, and frequently, the result is unreliability.

Another aspect of the problem is the complexity of present-day equipment and systems. Complexity is not only an attribute of the physical system but also of the process which creates the physical system. Within the physical system there is an interdependency between subsystems and components, and it is here that the probability theory enters in its simplest form.

There is another aspect of complexity of the physical system, and that is subsystem interaction, which may be environmental or functional. For example, vibration of one part might cause an electronic failure in another, or the output surges of one component might overload another.

In addition to the physical complexity of this system we must also deal with a very complex organization. The design and production of a complex physical system demands a very well-organized but equally complex organization of human beings. This, in turn, immediately develops into a requirement for complex communications. Some of the major troubles with the communication system include the inability to provide a complete interchange of information, the impossibility of transmitting proprietary or classified information, the misinterpretation of facts by recipients, and the impossibility of drawing on all pertinent existing knowledge as needed.

Finally, since organizations of human beings are involved, human error must be taken into account. Failures from this source occur not only because a person does not understand what he is doing, but also because people are sometimes simply careless or forgetful.

Reliability is concerned with the elimination of unreliability, and it involves all elements of the organization, particularly the engineering organization. No matter how well the manufacturing organization makes a poorly designed product, it is unlikely that it ever will be reliable. It has often been said, "You must design and build reliability; you cannot inspect it into the product." This emphasizes the fact that inspection is merely the process of comparing the product with applicable specifications and withholding those units that fail to meet these requirements. Inspection is an acceptance function, nothing more.

Related to inspection is another function well-known within industry, and that is quality control. Quality control is the function which plans and implements the criteria used in inspection. Quality assurance is concerned with integrating all functions which are directed towards satisfaction of customer requirements. It is no substitute for reliability.

Zero Defects

Zero Defects is a revivalist approach to solving one of the defense industry's toughest problems, the elimination of defective parts from products that have become increasingly complex and sophisticated. Since its inception in 1962, the Zero Defects program has been adopted by hundreds of defense contractors and subcontractors as well as by many non-defense companies. It is not a substitute for reliability engineering, but rather an adjunct or supporting technique.

Zero Defects is essentially a psychological approach to motivate employees to work more carefully. The idea is to make the employee feel personally responsible for the products he makes. Employees are told that they are better than they had thought, that they don't *have* to make mistakes, that all they have to do is to care more about what they are doing and to pay more attention to their jobs.

The message is carried by posters and bulletin boards to get the idea across to the employees. Workers sign cards pledging that they will try for perfection and receive Zero Defects pins to wear in the plant. Production units that are above average are given Zero Defects banners to hang up.

These methods seem to work. They always do if *used* with imagination and if *kept* to the forefront. This also means top management support of the effort. Martin Company's Orlando Division reduced hardware defects by 54 percent during the first year and 25 percent more in the second year and North American Aviation netted an 88 percent improvement in elimination of critical, or Class A defects which are defects that prevent a system from working at all.[3] It is generally estimated that $170 is saved for every $1 spent on Zero Defects.

The Defense Department is strongly pushing the Zero Defects campaign. The D.O.D. calls the program a comprehensive employee motivation project. It is aimed as much at the typist, whose single error on a specification could cause a major project defect, as at the assembly worker.

The Reliability Program

Military specification (Mil-R-27542) makes the following recommendations for the development of reliability programs:

1. Assign reliability goals for system
2. Concentrate maximum effort in design phase to achieve highest "inherent equipment reliability"
3. Determine reliability margins, apply basic statistics
4. Conduct design, specification, and procedure reviews
5. Formulate an adequate reliability testing program
6. Conduct a reliability review of all drawing and specification changes
7. Maintain controls in production via strong production control, inspection, and sample testing
8. Systematize closed-loop failure reporting, analysis, and feedback to engineers for positive corrective action aimed at nonrecurrence
9. Make a single group responsible for reliability and reporting to adequate authority
10. Organize an on-the-job training program.

To these should probably be added vendor control from a reliability and quality viewpoint.

These steps are taken to achieve the objectives of the reliability program:

1. Establishing the desired reliability in the design
2. Verifying the reliability through analysis, testing, and auditing
3. *Assuring* reliability through properly integrated engineering and manufacturing design and a good quality control program
4. *Maintaining* reliability through proper support by all elements of the organization
5. *Improving* reliability by accumulation of data, research on reliability, and dissemination of results.

[3] "Revivalist Zeal in the Drive for Perfect Parts," *Business Week*, May 8, 1965.

The elements or functions of a company more or less directly concerned with designing and producing the product are the following:

1. Management
2. Engineering
3. Testing
4. Manufacturing
5. Quality control and inspection
6. Purchasing and contracts.

It can readily be seen from the foregoing that the activities of reliability overlap and enter into all of the major departments or functions of a company. Moreover, management has the ultimate responsibility for all major decisions and policies, and the adequacy and firmness of its decisions is reflected in the quality of products produced and in customer satisfaction. Reliability is merely one quality of the product; others are performance, style, convenience, economy, etc. The problem is that reliability differs from the other qualities in a major respect, i.e., it is not an obvious attribute. It is a most abstruse quality and is open to many interpretations. Possibly this is because reliability as a subject is not well-defined. Some view it merely as the simple statistical estimation of numerical reliability, whereas those at the other extreme think of it as encompassing the whole development program.

It has been stated that reliability overlaps and enters into most major functions of the company. One approach that might be taken is that the responsibility for reliability be divided among the appropriate departments. Experience has proven that this is not the correct answer to organizing for reliability. It is now a subject in its own right and has methodologies with which most engineers are unfamiliar. It demands full-time attention and adequate recognition which it would not receive if it were divided among the various functions of the organization.

It has been generally agreed that best results are obtained when a single group has reliability as its responsibility. This group must be highly placed, and it must be essentially independent. In deciding where to place a reliability organization, it should be borne in mind that it must overlay all of the functions essentially concerned with designing and producing the product. To be effective, the reliability organization must possess sufficient authority over these functions.

Often the reliability group is established in conjunction with the quality control organization since its statistical techniques are similar. Certainly, Quality Control as a function can operate the data reporting system, vendor control, provide statistical services, set the guide lines for inspection, etc.; nevertheless, it must be the responsibility of a reliability group to review designs, provide for test planning, etc. This emphasizes the necessity for this group to be independent and points up the fact that they should have top management backing.

The reliability group should consist of people who are experienced and have backgrounds in the following:

1. Systems engineering
2. Operations research
3. Component design
4. Development of meaningful specifications
5. Quality control
6. A knowledge of manufacturing techniques and operations
7. Test planning
8. Environmental testing
9. Probability theory
10. Data collection, evaluation, analysis, and follow-up
11. Project management and/or coordination.

A typical reliability organization is shown in Fig. 12-6.

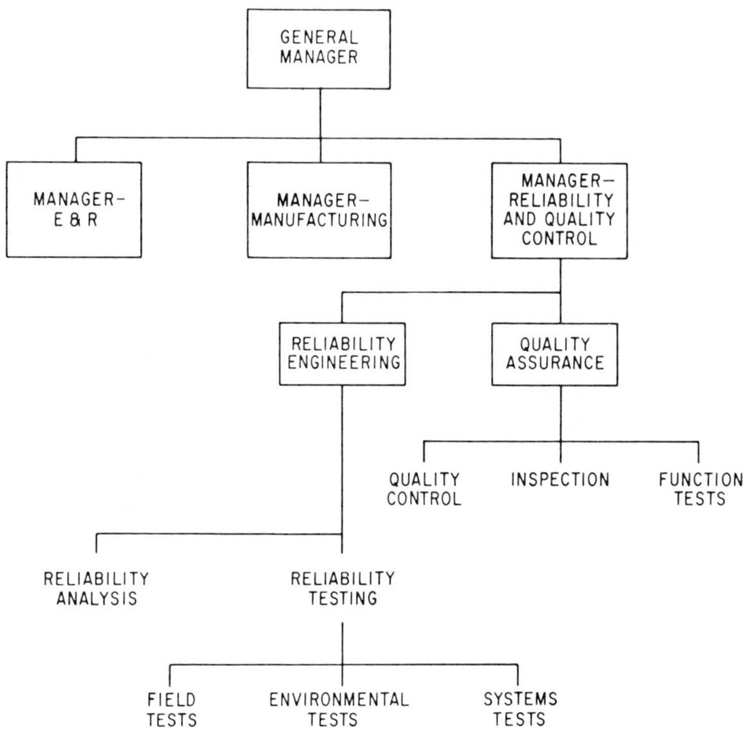

Fig. 12-6. Reliability organization.

Component Failures

Components may fail for one of six reasons. These are: (1) inadequate design, (2) random or chance effects, (3) improper manufacture, (4) unsuitability to the operational environment, (5) failure to use the component within a specified time period, and (6) wear-out. One of the greatest causes of failures in the development of missiles was due to lack of appreciation of environmental factors such as:

stress	humidity	erosion
vibration	dirt, sand, or dust	pressure
shock	noise	atomic radiation
acceleration	fungus	magnetic fields
temperature	chemical reaction	electrical fields

Component failures in a system may be classified as:

1. Independent
2. Dependent (caused by failure of another component)
3. Compensating (failure of the component compensates for failure of another)
4. Partial failure (usually deterioration)
5. Partial failure in applications which involve redundancy.

Raising Reliability

Despite all attempts throughout the design process, the tests of the final product may show that it does not meet reliability requirements. Although complete redesign is one alternative, it is not an attractive one. Some other possibilities involving partial redesign are as follows:

1. Derate the parts—Derating amounts to reducing the load in order to prolong the life of the part. This may in turn necessitate redundancy or rebuilding on a larger scale.
2. Substitute parts with lower failure probability for those parts which have known high failure rates.
3. Provide environmental isolation such as shock mounts, heat sinks, acoustic insulation, imbedment, heat controlled chambers, etc.
4. Redesign circuits or subsystems.
5. Employ redundant circuits or standby components.
6. Use wide-tolerance circuitry or mechanisms based upon the worst cases anticipated.

A design check list for reliability is given in Fig. 12-7.

Reliability Audit Approach

Just as the accounting function may audit all financial operations and reports in process, the reliability group should audit the engineering design

A. Product Requirements

1. What are the environmental requirements? Are they reasonable? Based on experience? Are they based on measurement or conjecture?
2. What are the reliability requirements?
3. Have all functional, reliability, and other requirements been specified?
4. Are the requirements in line with the customer's needs? Are they too severe? Are they consistent as to severity, completeness, level, detail, etc.?

B. Preliminary Design

1. Have proven designs been used wherever possible?
2. Has full usage been made of standard components and assemblies?
3. How much environmental extrapolation is necessary to use the above?
4. Has full usage of expert advice been made?
5. Have alternate approaches been fully explored?

C. Design Analysis

1. How does each component and material behave under the specified environments?
2. Is available life data realistic and factual?
3. Can reliability be calculated from available data?
4. If reliability can not be calculated, can the gaps be closed by building and testing relatively inexpensive components or breadboarded systems?
5. What are the weakest links in the design?
6. Is the anticipated or calculated reliability high enough, or is redesign indicated?

D. Corrective Action

1. Can expert consultants help?
2. Can Manufacturing or QC help?
3. Is low reliability mainly due to a few components? If so, can they be redesigned or used in a derated fashion? Is redundancy the answer?
4. Can the operating environment of critical components be changed so as to increase reliability by heating, cooling, shock mounting, shielding, etc.?
5. Is redesign indicated?

(Steps C and D may need to be repeated several times)

E. Final Design

1. Have Production, QC, and Purchasing helped by reviewing or writing specifications?
2. Can specs be written to assure 100 per cent test and inspection?
3. If component characteristics cannot be 100 per cent tested, can suitable manufacturing and QC procedures be substituted?
4. Are previously approved vendors available for items that must be subcontracted or purchased?
5. Is design such as to permit inspection and test for critical characteristics early in the manufacturing process?
6. Must all characteristics be tested at each stage?
7. Would "shakedown" test eliminate substandard units?
8. Can testing be accomplished without cutting product life appreciably?
9. Would temperature or other kinds of preconditioning of parts and/or components make possible the elimination of probable failures?

F. Redesign After Pilot Run

Carry back to Step C

Fig. 12-7. Design check list for reliability.

RELIABILITY—DESIGN AUDIT CHECK SHEET
TRW INC.

Drawing Name ________ Reviewed by ________ Project Name ________

Drawing No. ________ Next Assy. No. ________ Date Reviewed ________

Part purpose ________ Date completed ________

________ Time allocated ________ Hrs.

Reference data ________

____

____

____

ADEQUATE | RECOMMENDED MODIFICATION

1. IDENTIFICATION
   1. Requirement met
   2. Method of attachment

2. DESIGN CONSIDERATIONS
   1. Material specified
   2. Material satisfies design reqr.
   3. Minimum weight considered and wt. spec.
   4. C.G. specified
   5. Lubrication-method & points considered
   6. Static & dynamic loads considered
   7. Critical fatigue or stress pts. consd.
   8. Envelope dimensions specified
   9. Standard parts, specified per ABMA, MIL, MS, AN or Jan. Spec.
   10. Parts utilized within design limits and adequately derated for load.
   11. Electrical/Electronic Circuit considerations
       a. Parts list
       b. Design standardization
       c. Derating
       d. Redundancy
       e. Ambient and surface temperature
       f. Adjustments
       g. Complex circuitry
       h. Transient response
       i. Fail-safe response
       j. Operating life without failure
   12. Electrical Packaging Considerations
       a. Large parts secured

ADEQUATE | RECOMMENDED MODIFICATION | NONPERTINENT

       p. Heat treat necessary & specified
       q. Proof test
   15. Interchangeability considerations
   16. Clearances provided for assy. & service tools
   17. Accessibility to equipment for install., adjustment or replacement.

3. HUMAN ENGINEERING
   1. Human factors spec. ABMA-XPD-844 met
   2. Design precludes improper install.
   3. Delicate parts protected from damage
   4. Handling & installation damage potential minimized
   5. Minimum number of special tool reqd.

4. MANUFACTURING CONSIDERATIONS
   1. Alternate methods of fabrication considered
   2. Starting dimensions specified
   3. Drawing scales specified
   4. Spelling and numbers corrects.
   5. Edge break requirements
   6. Tolerances clearly specified
   7. Surface finish req. specified
   8. Highly finished surfaces minimized
   9. Extremely close tolerances minimized
   10. Fit between mating parts
   11. Inspection capability
   12. Manufacturing processes reqd. specified in sufficient detail
   13. Specification of equipment requiring assembly in a controlled area

ADEQUATE	RECOMMENDED MODIFICATION	NONPERTINENT	
			b. Vulnerable assemblies supported
			c. Stiffness in structures
			d. Enclosures, structures and chassis designed for minimum weight
			e. External metal parts grounded
			f. Cable routing and attachments
			g. 3 connections per solder terminal
			h. Bend radii specified
			i. Accessibility to equip. for install. adjustment or maintenance
			j. Fungus protection/Mil-V-173, Type I
			k. Cables protected/Mil-C-13777
			l. Solder joints stress-free/ABMA-PP-S-1
			13. Minimum type of materials, gages, etc., utilized
			14. Detail Considerations
			a. Lockwiring specified
			b. Torque requirements specified
			c. Shim clearances specified
			d. Shock mounts specified
			e. Cantilever mountings
			f. Rivets and spotwelds specified
			g. Mounting points accessible
			h. Undercuts & reliefs specified
			i. No loose or non-secured parts
			j. Adequacy of locking devices
			k. Adequacy of fasteners
			l. Bend radii specified
			m. Edge distance for holes specified
			n. Fillets & chamfers compatible for mating parts
			o. Weep and drain holes
			SUB-TOTAL

ADEQUATE	RECOMMENDED MODIFICATION	NONPERTINENT	
			14. Consideration of fabrication methods effect on physical & dimensional properties of equipment.
			15. Specification of inspection seals at set adjustment points
			16. Consideration given to special mfg. tooling required
			17. Sufficient clearances to avoid malfunction due to shock, vibration, noise, rubbing, fraying, etc.
			18. Interference & running fits properly specified
			19. Welds and classes of welds
			5. ENVIRONMENTAL CONSIDERATIONS
			1. Call-out of spec. requirements
			2. Elimination of non-required specs.
			3. Corrosion or galvanometric action considered
			4. Consideration given to previous environ. data or similar related test data
			5. Consideration given to deterioration of parts (rubber, plastic, etc.)
			6. Determination of parts or circuits to which envir. is detrimental
			7. Storage
			6. RELIABILITY CONSIDERATION
			1. Equipment life and wear rate considered
			2. Rel. failure rate considered
			7. QUALITY CONTROL
			1. Critical dimensions
			2. Test requirements
			3. Material
			SUB-TOTAL
			TOTAL

No. of dimensions less than .004 T.I.R. or TOLERANCE ______ No. of detail parts ______ % Reviewed ______

Fig. 12-8. Design audit check sheet for reliability. *Source:* TRW, Inc., Mechanical Products Div.

and the manufacturing process at every step. Such a process called the "reliability audit" has been worked out in elaborate detail and put into practice by R. R. Landers of TRW, Inc., who describes the process as follows:

An audit consists of the organized investigation and appraisal of a product during all phases of conception, design, production and usage. Its purpose is to assure the Customer a given level of performance and endurance at the lowest possible cost. Design and manufacturing parameters, activities and procedures collectively are called standards. A design and manufacturing audit consists of the continuous, critical review of these standards and their supporting data for the purpose of determining that these standards reflect the end objective expected by the Customer, and assuring that the product complies with these standards.

To insure efficiency and completeness, a plan specifying detailed procedures is formulated for each audit. This plan includes listing and procuring the items to be used in the audit such as:

1. Historical data, usually failure and analysis reports.
2. Drawings and supporting data, such as stress analyses, circuit analyses and test results.
3. Check lists and supporting forms.
4. Governing specifications, design criteria and the operating procedures of the department being surveyed.

The design audit is implemented with the aid of the check sheet shown in Fig. 12-8.

By having these items readily available, conflicting opinions can be factually supported and the differences satisfactorily resolved should an inconsistency arise.

The plan also determines:

1. Time allocated for each step of the audit
2. Persons to be contacted
3. Nature and extent of final report.

While a complete description of the details of the procedure cannot be given here, the design audit check sheet is shown in Fig. 12-8 because of the wealth of data it covers.

A Modern View of Reliability Management[4]

Since prevention of all failures is almost physically and economically impossible, the aim of reliability management from a practical basis is the control of the occurrence of failures. According to MIL-STD-7213, reliability is a probability, not necessarily related to the ultimate use environment (which may be unknown). Dependability is the generally accepted sense of reliability, rather than the restricted numerical usage.

[4] This section is a view presented by Peter H. Fowler in an article, "System Pathology," *IEEE Trans. on Reliability,* September 1968, and used by permission.

The restricted definition of reliability plus the techniques that have been developed for its measurement tend to distract attention from the consideration of a more scientific and meaningful basis for many assumptions of current reliability engineering. Control and prediction of failure must start from a full understanding of failure sources, particularly the broad policy and procedural failure sources that tend to plague many projects for long periods.

Peter H. Fowler has developed the following classification of failures. (The possibility that failures arise randomly, i.e., without understandable cause, is excluded; but the stochastic element in failure observation is accepted.)

Type I

The system failed because it could not have worked in the first place. The two major subdivisions of this type of failure observed in practice are as follows:

a. The design is inherently incapable of performing the actual mission, either because there is an unworkable combination of parts, or because the system's functional logic does not correspond with the requirement.
b. The use environment was beyond the capability of the system either because it was never qualified for the actual environment, or because the environment was misestimated.

Type II

The system equipment could have worked if it had remained just as in the drawing, but it did not, and hence, failed. There are two major subdivisions which are as follows:

a. A faulty part was built into the hardware.
b. The hardware was damaged either in manufacture, test, repair, or handling.

Type III

The system could work and did work, but has now worn out. The principal subdivisions of this class are as follows:

a. Some part of the hardware returned far enough toward thermodynamic equilibrium so that the hardware no longer operates.
b. Some part of the system has accumulated environmental damage to the point that it no longer performs its function.

Fowler suggests policies and procedures for controlling each type of failure above and concludes:

> The present goals of reliability engineering, from the point of view presented here, should be:

1. To collect data relating the occurrence of failures to the specific policy which generated them
2. To tailor prediction, contracting, and demonstration methods to correspond more directly with the realities of failure occurrence
3. To train a new generation of reliability engineers who both understand their job in meaningful terms and have the engineering, management, and mathematical background to predict and control the cost effectiveness of their own activities and the systems to which they contribute.

PRODUCIBILITY

Development of the Concept

Producibility, like reliability and standardization, represents an aspect of engineering design which has become highly specialized. Before World War II little attention was paid to this problem as a separate function, and the design engineer was generally presumed to possess adequate knowledge of the subject so that he could incorporate such qualities in his designs. Following the war, the development of Value Analysis created general recognition of the fact that specialized materials, techniques, and processes could be applied to products after they were designed to lower their manufacturing costs significantly. This in turn emphasized the fact that these accomplishments were wholly or partially due to original poor design from a producibility viewpoint.

Designing for Producibility

The design engineer's work may be considered to be divided into four strata:

1. Design for function
2. Design for standardization
3. Design for reliability
4. Design for producibility.
5. Design for maintainability.

Design for function is the work which leads to the layouts and is elsewhere described in this book.

Design for producibility is normally considered that portion of design in which materials, tolerances, finishes, and design configurations are selected and specified to yield minimum manufacturing costs—other factors being adequate and satisfactory. Producibility engineering involves (1) the introduction of manufacturing process knowledge (2) early in the product design cycle so that (3) the product can be produced at optimum cost. Producibility is:

1. A design attribute
2. Identifiable
3. Present in varying degrees in all products.

Product design involves taking into account functional engineering considerations, marketing considerations, and manufacturing considerations—the latter is concerned with the effect of materials and physical configuration upon manufacturing processes. The material used, the physical configuration of the part, and the manufacturing process to be used are all interrelated.

With respect to process selection, this is best handled or considered as a two-step procedure consisting of (1) basic process selection and (2) detailed process selection. The major impact upon cost results from the first step which is greatly dependent upon configuration and material specifications. Because of this, it is extremely important that producibility be considered from the very beginning of the design process.

Mr. R. L. Berg of General Electric has been a strong promoter of the use of Process Applications Specialists in producibility engineering activities. This specialist would be an expert on when a given process could be used, and what the relative cost effect is between one process versus another.

The actual manufacturing methods and processes are usually the responsibility of Manufacturing. Since Manufacturing is responsible for establishing manufacturing methods and processes, the design engineer and a manufacturing representative must work closely together in designing for producibility to avoid costly changes later.

Manufacturing's Part in the Producibility Program

The manufacturing organization performs four basic functions in the producibility program:

1. Searching for all kinds of information on new manufacturing processes and methods.
2. Reviewing, classifying, and documenting this information.
3. Providing research on new manufacturing methods.
4. Assisting engineering in the application of such manufacturing information to product designs.

R. L. Berg of General Electric points out further that there are two types of searches which may be made to keep abreast of new processes:

1. Directed search—finding a solution to a specific problem.
2. Random search—searching of manufacturing innovations used in other businesses and areas of technology unfamiliar to the company. This type of search may lead to major changes in manufacturing methods, processes, or materials.

Here, we are again involved in a function that must "cut across" two other activities. All previous remarks pertaining to the organization and operating of such activities apply to producibility engineering.

MAINTAINABILITY

In the past decade great strides have been accomplished in the field of reliability, and now a greater emphasis can be placed on the optimization of all the system parameters. One of the most important of these parameters is that of maintainability. The word "maintainability" is so newly coined that it is not yet defined in most dictionaries, reference books, or reference indexes. The Electronic Industries Association Maintainability Subcommittee M-5.5 has adopted the following as a definition:

> Maintainability is a quality of the combined features and characteristics of equipment/system design and maintenance resource planning which contributes to the rapidity, economy, ease, and accuracy with which the system can be kept in or restored to specified operating condition in the planned maintenance environment.

Maintainability is a design parameter and the primary responsibility for its achievement rests with the design engineering team. The distinction between maintainability and maintenance is very important. Too many firms place their efforts on maintenance and not on maintainability.

Why Maintainability?

Here are a few of the reasons why maintainability is receiving increased attention in design:

1. Some companies seem to have forgotten about it when they designed and developed their products.
2. More customers are considering the total cost of the product before buying.
3. Maintenance costs can be huge. The costs associated with maintaining some products vastly exceed their original price.
4. Manufacturers are increasingly extending warranties as a means of increasing sales.
5. New weapon systems are becoming so complex that maintenance costs are becoming prohibitive.
6. Maintenance down time and inadequate maintenance quality control often seriously impair operational effectiveness.
7. There is an ever-increasing necessity for large numbers of highly trained technical personnel to maintain complex equipment.
8. The complexity and high cost of test and check-out equipment is a significant portion of a system's total cost.

The military services are now including certain quantitative and qualitative maintainability requirements in many of their contracts. Those firms with this type of contract indicated that this approach was necessary and desirable for their product.

MIL-STD-470 outlines basic Maintainability Program Requirements for military contracts. It was designed to function as a standard of reference and document on maintainability in contracting. It outlines requirements or elements of a maintainability program and guidelines for preparation of a maintainability program plan. MIL-STD-470 is the result of efforts to consolidate the various positions with respect to maintainability.

The maintenance man hours required on a standard unit of ground equipment amount to 30 man hours for every 1,000 operating hours for each 1,000 parts. Figure 12-9 illustrates an interesting approach to displaying and/or comparing maintenance man-hour requirements versus equipment complexity as given by J. A. Gafaro and H. D. Voegtlen in "Measurement and Specifications of Product Abilities," in *Industrial Quality Control,* Vol. 18, No. 9, March, 1962. The solid line labeled, "Observed Level," represents the man hour rate that was required for the three classes of equipment

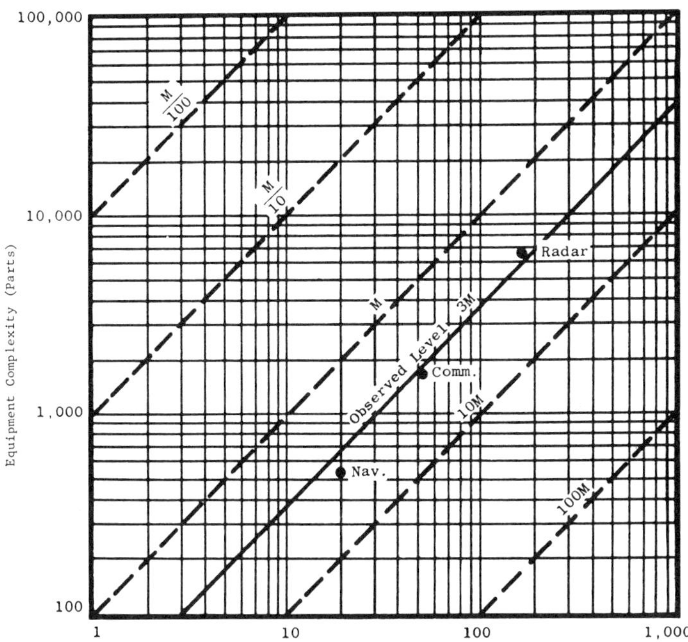

Fig. 12-9. Observed maintainability for ground electronic equipment. *Source:* J. A. Gafaro and H. D. Voegtlen, "Measurement and Specification of Product Abilities," *Industrial Quality Control*, Vol. 18, No. 9, March, 1962. Reprinted by permission of American Society for Quality Control.

studied. Although the equipment differed in complexity and function, the maintenance rate was almost the same. The dotted lines indicate various estimated maintainability levels and provide a reference for prediction of man hour maintenance requirements for other equipment. For instance, according to the referenced authors, airborne electronics will normally be between 10 M and 100 M.

The Integrated Concept

To solve maintainability problems, an integrated concept is being evolved which will interrelate maintainability with the various factors that determine the availability of the system. The electronics industry and the military have provided most of the initiative in attempting to come to grips with the elusive constituents that must be taken into consideration.

The approach is to choose specific objectives on the basis of the relative importance of representative maintenance functions in terms of maintainability, design concepts and principles. This approach is based upon an analysis of maintenance requirements in which maintainability is related to both quantitative and qualitative analysis evaluation. The quantitative goals require that techniques be available to measure, to specify, to predict, to trade-off, and to improve. Terms such as "mean time to repair" ("MTR"), and "maximum time to restore" have come into being.

Some of the requirements being specified and/or recommended by the military[5] in their contracts are as follows:

1. Availability and operational readiness goals are to be derived from an analysis of the System Operational Requirements.
2. The reliability and maintainability goals will be quantitatively stated in terms of *MTBF, MTR,* or similar or equivalent terms.
3. There will be periodic reviews of the reliability status during R & D.
4. The achieved reliability must be demonstrated by tests, by specifically designed demonstrations, etc.
5. The program must include a reporting of malfunctions and failures, the analysis of these data, and a corrective action plan.
6. A maintenance philosophy for the system and its components must be described.
7. Numerical measures of maintainability in such terms as mean time to repair, and maximum time to restore must be developed and used.
8. The maintainability of the weapons must be analyzed in terms of systems and subsystems.
9. There must be an analysis of the maintenance tasks and skills required to support the system.
10. There must be maintainability design reviews.
11. There must be maintainability demonstrations.

[5] See MIL-M-26512A for more information.

Probably the most difficult constraint that the design group must define is the maintenance technician that will be provided by the customer. The human technician is a complicated system. His capabilities, limitations, improvement of his effectiveness must be evaluated as an integral part of the design task. As far as the military is concerned, and to some extent in the civilian environment, the most pressing problem in this area is the availability of the technician: retention of the trained man today, and his replacement with the man of superior qualifications tomorrow.

The documents (maintenance manuals and instruction sheets) that have been provided the maintenance technician in the past have failed in many respects. The technical writer who prepared the manual received little attention from the designer, and as a consequence, wrong and misleading information often finds its way into the publications. The gap between the technical writer and the technician was in many cases, too wide for the communication to bridge. Writing at the engineer's level of comprehension means that the result is of little use to the man who actually needs it.

In order to overcome these obstacles the following steps need to be taken:

1. Work on the manual must be initiated early in the equipment design stage.
2. The design engineer, test engineer, technical writer, and a representative technician should work together as a team on maintenance instructions.
3. Manuals should be evaluated at several points during their development to insure that the information is correct and adequate.
4. Manuals must be written at the maintenance technician level. Care must be taken that a technician who is representative of the actual users of a manual reviews the manuscript.

Maintenance testing techniques and equipment place constraints on maintainability design. The isolation, identification, and location of a malfunction or failure and the factors affecting the selection of testing technique all must be considered by the design group, relative to maintainability.

The testing system to be specified is only important to the extent that it contributes to the optimum performance of the overall system. Testing and maintainability goals should be characterized by: minimum down time, maximum availability, and minimum cost.

The external maintenance factors can be subdivided into three areas: concept, environment, and personnel.

Consideration should be given to the utilization of test gear already in the customer's possession.

The proper selection and location of test points can greatly enhance the maintenance, repair, calibration, alignment, or monitoring of the prime equipment.

The type of test gear to be utilized, the testing environment, the technician, and the degree or amount of testing to be performed are all interrelated with the selection and placement of the test points.

The analysis of the applicable testing techniques is the third factor that should enter into maintainability considerations. The type of system, cost, personnel training and skill, time allowed for testing, test data required, maintenance levels at which the tests will be performed, test equipment availability, sequencing of tests, and the environments in which the maintenance is to be carried out are all relevant factors in determining what testing techniques should be employed.

The design team has to evaluate the relative merits of the different types of testing equipment and their relationship to all of the foregoing factors. There are four general types of testing equipment whose relative merits vary in accordance with the circumstances:

1. Automatic test equipment—automatically tests and evaluates the prime equipment.
2. General purpose test equipment—can be used in a variety of circumstances on different types of equipment. Generally available off-the-shelf.
3. Special purpose test equipment—designed for a specific application.
4. Built-in test equipment—built in as an integral part of the prime equipment.

Space does not permit an analysis of one type of test equipment versus another. However, the facts involved here are extremely important if test equipment is involved.

One of the major obstacles to be overcome is to establish procedures defining the methods whereby maintainability can be quantitatively measured. Historical precedent, past systems and their failures, may not be applicable to the newer systems and cannot provide reliable comparisons on which to make predictions. In order to help alleviate the situation, many handbooks, check lists, specifications, and papers are available with empirical data on relative trade-offs under certain circumstances. Most of the guides now available are not quantitatively oriented and do not provide for decision making when it is impossible to follow all of the facets of the check list.

Considerable effort is being expended by the Government and by industry to arrive at a procedure whereby all of the variables with their relative weights under different conditions can be easily and simply integrated to arrive at the optimum solution. The techniques that are available at this time only give an approximation to an optimum answer, but do not meet the criterion of being easy to use.

Most of the methods now used require that weighted values be assigned to each variable. Through various manipulations a quantitative result will emerge that indicates which of the various alternative design features under consideration should be incorporated.

The state-of-the-art is still in its infancy and is in the same relative position as reliability was only a few short years ago.

BIBLIOGRAPHY

ADAMS, R. M., and BROCK, G. N. 1963. Where the Maintenance Money Goes —And What Can Be Done About It. Paper given at the National Aeronautic and Space Engineering and Manufacturing Meeting, September 23–27, 1963, at Los Angeles, Calif.

BARBER, CARLTON F., JR. "Expanding Maintainability Concepts and Techniques," *IEEE Transactions on Reliability*, Vol. 8–16, No. 1, May, 1967.

BARLOW, R. E., and PROSCHAN, F. *Mathematical Theory of Reliability.* New York, N.Y.: John Wiley & Sons, Inc., 1965.

BAZOVSKY, I. *Reliability Principles and Practices.* New York, N.Y.: McGraw-Hill Book Company, 1962.

BLANCHARD, BEN S. "Cost Effectiveness, System Effectiveness, Integrated Logistics Support, and Maintainability," *IEEE Transactions on Reliability,* Vol. 16, No. 3, December, 1967.

BODNE, THOMAS A. "Basic Philosophies in Reliability," *Industrial Quality Control,* September, 1961.

BOEHN, GEORGE A. W. "Reliability Engineering," *Fortune,* Vol. 67, April, 1963.

BOLZ, ROGER W. "Engineering for Producibility," *Machine Design,* August, 1951.

BONOSEVICH, M. I. "Maintenance Testing Techniques." In *Maintainability Design.* Elizabeth, N.J.: Engineering Publishers, 1963.

BUSSIERE, RENE. "Product Reliability First—Build It Later," *SAE Journal,* July, 1961.

CALABRO, S. R. *Reliability Theory and Practice.* Englewood Cliffs, N.J.: Prentice-Hall, Inc., 1961.

CHORAFAS, D. N. *Statistical Processes and Reliability Engineering.* Princeton, N.J.: D. Van Nostrand Co., Inc., 1960.

"Commercial and Military Reliability," *Industrial Quality Control,* April, 1962.

CROSSAN, RICHARD M., and NANCE, HAROLD W. *Master Standard Data.* New York, N.Y.: McGraw-Hill Book Company, 1962.

CUNNINGHAM, CLAIR E. "Opening Comments," *IEEE Transactions on Reliability*, Vol. R-16, No. 1, May, 1967.

DAVIS, JAMES N. "Reliability—Where Do We Go From Here?", *Industrial Quality Control,* September, 1961.

DOVE, G. A.; MUNDELL, D. P.; and JOHNSON, E. E. "Program Management at the Subsystem Subcontractor Level for Product Reliability and Maintainability." In *1966 Annals of Reliability and Maintainability.*

European Productivity Agency of the Organization for European Economic Co-Operation. *Simplification, Standardization, Specialization.* Paris, France, 1958.

FARRELL, J. J., JR. "Reducing Item Varieties," *The Magazine of Standards,* (Amer. Stds. Assn.), October–November, 1960.

Fowler, Peter H. "System Pathology," *IEEE Transactions on Reliability*, Vol. R-17, No. 3, September, 1968.

Franks, P. E., and Furnish, C. W. *Automated Maintenance: Theory, Practice, and Implications for Training.* Washington, D.C.: Office of Technical Services, U.S. Department of Commerce, 1960.

Gafaro, J. A., and Voegtlen, H. D. "Measurement and Specifications of Product Abilities," *Industrial Quality Control*, Vol. 18, No. 9, March, 1962.

Goldman, A. S., and Slattery, T. B. *Maintainability: A Major Element of System Effectiveness.* New York, N.Y.: John Wiley & Sons, Inc., 1964.

Gray, Lee B. "The Great War for Reliability," *Industrial Quality Control*, November, 1961.

Greenberg, S. N., and Zwerling, S. "Reliability, Both a Tool and Objective in Design," *Industrial Quality Control*, July, 1961.

Halacy, D. S. "Reliability—Space Age Requirement," *Electronics World*, Vol. 66, No. 6, December, 1961.

Hilton, Peter. *New Product Introduction for Small Business Owners.* Washington, D.C.: Small Business Administration, U.S. Government Printing Office, 1955.

IEEE Transactions on Reliability. Special Issue on Maintainability. New York, N.Y.: Institute of Electrical and Electronics Engineers, May, 1967.

Jerger, Joseph J. *Principles of Guided Missile Design.* Princeton, N.J.: D. Van Nostrand Co., Inc., 1960, pp. 38–75.

Johnsen, K. "Zero Defects Campaign Gets DOD Impetus," *Aviation Week*, Vol. 81, No. 22, November 30, 1964.

Jones, David R. "Warranties May Grow in Length," *The New York Times*, April 5, 1964.

Landers, Richard R. "Reliability Audits," *Machine Design*, March 2, 1961.

Lanier, Ross E. "The Impact of the A-7A Maintainability Requirement on Management and Design." In *1966 Annals of Reliability and Maintainability.*

MacNiece, E. H. *Industrial Specifications.* New York, N.Y.: John Wiley & Sons, Inc., 1953.

Martin, H. W. *Variety Reduction, Simplifications, Standardization, Specialization.* London, England: British Standards Institute and Institute of Production Engineers, 1956.

Martino, Robert A. *Standardization Activities of National Technical and Trade Organizations.* Washington, D.C.: U.S. Government Printing Office, 1941.

"Mathematical Research on Reliability Prediction," *Industrial Quality Control*, July, 1960.

Mazzola, Frank D. "Maintainability Demonstration," *IEEE Transactions on Reliability*, Vol. R-16, No. 1, May, 1967.

Meykar, Orest A. "Maintainability Terminology Supports the Effectiveness Concept," *IEEE Transactions on Reliability*, Vol. R-16, No. 1, May, 1967.

Milek, John T. "Role of Management in Company Standardization," *The Magazine of Standards*, Vol. 33, April, 1962.

Military Standard 470, *Maintainability Program Requirements.* March 21, 1966, p. 2.

Military Standard 471, *Maintainability Demonstration.* February 15, 1966.

Mohr, Ernest E. "Starting a Standards Program," *The Magazine of Standards*, August, 1960.

National Industrial Conference Board. 1957. *Industrial Standardization, Company Programs and Practices.* Conference Board Reports. New York, N.Y.

O'CONNELL, E. P. "Trade-Off Techniques," In *Maintainability Design.* Elizabeth, N.J.: Engineering Publishers, 1963.

Office of the Assistant Secretary of Defense (Research and Engineering), Advisory Group on Reliability of Electronic Equipment. *Reliability of Military Electronic Equipment.* Washington, D.C.: U.S. Government Printing Office, June, 1957.

Office of the Assistant Secretary of Defense (Supply and Logistics), Ad Hoc Study Group on Parts Specification Management for Reliability. *Parts Specification Management for Reliability.* Washington, D.C.: U.S. Government Printing Office, May, 1960.

PANTELIS, SGOURCE, and CALSBRO, S. R. "Maintainability Prediction in the Department of Defense Development Programs," *IEEE Transactions on Reliability,* May, 1967.

Ratio-Electronics-Television Manufacturers Association. *Proceedings, Systems Reliability Analysis Task Group of the Electronic Applications Committee (Reliability).* A General Guide for Technical Reporting of Electronic Systems Reliability Measurements, Third National Symposium of Reliability & Quality Control in Electronics, January, 1957.

RECK, DICKSON. "The Role of Company Standards in Industrial Administration," *Advanced Management,* April, 1954.

———, ed. *National Standards in a Modern Economy.* New York, N.Y.: Harper & Brothers, 1956.

REDFERN, R. E. "Design Reviews." In *Maintainability Design.* Elizabeth, N.J.: Engineering Publishers, 1963, pp. 195–248.

RETTERER, B. L., and MCLAUGHLIN, R. L. "Maintainability Prediction and Measurement," *Industrial Quality Control,* December, 1963.

"Revivalist Zeal in the Drive for Perfect Parts," *Business Week,* May 8, 1965.

ROSSNAGEL, W. B. "Methods of Solving the Reliability Problem," *Product Engineering,* September 2, 1963.

———. *1967 Guide to Governmental Assurance Documentation, Annals of Reliability and Maintainability—1967.* New York, N.Y.: Society of Automotive Engineers, Inc., July, 1967.

SANDERS, T. R. B. "Variety Reduction, Its Importance in Industry," *The Production Engineer,* London, February, 1960.

SCHULTY, ANDREW S. "Impact of Standardization," *The Magazine of Standards,* Vol. 34, November, 1963.

SMITH, T. E. "A Consolidated Decentralized Reliability and Quality Control Program," *Industrial Quality Control,* August, 1961.

SOHN, HUNTER M. "C-5A Quantitative Maintainability Program." In *1966 Annals of Reliability and Maintainability.* New York, N.Y.: American Institute of Aeronautics and Astronautics, July, 1966.

STANTON, RICHARD R. "Maintainability Program Requirements, Military Standard 470," *IEEE Transactions on Reliability,* Vol. R-16, No. 1, May, 1967.

Thompson Ramo Wooldridge, Inc. *Reliability Audit Procedures.* A manual for reliability procedures used by the Tapco Group, Reliability Office, Tapco Group.

WARNER, C. E., and BERG, R. L. "Producibility—Designing for Production," *Mechanical Engineering,* May, 1961.

WUJEK, J. H., JR. "Basic Principles of Reliability," *Electronics World,* Vol. 73, No. 2, February, 1965.

ZAREMBA, W. A. "A New Approach to Size Selection," *Mechanical Engineering,* February, 1968.

CHAPTER 13

Measurement of E & R

INTRODUCTION

Measurement, Evaluation, and Controlling

Controlling is correcting after the fact for deviations from established values or limits of standards for performance. Measurement of performance versus standards is therefore important and an essential element of management control. While control is a prime characteristic of management, the term "control," which involves measuring and taking corrective action, has semantic overtones which tend to make it somewhat undesirable to professional personnel. In research work, in particular, scientists in a well-managed laboratory should be able to work towards their agreed-upon goals expeditiously if they are kept informed of measurements of their progress in terms of costs, time, and progress in related technical areas. Directive action by management to correct variances should be the exception for professional personnel.

It is obvious that measurement is essential to the management of any enterprise. What is often not so obvious is that generally, and particularly in E & R, the results of measurement should be made available to the man whose performance is measured for his own self-appraisal and creative action rather than merely offered to his manager for control action.

Control as such will not be discussed here since it involves factors discussed throughout this work. Measurement, which is a prime requisite of good management and control, will be explained in this chapter. Various approaches to methods of measurement are suggested. E & R management cannot take the attitude that engineering and research cannot be measured merely because it is a difficult task.

Engineering and research are costly activities which, while essential in some form and to various extents, nevertheless represent an expense and consequent diminution of profits. Management anticipates that the cost of engineering and research over one period of time will result in either continuing profits or greater profits at a later period. Measurement is, therefore, necessary to assure management that the engineering and research activities are contributing adequately in view of their cost. As engineering expenditures increase in relation to other factors, decreasing returns will eventually become prevalent. If an adequate measurement of engineering and research were possible, an optimum point might be found.

Any system of measurement and evaluation must be based on the following principles:

Measurement and evaluation should be

1. Related to company goals
2. Based on technical plans and organization
3. Partially based on standards related to the industry, the nation in which the organization is located, and on similar performance standards in other nations
4. Readily understandable by everyone
5. Limited to key points and events
6. Objective and quantitative, if possible
7. Able to detect variances and trouble spots quickly
8. Economical
9. Provide a stimulus to action.

Measuring is considered by General Electric to be a part of the manager's job and to consist of:

1. Devising and establishing measuring systems and media
2. Recording and reporting performances of people and components
3. Analyzing, appraising, and interpreting measured results
4. Making known the measuring systems, media, and results
5. Using results of measuring to readjust continually the work of measuring
6. Exercising judgment and making reasoned, objective, and timely decisions to effect the measuring work and progress.

General Approaches to Measuring E & R

Measurement of E & R may be either internal or external. Internal measurement consists of comparing accomplishments against plans, standards, or goals. It is this kind of internal measurement that is too often of primary interest to E & R managers and their staffs. The inherent weakness in internal measurement is that plans, standards, and goals are prone to be established on a realistic basis with regard only for what the present organization can accomplish. A poor organization might do as well as a good organization with regard to successful achievement of such goals since the former's management would tend to set lower goals.

External measurement evaluates E & R in terms of its objective worth to an outsider. While the general manager may be primarily interested in the short-range economic productivity of E & R (how much it is apparently bringing in), from the ultimate viewpoint, it is the long-range measurement that counts. In addition, measurement can and should be compared to both internal and external standards. All measurements should certainly consider performance against the initial three principal criteria previously mentioned. The external comparison standards should be for the industry that the company represents and also, if possible and meaningful, measurement should be checked against national performance. While it is difficult to obtain external comparison data, usually enough external data can be secured to establish some external measurement standards.

To summarize, then, the basic approaches to measuring E & R consist of establishing criteria in the form of objectives or standards and comparing some or all of the following against the criteria. These factors may be measured:

1. Inputs
   a. Money
   b. Personnel
   c. Facilities
   d. Time for major company program or growth
2. Processes (performance efficiency of individual activities making up the whole)
3. Output as a contribution to the business
4. Value-in-exchange (this is the in-house versus purchase comparison).

Other indirect approaches involve finding some index or indexes that correlate with quality of E & R such as:

1. Patents—quantity and quality
2. Publications—quantity and quality
3. Citations of work or publications.

Quantitative and Qualitative Measurement

Whatever criteria may be used, the measurement of E & R may, to a large degree, be in quantitative terms such as profits, time, value added, return on investment, etc. Alternatively, the measurement of E & R can be in qualitative terms based upon judgments. Some qualitative measurement should always be used. The difficulty lies in the fact that if quantitative measurements are used, there is a very strong tendency to use no qualitative ones or to ascribe to them a very minor role.

Levels of Measurement

E & R may be measured at each organizational level provided responsibility is properly delegated. For example, E & R in a particular organization might be measured at the following levels of existing management:

1. Engineer or scientist as an individual contributor
2. Group leader or first-line supervisor
3. Next higher management level
4. E & R as a whole.

Measurement at each level is particularly useful for internal control or directing activities at the corresponding levels, as well as for top management control, evaluation, and coordination of E & R activities.

MEASURING THE INPUT

Use of Indexes

In measuring E & R by measuring the inputs, the basic assumption is that if a company hires high quality (as judged subjectively) people, supplies them with superior facilities and adequate funds, the output will be of high quality. The quality of the input may be measured by indexes which allow the company to make key comparisons. For example, the distribution of manpower among the functional components may be compared with the industry or with the national average. Figure 13-1 shows such distributions for certain SIC industries.

Another supplementary index might be the ratio of technicians to engineers to measure the efficiency with which engineers are being used. This ratio could be compared with the industry ratio illustrated in Fig. 13-2.

Other indexes of quality of input might be:

1. Ratio of clerical support to engineers and scientists
2. Square feet of lab and office space per engineer/scientist
3. Performance cost per engineer/scientist
4. Average age of research equipment and instruments
5. E & R expenditures/sales per year
6. E & R expenditures/profits per year
7. E & R expenditures/sales versus national E & R expenditures/GNP
8. Dollar backlog of projects
9. Man-years backlog of projects
10. Average salary per engineer/scientist
11. Average salary per manager in E & R.

Measuring the Individual

Measuring the performance of individuals engaged in development engineering appears to be somewhat more feasible than measuring perform-

	EXTRACTING, PRODUCING	MANUFACTURING, PROCESSING	TRANSPORTATION	RESEARCH & DEVELOPMENT	MARKETING	GENERAL ADMINISTRATION
	% of total workforce engaged in each function					
Ordnance	0	47.0	.5	27.7	5.7	16.2
Food	0	60.1	1.6	2.7	16.0	11.4
Textile	0	81.3	.5	1.8	6.3	4.7
Paper	3.6	75.5	1.1	2.6	5.9	7.1
Chemicals	.2	58.5	.6	12.1	9.8	11.5
Drugs	0	48.2	.2	13.0	24.0	13.3
Oil	14.9	21.9	11.5	4.2	18.5	17.8
Rubber	0	48.2	.2	13.9	12.2	9.6
Stone, Clay & Glass	0	73.1	.4	4.8	9.7	7.4
Primary Metals	0	76.1	.8	2.6	5.0	8.1
Fabricated Metals	0	68.6	.3	6.2	10.8	9.8
Machinery (Nonelectric)	0	67.2	.2	8.3	13.0	10.9
Machinery (Electric)	0	62.0	.2	12.6	6.8	10.0
Electronics	0	55.7	.2	18.8	6.3	10.0
Transportation Equipment	0	65.5	.4	17.2	3.9	10.5
Aerospace	0	56.4	.4	23.2	3.8	11.0
Instrument	0	48.3	.2	26.5	10.7	11.2

Figures represent medians. They do not total 100 percent because a few accessory functions are omitted.

Fig. 13-1. Distribution of manpower. *Source:* "Check Your Management Costs," *Nation's Business*, Chamber of Commerce of the United States, Washington, D.C., January, 1962.

All industries	.71
Aircraft	.41
Chemicals and allied products	.39
Commercial laboratories	.76
Construction	.64
Electrical machinery	.70
Engineering and architectural services	1.52
Instruments	.57
Machinery (except electrical)	.82
Motor vehicles and parts	.67
Ordnance and missiles	.32
Total, selected industries	.67
All other industries	.79

Fig. 13-2. Ratio of technicians to engineers and scientists. *Source:* United States Department of Labor, Bureau of Labor Statistics, 1966.

ance of those engaged in research. Goals and schedules are more specific and shadings of quality are easier to detect for engineers. The measurement of the creativity of scientists engaged in research has been based upon indexes such as quality and quantity of publications and estimates of potential value of discoveries to the company.

Some index or number of points was assigned to the individual and Chapter 6 discussed methods of apprising him of these. The totality of points assigned to all individuals in the E & R organization year-by-year might be considered a measure of the quality of input.

It is not feasible, in general, to attempt to measure quantitatively an individual's contribution to profit as a function of his cost except in the case, perhaps, of a brilliant scientist or highly creative engineer. However, a discussion of those elements which must be considered for measuring the value of an individual may lead to an eventual solution of the problem.

The output of an individual is the amount and quality of work he performs per unit of time multiplied by the time he works. This could be expressed as:

$$O = R \times Q \times T$$

Where

O = output in quality units
R = rate of work
Q = quality of work expressed as a percentage
T = time worked

Based upon observations of factory production workers and upon "common sense" reasoning, it can be said that the quality of the work begins to deteriorate as the rate of work begins to significantly exceed the capabilities of the individual, as shown in Fig. 13-3. The optimum rate of work, R_o, would be that at which $R \times Q$ is maximum which will occur some-

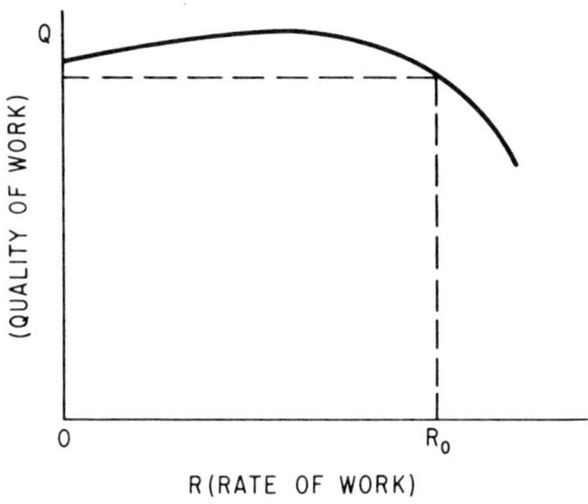

Fig. 13-3. Quality of work versus rate of work.

where after Q begins to drop. Whether this is an overall advantageous rate for E & R work can legitimately be questioned.

The time required to complete a job depends not only on the rate (modified by quality) but also on the difficulty. That is, the output is a function of rate of work, quality, and also time as a function of difficulty. The approximate relationship between the time and job difficulty is shown in Fig. 13-4.

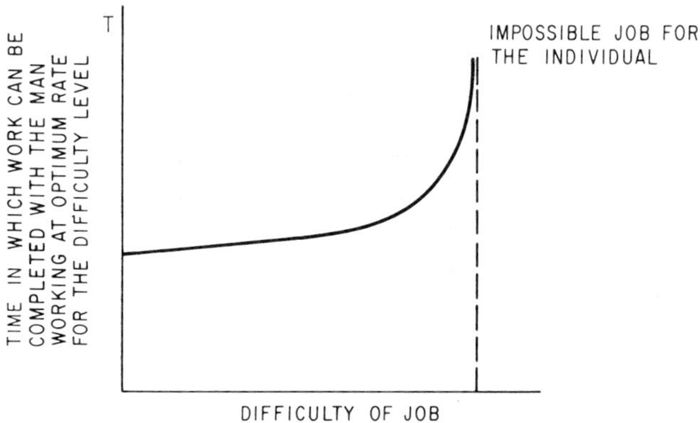

Fig. 13-4. Individual's time-difficulty curve.

It is best to assign a man a job at as high a level of difficulty as possible before rate of performance begins to rise rapidly. There is no specific point, but rather at the "knee" of the curve. From this curve it can be seen that assigning a man a job of very low difficulty for him saves relatively little time. Since the cost of the job bears a linear relationship to the man's time, it is economical to assign a job requiring less skill to an individual with less ability and therefore with a different time-difficulty curve. The assumption is made that each individual's pay is proportional to his most effective output.

It is now possible to examine the efficiency and productivity of the engineer if the above measurements and data are established. The efficiency of a machine or of an engineer is the ratio of his output to his input expressed as a percent. A measure of his productiveness would be the value of the output divided by the cost of the input. The trouble here is that the value of the output is usually difficult or impossible to state in definite quantitative terms. One approach would be to estimate what it would cost to pay another company to perform the job since this price would include a profit corresponding to the risk.

An expression of the individual's efficiency in the terms previously used is as follows:

$$\text{Efficiency} = \frac{t \times D}{T \times D_o} \times 100$$

Where

E = efficiency
T = time actually spent on the job by the engineer
D = difficulty level of the job
D_o = capability of the engineer expressed in same difficulty units as D
t = time required to do the job at its rated difficulty level

$$\text{Productivity} = \frac{\text{value of output}}{\text{cost of input}} = \frac{V}{T \times e}$$

Where

e = engineering costs in \$/unit of time
V = value of the job

The ratio D/D_o has been called the "challenge" of the job by E. O. Klint.

Just as qualitative measurements involve some quantitative thinking, quantitative measurements involve some judgment of value. The quantitative approaches try to formalize the measurement process and break it up into elements so that judgments may be made on small parts of the whole.

The question as to whether an individual contributes to the profit and other objectives of the company, relative to his cost to the company, is difficult to judge except in the case of the highly competent and the least competent individuals.

MEASURING THE PROCESS

Measuring the E & R process refers to measuring the group and its activities. It is actually measuring the managed group in action and involves the manager and the synergistic effects. The measurement of the contribution of the manager may be based on evaluation of the following:

1. How many junior engineers have been hired who have been developed to senior or other higher status?
2. How many engineers have been recommended for promotion to higher positions in other managed units? How many have actually been so promoted?
3. How many of his more junior men have proven their creative talents through inventions and patents? How many senior men have continued to produce? How many have "dried up?"
4. Are the group manager's men enthusiastic about him? His leadership? His technical "savvy?"
5. Does his group work together smoothly as a team? This is almost a

wholly qualitative measurement except for the very poor or very good men.

6. How well does he meet his objectives and goals?

This last can be left as a purely subjective measurement. However, one could tabulate the number of times his group meets its schedule dates and also how many times it misses them. One can even go further and calculate these achievements, or lack of them, on a percentage basis.

The ultimate factor to be evaluated is how great a contribution this group makes in achieving E & R objectives. Some criteria related to this aspect are:

1. Actual development time for a project compared with a projected time based on standards established for the class of product involved
2. Percentage or dollar change (plus or minus) in average yearly development cost per project by class
3. Number of new and/or products improved per year (or month)
4. Number of new products completed per year (or month)
5. Change (plus or minus) in the average yearly pay-off per project for a class of products
6. Change (plus or minus) in total pay-off or profit earned on products designed by the group
7. Square feet of new design drawings per month for a section
8. Estimated or actual total pay-off for all products the section has developed
9. Actual total pay-off for all products developed and put in use on the market
10. Development cost per person
11. Development project cost per engineer or scientist
12. The trend of the ratio of the cost of the E & R unit's cost to the sales volume of its product line, providing this is applicable.

Another more objective quantitative approach to measuring the working tempo of a group is Northrup Corporation's PACE Program. An observer tours a number of departments several times a day and observes the work being performed. He takes different routes in order to arrive in a particular area at somewhat random times. If a person is at the water fountain, doing crossword puzzles, or otherwise engaged in something unrelated to his work, he is considered idle. If a secretary is gazing out of the window, for example, it is assumed that she is idle. Conversely, if an engineer who has his work in front of him is staring at the ceiling, he is given the benefit of the doubt, since much of his work requires abstract thinking. A skilled observer gets to know the nature of the departments and the probable number of people to be out of the office. He can cover about 750 employees in his rounds. The tempo of the group is calculated as:

$$\frac{[N \pm L - (I + A)] \times E \times 100}{N \pm L}$$

Where

E = effort factor (group effort rating)
N = number of people assigned
L = loans, in or out
I = number idle
A = number absent from the area in excess of the "normal" for the group as judged by the observer.

With the development of sophisticated project management, the use of PERT/cost and other programming techniques provide good evaluation of work in progress. Various key supervisors are given responsibility for tasks and funds. Through the use of monthly, or even weekly computerized reports, information is made available. In such "responsibility reporting," the manager is supplied with schedules of costs, budgets, and variances on monthly, year-to-date, and a projected fiscal year basis for every account over which he has control. The quantitative summary index for evaluation is:

$$\frac{\text{Progress}}{\text{Schedule}} \times \frac{\text{Budget}}{\text{Expenditures}} \times \frac{\text{Quality (index)}}{\text{Specifications } (= 100)}$$

MEASURING THE OUTPUT

Measuring the output of E & R is based on one of two assumptions:

1. The cost of the input is fixed so that the question to be answered is: How good is its output?
2. Standards of performance may be established so that cost-per-unit output of specified quality may be determined.

One of the most general set of standards would consist of qualitative objectives of E & R as follows:

1. Follow competitors
2. Improve products to remain abreast of competitors
3. Improve products to lead the field, at least some of the time
4. Diversify but maintain technical continuity
5. Diversify beyond maintaining technical continuity
6. Conduct basic research.

Another set of criteria might be established by listing the planned, direct results of research and development, and the indirect results of research, as shown in Fig. 13-5.

Direct Products

1. The sum of all direct results of offensive, defensive, and fundamental research.
2. A pool of experienced and skilled scientific persons who may solve technical problems encountered by the remainder of the concern.
3. Knowledge for the general good of society.
4. Increased knowledge and skill with which to solve future problems of the concern.
5. Publications from experimental work.
6. Improved technical planning, i.e., anticipation of future technical difficulties of the concern and the prevention of such difficulties.
7. A pool of technical knowledge for dissemination throughout the concern and society.

Indirect Products

1. The sum of all indirect results of offensive, defensive, and fundamental research.
2. The protection of the reputation of the concern as a reputable manufacturer of a quality product.
3. Good will which assists sales of present or future lines.
4. A favorable reputation among technical people which facilitates hiring and keeping required personnel.
5. A continuously highly profitable business.
6. Trained men for operating and administrative positions.
7. Survival in a rapidly changing market or competitive technological situation.
8. Enhanced prices for capital stock.
9. A larger return on dollars invested in the concern.
10. The planned and coordinated growth of the enterprise.
11. Stabilization of sales and profits.

Fig. 13-5. Products of the overall research effort. *Source:* James Brian Quinn, *Yardsticks for Industrial Research* (New York: The Ronald Press, 1959), p. 45.

How the E & R organization performs overall with respect to guiding the company into the best technologies, to selecting and developing specific products, and conducting its work at a cost appropriate to its productivity is not easily stated in quantitative terms. There are also side benefits or indirect results that are highly intangible. Consequently, most companies are forced to rely heavily on qualitative measurements of the effectiveness of the E & R organization.

One E & R director, the head of this activity at General Mills, recognized the importance of project selection and, therefore, in addition to using the market research in other elements of the organization, established a small market research group reporting to him directly. While it may not be practical or possible for the E & R manager to have his own market research group, he can and should make full use of the company's market research staff and/or consultants.

Most of the group measurements discussed in the previous section can be applied to the total E & R organization. Some additional measurement criteria are:

1. How well is E & R doing in relation to competitors regarding the improvement of products and the finding of new ideas?
2. Are the products reliable, easily produced, and maintainable?
3. Do the products fit the market needs as interpreted by Marketing?
4. Does the E & R organization always have a backlog of potentially profitable projects which it has proposed?
5. Is the E & R organization building a reservoir of knowledge and attracting talented new people?
6. Are good technical reports of progress issued periodically?
7. Are costs of E & R controlled reasonably well?
8. Is there a steady flow of patents being issued?
9. Is the research group "lucky" enough to come up with a very valuable discovery from time to time?

Quantitative measurements of the total E & R output may be based on expected payoffs from projects. Methods for evaluating projects and products that estimated the return over the years, were given in Chapter 8. The present value of the cash flow due to a project was also mentioned. If the estimated probability of the success of a project is multiplied by the present value of the estimated cash flow, an "expected" present value of the project may be obtained.

If all proposed projects are ranked in order of expected present value, eventually projects will be listed which have no expected present value. The cumulative expected value by project of all present projects having a positive value could be plotted as in Fig. 13-6. Since all functions including top management participate in evaluating the commercial aspects of a project, it stands to reason that the valuation of a project is not overly biased by the E & R viewpoint. The total value of these projects may not be attributable to E & R; however, the total value and the profile does provide a measure of the quantity and quality of projects which the E & R organization is producing in terms of profits to the company. Actual results may be plotted as time passes to compare with these expected present values providing a further measurement. Figure 13-7 shows how such a plot might appear.

Another approach is to look at costs and profits from a functional viewpoint. It can be fairly easily seen that profits result from the application of the factors of production grouped according to the functional organization of the business.

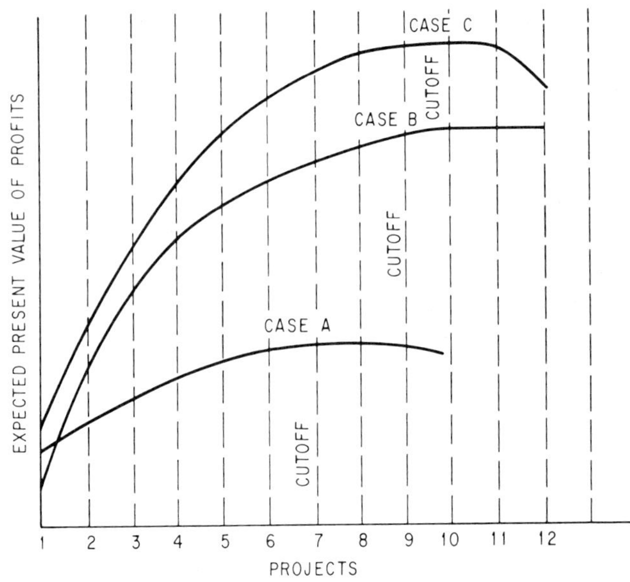

Fig. 13-6. Three situations showing accepted present value of projects available.

As the amount of one factor of production is increased while all others are held constant, there is initially an increase in returns and later a decrease in returns per unit added. It seems logical to assume that if increasingly more resources are poured into engineering, while the amounts devoted to all other functions of the business are held constant, there will be at first an increase in return and eventually a decrease in return per engineering dollar. Therefore, profits may be approximated by a quadratic function of engineering costs plus an interaction due to all other resources which

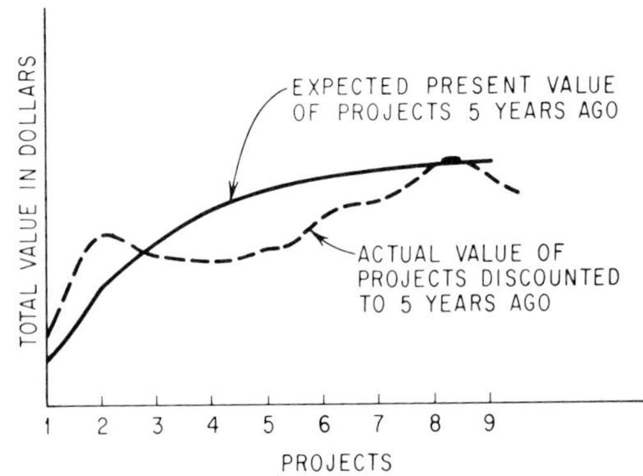

Fig. 13-7. Comparison of actual versus expected present value of proposed projects.

may be applied. A simple form of such a function might be the sum of two functions.

Therefore, the net profits may be approximated by:

$$P = (aE^2 + bE + c) + (dZ^2 + eZ + f)$$

Where

E = costs for engineering for one year
Z = all other business costs for the same year

Over a six-year period, it would be possible to obtain six pairs of values of E and Z and, therefore, six equations in the unknowns a, b, c, d, e, f. These equations can then be solved for values of the six parameters. Actually, over a number of years, it would be possible to plot the value of a calculated for several six-year periods and obtain an average or else a trend estimate. This is similarly true for the other parameters.

With the profit equation thus defined, it would be possible to calculate the anticipated profit of the expenditures for E & R if all other activities were held constant. The theoretical contribution to profit is given by the first term on the right side of the equation. The theoretical change in profit could then be compared with the actual change to measure the E & R function.

Summary

Obviously, there are many specific criteria which can be used for qualitative and quantitative evaluation of E & R. Top management should be the judge, and the use of all the various forms of measurement should be encouraged. Managers of E & R who try to prevent additional measurements in areas where these are possible are trying to build up a wall to prevent interference with their operations.

It can be seen that considerable work is required to develop any form of measurement of E & R, and this is especially true for the theoretical approaches discussed. Those mentioned would be only the first steps, and the more difficult ones to follow would be the determinations of inputs for such conceptual models.* Top management must use whatever tools are available today—qualitative and quantitative—to measure E & R. The fact that the tools may be poor does not negate management's responsibility (including the manager of E & R) to measure engineering and research as best it can.

* Some additional insights to the measurement of E & R can be found in a doctoral thesis by Paul Croke at Rensselaer Polytechnic Institute titled "Research on Research: (1) The Management Planning and Control of Research and (2) The Attitudes of Industrial Research Scientists."

BIBLIOGRAPHY

COTTON, JO, and STOLZ, ROBERT E. "The General Applicability of a Scale for Rating Research Productivity," *Journal of Applied Psychology*, 1960, pp. 276–77.

ENGLES, EARL F. "Evaluating a Company's Research Program," *Research Management,* May, 1967.

GORDON, GERALD. "The Problem of Assessing Scientific Accomplishment: A Potential Solution," *IEEE Transactions on Engineering Management,* December, 1963.

HODGE, MELVILLE H., JR. "Rate Your Company's Research Productivity," Vol. EM–10, No. 4, *Harvard Business Review,* November–December, 1963.

HUGHES, E. C. "Evaluation of Research," *Research Management,* November, 1967.

JACKSON, T. W., and SPURLOCK, J. M. *Research and Development Management.* Homewood, Ill.: Richard D. Irwin, Inc., 1967.

KLINT, EUGENE O. "How to Measure and Improve Engineer Effectiveness," *Product Engineering,* January 25, 1960.

KNUTILA, CHESTER. "A Tool For Evaluating Performance of R & D Engineers," *Management Services,* May–June, 1966.

NEWMAN, MAURICE S. "Accounting for Research and Development Expenditures," *Research Management,* July, 1965.

———. "Evaluating Research and Development Activities," *Management Services,* March–April, 1966.

QUINN, JAMES B. "How to Evaluate Research Output," *Harvard Business Review,* March–April, 1960.

———. *Yardsticks for Industrial Research.* New York, N.Y.: The Ronald Press Company, 1959.

REYNOLDS, WM. B. "Research Evaluation," *Research Management,* March, 1965.

ROCHE, A. F. "Measuring the Profits From Research," *Research Management,* May, 1967.

ROMAN, DANIEL D. *Research and Development Management: The Economics and Administration of Technology.* New York, N.Y.: Appleton-Century-Crofts, 1968.

SMIDDY, HAROLD F. *"Measuring" as an Element of a Manager's Work of Leadership.* New York, N.Y.: Management Consultation Services, General Electric Company, 1957.

STOLZ, ROBERT E. "Assessing Research Productivity," *Personnel Administration,* January–February, 1962.

YOVITS, M. C. et al., eds. *Research Program Effectiveness.* New York, N.Y.: Gordon and Breach, Science Publishers, Inc., 1966.

CHAPTER 14

Support Activities: The Administration Component

NATURE OF E & R ADMINISTRATION

E & R organization is changing rapidly as it adapts to the complex problems of large development and research projects. Such projects require continuous and close teamwork involving thousands of people. Even for small projects it is difficult to get everyone to work together at top efficiency. Only by shedding nontechnical chores can E & R managers hope to accomplish their job. This has led to the concept and introduction of the engineering and research administration component to handle required but subsidiary functions.

Administration conducts those activities which *aid* the E & R organization to proceed smoothly towards the accomplishment of its main purpose. The philosophy of E & R administration personnel must be to simplify the work of the technical staff in the administrative areas, even though it means more work for the administrative people.

It is not true, however, that engineers and scientists can live in a dream world without contact with the facts of business life. Planning and measurement are dependent upon basic thinking and information supplied by all levels of the technical and managerial staff. The people in administration can gather, correlate, and integrate such basic data. But the engineers and scientists must contribute to the raw data and, also, be made aware of the significance of their individual contributions in this area.

THE ADMINISTRATION ORGANIZATION

While the E & R administration services must be adapted to meet the needs of the particular organization it services, it is still possible, however, to make a fairly comprehensive list which covers almost all the appropriate functions found in representative E & R administration components. These functions may be divided into four major classifications:

1. Operations
2. Personnel
3. Facilities and Supporting Services
4. Programming.

The administration component can be established within either the functional or the project-type engineering or research organization. In large E & R organizations, the E & R administration work may require one or more people assigned to each major activity, Fig. 14-1. In a smaller organization, Fig. 14-2, some of the functions may be grouped together

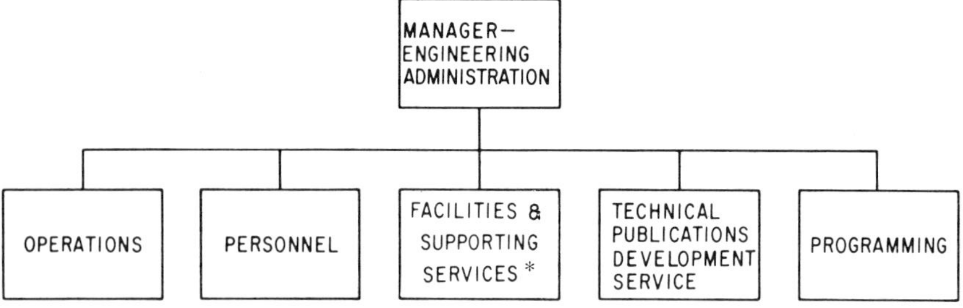

Fig. 14-1. E & R administration in a large organization.

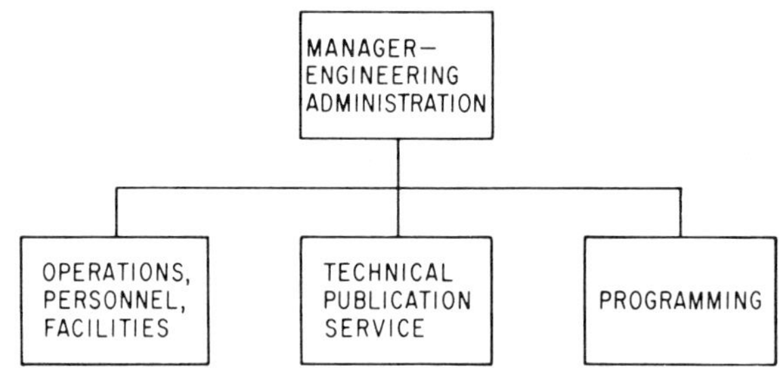

Fig. 14-2. E & R administration in a small organization.

with one person responsible for operations, personnel, facilities and supporting services; another person assisting the manager of E & R administration with the programming function; and a third, handling technical publication service. Other combinations are, of course, possible. As noted in Chapter 9, the programming group may report directly to the manager of E & R.

* Each major supporting-service head normally reports directly to the Manager of Engineering Administration, but sometimes to the Manager of E & R.

OPERATIONS

Operations work deals mainly with the planning, procedures, and numerous miscellaneous administrative matters which are necessary to keep the E & R organization going with some semblance of order. Such functions as organization planning, preparation of policy guides, and development of procedures are the most important. They form the structure of the organization and put it on wheels. However, the administration component also must carry out a number of other functions such as:

A. *Budgeting and Financial Functions*
1. Prepare, with the aid of component managers, capital and operating budgets and annual program summaries.
2. Integrate component budgets into total E & R budgets.
3. Reconcile the E & R budgets and annual program summaries with the proposed amounts allocated to E & R by the company's top management.
4. Prepare rolling forecasts of expenditures on a monthly or quarterly basis.
5. Distribute financial reports received from the accounting department and advise appropriate levels of management of significant deviations from financial plans.
6. Develop shop order control procedures.
7. Maintain E & R financial records.

B. *Engineering Area Floor Space Planning*[1]
1. Determine the total area needs of E & R—office, test, and storage —and reconcile with the company's allocation to E & R
2. Plan long-range requirements for floor area and special work areas
3. Prepare detailed layouts of office and other areas for approval by appropriate levels of E & R management
4. Plan long-range requirements for office furniture and equipment
5. Order office furniture and equipment and arrange for transfers of equipment between offices as needed
6. Plan and arrange for proper office services such as telephones, light, power, and temperature control.

C. *Miscellaneous*

1. Develop improved E & R procedures including possible mechanization or automation of technical functions through the use of computers

[1] These functions are often handled by the company's industrial engineering or plant engineering department in cooperation with E & R.

2. Conduct cost improvement program of engineering functions
3. Maintain emergency evacuation plan
4. Conduct suggestion system program in accordance with policies prepared by the employee relations staff
5. Process test reports including notification of contributors, calculation of test costs, preparation of reports, approval processing, and distribution
6. Process and maintain records relating to attendance at technical meetings
7. Process and follow-up miscellaneous surveys, requests for information, etc.
8. Guide visitors on plant tours.

Automation in E & R Work

The work of the E & R organization in pursuit of its objectives consists of creating and processing information. Processing of information can be divided into two classes:

1. Computing
2. Data processing
   a. Converting
   b. Transporting
   c. Reproducing
   d. Sorting
   e. Storing
   f. Retrieving.

The creative work can only be performed by human beings, but the above technical functions can be performed by machines in varying degrees. In addition to E & R, significant engineering information outputs are prepared for top management, i.e., in finance, manufacturing, and marketing.

Automation can be considered as any significant step towards the replacement of human labor by machine labor. For convenience in analyzing the E & R function, it is desirable to define various levels of automation. A simple division of the spectrum of automation developed by a large company is shown in Fig. 14-3. These definitions are very useful in analyzing E & R operations. Each step in the technical process can be listed and a level of automation assigned. It is then possible to draw a profile chart of the entire process in terms of automation level. Activities at low levels of automation will be highlighted.

Certain areas lend themselves more readily to automation than do others. In particular, the engineering and research administrators should look for:

1. Repetitive work
2. Work requiring constant revision which *routinely* affects much information output

3. High cost physical operations
4. Poor or slow communication processes.

In E & R organizations with a general low level of automation, greatest gains will generally be made by mechanization of output processes. Following this, mechanization of entire systems offers the next greatest gains.

	Function Performed by Machine	Characteristics
L 1	None	All work performed by humans. Manual aids are used.
L 2	Supplies action energy	Mechanical or electrical energy is supplied for the basic process action.
L 3	Supplies all action energy	Energy is supplied for all control functions, auxiliary functions, and basic functions.
L 4	Stores the control instructions	Machine follows established step-by-step stored instructions.
L 5	Controls intermediate and auxiliary actions	Feedback in minor loops assists in control.
L 6	Controls output by main loop feedback	Closed loop feedback produces controlled output by iterative process.
L 7	Modifies or creates control instructions	Machine determines what to do and requires no human control.

Fig. 14-3. Seven levels of automation in engineering work.

One major step in all research, design, development and general engineering work is the expression of creative (mental) effort in the form of drawings. From a system viewpoint, these drawings first must be produced, and secondly, reproduced, then distributed, studied, and returned to the researcher, engineer, or draftsman for revision. They are altered and again distributed to E & R, as well as Manufacturing and Purchasing, and finally stored in various files. In addition, records of each step must be established and maintained. It can be seen that almost all of these steps fall within the six classifications of data processing given earlier and are, in fact, automated to some degree in many organizations.

The automation of drawing processing, however, is relatively only a small step forward. Many companies have tackled their design processes with considerable success. When automating design processes, be willing at the start to provide for human decisions at various points when it appears appropriate.

PERSONNEL

Responsibility for personnel functions is often a matter of some confusion. Three groups have responsibilities in this area, and these responsibilities may be very simply separated. First, E & R management is responsible for seeing that only the right men at the right time are added to the E & R organization. E & R management is also responsible for the development and progress of its personnel and for control of their activities according to the limitations of company policy.

E & R administration provides a service to technical management by maintaining records and controls and making recommendations to management to take certain actions at appropriate times.

Similarly the central employee relations organization performs a service to E & R management by supplying candidates, advising on hiring, maintaining wage and salary administration policies, and processing such paperwork as is required for records and control. Together these service organizations often present information and recommendations in such full form that the E & R manager can easily and quickly make decisions. In a small company, these functions are usually performed by the company's personnel department.

Therefore, the administrative component in the larger companies:

1. Assists and at times advises on hiring, placement, transfer and severance of engineering personnel in conformity with organizational plans
2. Works with the company employee relations department and E & R managers in recruiting, selecting, and training personnel
3. Integrates manpower requirements with financial budgets
4. Plans and assists with the implementation of methods for developing higher skills in E & R personnel
5. Makes recommendations for integrating all salary actions within E & R
6. Maintains records of all salary actions
7. Maintains personnel data sheets on each individual
8. Prepares statistics relating to salary structure and level of technical and semiprofessional personnel for E & R
9. Prepares, with the assistance of E & R managers, job descriptions for all positions
10. Prepares monthly roster of personnel by organization component
11. Assists employees in obtaining information relating to all fields of personnel activity such as employee benefits, vacations, leaves of absence, and transfers.

FACILITIES AND SUPPORTING SERVICES

Engineering and research require a number of technical supporting facilities and services in their everyday conduct. A typical group of these is shown in Fig. 14-4. As noted in Fig. 14-1, the head of a major supporting service and/or facility usually reports directly to the Manager of Engineering Administration, rather than to a Manager of Supporting Services. In some cases he may report to the Manager of E & R.

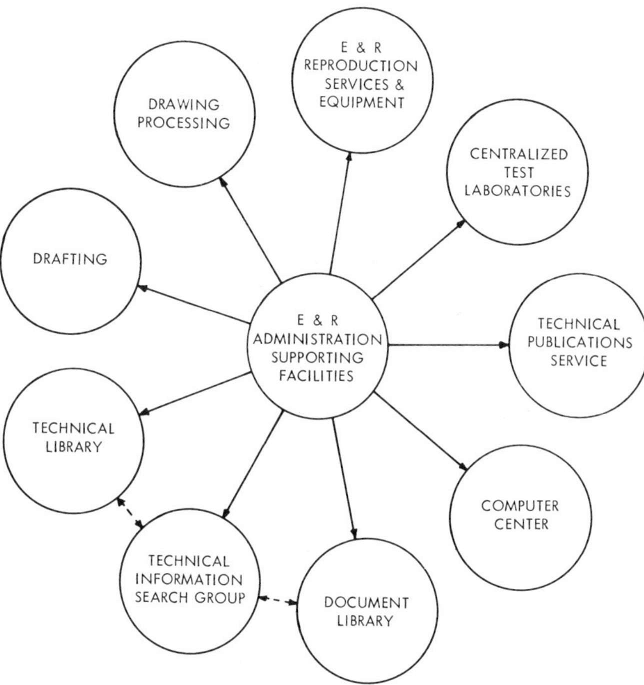

Fig. 14-4. Engineering administration supporting facilities.

Reproduction Services & Equipment

Reproduction of tracings of drawings and sketches, letters, and miscellaneous short documents and engineering reports is an essential function in engineering today. There is a need for reproduction facilities to be located close to the technical personnel and operated with a minimum of formality. "Open shop" machines with which the secretaries or the technical personnel themselves can reproduce from one to a few dozen copies are desirable. For long runs or high quality offset work, there is likely to be a central printing production group for the entire plant. For large volume reproduction of drawings, large diazo process machines, Xerographic machines, or the equivalent should be maintained in and operated by the E & R administrative component.

Technical Library

As the E & R organization grows in size, it is advisable to establish and maintain a technical library. As a minimum, enough engineering and scientific reference books should be kept on hand so that the E & R personnel is not crippled by lack of source information. It is preferable to maintain a library which permits engineers and scientists to keep abreast of their fields and to extend their knowledge. Some of the items which a technical library should contain are:

1. New technical books
2. A comprehensive group of handbooks
3. Magazines and periodicals
4. Pamphlets
5. Government publications
6. Indexes to publications and abstract reports
7. Dictionaries and encyclopedias (general and special)
8. Society proceedings
9. University brochures
10. Manufacturers' catalogues
11. Standards (USASI, ASTM, technical society, government)
12. Specifications (commercial, government)
13. Surveys (technical, industrial)
14. Codes (municipal, state, national)
15. Telephone directories (out-of-city)
16. Maps, city directories
17. State industrial directories.

In addition to a technical library, many firms which are engaged in defense work find it necessary to maintain a separate document library. This is because it is necessary to maintain careful control over a large volume of classified engineering reports received from external sources. Unclassified technical reports as well as classified documents are usually held in the document library. Copies of internally produced classified and unclassified reports are also maintained by the document library.

The two libraries are depositories, and the librarians—to a large extent—are custodians. The addition of a technical information group consisting of several engineers and scientists with a broad knowledge of pertinent engineering fields will often save a company many thousands of dollars. The technical information group is concerned with what information is accumulated and stored in the library and how to search out technical information in response to the needs of the engineers and scientists. It develops information-need "profiles" of engineers and scientists so that appropriate reports and information will be sent to them automatically.

Technical Publications

Technical personnel often are burdened with certain semi-technical and technical publications activities. These acitvities usually can be carried out in better fashion, and more inexpensively, by specialized personnel in E & R administration. The main administration publications' activities which relate directly to the product are:

1. Preparation and/or editing and production of administrative and technical reports
2. Preparation, production, and distribution of instruction books, technical manuals, and training manuals
3. Processing of technical papers and speech approvals
4. Assisting with the preparation and processing of patent applications.

Engineering administration can perform a considerable service for the research, development, and design personnel by editing and producing technical reports, progress reports, and technical proposals. The researchers and design engineers must, of course, supply the raw material and review the final work for technical accuracy. However, the writers and editors in engineering administration, many of whom hold engineering and science degrees, can help with the organization of material, the writing and/or editing, the preparation of graphics, and the expediting of each phase of the reports or proposals to meet established deadlines.

Instruction books are essential for operation and maintenance of equipment. Since equipment today is more complex to operate and maintain, such books cannot be second-rate, incomplete, ambiguous, or otherwise inadequate. The Armed Services have recognized this need by developing better and more rigid specifications for all phases of instruction-book preparation for all types of equipment. Using such MIL specifications as a guide, the technical writers can prepare good commercial specifications, better estimate costs, and produce instruction books which will aid immensely in building customer good will. It is the specialized know-how for either preparing the books and training manuals or subcontracting the work that engineering administration supplies. A typical flow of such work is shown in Fig. 14-5 to illustrate the relationship between the engineers and the engineering administration personnel.

DRAFTING AND REPRODUCTION

It would not be realistic or practical to discuss the problems of E & R management without some consideration of one of the principal forms of

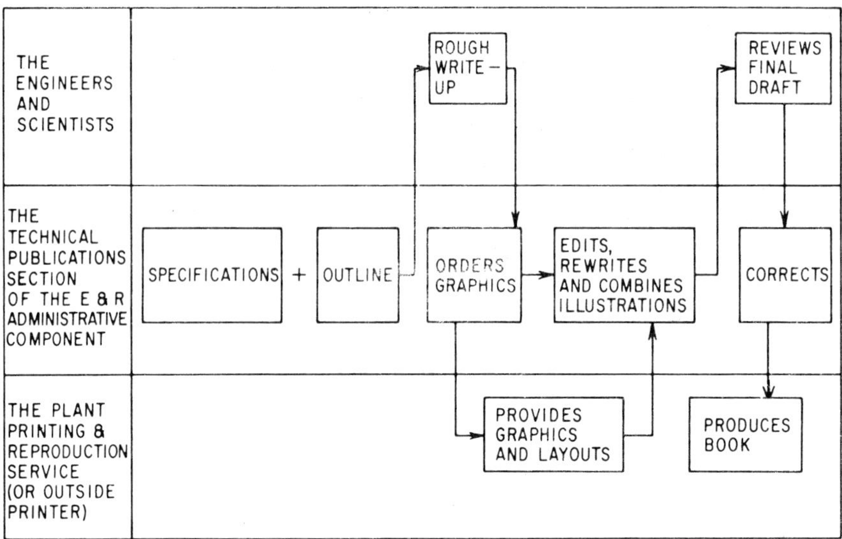

Fig. 14-5. Flow of work for instruction books. *Source:* R. G. Murdick, "Engineering Administration," *Machine Design* (July 7, 1960).

communication used by engineers and scientists. The two major activities in E & R, (1) designing, and (2) drafting, require specialized forms of communication.

Generally, the work of *designing* is the development, primarily through visualization by graphical methods, of patterns and arrangements of ideas which ultimately establish the form and function of physical systems or objects. The work utilizes skill in graphical presentation; geometry and mathematics; knowledge of engineering and manufacturing methods, processes, and materials; in conceiving, creating, refining, adapting, and improving components, products, and systems.

The work of drafting involves the definition of dimensions, shapes, and special arrangements; the physical objects and combinations thereof, using information and data supplied by designers and engineers, or that is otherwise available from standard sources. The work utilizes skill in graphical representation, geometry, and mathematics; knowledge of standardized and established drafting techniques and practices; and a knowledge of manufacturing methods, processes, and materials.

Drawing Control System

Drafting and drawings of any kind are expensive, and this activity is a major cost of any E & R operation or project. However, there are many reasons, other than cost, for maintaining strict control over all drawings. Other important reasons include safety against loss or against time-consuming damage. Establishing tight control over the drawing as it progresses from the idea to the finished print is not a simple task because there are many steps, the most important of which are the following:

1. A group leader works with a designer in establishing what is to be shown on the drawing.
2. As the designer progresses in developing the idea, detailers are called in to work out specific details.
3. When the drawings are completed by the draftsmen and detailers, they usually go to a clerk-typist for the addition of such notes and comments as are needed.
4. The drawings or tracings then proceed to a checker for review.
5. It is usual for the checker to send some or all of the drawings back to the designer and/or detailer for necessary corrections.
6. The drawings or tracings are again returned to the checker.
7. If no further inaccuracies are found, they are passed on to the group leader and the project engineer for authorization to have reproductions made.

The above is a generalized view of the steps involved, and it is quite easy to see that there are many opportunities for the drawings to be defaced, mislaid, or lost. If photographic storage should be involved, the process is complicated by further steps.

The following goals or objectives should be set for a drawing control system:

1. Keep accurate and up-to-date records of the locations of all drawings
2. Keep accurate and up-to-date records of the current status of all drawings
3. Minimize handling of original tracings to prevent damage, deterioration, or loss
4. Minimize the number of times the original tracing must be reproduced.

Accomplishing these tasks usually requires the development and application of drawing schedules, drawing number assignments, maintenance of location records, maintenance of work progress records, record cards for each drawing, etc. A typical drawing record card is shown in Figs. 14-6a and 14-6b.

Engineering Changes: Configuration Management

Configuration management which deals with engineering changes is neither a new concept nor a new management innovation. However, in the past few years this particular area of management has received major attention largely through the efforts of the Department of Defense.

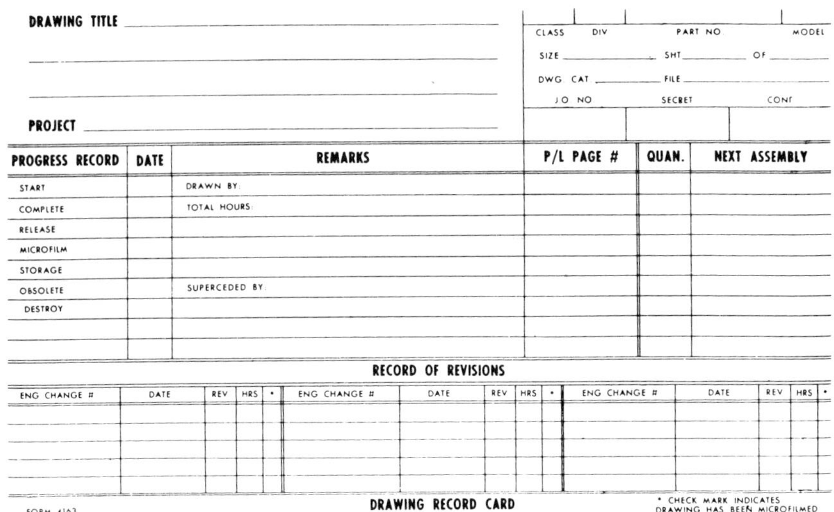

DRAWING TITLE

PROJECT

CLASS | DIV | PART NO | MODEL

SIZE ____ SHT ____ OF ____

DWG. CAT. ____ FILE ____

J.O. NO | SECRET | CONF

PROGRESS RECORD	DATE	REMARKS	P/L PAGE #	QUAN.	NEXT ASSEMBLY
START		DRAWN BY:			
COMPLETE		TOTAL HOURS:			
RELEASE					
MICROFILM					
STORAGE					
OBSOLETE		SUPERCEDED BY:			
DESTROY					

RECORD OF REVISIONS

ENG CHANGE #	DATE	REV	HRS	•	ENG CHANGE #	DATE	REV	HRS	•	ENG CHANGE #	DATE	REV	HRS	•

FORM 4163 DRAWING RECORD CARD

• CHECK MARK INDICATES DRAWING HAS BEEN MICROFILMED

Fig. 14-6a. Drawing record card (front).

TRACING CHARGE OUT RECORD

DATE	CHARGED TO	DATE	CHARGED TO	DATE	CHARGED TO	DATE	CHARGED TO

RECORD OF DISTRIBUTION

PROJECT SECTION			CUSTOMER			MANUFACTURING								
QUAN/TYPE	REV	DATE	QUAN/TYPE	REV	DATE	QUAN/TYPE	REV	DATE	QUAN/TYPE	REV	DATE	QUAN/TYPE	REV	DATE

CLASS	DIV	PART #	MODEL

Fig. 14-6b. Drawing record card (back). *Source:* American Machine & Foundry Co., Research and Development Division, Springdale, Conn.

Configuration management has existed within industry for many years under various names and phrases. Sometimes it is centrally located in the engineering department, in other organizations it may be divided—in terms of responsibility—among the drafting, engineering, and, possibly, the accounting departments.

Configuration management is an organized and systematic method whereby a particular group (or groups) has the responsibility to prepare, accumulate, and control engineering changes. These methods assure: (1) that the proper personnel in engineering, manufacturing, drafting, sales, etc., have reviewed the change and have given their approval or disapproval; (2) that the engineering documentation which is associated with or affected by the change is properly updated; (3) that similar units in production or in field usage receive the necessary attention demanded by the change; and (4) that related or interfacing equipments, subsystems, and systems affected by the change are compatible with the engineering change. It is a process designed to "bring order out of chaos" by considering the impact of the change on operations as a whole system instead of as an equipment entity.

An engineering change is any change to the product from the way in which it has been produced in the past. The military services recognize two change categories: Class I and Class II, a classification method that meets most civilian requirements as well.

Class I changes are:

1. Those affecting interchangeability of units as a whole and include service and repair parts
2. Those affecting performance
3. Those affecting price or other contractual particulars involving the customer and ultimate user.

Class I changes frequently require the customer's approval and must be backed up by engineering substantiation. Such changes must be segregated by the use of new part numbers and require a change in the parts list defining the article.

Changes which fall in the Class II category are usually identified only by change letters following the drawing or part numbers and may not be identified in the parts list. Class II changes concern, for example, tolerance modifications unrelated to interchangeable fits; material changes unrelated to physical properties; changes in process sequence; and other similar modifications.

Why has so much attention been given to this subject in recent years by the defense industrial community? A significant characteristic of the defense industry is that a great majority of products undergo continuous change throughout their development and service life.

Configuration management is divided into the two major activities: configuration control and configuration accounting. Configuration control concerns the procedures and practices employed in preparing, evaluating, and implementing engineering design changes. It assures that the necessary personnel have reviewed, evaluated, approved, and/or disapproved the change. This includes the customer and all interfacing equipment personnel. Configuration accounting concerns the process of accumulating, documenting, and reporting engineering changes according to designated procedures. It is the means by which accurate lists and reports keep track of the status of engineering changes for each equipment, subsystem, and system affected by the change. Configuration accounting is the "bookkeeping" activity of configuration management.

There are many Department of Defense regulations, manuals, and directives which provide policy, direction, and guidelines. Some of these documents are the DOD Standardization Manual (M205); Air Force-Navy Aeronautical Bulletin 445, which establishes policy for engineering changes to systems and equipment; and the Air Force Systems Command Manual 371-1 through 375-6. The latter series establishes policy, provides guidance, and assigns responsibilities to all contractors and Government agencies for the configuration management of Air Force design and development contracts. A new "all encompassing" DOD regulation is in the review stage.

Handling Changes in Drawings

The requirement for changing drawings, as previously outlined, is a major problem and also a costly one. While many drawing changes are the result of technological progress, improvement in products, and even in the process of standardization, there exists another area requiring drawing changes that cannot be chalked up to progress. This is the area which includes design and drafting errors. Whatever the cause of the change, the handling of drawing revisions is a function of major importance.

All changes, no matter how insignificant, must be formally recorded to ensure that the necessary data is perpetually available for reconstructing the product at any stage during its life. This calls for the use of drawing records plus an alteration or change notice such as Fig. 14-7. There is no single optimum method for recording drawing revisions which is applicable to all drafting operations. Involved is the size of the enterprise, its organizational structure, the nature and diversity of its products, etc. However, as a basic principle, the change record should appear on the drawing in a block or space provided for such purpose. Each revision should be identified by consecutively applied numerals or letters or by some other appropriate code. Some companies completely describe each revision by placing all the required information in the drawing change block. Many companies merely enter in the change block a reference to the engineering change notice responsible for the drawing revision.

In order to ensure that necessary revisions will be made to drawings, to control production, purchasing, tool application, cost, etc., it is necessary that a well-planned alteration or change notice system be established. The following principles may be used in the establishment of an acceptable engineering change notice system:

1. The engineering change notice:

ALTERATION NOTICE

No. 996-B
Sheet No. 1 Cont'd On Sheet —

Component 04
Status Part already machined S.O. 59-027-02 - KD-2019
Disposition Use part as made Draft Req. Yes

NAME OF PART	DRAWING No.	Sh. No.	Chg. No.	Change Reason	Responsibility Numbers		
Asm. Support Brace	T-7A7218	2	A-24	H	1. Eng. 2. Dftg. 3. Manuf.	X	4. Other Dept. 5. Outside Manuf.

Description of Change:

In Zone 11-H, changed the $1.927 \begin{smallmatrix} +.000 \\ -.002 \end{smallmatrix}$ dim. to $1.927 \begin{smallmatrix} +.002 \\ -.000 \end{smallmatrix}$

Submit for Information ______
Submit for Approval ______
Not to be Submitted ✓

Notice Issued By W.B. Sim Date October 15, 1969
Drawing Changed By ______ Date ______
Engineering Approval D. W. Darling Date October 15, 1969
Distribution
Engineering 3
Production
Drafting 2
Legal File 2

Fig. 14-7. Alteration notice.

a. Should verbally and/or graphically describe the change(s) in a previously issued engineering instruction, drawing, parts list, test instruction, etc. It should be in sufficient detail so that upon receipt of the notice the appropriate functions of the business can take prompt action, necessary for controlling and correcting or otherwise changing the ordering, planning, processing, inspection, pricing, and shipment of materials, parts, components, tools, or other products and equipments, and for computing necessary re-work and cancellation costs and charges

b. Should not be released until the status of the affected material, work and process, stock, tools, etc. have been determined and disposition of same agreed upon
c. Should instruct appropriate functional units as to disposition of affected material
d. Should be flexible to accommodate all kinds of engineering instructions, including test and inspection documents
e. Should specify reason, responsibility, and authorizations for the change
f. Should be individually identified, preferably in some form of consecutive serially numbered system to permit detection of missing notices in a given series
g. Should serve as a permanent record of the change and should be permanently filed to permit future reconstruction of documents as they existed at any particular point in time.

2. The system should incorporate a stop-work provision which can be made operative when required.
3. The system should ensure retrieval and destruction of obsolete and/or superseded engineering documents.
4. The procedure should be as simple and practicable as possible, consistent with objectives and requirements.
5. The procedure should encompass all concerned functions of the company such as purchasing, sales, industrial engineering, production control, quality control, inspection, etc.
6. A formal description of the complete system, its objectives, requirements and detailed procedures should be expressed in writing and jointly approved by all concerned functions of the business. Copies should be issued to all concerned functions.
7. Responsibility for action at each stage should be delegated to the individual positions.

Using the above principles, a change or alteration notice system can be constructed to meet the exact needs of each company. With the exception of those changes which must be processed promptly to maintain quality or to satisfy customer requirements, the timing of the release of the change notice has an important influence on inventories of finished parts and materials as well as on work in process. If the actual change can be deferred until inventories are brought into balance or until present stock is exhausted, substantial cost savings can be realized.

Organizing the Drafting Function

Since the organization of the drafting operation is directly related to and inevitably influenced by the organization of the total E & R function, the drafting organization cannot be dealt with as a separate entity. What will fit one company will not fit another in its entirety.

Simplified Drafting

Today, more than ever before, the challenge of modern industry is to produce more and better goods with less effort. As a key function, drafting, therefore, must meet the challenge. The old concept of drafting which permitted, or even demanded, that professional pride find expression in beautiful and artistically executed mechanical drawings with numerous accurately projected views and sections, many of which are unnecessary, is today as outmoded as the horse-and-buggy. A new yardstick for the measurement of drafting values is needed. Drafting must be stripped of its frills, yet surrender nothing in either clarity of presentation or accuracy of dimension.

Three of the easiest and most effective practices that can be applied to reduce drafting costs are the following: (1) simplification of delineation, (2) elimination of nonessentials, and (3) extensive use of freehand drawing. All of these practices have been used to some degree, but not all of them are used by every draftsman, and certainly they are not used to the extent that they should be by most drafting organizations.

The use of automation techniques is invading the drafting room and must be utilized to keep up with demands as well as to keep costs "in line."

Production and quality standards must be established and used for measurement. Related to such standards are objectives. These, too, need to be identified, communicated, and used effectively to direct the organization into those activities that will maximize the contribution of the drafting function to the success of the E & R organization.

CENTRALIZED TEST LABORATORIES[2]

The fundamental basis for all engineering and research is experimental. Also, testing must be considered as much a tool for the scientist or engineer as is a hammer or saw to the carpenter. This then requires the establishment, maintenance, and operation of test facilities. In medium and large companies many of these facilities and their operation are a separate responsibility. In such cases, the design engineer and/or scientist is the ultimate customer for the output of the experimental facility and the manager of the laboratory must always bear this in mind in all his planning and scheduling. A word of caution is appropriate at this time. Because the engineer or scientist is the customer does not necessarily mean that he

[2] The material under this title is largely paraphrased and condensed from Chapter 21 in the first edition of "Managing Engineering and Research," which was authored by Dr. Robert J. Hoe, Manager, Experimental Engineering, Knolls Atomic Power Laboratory, General Electric Company, Schenectady, New York.

knows best what information he should be getting from tests. In some cases he obviously will, but in others it may very well be that the experimental group has a better grasp of what tests should be conducted. The manager of the engineering laboratory must exercise diplomacy as well as salesmanship in determining the testing to be conducted in his facility.

In the field of E & R, the types of tests may be broken down into several categories, depending upon their applicability to the design. In general, the two main categories of tests are first those which might be considered as engineering tests, and second, research experiments. The division between the two basic types of tests depends upon whether the information is to be used for a specific design or whether the information is of a general nature to be used as a basis for future designs.

Testing which would fall into the category of applied research—that is, basic data experiments—include the measurement of the basic properties of materials and the interaction of physical phenomena which are necessary in order to establish the basic design criteria and design equations.

The tests to be considered under the category of "engineering design" are conducted to obtain information applicable to a specific engineering design. Such tests include tests of models and configurations mocking up the conceptual designs conceived by the designer. While a basic test of the strength of a material would be made on a standard test specimen, the engineering or development tests would be conducted on a model of the component to determine the regions of stress concentration and the soundness of the design.

In the development test stage, extensive use can be made of models, either scaled models—those made smaller or larger than the actual design—and/or models made of other than the design materials.

The purpose of engineering design or development testing is to provide the designer with information during the evolution of the design which will allow him to make modifications and improvements before the final product design is fixed.

After a design has been completed, extensive tests are conducted on the first component or system of that particular design. Such tests may be designated as prototype, proof, or operational tests. The prime purpose of these tests is to prove that the final product meets all the requirements of the design objectives and specifications.

Normally, the E & R series of tests would be completed with the successful conclusion of operational-type tests. However, there are additional tests which are carried out as part of the manufacturing and acceptance cycle of production components. In the medium and large companies, these tests would be entirely separated from the E & R laboratories. In a small company, however, it might be more reasonable to include the types of testing carried out in production and quality control in the same engineering laboratory in which the development and operational tests are run.

Evaluation of Needs

The responsible manager must evaluate the needs of the E & R organization in terms of the range and the character of the experimental work. Regardless of whether the laboratory is to consist of three or four men or several laboratories having scores of people, the character of the laboratory work must be matched to the needs of E & R and the company's products.

With these basic concepts in view, the individual responsible for experimental tests and research may then evaluate E & R needs in terms of the following, to establish requirements, objectives, and policies:

1. Present and planned products
2. Usefulness of test data for product development versus cost of obtaining data
3. Policy of company with respect to seeking technical breakthroughs, new developments at the frontiers of engineering knowledge, or incremental advances
4. Type of tests required by functional field
5. Type of test required by design engineering including tests to verify construction, proof tests, product quality control tests, and tests for operation
6. Promptness with which data will be required
7. Scope of supporting analytical work or interpretation required
8. Diversification and complexity of experimental work required
9. Degrees of refinement of data which will be required—this affects the choice of equipment needed
10. Degree to which literature searches and analyses may be substituted to obtain equivalent or satisfactory data
11. Need for models and simulation work. Often analog computers for simulation of operation of systems are included in the laboratory.

Laboratory Organization

The organization of the laboratory must, of course, be suited to handling the immediate work. There must be flexibility in the organization, and plans should be prepared for changing structure as either the laboratory grows or the direction of the work changes. The organizing principles discussed in earlier chapters apply here and to the other components of E & R administration as well.

The engineering laboratory may be organized along any of the following lines:

1. By technical function or field
2. Product project
3. Departmentalization according to facilities
4. Parallel to the engineering design organization

5. Combination of the above
6. Divided by the classification of tests into short-run and long-run tests
7. No formal permanent organization. People are assigned to a test when the test is scheduled.

Planning Test Equipment

The laboratory manager can do a much better job of planning for test equipment and associated instrumentation if he first analyzes the characteristics of these items. Consider some of the possible *classifications* of test equipment which affect the selection decision:

1. Essentially "permanent" equipment or "one-shot" equipment
2. General-purpose equipment or special-purpose equipment
3. Crude equipment for surveying or scoping investigations or refined, accurate, scientific equipment
4. Static or dynamic test equipment
5. Manually controlled or automatically controlled test equipment
6. Equipment designed for tests of the following types:
   a. Mechanical
   b. Electrical
   c. Electronic
   d. Chemical
   e. Metallurgical
   f. Thermal
   g. Nuclear
   h. Optical
   i. Sonic
   j. Aerodynamic and fluid flow
7. Fixed test equipment, semifixed equipment, mobile (around the laboratory), or field test equipment
8. Centralized test equipment or facilities whereby other test equipment is brought to the test equipment or decentralized test equipment. Examples of the former are nuclear reactors with test ports for equipment, cold chambers, or autoclaves
9. Test instrumentation.

Instrumentation

The necessity of instrumentation to collect experimental data is obvious. The reasons for using or *not* using instrumentation for control purposes in an experiment are not as obvious. A human may respond more quickly to changes in the experimental conditions than would an instrumented control system. This is particularly the case when many variables are involved, and any automated control system would be very complex.

Other factors which should be evaluated in selecting test instrumentation are interchangeability, flexibility, maintainability, reproducibility (precision), cost, anticipated future instrumentation that will be available and which will make the selected units obsolete, and calibration methods and requirements.

Besides test and control instrumentation, the laboratory manager must be concerned with calibration instrumentation. Some basic questions he must consider with regard to the purchase of calibration instrumentation are:

1. What is the cost of the calibration equipment under consideration?
2. What is the degree of difficulty of the calibration procedure? Are competent personnel available to do the job?
3. With what frequency must the instrumentation be calibrated?
4. Does the equipment need to be calibrated? Are relative readings, rather than absolute readings, of prime importance?
5. Should the calibration be contracted to an outside firm? What are the advantages and disadvantages of this action?

Budgeting

While budgeting principles for E & R are discussed in some detail in Chapter 10, there are a few special aspects of budgeting for E & R laboratories. In general, budgets for E & R laboratories should be prepared so that it is possible to measure performance against plans according to:

1. Each specific test (Avoid "open ended" test programs.)
2. The originating organization in design engineering. It should be possible to measure how well requestors are adhering to plans and how well they are planning. Poor planning on the part of design groups can thus be distinguished from poor performance of laboratory personnel.
3. The performing sub-component or individual in the laboratory
4. Labor costs, materials, subcontracts, and indirect costs. Location of any variance in these items narrows down the area where problems are occurring.

Procedures

Given an annual plan of work, a budget, and a schedule, what procedures need to be established for conducting work to implement the plan? It is apparent to anyone who has worked in engineering that tests will not be initiated on schedule or terminated as planned. Additional tests will be demanded by engineers, and requests to extend planned tests will often be received. Tests in some laboratories are operated on a day-to-day basis with no planning of procedures or specifications of the test. Is this an efficient way to operate even a small laboratory? The answer suggested here is that it is not! Formal procedures of some kind will lead to better implementation of plans. Plans, after all, should represent careful thinking and are worthless if they are not carried out with equal care.

Recording Test Results

Procedures should be established for this very important step in experimental work. If the test results are not properly recorded, the entire test may be worthless. In fact, improper recording of data may lead to misinterpretations which are very costly to the designer.

Test personnel should be indoctrinated with the idea that data should be recorded exactly as it appears. *Interpretation is a step which follows data recording; it does not precede data recording.* Too often, data takers in engineering laboratories make entries so that an erratic reading conforms to previous data, or they omit readings which do not seem to fit, or they may even add readings which they have never taken. Above all, honesty is a necessity for science and engineering.

Interpreting Results

As mentioned above, interpreting should be a separate and subsequent operation in relation to recording. There are two distinct aspects of interpretation. One is the objective interpretation of the raw data in terms of the conditions of the test. The other aspect of interpretation is not based on anything which appears on test result data charts.

The latter is represented by the subjective views of the operator. For example, did the operator notice that the recorders fluctuated or oscillated between readings? Did some parts of the equipment not appear to be working well? Did the operator hear unexpected noises during operation? Did some readings appear to result from erratic behavior of the recorder?

A very common problem in interpreting data occurs when a single reading is missing or is far out of line with all other readings. The common and improper procedure is to "fudge" the data. The proper procedure for the test engineer is:

1. To develop various hypotheses which could explain the out-of-line reading
2. To determine a value, by statistical methods, for the peculiar reading which minimizes the sum of the squares of the errors in the data representation
3. To present the actual data point, the calculated data point, and the hypotheses advanced for the explanation of the erratic reading.

Reporting Results—The Test Report

The greatest lack in engineering test groups is the failure to write reports, or, to write them in time to be useful. Research laboratory people share some of this failing. Because of stronger professional feeling, scientific researchers tend to write elegant reports, but these are often too late to be of use to the immediate customer.

The engineering job is not done, and the test is also incomplete until the results have been documented and sent to the customer—the design engineer.

Relationships With Design Engineers

The E & R laboratories are service groups, and the members of these staffs must so conduct themselves. In most companies, the income to the company is from the sale of products—hardware—rather than from the extensive sale of research alone. Responsibility for the design of hardware is vested in the design engineering organizations; laboratories are established to provide information and consultation. This philosophy must be accepted by laboratory personnel.

In the performance of their services, however, laboratory workers are entitled to be given the opportunity of doing a professional job. Within the scope of their responsibility, they have the right to, and should, conduct their work on a scientific basis according to the practices of their particular discipline. Not to do so would be a disservice to the engineering designer.

It is recognized that the value of experimental facilities lies in their ability to produce design information. To do this they must have adequate flexibility to adjust to modifications in current test programs.

THE COMPUTER CENTER

Engineering and research are each concerned with identifying or recognizing problems, defining the problems, conceiving and developing solutions, and evaluating results at each stage. Until the advent of electronic computers, the line dividing the creative and the decision processes in E & R from the mechanical and routine processes—the human from the machine processes—was fairly obvious. In engineering work in particular, electronic equipment of all types has begun to take over engineering functions such as conversion of data, computation, storage, retrieval of past experiences, reproducing, sorting, transporting, and printing or other recording of engineering data and results. Not only do the machines perform many of the functions formerly performed by engineering labor, but they perform them faster, more accurately, more cheaply, and in a quantity surpassing the human efforts of a lifetime.

Electronic computers now come in sizes to fit every budget and size of operation. Time sharing is becoming a common practice, and many E & R activities not only have their own computers, but they also have access to others on a time-sharing basis.

It is likely that engineering decision processes and control and the conduct of engineering work will be taken over more and more by computers. Engineers and scientists will be concerned with identifying problems, determining inputs to set the computers in action, and developing more complex programs. The more modern large computers will develop some of their own programs, and the trend in this direction will probably accelerate.

At the printing of the first edition of this book, the computer was still a novelty to many. Today it is a necessity—a commonly used tool. Tomorrow it will be a more sophisticated and an even more heavily used tool. Analog and digital computers will be more closely merged to provide more varied services.

Operation of a Computer Center

In actual operation of a computer center, the manager will face a number of unique problems. Housekeeping has been mentioned before. There are literally thousands of punched cards passing through a computer center, many of which are destined to become scrap and end up on the floor or on top of cabinets. Listings of data running into the hundreds of feet of paper are run off, and much of this paper is read and discarded. Some computer programs are filed and left to become obsolete, whereas others are taken out and then left on top of equipment. Computer manuals, miscellaneous notebooks, old program write-ups, etc., can all contribute to making the computer area resemble a rubbish heap unless tight housekeeping control is exercised. Adequate filing space for card programs, for tapes, and for supplies is necessary. Formalized treatment of program write-ups and facilities for storage of such records should be planned.

Computer programs should not be considered complete until they have been written up and bound in a notebook. Therefore new programs should not be taken on by a programmer until his previous ones have been completed. A completed record of a program should contain, as appropriate:

1. Systems chart
2. Computer flow chart
3. Detailed coding with explanation
4. Computer operating instructions
5. Final machine listing of the program and test results.

Procedures and methods are very important in such operations as card punching, verifying, duplicating, and card handling in general. Realistic time standards should be set for as many of these jobs as is possible, and a record of the backlog should be kept and analyzed.

When a computer is first put into operation, there is usually considerable excess capacity. If total costs of the computer center are distributed to the users, the charges may discourage other engineers from using the computer. In order to avoid this, the manager of the computer center should try to absorb excess capacity charges in his group by renting computer time to outsiders, and by personally seeking out major problems of the engineering groups which should be computed on the machine. Small amounts of excess capacity may be used for training purposes.

As the computer becomes a fixture in the E & R organization and engineers and scientists become aware of its usefulness, a backlog of problems begins to grow. Large problems will take up much of the machine time, particularly those machines which do not have "interrupt ability," thus, a problem once started cannot be taken off without losing all the work already done. The manager of the computer center must work out a system of priorities with the engineering managers. It is often advisable to establish one hour each day for short jobs of a few minutes and for debugging work. It should not be necessary to wait several days to get on the machine for this work. Debugging in particular should be practiced on a day-to-day basis.

Programming

A good, technically competent E & R administration group can provide its most valuable service by aiding technical management to plan, coordinate, and control the large projects. Management has been defined as the science of establishing proper objectives and efficiently utilizing human, material, and time resources to achieve the objectives. During each stage of a technical project, different numbers and kinds of people plus varying facilities and equipment are needed. Careful coordination is required to complete a project on time and within the budget.

What can an E & R programming group do to meet this critical need? It can perform the arduous task of gathering information, estimates, and background experience bearing on each new product. It can forge this voluminous detail into charts, time schedules, task descriptions, cost schedules, etc.

Programming is both an art and a science as discussed in Chapter 9.

THE ADMINISTRATOR

The E & R administration component must be headed and staffed by competent people having technical backgrounds and skills, in addition to required business and other necessary backgrounds and interests. They must have the common sense to avoid one major hazard—Parkinson's Law. Services should not be provided just because they are "nice to have." Records should not be kept just to be on the safe side.

The administration component should be headed by a man who has a deep understanding of, and sympathy with, the real needs of both technical personnel and management. At the same time, he must have the vision and boldness to streamline procedures, reduce red tape, and destroy obsolete records. In the latter connection, moreover, most *administrative* correspondence is as outdated as yesterday's newspaper. A dynamic organization moves ahead too fast to be bothered looking behind and getting involved in legalistic recriminations. *Technical* records are important and must be maintained in a discriminating manner.

The E & R administrator must be future-oriented. He must be concerned with means of expediting today's technical job and making tomorrow's job easier.

BIBLIOGRAPHY

"Automation in Research and Development," *Research/Development,* March, 1962.

DAMIANI, A. S. "Experience—Proven Technique to Guide R & D Planning Facility," *Plant Engineering,* October 2, 1968.

HISCOCKS, E. S. *Laboratory Administration.* London: Macmillan, 1956, and New York, N.Y.: St. Martin's Press, Inc., 1956.

IRVING, JAMES R. "Setting Up a Quality Control and Technical Development Laboratory." In *Technical Aids for Small Manufacturers.* Washington, D.C.: Small Business Administration, 1959.

KUSTANOWITZ, ALVIN L. "What Computer Service Centers Offer Engineers and Managers, *Chemical Engineering,* July 15, 1968.

LINVILLE, T. M. "Managing Research Labs," *Electrical Engineering,* November, 1958.

MEES, C. E. K., and LEERMAKER, JOHN A. *The Organization of Industrial Scientific Research.* New York, N.Y.: McGraw-Hill Book Company, 1950.

MURDICK, R. G. "Engineering Administration," *Machine Design,* July 7, 1960.

"Outlook in Lab Instrumentation," *Research/Development,* April, 1961.

SCHENCK, HILBERT, JR. *Theories of Engineering Experimentation.* New York, N.Y.: McGraw-Hill Book Company, 1961.

SMITH, RUTH. "Expansion Built into R/D Center," *Research/Development,* December, 1961.

STOETZEL, RALPH. "The Architect and the R & D Center," *Research/Development,* January, 1961.

CHAPTER 15

Packaging Engineering and Industrial Design

Industrial design, packaging, and packages themselves perform multiple services. Principal among these services are the containment, protection and enhancement of the product, and advertising. The cost of packaging America's products easily exceeded 20 billion dollars in 1962, while in 1968 it is estimated to have cost 35 billion dollars. Almost all of the packaging costs are ultimately passed on to the consumer.

The package is an indispensable item, and in many cases, a product in its own right. It is a necessity for liquids, powders, and granules; in fact, nearly every manufactured product, whether for industrial use or consumer use, must be packaged. There are also combinations of packages. For instance, some products require first, a bottle; next, the bottle is surrounded or contained within a carton; the carton is then placed with other bottles and cartons in cases and shipping devices, which are also essentially packages. Examples of these shipping devices are unitized loads on pallets, truck trailers, and unitized cargo cases.

A majority of consumer products must now fulfill both functional and aesthetic purposes if the manufacture and sale of the product is to be profitable. Satisfaction of ownership stems from both the utility of the product and the beauty that it contributes to its surroundings. In doing this, the package must create sales appeal.

To sell a product, the package must readily identify to the shopper the product's character and nature. Packaging is even affected by the age and sex of the user. Cigars, for example, are packaged for masculine appeal—at least up to the present, in the U. S. Cigarettes are packaged to appeal to both men and women. Other products are packaged to appeal to children; for example, the cartons containing breakfast foods.

Some products remain in the customer's home for long periods—weeks, months, and even years. This type of packaging must naturally be decorative and must be designed to give long-lasting service, offer pleasure, and win admiration. Packages which contain perishable products, on the other hand, usually are designed for a short life span. The customer derives only as much direct benefit as their primary function demands.

There are four main factors affecting packaging. First, the fundamental functions of the package are the protection and containment of the product, a factor which can be successfully attacked by well-understood techniques and engineering principles. Second, messages can be incorporated as part of the package which permits the package to carry a portion of the advertising burden. In fact, it is conceded by many that the size, shape, and feel of the package, plus its printed message, has as great an effect on the consumer of shelf goods as all the rest of the advertising effort. Third, the cost of the package ranges from a fraction of a percent to nearly the entire cost of the material sold. Fourth, is the fact that there is not, as yet, a clear-cut profession of industrial design and packaging Everyone with legitimate interests in packaging, even the consumer, feels he has some competence in the field. Many interests must be served and the central issue is how to do this most effectively.

MANAGERIAL CONSIDERATIONS

Problems Concerning the Package

In addition to the broad general purposes previously stated, there must be added some particular considerations of great importance to management.

A factor closely associated with protection is that of convenience to the producer, to the intermediate handler, and to the consumer. If convenience is increased, the costs of handling, transportation, and related problems are reduced. One of the largest cost components of a manufactured product is that of material handling. The package has a direct influence on the amount of material handling required in production, in distribution, and in the use of many products.

Convenience also enters into self-service selling. Here the product, or its containing package, must do practically all the work which was previously performed by the salesman of not more than a decade ago. It is not surprising that many manufacturers have over-reacted to this situation. For example, some firms have produced packages which "scream" to attract the attention of the purchaser. This approach works only as long as all of the other packages on the adjacent shelves are not "screaming" with equal vigor. Inversely, the same would be true for a "whispering" package. The "whispering" package surrounded by "screaming" packages would attract attention; however, if all the other packages "whisper" then no attention is gained.

Changing package designs rapidly is not the road to long-run profits. It leads, instead, to confusion on the part of the buyer who holds the key to successful selling. Managers generally agree that they do not want to create confusion in the minds of their customers.

It must be understood by the E & R manager that the greatest overall satisfaction is not necessarily found exclusively in the use of the product. Satisfaction can also come from pride of ownership, from the knowledge or having made a satisfactory business transaction, and from the feeling that the buyer has received an honest return for his investment. Ease of use and good performance are important. Related to this are the instructions, for example, for the making of a cake, or for the assembly of a wagon.

The entire field of industrial design in packaging is open to enormous possibilities for development and research. New materials open new approaches and at the same time pose new problems. For example, when dry cleaners ceased using the conventional paper cover on dry-cleaned articles and replaced it with a polyethylene bag, it seemed that a wonderful improvement had been made. Truly there had because the clean garment could then be displayed in all its beauty. However, the "fly in the ointment" was the fact that the polyethylene bag was something that children apparently liked to play with, and, unfortunately, many of them suffocated before manufacturers began putting holes in the bags to reduce this hazard.

A long-felt need is the easy disposal of discarded packages, one of the principal ingredients of garbage, which has become a problem. Here is an almost untapped mine of potential customer satisfaction. Thus, management's problem is not whether new concepts should be sought, but rather how they should be sought and how the new concepts are to be used.

Unity between the product and its package appears to be one of the most important needs in the field of packaging.

The Problem Related to Required Skills

It can be seen from the previous discussion that the basic physical considerations of package selection are: the nature of the product; service features associated with the package; the product's shelf life; package disposability; re-usability by consumer and/or manufacturer; necessary reclosing features; beauty; and the materials availability for use in making packages. It is easily apparent that the industrial design and packaging problem is compounded of technical matters concerning the products, the package, and the package's interaction with the product; of marketing and selling factors; of customer utilization and satisfaction; and of cost factors. Not only are all of these items closely related, but they also interact. For example, providing a window in the face of a box will require a change in advertising copy, a possible change in the product in order to retain color on exposure to light which, in turn, may affect the product's shelf life, plus a change in the machinery required in the plant. All of these affect costs as well as the advertising and merchandising functions.

All of these factors point up the need for a variety of skills required by industrial designers and packaging personnel. It is also rather obvious that engineering skills are needed. Not only is mechanical engineering skill needed, but chemical engineering as well, in the case of many products. In fact, it is not difficult to find some need for almost all of the basic kinds of engineering skill.

Cost has been mentioned on many occasions and also problems related to manufacturing and material handling. These call for a high degree of skill in cost estimating, plant layout, material handling, and similiar activities—all of which are encompassed within the relatively new field of industrial engineering.

In many cases the reaction of the customer is of prime importance, and skill in human engineering and motivation research in addition to conventional market research and marketing are required.

Coordination of the activities of the product design staff, the package and industrial design personnel, and the consumer research group, is necessary. Therefore it is desirable to have on the package and industrial design staff at least one person who has had experience in the design of the company's product and who has been associated closely enough with the users to know the most wanted features of the package and the product. A product engineer with field experience might provide this required background and skill.

It is obvious that no one individual can fill all the requirements and that probably a minimum of four people would be needed to provide the required skills. Finding people with the requisite skills is indeed a major problem.

THE ORGANIZATION PROBLEM

Organizational Development Patterns

Since E & R always has some industrial design and packaging responsibility, the manager of E & R needs to be acquainted with the commonly encountered ways of handling this problem. He must realize from the outset that industrial design in packaging is a service function. The industrial design group must serve all of the functional points of engineering as well as work with and perhaps serve other organizational elements entirely outside of the field of engineering.

That packaging and industrial design is important to American industry and that it has been recognized by some people, at any rate, as a profes-

Degree of Professional Approach to Packaging

Industry	Rank	No. of Answers	Av. Score	Percent
Cosmetics	1	8	16.6	69.2
Tobacco products	2	5	14.4	60.0
Food processors	3	41	14.3	59.9
Pharmaceuticals	4	12	13.2	55.3
Paper products	5	5	12.0	50.0
Appliances	6	8	11.5	48.0
Building materials	7	9	11.3	47.3
Variety stores	8	4	11.0	45.9
			10.9	45.4 (Average)
Industrial chemicals	9	13	10.6	44.2
Oil products	10	8	9.7	40.5
Industrial equipment	11	33	9.2	38.5
Industrial devices	12	16	9.0	37.7
Furniture	13	6	8.6	36.0
Automotive products	14	8	8.6	35.8
Clothing	15	10	7.7	32.0
Packaging suppliers	16	16	5.5	22.9

Maximum possible score: 24.00

Fig. 15-1. Results by industry of survey covering degree of professional approach to packaging. *Source:* Research Project reported in *Company Organization for Packaging Efficiency*, by Professor Donald D. Deming of Rensselaer Polytechnic Institute's School of Management, and sponsored by the American Foundation for Management Research, New York.

sional and separate problem is illustrated by Fig. 15-1 which tabulates the degree of professional approach to packaging. It is extracted from "Company Organization for Packaging Efficiency" by Professor Donald D. Deming of Rensselaer Polytechnic Institute and it describes a research project conducted for the American Foundation for Management Research.

The degree of professional approach to packaging was measured by the following six criteria:

1. Use of a formal packaging organization. (No = 0; Yes = 4)
2. The firm does its own research. (No = 0; Yes = 4)
3. The firm uses professional consultants. (No = 0; Occasionally = 2; Frequently = 4)
4. The firm uses package suppliers' services. (No = 0; Occasionally = 2; Frequently = 4)
5. The firm uses market research to assist in the selection of a proposed package. (Never = 0; Seldom = 1; Occasionally = 2; Frequently = 3; Always = 4)
6. The firm uses market research to assess the effectiveness of existing packages. (Never = 0; Seldom = 1; Occasionally = 2; Frequently = 3; Always = 4)

Each of the above criteria was given equal weight. Figure 15-1 lists, from top to bottom and by industry, the more professional approaches. The average score by industry groups indicates the number of points out of a possible 24.

Even though the packaging problem has been approached on a professional basis, industry is not agreed as to how it should be organized; neither have our educational institutions agreed upon how to educate men for this activity.

While there is no well-recognized and best way of handling the packaging and industrial design problem, certain evolutionary forms or approaches can be noted. Initially a manufacturing firm may have no packaging specialist. All activities relating to packaging and industrial design are handled by the various existing departments in the course of their regular assignments. Each department gives the industrial design and packaging function a portion of its attention. Thus, Manufacturing, Engineering, Advertising, Purchasing, Traffic, Quality Control, and even Legal Counsel may be involved. At this point it is not uncommon for top management to eventually decide that a coordinator is needed to blend properly these various interests, and a packaging specialist position is established to make sure that the work gets done correctly. This approach makes it possible for management to look to one person for getting results in a packaging and industrial design area.

Another approach which often occurs in the handling of the packaging problem is the establishment of a packaging committee with membership consisting of all departments having responsibilities in this area of endeavor. A committee often exists, even where a formalized packaging department has been established. It can serve the valuable purpose of unifying viewpoints, increasing understanding, and achieving positive support for an agreed-upon course of action. If it is expected to function in lieu of a manager of Packaging and is therefore to be an action group, it is subject to all of the limitations of any committee. The usage of the packaging committee is quite popular as illustrated in Fig. 15-2.

Still another developmental form occurs when a manager—he may be the E & R manager, a marketing manager, or the company treasurer (as in one medium-sized bakery firm)—is assigned authority and responsibility for most package decision-making and administration in addition to his regular duties.

An advanced form of organizational development involves the creation of an entire industrial design and packaging (IDP) department. This approach is most often found in large companies. In this centralized department is placed a majority of the activities formerly carried out by other operating and staff units, such as package design, industrial design, art work, testing, engineering, and general administration of package planning and

Do You Have a Packaging Committee?

Industry	Rank	No. of Answers	Percent of Yes Answers	Weight
Cosmetics	1	8	75	3.00
Tobacco products	2	5	60	2.40
Appliances	3	8	50	2.00
Oil products	4	8	50	2.00
Food processors	5	41	39	1.56
Industrial chemicals	6	13	31	1.23
Automotive products	7	8	25	1.00
Building materials	8	9	22	0.89
Industrial equipment	9	33	21	0.85
Clothing	10	10	20	0.80
Paper products	11	5	20	0.80
Industrial devices	12	16	19	0.75
Package suppliers	13	16	19	0.75
Pharmaceuticals	14	12	17	0.67
Furniture	15	6	0	0.00
Variety stores	16	4	0	0.00

Fig. 15-2. Tabulation by industry of answers to question: "Do you have a packaging committee?" *Source:* See Fig. 15-1.

control. Figure 15-3 illustrates how various industries have reacted to the establishment of a formal packaging and industrial design organization.

Does Your Firm Have a Formal Packaging Organization?

Industry	Rank	No. of Answers	Percent of Yes Answers	Weight
Variety stores	1	4	100	4.00
Cosmetics	2	8	87	3.50
Pharmaceuticals	3	12	83	3.33
Industrial devices	4	16	69	2.75
Furniture	5	6	67	2.67
Industrial equipment	6	33	64	2.55
Appliances	7	8	63	2.50
Industrial chemicals	8	13	62	2.46
Food processors	9	41	61	2.44
			56	2.23 (Average)
Building materials	10	9	56	2.22
Automotive products	11	8	50	2.00
Package suppliers	12	16	44	1.75
Paper products	13	5	40	1.60
Oil products	14	8	25	1.00
Tobacco products	15	5	20	0.80
Clothing	16	10	0	0.00

Maximum possible score: 4.00

Fig. 15-3. Tabulation by industry of answers to question: "Does your firm have a formal packaging organization?" *Source:* See Fig. 15-1.

When Should an IDP Department Be Established?

The key problems are questions in the minds of management such as: When, if ever, should a separate packaging department be established? To whom should it report? At what level in the organization does it properly belong? What functions should be centralized in this department?

Some of the factors and conditions which tend to make it advantageous to create a separate industrial design and packaging department are when:

1. The package is an important factor affecting the sale of the product.
2. Packaging costs are significant in relation to the cost of the product.
3. There is enough packaging work to be performed to occupy at least one person full time. (This condition is not usually met for the small manufacturer.)
4. Excessive complaints, delays, damage to product, and inadequate attention to packaging results from having duties divided among several departments.
5. Specialization of knowledge and skills is desirable. A full-time specialist who concentrates upon a particular field of work often is able to solve problems more quickly and better because he has the necessary information and know-how which a non-specialist does not.
6. Top management desires to place greater emphasis upon packaging.
7. Problems of coordination among several departments involved become excessive. "Buck-passing" may exist among such functions as advertising, market research, purchasing, traffic, and production.

The "opposite side of the coin" occurs for companies that do not have enough work to justify a full-time person for this activity, when packaging and industrial design is of only moderate importance to the promotion and sale of the product, protection problems are simple, and when the work is being carried out smoothly and successfully by each of the various individuals in other functional areas. Centralization may lead to a lack of consultation among those groups having a legitimate interest in the industrial design and packaging decision.

Where in the organizational structure of a company should the packaging department be situated? A survey of actual organizational arrangements indicates a great variation in practice, and it is almost impossible to detect any fixed pattern even for a given industry. This is illustrated by Fig. 15-4 which quotes the previously cited packaging research project. Figure 15-4 illustrates the manner in which various industries have fitted packaging responsibilities into their organizational structure. In reading this table we can see that a higher percentage of the appliance industry places the packaging responsibility within Engineering. However, the same industry also places the packaging responsibility under Marketing. In placing it under Marketing the paper industry is first and the appliance industry

Various Company Departments in Charge of Packaging

Rank	Engineering	Marketing	Purchasing	Production
1	Appliances	Paper	Food	Pharm.
2	Building	Oil	Furniture	Ind. chem.
3	Oil	Appliances	Cosmetics	Paper
4	Furniture	Ind. equip.	Ind. devices	Building
5	Ind. devices		Ind. chem.	Furniture
6	Cosmetics		Ind. equip.	Ind. equip.
7	Package			Ind. devices
8	Ind. chem.			Package
9	Ind. equip.			Food
10	Food			Auto prods.
11				Appliances
12				Cosemetics

Rank	Manager	President	Advertising	Sales
1	Auto prods.	Tobacco	Variety	Appliances
2	Variety	Package	Cosmetics	Package
3	Oil	Building	Ind. equip.	Food
4	Ind. equip.	Food	Furniture	
5	Cosmetics	Ind. devices		
6	Pharm.	Cosmetics		
7	Package	Pharm.		
8	Furniture	Ind. chem.		
9	Food	Ind. equip.		
10	Ind. devices			
11	Ind. chem.			

Fig. 15-4. Tabulation by industry of various company departments in charge of packaging. *Source:* See Fig. 15-1.

falls into third place. No cases were found in the appliance industry where packaging was placed under Purchasing; however, it was found that the appliance industry did occasionally place it under Production. Among those firms in which packaging was placed under the production function the appliance industry ranked eleventh, whereas pharmaceuticals ranked first.

Another problem associated with the organization of the IDP function is that of level. The head of IDP functions usually is a member of middle management. The proper level in the management hierarchy for the placement of the man in charge of IDP is dependent upon how important this function or activity is to the over-all objectives of the company and the amount of money involved in packaging.

Clearly top management decision-making is necessary where questions of corporate identity are involved and where the package can have a serious effect upon the ultimate success of the business. The packaging department can do the planning, the creating, and the proposing, but it obviously cannot make the final decision.

At the other extreme, it is inadvisable to place the activity at the lowest rung of the management ladder. If this is done, the head of the IDP function cannot work effectively and hold his own in discussions and decision-making activities among the directors of Marketing, Advertising, Purchasing, Engineering, and Manufacturing. He must have sufficient power and status; otherwise, his voice will become lost.

Suggested Approach to Organizing for Packaging

Most companies have found it difficult, if not impossible, to resolve the conflicts in interests that occur if a separate packaging department is established with every possible packaging and industrial design responsibility seated within it. In fact, it is doubtful that this ever will be the "pattern of the future," especially where the package can affect customer action at the point of sale. The suggested approach to organizing IDP which now follows is believed to be appropriate and applicable in medium to large and in both industrial and consumer product companies. What is suggested is that it is appropriate to establish a packaging and industrial design function in E & R. It should normally be assigned the following functions:

1. Designs packages, giving adequate consideration to primary function, utility, cost, protection, advertising, and graphic arts aspects. It involves considerations of size, shape, strength, weight, chemical and physical properties, as well as color and form. Provision must be made in the design for problems involved with filling, closing, handling, transporting, and use of containers.
2. Conducts or arranges for appropriate physical and chemical tests of packages, packaging materials, inserts, cushioning, containers, wrappings, etc. This may involve utilizing services of the company's own testing facilities or outside testing organizations. Test shipment of goods may also be made.
3. Prepares, distributes, and maintains written package specifications.
4. Evaluates proposed and existing packages. This will involve using information obtained from departments such as consumer service, market research, manufacturing, engineering, traffic, legal, and cost accounting.
5. Keeps fully informed of new developments in the field.
6. Provides counsel and information to other units in the company.
7. Maintains an adequate library of technical information on packaging, including samples of packaging materials and data on their characteristics.
8. Maintains equipment necessary to build sample packages. Builds sample packages for evaluation for own group and others concerned with the packaging and industrial design problem.
9. Performs the packaging activities with adequate regard for costs.

The purchase of packaging materials usually is best handled by the same department which buys all other materials—the purchasing department. However, Purchasing must recognize that its responsibility for buying is equally subject to problems stemming from Advertising (if the package has a major affect upon sales) as it is from the package design function. It is this multiple responsibility that has brought about the popularity of the packaging committee, whose primary responsibilities are the dissemination of information and the unification of viewpoints. Such a committee would be advisable in most companies using the approach suggested. Marketing, including its arm of Advertising, should usually handle all things related to the impression that the package makes upon the customer. Marketing also is involved in market research, whether conducted internally or subcontracted to outside organizations. That marketing research as related to the packages used is important to industry in general is illustrated by Fig. 15-5. In addition, marketing research is used to assess the effectiveness of existing packages as illustrated in Fig. 15-6.

How Often Do You Use Market Research to Select the Proposed Package?

Industry	Rank	No. of Answers	Score	Percent
Cosmetics	1	8	2.75	68.8
Food processors	2	41	2.44	60.6
Paper products	3	5	2.20	55.0
Tobacco products	4	5	2.00	50.0
Pharmaceuticals	5	12	1.92	48.0
Building materials	6	9	1.67	41.8
Clothing	7	10	1.30	32.5
Oil products	8	8	1.25	31.3
Variety stores	9	4	1.25	31.3
Industrial chemicals	10	13	1.23	31.2
Industrial devices	11	16	1.19	29.8
Appliances	12	8	1.00	25.0
Automotive products	13	8	1.00	25.0
Furniture	14	6	1.00	25.0
Industrial equipment	15	33	0.97	24.3
Package suppliers	16	16	0.69	17.3

Fig. 15-5. Tabulation by industry of answers to question: "How often do you use market research to select the proposed package?" *Source:* See Fig. 15-1.

It will depend upon cooperativeness of personnel, employee's morale, employee's loyalty, and the personality of concerned managers as to whether an over-all packaging coordinator should be established. If such an individual is established, he should function as a staff coordinator and should be attached to the chief operating executive. He then becomes essentially responsible for, and serves as the administrative unit, through which packaging ideas, problems, questions, plans, and procedures are resolved.

How Often Do You Use Market Research to Assess Effectiveness of Existing Package?

Industry	Rank	No. of Answers	Score	Percent
Cosmetics	1	8	2.38	59.5
Food processors	2	41	2.10	52.5
Tobacco products	3	5	2.00	50.0
Building materials	4	9	1.89	47.3
Pharmaceuticals	5	12	1.88	47.0
Oil products	6	8	1.50	37.5
Paper products	7	5	1.40	35.0
Industrial chemicals	8	13	1.39	34.5
Appliances	9	8	1.25	31.3
Variety stores	10	4	1.25	31.3
Clothing	11	10	1.20	30.0
Automotive products	12	8	1.13	28.3
Industrial devices	13	16	1.13	28.3
Industrial equipment	14	33	1.06	26.7
Furniture	15	6	1.00	25.0
Package suppliers	16	16	.79	19.8

Fig. 15-6. Tabulation by industry of answers to question: "How often do you use market research to assess effectiveness of existing package?" *Source:* See Fig. 15-1.

Services Offered by Package Manufacturers and Machinery Suppliers

The manufacturer of packages can usually provide a certain amount of technical assistance to the user. As a general rule such services fall into two categories: (1) the selection of material and the package design for economical functioning of the package as a protective and containing device, and (2) services dealing with the service treatment of the package such as its communicative features and art work.

Package material manufacturers frequently provide service to both the converter and to the ultimate manufacturer. This service has broadened in scope as a result of the introduction of many new and unfamiliar packaging materials. It has become a virtual necessity to familiarize the converter and the user with the physical specifications and limitations of the new materials.

Packaging machinery manufacturers offer customers a variety of services concerned with the installation and proper adjustment of equipment and the training of personnel to operate the machinery. A few machinery manufacturers can provide additional services such as research and development and contract maintenance.

Contract packaging companies are equipped to fill packages and put them into cartons which in turn can be placed in shipping containers for shipment to the ultimate destination. Such service can make possible the elimination of handling the packaging problem internally.

Packaging laboratories have been set up for testing packages on a contract basis. Package materials, package designs, the interaction of such factors as compatibility of package materials and product, the effect of climatic conditions on packaging materials and designs, and the physical strength of basic packaging structures are but a few of the services offered by such laboratories.

The scope of packaging design services offered by package manufacturers varies greatly. The nature of the basic packaging material is a major controlling factor. For example, the services that the manufacturer of basic polyethylene offers are directed towards expanding the use of his product. To achieve this objective, the makers of such products have found it necessary to assist the packaging industry to learn the methods of developing the machines and techniques which will permit the most effective use of this material. On the other hand, they offer little if any service in the area of packaging design and art work. Paper box manufacturers, on the other hand, provide design service which will make the most effective use of the materials and printing processes which they have to sell.

Some of the very large manufacturers of packages and packaging products offer services which can even challenge the best of the industrial design firms in terms of breadth of service, quality of specialized personnel, and testing facilities. One such company maintains a large laboratory facility, separate in organization from the other branches of the company. The laboratory maintains a staff of qualified package designers, artists, and research personnel who use all of the laboratory devices for measuring the perceptual effect of various packages and the surface design and any other feature of the package which might affect its ultimate success. This same firm, in addition to its research staff and newest testing equipment, also has a small auditorium for use in presenting design work and research findings. It is here that customers are shown the work in process, the recommendations, and general displays of staff efforts.

While a few package manufacturers have design staffs of more than 100 people, it is more usual to find firms with ten or fewer employees in this category. Some package producers have very small staffs and have no marketing or motivational research as part of their service.

It is quite common to use suppliers' services as is illustrated by Fig. 15-7.

THE INDUSTRIAL DESIGN AND PACKAGING CONSULTANT

Most of the discussion so far in this chapter has emphasized the term "packaging." When going to outside firms for help in packaging and industrial design, such outside firms tend to emphasize the term "industrial design." In its more limited sense, "industrial design" means only the

How Often, if at All, Do You Use Supplier Services?

Industry	Rank	No. of Answers	Score	Percent.
Tobacco products	1	5	4.00	100.0
Appliances	2	8	3.75	93.8
Building materials	3	9	3.56	89.0
Food processors	4	41	3.42	85.6
Industrial chemicals	5	13	3.39	84.9
Furniture	6	6	3.33	83.3
Phamaceuticals	7	12	3.33	83.3
Paper products	8	5	3.20	80.0
Automotive products	9	8	3.00	75.0
Oil products	10	8	3.00	75.0
Variety stores	11	4	3.00	75.0
Clothing	12	10	2.80	70.0
Cosmetics	13	8	2.75	68.9
Industrial equipment	14	33	2.73	68.3
Industrial devices	15	16	2.25	56.2
Package suppliers	16	16	1.50	37.5

Fig. 15-7. Tabulation by industry of answers to question: "How often, if at all, do you use supplier services?" *Source:* See Fig. 15-1.

shaping and coloring the product or packaging. In its widest sense, the term "industrial design" involves a whole philosophy.

"The designer aims at having a complete view of the product from all aspects, which among other things cover the following:

The application of:	Creative imagination Discriminative judgment
In terms of:	Form Color Texture
In relationship to:	Use User Environment
With consideration to:	Performance Structure Materials Manufacturing process Distribution

"The Industrial Designer is fully aware that he cannot be an expert in all these fields. His principal aim, therefore, is to coordinate the various aspects of the work and bring up questions for discussion. He tries to get the people normally working with the product out of their traditional way of thinking and open their eyes to matters in which they are professionally blind. In other words, he tries to get them to produce new ideas themselves. However, the Industrial Designer must be able to master at least two things by himself: judging shape and judging colour combinations."[1]

The successful independent industrial design consultant is a strange mixture of artist, architect, engineer, market and consumer research worker and, last but not least, a business man, both for himself and for his clients. Most industrial designers appear ready to cope with everything in the design field from trade-marks and letterheads to packaging, window displays, and consumer goods. Some will also tackle producer goods such as heavy industrial equipment, as well as military equipment. Many of the major industrial design firms have been involved in designing even the interiors of atomic submarines as well as designing tanks and other similar military equipment.

The consultant, without exception, will work closely with the client's own design and engineering facilities. It is rare that an industrial designer will supply the client with production engineering drawings.

In regard to payment, the industrial design consultant rarely, if ever, will accept royalties as part of his fee. Usually, the consultant is paid a retainer or fixed fee.

If a retainer is involved, the client pays the consultant a yearly amount for his advice and work; however, the work provided must be within cer-

How Often, if at All, Do You Use Consultants?

Industry	Rank	No. of Answers	Score	Percent
Tobacco products	1	5	3.20	80.0
Paper products	2	5	2.80	70.0
Food processors	3	41	2.44	60.5
Cosmetics	4	8	2.25	56.3
Pharmaceuticals	5	12	2.17	54.1
Clothing	6	10	1.60	40.0
Variety stores	7	4	1.50	37.5
Building materials	8	9	1.11	27.8
Industrial equipment	9	33	1.09	27.3
Appliances	10	8	1.00	25.0
Industrial devices	11	16	1.00	25.0
Oil products	12	8	1.00	25.0
Industrial chemicals	13	13	0.92	23.0
Furniture	14	6	0.67	16.8
Package suppliers	15	16	0.63	15.8
Automotive products	16	8	0.50	12.5

Fig. 15-8. Tabulation by industry of answers to question: "How often, if at all, do you use consultants?" *Source:* See Fig. 15-1.

[1] "Industrial Design in the United States," published by The European Productivity Agency of the Organization for Eurpoean Economic Co-operation, Paris, France, 1959.

tain limits which are fixed by contract. If the client calls upon the consultant to do a specific job outside the terms of the contract, he must pay an additional sum to cover all the direct and indirect expenses involved. It is quite common to find industrial design consultants paid on a retainer basis.

A second approach is the fixed fee basis where the consultant agrees to do a specific job. Hourly rates charged by consultants vary from around seven to ten dollars for a junior assistant to a maximum of 30 to 40 dollars per hour for a senior industrial designer. That consultants are often used is illustrated in Fig. 15-8.

CONCLUDING REMARKS

The various considerations involved in industrial design and packaging have been discussed, and the organizational problems have been treated in considerable depth. Appendix 15-A is an attempt to provide basic concepts in outline form and more importantly a packaging and industrial design check list of the various factors that must be considered in handling the important functions of packaging and industrial design.

APPENDIX 15A

Packaging Engineering and Industrial Design Check List

THE FUNCTIONAL PACKAGE

1. Packaging and industrial designers, as well as marketing, manufacturing, purchasing, and engineering personnel must participate in the design of the product.
2. Human engineering studies should be made when panels or controls are involved.
3. Mechanical, electrical, chemical, and cost considerations in designing functional packages (casings).
   a. Protective requirements
   b. Appearance requirements
   c. Material handling requirements
   d. Operational or functional requirements
   e. Cost factors
   f. Labeling factors such as trade-mark, patent number, electrical or physical limits, weight, warnings, etc.
   g. Standardization.

THE CONTAINER-PACKAGE

1. Packaging and industrial designers, as well as Marketing, Manufacturing, Purchasing, and Engineering participate not only in the design of the product, but also the package.
2. Types of containers:
   a. Paper, paperboard, and casings
   b. Films, foils, and laminations
   c. Adhesives and tapes
   d. Paperboard packages
   e. Flexible packages
   f. Plastic packages—molded and sheet
   g. Metal packages
   h. Glass packages, closures, and caps.
3. Mechanical, electrical, chemical, labeling, packaging, legal, and cost considerations in designing containers:
   a. Protective requirements
   b. Appearance requirements and importance of color
   c. Labeling requirements
   d. Packaging requirements
   e. Legal considerations
   f. Material handling considerations and shipping regulations.

g. Reusability of container
h. Standardization and preferred sizes
i. Aerosols, valves, and propellants.

PRODUCT AND PACKAGE

Product Characteristics

Physical form

Fragile	Oily or greasy
Gaseous	Powder
Granular	Solid
Liquid	Viscous.

Is water-vapor protection needed in:

Manufacture
Marketing and distribution
Use by consumer?

Does the product face hazards from:

Light	Handling	Sifting	Fungi
Bacteria	Cold	Leakage	Odors
Mold	Heat	Insects	Vapors
Corrosion	Thermal change	Pilferage	Chemicals
Rodents	Barometric change	Impact	Oils
Shipment	Humidity change	Shock	Greases?

Other considerations:
Must seals on package material give same protection as package material?
Is reclosure needed to protect unused portion?
Will product and package interact chemically?

Material Selection

Appropriateness
Is structural strength sufficient and consistent with intended use of the product and/or packages?
In "producibility," will the product and/or package lend itself readily to the forming processes of fabricating, graphic arts, etc.?
Are inks, adhesives, etc., properly selected for use on the package material and for resisting all hazards that will be encountered?
Is the material used familiar to consumers in form, shape, and texture or will it require "selling"?

Adequacy of structure
Will it permit mechanized production?
Can it withstand the extremes of temperature encountered in storage and shipment?
Will it physically "withstand" the handling in warehouses, transportation, and retail stores?

Must the package prevent the loss of:
Aroma, flavor or any other volatile components?

Color?
Physical shape of product (breakage of tablets, etc.)?

Will the package:
Protect against odors?
Prevent oxidation or chemical reactions?
Permit vacuum, gas or hermetic packing, if this is required?
Maintain the product in a sterile condition where this is required?

Availability
Is steady supply of material assured?
Are delivery dates timely?
Do prices fluctuate?
Are prices in line with all other factors?
Have all possible sources of supply been listed and checked?

COORDINATION IN PLANNING

Internal
Are all concerned departments represented?

E & R	Production
Market Research	Legal
Purchasing	Sales
Art	Advertising
Marketing	Other.

In respect to package size, appearance and/or structure, are there any conflicts to be compromised?
Have all specifications—color identity, dimensions, special fabrication, material, instructions, etc. been established and recorded?

External
Have all possible steps been taken to ascertain dealer attitudes?
Has Market Research established that there will be good consumer acceptance for product *and* package?

PRODUCTION AND HANDLING

MANUFACTURING CONSIDERATIONS

Equipment
Can package be formed, filled, weighed and closed on existing equipment?
Would a change in the package avoid need for new equipment?
Would a modified package form make it possible to use new types of equipment to increase efficiency and reduce cost?
Has an anticipated production schedule been planned, and can it be accomplished?
Will the package readily adapt itself to changing demands in volume?
Does package lend itself to standardization?

Personnel
Will the package(s) permit standardized operations?
Will it require special personnel?
Does construction make possible minimum personnel in packaging operations?

Does the package impose unusual difficulties of breakage or inspection?
Will production involve hazards to personnel?

Design and structure
Is the container of the right size and shape to make possible the movement through packaging line at right speed?
Is the closure suited to efficient line operations?
Are package openings adapted to filling devices?
Are there suitable surfaces or spaces for labeling?
Is the package and/or shell "engineered" for sufficient shock resistance in machine handling?
Does the design permit proper storage and handling?

Pre-production factors
Will fabrication involve standard or unusual methods and equipment?
Can packages be shipped and stored readily before delivery to production line?
Are convenient sources of service and supply available?
Are adequate alternate sources of supply available?
Are materials and containers packaged so as to permit automatic feed to the packaging line?
Have problems of inspection, quality, and inventory control been considered regarding incoming supplies?

Convenience Factors

Packing and shipment
Can the various packaging materials be conveniently and easily assembled for packaging?
Is the package of proper weight or capacity in relation to the bulk container?
Can the package be adapted for shipment in end-use cases?
Is there an accepted method of packing the product for shipment? Can it be used?
Is the unit package properly adapted for convenient bulk packaging and handling?
Have packages been considered in relation to over-all problems of materials handling?

Economic Considerations

Has material used been kept to a minimum?
Does the package comply with standardization practices that make for economy in all operations?

Is container cost in proper proportion with:
Product price and/or cost?
Market to be reached?
Class of product?

Does price paid for packaging material assure a minimum number of defects?
Does the package protect for normal product life plus providing an adequate margin of safety?
In weight, size, and structure, will the package be economical to the shipper and intermediate handlers?

MERCHANDISING

The Package and Its Target

The product
- Is it a new product?
- Has its relative quality been analyzed competitively?
- Have its special points been listed?

Have all potential package choices been listed and studied in regard to:
- Which packages will reach what markets best?
- New or improved materials or packages that may permit longer shelf life and distribution over a wider area?
- Additional package forms (such as aerosols) and sizes (such as unit packs) that may open new outlets, permit greater market penetration?
- Special markets: do-it-yourself, juvenile, senior, suburbanite, dietary, etc.?

The market

Has it been determined who the ultimate consumer is with regard to:

Age	Geographical location
Income	Socio-cultural level
Sex	Export potential
Race	Ethnological background

The distribution plan—what channels will be used to sell:

Independents	Chains
Self-service	Mail order
House-to-house	Other

Buying habits
- Have you checked retailer buying and usage habits with regard to:
  - Size of purchase?
  - Storage prior to sale?
  - Display on shelf, counter or window?
- Is package adapted for mass display?
- Is a single unit attractive?
- Will package be seen above and/or below eye level? Will the label panel be displayed?
- Will point-of-sale support be expected?

Size considerations
- Is package size adapted to:
  - Distribution methods,
  - Consumer habits?
- Will changes of package size affect:
  - Consumer convenience,
  - Quantity of purchase?

Competition
- Has the product and its package been compared with that offered by competition?
- Have competitive packages been compared relative to:
  - Materials used,

Sizes,
Shapes,
Colors,
Designs?

Has it been considered whether the package should resemble competing packages or be distinctively individual? (Consider this question from the viewpoint of the manufacturer, wholesaler, retailer, and the consumer.)

PACKAGE APPEARANCE

Identification

Are all necessary features present, properly positioned, and emphasized?
Is the brand name unmistakably in position and style?
Does the package adequately feature trade name?
Is the name of the manufacturer given due prominence?
Is the product name featured for quick identity?

Does the package reflect:
The outstanding qualities of the product?
The maker's integrity?
Is an advertising tie-in possible?
Is the package, including the colors used, adapted to TV—both color and black-and-white?

Information

Does package carry all mandatory information in an acceptable manner?
Are there special legal regulations that must be observed?
Are instructions and uses legible?
Can directions and instructions be clarified, shortened, or improved?
Do the illustrations instruct, interest and/or attract the consumer?
Should a price panel be provided?
Is code marking needed?

Inviting attention

Does the package make a pleasing impression on the consumer:
From a distance?
From a close view?
On the shelf, counter or window?
In the consumer's home?
As a gift?
Does it carry a self-selling story?
Can visibility and appeal labeling be combined?
Is its remembrance value high?
Is the package a self-sufficient advertising unit?

DISTRIBUTION FACTORS

Is the package size and shape convenient for both the wholesaler and the retailer?
Is the package convenient for storage, stacking, display, sales handling, price marking, check out and delivery?
Is the package designed to expedite self selection, self-service, and quick turnover?

Does package perform well in retail outlet from standpoint of:
Breakage,

Pilferage,
Soilage,
Seasonal or holiday turnover,
Dealer problems in regard to tie-ins or special promotions?

USE FACTORS

Consumer needs
Are the unit sizes the proper ones?
Is inspection prior to sale desired and/or possible?
Is the package safe to handle and use?
Can the package be opened easily and then closed for further use?
Can a dispensing device be effectively used?
Can the consumer measure out required use quantity easily and accurately?
Is there a disposal problem?
Is container re-use a possibility?
Have hand-grip features, etc. been considered?
Is package size appropriate for consumer storage?

BIBLIOGRAPHY

DEMING, DONALD D. *Company Organization for Packaging Efficiency.* New York, N.Y.: American Foundation for Management Research, 1960.

The European Productivity Agency of the Organization for European Economic Co-Operation. *Industrial Design in the United States.* Paris, France, 1959.

FRIEDMAN, WALTER F., and KIPNEES, JEROME J. *Industrial Packaging.* New York, N.Y.: John Wiley & Sons, Inc., 1960.

CHAPTER 16

Buying and Selling E & R

ROLE OF OUTSIDE E & R

Outside research encompasses scientific, technological, and engineering development as well as economic evaluation of technical alternatives, the performance of special tests, and a large variety of associated work. Such work is predominantly directed towards a specific objective; that is, it is usually *applied* research, *specific* engineering development, advice on a *particular* subject, or evaluation of a *particular* proposition.

The scope of outside work ranges from million dollar projects to those costing only a few hundred dollars for a few days of advice from a consultant. Typical projects may involve the complete handling of a large R & D project; the investigation of a highly technical and specialized problem; management guidance of a contractor's E & R; testing of a part or process; or simply some technical counsel.

WHY GO OUTSIDE?

Cost

A major reason for seeking outside assistance is that the company may not be able to afford or justify a permanent research facility and staff. Another reason for going outside, based upon cost, is that a specialist's service may be needed for a short period of time, and such service can be obtained at less cost from an outside group for a short period than by attempting to hire a specialist on a permanent basis. While cost is also involved in some of the other reasons, it is not an overriding factor.

To Get the Right People

There are various reasons why outside research could provide the right people. The outside firm may have a great deal of pertinent know-how acquired at the expense of another company. In fact, it may have been working consecutively on problems that need the same techniques, equipment, and know-how.

A fresh viewpoint might be desired so that the company's problem will be examined on an entirely different basis. There may be jobs requiring a technical specialty that the company staff does not possess. The company may wish to hire a certain kind of specialist that it has been unable to employ directly for various reasons, and he can be obtained on a full- or part-time basis from an outside firm.

Facilities

There are few companies whose R & D facilities entirely fulfill their needs. Many outside research organizations were formed specifically to provide specialized facilities (including the personnel to operate them) not ordinarily available in the average laboratory. It may be appropriate to use an outside E & R firm to obtain access to such specialized facilities on a continuing basis whenever the need arises. Also, if there is only temporary interest in the usage of a given facility that the firm does not have, they may go to an outside E & R firm. In addition, they may use an outside facility if the corporation wishes to defer the capital expenditures associated with the acquisition of major, specialized laboratory facilities.

Overflow Work

The normal size of the company E & R staff should be fully utilized when work is low. Therefore, at peak loads it becomes impossible for the staff to maintain required progress. Consequently, many companies find themselves facing deadlines that cannot be met in the in-house effort. Also, such situations may be caused by a crash military program or by a highly competitive situation where the competitor is suspected of coming up with a breakthrough which could cause embarrassment. Outside facilities are frequently used to solve such problems.

Information

An outside E & R agency, which has performed certain work for another firm in the past may have developed information which has been kept restricted but which might help solve a particular problem. While reputable research organizations cannot be in the position of freeing such information, they can conduct research based on such information where the conclusions themselves will not jeopardize the restricted data for their first client. Also, while they will not work on a similar project for a second firm until after a period of time, they may be willing to do so at the end of that period.

Industry-wide problems often arise where it is logical to establish a cooperative project sponsored by several firms. Under such circumstances it would be inappropriate for the work to be conducted in the laboratory of a single participating company. For example, there might be a problem involving the wear of bearings which is of mutual interest to a ball-bearing manufacturer and a producer of lubricants. A second example would be where two or more bearing manufacturers had to agree on standards such as shaft dimensions or hardness of materials. Such firms often jointly sponsor the required research. It is typical in such cases to go to an outside E & R firm. In some cases industry associations set up a separate organization to handle such work.

Acquisition of E & R Management

Organizations who are specialists in a particular industry and who want to diversify often are reluctant to enter into a research program foreign to their background, simply because they do not thoroughly understand it. The most practical way for such organizations to acquire competence quickly is to team up with an outside E & R organization.

Subjective Factors

The internal E & R organization sometimes lacks the necessary prestige in its own company to "sell" management on a particular program. The E & R manager, under these circumstances, sometimes recommends accepting a solicited proposal from an outside group to encompass the desired program. Occasionally, this tactic is pursued even further where the internal organization has partially developed an idea and wants to strengthen its hand by bringing in an outside organization to complete the work. This makes it possible to go to the company's top management with the recommendations of the outside organization.

To Pursue Alternate Solutions

At times a company recognizes an area as being so vital to its existence that it must pursue every possible solution. Parallel approaches, however, often do not get a fair trial when conducted in a single laboratory. There is a tendency for personnel to find glamour and attraction in one of the programs and to neglect the other which may not match their personal inclinations or training. It is often best to try the alternative approach by using an outside E & R group which will not only be remote from the in-house organization, but perhaps even competitive with it. When properly handled, this can act as an effective spur to both organizations.

Corroboration

Sometimes a company's research staff will turn up highly significant results which affect both the product and its advertising. An independent check by an outside group under such circumstances may be desirable. Similarly, a research staff may propose that the company go into a new line of products based on some discovery made in its research. Under these circumstances, however, the corporate management is usually skeptical as to the value of such products and/or the soundness of the technology since it is foreign to their normal corporate interests. Again, outside E & R organizations are often used under such circumstances by corporate management to obtain an independent evaluation of such work against a broader backdrop of competence, in both marketing and technology.

Critical Mass or Size

Research in almost any given field of endeavor requires an approximate minimum number of people for it to be successful and reasonably efficient: However, the number varies with the field and somewhat, with the backgrounds and motivation of those involved—the minimum usually varying between two to twenty-five. A company may not be able to afford the required number on a full-time basis or even find the required number. The solution to this kind of problem often dictates joining forces with an outside E & R group.

Parallel Programs

When time is of the essence, it is sometimes wise to approach the problem on a parallel basis—one being an in-house effort and the other using an outside research group. This approach can also encourage more intensive action in both organizations.

Industry Data

Most industrial groups or associations are suspicious of proposals emanating from one of the companies in the industry group. They prefer using an independent source which is technically competent to understand the problem, has no incentives to endorse a particular solution, and which is in a position to review all of the alternatives. Because of this, industry-wide programs generating test data, standards, or technical data are often placed in an outside E & R group.

SOURCES OF OUTSIDE E & R

Sources of R & D available to companies today are numerous, and the number increases yearly. Their capabilities and specialties extend from one end of fundamental or basic research, through applied research and engineering, and simple consultation, right down to market research and production engineering. Most organizations have a range of interests and specialties and are, frequently, stronger in some than in others.

Listings of many R & D organizations can be found in: *Research Centers Directory,* Archie N. Palmer and Anthony P. Kruzas (eds.), Gale Research Company, Detroit, 1965, and *New Research Centers* (Quarterly supplement), Archie N. Palmer, Gale Research Company, Detroit. Large universities can supply the names of specialists on their staff.

Universities and Colleges

In general, universities conduct research in support of their teaching programs. Such research may be supported by either grants or contracts. While there are some full-time university researchers, most university research is a part-time effort of the professors and of talented graduate students who are working on theses. Also, in most universities there are provisions for permitting the teaching staff to enter into private consulting arrangements with outsiders.

While some universities simply permit these activities and leave it to individual schools, departments, or professors to find such support, others have specific channels to create the opportunity for the outsider and the teaching staff to work together. These research and consulting activities are vital to the existence of universities. They deserve support wherever possible because industry and government must depend upon such men to produce our future technical personnel.

Extremely well-qualified researchers are available from this source, but the sponsor must realize that there are some limitations. Universities usually reserve the right of free publication; therefore, the accomplishments are not the exclusive property of the sponsoring organization. This statement, of course, does not hold true if it involves a purely consultant arrangement between the professor and the company. The sponsoring company should also understand that the work is usually pursued on a part-time rather than on a full-time basis. However, this can mean up to one-half time for the professor and sometimes up to full-time for a doctoral student. Then too, during summer or other vacation periods, the professors and students are often available on a full-time basis. In general, basic research rather than applied research is conducted in university laboratories.

Nonprofit Research and Development Organizations

Nonprofit E & R organizations as a source of outside research are dominated by ten institutes or foundations which have a combined sales volume of over $200,000,000 per year. Some of these organizations have offices and/or facilties in various locations in the United States and also in foreign countries. Many are endowed and some are sponsored by universities; however, all of them are substantially independent and are chartered as not-for-profit corporations. Some of the largest firms and their main locations are as follows:

1. Battelle Memorial Institute, Columbus, Ohio
2. Stanford Research Institute, Menlo Park, California
3. Cornell Aeronautical Laboratory, Buffalo, N. Y.
4. I. I. T. Research Institute, Chicago, Illinois
5. Mellon Institute Research Foundation, Pittsburgh, Pa.
6. Southwest Research Institute, San Antonio, Texas
7. Franklin Research Institute, Philadelphia, Pa.
8. Midwest Research Institute, Kansas City, Missouri
9. Southern Research Institute, Birmingham, Alabama
10. Research Triangle Institute, Durham, N. Carolina.

In addition to the institutes listed above, there are some non-profit organizations that began as essentially captive R & D organizations of one or more government agencies or departments. Examples of these are:

1. Aerospace Corporation, El Segundo, California
2. Institute for Defense Analysis, Washington, D.C.
3. Mitre Corporation, Bedford, Massachusetts
4. Rand Corporation, Santa Monica, California
5. System Development Corporation, Santa Monica, California.

These companies have highly-qualified staffs and are renowned for their advanced research on all kinds of complex problems and projects. The common feature which distinguishes them from many other research corporations is their knowledgeability in systems work. It should be emphasized that this group serves a broad range of customers including military, public, commercial, and educational clients.

Finally, there are some organizations that are slightly different from those already named. An example of these would be the Michigan Research Institute of the University of Michigan which accepts both commercial and government-sponsored work.

These groups are equipped to handle large interdisciplinary research projects. In addition, they will carry out small projects and, at times, will even serve as consultants. In order to use this group effectively, one must know their specialties, their immediate programs, and available facilities. While some of these institutes endeavor to specialize in a particular field, specific programs going on "in-house" may qualify one of the organizations, not normally specializing in the subject.

Profit-Oriented Research, Development, and Testing Organizations

An increasing number of organizations, some specializing in particular fields, with others covering a broad range of interests, have appeared on the American scene. They differ from the consultants in that they have laboratory facilities; they differ from the university research effort in their full-time pursuit of E & R projects; they differ from the research institutes and foundations which sometimes tend more to the solving of classes of problems rather than "How do we solve this particular problem?" approach. Most of them are profit-oriented.

One extremely well-known firm can be emphasized as the prime example for the research and development oriented organizations of this general group classification. The oldest and probably the most distinguished such organization, The Arthur D. Little Company, Inc., started as a corporation of consulting chemists and expanded into such fields as chemical engineering, chemical processes, economics, automation, and management consulting. Some other substantial engineering firms which are engaged in consulting, but which also have technical talent available on a contractual basis, are Stone and Webster, Bechtel Corporation, and The Fluor Corp., Ltd.

Some organizations specialize in testing and if your problem is primarily related to testing, they should be considercd. However, many of the non-profit organizations will also accept the "testing only" projects.

Don't be misled as to relative costs by the profit versus non profit aspect of the organization. Each has an overhead and the nonprofit must recover its total costs and hence must bid to assure eventual recovery. Finally, the overriding factors should always be competence, required facilities, and the probability of success. The latter two factors are far more important than any minor difference in indicated or quoted cost.

Industry-Sponsored Laboratories

Three groups are found in the category of industry-sponsored laboratories:

1. Those sponsored by industry trade associations
2. Those sponsored by professional associations
3. Those sponsored by co-operatives.

A report summarizing this type of activity has been published by the National Science Foundation and is entitled *Research by Co-Operative Organizations*. Examples of the sponsors include: American Gas Association, American Institute of Banking, the Portland Cement Association, Structural Clay Products Institute, American Farm Bureau Federation, the Florida Citrus Canners Co-operatives, Sunkist Growers, Inc., and the

Hawaiian Sugar Planters' Association. Moreover, the American Chemical Society, the American Medical Association, and the National Geographic Society also conduct research.

These organizations are primarily concerned with industry-wide problems, and they are generally careful to avoid profound research which would lead to an abolition of their industry or to a patent structure which might be deemed a monopoly. Therefore, many of the organizations exist largely to preserve standards or quality, or they exist as a protective association to assure the stature of that particular industry or professional group. While the services in such organizations are generally available only to associated companies or members, a company whose normal field of endeavor might not qualify it for membership will usually receive a cordial reception to any inquiry it may make.

Government Laboratories

Examples of government service laboratories include: The Bureau of Standards, the Naval Research Laboratory, Naval Ordnance Laboratory, Naval Electronics Laboratory, various laboratories of the Air Research and Development Command, laboratories of the Signal Corps (such as Fort Monmouth), and the Harry Diamond Laboratories. The Department of Agriculture, through its extensive research program, dominates agricultural research to the point where it is imprudent for private organizations to conduct their operations without reference to its work. Independent governmental agencies also conduct research. Examples of this latter category include the Atomic Energy Commission and The Civil Aeronautics Authority.

Most of the above research facilities are unavailable for work on specific industrial problems; nevertheless, their work is of considerable interest and importance. Their programs are also quite responsive to suggestions by industrial groups, and they frequently can be persuaded to carry out work on problems which are of national interest but which cannot be afforded by a single company. These laboratories conduct about one-third of the total volume of research in the United States; therefore, it is unwise for any company to ignore this tremendous reservoir of knowledge which is available except where the results of such activity are classified for security reasons.

Consultants

One of the principal sources of consulting talent in this country is from the staffs of universities. Such men are usually reached by personal contact or by getting in touch with the appropriate dean or department head. In addition, there are myriad professional consultants, some of whom act as individuals while others represent organizations of considerable magnitude. One directory of such organizations has been published by the

American Management Association, Inc., and is entitled *Directory of Consultant Members.* The Association of Consulting Management Engineers (ACME) with offices in New York will also provide a list of their members, some of whom have entered the new product development area.

Consultants are used to bolster the technical and/or managerial know-how of an organization. They are also used when persons who are unavailable for full-time employment or when an independent outside look is needed at a particular aspect of corporate endeavor. Per diem rates usually range between $150 and $500 per day plus out-of-pocket expenses.

Supplier's (Captive) Laboratories

No company is fully self-sufficient and often must depend upon suppliers and users to do some of their research. Many companies pursue policies which stimulate other organizations to investigative work and development of their own problems. Such activity includes "not-too-subtle hints" to component manufacturers that the company is seeking substitutes for their products. This will sometimes prod them into action. Also, doing a little research on the component manufacturer's problem will often help to secure his assistance.

Captive research organizations may have the capability of solving the company's problem but may lack the financial incentive to do so. One way for the company to solve this problem is to enter into an arrangement involving the transfer of funds and/or people.

Another way of getting attention is for the user or a class of users to take matters into their own hands and attempt a few breakthroughs in laboratories outside of the supplier industry. Merely getting together to define the problem will sometimes cause action. An example of the use of this technique is the banking industry.

SELECTING AN OUTSIDE E & R SOURCE

The most important prerequisite for selecting an outside E & R facility is for the company to understand its own problem. The better it is able to define its own problem, the more effectively the outside research organization can function. Also, it must know its own capabilities so as to determine exactly where the research is needed, when it must be started, and when it can be stopped.

Some typical questions that should be explored are the following:

1. *How much work has been done on the problem area and where?* Assuming that some work is being done you may decide to buy into an appropriate program if it is possible. On the other hand, for ethical or proprietary reasons you may wish to avoid laboratories

that already have programs in your problem area. Also, if someone has already started an effort two or three years ago in your problem area, perhaps you had better consider abandoning your own effort, since it will be difficult to catch up with them.

2. *What laboratories are working for competitors?*
   Research institutes and most of the consultants will decline to work on the same subject for competing companies. Universities, government, and co-operative laboratories endeavor to be impartial.
3. *Is it a problem of extending the art or merely a problem of exploiting existing know-how?*
   Pick the outside laboratory most suited to your needs, remembering that such laboratories specialize in doing different things in different areas. For example, in some areas they may only conduct basic research, whereas the same laboratory in another area is doing applied research and engineering.
4. *Will proprietary information be needed?*
   If so, you must hire an organization that maintains the confidence of the client.
5. *Will proprietary information be generated?*
   The research institutes, profit-research organizations and consultants will respect your need to maintain secrecy about both furnished proprietary information and that which is generated as a result of a project. However, if you want the know-how disseminated, the same organizations can be of assistance in spreading acquired knowledge.
6. *Will patent problems arise?*
   In government and co-operative laboratories, as well as in most universities, patents are not assigned to the client or sponsoring organization. The exact opposite is true concerning research institutes, profit-research organizations and consultants. It should also be understood that contract research organizations and consultants cannot guarantee that they will not use someone else's patent structure in arriving at a solution to your problem.
7. *Does your problem require the development of a general solution or a narrow and specific one?*
   The research institutes are outstanding if your problem requires the development of a general theory behind a class of problems, whereas the profit-research groups may be more appropriate if a one-shot solution is the answer.
8. *Is the problem peculiar to a specific industry?*
   If so, go to a company in the industry or to an industry laboratory. Companies will do research for another firm if time is available and the contract provides enough potential profit.
9. *Will industry standards become involved?*

If so, the source of the research information must be respected and above reproach.

10. *What is the size of the project?*
Universities can usually handle grants up to $100,000 without major problems, and some can handle much larger projects. Research institutes can often handle projects that range in cost up to several million. A project of less than $5,000 is obviously a short-range project and usually a one-man effort. Research institutes and foundations are geared to handle long-range problems. At times, universities have continuity problems because research is usually geared to an individual rather than to a whole department or organization.
11. *Will the solution involve various disciplines?*
If two or more disciplines are involved in developing the solution to your problem, be sure that the research source selected is competent in the required areas.
12. *Will special equipment be needed?*
Involved in this problem is finding a contract research source that either has the equipment or is willing to secure or build it. Also, keep in mind that you will need to settle the question of ownership of equipment when the program ends.
13. *Is security involved?*
This question not only involves military security but also the question of keeping the results secret. Universities can handle military classified projects, but they generally will refuse to accept projects for which the sponsor will not allow the results to be published.
14. *What amount of follow-up will be required?*
To a degree this depends upon the problem, and it also depends upon the personnel doing the research. This question can only be explored through discussion with the contract research organizations.
15. *Will there be a continuing need for outside research in this particular problem area?*
Contract research organizations do require some indoctrination, and when you have a continuing need for help it is advisable to stay with one organization. This reduces the training problem, and ultimately a trained group within the contract organization will be generated.

In choosing an outside E & R source, the company should send a representative to visit several potential sources. He should be a knowledgeable person capable of discussing not only the problem area but also able to negotiate with the contract source. He should not only meet the department head, but he should also tour the laboratory and secure introductions to the men who would be assigned to work on the problem. This holds true regardless of the organization involved. It is important to remember that the research actually must be performed by individuals and the greater their competency, the greater the chances for success. If the contract to be placed is large, the buyer will find it advantageous to request proposals from several firms.

The following questions may help in narrowing the choice:

1. What experience has the particular organization had in the problem area?
2. How successful has their research been for other clients? Try to talk to some of them.
3. What are the library facilities available to the contract research group? Does it have a well-developed and efficient search system?
4. Does the contract research organization do any research work of its own? This can be a measure of its initiative and creativity.
5. Are the contractual arrangements sufficiently flexible to serve your particular purpose?

SOME DON'TS FOR OUTSIDE E & R CONTRACTING

It would be inappropriate not to mention at least a few of the things that we should not do in utilizing outside research facilities.

The members of contract research organizations are generally both intelligent and well-trained, and they have a scientific curiosity about things and how they work. The company cannot expect good performance if it does not give the contract organization the *whole story*. Because of this inherent curiosity or need to know, the company should give the contract group a considerable amount of background information on its problem. Research institutes, consultants, and profit-research organizations are prepared to keep secrets as well as would the company's own staff. If consultants are not given full information, the company may end up with results that it cannot use. This will not only waste the consultants' time but also the company's time and money, as well.

Approach the contract organization with an open mind. Frequently these groups will have a viewpoint that will indicate an entirely different approach than the company had conceived. Don't be upset if the contract group suggests that the wrong problem is being tackled or that the problem is being started at the wrong point. Eventually, the E & R manager must make a judgment, but he would be well-advised to be open-minded if he is to make the most effective use of outside talent.

Conferences and report-writing cost money. The company can save money and also a lot of time if it provides a competent liaison with the outside E & R group and endeavors to minimize the conference and report-writing time.

Preordained results for advertising or for any other purpose cannot be expected. Research organizations will not lend their names to the underwriting of a process or scheme unless it really measures up. Also, it is often a year or two after the research has been completed and further work done that the correctness of the result is finally known.

Don't start and stop research for any reason. The most effective way to handle any research problem, either in-house or contract, is to let it run to its conclusion at a steady pace to avoid the necessity of reorientation or replacement of personnel. While many contract research organizations are geared to the replacement of personnel as projects phase in and out, their effectiveness will suffer from starts and stops.

Do not assume that because no one in the company's E & R staff has ever heard of anyone in the contract organization or that the contract firm is a thousand miles away, or that they have a 200 percent overhead rate, that the organization is unsuited to your needs. The real questions are: "What are they doing that is pertinent to your problem? How soon can they deliver? What is the probable quality of their results? Can the task be accomplished within budgetary limitations?"

Initial cost quotations can be grossly misleading. Large differences are apt to be due to different understandings or experiences in the field rather than to differences in organizational efficiency. One can hope for bargains; however, research on the wrong subject, or by the wrong people, or at the wrong time is terribly expensive.

THE SMALL COMPANY VIEWPOINT

Contract E & R can be especially valuable to the small firm. Remember that most small companies probably started with one product which was developed by one of the founders. Although they may be fortunate in having added several related products, there comes a time when these original products must be replaced by new products.

A very small firm cannot afford to maintain a research staff and adequate facilities. While the "larger" companies can conduct some of their own research, they usually endeavor to utilize some contract research organizations.

Often small businesses fail to utilize outside E & R because:

1. They do not understand the need for continued product development and the proper role for E & R
2. They are unaware of the uses, sources, and costs of outside E & R.

Fear of high costs for contract research is largely unjustified. Many contracts are under $10,000. The company may investigate using outside E & R only to be appalled at the idea of paying a top technical man $250 a day or finding that a small project may cost $25,000. However, intelligent use of outside E & R actually may determine whether the small company will grow or even survive.

Small companies have special problems in utilizing outside E & R. First of all, the risk in the investment increases as the number of projects decreases. The company which can support only one or two projects at a time runs a substantial risk that there may be no return for a long period of time or no return at all. Conversely, the company supporting many projects needs only one good commercial success to cover the losses involved in many less-successful projects.

The small company may still develop a good new product, but it may not have the capability for turning it into a commercial success. This may be due to lack of adequate or appropriate manufacturing facilities, lack of the right kind of marketing organization, or lack of financial resources.

Small firms may also lack a scientist or engineer of their own who has the background needed to follow the projects. Effective liaison is required to keep the contract organization informed of company interests and capabilities. The person responsible for liaison must also be able to recognize when to shut off the outside effort and allow his own company to take over.

The expense of contract E & R is deceptive. For a number of reasons, it is usually more expensive to have the work done outside for a single job than it would be if the company were capable of doing the job itself. However, what really matters in the total view is not its cost, but the profit derived from the outside E & R effort.

OUTSIDE E & R OPERATIONAL CONSIDERATIONS

Contracts

A surprisingly large number of contracts are simple letters of agreement where the sponsor depends upon the ethical standing and procedures of the contract research group, and they in turn depend upon the company in a similar manner. Another procedure is to use a simple standard contract form originating with either one of the parties. If the contract is of considerable size or is undertaken for the government, a carefully drawn legal document will be necessary.

As previously mentioned, the details of the project should be spelled out and defined in a very careful manner. Preliminary conferences should be held to determine whether there will be personality or philosophy clashes which could prevent a group partnership from developing.

In order to protect both parties, agreements usually provide for cancellation of the contract by either party upon reasonable notice. Results cannot be guaranteed in research so that most contracts are on a "best efforts" basis. If the work is not pure research and is at the engineering end of the spectrum, fixed price contracts are possible.

It may be advisable to initially contract for a preliminary survey of a particular problem and later establish the final contract after the organization has been able to look into the problem at some length.

Some of the key topics that may be included in a contract for outside E & R are as follows:

Scope. The scope can originally be defined by either the company or by the contract organization. It should occur after conferences and discussions between both parties. Included in the statement of scope should be such items as objectives, the approaches to be investigated, the extent of the personnel and facilities to be applied, and any limitations regarding areas to be investigated.

Schedule. Usually a time schedule is not included; however, the contract will usually establish a specific ending date based upon funds available, or the completion of the project, or until one of the parties cancels the contract. The more clearly the work is defined, the more detailed the schedule can be.

Cost. The contract or agreement should define the rate at which charges are to be accumulated, the maximum amount that can be spent without written permission from the sponsor, the frequency of billing, any advance payments that may be required, etc.

Reporting. The agreement should specify the frequency and type of reports. A short project probably only requires a final report. For projects lasting one or more years, reports of milestone completion are desirable. In addition it may also involve monthly progress reports as well as technical topical reports on completed phases of the work.

Liaison

Once the contract has been signed, the matter of liaison between the company and the outside E & R agency requires special attention. Although the contract organization has a basic responsibility for carrying out the program, the sponsor company must act as a partner in the venture. The sponsor must share its background and experience and yet allow freedom of investigation.

Any technical program of more than minimum size cannot be laid out in complete detail in advance. Technical and administrative decisions must be made along the way. Consequently, a responsible technical representative should be established by both parties for the official transmission of decisions and information.

The mere fact that an official representative is established does not mean that there should not be freedom of contact and sharing of ideas. This should be encouraged at all levels of the organization and can be helped a great deal through scheduled meetings. It is well to maintain a close partnership.

The success or failure of the program depends largely upon the compatibility of the two parties and the degree of freedom given to the outside E & R organization. Interchange of information and discussion of objectives are helpful, but over-zealous interference on the part of the sponsor can be fatal to the project. The sponsor must be patient and understand the limitations of the research process. If the sponsor follows and understands the details of the research, he can even profit from the failures.

The E & R Manager and Contract Research

Typically, the contract research organization reports to the manager of E & R but he may use other company personnel to monitor the techniques, to watch the financial aspects, or handle the problem of integrating the work into the company. Also, the outside research organization can in fact be working for top management, rather than for the manager of E & R. The outside research organization sometimes also works for another part of the organization which will be the user of the desired information. Both political as well as technical factors need to be considered.

From a corporate viewpoint, it is sometimes wise to include, as part of the E & R budget, a portion for outside research. This may vary from one or two percent to 50 percent of the total research budget available to the manager of E & R. Companies without such budget consideration usually must go to the board of directors to obtain funds for contract research. Such inflexibility and lack of foresight can not only be embarrassing, but it can also greatly hinder progress towards the solution of a particularly knotty problem.

SOME PARTICULAR CONSIDERATIONS IN CONTRACT E & R

Some common questions which may be asked in regard to employing outside E & R are given as further guides for consideration:

Q. What effect will the management of my company have upon achieving results through contracting for E & R?

A. A very significant effect. Stop-and-go research, inadequate explanation of the real problem, and lack of effective liaison may result in solution of the wrong problem or an unsatisfactory solution of the right problem. Consultants cannot substitute for general incompetence in management, but they may supply good research management to companies with good general management.

Q. Is it wise to engage an E & R group which may have worked for my competitors?

A. Yes. Just as wise as employing an executive, engineer, salesman, or any other worker who has had previous valuable experience. The effective research consultant brings a breadth of experience from having served many clients in many situations. Both expertise and breadth of experience are valuable for research projects.

Q. What happens if the consultant I engage works for one of my competitors in the future?

A. Reputable E & R consulting groups have ethical standards which would prohibit their disclosing confidential information. Often, they will not take on a job with a competitor if it involves the same area of research until a specified time, e.g., one year has elapsed. Thus, you will not be paying for research which your competitor can buy cheaply afterwards. A consultant protects his clients' interests, and goes to great lengths to do this.

Q. If I have what I think is a big project, can E & R costs be estimated in advance?

A. Yes, it is advisable to consider approaching your problem in two phases. In the first and low-cost phase, have the consulting organization analyze your problem, make some exploratory investigations, and submit a proposal for the completion of the project. This proposal should list what will be done, when it will be done, who will do it, and how much it will cost.

Q. What size firm will serve me best?

A. If your company is large, you will be able to select a firm to suit your problem. An integrated E & R organization will be able to handle each stage of the investigation itself and bring to bear a diversity of talent that will provide solutions which are sound from all viewpoints. If your company is small and money is tight, it may be that you will do better by using small E & R groups or individuals to solve very specific problems. Some large consulting firms do not like to handle work for small companies because they feel that: 1. Small firms do not understand what may be expected from consultants, and 2. To achieve any significant results, costs will be higher than small firms are prepared to pay.

Q. Can the small firm obtain outside E & R "free"?

A. Occasionally. If the small firm is a steady supplier to one of the giant corporations, the large corporation may supply advice or technical assistance to improve the product. If the small firm buys components regularly from a well-established supplier, the firm may be able to obtain technical assistance from the supplier. The small firm is in a better position to obtain free E & R if it has in its employ highly competent E & R individuals who can "pick the brains" of people in other organizations and keep abreast of technical developments in government and private laboratories.

SELLING THROUGH TECHNICAL PROPOSALS

A technical proposal is a bid (usually directed to a governmental agency or department) for undertaking technical research, engineering design, and/or supplying equipment of an advanced or novel nature. Technical proposals may be classified as:

1. Internal
2. External—solicited or unsolicited
   a. Directed to a government agency
   b. Directed to a prime contractor or subcontractor for government work
   c. Directed to a private firm for its own commercial purposes.

While both major classifications have much in common, the external technical proposal is broader as well as more significant in industry. The growth of government E & R over the past ten years has resulted in a parallel growth in the number of technical proposals. Since "sole-source" awards of contracts by government agencies are generally avoided, there are usually three or more technical proposals submitted for each contract and usually also, for each subcontract of significant cost. The preparation of technical proposals for the government is a legitimate and allowable charge against the company's overhead costs, under both the tax laws and Armed Services Procurement Regulations.

Proposals may also be classified as "solicited" or "unsolicited." The solicited proposal is prepared in response to an invitation to bid on the research, engineering, and/or production of equipment. The proposal may be solicited by public advertisement or by mailing the request to bid, along with specifications, to a selected list of qualified companies.

The unsolicited proposal is prepared through the initiative of the company. A company, because of its technical competence, recognizes that a specific item is needed by the military and believes the state of the art has advanced enough to make the design of such equipment feasible. The unsolicited proposal involves the higher risk of showing that the need covered by the proposal really exists. In addition, such a proposal may be subject to review by more people than a solicited proposal with consequent difficulties in being accepted. The advantage, of course, is the winning of a contract without competition.

Strategy

The strategy in bidding on a government contract or subcontract determines the investment of money and time in producing the technical proposal.

Briefly, the following conditions and consequent appropriate strategies may coexist:

A. The company plans to bid.

1. Real competition exists; that is, the government project officer or the prime contractor does not have a favored vendor and is, therefore, not just going through the motions.
    a. The bidder really wants the contract.
    b. The bidder does not really want the contract but wishes to establish or maintain a good relationship with the contracting agency.
2. Real competition does not exist, and the contracting officer is merely obtaining three bids to maintain an appearance of competitive bidding.

B. The company declines to bid for one or more of the following reasons:

1. The company knows that the situation is not really competitive in that the contractor has really selected a vendor.
2. The company knows that there is one outstandingly qualified competitor bidding.
3. The company is not qualified to do the job.
4. The company's previous dealings with the contracting agency have been unsatisfactory, or the contracting officer has a reputation which indicates the impossibility of a satisfactory working relationship.

HOW TO PREPARE THE PROPOSAL

Proposal Team

Technical proposals are usually prepared by a team made up of representatives from: (1) Marketing, (2) Engineering and/or Research, (3) Manufacturing, (4) Finance and/or Accounting. While the nominal leader of the team is the marketing representative, this job very often becomes a cooperative undertaking shared by both the marketing and the engineering representatives.

This team concept is illustrated by the organization chart in Fig. 16-1. Such proposal groups or bid teams are usually temporary arrangements, and the individuals only spend part time on proposal work.

Responsibilities of each team member should be clearly defined. The engineering representative is responsible for the technical content of the

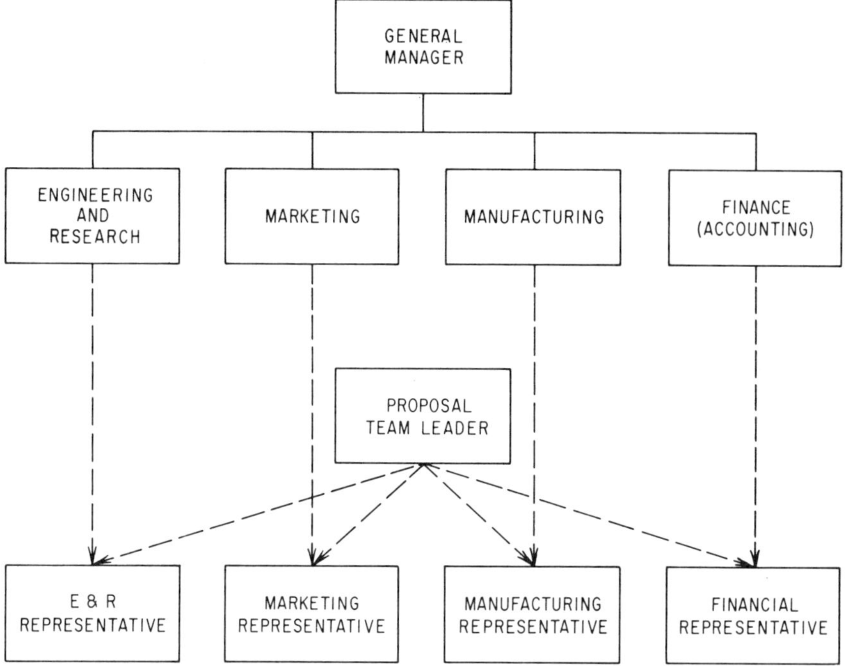

Fig. 16-1. Organization of a proposal team.

proposal; however, this responsibility is shared with the research representative when research activity is involved. The manufacturing representative is generally responsible for all facts relating to production of hardware, including schedules, related cost details, tool lists, facility lists, extent of production know-how and skills, etc.

The finance representative usually has a twofold responsibility: (1) Compilation of all cost data and (2) Fulfillment of auditing requirements. His auditing activity is basically concerned with the compilation of costs. Since much of this information is not directly available from his own activity and must be drawn from Engineering, Purchasing, and Manufacturing, he must be responsible for the accuracy of the data. To meet this requirement, he must serve as an auditor in the truest sense. Not only must he audit the basic data but also the overall financial aspects involved in the pricing of the bid. Often, the financial officer also takes part in establishing bid prices.

The Sales or Marketing representative is responsible for the tenor and tone of the proposal wording; the production of the actual proposal, including art work; and the final pricing of the bid, subject to general top-management approval. As nominal leader of the team, he is also responsible for seeing to it that the team members complete their jobs on schedule.

In larger companies, most of the basic work in producing the proposal and art work is performed by the technical writing and graphics groups. The marketing representative merely reviews their output, initiates changes where necessary, and, in general, makes sure that deadlines for the production of the bid are met.

The purchasing function is not always represented on the bid team. However, a purchasing representative may be included when production of actual hardware is involved and/or purchased material represents a high percentage of the manufactured cost of the resultant product.

Preliminary Steps

A bid team's first step in preparing a proposal is to study and evaluate the request to bid. The specifications involved may be either general or detailed. If they are extremely general, it is up to the bidder to fill in any necessary detail and to see to it that he is properly covered against the eventuality of detailed specifications being produced later by the contractor. If the specifications are detailed, each item should be carefully examined. Acceptance or rejection of a proposal may hinge on the attention given to some obscure requirement in the "fine print."

The problem in preparing proposals is not one of getting too much information but, rather, getting enough. Members of the bid team should take advantage of every possible opportunity to discuss the bid invitation with representatives of the contractor, particularly the ones concerned with technical requirements. In addition, the possibility of having a specialist consultant to assist in the preparation of the bid should not be overlooked.

Once the detailed information has been obtained, company management must take stock of the various factors that govern its bidding position:

1. Available technical competence in terms of estimated requirements
2. Work load and job-priority assignments
3. Required facilities and working capital
4. Strength of known competitors
5. Possible profit in view of competition, nature of the job, and forecast of future requirements.

From such an evaluation, management must decide either to continue with the development of the proposal or to drop the effort. If the decision is to go ahead, Engineering draws the first assignment.

Technical Aspects

In preparing the engineering and research portions of the proposal, the engineers must keep the specifications closely in view. By looking at past history and making conservative extrapolations of technological advances, the engineers start to examine the possible technical approaches for developing equipment to meet the specified operational requirements. More specifically, these steps are as follows:

1. Review previous successful and/or unsuccessful efforts to solve similar problems
2. Attempt to develop new, economical, and technically sound approaches to the problem
3. Analyze thoroughly all alternative approaches and prepare reasons why these are not as favorable as the company's approach.

Step 3 of this procedure is dependent upon the successful accomplishment of Steps 1 and 2. In practice, its importance is very often underestimated; moreover, bids are frequently eliminated because a concept involved had one or more of the following characteristics:

1. Development would involve high risk with insufficient compensation
2. Resulting product would be larger, heavier, less accurate, slower in operation, etc., than one using an available alternative
3. Design would not provide for future increase in capacity or power·
4. Project would be committed to a single design approach with no apparent support in the form of alternate design concepts and/or hardware.

Management should review the final proposal from the viewpoint of the procurement officer by asking these questions: Does the proposal show that the company understood and attacked the correct problem? Are alternate solutions offered? Is the technical analysis mature? Are advanced but realistic concepts offered? Are substitute specifications provided when exception is taken?

In most equipment today, greater emphasis is being placed on reliability of components and systems because reliability is now measured in quantitative terms. Suppliers who claim their prospective equipment will have "high reliability" are really saying nothing. Reliability is measured by stating how long each part or system will function at some specified condition. The probability of system failure under specified operating conditions may be calculated from the reliability of components.

Quality control is, of course, important to the buyer. Vendors may be urged to present information on their quality control organization and operations. With government work it is convenient to require submission and approval of the quality control manuals and procedures — both of the contractor and major subcontractors.

Related information on existing Value Engineering and Zero Defects Programs are important. Also, the proposal should delineate how the bidder expects to handle configuration management and control.

The bidder should be aware that he may be judged by such things as the following:

1. His reputation in the field
2. Experience of his previous clients
3. General quality of the proposal, particularly the technical sections
4. Reputations and stated backgrounds of key managerial, technical, and other professional personnel described in the proposals, including technical supporting personnel and research staff
5. The firm's technical facilities and equipment
6. Length of time they have been engaged in technical work of the nature and scope on which they are bidding.

Management Aspects

The purpose of the management section of the technical proposal is to convey the vital message of exactly how the contractor plans to do the job. The management section of the proposal is broken down here into seven parts for convenience of discussion:

1. Master plan for doing the job
2. Organization for doing the job
3. System of management procedures and controls for execution of the plan
4. Management and technical reports
5. Company's policy on relationships with its customers
6. Financial responsibility
7. Management competence.

A master plan is required for proposals for systems or project work for the government because of the great increase in scope and depth of such work. The contractor must show how he will tie together the overall configuration, the performance requirements, the operational dates, and economic considerations. He must show how he will approach new problems for which no precedent exists.

In the area of the unknown, the contractor may show sufficient parallel effort or back-up programs which will prevent the entire project from collapsing because of failure in one area. The contractor should be in a position to redirect efforts quickly if program changes are required because of unexpected developments which cause the customer to modify his objectives.

Checkpoints or milestones must be clearly defined so that it is apparent that the contracting agency will be in a position to observe how the project is going and be able to take appropriate corrective action.

In a large project, teamwork and strong motivation of all concerned are essential ingredients for success of the project. The success of the project depends largely on the personality, ability, and experience of the project manager and his management team. He must provide the drive which will permeate the entire organization. When setbacks occur, as they inevitably will, he must instill confidence in and inspire his men at such times. The project manager must have the complete confidence of top management and ready access to top management. Due to the importance of the management team, their qualifications should be presented in the best possible manner.

Management controls and procedures for accomplishing projects should make appropriate use of both the conventional and the new sophisticated systems such as PERT. (See Chapter 12.) Record control, flow-of-work procedures, financial planning and control are critical to successful operation of complex projects. Where production of hardware is involved, the elements of production and material control should be thoroughly covered.

A special problem today is control of the activities of many subcontractors. Large prime contractors now subcontract up to 60 percent of the work in many instances. Management techniques of the highest order are required to follow the technical work, schedules, and integration of results for over a hundred subcontractors on a single project. A clear definitive plan for such followup provides a measure of the contractor's management.

The quality and type of management reports and their relationship to each other have a bearing upon the effectiveness of communication between the contractor and the customer. They also play an important part in the coordination of work within the company. The proposal will be enhanced if it demonstrates the ability of the company to provide effective reports. Samples of past reports could be appended, for example, along with the discussion.

The contractor relationship, another aspect of management very important to the customer, may vary considerably according to the philosophy of the management and the attitude of the customer. Some customers will place heavy reliance on the competence of the contractor to perform according to the contract. Most government agencies, however, maintain close supervision over the contractor with practically a one-to-one matching of supervisory personnel. Colonel R. A. Zais, Air Force Systems Command, stated: "A final topic worth mentioning here is the matter of how the contractor proposes to respond to Air Force direction and control. This is a matter of recognizing first the true position of the contractor in that he is acting as an extension of the Air Force effort by contractual arrangement and that he must demonstrate the system of controls which ensures that government policy is carried out." [1]

[1] Colonel R. A. Zais, "Management Section of a Proposal," *Proceedings of Air Force Systems Command Management Conference,* May 2–5, 1962, p. 2–11–6.

The bidder must be prepared to show financial responsibility in the proposal. Items to be considered are:

1. Capital structure
2. Liquidity
3. Retained income, credit, and availability of capital
4. Flexibility of fiscal policies—does he have stated policies?

Lack of sufficient working capital as well as doubtful over-all financial responsibility can be logical grounds for disqualification.

The competence of the management of the firm may be judged from the following information determined from the proposals or outside sources:

1. The general reputation of the firm in the industry
2. Profit position and growth of the firm
3. Age, experience, special talents, and length of service with the company of its management
4. Depth or "backup" of management talent
5. Extent of decentralization of individual responsibility
6. Management's proposed approach to fulfilling technical, time, and financial aspects of the project.

Costing and Pricing Basics

The E & R manager early in his career as a scientist or as an engineer learned that cost estimates on future and existing products must regularly be developed. It is impossible for the successful manager to turn this onerous chore completely over to the accountants because they can only summarize the information which he provides. Also, it will be impossible for him to intelligently assist the accountants in summarizing a cost estimate unless he fully understands the cost elements going into the estimate and in addition, knows how they will be handled and how they enter into the costing and the pricing of the product or service to be provided.

The many cost elements entering into an overall cost estimate necessitate the use of a separate cost analysis form such as the one illustrated in Fig. 16-2. This kind of cost analysis form can be used to re-cost an old product, to cost a new product, or a technical proposal. The example shown, illustrates how it can be used to cost a fictitious product. It will usually be supplemented by a separate E & R cost estimating form which permits a logical breakdown of E & R costs.

Costs in excess of those used in determining bid price are often experienced for the following reasons, especially where the scope of the work required has been poorly defined:

1. Deliberate underbids may be made by a contractor who expects to make up the discrepancy through changes in the scope of the work

__Cost Estimate
__Bid Estimate
__Engineering
__C.P.F.F.
__Fixed Price
__Cost Indication
__Make-Buy

THE NEW PRODUCT COMPANY
Plant - New York, New York

BR. or Est. No. 2536
Date January 5, 1969
Page 1 of 1

Distribution	Customer: Manufacturers of Military Electronic Equip. Customer No.:				
	Article:	Item #	Qty.	At	Amount
H. B. Allen	Special high-temperature electrolytic capacitor having extremely low electrical leakage			(unit cost)	
G. M. Clark					
J. E. West					
I. Newman	Representative unit	1	150M	$6.70	$405,000.00

		%	1					
1	Material		2.78					
2	Shrinkage	2	.06					
3	Procurement	5	.14					
4	Transportation	1	.03					
5	Total Material		3.01					
6								
7	Labor		.34					
8	Efficiency	90	.03					
9	Total Labor		.37					
10								
11	Overhead	181	.67					
12	Pre-Prod. Engr.		not charged					
13	Tools Etc.		.19					
14	Prod. Support Engr.		.13					
15	Engineering Labor		4.37					
16	Engineering O/H							
17	Total Mfg. Cost							
18	Interest							
19	Gen. & Admin.	5	.22					
20	Institutional Adv.	1	.04					
21	Royalties							
22								
23								
24	Total Cost		4.63					
25	Desired Profit		2.07					
26	Des. Selling Price		6.70					
27	Actual Profit		2.07					
28	Act. Selling Price		6.70					

Delivery and F.O.B. Point: New York, N. Y.

Comments: The above cost estimate is for a typical capacitor with a current selling price of $6.70 each.
Pre-Production engineering is considered as a legitimate charge against company R & D budget.
Pre-Production engineering is amortized over estimated first year's production for costing purposes.
Tool and Facilities are lumped into one charge and amortized over a three-year period for costing--therefore one-third (1/3) of total charged to first year's production.

J. Blow, Product Manager — J. E. West, Engineer — G. M. Clark, Cost Estimating — J. Adams, Estimator

4G1319-2 M-1705-2

Fig. 16-2. Cost analysis form for costing new products. *Source:* Delmar W. Karger, *The New Product* (New York: The Industrial Press, 1960).

as it progresses, or who hopes to obtain a favored position in future related projects

2. Honest lack of understanding by the inexperienced bidder who does not realize the scope of the research and engineering involved or the cost of producing the technical breakthroughs which may be required
3. Lack of adequate funds in the hands of the procuring agency to meet the requirements of the technical job, a situation implicitly recognized by both the procurement agency and the contractor

4. Lack of technical or management capability on the part of the contractor.

Alternative bids, one giving a low-cost approach and the other a deluxe approach, are usually held to be non-responsive. On the other hand, a single approach priced to be in accord with the invitation will usually enhance the bidder's chance of success. While cost is a prime factor in determining the order of acceptability of bids, other considerations can and do loom equally as large. Naturally, contractors wish to stretch their funds as far as possible.

Various Operations Research approaches to bidding have been proposed. An earlier good example is Lawrence Friedman's article in *Operations Research,* February, 1956. Others that are more recent have appeared in appropriate journals. However, few, if any, have really been applied, but those that were, seldom represented the ultimate decision. This is not to imply that a study or approach of this kind is to be ignored. As we gain more knowledge, Operations Research will acquire a greater practical value.

In spite of all the detailed government instructions and regulations relative to costing, bids are still submitted in which the bidder has omitted some element of cost. A check of cost elements in the selling price structure such as that shown in Fig. 16-2 might be used in a final overall review.

Proposal Content

A good proposal should include the information shown in Fig. 16-3, "Proposal Content."

PROPOSAL CONTENT

1. Introduction
   It is usually advisable to present a brief, clear, concise statement of the problem or technical requirement (particularly for unsolicited proposals), a brief analysis of the problem and a summary of the proposed method of solution. In addition, it is usual and advisable to include a statement relating this particular proposed achievement to the over-all system or related involved concepts, a conservative estimate of performance, realistic time table, cost estimate, and a statement of the company's ability and willingness to devote its resources to the proposed work.

2. What is Offered?
   If the proposal involves the solution of a technical problem, the solution should be developed by using as many chapters as there are significant parts to the solution. If alternate solutions are known, give their advantages and

Fig. 16-3. Type of information that should be included in a good technical proposal.

disadvantages, being sure to state why they were not chosen. When a proposal primarily covers "hardware," then the proposal should next list the equipment to be supplied, comments on adherence to specifications (especially in a place where they will be improved upon) and an item-by-item comment on the "Request to Bid" listing.

3. Supporting Statements
Indicate the company's understanding of the problem and its ability to solve it by identifying the more difficult areas and outlining how solutions will be attained, especially pointing out alternative approaches that will be used if the primary attack fails.

4. Company Qualifications
Establish in as fair and concise manner as possible why the company is best qualified to accomplish the required tasks. This argument should be related to the company organization, key personnel, facilities, prior work in the field, availability of skilled labor, company know-how, etc.

5. Method of Approach
Outline the plan of attack including personnel assignments, facilities, procedures, scheduling and scheduling techniques, etc. Establish the fact that the company has a practical approach and knowledge of the problem and will be able to develop the solution and/or manufacture the hardware.

6. Supply Cost Data in the Form Requested by the Contractor
Supplementary data can be supplied, but make sure that the primary data is supplied in the exact form requested.

7. Conclusion
Often this is not required and would merely be redundant. However, for complex proposals a concluding statement in which a summarization is presented with an emphasis of the strong points of the proposal is often advantageous.

8. Appendixes
Practically all firms utilize this device to present such items as an Annual Report of the company, facility lists, general organization charts, and any other material which would help support the proposal.

9. Preliminaries
It is usual to package proposals in some form of cover, and the proposal itself will usually include a Title Page, a Table of Contents, identification of sections of the text, a list of charts and/or tables, a list of illustrations. Occasionally security, legal and proprietary notices are also included.

10. Reliability Considerations
Outline current company activity and organization for reliability and state what exactly will be done to assure the required level of reliability for the system or equipment to be developed and/or produced.

11. Quality Control
Establish the company's ability to control quality at the level required for this task, indicating acceptance methods, availability and usage of calibration standards, important check points which are to be established, and pertinent comments concerning the quality control manual, especially whether it has been approved by one or more of the military services.

Fig. 16-3 (*Continued*). Type of information that should be included in a good technical proposal.

One of the most important sections in a technical proposal is the initial summary. It is read by more persons in positions of authority than any other part of the proposal. Its objective must be to convince the contractor that the bidder is fully capable of meeting his needs. The summary should be brief, i.e., no more than two or three pages in length. In unsolicited proposals, the summary should include a statement of the technical requirement which the proposal fills. For solicited proposals this statement can be omitted.

Dressing up the Proposal

A beautifully adorned proposal elaborately illustrated with isometric drawings and colored overlays will not overcome technical deficiencies. On the other hand, a sloppily prepared proposal with insufficient charts and illustrations, poor reproduction, and generally unprofessional appearance may result in the bidder's losing out despite a technically superior approach. It is not unknown for contractors to take advantage of information obtained in all bids in guiding a second round of bidding. For these reasons, the proposal should be prepared on standard-size paper, neatly typed (double spaced unless it makes the proposal too voluminous), adequate margins for notes, black-and-white line drawings and photographs unless color is necessary for clarity. Conservative inexpensive covers are appropriate.

Cover Letter

The letter transmitting the proposal or bid will be the first item read and can be a potent selling aid. If the cover letter includes an important "sales pitch," a copy of it should be attached to each copy of the proposal. Otherwise, the contents of the letter may never be seen by the people who receive the extra copies of the proposal for evaluation. This letter is also the ideal place for personalizing a proposal or bid through mention of specific individuals, situations, or other appropriate references which do not fit in the bid itself.

Negotiated Contracts

In contrast to competitive-bid contracts in which the award is the result of open competition of anyone interested, negotiated contracts may be awarded to selected contractors based on either past performance for the purchase or a study of the qualifications of one or more candidates. Just because a contract is negotiated does not mean that any particular pricing arrangement must be followed.

Bidding to the Government

If you expect to do business with the government, develop or hire an expert on procurement regulations and make it possible for him to maintain his knowledge on a current basis. His office should be responsible for maintaining the file of the Armed Services Procurement Regulations (ASPR) as well as the special regulations pertaining to the agencies and departments normally serviced. Not only should he be familiar with what they say, but (sometimes more importantly) how they are currently being interpreted. Legal and accounting training are both helpful in this position.

BIBLIOGRAPHY

Air Force Systems Command. *Proceedings, Air Force Systems Command Management Conference,* Monterey, California, *May 2–5, 1962.*

BALDWIN, WILLIAM L. *Contracted R & D for Small Business.* Tuck Bulletin 27, The Amos Tuck School, Dartmouth College, 1962.

BERDICK, MURRAY. "Outside Research." In *Handbook of Industrial Research Management,* edited by Carl Heyel. New York, N.Y.: Reinhold Publishing Corp., 1959.

BOOSE, WM. R. "Marketing to the Navy," *Journal of Marketing,* July, 1962.

CARMICHAEL, COLIN. "Wasted Engineering Manpower," *Machine Design,* May 10, 1962, p. 113.

CLARKE, RALPH E. *A Guide to Aerospace-Defense Contracts.* New York, N.Y.: Industrial Press Inc., 1969.

DEAN, BURTON F., and CULHAN, ROBERT H. "Contract Research Proposal Preparation Strategies," *Management Science,* June, 1963.

DIVITA, SAL F. "Selling R & D to the Government," *Harvard Business Review,* September-October, 1965.

EDDMAN, FRANZ. "The Art and Science of Competitive Bidding," *Harvard Business Review,* July-August, 1965.

"Free R & D Pays for All," *Business Week,* June 16, 1962.

FREMED, RAYMOND F. "Profile of Propulsion Proposal Team," *Chemical Engineering,* October 17, 1960, p. 198.

FRIEDMAN, LAWRENCE A. "A Competitive-Bidding Strategy," *Operations Research,* February, 1956.

GEISLER, MARGARET S. "Getting Your Product on a Qualified Products List." In *Management Aids for Small Business.* Washington, D.C.: Small Business Administration, 1959.

"General Procurement Policies of DOD Agencies," *Aviation Week & Space Technology,* Marketing Directory Issue, December, 1960, (1961 Buyer's Guide).

GINDER, S. P. "Optimizing R & D Bids," *Machine Design,* April 26, 1962, p. 19.

GOLAND, MARTIN. "The Effective Use of Outside Research Facilities." American Management Report No. 39, *Developing a Product Strategy.* New York, N.Y.: American Management Association, Inc., 1959.

HARTMAN, FREDERICK, and MOGLEWER, SIDNEY. "Allocation of Resources to Research Proposals," *Management Science,* September, 1967.

HOLST, HELGE, and JEWETT, CHARLES L. "Government Contracts." In *Handbook of Industrial Research Management,* edited by Carl Heyel. New York, N.Y.: Reinhold Publishing Corp., 1959.

KARGER, D. W. *The New Product.* New York, N.Y.: The Industrial Press, 1960.

KARGER, D. W., and MURDICK, R. G. "Technical Proposals for Contract Projects," *Machine Design*, February 16, 1961.

KRAJEWSKI, EUGENE W. "To Win That Defense Contract You Must Prove Capability," *Machinery*, February, 1962.

LARSEN, JEANNE E., and STEVENS, WILLIAM D. "A Basic Guide to Defense Marketing," *Industrial Marketing*, August, 1961.

LE BARON, I. E. "Using Outside Research Facilities: A Management View." American Management Report No. 13, *How to Plan Products that Sell.* New York, N.Y.: American Management Association, Inc., January, 1958.

MCGUIGAN, WM. D. "The Role of Outside Research Facilities." Paper presented in New York, N.Y., to an American Management Association Orientation Seminar, "Organizing and Controlling Research and Development," No. 715–92, April 16, 1958.

"Military Sales: Where to Go, Whom to See," *Aviation Week & Space Technology*, Marketing Directory Issue, December, 1960.

MURDICK, R. G. "How to Evaluate Engineering Proposals," *Machine Design*, September 28, 1961.

———. "Using Outside R & D," *Machine Design*, May 11, 1961.

"Research Talent Everyone Can Use," *Nation's Business*, March, 1959.

"Selling to AASA," *Aviation Week & Space Technology*, Marketing Directory Issue, December, 1960.

"Selling to ARPA," *Aviation Week & Space Technology*, Marketing Directory Issue, December, 1960.

SOPER, GOODREAU, and KELLY, LINUS A. "Research and Development Opportunities with the Federal Government." In *Management Aids for Small Business*. Washington, D.C.: Small Business Administration, 1960.

STEVENS, RAYMOND. *Frank Words on Contract Counsel and Research.* Pamphlet. New York, N.Y.: Arthur D. Little, Inc., undated.

CHAPTER 17

Legal Considerations in Engineering and Research

MECHANICAL PATENTS

The Basic Patent Issued by the U. S. Patent Office

Ideas are not inventions. Neither are patents inventions. Ideas are the prelude to invention. Therefore ideas themselves are not patentable. Patents are merely the legal documents that claim and describe inventions.

Invention is generally understood to be the creation of something which did not exist previously. Furthermore, invention does not include the revelation of something which exists but was unknown. For example, the discovery of a law of nature or a scientific principle is not regarded as constituting an invention since it had existed but was merely unknown. Invention is the requirement which constitutes the foundation of the right to obtain a patent. Other requirements are that the invention (a) must be new, (b) must be useful, (c) must be fully disclosed, and (d) must never have been abandoned.

A patent is a contract between the government and the inventor. Since there must be a consideration binding any contract, there must be one in a patent. Here the consideration is the public disclosure of the invention. In exchange for this consideration, the government promises the inventor the following exclusive rights:

1. The right to manufacture, to use, and to sell the invention—and the right to exclude all others from doing any one or all of these
2. The right to sell his patent
3. The right to license others to do any or all of these things.

The rights to the inventor's invention are his exclusive property for a period of seventeen years from the date of issuance of the patent. At the close of this period the contract terminates, and the public has free access to the invention.

A patent, just like any other business contract, may be invalid or unenforceable due to fraud in its inception, failure of consideration, or a mistake of fact. Since a patent is essentially a contract with the government the inventor has the right to expect it to be valid; however, it is a fact that patents are often proven invalid.

This fault in the patent contract arises naturally because everyone, including businessmen, when they are confronted with something that interferes with their interests will look for "a way around." In the case of an adversely held patent it is natural to question its validity on legal grounds or to seek a way of avoiding the patent by "designing around it"—going to a type of construction that achieves the desired result without infringing or using the invention.

The Rights of a Patent Owner

Anyone may obtain a U. S. patent on a bona fide invention, no matter where the idea was conceived or developed. He does not have to be a U. S. citizen, and age or sex has no significance.

A patent owner can enforce his exclusive rights by suing infringers in the federal courts to recover money damages and/or to obtain a court order enjoining and restraining acts of infringement. He may even obtain an injunction to restrain a threatened infringement.

The patent owner can "mortgage" his patent by using it as collateral for a loan or rent it by licensing others to make, use, and/or sell the invention in exchange for payment. The payment may be any legal consideration including a cross-licensing arrangement with another firm. He may bequeath it in his will; otherwise, upon the owner's death, the patent will pass to his heir or successors as part of his personal property. Also, the patent owner, if he wishes, may give away his patent during his lifetime or he can dedicate it to the public.

The rights of co-ownership of a patent are somewhat unusual. An heir, legatee, or other owner of an undivided fractional interest in a patent, in the absence of a limiting agreement, has unrestricted power to sell or license a patent and thereby create in his assignee or licensee the right to make, to use, or to sell the entire invention without the co-owner's consent and without accounting to him for any of the profits or royalties that are received. Except in infringement suits and where no agreement to the contrary exists, the amount of undivided interest owned or assigned is of no importance.

Patentable Inventions

Invention is ordinarily defined as something new; however, the line of demarcation between invention and non-invention is difficult to ascertain. Generally speaking,if the device produces a new result or an old result in a new or more efficient manner, it is regarded as involving invention and may be patented. The courts and Congress, however, have not defined this term exactly, except in a negative way. They have done this by establishing some of the things which an invention is not.

For example, a new item or result is not invention if it is obvious. Since obviousness cannot be determined in the abstract sense, it must be evaluated in terms of a particular instance in a particular time period—the time period in which the invention was made. Related to the problem concerning obviousness is the fact that certain phenomena are obvious today, whereas years ago they were not.

If the device is new, but anyone skilled in the art could have readily designed it if the need existed, it is not invention.

Substitution of equivalents is not invention. Yet, if the substitution of an item accomplishes the same result in a different manner or performs a different function, it can be classed as an invention.

A new combination of old elements (these elements may be those of an electrical circuit, chemicals, materials, etc.) can be invention if it produces a new result or an old or desired result in a new manner. Therefore, a combination of known and even patented items can still be patentable if the requirements of invention, such as described above, are met.

The combination of elements cannot be mere aggregation. The elements or parts must coact or cooperate with each other in producing the final result, either simultaneously and/or successively. If the result is attained by the separate action of each part performing its own separate individual function, the combination cannot be classified as invention. The classic illustration of an unpatentable combination is a lead pencil with eraser. The courts[1] held that there was no cooperation or joint action between the pencil or rubber eraser, that each performed its own function in exactly the same way as before the elements were joined. Hence the combination could not be patented.

The substitution of a different material is not invention unless a new function or result is obtained. For example, the substitution of synthetic for natural rubber as a gasket material has been held by the courts as no invention. Had this substitution produced a significantly new result, it would have been an invention.

Changing the size, shape, or speed of one or more elements is not invention unless the result is different or the same result is arrived at through a

[1] Reckendorfer v. Faber, 29 U. S. 347.

different mode of operation. Edison achieved a patentable invention by reducing the size of the incandescent-lamp filament because it produced a new mode of operation and a new result. However, the courts have held, in another case, that increasing the vacuum in a high-vacuum tube is not invention since it is merely a natural improvement in this device.

The mere addition or omission of parts is not invention. The added parts or part must cooperate with the remaining parts to produce a new function or result. The omission also must produce a new result. For example, if one part can be made to perform the function of one or more omitted parts which previously were essential to the original invention, then the omission could be classified as invention.

The fact that the quality of invention is present does not guarantee patentability. While the quality of invention is essential, certain other requirements must be met. These basic requirements are summarized in Fig. 17-1 —Check List of Patentability.

WHAT ARE THE CONDITIONS OF PATENTABILITY?

Here are ten basic requirements that must be met in addition to invention:

1. The applicant must be the original and first inventor and must make an oath (there is a prescribed inventor's oath) that he verily believes himself so to be.

2. His invention must be useful, not frivolous, nor contrary to public policy, nor inimical to the public welfare. The degree of utility required is not great since such items as "bouncing putty," toy "flying saucers," new species of roses, etc., have been patented. One can patent most anything falling in this general requirement (providing it meets the other tests) except mental processes, mathematical systems, methods of doing business, printed matter, and products of nature such as the chemical elements — however, the process of detecting and/or isolating a chemical element can be covered. Other coverable items by statute are chemical compositions, processes of all kinds, mechanical devices, and electrical circuits.

3. The invention must not have been previously known or used in the U.S. nor described in <u>any</u> printed publication anywhere in the world prior to making the invention. This emphasizes the importance of keeping up with professional and trade journal publications. As to what constitutes "prior knowledge" in the restricted legal sense, it is knowledge of a completed and operable device or system — mere knowledge of the conception of an idea is not enough to prevent the obtaining of a patent by the true "first inventor" who makes or completes the invention in operable form.

4. The invention must not have been patented or described in any printed publication anywhere more than a year before the filing date of the patent application. Many foreign countries require that there be no prior publications anywhere before the application is filed in those countries.

5. The invention must not have been in public use or on sale in the U.S. by others before the applicant made the invention or more than one year by the applicant prior to filing the U.S. patent application. The moral from the above

Fig. 17-1. Conditions of patentability.

is to be prompt in filing. Using experimental models to test the invention is not considered as use in this rule. Use by the government or contractors to the government in "classified" work is considered as use.

6. The invention cannot at any time have been abandoned — ceasing to work on it for a time and then later finishing it is not considered as being sufficiently diligent in completing the invention to permit patentability. This does not bar the "part time" inventors from securing a patent since such a person will only be presumed to be able to work on the invention part of the time. However, he still can't abandon it for several months and still prove diligence in completing it.

7. The inventor may not, prior to filing in this country, obtain a patent in a foreign country on any foreign application filed more than twelve months before the U.S. filing date.

8. The invention must not have been described in a U.S. patent. A filed and issued patent is a bar to the granting of a patent to a second applicant. The bar can only be overcome by sworn proof that the second inventor actually completed his invention before the first inventor.

9. The invention cannot be something that is obvious to anyone having ordinary skill in the art. Just what constitutes ordinary skill has not clearly been established, especially for our complex technology. Because of this, it is possible for patents to be issued without complete compliance with this requirement and it therefore becomes important for companies engaged in complex E & R work to seek patent protection on all ideas, even those that often appear obvious to the experts and pronounced by them as not being patentable.

10. "A person shall be entitled to a patent unless before the applicant's invention thereof the invention was made in this country by another who had not abandoned, suppressed, or concealed it. In determining priority of invention there shall be considered not only the respective dates of conception and reduction to practice of the invention, but also the reasonable diligence of the one who was first to conceive and last to reduce to practice, from a time prior to conception by the other."*

The actual date of conception is most difficult to establish since it basically is a personal mental event. Because of this, the inventor should, as quickly as practicable, record and write out a description of the invention including related drawings. It should then immediately be explained to someone who will understand it and who will sign and date the description, acknowledging the explanation.

Reduction to practice means completion and satisfactory operation of a working model. Where the expense of building such a model is too high, he may make a "constructive reduction to practice." This involves making and filing a patent application and detailed specification so complete that one could build an operable device in accordance with the patent specification and that it would work or perform as described.

Diligence related to the effort put forth from the time of conception to the reduction to practice of filing of the patent application — any lack of continuing effort might be in favor of a second inventor working on the same idea.

*Section 102 (g) of the revised statute of 1952.

Fig. 17-1 (*Continued*). Conditions of patentability. *Source:* Delmar W. Karger, *The New Product* (New York: The Industrial Press, 1960).

The Patent Application

The claims in a patent application are by far the most important items in this document since they are the only basis of patent protection. The allowed claims, of course, have this same importance in the issued patent. Claims should be stated in as broad terms as possible so that it will be impossible, or at least very difficult, for someone else to design around the patent. If another person is able to produce a comparable device by eliminating one part of each claim, he will not be infringing the patent. This is known as designing around the patent.

Merely adding something to the combination of a prior patent claim does not avoid infringement. Also, omission cannot be achieved by merely substituting an equivalent element such as a synthetic gasket for a rubber gasket. A patent is infringed when every element of one claim is included in the so-called infringing structure. It is for this reason that long and detailed claims are said to have a narrow scope since they tend to be easily avoided by omitting one of the claimed elements.

After the patent office receives the application, its first major action is the review of the application in which it identifies and cites known prior art by referencing prior or related patents and indicates which, if any, of the claims it will allow. This initial operation of the patent office is generally known as "first action." The patent attorney and the inventor must then review this "first action" material as supplied by the patent office, make corrections and/or additions, rephrase the claims where required, present contrary arguments where appropriate, and then resubmit the application. Six months are allowed the inventor to reply to the "first action."

The question of what is an equivalent element is a troublesome problem in infringement. The courts have ruled that an equivalent not only must perform the same function, but that it must do so in the same mode of operation. If it performs the same function but in a different mode of operation, then it is not an equivalent and a device using such a structure does not infringe the patent claim. The general rule is that one cannot employ a mechanical equivalent where the mode of operation is the same as that of the patent. In chemical cases, one cannot substitute a chemical which will perform the same function as the chemical cited in the patent claim. An example of this which was ruled upon by the court was that cellulose acetate could not be substituted for nitrocellulose to circumvent a plastic wood patent, since the substitution was viewed as being an obvious equivalent.

Determination of Inventorship

Determination of inventorship can be a real dilemma and must be faced in almost every company today due to the many group research projects.

The patent laws are explicit in requiring that the patent application be filed in the name of the inventor, or inventors, whose contribution to the arts or sciences is represented by the invention.

The courts will normally find a patent to be invalid where the wrong inventor or inventors have been designated. Both the law and the courts are consistent in requiring a patent to be granted only to that person or persons who exercised an inventive faculty.

There are no exact rules by which the matter of inventorship can be determined where a cooperative effort has produced an invention. While exact rules are absent, there are both negative and positive guides.

An attempt will be made to clarify this situation by reference to typical examples encountered in E & R laboratories.

If there has been a group assignment to solve a particular problem or to achieve a given result and the conception of an idea for achieving the result or solving the problem clearly represents the contributions of one person, then that person is the sole inventor.

The mere isolation of a problem may constitute invention. This can be illustrated by a situation in which considerable trouble was experienced in the operation of a compressor under certain operating conditions. The inventor analyzed the problem and traced it to a failure to vent properly a particular portion of the compressor system. Thereafter, a co-worker performed the routine of designing a suitable vent. This is a clear case of a sole or individual invention which was made by discovering the cause of the problem.

In a similar vein, the efforts of many people working in concert may be brought to fruition by the insertion of the inventive key by one of their number after the others have provided all but the missing element. Again under these circumstances, a sole invention may result.

It is not necessary that joint contributions be equal in magnitude. In cases of joint invention it is necessary to appraise the contribution of each of the several parties involved to ascertain whether one or several supplied that quantum necessary to constitute invention. It is possible that one inventor may have made a relatively minor contribution and still be considered a joint inventor.

Related to the problem of joint inventors is the fact that they need not contribute in the same way to a common invention. One party might conceive the solution to a problem and another the means for implementing the solution. The fact that one party had no part in the actual construction of a machine has not been held to negate joint invention. An extension of this idea is the case of a party having an idea but not being technically or scientifically equipped to express it in workable form. This party therefore collaborates with a technician or a scientist who gives physical or practical expression to the idea. It depends upon the extent of the contribution of the technician or scientist, whether a sole or joint invention has occurred. This is almost the exact reverse of the previously cited example involving a compressor problem.

Obviously, a supervisory status does not entitle such a person to pre-empt entirely or even to share as co-inventor of his subordinate's invention. The mere assignment of a problem for solution does not constitute one as an inventor unless a solution is also presented in such a way as to make the detailed execution obvious to one skilled in the art. On the other hand, it is a dangerous error for the creative supervisor, out of a misplaced sense of modesty or loyalty, to credit his part in an invention, in whole or in part, to a subordinate. This could jeopardize the protection system (system of patents and patent claims) that could be built around the invention. This is another reason why it is very important to have patents, and competent patent attorneys work with engineers and scientists as the ideas are conceived. The longer one waits to determine inventorship, the more difficult it is to establish.

File-Wrapper Estoppel

Frequently an allowed patent claim is subject to a restricted interpretation. This condition occurs if, during the prosecution of the patent application, the inventor or his attorney has to define the meaning of certain elements in a claim or claims to the point that only a restricted interpretation could result. This kind of argument and resultant action can create what is known as "file-wrapper estoppel." Stated another way, the inventor is estopped from any but the restricted interpretation by the documents and material contained in the patent-office filing folder or file wrapper. The net result is that a claim may appear to be infringed; however, due to the file-wrapper estoppel action, any infringement proceedings would compel a finding of no infringement.

If a patent is blocking a product or process for a company, it is often worth examining the patent-office filing folder for an "out" via a file-wrapper estoppel.

COMPANY PATENT PROGRAM

A well-planned and executed engineering and research program must include the identification of inventions and their legal protection.

Good records not only are a valuable asset but almost an absolute necessity in any patent prosecution. Often it is disastrous not to have them. Every knowledgeable firm employing engineers and/or scientists provides notebooks to record experiments, technical decisions, statements of problems, etc. Recommended practice dictates that each page be dated, signed, and witnessed. Notebooks with stitched-in pages do not absolutely require each page to be witnessed. However, the individual-page approach has an important advantage in a patent action. Only selected pages need to be brought into court, rather than the whole notebook which could disclose other data the company desires to retain on a confidential basis.

In addition to engineering notebooks, a separate form, ordinarily known as a patent disclosure, can and often is used to record potential inventions. Disclosure forms normally provide space for dates, a verbal description of the invention, required drawings, the inventor's comments regarding known prior or related "art" (knowledge), and provision of space for the oaths and signatures of witnesses.

Usually provision is made for two people to sign. The inventor describes his invention to witnesses who should have the technical knowledge and ability needed to understand his explanations so that they can swear to the explanations and make an attestation similar to that in a typical witness oath as shown in Fig. 17-2. Such forms usually are of the type that will permit easy reproduction.

WITNESS OATH

The invention was first explained to me by the above identified inventor(s)

on____________________, 19_______.

______________________________ ________________________

Signature of Witness Date of Signature

Fig. 17-2. Witness oath. *Source:* Delmar W. Karger, *The New Product* (New York: The Industrial Press, 1960).

Where each page of the engineer's notebook is signed, a separate patent disclosure form is not needed if individual notebook pages are reproducible and generally removable from the binder and if space is provided for supplementary information needed by the patent attorney.

Most firms, however, require both notebook pages to be witnessed and signed and also the use of the separate form previously described.

The witness provision is often misunderstood. This is illustrated by the common misconception that a person secures protection for his invention by sending a registered letter to himself in which the invention is described and his signature has been notarized. Such a letter is generally meaningless since the inventor has not established proof, by explanation to witnesses, of his real understanding of the invention. Such a letter could only help in substantiating the date of conception of the claimed invention.

Patent applications, as previously stated, should only be developed by competent patent attorneys.

The manager of E & R should align himself closely with the patent attorney or patent department. Each will benefit from the other's activity, and a close relationship is essential to success in this area. The discussion preceding this paragraph implies that inventions made on the job are company property. Courts have generally upheld this view; however, in order to eliminate problems and difficulties, most companies require at least their technical and other possibly creative personnel to sign agreements to assign their inventions to the company and also to protect the company trade secrets. Involved in this problem is the fact that an invention cannot be assigned until it can be identified; therefore, it must be identified by description or by reference to the serial number and filing date of the patent application, or the patent number if it has already been issued.

That it is difficult to recognize patentable inventions and even the inventors in many cases should be clear from the previous discussions. All supervisory engineers should therefore be given at least some rudimentary training regarding the identification of inventions and what needs to be done concerning them. Such information not only should be in written form, but it should also be thoroughly and personally explained to each and every one of the involved persons. Retraining should be on the agenda about every six months.

If invention is not recognized, it will be lost to the company. This emphasizes the need for having people who are trained to recognize invention review engineering notebooks. People without the proper training or motivation tend to take the "easy way out" by claiming an invention is "old art" and can't be patented, or that any patent obtained would be too weak to be worth the effort. Aside from the patent problem, invention recognition is necessary to any exploitation. Penicillin was discovered years before it was improved; the first man didn't recognize it as an important development.

Most large companies have a patent committee consisting of the engineering and research managers, the head patent attorney, and the manager of new product development, if this latter person exists. In other companies, the sales manager and/or the factory manager are added to the committee. The patent committee normally reviews disclosures of invention and decides what action should be taken concerning them; that is, should a patent application be filed, should an initial search or novelty search of "prior art" be made to determine related patented inventions, etc.? A new term, an "initial or a novelty search" was mentioned. In many instances, the patent attorney makes or has made what is known as novelty search of "prior art" in the patent office to determine whether the invention is in fact probably new and thus patentable.

However, it is virtually impossible to be absolutely sure that a worthwhile patent will ultimately be issued.

Occasionally, because of the diverse and broad art apparently existing or because of other factors such as cost involved and/or the real value of a novelty search, the attorney will draw up a patent application and start prosecution of the patent without a novelty search. Final decision will then be based on the first action received from the patent office on the patent application. Making the correct decision as to what to do at each point in the protection of an invention requires experience and sound judgment.

Because of the long processing time required in the U. S. Patent Office, companies frequently manufacture and sell a product before a patent is obtained. In such situations, they usually attempt at least partially to protect their interests by marking the product with "patent pending" or "patent applied for." Actually, a patent applicant has no rights under the patent statute until the patent is issued; furthermore, the rights are not retroactive. Nevertheless, this practice usually serves as an effective deterrent to competition. However, it should also be understood that the law counts it a punishable misdemeanor to so mark a product if a patent application is not actually in process by the patent office.

Two helpful publications available from the Superintendent of Documents, Government Printing Office, Washington 25, D. C., are first a compilation of patent laws and second a roster of attorneys and agents registered to practice before the U. S. Patent Office. A brief description of each patent issued is contained in the weekly government publication, the *Patent Gazette*. These and other useful publications regarding patents can be obtained from our government.

Outside Inventors

Ideas from outsiders can be dangerous. If such ideas are incorrectly handled, an unasked-for brainstorm can easily cost tens of thousands of dollars in legal costs, and associated damage claims have often exceeded one million dollars. The incidence of such occasions is growing every year, and any management man from board chairman down can have an unsolicited idea unexpectedly foisted upon him. Watch out for the letter that begins "Dear Sir: I have an idea that will make a million dollars for your company . . . "

If an inventor or "would-be" inventor discloses his secret in confidence to another, that person receiving the confidential information assumes an obligation neither to disclose the secret to anyone else nor to use it for his own benefit without the permission of the inventor. The obligation of confidence remains even if the item disclosed is not valuable or patentable, or if it is patented by the inventor after a disclosure. The courts have steadfastly upheld this viewpoint; consequently, manufacturers should be wary of accepting *any* confidential disclosures. There are cases on record where the courts have held both for and against the person disclosing the idea, even though the disclosed idea was from an expired patent and therefore was actually in the public domain.

The formulation of a company policy on the subject of ideas from outsiders must be looked at from two viewpoints:

1. The possible values that such ideas may have
2. Whether customer good will is involved.

With the heavy emphasis on new product development one hesitates to overlook the valuable idea. Secondly, it is not hard to conceive that in a consumer-product-oriented company, the customer good will could be involved. Certainly, a policy should be formulated and most definitely should be communicated to management at all operating levels who in turn should communicate it to any employee who could possibly be exposed to the problem. This policy and any associated system and/or procedure should be recirculated and republicized at least every six months. Many companies distribute pamphlets or booklets that not only summarize policy on the subject but also include an agreement form which the idea man is asked to sign. Such booklets are sent to anyone who offers an idea and are also distributed throughout the company.

One preventive measure is that the company maintain a complete collection of samples of the company's present and outdated products, labels, product names, slogans, containers and other items usually involved in the area of inventive ideas. By doing this one can easily settle whether an idea is relatively new to the company.

A second preventive measure is the maintenance of dated, signed and well-filed notebooks and invention records. This aspect of the engineering and research operation cannot be overemphasized.

Nearly all manufacturers from time-to-time receive unsolicited disclosures. The receipt of such materials poses a serious problem, especially if it is read by any of the company's engineers or technical personnel. Most company policies require the incoming mail department to route all such correspondence to a designated individual. This individual is generally a nontechnical employee who is instructed to seal the disclosure and to place it in a company vault. Then as a general rule a form letter is sent to the person who submitted the disclosure asking him to sign the disclosure statement. Other actions are possible; in fact, there are eight feasible, sound courses of action:

1. Refuse to accept the idea in confidence.
2. Return all papers, drawings, and letters with a statement that no copies have been made.

3. Keep all papers in a closed file until the solicitor signs an agreement with the company.
4. Cite references if the correspondent's information is already known art.
5. If the publication of the idea is not known, refuse to admit that the information is new and novel.
6. Send an agreement form if management thinks the idea is worth consideration.
7. Request that the information be resubmitted in the form of a patent application or as a witnessed, full disclosure.
8. If management wants to negotiate, request that the correspondent meet with company officials.

Suggestions 2 and 3 are used effectively by many companies; however, there is conflicting opinion in legal circles as to which of these measures is the best safeguard.

Disclosure statements which correspondents are asked to sign usually contain several or all of the following ideas:

1. The submitted information must be in writing, preferably a copy of a patent application that has been submitted to the patent office or, at least, a dated and witnessed, full disclosure.
2. The company does not have to agree to hold a correspondent's information in confidence.
3. The sender is requested to keep an exact duplicate of all materials submitted.
4. The company is not obligated to reveal its own knowledge on the subject.
5. The company is allowed to reserve the right to negotiate for payments after it sees the correspondent's full information; in fact, maximum payment may even be specified.
6. The company is not bound either by contract or by a confidential relationship if a patent issues except under the term of future agreements on licenses.
7. The company is under no obligation to consider the information other than to say whether it is interested.
8. The company is not asked to admit that the idea is new, novel, and concrete.

If this kind of case gets into a court of law, the court will examine the facts in every case to determine:

1. What was submitted and was the inventive idea the outsider's property?
2. How the idea was submitted and was a contract made or implied or was a confidential relationship established?

3. Who received the idea? Did an "agent" of the company commit the firm?
4. What may be recovered as compensation?

DESIGN PATENTS

The types of patents issued to protect inventions relating to mechanical devices, electrical circuits, chemical processes, etc., are of the general type known as mechanical or utility patents. This is the type of patent covered in the previous discussions. Utility patents having very broad claims are sometimes referred to as basic patents.

The U. S. patent law also provides for the issuance of design patents for certain types of new and/or ornamental designs. The theory in back of this section of the patent law is that a unique and aesthetically pleasing design of an article may be an important factor in its commercial success and should be accorded some protection from copying. Design patents only cover the exterior appearance of an article, not its internal structure, workings, functions, or functioning. Because of the limited scope of design patents, they are usually less valuable than mechanical or utility patents.

Design patents are obtainable for periods of three and one-half, seven, or fourteen years, depending upon the fee paid by the applicant and the time period for which he requests or elects to apply. It is only possible to cover one part in a design patent. If two or more parts are to be protected, separate design patents must be obtained for each part. For example, two design patents must be obtained if complete protection is desired for a desk pen-set, one for the holder, and one for the pen which is separable from the holder.

Design patents are usually obtained to protect items such as wallpaper patterns, chinaware, cabinets, bathroom fixtures, etc. While they can be used to cover parts such as machine screws, here one normally can and should obtain a utility patent unless only an ornamental design is involved. When an item can be covered by either a utility patent or a design patent, the utility patent protection is usually the kind to obtain, if for no other reason than that the utility patent is issued for a longer period of time.

Even without a design patent, the law does provide some protection against copying products by competitors. Such protection stems from the sweeping monopoly granted by the law of unfair competition. Unfortunately, the layman is faced with a difficult task in trying to interpret or predict just what is protected by this sweeping monopoly; in fact, attorneys have a difficult time doing so. Sometimes, a "Chinese copy" is legal whereas in other cases the mere similarity in appearance of a competitor's product may be ruled illegal.

In one situation the court not only pointed out a danger lurking in a combination of mechanical and design patent applications for the same subject but also stated some of the "ground rules" in the following extract from its ruling:

> Where one procures a design patent and subsequently procures a mechanical patent, the second patent is not void for double patenting unless it is necessary to use the design disclosed in the design patent to make use of the mechanical invention defined in the patent claims or the latter mechanical patent.
>
> If the design includes ornamental features which go beyond and are patentable over the structural features as defined in the claims of the mechanical application, the inventor is entitled to two patents.[2]

In another case the court further stated:

> It is also well established that while, as a matter of law one may have a mechanical patent and a design patent on the same subject matter, there must be a clear patentable distinction between the two; or, in other words they must involve different functions. When the two ideas are indistinguishable in their characteristics and manifestly the result of the same inventive idea, a second patent will not be granted.[3]

GOVERNMENT CONTRACTS AND PATENTS

The procurement policies of federal agencies affect the patent rights of industry and the basic structure of E & R organizations. This problem is highlighted by the fact that the Government is sponsoring the major portion of our country's research and development and by the fact that the Government does not operate under one uniform policy. At present the Atomic Energy Commission (AEC), the National Aeronautics and Space Administration (NASA), and the Federal Aviation Agency (FAA) take title to inventions associated with their contracts, whereas the Department of Defense (DoD) takes a free license.

There is a difference of opinion, both in and out of the Government, as to the most desirable ownership policy regarding Government-sponsored inventions. One group proposes that title to inventions made under the Government contract should be in the Government to assure that the public does not pay twice for such inventions (once in taxes and again in monopoly). The opposite view is that the Government should take only a free license, thereby leaving the inventor with the right of commercial

[2] Regent Jack Mfg. Co. v. U. S., 130 U.S.P.Q. 235, July 19, 1961.
[3] In re Barber, anyone Fed.-2d 231, Jan. 27, 1936.

exploitation since this will serve as a very powerful incentive for future technological advancement.

In connection with government contracts, three big classes of property rights must be considered. They are:

1. Patents on inventions
2. Trade secrets
3. Industry know-how.

Patents on Inventions

Patents on inventions pose no particular problem if the invention is made using private funds. The problem arises in the Patent Rights Clause used in government contracts which says that the Government shall have title (AEC, NASA, FAA) or a free license (DoD) in inventions *"first actually reduced to practice"* in the performance of a contract. It therefore makes no difference whether the invention actually had been conceived prior to the receipt of the contract, the government gets whole or partial ownership in all inventions reduced to practice in performance of the contract regardless as to when, where, or how they were conceived. While industry can object, Government procurement agencies, however, require it as a condition of obtaining a research contract. It is the inclusion of the "first actually reduced to practice" provision in the government contracts that poses a very serious problem to industry.

A second problem regarding patents is that concerning security. A patent may be withheld from issue because of security classification or considerations; therefore, the company is prevented from exploiting it commercially. The delays caused by security clearance can cause the invention to become obsolete and in some cases the term of the patent has even expired. A second problem concerning security, involves the inventor's right to obtain foreign patents for exploitation. An inventor is not permitted to file applications abroad until the subject matter has been declassified. Consequently, the opportunity to obtain a valid foreign patent has often passed. The only relief offered him is that he may petition the government for a modification of secrecy to permit him to file in a specified country or countries. Such a petition is not ordinarily granted unless the government has disclosed the invention to the foreign government. Even if the subject matter is not classified, security measures often impede the opportunity to obtain valid patents abroad since the patent application cannot be sent to a foreign government within six months after filing in the United States unless a Commerce Department permit is obtained; moreover, delays in obtaining such permits are quite usual.

Trade Secrets

Another problem concerns itself with trade secrets. A trade secret is "know-how" held confidential in a company, of which a good example is the formula for Coca-Cola. If the company maintains a trade secret, it can through court action enjoin any individual who obtains knowledge of the trade secret in confidence from improperly using said knowledge, as well as anyone else or any company which obtains said knowledge from said individual. The right to protect trade secrets, which arises in common law, is recognized by all of our courts. The Department of Defense includes in its procurement regulations a provision for obtaining trade secret data from contractors in return for a reasonable compensation. The problem arises, however, from the fact that no company wishes to part with trade secret data even if compensated; yet, it must do so if it wishes to bid on certain government contracts. This again is a practice of the government that must be understood by E & R managers.

Know-how

"Know-how" encompasses other items in addition to trade secrets. Such items range from the skills of workmen to detailed manufacturing specifications. Know-how is unpatentable and inherently cannot be kept secret. It can only be protected by restricting its dissemination. When a company sells a product, the customer could attempt to duplicate it by dimensioning the product, analyzing it, and eventually trying to produce a copy; however, the vendor does not supply the customer with manufacturing drawings and specifications. The problem arises under a Department of Defense ruling which makes it a requirement in certain contracts that manufacturing drawings, supporting specifications, and much other generally considered private know-how be released with the product.

While industry must and should cooperate with the government procurement agencies, even though the situation is confused, it nevertheless needs to take those measures still left to it to protect its own property rights in its designs, inventions, know-how, and trade secrets.

There is little that can be done by the sales department of any company to help the situation as it presently exists. While sales may object to a particular clause, their proposal runs the danger of being classed as being in noncompliance with the invitation to bid unless the clause is previously removed. The government agencies generally do not remove such clauses, and most sales departments therefore do not wish to run this danger since their bid can be and often is rejected if it does not comply with all of the requirements indicated by the invitation.

The only place where remedy can be achieved at least to a degree is in engineering. Some companies have taken the position that when manufacturing drawings are required, a minimum of drawings should be supplied —only enough to comply with the contract. In addition engineering should do everything possible not only to identify invention but also to reduce them to practice and file for patent protection prior to the invention becoming involved in a government contract. This places a great deal of responsibility on engineering and research management. Furthermore, it means that E & R should have sound patent policies and see to it that they are complied with in every respect by their personnel.

Legal Actions Concerning Patents

Engineering managers at times will become involved in litigation concerning patents. Usually they are involved because they must help the trial attorney prepare his case often by providing "expert" witnesses.

If the engineering manager does get involved and has any opportunity in influencing the selection of the attorney, then by all means he should get the most experienced and successful trial attorney that can be located. The total cost of a patent litigation is so great that the attorney's fees should never be the overriding consideration. Just as in criminal law, trial attorneys accumulate different records of success and those who have been really successful tend to continue to win far more than they lose.

With respect to providing expert witnesses in a patent litigation, the problem is to locate and use expert *testifiers* rather than expert engineers. This is the admonition of Emanuel Poznak, one of the country's most successful trial attorneys. In a speech at Rensselaer Polytechnic Institute he had the following to say concerning expert testifiers versus expert engineers and scientists:

> The choice of an expert in patent litigation is often a matter of critical importance. Because technical issues are often involved, there is the understandable tendency to select an expert solely because of his technical knowledge of the subject, with little regard for his experience as a testifier. In other words, he is often selected on the basis of his expertness and reputation as an engineer or scientist, rather than on the basis of his experience and skill as a witness.
>
> To clarify this distinction let me give you two examples taken out of my own trial experiences.
>
> In one of these cases involving the charge of infringement of a patent for a complicated medical camera, Albert Einstein appeared as a witness for the plaintiff. I was the attorney for the defendant. Professor Einstein stated that his interest in the case arose from his friendship with the plaintiff, that he had never served as a patent expert in litigation in this country, and that he was appearing in the capacity of a physicist.
>
> During his pre-trial deposition, Professor Einstein had testified to the effect that in the operation of plaintiff's camera there were two factors that had to be considered—focusing and aperture adjustment. Thinking only of the technical aspects, he placed emphasis on the relationship between these two factors, stating: "Only the combination works. One alone does not work."
>
> In emphasizing this relationship he spoke as a physicist. He did not speak as a professional testifier who must always bear in mind the purpose of his role, which is to dwell on the issues of the case as they would be expected to arise during the trial and as emphasized—in this case—by the plaintiff's attorney. One of the issues was, as I recall it, whether or not a certain claim of the patent in suit presented a structure that was operable—that is—workable—in the light

of the fact that the claimed structure contained only one of the two features referred to by Professor Einstein.

Under direct examination Professor Einstein had implied that it was operable with only one of the two features present, though not perfectly as he later admitted with full candor. It was now apparent to me that, through lack of trial experience, he was drifting into an error of emphasis. When, under cross-examination, I confronted him with his previous testimony that one without the other would not work, he frankly admitted that he had made a mistake!

And, if I may add this personal note, this frank admission resulted in an immediate stampede for the exit by the reporters who were covering the trial. And the next day there were front page headlines reading: "Einstein Admits He Could Err."

In the other case, where I also represented the defendant in a patent infringement suit, the plaintiffs had as their expert a professor of mechanical engineering with extensive experience as a testifier. He sought to support the plaintiff's contention that the accused device—the defendant's device—employed a nozzle which directed a jet of steam downwardly against a steam-deflecting flange that formed a juncture between two hemispheric shell segments. The accused device did indeed have a nozzle, but instead of a flange there was a slightly protruding bead. I sought to prove that the bead was not a flange and that it did not deflect the steam coming from the nozzle.

Since the accused device was in evidence as an exhibit, I started it going until there was a continuous jet of steam issuing from the nozzle. Then, in cross-examining the witness I said, "Professor, you testified that this bead—which you call a flange—acts as a deflector, did you not?" He answered, "I did so testify." "Then," I continued, "the steam issuing from this nozzle toward the bead must be deflected upwardly by the bead, and there should therefore be no steam below it. Bearing this in mind, would you then, Professor, kindly place your finger directly below the bead or flange? You don't have to, of course. If you prefer not to, just say so." I wanted that in the record.

The plaintiffs' attorney then jumped to his feet and said "Let him, if he wants to." It wasn't his finger.

The professor did put his finger below the bead—but quickly withdrew it—as I expected he would.

But, expert testifier that he was, he uttered not a sound, nor a word. He did not want the court stenographer taking the minutes of the trial to record any admission that would indicate his withdrawal of his finger, which could be construed as an admission that the bead was not a steam deflector. This was a situation where he knew he should remain silent. Here we had an expert testifier.

And, if I may, let me add another personal note. There are ways of handling such a witness. In that case I did it by saying, "Professor, I noticed that you quickly withdrew your finger!"

That went into the record.

Another interesting comment made by Mr. Poznak in his speech at Rensselaer Polytechnic Institute was that he believes the company should give company inventors some kind of continuing right in their invention rather than taking over the entire invention, either with or without a token fee. This same idea was mentioned under the subject of compensation.

Patent Law Problems and Changes

A presidential commission's report on ways to improve the U. S. patent system "kicked up a storm" in 1966 and early in 1967.

In general, the commission believed that something must be done to eliminate the long lag between the time of application for a patent and when action is taken upon it. Something needs to be changed, according to the commission, to speed the flow of new technical information into the public domain where it can be translated into goods and services. Further, they believe that if patents are to continue as the backbone of invention, something must be done to lower the prohibitive costs of obtaining and enforcing patents. Finally, U. S. patent law must be brought into harmony with patent laws throughout the world.

To achieve these ends the commission suggested that:

1. U. S. patents be issued on a first-to-file basis, rather than a first-to-conceive or first-to-reduce-to-practice. This, it is felt, would end most of the interference claims which now clog our courts.
2. A preliminary application, or instant form of disclosure to the patent office be substituted for the present "period of grace," the time between initial filing and submission of supporting evidence to prove that an idea is really patentable, is also recommended. This instant disclosure form is designed to cut costs and save the time of harried patent examiners.
3. An invention should be "unobvious" in technical literature anywhere in the world. This suggestion the commission sees as a necessary first step toward a world patent system.
4. Assignees as well as inventors be allowed to file for patent applications. This is a move to protect the interests of employers of inventors.
5. A patent office decision refusing a patent claim could not be reversed in the courts unless clearly in error. This would be a step to reduce the load on the courts.
6. A U. S. patent be considered valid for twenty years after its earliest filing date, instead of seventeen years after the issuance of the patent. This would end deliberate dallying between the first filing and final submission of claims.
7. Imports into the U. S. of licensed products made abroad by a process patented in the U. S. be considered a patent infringement. This would strengthen the validity of the U. S. patent system and U. S. patents.

There are those for and against the above recommendations and only time will tell whether Congress will get around to changing things.

The patent is a monopoly which is granted for public disclosure and is a just reward for invention. However, a patent monopoly must be managed with finesse in order to avoid antitrust violations. The Justice Department, from time to time, has attacked large holders of patents such as E. I. duPont de Nemours and Company. It seems that anti-trusters generally look with disfavor at patent holders or licensees if they do, among other things, the following:

1. Fix prices
2. Set territories for using the patents
3. Limit types of business in which the patent can be used
4. Limit sales volume
5. Let a licensee sell a product only if he buys it from the patent holder
6. Require buying other products from the patent holder
7. Insist on cross-licensing of patents.

It would be advisable for the engineering manager who is concerned with the legalities associated with patents, to keep an eye on business publications such as *Business Week,* The Financial and Business Section of the *New York Times,* etc., for articles dealing with patent problems and anti-trust actions associated with patents. What is under attack today, is not always under attack the following year. Also, each year usually sees anti-trust action aimed at a new area.

In a somewhat similar manner, the engineering manager should keep abreast of likely patent law changes to adjust his organization to be in accord with them before they become the "law of the land."

COPYRIGHTS

The design of certain articles can be protected by copyright registration rather than by means of a mechanical or a design patent if such articles are classified as works of art. Examples include artistic jewelry, enameled glassware, etc. Copyright registration offers some advantages since it provides protection for a longer period, namely twenty-eight years, and it may be renewed for a like period.[4] In addition, the work of art need not be novel or inventive although it must be original with the artist or author who claimed the copyright.

There are two kinds of basic copyrights—common-law and statutory. Common-law copyright is a fundamental right which stems from the common-law and will be upheld by the courts even without a certificate of copyright registration. This kind of copyright covers the results of an individual's personal efforts and intellectual labor. Everyone has an inherent common-law copyright on his private correspondence, speeches, etc.

[4] A proposed revision of the United States copyright law would add nineteen years to the term of existing copyrights, while any future copyrights would last until fifty years after the death of the author.

However, if such writing or speeches are published without restriction, then the common-law right is lost.

Statutory copyright has the same origin as the U. S. patent laws. Registration of copyrights is the responsibility of the Library of Congress instead of the U. S. Patent Office. The registor of copyrights is empowered to issue certificates of copyright registration to anyone who complies with the regulations. The application for copyright can be made by the original author, his legal representative, or by the company that publishes the work. There is no examination for novelty or originality.

The copyright is valid only if the work is original. The statutory notice—that is, "Copyright, (year), by (name of author)" must appear on the book or other material at the time it is printed and distributed; in fact, it must so appear before registration. All printed and distributed material becomes dedicated to the public unless the above action is taken.

TRADE-MARKS AND SERVICE MARKS

The philosophy of trade-mark law is based on protection of the public, whereas the patent law was created to protect the inventor. Since the "public interest" is involved in all legal cases dealing with trade-marks, the courts tend to be much stricter in the rulings on trade-mark infringement.

Trade-marks are used to identify goods. They are considered by many to be indispensable in sales promotion and advertising and offer many benefits. Registered trade-marks do not expire; however, they may be lost through nonuse or misuse.

The right to trade-mark protection, which stems from common law, is acquired by priority of adoption in use rather than by registration. Congress has, however, passed a number of federal laws which provide for registration in the U. S. Patent Office of trade-marks which are used in interstate or foreign commerce.

From a legal viewpoint the best trade-marks are those that are "coined" or made up as a fanciful combination of characters or symbols and convey no primary or generic meaning. Advertising managers, however, usually prefer trade-marks that do have some kind of meaning which is in direct contradiction to the suggested ideal from a registration viewpoint.

A trade-mark or brand name must be used before any rights arise. In fact, it must be used before registration can be effected. The mark should be applied to either the product or its container.

It is difficult to license or transfer trade-marks or service marks to another manufacturer. Any attempt to accomplish this will place the mark in jeopardy, and it is not recommended.

Service marks are similar to trade-marks, the only difference being that service marks are used to identify services rendered rather than a tangible and usable product. They have the same purpose as trade-marks and are acquired and protected in exactly the same manner. They normally appear on literature, brochures, stationery, advertisements, etc., since no physical product is normally involved and service is the thing being offered.

THE LAWS OF AGENCY AND CONTRACTS

Any manager should have at least an elementary knowledge of the law of contracts, agency, and negotiable instruments—the first two being the more important. While it is impossible to cover this material in a few paragraphs, some principles and facts are worth emphasizing.

E & R managers will surely act as an agent, and they usually become involved in consummating contracts. If an agreement with a consulting engineer is negotiated and he performs the desired services as a result of a manager's action, the manager has acted as an agent of the corporation (which is a legal entity) and has thereby committed the company to an employment contract.

No one can escape contact with the agency device, since it happens when one buys a loaf of bread or deposits money in a bank. Business could not exist without it. Basically, an agency is a relationship where one party acts for and under the control of the other; however, the control does not have to be exercised to ensure an agency relationship. An agent can do practically anything business-wise that a principal can do.

An agency can be created by (1) Agreement (compensation is not necessary), (2) Estoppel (principal may create an impression of agency and if a third party reasonably relies on it, the principal may be estopped from denying an agency), (3) Ratification (where a person acts for another without authority and the other confirms the act by work or conduct, he has ratified), and (4) By operation of law (an example would be a wife and/or child authorized to act as agent of husband and/or father who has failed to support them).

The principal has a duty:

1. Not to breach agency contract
2. To compensate except where agent acts gratuitously
3. To reimburse for sums spent on behalf of principal
4. To exonerate agent and save him harmless from liabilities incurred while acting as directed
5. To comply with statutory duties such as maintain safe and healthful working conditions, pay minimum wages, recognize qualified unions, etc.

Practically all managerial employees and hordes of others will occasionally or regularly act as agents. Be assured that the specific laws and principles are complex and should be studied.

In a similar vein, the law of contracts (of which agency law is a special case) also deeply affects the E & R manager. One definition of a contract is that it is an agreement between two or more competent persons, having for its purpose a legal object (an object that is considered lawful), wherein both persons agree to act or refrain from acting in a certain manner, and where such agreement is supported by a consideration. There are five, and sometimes six, essentials that must be present to have established a contract. They are the following:

1. There must have been an offer that was intended as an offer, and it must have been communicated.
2. The offer must be accepted, *and* the acceptance must be communicated—except where it is accepted by completion of the action requested.
3. The promises or actions must be supported by a consideration; however, the consideration cannot be something given gratuitously. It must be the thing bargained for. Adequacy is not important in court except in cases of fraud. Also, past consideration will not support a contract.
4. Parties must have legal capacity to contract; for example: infants, the insane, or intoxicated persons cannot form a binding contract.
5. The objective of the contract must be legal.
6. In general, contracts can be oral; however, some must be in writing such as the contracts covering the sale of real estate.

Many special rules and conditions attach to each of the six points, and the E & R manager is advised to read a good text on business law to be able to recognize danger areas. He should then consult the company attorney when they are encountered.

PRODUCTS LIABILITY AND RELIABILITY

If we take the time to analyze the problems associated with products liability and reliability (products liability and reliability are irretrievably and intimately related) we cannot help but arrive at the following general conclusions:

1. The firm's response to the problems of products liability and reliability must involve every department or function of the business; i.e., Engineering, Manufacturing, Advertising, Sales, Insurance, Service, and Legal.
2. Engineering must produce better designs for manufactured products so that they can be produced at a reasonable cost and yet meet new criteria for safety and reliability.

3. The elimination of products liability hazards in the manufacturing cycle must be aided by Engineering, beyond the mere specification of design. For example, they must aid Quality Control by helping produce testing guides which are most effective and yet keep costs within permissible limits. This may require the design of special equipment for the testing procedure.
4. Engineering must work with the insurance carriers in order that claims can be properly handled and thereby minimize liability on claims.
5. Since service and operating instructions are usually produced within the E & R function, they have a unique opportunity to minimize hazards by proper instructions. Also, if a hazard cannot be eliminated, the proper statements concerning a hazard in such instructions can often minimize future damage claims.

In the past, the liability of the manufacturer to the consumers of his product primarily arose from (1) Negligence in the design or manufacture of the product, and (2) Warranty. Here the emphasis was and still is on negligence with respect to the first point and to some degree to false representation with respect to the second point.

Today a new trend appears to be beginning—the imposing of liability *irrespective of fault.*

The law is changing in other respects. In the past the manufacturer was usually only liable to those who were parties to a transaction. According to one source the courts have used 29 fictions, subterfuges,and theories to avoid the effect of the "privity rule" in order to extend liability to persons who were not a party to the transaction.

Another primary reason why the engineering manager must be increasingly concerned with this general subject is the fact that the verdicts are increasing in size as well as number.

The old disclaimers and "hold harmless" agreements to limit the liability are now largely ineffective.

Engineers and designers must be made more aware of the problems in this area. These men must not only keep in mind that the device must work well and must be economically feasible, but they also must take into account that human beings will operate the device and will be in contact with it. The background of the user must be considered in this process.

One way the courts have circumvented the old privity concepts of a contract is by finding that an obligation runs from the manufacturer to a remote purchaser on the basis of an express warranty. Law in the past recognized express warranties, but had limited them to an affirmation of fact as to the quality of the goods. Anything other than this was categorized as "sales talk." Now the courts appear to be saying that advertising labels and sales literature constitute an express warranty on which an injured party can base a cause of action.

If one only considers liability under warranties as being between a manufacturer and the buyer (not liability to third party), it still appears to be the law that reasonable warranties that are freely negotiated will be enforced. Here it is extremely important, however, that the bargaining position of the buyer be approximately equal to the position of the seller. One final point: it appears that the desire and philosophy of the courts, and perhaps of society in general, is to place the burden of liability on the manufacturer since he is far more financially capable of paying the judgment. As to liability to third parties, there seems to be a tendency to bite the biggest entity, the manufacturer, rather than the sub-manufacturer.

Between the problems of patents, labor laws, government rules and regulations, contract law, the law of agency, and the problems of products liability and reliability, it would seem rather obvious that the E & R manager cannot afford to ignore legal problems and must in fact become reasonably familiar with the legal aspects of the business—enough to know when he needs to turn to an expert, the company's legal department, or an attorney. Also, here he will often find that attorneys tend to provide the pros and cons of a situation and leave the ultimate decision up to management.

BIBLIOGRAPHY

BRAINERD, ANDREW W. "Protecting Patents, Know-How and Trademarks Abroad," *Management Review,* December, 1964.

BUCKLES, R. A. *Ideas, Inventions, & Patents.* New York, N.Y.: John Wiley & Sons, Inc., 1957.

CATALDO, BERNARD F. et al. *Introduction to Law and the Legal Process.* New York, N.Y.: John Wiley & Sons, Inc., 1965.

"Clients, Contractors, and R & D," *Chemical Engineering Progress,* June, 1965.

CRONSTEDT, VAL. *Engineering Management and Administration.* New York, N.Y.: McGraw-Hill Book Company, 1961.

CROSBY, R. W. "Patent Hearings Flash Warning; Industry's 'Rights' at Stake," *Iron Age,* June 15, 1961.

DALRYMPLE, DOUGLAS J. "Patent Monopolies and the Law," *California Management Review,* Spring, 1967.

———. "Do You Know the Law? Implied Warranty," *Business Management,* (July, 1966), 30:8.

EATON, WILLIAM W. "Patent Problem: Who Owns the Rights, "*Harvard Business Review,* July–August, 1967.

ESHELMAN, R. H. "Patent Searches Pay Their Way in Design and Development," *Iron Age,* September 3, 1959.

GALLAGHER, JOHN T. "A Fresh Look at Engineering Construction Contracts," *Chemical Engineering,* September 11, 1967.

GRAY, A. W. "How to Handle a Breach of Warranty," *Purchasing,* (October 5, 1967), 63:60–62.

———. "What Are Company Rights . . . When an Employee Gets a Patent?", *American Machinist,* August 10, 1959.

GRAY, FRANCIS W. "The Drama of Patents," *Chemical Engineering,* February 26, 1968.

HUGHSON, ROY V. "Pros and Cons of Patent Legislation," *Chemical Engineering,* February 26, 1968.

KARGER, D. W. "Patent Fundamentals," *Machine Design,* August 20, 1959.

"The Lines Are Drawn for a Patent Law Fight," *Business Week,* January 28, 1967.

LUSK, HAROLD F. *Business Law, Principles and Cases.* 8th ed. Homewood, Ill.: Richard D. Irwin, Inc., 1966.

Machinery and Allied Products Institute and Council for Technological Advancement. *Products Liability and Reliability: Some Management Considerations,* Washington, D.C.: 1967.

"Patents in Pattern of Today," *Engineering,* Vol. 184, No. 4788:749, December 13, 1957.

PHALAN, R. T. *Introduction to Basic Legal Principles.* Scranton, Pa.: International Textbook Co., 1964.

"A Poke at the Power of Patent Holders," *Business Week,* February 18, 1967.

POPPER, HERBERT. "The Patent Chief Speaks Out," *Chemical Engineering,* February 26, 1968.

"Protecting Proprietary Information," *Chemical Engineering Progress,* June, 1966.

QUINN, H. "Warranty is Name of the (ad) Game in Detroit, Auto Makers Find; but U.S. is taking hard look at some nebulous wording," *Advertising Age,* (December 19, 1966), 37:3.

REDMOND, G. H., and WEBSTER, F. M. "How Chrysler Communicates Data on its Warranty Program," *Office,* (August, 1966), 64:69–72.

"The Riches in Dormant Patents," *Business Week,* April 15, 1961.

SCHER, V. Y. "Protecting Your New Ideas," *Textile World,* Vol. 110, No. 5, 38–39, June, 1960.

SCHMOOKLER, JACOB. *Invention and Economic Growth.* Cambridge, Mass.: Harvard University Press, 1966.

SHIPMAN, JOHN R. "International Patent Planning," *Harvard Business Review,* March–April, 1967.

SPANGENBERG, CRAIG. "You, Your Product and the Law," *Mechanical Engineering,* June, 1968, pp. 18–24.

VAUGHN, RICHARD C. *Legal Aspects of Engineering.* Englewood Cliffs, N.J.: Prentice-Hall, Inc., 1962.

VOTAW, DOW. *Legal Aspects of Business Administration.* Englewood Cliffs, N.J.: Prentice-Hall, Inc., 1956.

WADE, WORTH. *Patent Guide for the Research Director.* Ardmore, Pa.: Advance House Publishers, 1964.

WILCKE, GERD. "Practical Uses of Patents Lag," *The New York Times,* October 9, 1966.

CHAPTER 18

Professional Activities and Conduct

Technical and Professional Conduct

Technical society activities, attendance at technical meetings, the preparation of papers, and the writing of articles for publication are often considered to fall in the "nonproductive" category by E & R managers. There are, however, a number of strong reasons why management should go out of its way to encourage its technical people to participate in technical society activities and to write for publication.

TECHNICAL SOCIETIES

There are approximately 630 scientific, engineering, and technical organizations in the United States today of which 400 are concerned with areas of interest to people working in research and engineering of products.[1] These societies provide the principal means for technical people to communicate among themselves. Most advances in science are based upon the platform of previous knowledge. Cut off all communication, and science and engineering would stagnate. The technical societies, through the publication of journals, standing committees in specialized areas, and national and local meetings offer the principal medium for communication.

The function of technical societies in the scientific world is summarized well by Dr. C. G. Suits, former Vice President and Director of Research for General Electric:

[1] *National Organizations of the U. S.,* Volume 1, Gale Research Company (Detroit 26, Michigan: Book Tower, 1968). Section 4, Scientific and Technical Organizations.

The professional and technical societies comprise, in aggregate, a "supreme court" of informed scientific opinion. The verdict of this court concerning the importance of scientific work generally transcends the opinions of the author or the sponsors of the work. To be sure, the verdict may not be explicit nor prompt, but it is generally final and inescapable. It does what the author, because of his proximity to the work, usually cannot do—properly judge a new scientific result in relation to the work of others, to development in the whole field, and to important progress in related fields or fields that are competing in scientific interest with the author's field.

Problems and Policies

A policy of actively encouraging membership in professional societies probably will result in a broadened viewpoint for more of the staff. A much higher percentage of a manager's people will likely find themselves called upon to take an active part in societies and respond accordingly. They will become better known by other scientific and management people throughout the country. If the contribution of the company's engineers and scientists on standing technical committees is of a high caliber, the reputation of the company will be enhanced. It is well known that good engineers and scientists attract other top engineers and scientists. This represents a valuable recruiting factor.

One of the drawbacks of participation may be an appreciable loss of time spent on the main activities of the E & R organization. Correspondence is usually prepared during working hours so that scientific and secretarial time is diverted. A large number of days, in total, may be lost because the technical people must travel to special meetings, symposiums, or national meetings.

Perhaps a larger danger is having someone unintentionally "leak" news of the imminence of an important development to a competitor. This must be carefully guarded against by proper briefing of staff before attendance.

Major technical societies offer engineers an opportunity to participate in local meetings in the larger cities of the United States without imposing any burdensome traveling cost. For example, The American Society of Mechanical Engineers is organized into local groups or "sections," larger geographical regions or "divisions," and finally on an overall national basis. Papers which are presented at sectional or divisional meetings are indexed in the annual Transactions. The Transactions contain about 95 percent of the papers presented at local, divisional, or national meetings. As with most professional organizations, in order to present a paper at a national meeting, the engineer must submit an outline well in advance of the winter convention. If the publications committee accepts the outline, the paper, when written, may be preprinted and discussion invited.

Those who have attended many national or regional technical meetings may have observed that it seems as if 90 percent of those attending spend their time circulating around the halls outside the meetings in progress. It is here that people get to know each other on an individual basis and discuss specific details of their subject areas. Unfortunately, from the viewpoint of some companies, considerable recruiting goes on in the halls.

Before sending a man to a technical society meeting, his manager might have him make a request to attend based upon some particular papers in his area of interest. The engineer who attends should be expected to write a brief summary of the presentations and/or discussions not only of the papers, but also of the more important things seen and heard. Considering that the company may invest several hundred dollars in sending a man on such a trip, he should not consider this an imposition. At some meetings on new technologies, it is not unusual to see participants photographing the blackboard or data presented by slides to bring back the detailed results of new research.

Payment of Fees and Dues

Should the company pay a man's membership fee and dues in a technical society? One viewpoint is that the company should not pay dues or fees except under special circumstances. First, and most important, membership in an organization representing his profession is a requirement of the man who claims to be a professional. It is a professional and personal responsibility. As such, the nominal cost should not be borne by some other individual or organization. Second, if the company follows the policy of not paying membership dues, it has the opportunity of observing which men take an interest in their professional development. The true professional is a long-run asset to a company, although some companies may feel that professionalism conflicts with company operations at times.

There are circumstances when a company may consider paying fees and dues for membership in a society. When a new man is hired directly out of college, he must serve an apprenticeship before he can be considered a professional in his field. The company might encourage his development by paying his membership in a society for his first year of employment. This will acquaint the man with the purposes and advantages of society membership. Another reason for the company paying a man's membership is that the company believes it is in its own interests. For example, a senior engineer may belong to The American Society of Mechanical Engineers. The company, however, has a pressing need for someone in the E & R organization who is thoroughly familiar with some areas of materials testing. Therefore, the company pays for the engineer's membership in the American Society for Testing and Materials, sends him to the society meetings, and encourages him to take part in committee work of the society. In other words, the membership in this second organization is for the convenience of the company. Many companies take exactly the attitude just expressed in combination with the thoughts given in the previous paragraph.

A counterview of the above policy is that the company should pay fees and dues in technical societies for anyone who wishes to join. Those proposing this viewpoint believe that the company gains considerably by having as many as possible of its technical people as members of technical societies. The cost per individual is a very small fraction of his salary; however, the returns can be very great. Each man who joins his professional society personally receives a copy of the society's journal. He is much more likely to read it and keep up with new developments than if he had to go to the company's technical library during working hours. The more members of technical societies from a company, the greater the number of its personnel who are likely to be drawn into active participation in societies and in writing for the journals. These activities help develop leadership, to build the company's reputation, and to provide incentives for the younger men who wish to grow in professional stature. Morale will be improved because there is no discrimination among technical personnel as to who gets his membership paid. Furthermore, at salary review time, if it is known that the manager asks his men what benefits they have obtained from membership in their society over the past year, the men may feel motivated to try to obtain some worthwhile benefits through reading the journals and participating in other ways. From the above, it can be seen that a strong case on economic grounds can be made for the company to take the initiative in this area.

WRITING FOR PUBLICATION

Why Publish?

While top management of the company establishes policy regarding publication, the manager of E & R may exert his influence in its formulation. Not only should he encourage his men to write, but he should provide leadership through his own publication. Within the company policy, the manager of E & R also develops a more definitive policy for his organization. The first question to be answered when developing a policy is: Will there be a net benefit to the company if publication of work is encouraged or if it is discouraged? A second question which companies may not take so seriously is: Should publication be encouraged to advance the state of the art and contribute to the advancement of society?

The advantages to the company incurred through a policy and program of encouraging its technical personnel to publish are as follows:

1. The name of the company and type and quality of its technical work is placed before the potential customers, in the case of industrial and government products.
2. The prestige of the company is enhanced, in general.
3. Permanent records of results are obtained since periodicals are bound and stored in a large number of libraries throughout the country. Books, of course, are similar permanent records. This contrasts with internal company memos and reports which may not be retained beyond a fixed number of years. Microfilming of all reports for permanent storage is an expensive and time-consuming process.
4. The morale of the engineers and scientists is improved, because individuals feel pride in themselves and their organization when they have a high publication rate.
5. "Like attracts like," as was mentioned earlier. An organization which has a reputation built upon publications will attract other good personnel. Publication is a more effective way of building such a reputation to attract technical people than word of mouth or advertising. Consequently, recruiting costs may be lower, and the company may have better candidates from which to select.
6. If each company publishes the results of its research, progress can be accelerated. In most cases, a company publishes the results of its studies because if it doesn't, someone else will soon face the same problem, solve it, and publish the results. There is some advantage to being first in publication, but little advantage within the industry as a whole to withhold publication. Publication does not wipe out a technological lead, necessarily; it merely reduces the time lag slightly. This argument does not hold in some cases of process development as will be discussed under the disadvantages below.

The disadvantages of a program which encourages publication of technical advances are:

1. In the case of unpatentable devices, trade secrets, or secret processes for which patents would offer no protection, publication of such information could severely damage the company's competitive position.
2. A significant amount of the time of the professional people might be spent in preparing technical articles, and their efforts may be diverted from the main company projects.
3. The cost of a well-run program might represent a sum which could be better spent elsewhere within the company.

In general, it is possible for a company to establish a well-run program which will achieve the advantages and avoid the possible disadvantages. Some of the factors to consider in establishing a program for encouraging technical publications are given below.

Setting Up a Program for Technical Publication

The acceptance rate of articles submitted for publication can be greatly increased by having a technical editor and advisor available to the E & R organization. This individual should be thoroughly familiar with the requirements of many technical and trade journals. Over a period of time he has probably built up a personal acquaintanceship with the editors of many of these publications and can obtain frank criticism of articles.

The technical editor develops incentive programs, searches out areas of research on which articles should be written, and stimulates and assists the engineers and scientists in preparation of manuscripts. He usually provides editorial suggestions, makes sure typing and graphic services are available, and expedites internal approvals of articles.

The success of the technical publication program depends upon the backing of management and the competence and energy of the technical editor. Management may see to it that publications are listed in the individual's personnel record and considered when his salary is reviewed. Bonuses, awards, and publicity may be given in accordance with the number of articles, or for some especially valuable report on research. The technical person must be made to feel that considerable prestige and recognition is attached to a good publication record.

There are basically five types of publications in which the engineer or scientist may seek publication:

1. The pure research journals, usually published by a technical society
2. The business or trade magazine which is published by a private publishing house and contains applied science and engineering papers and industry news
3. Company journals such as those published by IBM, Westinghouse, and Battelle Memorial Institute
4. Periodicals and journals published by associations of technical groups with some common interest. Transactions of societies are included in this category.
5. Periodicals dealing with technical management or general industrial management.

The research journals generally have rigid requirements with respect to the format and length of articles submitted. Standards of quality are high, and the publications do not pay for articles. In fact, some journals charge the author according to the length of the article. On the contrary, trade magazines usually pay a fee for each printed page or a flat amount regardless of the length of the article. Some technical magazines provide considerable help to authors by giving editorial assistance and criticism, accepting rough text and illustrations, and preparing elaborate graphic art work. *Machine Design* is a good example of such a technical magazine.

If an engineer or scientist is faced with the choice of seeking publication of his results in a scientific journal or in a well-paying magazine, he may be tempted to seek the greater certainty, the lesser effort, the greater remuneration, the finer production job, and the broader circulation of the trade magazine in place of the possible prestige offered by the journal. This choice would occur only when the material could be adapted to either type of publication. Therefore, one important goal of a program for publication would be to achieve a balance among the various types of publications. This balance might be achieved by providing compensation to those who publish in nonpaying journals or magazines. Other motivation may be provided by purchasing reprints of the article for the author over and above the small number of complimentary copies the publisher may supply.

One aspect of a publication program which may negate all other efforts is the approval policy and procedure. Most companies do and should require some minimal review for legal, patent, copyright, proprietary information, and technical correctness. However, in some companies, the review is made by so many people and takes such a long time that authors become discouraged. Furthermore, technical reviews may be made by people without the technical competence of the author or by staff people who insist upon editorial changes and rewording for "political" reasons. It is better if there is a deadline of one week for key people to review the article, and the burden of proof that changes in the article are required should be on the reviewers. Arbitrary changes in technical content should be banned, but suggestions welcomed.

Company Programs

According to Leroy Pope, a feature writer for United Press International, literature (technical and professional) is becoming a big by-product of the industrial world.[2] Companies encourage employees by cash bonuses (examples: Convair Division of General Dynamics and Corning Glass), others encourage the writing on company time (examples: Detroit Edison and Dravo Corp.). Westinghouse even has a one week training course in writing, for technical and professional employees.

According to Mr. Pope, Studebaker-Worthington, Inc., queried 500 corporations and found 72 percent made an effort to get their employees to write. Mr. Karassik, a general manager for the firm has written over 1,000 articles for which he received about $65,000.

A number of major industrial companies were surveyed in the preparation for this edition, as to their publications practices and the results are shown in Fig. 18-1.

Figure 18-1, while it does not give a complete representation of the

[2] Leroy Pope, "Literature Big By-Products of Industrial World," *Schenectady Union Star,* Schenectady, N. Y., April 22, 1968.

Of 34 Companies Surveyed:

Number	Policy
23 (9—sometimes, 3—rarely)	Assign papers in order to present significant information.
34 (2—under certain conditions)	Permit the author to write on company time.
0	Require the author to write on his own time.
32 (5—minimal assistance)	Provide assistance for editing and rewriting.
33	Have a formal article review period. (Varies from one day to eight weeks.)
31	Provide art work and illustrating services to all employees.
10	Employ the public relations department as the author's agent.
15 (1—for internal cicrulation)	Have their own technical magazines.
8	Have an honorarium program.
25 (6—under certain conditions)	Permit the author to accept payment.

Number	Policy
29 (8—when appropriate, 1—in company newspaper)	Publicize the author.
31 (7—occasionally)	Distribute reprints.
23	Consider authorship on employees' personal records.
0	Discourage publication.
	Pay expenses associated with belonging to or participating in:
28 (12—when appropriate)	a) technical and professional society
18 (3—when appropriate)	b) community service organizations
18 (3—when appropriate	c) writing (technical and professional)
13 (4—when appropriate)	d) engineering licenses
34 (6—when appropriate)	e) attendance at conventions and seminars
33 (5—when appropriate)	f) participation in educational programs.

Fig. 18-1. Variety of company policies regarding employee writing.

integrated programs, does show that companies are actively encouraging participation in community activities and publication by their technical people. Companies that participated in the survey were: American Telephone and Telegraph Company, Armstrong Cork Company, Babcock and Wilcox, Beckman Instruments, Carborundum Company, Dravo Corporation, Du Pont, Emerson Electric Company, Fairchild Hiller Corporation, Ford Motor Company, General Dynamics, General Electric, General Motors, IBM, International Nickel Company, Merck and Company, Inc., Minnesota Mining and Manufacturing Company, Monsanto Company, North American Rockwell, Polaroid, RCA, Shell Oil Company, Westinghouse Electric Corporation, Worthington Corporation, Xerox, and nine others who preferred to remain anonymous. In some of the companies, different policies are followed at different plants or in different departments. Thus, Fig. 18-1 indicates the variety of practices followed, rather than a uniform or complete policy for the company.

Some of the policies need to be expounded upon. Emerson Electric Company, for example, elaborated upon its reply to the survey by stating that if an author is directed to prepare a paper, he is permitted to write on company time. If he generates an idea for presentation of information to a select or general media, he *may,* with the approval of the Publications Review Committee, be authorized to prepare the piece on company time. Du Pont allows the author to write on company time if the piece is work-related.

With regard to the author's accepting payment for his work, Du Pont will allow acceptance of payment only if the piece is non-work-related and written on the author's own time. Emerson Electric Company considers the circumstances individually and then permits authors to accept payment for their work only with prior approval of the Publications Review Committee. Dravo has no firm policy in this area, but added, "probably payment from publication would disqualify (the) employee from collecting under our Editorial Awards Program."

In the area of publicizing the author the "when appropriate" responses in the table refer to newsworthy or significant articles and papers. At Westinghouse Electric Corporation the normal publicity on authors is internal through "employee newspapers, periodic reports listing presented papers and published articles, and through presentation of honorarium checks to authors.'

None of the companies discouraged publication, *per se.* Some companies made specific reference to publication of proprietary information, and, of course, discouraged publication of such information.

When company representation is desired in a technical or professional society, at conventions or seminars, and in community service organizations, the associated expenses are generally paid by the company. Exception is made in some cases for technical and professional organizations. Some companies expect the employee to belong to and pay the membership dues of the professional organization of his field. Other job-related expenses are paid by the company. Usually the individual is expected to acquire his engineering license on his own, but Shell Oil Company will pay expenses associated with the license when a licensed engineer is required for a particular work location.

Participation in educational programs is sometimes restricted to: job-related programs (Armstrong Cork Company); officers, committee members, presenters, and "otherwise without reason" (Du Pont); or where appropriate to the man's work and development (Monsanto).

Some companies encourage publication by their engineers and scientists through communications such as that shown in Fig. 18-2.

Requirements for Position of Consultant-Semiconductor Applications

The following outlines the general requirements for promotion to the position of Consultant-Semiconductor Applications.

1) Professional Engineering License in the State of New York.

2) Senior Member of IRE and AIEE.

3) Active continued participation in local and national professional societies, industrial organizations, and similar groups including work on technical committees or in administrative positions.

4) At least ten papers presented at Professional Society Meetings and five papers published in Professional Journals.

5) At least 25 feature length articles published in trade magazines.

6) Author or major contributor to at least one technical book.

7) At least 15 patent disclosures submitted and three patents issued.

8) Instructor of at least two, 24 week (or longer) courses in semiconductor devices and circuitry.

9) Continued excellent performance in fulfilling the responsibilities of an Application Engineer (as described in the position guide) for at least five years.

10) Demonstrated competence in applying all types of semiconductor devices by means of one-or two-year assignments in the areas of power rectification, computer circuitry, communications, industrial control, and use of special semiconductor devices.

Exact details of the above requirements many be modified somewhat to meet individual cases, but satisfactory accomplishment of each of the ten points is obligatory.

Fig. 18-2. Requirements for high-level consulting position include presentation and publication of technical papers and articles. *Source:* General Electric Co.

GUIDELINES FOR PROFESSIONAL CONDUCT

Nature of Ethics

The engineer is thoroughly oriented towards the physical world where "facts are facts" until proven otherwise. Ethics is concerned with the world of values in human conduct. What are the rights of man in society and the rights of society with respect to the individual? Are there natural human rights? How should man conduct himself to respect the rights of other individuals? These are the kinds of questions which are the subject of ethics.

The question of what is "right" and what is "wrong" can basically be only subjective. Right and wrong depend upon value judgments and there are no scientific answers to value questions. An act in order to be "right" must be based upon "good" intentions, must be accomplished by "good" means or actions, and must have a "good" end result.

The ethical codes of society arise to protect the individual. They are based upon religious beliefs imbedded in the particular culture, the legal concepts which, in turn, have grown out of earlier ethical concepts, and the characteristics and beliefs of the particular society in its everyday action. It is interesting to note that in a particular society, that which is ethical is not necessarily legal, and that which is legal is not necessarily ethical.

There are a number of confusing aspects about ethics to the person who first contemplates them. He, first of all, may have his own standard of conduct. The company in which he works may have a different set of values which he may consider as looser or more rigid than his own, or perhaps, just different. Then, in a society such as that of the United States, there may be a stated code of conduct which appears to deviate from the conduct of individuals in general.

The conflicts in American ethics have been clearly projected by John M. Brewster of the U. S. Department of Agriculture. According to Brewster, the desire for status developing from early American life unfolded into three main groups of value judgments: the work ethic, the democratic creed, and the enterprise creed.

According to the work ethic, a man fails to deserve the esteem of self, family, and country if he prefers an easy life to excellence in employment of his choice. According to this American folklore, individuals and nations alike possess the means to achieve their aspirations. "To believe less puts a ceiling on the American Dream and belittles the promise of American life."

The value judgments of the democratic creed are: (1) All men are of equal worth and dignity, and (2) No man, however good and wise, is wise enough to have dictatorial power over any other.

The enterprise creed, however, embodies an opposite and negative meaning of freedom. It states that owners or their legally delegated representatives deserve exclusive right to set the working rules of their production plants. Therefore, according to this view, a prime function of government is to prevent anyone, including government itself, from restricting the power of proprietors from running their business in any way they see fit (the socialistic oriented governments of today certainly do not function in this manner).

The engineer who first considers the value judgments of his society and his company will be in a better position to crystallize his own code of personal values and behavior. Herbert J. Taylor, a former President of Rotary International, suggested four guides to evaluating the rightness or wrongness of an action in his business life. He asks himself these four questions:

1. Is it the truth?
2. Is it fair to all concerned?
3. Will it build good will and better friendship?
4. Will it be beneficial to all concerned?

Unfortunately, the engineer who seeks a positive response to all these questions before acting might never take any action at all.

Another basic rule of conduct which is often proposed is the Golden Rule. Psychologists point out that all men are different, and what pleases one man may offend another. Therefore, some psychologists believe the rule should be rewritten to read: "Do unto others as they would have you do unto them."

For the engineer, his behavior in business is closely connected with his status as a professional. Therefore, engineering leaders and engineering societies are continually trying to set forth a standard code of ethics. One example is shown in Fig. 18-3. Can the various ethics of many individuals be made to conform to a single standard? Are the value judgments of those who prepare a standard code "good" or "bad," "right" or "wrong?" Do the ethics of the profession transcend the ethics of the company? The engineer in real life must, at some time, face this latter question in the form of a conflict between company instructions and professional behavior.

From the above discussion, it is apparent that this chapter will not propose any standard of ethics for the individual. The purpose of the above discussion is to clarify the problem for the individual who wishes to formulate his own code of ethics. As a value judgment, it is recommended here that each engineer formulate such a code for several reasons. First, he will then be able to act with greater consistency in the face of varied problems. Secondly, he will more likely be able to evaluate his alternative courses of action by using his code as a yardstick (where other than technical judgment is required). Thirdly, he will create a dependable and clear image of himself in the eyes of his associates; a characteristic of a leader.

Professional Aspects of Engineering

Engineering, because of its relationship to the public welfare and its inherent intellectual and educational requirements, properly deserves to be a profession. It has been but a few decades since doctors have advanced from unlicensed barbers to a professional group with strict requirements, both technical and ethical. Engineers today are on the verge of establishing themselves as a professional group through similar development. Many engineers and societies take the position that engineering is now a profession with a set of standards and canons of ethics.

CANONS OF ETHICS FOR ENGINEERS

(Adopted by the Engineers' Council for Professional Development, October 25, 1947)

Foreword

Honesty, justice, and courtesy form a moral philosphy which, associated with mutual interest among men, constitutes the foundation of ethics. The engineer should recognize such a standard, not in passive observance, but as a set of dynamic principles guiding his conduct and way of life. It is his duty to practice his profession according to these Canons of Ethics.

As the keystone of professional conduct is integrity, the engineer will discharge his duties with fidelity to the public, his employers, and clients, and with fairness and impartiality to all. It is his duty to interest himself in public welfare, and to be ready to apply his special knowledge for the benefit of mankind. He should uphold the honor and dignity of his profession and also avoid association with any enterprise of questionable character. In his dealings with fellow engineers he should be fair and tolerant.

Professional Life

Can. 1. The engineer will cooperate in extending the effectiveness of the engineering profession by interchanging information and experience with other engineers and students and by contributing to the work of engineering societies, schools, and the scientific and engineering press.

Can. 2. He will not advertise his work or merit in a self-laudatory manner, and he will avoid all conduct or practice likely to discredit or do injury to the dignity and honor of his profession.

Relations With the Public

Can. 3. The engineer will endeavor to extend public knowledge of engineering and will discourage the spreading of untrue, unfair, and exaggerated statements regarding engineering.

Can. 4. He will have due regard for the safety of life and health of the public and employees who may be affected by the work for which he is responsible.

Can. 5. He will express an opinion only when it is founded on adequate knowledge and honest conviction while he is serving as a witness before a court, commission, or other tribunal.

Can 6. He will not issue ex parte statements, criticisms, or arguments on matters connected with public policy which are inspired or paid for by private interests, unless he indicates on whose behalf he is making the statement.

Can. 7. He will refrain from expressing publicly an opinion on an engineering subject unless he is informed as to the facts relating thereto.

Relations With Clients and Employers

Can. 8. The engineer will act in professional matters for each client or employer as a faithful agent or trustee.

Fig. 18-3. Engineers' Council for Professional Development Canons of Ethics for Engineers.

Can. 9. He will act with fairness and justice between his client or employer and the contractor when dealing with contracts.

Can. 10. He will make status clear to his client or employer before undertaking an engagement if he may be called upon to decide on the use of inventions, apparatus, or any other thing in which he may have a financial interest.

Can. 11. He will guard against conditions that are dangerous or threatening to life, limb, or property on work for which he is responsible or, if he is not responsible, will promptly call such conditions to the attention of those who are responsible.

Can 12. He will present clearly the consequences to be expected from deviations proposed if his engineering judgment is overruled by non-technical authority in cases where he is responsible for the technical adequacy of engineering work.

Can. 13. He will engage, or advise his client or employer to engage, and he will cooperate with, other experts and specialists whenever the client's or employer's interests are best served by such service.

Can. 14. He will disclose no information concerning the business affairs or technical processes of clients or employers without their consent.

Can. 15. He will not accept compensation, financial or otherwise, from more than one interested party for the same service, or for services pertaining to the same work, without the consent of all interested parties.

Can. 16. He will not accept commissions or allowances, directly or indirectly, from contractors or other parties dealing with his client or employer in connection with work for which he is responsible.

Can. 17. He will not be financially interested in the bids as or of a contractor on competitive work for which he is employed as an engineer unless he has the consent of his client or employer.

Can. 18. He will promptly disclose to his client or employer any interest in a business which may compete with or affect the business of his client or employer. He will not allow an interest in any business to affect his decision regarding engineering work for which he is employed, or which he may be called upon to perform.

Relations With Engineers

Can 19. The engineer will endeavor to protect the engineering profession collectively and individually from misrepresentation and misunderstanding.

Can. 20. He will take care that credit for engineering work is given to those to whom credit is properly due.

Can. 21. He will uphold the principle of appropriate and adequate compensation for those engaged in engineering work, including those in subordinate capacities, as being in the public interest and maintaining the standards of the profession.

Can. 22. He will endeavor to provide opportunity for the professional development and advancement of engineers in his employ.

Fig. 18-3 (*Continued*). Engineers' Council for Professional Development Canons of Ethics for Engineers.

Can. 23. He will not directly or indirectly injure the professional reputation, prospects, or practice of another engineer. However, if he considers that an engineer is guilty of unethical, illegal, or unfair practice, he will present the information to the proper authority for action.

Can. 24. He will exercise due restraint in citicizing another engineer's work in public, recognizing the fact that the engineering societies and the engineering press provide the proper forum for technical discussions and criticism.

Can. 25. He will not try to supplant another engineer in a particular employment after becoming aware that definite steps have been taken toward the other's employment.

Can. 26. He will not compete with another engineer on the basis of charges for work by underbidding, through reducing his normal fees, after having been informed of the charges named by the other.

Can. 27. He will not use the advantages of a salaried position to compete unfairly with another engineer.

Can. 28. He will not become associated in responsibility for work with engineers who do not conform to ethical practices.

Fig. 18-3 (*Concluded*). Engineers' Council for Professional Development Canons of Ethics for Engineers.

Almost any concept of the professional worker is based upon a philosophy of service. Mary Parker Follett, the illustrious management scholar, wrote:

> . . . For most people the word "profession" connotes a foundation of science and a motive of service.

George Pettee in writing about operations research expresses his ideas on the meaning of profession simply:

> There is no mystery about the word "profession" as it is used here. A profession is an identifiable group of people who earn their living in a common manner. It is something for which people can be trained. If it is an old and established profession, young people in college can decide that they want to belong to it and can prepare for it accordingly. A profession is a classifiable special skill, and its members can be readily identified by prospective clients. If it is a real profession, it is a career which a person can enter, where he can earn his living, and from which he can eventually retire with a sense of accomplishment[3]

William Wickenden expressed this concept of service by saying:

> Every calling has its mile of compulsion, its daily round of tasks and duties, its standard of honest craftsmanship, its code of man-to-man relations, which one must cover if he is to survive. Beyond that lies the mile of voluntary effort, where men strive for excellence, give unrequited service to the common good, and seek to invest their work with a wide and enduring significance.

[3] G. S. Pettee, "Operations Research as a Profession," in *Operations Research for Management,* J. F. McCloskey and F. N. Trefethen, eds., Baltimore: The John Hopkins Press, 1954, pp. 36–37.

It is only in this second mile that a calling may attain the dignity and the distinction of a profession.[4]

The characteristics of a profession are, of course, a matter of definition. The baseball player, the "pro" golfer, and the white-collar clerk all consider themselves professionals. Anybody who earns his livelihood through some special skill might consider himself a professional. It is important for engineers, therefore, to define clearly what they mean when they claim that their calling is a profession, to state what sets their group apart and in what respects. The National Society of Professional Engineers (NSPE) and authors writing for its publication, *The American Engineer,* have devoted much effort to this subject. Wickenden's work cited earlier gives a very valuable discussion of the nature of engineering professionalism. Students of management have followed a parallel course and have written much on the subject. The following criteria for an occupation to be a profession is proposed here:

1. Professional work requires knowledge obtained through advanced study in a field of science or learning customarily acquired by a prolonged *formal* course of *specialized* study as distinguished from *general* academic education and from an apprenticeship.
2. Professional work requires consistent exercise of discretion, judgment, and personal responsibility in its performance.
3. A profession must be regulated by a national-level association of its members which:
   a. Establishes minimum levels of skill and knowledge
   b. Establishes standards of ethical practice to guide the relations of members with each other, the client, and the public
   c. Standardizes terminology
   d. Sets policies and standard practices and procedures to be followed in appropriate cases
   e. Publishes the official journal for the profession
   f. Promotes the advancement of the science and art of the profession.
4. An in-training of internship period is required before professional status is achieved.
5. Practitioners are expected to extend the knowledge upon which the profession is based.
6. Practitioners make their knowledge and contributions freely available to others in the profession and take responsibility for assisting and developing the newer and younger members of the profession.
7. Members are required by law to be licensed in order to practice the profession.

[4] William E. Wickenden, *A Professional Guide for Junior Engineers,* G. Ross Henninger, ed., New York: Engineer's Council for Professional Development, 1949, p. 44.

8. The professional man at all times maintains an attitude towards his work and society characterized as follows:
   a. A social consciousness, a desire to contribute to rather than simply benefit from civilization; a resolve to place the public welfare above other considerations
   b. The continued acquisitions of special skills on a high intellectual plane, generally evaluated by means of self-imposed standards of excellence
   c. A sense of trusteeship—personal responsibility to protect the employer's interest
   d. Individual initiative and acceptance of individual responsibility, both of the highest order
   e. A right to expect and receive adequate financial recognition.

Problems of Engineering as a Profession

Three current problems face the practitioners of engineering in establishing their profession on a recognized basis:

1. Unity
2. Registration and minimum standards
3. The engineer as an employee.

There are a number of major engineering societies in this country, each representing a different discipline. Some such as the NSPE and Engineers Joint Council cut across all disciplines. As a result, engineers speak with many voices on subjects bearing upon legal and social matters affecting them. In recent years, efforts have been made to unify the engineering societies by having existing cross-discipline societies coordinate matters in particular concerns of a legal, educational, and professional nature. When this situation becomes effective, engineers will have made a big step towards presenting a clear and united picture to the public and politicians.

If engineering is to be a profession, it must establish minimum educational and competence requirements. One way of achieving this goal is to have state laws passed which provide for registration on the basis of standardized examinations and a required minimum practical experience.

All of the states, territories, and possessions of the United States have engineering registration laws. These laws vary in detail, but in general they follow a pattern which is indicated by the Model Law issued by the National Council of State Boards of Engineering Examiners. It is within the discretion of the state board whether an applicant is required to take an examination, but all of the state laws authorize such examinations when the Board feels that it is required. The trend is definitely toward mandatory written examinations, although in some states it is still possible for an engineer with extensive responsible experience to obtain registration without examination.

Admittedly, registration does not guarantee competence, but it undoubtedly eliminates many people from practicing who are certainly incompetent. There are engineers who feel strongly on each side of this question of registration so that the group as a whole is far from unified on this key aspect of professionalism.

Engineers, unlike doctors, are not usually self-employed. The patient who goes to a doctor places himself unreservedly, one may even say blindly, in the doctor's hands. The client of the engineer, whether it be his employer or an outside concern, may question the engineer at each step of the way. In much government defense work, even the most competent engineers are usually required to justify every step of their technical work to the government agency. Engineers may be told to adopt an alternative technical approach, often for political reasons, far different from the one they would take if they had complete professional freedom. In the face of this situation as it exists, Rear Adm. H. G. Rickover, U.S.N., exhorted the graduating class at Stevens Institute of Technology in 1958 as follows:

> Service ceases to be professional if it has in any way been dictated by the client or employer. The role of the professional man in society is to lend his special knowledge, his well-trained intellect, and his dispassionate habit of visualizing problems in terms of fundamental principles to whatever specific task is entrusted to him. Professional independence is not a special privilege, but rather an inner necessity for the true professional man, and a safeguard for his employers and the general public. Without it, he negates everything that makes him a professional person and becomes at best a routine technician or hired hand, at worst a hack.

A difficult dilemma, from a professional viewpoint, may occur when engineers are working for a manager who is not an engineer. If the lay manager *directs* an engineer to adopt some line of approach which is contrary to what the engineer believes is in the best interest of company or society, what action should he take? If it is a minor technical design point, should he make an issue of it? How major does a question of professional belief have to be? It is easy to see the possible dilemma of the engineer who works for a lay employer and who also desires to be identified with his profession.

Another problem of the engineer as an employee is the conflict between professionalism and unionism. An excellent discussion of the problem, is given by Solomon Barkin who is a labor economist, in his writing *The Decline of the Labor Movement* as published by The Center for the Study of Democratic Institutions, Santa Barbara, California.

POWER AND CONFLICT

Any manager or aspiring manager should not only be familiar with the nature of ethics, but he should also be aware of the nature of power and conflict for his own protection. The utilization of power tactics represents an opposite extreme of values to those expressed under professionalism.

In spite of modern bureaucracy, emphasis on group effort, human relations, and democratic leadership, there is a belief by many authorities that all social relations are power relations. There are inner-directed men who, appearing to conform superficially, are engaged in a constant striving for power over their associates. Ethics are excluded from consideration as to their means of reaching their goals; manipulation and maneuver characterize their processes. Machiavelli set down many of the principles which power-seekers follow. A modern discussion which every manager should read is *The Anatomy of Leadership* by Eugene Jennings.

A basic power principle is that the individual in order to survive in the struggle for power must act in such a way that he increases his power to act. As the individual gains power, he must increase or expand further his power to take action beyond that required for the regular established activities. As a second basic principle, the structure of power and authority is inseparable from its communication structure. Without communication, the leader can command nothing but his desk. Many specific rules may be developed from these two principles, and some of the more important ones are given below in the convenient form of advice on conduct.

1. Establish alliances with key people at all levels of the organization.
2. Don't identify with one clique. Power relationships are fluid and the ruling clique may be overthrown.
3. Aggrandize by taking on responsibilities in gray areas or those that other managers wish to discard.
4. Dramatize yourself. Try to avoid situations where you must act extemporaneously. Prepare well for meetings and conferences in order to avoid surprise. It is well to have formulated your philosophy and strategy in business so that when crises arise, you can appear decisive. Adopt an air of confidence in your speech and action.
5. The proper use of channels of communication is essential to retain and increase power. Do not tell all you know at all times, but look for the most advantageous timing in the release of information. In dealing with subordinates, communicate in symbols, which they understand. For example, the word "team" is an excellent word to use in employer-employee relations, particularly when much of the work is tedious and not likely to lead to rapid advances in grade.[5]
6. The skillful leader retains maneuverability. Always retain an escape hatch with regard to the failure of programs you undertake or with regard to your job. In any consideration of maneuverability, timing

[5] Joseph F. McCloskey and Florence N. Trefethen, eds., *Operations Research for Management* (Baltimore, Md.: The John Hopkins Press, 1954), p. 75.

is an important dimension. There is the right time to identify your firm position. There is the wrong premature time to take a stand, to resolve a conflict. There is a right time to appear on the stage as credit is being handed out. Do not be pressed into making a decision involving people; usually time is on your side and problems will work themselves out.

Conclusions on Professional Conduct

A manager, whether in E & R or some other function, must create his own system of values. This chapter has provided an introduction to two extremes of value systems. The E & R manager will gain an understanding of the diversity of beliefs and their rationale by a study of the few selections in the bibliography of this chapter. As any manager soon realizes, technical training and knowledge alone are not sufficient to make him a capable manager.

BIBLIOGRAPHY

BREWSTER, JOHN M. "Value Judgments as Principles of Social Organization." In *Proc. Papers of the Agricultural Economics and Rural Sociology Section, Annual Meetings of the Southwestern Science Association.* March 27–28, 1958.

FULLER, NELSON. "How We Encourage Engineers to Write," *Chemical Engineering,* October 5, 1959.

HEYNE, PAUL T. *Private Keepers of the Public Interest.* New York, N.Y.: McGraw-Hill Book Company, 1968.

"Is Managing an Art or a Fight?", *Business Week,* August 19, 1961.

JAY, ANTONY. *Management and Machiavelli.* New York, N.Y.: Holt, Rinehart & Winston, Inc., 1967.

JENNINGS, EUGENE E. *An Anatomy of Leadership.* New York, N.Y.: Harper & Brothers, 1960.

MACHIAVELLI, NICCOLO. *The Prince.* Edited and translated by Thomas G. Bergin. New York, N.Y.: Appleton-Century-Crofts, 1947.

MAGOUN, F. A. *Cooperation and Conflict in Industry.* New York, N.Y.: Harper & Brothers, 1960.

MANDEL, SIEGFRIED, ed. *Writings in Industry.* Vol. I. Brooklyn, N.Y.: Polytechnic Press of the Polytechnic Inst. of Brooklyn, 1959.

MCELWEE, E. M. "Communication: A Responsibility and a Challenge," *Proceedings of the IRE,* May, 1962, pp. 1113–15.

MILLS, JOHN. *The Engineer in Society.* Princeton, N.J.: D. Van Nostrand Co., Inc., 1946.

National Council of State Boards of Engineering Examiners. *A Model Law.* Adopted at the annual meeting of NCSBEE in Portland, Oregon, August 18, 1960. Clemson, S.C.

Pope, Leroy. "Literature Big By-Product of U.S. Industrial World." UPI feature, *Schenectady Union-Star,* April 22, 1968.

"Publications: Where They're Going," *Chemical Engineering Progress,* March, 1967.

Schelling, Thomas C. *The Strategy of Conflict.* Cambridge, Mass.: Harvard University Press, 1960.

Schmitt, R. W. "Why Publish Scientific Research From Industry?", *Management Research,* Spring, 1961.

Turbett, Frank J. "When Are P.E.'s in Industry Acting Unethically?", *The American Engineer,* April, 1958.

Wickenden, William E. *A Professional Guide for Junior Engineers.* New York, N.Y.: Engineers' Council for Professional Development, 1949.

CHAPTER 19

From Engineer to Manager

The Two Jobs of the Engineer

The young engineering graduate should realize clearly at the outset that he must always work at two distinct jobs. The first is the functional technical job (or, possibly later on, a managerial job) of his everyday work. In this job(s), he must work to gain the technical competence and the skill required to utilize all his talents.

The second and equally important job that he should carry out is the management of his career. In this latter job he must soon decide whether his interests and talents mainly lie with the technical or engineering aspects of his profession, or in the field of management as the source of his self-fulfillment. The earlier the beginning engineer can determine in which of these general areas his talents and interests lie, the better off he will be.

A word of caution and advice is appropriate: Don't, under any circumstances, decide upon one career or another because the wife, family, associates, or the "world at large" looks more favorably upon one choice of action rather than another. Also, although it may be difficult, under no circumstances allow possible financial return be the sole or even the most important factor in selecting a particular kind of a career. In a similar manner, avoid letting the combination of prestige and possible financial rewards be the only factors determining a choice of action. A man spends well over 50 percent of his waking hours either on the job or under its influence away from the work scene. If he is trying to do work which is distasteful and/or uninteresting, his professional life will be unfulfilled and under these circumstances, not only will he probably fail to achieve job success but he will generally end up leading an unhappy life.

If a person's real interests lie in the direction of management (not just a belief that this is most desirable), but he does not appear to have the spontaneous leadership qualities of some of his colleagues, he need not be discouraged. The ability to lead in a business organization can largely be learned through diligent study and practice, provided the required work does not clash with a person's basic personality traits. For example: He must now often make quick decisions with only partial data, which affect himself, his associates and/or his company; a procrastinator practically never succeeds in managerial work. If this is difficult and/or disturbing, managerial work is not for you! It is usually necessary to "stick your neck out" several times a day, and with the person who ends up worrying about such actions later, at home, this means that his tensions will be reflected on the job in both his technical and personal relationships.

The engineer or scientist must remember that his background and previous training have oriented him to a consideration of *things* rather than people. It is generally recognized as a result of sociological studies of engineering students that the more satisfied men with this career choice tend to be "inward looking" rather than "outward looking." They are not greatly interested in the world about them, the sociological changes that are taking place, the social scientists' and psychologists' view of people, etc. In a managerial job the primary emphasis will be on people, not only on the technical jobs to be accomplished. Although the success of many technical assignments depends heavily on careful planning and organization, most of the technical managers' problems will be "people oriented." Successful managers realize that the human factors can make or break a project.

If no fundamental conflicts exist and the person wants to learn the practice of management, it can be done. One company that has done considerable practical research into this matter states:

> Unquestionably, some individuals show attributes of leadership very early in their personal growth. They have ideas and plans which make sense to others. They have beliefs, energy, and emotional drive which prompt them to strongly promote such ideas and plans and which engender confidence in others that the plans are worth following.
>
> We continue to follow the lead of those who seem to us to be wisest in their counsel and who advocate actions in our own best interest and also in the overall, long-time best interests of others in our society. On the other hand, we eventually repudiate the leadership of those who would tear down institutions and social practices which are cherished because they are just and are productive of general well-being.
>
> The thesis at this point is that one can learn how to be an effective leader, and that those who continue to be leaders among us have learned and have consciously exercised practices which result in voluntary following of such leadership by others. Thoughtful persons often become convinced that they have insights which not only will lead to satisfactions for themselves but, even more importantly, will also be of lasting benefit to others as well. A desire to contribute in the general social good is very real though it may sometimes be hidden deeply from public view behind an exterior of apparent hard-shelled self-sufficiency. For most men, the deepest and the most lasting satisfactions come

not so much from a feeling of power over others but rather from a belief in lasting contributions to the welfare of others.[1]

THE UNMAKING OF AN ENGINEER

Recent studies show that the technically competent individual contributor is receiving greater recognition and remuneration than ever before. Nevertheless, engineers as a group are aware that the greatest financial rewards are given to those who make the transition to management work. The engineer who considers making such a change in his career should recognize that it is a drastic move and one that is usually irreversible. From the viewpoint of society, no really creative worker should be diverted as long as he can continue to be productive in his special field. However, it is also true that there are many who serve an engineering apprenticeship, yet are more interested in management, and who are better equipped to do executive work than creative work. For such engineers just starting their careers, the main question is, "What should I do to move up from the ranks to first-line manager?" For engineers or low-level managers who have been offered promotion to the broadly responsible job of engineering manager, the main question is "What specific, practical, systematic approach can I make in my new job to show that I can handle it?" This chapter presents the thoughts of some experienced managers and observers, which bear upon these questions.

Basic Routes From Engineer to Manager

The would-be manager, starting his career with an engineering organization, should first examine the organization hierarchy since it is usually difficult to skip steps. It is probable that he will find something similar to the following:

First, Top Level—Engineering Manager	....
Second Level—Function or Project Managers	Consulting Engineers
Third Level—First-line Managers	Consulting Engineers
Semiformal Level—Team of Group Leaders	Specialists
Individual Contributors—Engineers	....

The goal for the ambitious engineer is to get off the ground and onto the ladder. Once he is on the ladder, he has joined a new group and should begin the process of establishing himself as a manager—*not as an engineer.*

[1] *Professional Management in General Electric,* Book 3, The Work of the Professional Manager, p. 186, with permission from General Electric Company.

This concept is important, and he should not fall into the trap of claiming and believing that he is primarily doing engineering work. There are those who bear the title of "manager" who still claim to be doing engineering work; nevertheless, there is ample evidence provided by engineering leaders as well as management analysts, to show that a manager who is doing his job correctly does little or no engineering work himself.

Discussions with a number of high-level E & R directors having the status of vice president in their respective organizations, indicated that they and many others like them held some belief that their work as a manager was not as important as the work of the individual technical contributor. To some extent they held the feeling that the managerial work was demeaning and that this was also the view of their subordinates. If the reader has any feelings along these lines, it is suggested that he abandon the managerial route. He will not be happy in it and the odds are great that he will not be too successful.

In a somewhat similar fashion the technical manager should recognize that the management of Engineering and Research might be difficult, but that the task is not impossible. There are some who attempt E & R management who hold to the belief that it is not really possible to manage the function. Again, if this is the belief of the reader, he should not move into the management of the technical function.

The manager must spend full time in planning, organizing, guiding, coordinating, and measuring the work of his men. He utilizes his technical knowledge in these processes and in making decisions involved in these processes. He must accomplish his goals through the technical efforts of his people. This point is so fundamental that the rising engineer should not be led astray by any illusions.

Nine primary routes to managerial positions that are open to the engineer (excluding nepotism or buying into control of the company) are listed below. A combination of two or more of these obviously will hasten the process. It is not an object here to pass value judgments on the merits of any method but simply to point out what exists in fact. These routes are:

1. Showing outstanding technical competence and some organizational ability
2. Aggressive and effective analysis, summarization, and presentation of work segments larger than his own
3. Producing required work on time and in an outstanding manner
4. Demonstrating an understanding of the total factors involved in his work activity
5. Sponsor-protégé arrangements
6. Job-jumping
7. Moving to consulting engineer and switching over to manager at a corresponding level in the organization

8. Dependable engineering work plus outside leadership in important community and professional activities
9. Doing a reasonably good engineering job and earning a graduate degree in management or business administration.

Technical Competence

There is not much the individual can do about his native ability; either he is gifted or he isn't. However, anyone who has successfully completed an engineering and/or scientific education has more intelligence than the average. This means his knowledge and ability can always be improved upon by self-education and by participation in graduate or extension classes. If a man does not have enough self-discipline to pursue a plan of self-education and if extension or graduate classes are not available, a compromise course is always available—correspondence study.[2]

Improving his technical competence does not make a person creative, but it certainly improves his ability to do good "straightforward" engineering. Doing well at the professional specialty is one of the best ways to reach the managerial ranks. By seeking broader technical responsibilities, the engineer can get started on the way to the management ladder.

Evaluation, Summarization, and Presentation

If the engineer recognizes his limitations in creative work or his lack of technical superiority, he still must be technically competent if he wishes to rise to engineering management. The lack of technical competence, however, is not a bar to performing management work in other functions of the business. He may be able, by extra effort or special talent, to grasp a larger part of the picture than his colleagues. He may be able to organize and communicate the problems and implications of the results of the work group and be outstanding in expressing group opinions. If he also proposes sound plans for future action, takes on the work of scheduling (distasteful to most engineers), cost estimating, and small administrative tasks at every opportunity, he may be able to obtain responsibility for small projects as a start.

Reference was made earlier in this chapter to possible extra effort. It should be understood that advancing *either* through the technical or the managerial route means much extra effort; for such people the work-week is fifty to sixty hours. Certainly, these hours are not all put in at the office—much of it is at home; reading, dictating, writing, computing, analyzing data, etc. Additional extra hours may also involve traveling and entertaining.

In connection with entertaining, the man who really wants to get into

[2] The *Guide to Correspondence Study* of the National University Extension Association, whose secretary is located at Bloomington, Indiana, is a booklet listing a host of college credit courses available from approximately thirty colleges at very moderate fees.

the top managerial ranks would do well to pick a wife who can help him in his career. She must be willing to let him place his work in the position of greatest importance, and must also be able and willing to entertain, successfully, both upper *and* lower level personnel, professional associates, etc. Most companies today look carefully into the wife's qualifications when hiring a top executive.

Sponsor-Protégé

The shadowy sponsor-protégé relationship exists more frequently than engineers suspect. Most organizations are complex networks of sponsor-protégé relationships. Each manager wants men working for him whom he likes and upon whom he can *depend*. This means that the man must be competent and valuable in a work sense to the manager. No one but a fool would take to a new job an incompetent individual—certainly an ambitious and rising manager can't afford this luxury. As he moves up, he seeks promotion of these men to work for him in his new position. They in turn work as one on his team and never as rivals. The engineer who attaches himself to the competent rising manager through close personal relationships may not only obtain his start but also his career by this means.

One of the most important steps the engineer takes is that of picking the right manager to work for. The good manager will train his men well and help them take advantage of opportunities.

Job-Jumping

In the early stages of a man's career, he may find it advisable to build up a technical specialty over a period of two or three years and then go into the market for a better job elsewhere. In most companies, progress is slow and not always steady—certainly promotional job openings are limited in any one given company. On the other hand, the company which is expanding and requires experienced engineers, must be willing to offer more than such engineers are getting to attract them away from their old company.

The engineer who is mobile has a considerable advantage over his more stable colleagues. The pitfall which the engineer must avoid is accepting promises of opportunity in lieu of hard cash and/or an immediate leadership assignment. Changing jobs and/or companies can also be used to advantage in another way. One can deliberately change jobs, not for a higher salary, but in order to learn a new specialty or acquire managerial experience (albeit at a low level). Often such moves are not immediately financially advantageous; however, they can be made to "pay off" over a period of years. If a man changes jobs only three or four times in his first ten years, he need not worry about being classified as a "floater" by even the more conservative companies. At the same time, two or three years on each job allows him to grow in spurts, so to speak.

One word of warning—don't expect every new job to be personally satisfying or even reasonably satisfactory. If you change jobs several times, expect at least one of them to be completely wrong for you—one that you will have to write off as a bad experience. When it happens, get out fast! Admit the error to yourself and to your next prospective employer. One way to keep such incidents to a minimum is to apply in reverse some of the advice given in Chapter 5.

From Consultant to Manager

The aspiring engineer may take the indirect path of developing a reputation for a specialty and becoming a consulting engineer within his company or with a consulting firm. If he wishes to follow this route he should select his specialty as one that is not too specialized but rather, is basic to the main engineering work. For example, in a company devoted to pressure vessel design and manufacture, the engineer might build his reputation in stress analysis and material application. This would be more appropriate than becoming a specialist in, say, fasteners or finishes. After the engineer has risen to the level of consulting engineer by default of competition, he is then in a position to broaden both his knowledge and his relationships, and remain on the lookout for first-line managerial openings.

Demonstrated Leadership Outside the Company

By long, dependable service with the company, combined with active leadership in professional activities such as writing books and articles, and by securing election to local and national offices in professional and trade associations, and/or in community service organizations, and activities such as Chamber of Commerce, Kiwanis Club, Rotary Club, Lions Club work, and Community Chest drives, municipal and educational study groups, etc., the hardworking engineer can, in this manner, develop management and personnel relationship skills. His contacts with officials of his company in such activities give him "high visibility." While this method provides, perhaps, the greatest development of the whole man, it can be a lengthy route. Certainly it is uncommon for an engineer because he usually feels more comfortable and happy dealing with things—unfortunately, management is mostly concerned with people, and here are people upon whom you can practice your embryo management skills with no work environment penalty for failure.

Earning a Graduate Degree in Management

One route to managerial responsibilities that many engineers take is to return to the campus and earn a graduate degree in management or business administration. It seems that this road is becoming increasingly popular.

Two possibilities are open—to go back for full-time study or else earn a degree by working during the day and going to school at night. The latter route is usually only open to those in the larger metropolitan areas.

That such action has its financial rewards is borne out by surveys of Rensselaer Polytechnic Institute graduates. The men who earned their master's degree in management, within one to three years of the undergraduate degree in engineering or science, had an average salary that was 17 percent higher than those who held a master's degree in an engineering area (the comparison engineering salaries were those disclosed by Engineering Joint Council salary surveys). If the master's degree in management or business administration was earned four or more years after the undergraduate degree, they still were about 7 percent ahead of those in the E. J. C. survey.

There is ample reason for the popularity and effectiveness of this route. First, our increasing dependence upon science and engineering makes an undergraduate in this area valuable. Secondly, management is becoming increasingly complex and there is less dependence upon the art of management and more dependence upon basic principles and scientific techniques.

One final comment, a few graduate programs at the masters level permits the development of a major in engineering and research management.

ESTABLISHING A PLAN

A highly successful young engineer in a large bureaucratic, decentralized organization set down a plan when he joined the company. He established a schedule of dates at which he planned to achieve certain positions and approximate salaries. He took every opportunity to travel and to talk with engineering managers in different plants within the company. This included vacation trips as well as business trips. He recognized that because he was young and just starting, managers would be interested in talking with him about his future, since managers must continually be on the lookout for good talent. If this young engineer's progress showed signs of falling behind his timetable, he arranged a conference with his manager to determine what he should do to bring himself up.

The moral of this story is that every engineer should establish a career plan. He may change the plan from time-to-time. He may find that his abilities or his drives do not match up to his aspirations. In any case, he gains knowledge about himself, his potential contributions, and his place in the scheme of life.

Here are some guidelines for the young engineer who seeks to establish his worth early in his career:

1. Give your best effort to every assignment. When you first start out you may well be given very simple assignments which you feel don't utilize all your talents. If you accept small jobs cheerfully and perform them to the best of your ability, you will be given successively

larger and more important jobs. On your first jobs you will be very carefully observed.

2. Find out specifically when each job must be completed and get it done on time. There is a premium upon the ability to get jobs done on time or ahead of time. Build a reputation for getting your work done right and on time. As a professional worker, you have the responsibility to work beyond the scheduled hours when the task demands. Managers are selected from those who put company obligations above personal convenience.
3. Follow up and be tenacious. Continually check to see that others who must supply you with information, equipment, and shop work will meet the required schedules. Keep after those who fall behind in their commitments. Try to avoid irritating these people, but let them know firmly that you are going to meet your schedules at any cost. Try to work out your mutual problems and avoid complaints to higher-ups except as a last resort. Confirm instructions and commitments in writing.
4. Promote "high visibility." "High visibility" means that managers see you often. Promote your ideas, speak up, and "be around" when you know new jobs are about to break. When your manager wants to give out a special assignment, he may think first of the engineer he sees most often. Get yourself known by other managers through personal meetings.
5. Be accurate in your statements and thorough in your preparation of presentations. One inaccurate statement can make your report valueless from a career-building viewpoint.
6. Keep your manager informed of your progress, problems, and significant relationships with other organizations both internal and external.
7. If you are highly ambitious, be courageous. When you have mastered the work in any position—technical or managerial—ask for a promotion. If you don't get it, look around elsewhere. In other words, move up or get out! It is very typical in large organizations for men to spend two or three years in a position after the work has become routine to them. This time is lost forever from a man's career progression.

GETTING OFF TO A GOOD START AS MANAGER OF ENGINEERING

Being an Effective Manager

There are some guidelines that can assist you in being effective as a manager. Those which immediately follow are essentially paraphrased from portions of Peter F. Drucker's book, *The Effective Executive.*[3] Great wisdom and intelligence that is not applied to action and behavior is meaningless and of no practical value.

It is important to accomplish the tasks that must be finished in order to make a contribution, and this requires the manager to be effective. According to Peter Drucker, effectiveness is a complex of practices. Practices can be learned, although the practices involved with being effective are deceptively simple.

Certain necessary habits are outlined by Mr. Drucker and one of the first of these is that the manager must know what he does with his time. Once he knows what he does with his time, he can begin to manage it. It is important not to guess at how one's time is spent, rather keep a log and find out, or have your secretary do so. Time is totally un-elastic, it is totally irreplaceable, and everything we do requires time.

Before you do anything, make sure you know what contribution is expected of you toward the success of the organization. By contribution, something more specific is meant than being in charge of XYZ engineering, supervising twenty engineers, managing the drafting room, etc. What exact contribution is expected? This should be the overriding question.

Be primarily concerned with the strengths your staff has to offer. The manager cannot get a job done with their weaknesses, he can only accomplish it through their strengths.

Subordinates do not, as a rule, rise to positions of importance over the prostrate bodies of incompetent bosses. Making the strength of your boss productive is a key to your own effectiveness. If the boss is relieved of his job for incompetence or failure, the successor is rarely the bright young man next in line, or anyone else working for the man who was relieved of his job.

Concentrate your efforts. Do not try to do two or three things at one time. Most of us find it hard enough to do well even one thing at a time. This is easier said than done because the manager faces so many tasks clamoring to be done at once.

Establish priorities for the tasks which need doing.

> Courage rather than analysis dictates the truly important rules for identifying priorities:
>
> 1. Pick the future as against the past
> 2. Focus on opportunity rather than on problem
> 3. Choose your own direction—rather than climb on the bandwagon
> 4. Aim high, aim for something that will make a difference, rather than for something that is "safe" and easy to do.[4]

While decision making is only one of the tasks of an executive, it usually

[3] Peter F. Drucker, *The Effective Executive,* New York, N. Y.: Harper & Row, Publishers, 1967.

[4] *Ibid.*

takes but a small fraction of his time. However, it is the specific executive task and therefore a managerial task.

Be well aware that decisions concerning people are time consuming. Unfortunately, people do not come in the proper sizes, shapes, character, and with the proper characteristics needed to accomplish the tasks posed by an organization. Neither can people be machined down or recast for the accomplishment of required tasks. According to Drucker, people are always "almost fits, at best." [5]

Taking Over a Going Organization

Taking over a going organization may represent a tremendous opportunity or a grand frustration for the new manager. If the organization is one of low morale, inefficient methods, and poor working relationships, it may offer a challenge which the new manager can meet. On the other hand, if the engineering organization consists of old-time, long-service engineers set in their ways, divided into cliques, sprinkled with prima donnas, and resentful of a new manager, major surgery may be required which only the general manager can perform.

In either case, the new engineering manager should go through much of the thinking and planning processes described in the first part of this chapter. It should serve as his blueprint of the future. He should be careful about bringing his plans out into the open at once, because changes in such a rigid environment will probably need to be introduced gradually.

Immediate operating improvements may well be possible in any going organization. For example, in one business which was grossing a little over ten million dollars a year, the newly appointed manager of engineering found from a routine manufacturing report that manufacturing losses amounted to about one million dollars per year. He investigated and found that most of these losses were due to poor communications between the engineers and the factory, engineering drawing changes, unnecessarily tight tolerances, and other engineering practices. He immediately instituted an educational program for the engineers and within months the losses were reduced to a rate of 6 percent of their former amount. Other examples from the experiences of other managers could be cited.

Check List of Key Points for Good Management

This chapter has reviewed some guidelines for the new manager of engineering, in adopting a systematic approach to selecting engineering activities, defining objectives, establishing the engineering organization, and obtaining his charter. In short, it attempts to answer the primary question on the mind of the new manager, "How can I make an organized start on my new job?"

[5] *Ibid.*

There are some engineering managers whose success is conspicuous for the following reasons:

1. They move on upward, regularly, to manage larger engineering organizations which also represent considerably larger company investments.
2. The people who have worked for these managers, either permanently or in passing, both respect and admire them.
3. They combine new theory and techniques with realistic understanding of people and operations.

One such outstanding engineering manager was interviewed three months after he had taken over a going organization and made his mark again. This manager was asked to give off-hand, just as they came to his mind, some guides to taking over and operating an engineering organization. The notes given below, Fig. 19-1, might well be pasted on the top of the desk for daily reading.

Now You're A Manager

SET UP THE ORGANIZATION

Get a charter which spells out your duties and relationships with other individuals and departments.

Be sure that your department is well-organized, with all subordinate jobs well-defined.

Make sure that your immediate subordinates, and also the next lower echelon, understand their responsibilities.

If there are any cliques, former managers, etc., make it plain that all major decisions are to be yours.

In hiring subordinates, place a premium on a combination of experience and potential, rather than on experience alone.

Be sure the people in lower-echelon management spots are capable of managing properly. Personality and psychological tests are often misleading.

EXPECT A GOOD JOB

If the people you hire are not doing a satisfactory job, tell them. Outline the standards you expect, and let them know that if they fail to deliver, you have no choice but to replace them.

Don't supervise your lower-level managers too closely, but meet with them individually for a short time each week.

Make it plain that you expect a good job. In most cases your men will live up to your expectations.

Be "tough," but don't be brutal.

LEARN TO HANDLE PROBLEMS

Keep your own superior notified of what problems arise, but don't call him

Fig. 19-1. Some guide points for an engineer assuming a managerial position. *Source:* R. G. Murdick, "From Engineer to Manager," *Machine Design* (March 30, 1961).

unless necessary. If you think a problem warrants his attention, leave a message for him. This gives him the option of getting in touch with you or not, as he sees fit.

When an urgent problem comes up, move in fast and follow the details closely. Leave no doubt that you have taken charge. If necessary, work yourself and your men around the clock.

Don't be afraid to ask questions when problems come up.

Learn to evaluate accurately any information that comes your way. A good manager doesn't have to be a good engineer, but he should be able to sift evidence and come up with a decision.

GET THE JOB DONE RIGHT

When a new job comes up, analyze it and start making your plans. See that current jobs are carried on by delegation, and spot check to see that things keep running smoothly.

Keep in touch with major reports on manufacturing, finance, marketing, etc., which may have an effect on engineering. Try to find areas where engineering's contribution may be extended.

Anticipate problems. Avoid the possibility of having to push the panic button. See that jobs are done on schedule. Be sure that all specifications are met and that nothing is shipped out that doesn't meet engineering specifications.

TREAT YOUR MEN RIGHT

Don't short-circuit or override your men - work with them.

Don't criticize a man in front of others; feel free to reward a man in front of others.

Try to get your men advanced in salary and responsibility as rapidly as they deserve it. Don't hang on to a man who is offered a better opportunity than you can offer him.

Accept full responsibility for the mistakes of the group: don't unload them on to the individual when discussing these errors.

Don't let yourself become obligated to your subordinates through outside favors.

Keep your men informed and let them know where you stand with respect to them.

Fig. 19-1 (*Continued*). Some guide points for an engineer assuming a managerial position.

BIBLIOGRAPHY

BASSETT, GLENN A. *Management Styles in Transition.* New York, N.Y.: The Presidents Association, American Management Association, Inc., 1966.

BATTEN, J. D. *Beyond Management by Objectives.* New York, N.Y.: The Presidents Association, American Management Association, Inc., 1966.

———. *A Tough Minded Climate for Results.* New York, N.Y.: The Presidents Association, American Management Association, Inc., 1965.

GIVEN, W. B., JR. "The Engineer Goes Into Management," *Harvard Business Review,* January–February, 1955.

———. "The Management Function of the Engineer in Industry," *Chemical Engineering,* November 14, 1960.

———. "What It Is To Be Boss," *Product Engineering,* December 25, 1961.

HEALEY, FRANK H. "Job Status for the Research Scientist," *Research Management,* Winter, 1960.

HINRICKS, JOHN R. *High Talent Personnel: Managing a Critical Resource.* New York, N.Y.: The Presidents Association, American Management Association, Inc., 1966.

KELLOGG, MARION S. *Closing the Performance Gap.* New York, N.Y.: The Presidents Association, American Management Association, Inc., 1967.

KELTON, GILBERT. "So You Want to Be a Technical Manager?", *Industrial Laboratories* (now *Research Development*), March, 1959.

KING, W. J. "The Unwritten Laws of Engineering," *Mechanical Engineering,* May, June, July, 1944.

LEAMER, FRANK D. "Professional and Administrative Ladders: The Advantages of Broad Job Classification in a Research Organization," *Research Management,* Spring, 1959.

MORGAN, JOHN S. *Managing the Young Adults.* New York, N.Y.: The Presidents Association, American Management Association, Inc., 1967.

MURDICK, ROBERT G. "From Engineer to Manager," *Machine Design,* March 30, 1961.

NEWMAN, LOUIS E. "Some Philosophies of Management," *Advanced Management,* February, 1959.

Resource Publications, Inc. *Index of Opportunities for Engineering, 1968–9.* New York, N.Y.: The Macmillan Company, 1968.

SHEPARD, HERBERT A. "The Dual Hierarchy in Research," *Research Management,* Autumn, 1958.

SKIFTER, HECTOR R. "The Art of Engineering Management," *Proceedings of the IRE,* May, 1962, pp. 1102–09.

TANGERMAN, E. J. "Which Way Up . . . Technical or Management?", *Product Engineering,* August 14, 1961.

WILSON, G. J. "Scientific and Administrative Position Titles and Levels Descriptions," *Research Management,* Autumn, 1951.

Index